Marx, Engels, and Marxisms

Series Editors
Marcello Musto
York University
Toronto, ON, Canada

Terrell Carver
University of Bristol
Bristol, UK

The volumes of this series challenge the 'Marxist' intellectual traditions to date by making use of scholarly discoveries of the *Marx-Engels Gesamtausgabe* since the 1990s, taking on board interdisciplinary and other new critical perspectives, and incorporating 'reception studies'. Authors and editors in the series resist oversimplification of ideas and reinscription of traditions. Moreover, their very diversity in terms of language, local context, political engagement and scholarly practice mark the series out from any other in the field. Involving scholars from different fields and cultural backgrounds, the series editors ensure tolerance for differences within and between provocative monographs and edited volumes. Running contrary to 20th century practices of simplification, the books in this innovative series revitalize Marxist intellectual traditions.

More information about this series at
http://www.palgrave.com/gp/series/14812

Xavier Lafrance • Charles Post
Editors

Case Studies in the Origins of Capitalism

palgrave
macmillan

Editors
Xavier Lafrance
University of Québec in Montréal
Montréal, QC, Canada

Charles Post
Graduate Center and Borough
of Manhattan Community College
City University of New York
New York, NY, USA

Marx, Engels, and Marxisms
ISBN 978-3-030-07078-6 ISBN 978-3-319-95657-2 (eBook)
https://doi.org/10.1007/978-3-319-95657-2

Cover credit: fberti / Getty Images
Cover design by Akihiro Nakayama

This Palgrave Macmillan imprint is published by the registered company Springer Nature Switzerland AG
The registered company address is: Gewerbestrasse 11, 6330 Cham, Switzerland

To the Memory of Ellen Meiksins Wood, 1942–2016

Series Foreword

The Marx Revival

The Marx renaissance is underway on a global scale. Whether the puzzle is the economic boom in China or the economic bust in 'the West', there is no doubt that Marx appears regularly in the media nowadays as a guru, and not a threat, as he used to be. The literature dealing with Marxism, which all but dried up twenty-five years ago, is reviving in the global context. Academic and popular journals and even newspapers and online journalism are increasingly open to contributions on Marxism, just as there are now many international conferences, university courses and seminars on related themes. In all parts of the world, leading daily and weekly papers are featuring the contemporary relevance of Marx's thought. From Latin America to Europe, and wherever the critique to capitalism is remerging, there is an intellectual and political demand for a new critical encounter with Marxism.

Types of Publications

This series will bring together reflections on Marx, Engels and Marxisms from perspectives that are varied in terms of political outlook, geographical base, academic methodologies and subject matter, thus challenging many preconceptions as to what 'Marxist' thought can be like, as opposed to what it has been. The series will appeal internationally to intellectual communities that are increasingly interested in rediscovering the most powerful critical analysis of capitalism: Marxism. The series editors will ensure that authors and editors in the series are producing overall an eclectic and stimulating yet synoptic and informative vision that will draw a very wide and diverse audience. This series will embrace a much wider range of scholarly interests and academic approaches than any previous 'family' of books in the area.

This innovative series will present monographs, edited volumes and critical editions, including translations, to Anglophone readers. The books in this series will work through three main categories:

Studies on Marx and Engels

The series will include titles focusing on the *oeuvre* of Marx and Engels which utilize the scholarly achievements of the on-going *Marx-Engels-Gesamtausgabe*, a project that has strongly revivified the research on these two authors in the past decade.

Critical Studies on Marxisms

Volumes will awaken readers to the overarching issues and world-changing encounters that shelter within the broad categorization 'Marxist'. Particular attention will be given to authors such as Gramsci and Benjamin, who are very popular and widely translated nowadays all over the world, but also to authors who are less known in the English-speaking countries, such as Mariátegui.

Reception Studies and Marxist National Traditions

Political projects have necessarily required oversimplifications in the twentieth century, and Marx and Engels have found themselves 'made over' numerous times and in quite contradictory ways. Taking a national perspective on 'reception' will be a global revelation, and the volumes of this series will enable the worldwide Anglophone community to understand the variety of intellectual and political traditions through which Marx and Engels have been received in local contexts.

Titles Published

1. Terrell Carver and Daniel Blank. 2014. *A Political History of the Editions of Marx and Engels's "German Ideology" Manuscripts.*
2. Terrell Carver and Daniel Blank. 2014. *Marx and Engels's "German Ideology" Manuscripts.*
3. Alfonso Maurizio Iacono. 2015. *The History and Theory of Fetishism.*
4. Paresh Chattopadhyay. 2016. *Marx's Associated Mode of Production.*

5. Domenico Losurdo. 2016. *Class Struggle: A Political and Philosophical History.*
6. Frederick Harry Pitts. 2017. *Critiquing Capitalism Today: New Ways to Read Marx.*
7. Ranabir Samaddar. 2017. *Karl Marx and the Postcolonial Age.*

Titles Forthcoming

Robert Ware. *Marx on Emancipation and the Socialist Transition.*
Jean-Numa Ducange and Razmig Keucheyan, eds. *The End of the Democratic State: Nicos Poulantzas, a Marxism for the 21st Century.*
Vladimir Puzone and Luis Felipe Miguel, eds. *The Brazilian Left in the 21st Century: Conflict and Conciliation in Peripheral Capitalism.*
John Gregson. *Marxism, Ethics, and Politics: The Work of Alasdair MacIntyre.*
George C. Comninel. *Alienation and Emancipation in the Work of Karl Marx.*

Acknowledgments

We would like to thank the organizers of the London Historical Materialism 2016 Conference, where the idea for this book surfaced. We are very grateful to Michelle Chen and John Stegner, our editors at Palgrave, for their continuing support at each stage of this project. Many thanks to Alexandre Lemay-Roche for his precious help with the preparation of our manuscript. Thank you also to the contributors and to the numerous people with whom we have discussed and debated these issues over the years.

Contents

Notes on Contributors

Chris Carlson is Ph.D. Candidate in Sociology at the Graduate Center of the City University of New York, United States.

Mark Cohen is Assistant Professor of Sociology at the Chinese University of Hong Kong, China.

Spencer Dimmock is Honorary Research Fellow in History at Swansea University, United Kingdom.

Eren Duzgun is Assistant Professor of International Relations at the Institute for History at Leiden University, Netherlands.

Jessica Evans is Ph.D. Candidate in Political Science at York University, Canada.

Christopher Isett is Associate Professor of History at the University of Minnesota, United States.

Xavier Lafrance is Assistant Professor of Political Science at the University of Québec in Montréal, Canada.

Nicole Leach is Ph.D. Candidate in Political Science at York University, Canada.

Stephen Miller is Associate Professor of History at the University of Alabama at Birmingham, United States.

Javier Moreno Zacarés is Ph.D. Candidate in Politics and International Studies at the University of Warwick, United Kingdom.

Charles Post is Professor of Sociology at the Graduate Center and Borough of Manhattan Community College, City University of New York, United States.

Michael Andrew Žmolek is Lecturer of History and International Studies at the University of Iowa, United States.

List of Tables

CHAPTER 1

Introduction

Xavier Lafrance and Charles Post

The Great Recession that began in 2007–2008 has brought a renewed interest in the study of capitalism.[1] The immense turmoil and human suffering caused by the deepest economic slump since the Great Depression of the 1930s underlined the urgency of understanding the logic of the capitalist system and its manifold impacts on our lives—its tendency to crisis,[2] its environmental impact[3] or the way it nurtures inequalities. Interest in the last has been clearest in the extraordinary success of Thomas Piketty's *Capital in the Twenty-first Century*[4] and the *Occupy* movement's pitting of the 1% against the 99%. A decade after the outbreak of the recession, these issues are still firmly on both the political and the academic agendas.

A renewed attention to capitalism as a system has led to the publication of several volumes on the history of capitalism in recent years.[5] In the United States, the "new history of capitalism" has by now become an established subfield, with its own programs, departments research chairs and book series. A number of important books on the history of US capitalism have also been published.[6] This historical interest is not

X. Lafrance (✉)
University of Québec in Montréal, Montréal, QC, Canada

C. Post
Graduate Center and Borough of Manhattan Community College,
City University of New York, New York, NY, USA

X. Lafrance, C. Post (eds.), *Case Studies in the Origins of Capitalism*, Marx, Engels, and Marxisms,
https://doi.org/10.1007/978-3-319-95657-2_1

surprising, given that how we approach the history of capitalism shapes our ability to comprehend the logic of this system and our capacity to act on it. To grasp the dynamics of capitalism, we must be able to differentiate it from preceding historical societies. This book's aim is to contribute to our understanding of capitalism by offering historical analyses of its origins in different regions of the world. We stress that capitalism is a distinct type of society and one that is very recent in the history of human civilizations. Because of this insistence on the historical, as opposed to natural, character of capitalism, the studies gathered here differ from most recent and older contributions on this topic.

Almost all past efforts at historicizing capitalism and at explaining its origins have ended up assuming the very things that need to be explained. Most historical explanations of its origins have been circular, suggesting that capitalism emerged out of pre-existing, if embryonic, capitalist dynamics. Most have focused on the quantitative growth of commercial activities progressively liberated from long-standing traditional constraints or a universal human proclivity to develop labor-saving technology (productive forces). This propensity to explain capitalism as an outgrowth of age-old and quasi-universal trading activities—the "commercialization model"—has its roots in the historical narratives developed by the Enlightenment and the classical political economists.[7] Here, ancient profit-taking commercial practices, typically involving buying cheap in one region and selling dear in another, are equated with capitalism and its restless drive to accumulate. We are left with historical explanations that essentially revolve around the removal of obstacles to timeless processes—an endeavor often attributed to triumphant urban merchants, sometimes involving violent revolutions. Historical lines of demarcation are blurred, with the unique imperatives of capitalism becoming naturalized.

Such teleological assumptions still permeate recent historical accounts. For instance, editors of the recently published two-volume *Cambridge History of Capitalism* claim that one of their main goals is to determine: "Why did capitalism and modern economic growth take so long to get started in the first place?"[8] Assuming that capitalist accumulation was bound to eventually happen, they claim that: "we look for the beginning of the 'rise of capitalism' as far back as archeologists have been able to detect tangible evidence of some human activity that was consistent, if not fully congruent, with the practices of modern capitalism".[9] The editors and contributors find evidence of capitalistic economic growth as far back of ancient Greece and Rome and even first millennium BCE Babylonia.

In another recent book, Jürgen Kocka offers a "history of capitalism from antiquity to the present".[10] While seeking "trace elements of a kind of proto-capitalism in small amounts" throughout history, he claims that merchant networks that developed in China, Arabia and parts of Europe are precursors of "modern capitalism".[11] Henry Heller has also lately tackled the issue of the birth of capitalism, from an ostensibly Marxist perspective. While assigning a key role of the "territorial state" in forging markets and directing colonial ventures, Heller maintains that late medieval class struggles between feudal landlords, on the one hand, and urban and rural producers, on the other hand, allowed the more "socially and economically ambitious" upper stratum of the urban population to play a "key role in the development of capitalism from the late fifteenth century". These "proto-capitalist elements", the small producers, eventually "formed the shock troops of the early bourgeois revolutions" and engaged in "[t]he development of productive means to enhance the extraction of relative surplus value and the ultimate emergence of the law of value in the competitive market".[12] In standard tautological fashion, economic behaviors stemming from the application of the law of value—cost-cutting strategies implying the productivity-enhancing development of means of production—are here presented as factors leading to the emergence of this very law. Never mind the fact that the presence of the law of value "distinguished capitalism from feudal systems in Europe and elsewhere", as Heller himself stresses, apparently unaware of any contradiction.[13]

A notable and stimulating exception among recent contributions is the work of Joyce Appleby, who claims that "there was nothing inexorable, inevitable, or destined about the emergence of capitalism".[14] Appleby refuses to read capitalism back into historical societies that preceded it or to present it as the logical continuation of trading activities. As she puts it, "capitalism is not a predestined chapter in human history, but rather a startling departure from the norms that had prevailed for four thousand years. Nor did commerce force capitalism into being. There have been many groups of exceptional traders—the Chinese, Arabs, and Jews come to mind—but they were not the pioneers either the Agricultural or Industrial Revolution. We could say that a fully developed commercial system was a necessary, but insufficient, predecessor to capitalism".[15] Moreover, "capitalism was not a general phenomenon, but one specific to time and place".[16] While Western European countries were eventually compelled to imitate their neighbor and rival, Appleby insists that only England experienced a capitalist transition at first.[17]

On these points, the perspective developed by Appleby is similar to our perspective. Indeed, the case studies gathered here stress the historical character of capitalism; none take for granted its emergence. However, whereas Appleby's theoretical inspiration is Weber's work which views capitalism as a "cultural system",[18] we rely on a historical materialist framework and an understanding of the capitalist system developed by Robert Brenner and Ellen Meiksins Wood. The approach advanced by Brenner and by Wood has often been dubbed "political Marxism" (PM). For reasons that become clear in what follows, we prefer to speak of "*Capital*-centric Marxism", whose roots are in Marx's mature critique of political economy.[19]

Classical Accounts of the Origins of Capitalism and Marx's Critique of Political Economy

Adam Smith offers one of the first systematic attempts at explaining the origins of capitalism and one that still informs—unwittingly or not—much of contemporary research on this issue. Smith developed the classical version of the commercialization model of the origins of capitalism. For him, the same fundamental factors producing economic prosperity in modern society also explain the historical development of human civilizations in general.[20] Seeking to better their condition, self-interested individual producers specialize and enter exchange relationships with others. Out of a natural human propensity to "truck, barter and exchange", a division of labor emerges and sustains economic development. An "invisible hand" thus not only organizes the activities of self-interested individuals in modern economies, but also propels a historical development going through four "modes of subsistence", from hunting and gathering, to pastoral society, to settled agriculture and, finally, commercial society. This evolution of the division of labor goes hand in hand with an accumulation of capital stock allowed by the parsimony of individual economic actors. Hence, an "accumulation of stock is previously necessary for carrying on th[e] great improvement in the productive powers of labour" that derives from the invention and usage of "a variety of new machines" in commercial societies.[21]

Another classical explanation of the origins of capitalism, and one that offers an influential alternative to the Marxist account, was developed by Max Weber. For Weber, the emergence of capitalism is a non-issue because profit-seeking commercial enterprises have existed throughout the history of civilization. What Weber sought out to explain was the emergence of "modern capitalism", under which the satisfaction of everyday-life needs by private businesses aimed at maximizing their profits became the rule. This form of economy emerged at first only in the Western world in the middle of the nineteenth century. According to Weber, modern capitalism possesses the following features: the privatization of means of production, rational accounting, wage laborers compelled to sell their labor in the market and free to do so without restriction, free commodity markets, "rational" technology reducible to calculation so as to facilitate the mechanization of production and "calculable" and dependable law.[22]

Weber addresses the origins of modern capitalism is his *Protestant Ethic and the Spirit of Capitalism*.[23] In this book, Weber postulates that the Protestant ethic, and more specifically Calvinism and its doctrine of predestination, created a deep anxiety among believers who were uncertain whether they were among the "elect" who would be saved by God. To alleviate this anxiety, Calvinists were diligent at work in order to secure entrepreneurial success, which was understood as a sign that one was saved. This Protestant ethic paved the way to a capitalist spirit that was eventually secularized and that outstripped the traditional economic ethic that had previously informed the motives of economic actors and acted as a fetter to capitalist development. For entrepreneurs imbued with the spirit of capitalism, profit maximization became an end in itself.

The transformation of the motives of economic actors under the influence of the Protestant ethic is part of Weber's broader consideration of institutional and cultural developments that led to the rise of modern, rational capitalism in the West. In subsequent works on the sociology of world religions, in his *Economy and Society* and especially in his posthumously published *General Economic History*, Weber developed causal chains to explain the rise of Western modern capitalism, as part of the larger process of rationalization specific to European civilization.[24] He specifies two central causal forces: the emergence of the rational-legal state and, the development of a new economic ethic which displaced substantive rationality, concerned with immediate needs related to the preservation of community ties, with a "formal" rationality involving mean-ends calculus aimed at maximizing returns.[25] Western European cities, where bourgeois producers gained increasing economic autonomy, acted as incubators of this new ethos.[26] The development of the latter culminated with the rise of Protestantism and the spirit of capitalism and unleashed a Smithian pattern of trade deepening the division of labor and sustaining economic development.

Smithian assumptions permeate Weber's work. Weber focuses on the unique ability of European civilizations to remove obstacles to the free movement and development of land, labor and capital.[27] In other civilizations, kinship systems, patrimonial states or religious demands constrained the development of a fully blossomed, modern capitalism. While Weber "found that many [factors] conducive to the unfolding of modern capitalism in China, India, and ancient Israel, [these] were in the end outweighed by a series of opposing constellations".[28]Again, the emergence of capitalism is assumed rather than explained. Weber fails to provide an account of the emergence of free and market-dependent wage laborers. He presents the proletarianization of labor as a precondition for the rational capital accounting that, according to him, sits at the heart of modern capitalism, under which "the optimum profitability of the individual worker is calculated like that of any material means of production".[29] Weber's explanation is functionalist: the separation of workers from the means of production is the necessary result of the use of technology in large-scale factories and the rational organization of modern economies, which call for a military-like discipline of labor under centralized and bureaucratized control.[30]

Karl Marx was the first to seriously address the issue of the transformation of class relations that led to the transition to a capitalist economy. There are, however, two distinct phases in Marx's understanding of the transition. In some of his earlier work and especially in *The German Ideology*, *The Poverty of Philosophy* and *The Communist Manifesto*, Marx essentially reproduces Smith and other classical political economists' analysis. Here, a transhistorical development of productive forces driven by an ongoing division of labor responding to the expansion of the market determines the evolution of class relations as well as a linear succession of modes of production. The rise of trade and technological development takes place in the urban interstices of a feudal society, where a bourgeoisie of merchants acts as a force of progress against feudal agrarian classes. The upshot is a bourgeois revolution that breaks down the remaining political obstacles to a fully developed capitalist economy and society. Yet, this revolution is less the starting point of capitalism than the culmination of a protracted process of capitalist accumulation. For the younger Marx, then, capitalism is already on the rise within the feudal mode of production and contributes to its desegregation. However, capitalism's presence is again presupposed rather than explained.[31]

Marx broke with Smithian notions and developed his truly original contribution on the origins of capitalism in his mature critique of political economy in the *Grundrisse* and in *Capital*.[32] There Marx unequivocally rejected classical political economy's notion of a "primitive accumulation" enabling a shift to a capitalist society. Smith's accumulation of capital "stock" and expanding trading activities could never, on their own, explain this shift. As self-restrictive and thrifty as wealth hoarders might have been, they did not create capitalism. As Marx puts it, "the *mere presence of monetary wealth*, and even the achievement of a kind of supremacy on its part, is in no way sufficient for th[e] *dissolution* [of earlier modes of production] *into capital* to happen".[33] On the contrary, Marx is insistent that the centralization of monetary wealth by usury in pre-capitalist societies "does not change the mode of production, but clings to it like a parasite and impoverishes it". The "usurer's capital impoverishes the mode of production, cripples productive forces instead of developing them, and simultaneously perpetuates these lamentable conditions in which the social productivity of labor is not developed". Whether or not usury can act as an element conducive to the formation of a capitalist mode of production depends not on usury's own logic but on "other conditions".[34]

Likewise, "taken by itself", the development of merchant capital—historically organically related to usury—"is insufficient to explain the transition from one mode of production to the other".[35] In fact, as a rule, "the less developed production is, the more monetary wealth is concentrated in the hands of merchants ... The independent development of commercial capital stands in inverse proportion to the general economic development of society ...".[36] Marx notes that waves of trade expansion have taken place at different points in history but resulted in the development of a capitalist mode of production only in the modern world. This leads him to conclude that, while commerce can have a solvent effect on traditional economic structures, whether or not "a new mode of production arises in place of the old, does not depend on trade [per se], but rather on the character of the old mode of production itself".[37]

Marx points to the historically specific character of each mode of production and leaves behind the notion of universal laws of historical development, whether anchored in a human propensity to truck and barter or to systematically develop productive forces. In his mature works, he breaks with the commercialization model while developing a theoretical perspective where the nature of class relations of exploitation defines the working logic of a given mode of production—rather than class relations being defined by the division of labor emerging out of the development of forces of production. Marx explains that, in pre-capitalist modes of production, because the "worker himself remains the 'possessor' of the means of production of his own means of production and the conditions of labour needed for the production of his own subsistence, the property relationship must appear at the same time as a direct relationship of domination and servitude".[38] Put another way, in non-capitalist modes of production, such as European feudalism, individual peasants and other direct producers formed communities that organized their self-reproduction by securing non-market access to their means of production and of subsistence.[39] Consequently, ruling classes appropriated labor surpluses by way of "extra-economic compulsion".[40] Whereas direct producers avoided market dependence and the competitive imperatives that stem from it, appropriators accumulated extra-economic means of coercion, as opposed to investing in the development of forces of production.[41] It follows that the feudal (and the other non-capitalist) mode of production led individuals and the classes that they formed to reproduce themselves in ways that were not conducive to Smithian patterns of growth but rather to the perpetuation of existing social and economic structures.

The expansion of commercial exchange and the accumulation of monetary wealth were necessary but never sufficient conditions for a transition to capitalism. Their impact varies according to the nature of mode of production in which they operate. As Marx explains, "[i]n themselves, money and commodities are no more capital than the means of production and subsistence are. *They need to be transformed into capital*".[42] "Capital is not a thing, but a social relation",[43] and for mere wealth to be turned into *capital*, a radical transformation of relations of class exploitation—or what Brenner calls "social property relations"—had to occur. This is not a matter of an incrementally growing numbers of individual merchants or artisans willingly saving before investing in production in response to market opportunity. Only through a radical alteration of *class relations* could a new mode of production conducive to sustained economic growth emerge. This implies social conditions in which economic actors become market dependent and are compelled by competitive imperatives to systematically develop the forces of production. Hence, for Marx, the secret behind the "so-called primitive accumulation" is "the historical process of divorcing the producer from the means of production".[44]

Marx discusses this process in the last part of the first volume of *Capital*, where he focuses on the mass expropriation of peasants in the English countryside. In the new agrarian context that emerged out of this process of expropriation, English landlords increasingly relied on economic as opposed to extra-economic forms of appropriation, as growing numbers collected rents out of the commercial profits of tenants who employed dispossessed wage laborers. This resulted in sustained economic development since, as Marx notes, "the revolution in property relations on the land was accompanied by improved methods of cultivation, greater co-operation, a higher concentration of the means of production and so on, and because the agricultural wage-labourers were made to work at a higher level of intensity".[45] While he did not provide an account of the causes of these transformations of the English agrarian sector in the early modern period, Marx's decisive contribution cleared the way for later Marxist historians.

The Dobb-Sweezy Debate on the Transition from Feudalism to Capitalism

For nearly eight decades after the publication of the first volume of *Capital*, the theorists of the Second and Third International ignored, for most part, the "late Marx's" account of the origins of capitalism. The discussion of the origins of capitalism after Marx reverted back to his earlier formulations was based on Smith's version of the "commercialization model". Most post-Marx discussions (Plekhanov, Kautsky, Lenin, Trotsky, etc.) of revolutions in the less developed regions of the world—initially Tsarist Russia and later the Global South as a whole—revolved around whether or not the "bourgeois-democratic revolution" had been completed in these areas.[46] While drawing radically different strategic conclusions about the possibilities and limits of working class struggles in these societies, all of the participants in the discussion assumed key elements of the "commercialization model". All embraced the vision that capitalism had developed in the urban 'interstices' of the feudal (or other pre-capitalist societies), diffusing to the countryside with the growth of markets, setting the stage for a "bourgeois-democratic" revolution which would destroy the remnants of pre-capitalist social relations through a radical land reform, parliamentary democracy and (where necessary) the achievement of national independence. When the question of the origins of capitalism was directly addressed, as for example by the Soviet historian M.N. Pokrovsky,[47] the Smithian narrative of *The German Ideology* and *The Communist Manifesto* was reproduced in its entirety.

The publication of *Studies in the Development of Capitalism*, authored by the leader of the British Communist Party's Historian Group, the economist Maurice Dobb,[48] marked a partial break with the Marxian variants of the "commercialization model".[49] Dobb rejected the notion that the reproduction of non-capitalist social property relations, in particularly those of European feudalism, was incompatible with the growth of trade and urban centers. Instead, feudalism, distinguished by lordly expropriation of rents (in labor, kind or cash) from an unfree peasantry (serfs) through political and juridical mechanisms, had its own distinctive, non-capitalist logic. The systematic obstacles to either the lords or peasants developing the productivity of labor through specialization, technical innovation and accumulation of land and tools resulted in an *internally generated* crisis of feudalism in the form of subdivision of landholdings and declining yields per acre and per worker. By the mid-fourteenth century, the feudal crisis produced a massive demographic collapse across Europe, which opened the road to the transition to capitalism. For Dobb, the abolition of serfdom and urban guilds marked the end of extra-economic extraction of surpluses. As the "petty mode of production"—rural and urban household production—was freed from feudal "super-structures", peasants and artisans were able to respond to market signals, specialize output, innovate and accumulate. As early industrial and agrarian capitalism spread, it confronted the remnants of feudal relations in the countryside and feudal power organized through the Absolutist States. The bourgeois revolutions in England (1640–1660) and France (1789–1799), led by urban and rural capitalists, overthrew Absolutism, established capitalist rule and eliminated the last vestiges of feudalism, completing the transition to capitalism.

The US Marxist economist Paul Sweezy's[50] review of Dobb's book in *Science & Society* initiated the first debate on the transition to capitalism among Marxists.[51] Sweezy insisted that feudalism, as a form of non-commercial "natural economy", was highly resistance to change. Instead, the impetus for the transition to capitalism had to come from *external* developments—most importantly the growth of towns and trade after c. 1000 AD. Relying on the work of Henri Pirenne,[52] Sweezy argued that the growth of trade and towns dissolved feudalism—monetarizing rents and undermining serfdom and promoting the growth of markets that destabilized guilds and other restrictions on production and trade. Sweezy[53] argued that the trade-induced collapse of feudalism initiated a period of "pre-capitalist commodity production" which was not governed by capitalist dynamics of specialization, innovation and accumulation. Instead, this distinct phase prepared the way for the emergence of capitalism in the seventeenth and eighteenth centuries. Dobb and the prominent medievalist R.H. Hilton[54] continued to insist that the source of the feudal crisis was *internal* to this mode of production and the liberation of the "petty mode of production" from relations of extra-economic coercion led to the emergence of capitalism. For Dobb, Hilton and most other participants in the debate, the bourgeois revolutions—the English Revolution of Civil War of the seventeenth century and the French Revolution of the eighteenth century—were essential to the removal of "pre-capitalist remnants" in the countryside and the consolidation of capitalism.

In many ways, the "Transition Debate" in *Science & Society* pitted an advocate of Marx's mature account of the origins of capitalism—Dobb—against a defender of his earlier, Smithian influence thinking—Sweezy. However, a close examination of Dobb and Sweezy's arguments reveals greater ambiguity. On the one hand, Sweezy does give explanatory primacy to the growth of trade in the dissolution of feudalism. However, he rejects the notion that the expansion of trade *alone* produced capitalist commodity production. On the other, Dobb and Hilton understood that the crisis of feudalism was rooted in the specificity of feudal social property relations, not in the growth of towns and trade. However, they defend the Smithian claim that once producers are freed from extra-economic coercion, they will become capitalist producers. In other words, capitalism remains present in the interstices of feudalism, awaiting its liberation from non-market constraints. As we see, this does not account for the persistence of "free" peasant production in most of Western Europe through the mid-nineteenth century because it cannot explain how producers become *dependent* on the market for their economic survival and are thus *compelled* to specialize, innovate and accumulate.[55]

Hilton and Dobb's arguments about the bourgeois revolutions also suffer from similar problems. On the one hand, historical research since the 1960s[56] confirms the thoroughly capitalist character of English agriculture before the English Revolution. Put simply there are no "feudal" remnants to be removed by a revolutionary bourgeoisie in England. On the other hand, there is voluminous evidence that the French Revolution was neither led by capitalists nor abolished non-capitalist social property relations.[57] The French "bourgeoisie" was not formed of capitalists but of merchants dependent upon royal monopolies and urban professionals seeking income-producing offices in the Absolutist state. The revolution's land reforms actually consolidated peasant proprietorship in France for well over a century, limiting the size of the domestic market for manufactured goods. Similarly, the abolition of the guilds did not "liberate" artisans to become capitalists but instead opened the way for new, municipal forms of the customary regulation of manufacture.

The Brenner Debate

The publication of Robert Brenner's "Agrarian Class Structure and Economic Development in Pre-Industrial Europe" in *Past & Present* in 1976 fundamentally transformed the discussion of the origins of capitalism.[58] While engaging the main non-Marxian explanations of the transition to capitalism in Europe—the "commercialization model" associated with North and Thomas[59] and the "demographic model" associated with M.M. Postan[60] and Emmanuel Le Roy Ladurie[61]—Brenner's essay also reshaped Marxian discussions for the next 40 years. While differing on the relative importance of the spread of markets or long-term population movements, both models assume that the early modern agrarian economy responded in a basically automatic manner to changes in the supply and demand of land and labor. Not only did these models assume that specifically capitalist dynamics—the necessity of producers to specialize, innovate and accumulate in response to market signals—existed transhistorically, but they were unable to account for the *divergent* paths of development across Europe in the fifteenth century. Brenner pointed out that the spread of towns and trade beginning in the eleventh century and the demographic collapse of the fourteenth century were *cross-European phenomena.* However, these relatively uniform processes produced very different outcomes—the reduction of a formerly free peasantry to serfdom in Eastern Europe, the emergence of a free, subsistence-oriented peasantry in most of continental Western Europe and the emergence of the distinctive relationship between capitalist landlords, capitalist tenant farmers and wage laborers in England alone.

Brenner's alternative explanation began, as did Dobb, with the specificity of feudal social property relations and its specific crisis tendencies. The ability of the lords to use extra-economic coercion to extract rents in labor, kind or cash from the peasantry and the peasantry's ability to reproduce their possession of land outside of market competition ruled out the systematic development of productivity through improved methods and labor-saving techniques. As population rose in the face of relatively stagnant agrarian productivity, the tendency toward the parcellization of landholdings through partible inheritance led to declining yields per acre and labor input and, eventually, to demographic collapse. The *outcome* of the feudal crisis, however, was not pre-determined. Instead the intensified struggle between lords and peasants in different zones of Europe shaped the *divergent results* of the crisis.[62] Across Europe lords and peasants struggled to *reproduce their existing class position*—the lords' access to peasant surpluses and the peasants' effective possession of landed property. The differing conditions faced by lords and peasants in varied parts of Europe produced *a variety of outcomes* of the feudal crisis, with the emergence of capitalist social property relations occurring in England alone, as the *unintended consequence* of the struggle of lords and peasants to reproduce themselves.

In Eastern Europe, where the legally free peasants possessed large plots of land but did not develop strong communal village organization, the lords were able to defeat peasant revolts and establish the "second serfdom". In Western Europe, the stronger peasant villages were able to free themselves from serfdom and monetarize rents. However, the "liberation of the petty mode of production"—the abolition of serfdom—did not lead automatically to capitalism. Instead, the peasants preserved their effective possession of their plots through stable, customary rents and taxes. The Western peasantry engaged in "safety-first" agriculture—marketing only physical surpluses after the consumption needs of household members and villagers were satisfied. The consolidation of Absolutist monarchies, whose main source of revenue was taxes on the peasants, short circuited lordly attempts to consolidate leaseholds and raise rents in response to increased agricultural prices. Only in England were the peasants able to gain their legal freedom, while the lords—in possession of larger *demesne* and backed by a more centralized state—were able to impose commercial, *capitalist* leases on their tenant farmers. Thus, the breakthrough to specifically capitalist social property relations—in which capitalist tenant farmers were *compelled* to specialize, innovate and accumulate in order to pay rising rents—was the *unintended consequence* of the feudal crisis.

The ensuing debate on Brenner's essay involved a variety of prominent medieval and early modern European historians, some Marxists but most not. While most criticisms focused on particular historical details, Brenner faced two major criticisms—one from Le Roy Ladurie,[63] in defense of the demographic model, and another from Guy Bois[64] and Rodney Hilton,[65] in defense of a canonical version of historical materialism. Despite their differences, both charged Brenner with conflating "political" and "economic" factors in his analysis. On the one hand, Le Roy Ladurie accused Brenner of conflating "surplus extracting" classes and "ruling classes" in pre-industrial Europe as if they were one in the same. While acknowledging that the demographic collapse produced a different result in Eastern Europe, Le Roy Ladurie continued to insist that objective-economic demographic trends produced uniform results across Western Europe, including England. As Brenner[66] pointed out, this left him incapable of explaining how England alone broke out of the Malthusian population cycle—supporting a growing population with an increasingly productive agriculture based on capitalist social property relations. Only the historic divergence in social property relations, between capitalist and peasant (independent household) production, could explain the difference.

On the other hand, Bois and Hilton accused Brenner of giving excessive weight to political factors—the class struggle—in analyzing the feudal crisis and its outcome across early modern Europe. It was Bois who first leveled the charge that Brenner's was "political Marxist". Specifically he argued that Brenner underestimated what Marx, in the 1859 *Preface* to *A Contribution to the Critique of Political Economy*, called the "contradiction between the forces and relations of production" under feudalism that manifested itself in a "falling rate of seigneurial revenue". Brenner pointed out[67] that Bois's was correct that rents and taxes were declining in Northern France in the thirteenth century. However, in the same period seigneurial incomes *rose* in England. Brenner argued that the relative organization and strength of lords and peasants in England and France—English lords possessed larger *demesnes* in relation to lands regulated by village communities than their French counterparts—explained the divergent trends in seigneurial revenues in the thirteenth century.

As Ellen Wood pointed out, "the criticisms levelled by Bois and Le Roy Ladurie were quite substantially beside the point, and both … took for granted a separation between the 'political' and the 'economic' that is specific to capitalism".[68] Under feudalism and other non-capitalist forms of social labor, surplus was extracted from the peasantry through *extra-economic* means—via political, juridical and military power. In these societies, there is no separation between the non-producers' *personal* political power and their extraction of surplus production, and this is why Brenner coined the phrase "politically-constituted property" in reference to non-capitalist modes of production. Thus, the relationship of class forces—the balance of power *between* classes and the level of solidarity *within* classes—plays a greater role in shaping the form of feudal, compared with capitalist crisis. By contrast, capitalism alone makes both producers and non-producers dependent upon successful market competition for their economic survival. Capitalism's unique laws of motion/rules of reproduction—the law of value which compels producers to economize labor time through productive specialization, labor-saving technical innovation and the accumulation of surplus value—operate through the mechanism of price competition. Put simply, capitalism is reproduced through the "dull compulsion of the market place" rather than through varied forms of extra-economic coercion. Only under capitalism do we see a separation of the "political" and the "economic"—the capitalists' state constitutes a *public sphere* of "impersonal power"[69] while exploitation is *privatized* in individual units of production (a point on which we come back later). The unique dynamism of capitalism—the constant development of the productive forces—and its crisis tendencies—falling profits as a result of the increasing mechanization of production—operate much more *independently* of the desires and goals of either individual capitalists or the capitalist state.[70]

"World Systems Theory" and the Critique of "Neo-Smithian" Marxism

At the same time Brenner was intervening in the wider debate among historians over the different trajectories of economic development in early modern Europe, he engaged a new work that had rekindled interest in the transition to capitalism among Marxists—Immanuel Wallerstein's *The Modern World System*.[71] Wallerstein's research on the political and economic evolution of post-independence Africa had led him to question much of the received wisdom of conventional social science on economic development and social change. Specifically, he came to see the limits of "modernization theory"[72] which posited a universal sequence of economic stages that each society, defined by the nation-state, would traverse over time. Instead, Wallerstein concluded that the tremendous social and economic inequalities between societies were not the product of their being at different "stages" of development but the products of the workings of a single, capitalist world economy. Wallerstein embraced the work of the

Marxian dependency theorist, Andre Gunder Frank,[73] who argued that "economic development and underdevelopment are the opposite face of the same coin. Both are the necessary result and contemporary manifestations of internal contradictions in the world capitalist system".

In *The Modern World System*, Wallerstein synthesized Sweezy's account of the transition to capitalism with Gunder Frank's analysis of the unity of development and underdevelopment in the capitalist world economy. At the center of Wallerstein's historical analysis is the distinction between *world empires* and *world economies.* While world empires like China often began at a much higher level of agrarian labor productivity, their single polity often appropriated the lion's share of surplus product and blocked the spread of markets. World economies like Europe, with their multiple states, left surpluses in the hands of local rulers who could reinvest them in productive activities and allowed the growth of a trade-based division of labor after 1000 AD. As had Sweezy, Wallerstein argued that the expansion of markets was the main solvent of feudalism and the development of capitalism. Following Gunder Frank, he argued that all of the varied forms of "labor control"—wage labor in the Northwestern European "core", sharecropping and serfdom in the European 'semi-periphery' and slavery and peonage in the New World "periphery"—were regional market responses to the relative supplies of land and labor. All of these forms were *capitalist* from birth, part of a world economy in which surpluses were transferred from the periphery and semi-periphery to the core. This process of surplus transfer, through mechanisms of "unequal exchange",[74] guaranteed the economic development of the core through the underdevelopment of the periphery and semi-periphery.

Brenner's essay, "The Origins of Capitalist Development: A Critique of Neo-Smithian Marxism",[75] located the roots of Sweezy, Gunder Frank and Wallerstein's arguments in the work of Adam Smith.[76] As mentioned earlier, for Smith, humans had a natural tendency to "truck, barter and trade". Historically, these tendencies produced the growth of the division of labor and greater trade. In the absence of "obstacles" (political and customary restrictions on trade) to the deepening of the division of labor, producers would take advantage of the *opportunities* presented by the market to specialize output, technically innovate and accumulate. Brenner, following Marx, demonstrated that producers could be compelled to respond to market signals in this way if certain social property relations existed. These property relations allow direct producers to move from one branch of production to another, let capitalists expel labor from production and compels them to introduce more efficient tools and machinery to lower costs through specialization, innovation and accumulation so that they won't face the loss of their means of production through market competition. Put simply, neo-Smithians like Sweezy, Gunder Frank and Wallerstein *assume* what needs to be *explained*—the existence of capitalist social property relations and their distinctive "rules of reproduction"/laws of motion.

In painstaking historical detail, Brenner demonstrates that different social property relations in different regions of the emerging world market of the "long sixteenth century" (1450–1640) were not regional responses to the relative supply of land and labor but the products of divergent class conflicts in various parts of Europe and the Americas. Neither the "underdevelopment" of the semi-periphery and periphery nor the "development" of the core was the product of surplus transfers through unequal exchange. Instead, it was the logic of their specific social property relations that shaped their pattern of development—with non-capitalist forms like sharecropping, peasant production, serfdom and slavery *structurally* ruling out the continuous development of the productivity of labor through technical innovation and the specifically capitalist agriculture in England *uniquely requiring* the continuous development of the productive forces.

Later Debates

Since Brenner's breakthrough contributions in the mid-1970s, his thesis on the centrality of the transformation of social property relations to the origins of capitalism has been challenged both by professional historians and by more "orthodox" Marxists. The professional historians have, for the most part, concentrated their criticisms on Brenner's account of the origins of capitalism in England in the fifteenth and sixteenth centuries. Two distinct currents have emerged among these historians. John Hatcher and Mark Bailey[77] and S.P. Rigby[78] have accused Brenner of a form of "class" reductionism that essentially ignores the role of demographic factors and the spread of markets in the dissolution of English feudalism and the emergence of capitalist agriculture. They defend a *causal pluralism* that gives equal weight to population collapse, the growth of commerce and changes in class relations. As Spencer Dimmock,[79] a contributor to this volume, points out, these arguments both misinterpret Brenner and face the same problems as the earlier demographic and commercialization models. On the one hand, Brenner did not dismiss or ignore demographic and commercial factors. Brenner acknowledged both the growth of markets since the eleventh century and the demographic collapse of the fourteenth century. However, he argued that different social property relations ultimately determined their impact in varied regions of Europe. Their failure to give *causal primacy* to social property relations leads them to be unable, as did Le Roy Ladurie as well as North and Thomas, to explain how *uniform* population and trade developments led to *divergent* outcomes in England, Western and Eastern Europe.

The second trend among historians critical of Brenner has been a new "Smithian" historiography that gives explanatory primary to the growth of markets in the origins of capitalist agriculture in England. Claiming that Brenner's analysis lacks a "prime mover" in explaining the emergence of agrarian capitalism, S.R. Epstein[80] argued that the removal of feudal political constraints on trade and the resultant centralization of political authority led to an unprecedented level of market integration in England. Epstein, along with J.R. French and R.W. Hoyle,[81] argued that the newly liberated peasantry seized the new opportunities presented by the growth of markets to specialize, innovate and accumulate. Like Epstein, French and Hoyle—and Dobb and Hilton before them—Jane Whittle also argued that the abolition of serfdom freed the peasantry to take advantage of new market opportunities and eventually "merge into capitalism". In Whittle's account, the peasantry "expropriated themselves" without any interference by landlords.[82] In other words, peasants *voluntarily* opted to specialize output, innovate technologically and accumulate land and tools, rather than being compelled to do so by increasingly insecure leases imposed by the landlords.

The new Smithian historians' claims reproduce many of the same problems of earlier versions of the "commercialization" model and, in the case of Whittle, are based on very weak historical evidence. As Wood points out,[83] all variants of the claim that capitalism emerges from the spread of markets fundamentally view the market as a realm of *opportunity* rather than *coercion*. This notion fundamentally ignores the *dangers* that come when producers specialize output in order to take advantage of market "opportunities". Put simply, rural producers who forgo the production of their own subsistence put themselves at the *risk of starvation* in the case of bad harvests, falling prices and the like. Except for a minority of wealthy peasants, rural households opt whenever possible, for safety-first agriculture—the marketing of physical surpluses after the subsistence needs of household members and neighbors are met—not out of cultural conservatism or the absence of markets but out of material *self-interest*. Whittle's historical claims about the predominant role of enterprising yeoman farmers consolidating landholdings are also open to challenge. It is not only based on an extremely small sample of manorial records from Eastern England, but her data actually contradict her claim. A careful examination shows that the lesser landlords of the region—the "gentry"—were the main forces evicting small peasants and consolidating landholdings that they then rented through commercial leases.[84] The minority of wealthy English peasants—the "yeomanry"—that took up commercial leases were coopted by a ruling class actively engaged in the capitalist restructuring of the countryside.

The main Marxian criticisms of Brenner have come from those, following Bois, who defend the "canonical" version of historical materialism outlined in the 1859 preface to *A Contribution to the Critique of Political Economy*.[85] Led by Chris Harman,[86] and joined after the mid-1990s by Alex Callinicos, the "productive forces" Marxists reiterate Bois's claims that Brenner's account of the origins of capitalism places too great an emphasis on "subjective" and "political" factors like class struggle, while giving insufficient weight to "objective" and "economic" factors, in particular the "contradictions" between productive forces (labor processes) and productive relations (class relations). From this perspective, history is driven by the development of the productive forces—a transhistorical tendency for humans to improve the productivity of labor through the introduction of new tools and methods. Eventually, these new productive forces run up against limits posed by the existing productive relations, leading to crises and the emergence, through a process of class conflict, of new class relations that are compatible with the new forms of the labor process.

Harman's original account[87] begins with the consolidation of feudalism around 1000 AD, which brought with it a sharp increase in agricultural productivity—both in terms of yield per acre and in terms of per labor input—as a result of the introduction of new plows and crop rotation systems. This growth of rural productivity allowed for the revival of towns, as the centers of both handicraft production and lordly consumption, and the spread of trade across Europe. In much the same way as Pirenne, Sweezy and Wallerstein, Harman argues that the growth of trade acted as a solvent of feudal social relations. However, Harman avoids Pirenne and Wallerstein's simplistic claim that the growth of trade was the equivalent of the emergence of capitalism. Instead, Harman opts for a version of Sweezy's argument that the dissolution of feudalism via commerce produced a "transitional society"—"pre-capitalist commodity production".

It was the outcome of class struggles in both the towns and the countryside, culminating in "bourgeois revolutions" led by urban merchants and manufacturers and capitalist farmers that overthrew Absolutism, abolished the remnants of feudalism and cleared the way for capitalist production. While Harman's later accounts[88] attempt to nuance his arguments, the essentials remain—the autonomous growth of the productive forces leads to the spread of markets, dissolving feudal social relations and creating the conditions for the emergence of capitalism.

As Brenner points out in a debate with Harman,[89] this thesis suffers from a number of major conceptual and empirical problems. The model assumes that feudal social property relations were amenable to a fairly continuous introduction and diffusion of new tools and methods slowed, at best, by "resistance in terms of cultural traditions". However, Harman never demonstrates how either lords or peasants were compelled or capable of continually adopting new techniques. Instead, the lords' inability to organize the peasants' labor process and the peasants' non-market access to land combined with the lords' extraction of most of the surplus product meant that neither lords nor peasants were either obliged or able to continually introduce new methods.[90] Nor can Harman and other "productive forces" Marxists identify the mechanism that guarantees that the new social relations of production that the new productive forces eventually create will be compatible with the continued development of labor productivity.[91] As Brenner argued, Harman's argument makes "it difficult to understand why human history on a global scale has not been to a much greater extent a narrative of progress and, in particular, why the onset of capitalist development did not take place much earlier and occur more broadly".[92] Harman and others can only overcome these problems by reintroducing a variant of the "commercialization model"—with all of its historical and theoretical problems.

More recently, a new Marxian critique of the "political Marxist" account of the origins of capitalism has emerged. In order to overcome what they view as Brenner and Wood's overly "internalist" account of the origins of capitalism (and the overly "externalist" account of Wallerstein), Alex Anievas and Kerem Nisancioglu in *How The West Came to Rule: The Geopolitical Origins of Capitalism*[93] utilize the notion of "uneven and combined development". Originally formulated in his magisterial *History of the Russian Revolution*,[94] Trotsky argued that the establishment of capitalism in Western Europe, Japan and the United States in the mid-nineteenth century profoundly altered the conditions of reproduction of the feudal-Absolutist autocracy in Russia. Faced with political-military competition from these more advanced societies ("uneven development"), Tsarist Russia attempted to adapt the most advanced social relations and labor processes from the industrial capitalist West while preserving "archaic", non-capitalist forms in agriculture ("combined development"). According to Trotsky, the breakthrough to capitalism in the West subjected Tsarist Russia to the "whip of external necessity". However, because Russia enjoyed the "privilege of backwardness", it was able to "jump over" the varied phases of capitalist development (handicrafts and manufacturing) and establish modern capitalist industry in the midst of a sea of peasant producers.

For Anievas and Nisancioglu, uneven and combined development is not *specific* to capitalism but a *general law of history* that allows them to introduce a greater degree of *contingency* into Marxian accounts of history, while making these accounts *global.* Anievas and Nisancioglu argue that uneven and combined, as manifested through *inter-societal* relations, is central to accounting for the emergence of capitalism in England and parts of Western Europe in the sixteenth and seventeenth centuries. *How The West Came to Rule* provides a sweeping history of the varied impacts of inter-societal interactions that created the conditions for capitalism. In this account, it was the expansion of the Mongol trading empire in the thirteenth century leading to the European demographic collapse, the Ottoman tributary empire's wars in Southern and Eastern Europe allowing the relatively isolated English aristocracy to demilitarize, the European colonization of the Americas and the establishment of plantation slavery, the Dutch colonization of Southeast Asia and the British colonization of India that are the crucial moments in the emergence and consolidation of the capitalist mode of production.

While claiming to transcend the limits of existing accounts, including that of Brenner and Wood, *How the West Came to Rule* is deeply flawed, both conceptually and historically.[95] First, the "law of uneven and combined development" is *specific* to capitalism. While *uneven development* characterizes all of human history, the process of more "backward" groups appropriating productive methods from more "advanced" groups did not lead to "combination"—the introduction of the capital-wage labor relation and the *systematic* development of labor productivity through labor-saving devices—before the advent of industrial capitalist production.[96] Attempts to use uneven and combined development to explain the *origins* of capitalism reproduce the errors of the "commercialization model"—*assuming* the existence of capitalist rules of reproduction to *explain* the emergence of capitalist social property relations. The result is a *causal indeterminacy* where all factors—from the rules of reproduction and crisis tendencies of feudalism, to the outcome of peasant-lord struggle in different regions of fourteenth-century Europe, to the spread of markets, and various forms of inter-societal interaction—are of equal importance in explaining the origins of capitalism. However, without a clear ordering of determinations—the heart of materialist social theory—we are left with mere historical *description*, not *analysis* or *explanation*. *How the West Came to Rule* is also filled with a variety of problematic historical claims that, again, reproduce many of the questionable assertions of both the demographic and the commercialization models.

Political Marxism and the Renewal of Historical Capitalism

What are, then, the implications of Brenner's defense and deepening of Marx's analysis of the origins of capitalism to our understanding of the basic tenets of historical materialism?

Ellen Meiksins Wood has made a major contribution to renewing historical materialism from a "political Marxist" perspective.[97] Since there are no transhistorical laws of development, each mode of production has a singular logic that stems not from an abstract economic logic but from a given configuration of social power. At the most fundamental level, historical materialism explores social, political and cultural life by analyzing the specific ways in which human beings establish social relations among themselves and with nature in order to produce their material conditions of existence. In other words, we begin with the ways in which humans establish social relations of reproduction with nature and then try to understand how the distinct character of these specific social relations structures historical processes and shape other sets of social, political and cultural relations. As Wood explains, a basic precept of Marx's historical materialism is that "the forms of [social] interaction [with nature] produced by human beings, themselves become material forces, no less than are natural forces".[98]

For *class* societies, the analysis moves to the ways in which classes reproduce themselves and how this affects social and political reality. As Marx explains, the "relationships between the rulers and ruled", the "specific form of the state" and of the "entire social structure" are determined by the specific form in which "unpaid surplus-labor is pumped out of direct producers" by an exploiting class. This is a crucial point: class relations are not an epiphenomenon responding to the development of forces of production. On the contrary, it is the way in which class relations of exploitation are configured that orients the development (or non-development) of productive forces within a given mode of production. Put another way, the concept of a mode of production does not refer to the technical or even the social organization of the immediate process of production. Modes of production are always simultaneously *modes of exploitation*. The distinct "laws of motion" attached to a mode of production derive from distinct social property relations, which Brenner defines as "the relations among direct producers, relations among exploiters, and relations between exploiters and direct producers that, taken together, make possible/specify the regular access of individuals and families to the means of production (land, labour, tools) and/or the social product per se".[99] In other words, when speaking of a mode of production or a set of social property relations, we refer to a multilayered and complex configuration of social power that orients how classes reproduce themselves while also allowing a class to appropriate a surplus at the expense of another (or several others). This, it should be stressed, is by no mean a reduction of Marx's concept of a mode of production to relations of exploitation, leaving out a whole series of social spheres, as some critiques of PM have argued.[100] The specific type of surplus appropriation that forms the kernel of a given mode of production is made possible by, and exists through, a dense configuration of economic, political, legal, cultural, and ideological relations and institutions. As Wood has explained, many institutions and relations that have been confined to a "superstructure" by "orthodox" Marxists are in fact directly involved in the form of class exploitation that defines the material "base" of social life.[101]

Brenner's concept of social property relations always involves *horizontal* relationships of competition and collaboration *within* classes as well as vertical conflicts *between* classes. Both these horizontal and vertical class relations are structured by the "rules of reproduction" established by distinct social property relations. Human beings do make their own history, but they do so in a material context that imposes limits to their social action that can only be transcended by exiting an existing mode of production. In non-capitalist modes of production, class exploitation took an extra-economic form, and this implied distinct rules of reproduction. Under feudalism, it was the superior legal status of exploiting European landlords that provided them *personal* political power and access to the state's means of coercion that they wielded to appropriate a surplus from direct producers. In the context of "parcellized sovereignty" that characterized European feudalism, landlords were compelled to compete with one another (horizontal class relation) to extract labor surpluses produced by peasants (vertical class relations) through the accumulation of means of coercion and of land. While the balance of power between classes played a crucial role in shaping the evolution of non-capitalist class societies and polities, members of the feudal ruling classes faced "rules of reproduction" that constrained them to systematically build military states, thus engaging in a process of "geopolitical accumulation".[102] As Brenner has it, "the drive to *political accumulation*, to *state-building*, is the *precapitalist analogue* to the drive to *accumulate capital*".[103]

Under capitalism, by contrast, exploitation takes place via the "dull compulsion of the market place" rather than through different types of extra-economic coercion. This implies a separation of the moments of appropriation and of coercion—appropriation takes place in the privatized sphere of production by individual capitalists subject to market competition, while coercion takes place in a public sphere where the state safeguards private property and maintains social peace. This tendency toward a separation of economic and political spheres is unique to capitalism.[104] In Karl Polanyi's terms,[105] economic relations are no longer socially embedded under capitalism—they cease to be subsumed under social, political or cultural regulations and are now organized through the operation of competitive markets and the logic of profit maximization and capital accumulation. Both direct producers and the exploiting class must successfully compete on the market in order to reproduce themselves. This market dependence leads to "rules of reproduction" that constrains capitalists to systematically cut costs and to maximize profits by investing in productivity-enhancing technologies.

The state, of course, must intervene to regulate the economy in different ways. However, these interventions depoliticize crucial dimensions of social life by assigning them to the economic sphere. Meanwhile, because surplus appropriation takes place "economically", the state can now become public. In the absence of popular struggles, the capitalist state of liberal democratic regimes appears to be an impersonal and autonomous entity that represents formally equal citizens. Nevertheless, this formally autonomous state continues to depend on sustained capital accumulation in order to access tax resources and to maintain its legitimacy. Consequently, the apparently autonomous state of "all citizens" is in practice compelled by accumulation imperatives to act as the "executive committee" of the capitalist class.

Description of the Chapters in the Book

Political Marxists have been criticized for relying on a concept of capitalism that is so abstract, that it can never explain concrete reality.[106] Yet, it seems to us that the identification of the basic characteristics and logic of the system are crucial in order to study the processes that led to its emergence in different parts of the world. If we don't know what capitalism is, how will we know what we should be looking for when studying its origins? Without a clear conception of what it is, we run the risk of seeing capitalism (or embryonic forms of "proto-capitalism") everywhere and at all times. We insist that capitalism as a historically specific social system—as opposed to a universal phenomenon anchored in human nature that manifests itself in a more or less repressed form—really does exist.

Our conception of capitalism has not simply been derived from Marx's theoretical insights, but also from meticulous empirical observations. It has now been used for new historical inquiries. Political or *Capital*-centric Marxism provides tools for the study of historical processes—tools that can be used to observe how and when capitalism is actually *happening* in concrete historical processes taking place in distinct countries or regions. Our understanding of capitalism provides important clues to do this. For instance, since we know that capitalism is not the culmination point of an abstract and transhistorical logic, we know that we will be studying deep and broad *social* transformations—not simply the emergence of a narrowly conceived "economy". We know that we won't simply be searching for a quantitative extension of trade but for a qualitative conversion of class relations and of the legal and political institutions that make possible surplus appropriation. Since we assume that the emergence of capitalism is not a natural phenomenon but a radical transformation of the configuration of social power, we can expect that the state will be playing a key role in its formation. Unprecedented economic dynamism and sustained growth are also to be expected.

We believe Anwar Shaikh's assertion that "capitalism's sheath mutates constantly, but it's core remains the same"[107] also applies to the origins of the system. After its original apparition in the English countryside, capitalism never emerged in the same way in other regions. Everywhere it did, similar *basic transformations of social property relations* occurred, but the processes that led to these transformations were necessarily historically and geographically specific. The chapters assembled in this book offer examples of the unique ways in which the capitalist system emerged in different parts of the world. We address the issue of the international propagation of capitalism over the last two centuries in the conclusion of the book, in light of the rich chapters that we now briefly summarize to complete this introduction.

In the first chapter, Spencer Dimmock comes back on the original surfacing of capitalist social property relations in the English countryside. He explains how waves of evictions of peasants and the generation of large-leased, competitive, farms out of a previously communal, customary agriculture first took place in England in and from the fifteenth century. Dimmock responds to studies that have played down the role of violence and political and class conflict in the passage to agrarian capitalism and placed much greater emphasis on market-centered forms of causation. The chapter focuses on the evidence for the violent eviction of peasants from their homes and livelihoods and on the agents of that violence. Emphasis is placed on the changing political context of the fifteenth and sixteenth centuries—that is, on the changing balance in the structure of power in England that enabled these changes to take place.

Building Dimmock's chapter, Michael Zmolek explores how the emergence of agrarian capitalism created a general condition of market dependence as well as new market imperatives which would subsequently transform English manufacturing, giving rise to a capitalist industry in the form of the first Industrial Revolution. Zmolek argues that whereas the emergence of agrarian capitalism required, primarily, the subsumption of land to capital, the emergence of industrial capitalism required the subsumption of labor to capital. He shows how, once the imperative for "improvement" caught hold of manufacturing, employers began to introduce innovations in labor organization and in machinery. The chapter stresses on how the coercive support of the state, both legislative and military, was crucial for capitalist employers to prevail.

The agrarian and industrial transitions in France are also treated in two distinct chapters. Stephen Miller deals with the agrarian case. Miller challenges historians that assume that capitalism had been latent in France until the towns aroused farmers to specialize in lucrative commodities and make improvements to capitalize on the market opportunities. He argues, in contrast, that conflicts of the feudal period left a configuration of peasant parcels of land and seigneurial classes backed by the monarchy. In this context, peasants labored intensively and deprived themselves to obtain more land while noble and bourgeois landowners exploited peasant labor through seigneurial and sharecropping rents but did not invest in agriculture. The peasant revolution in 1789 and continued labor-intensive husbandry further entrenched farming for use value despite the growth of industry and cities in the 1800s and 1900s. Miller shows how it was technocrats under de Gaulle in the late 1950s that finally transformed this system into capitalism by regulating access to land and pressuring farmers to take out loans, in order to improve husbandry on account of market competition.

Xavier Lafrance's chapter shows that capitalism did not emerge endogenously in France and emerged as a state-led process in response to geopolitical pressures originating from capitalist Britain. Sectors of French elites envisaged emulating the British model already from the mid-century but concrete attempts to do so largely failed. While, as demonstrated by Miller, the 1789 Revolution consolidated small peasant agriculture, it also allowed artisans and industrial workers to make substantial gains and to preserve the customary regulations of their trades. A non-capitalist economy remained in place over the half-century that followed the revolutionary period. The capitalist restructuring of France's industrial sector was finally initiated under the Second Empire and the Third Republic. In order to maintain the country's geopolitical standing, these regimes stimulated industrial development by building a competitive national market, exposing the country to foreign capitalist competition and decisively acting to eliminate customary regulations of labor relations and industrial production.

In one of his early publications, Robert Brenner left a passing claim that Catalonia had experienced an agrarian transition to capitalism in parallel to England, a claim that has been dismissed by Catalan historians and forgotten by his followers. Javier Moreno Zacarés revisits the question of the Catalan transition while teasing out its broader implications for the Transition Debate. In contrast to Brenner's claims, this chapter argues that pre-capitalist social property relations persisted in Catalan agriculture throughout the period of transition. Instead, the locus of the capitalist breakthrough is situated by Moreno Zacarés in the proto-industrial textile sector that thrived in the eighteenth century. The chapter also attempts to show how the Catalan transition highlights the distinct importance of changing subjectivities around production and labor and to show how the capitalist production ought to be socially constructed.

Moving on to the other side of the Atlantic Ocean, Charles Post follows the American road to capitalism. His chapter challenges the notion that North America was capitalist from the beginnings of English colonial settlements in the seventeenth century. While English colonialism in the seventeenth and eighteenth century was fuelled by the dynamics of capitalism, the inability to establish a social monopoly of land led to the establishment of two distinctive non-capitalist forms in colonial North America—independent household ("peasant") production in the North and plantation slavery in the South, bound together with England through the activities of sea-board merchants. Post shows how the unintended consequences of the American Revolution transformed Northern agriculture into petty-capitalist farming through the establishment of a competitive market for land, while preserving and reviving Southern plantation slavery. The chapter ends with an analysis in the ways in which the contradictions between the expanded reproduction of plantation slavery and Northern capitalist agriculture and manufacturing set the stage for the political conflicts that culminated in the US Civil War.

A common critique facing those working within PM is that it is unable to account for the contributions and persistence of racialized, gendered, colonial and otherwise unfree labor relations within capitalist modernity. In her chapter, Jessica Evans argues through a PM approach that race and changing colonial relations were, in fact, central to the spread and reproduction of capitalist social relations, through an examination of the transition to capitalism in Central Canada toward the end of the nineteenth century. Evans shows how the transition was importantly stimulated by the global conditions generated by the expansion of British industrial capitalism which led to the emergence of a global agricultural commodity market. This shift relied on self-governing economies who needed to build their own state institutions, rather than rely on the governing structures of the metropole. Looking to the central tension surrounding the intersection of a need to build state coffers, legitimate centralized administration and monopolize land through indigenous dispossession, Evans shows how the state turned to the coercive and ideological organization of political subjectivities by mobilizing a "national identity" predicated on white supremacy.

Mark Cohen addresses the case of Japan during the Meiji era (1868–1912). He explains that this case has often been held up as a paradigmatic case of capitalist development "from above", in which industrial capitalism did not emerge from a revolution in the production relations of the rural majority. Instead, state elites used fiscal policy to nurture the development of capitalism on top of a fundamentally pre-capitalist agrarian economy. Cohen criticizes these accounts and provides an alternative explanation of the transition to capitalism. He first presents ample evidence of broadly based productive dynamism related to the rise of agrarian capitalism in the Japanese countryside. Cohen then argues, against many of the economic historians who have contributed to uncovering the dynamism of the Meiji-era rural economy, that this process of economic development was not simply a continuation of the commercialization of the preceding centuries. Instead, Cohen stresses that the changes to the legal enforcement of landlords' property rights enacted by the Meiji state in the 1870s, tied to its efforts to reform the land tax, fatally undermined the non-market access to the means of subsistence previously enjoyed by peasant cultivators.

Our next chapter focuses on a first case from the "Global South". Chris Carlson studies the emergence of Brazilian capitalism. His chapter challenges scholars who have long viewed the development of capitalism in Brazil as a product of the colonial division of labor and Brazil's insertion into the world economy, as well as scholars who see it as coming about with the transition from slavery to wage labor and the proletarianization of the peasantry that occurred several centuries later. Carlson argues that there are in fact significant regional differences with how and when the transition to capitalism occurred in Brazil and that these differences are key to explaining the vast divergence between the North and the South. In parts of the South, especially the Southeast, the transition played out somewhat like it did in the Northern United States, with an expanding frontier of family farms in which access to land came to be mediated by market mechanisms. In the Northeast, on the other hand, land appropriation was, and continues to be, dominated by wealthy and powerful elites that were not subject to the same market pressures as their counterparts in the Southeast.

Eren Duzgun takes issue with the common view that the Ottoman Empire and Turkey transitioned to capitalism during the late nineteenth and early twentieth centuries. He argues that there was no transition to capitalism in Turkey until the 1950s and that the late Ottoman Empire (1839–1918) and early Turkish Republic (1923–1945) actually followed a non-capitalist (and non-socialist) path to modernity. Furthermore, Duzgun explains that while the process of capitalist development began in the 1950s, the newly emerging agrarian/industrial classes and institutions remained either unwilling or unable to expand and deepen capitalist social relations. The chapter demonstrates that the Islamic "National View movement" (NVM), albeit unsuccessful to control the state from the 1970s to the 1990s, provided the blueprint for a novel capitalist modernity, which was taken up by Erdogan's Justice and Development Party in the new millennium.

In the last case study of this volume, Chris Isett focuses on Taiwan. Isett contends that, taken as a whole, the scholarship on East Asian developmental success underestimates the challenges that firms are facing when entering established markets. Moreover, it fails to understand that even before policy can affect development, the state must free itself of the control of the traditional ruling elites, whose economic interests run counter to the requirements of modern economic growth and the instantiation of which is the cause of underdevelopment in the first instance. Offering an alternative account of Taiwan's postwar performance, Isett explains that its success was only possible because of highly peculiar circumstances arising from the separation of one ruling elite from its base on the mainland and its willingness, on exile in Taiwan, to eradicate the existing landlord and merchant classes nurtured under Japanese colonialism. With no vested interest in preserving the domestic order, the leadership of the state in exile could then impose the social conditions necessary for capitalism.

Our last chapter addresses the gendered dimensions of the transitions to capitalism. Doing so, Nicole Leach offers both a political Marxist critique of Federici and a feminist critique of Brenner. Leach explains that the pre-existence and continuation of an organized system of gender oppression throughout the transitions from pre-capitalist modes of production to capitalism have been the topic of heated debates across socialist and radical feminist definitions of patriarchy and its relation to capitalism. In Caliban and the Witch, Federici makes a significant intervention into these debates by revisiting the transition from a specifically feminist lens and investigating the structural components that allow and facilitate the continuation of exploitative gender relations. Yet, Leach stresses that Federici's investigation relies on world systems theories' overly expansive geographic and temporal reading of the transition and, thus, does not spell out a historically specific account of the transition. Leach works with the best aspects of Federici's feminist intervention into the transition while recognizing and critically addressing the theoretical shortfalls that leave unfinished the project of accounting for both the emergence of capitalist social property relations and the continuation of women's oppression. She argues that critical engagement with PM provides an opportunity to build from the methodological work of social reproduction feminists, such as Federici, and to properly reorient feminist approaches to the question of capitalism's origins.

Notes

1. Among many recent contributions, see, for instance, Leo Panitch and Sam Gindin, *The Making of Global Capitalism: The Political Economy of American Empire* (London: Verso, 2012); Frederic L. Pryor, *Capitalism reassessed* (Cambridge: Cambridge University Press, 2010); Anwar Shaikh, *Capitalism: Competition, Conflict, Crises* (New York: Oxford University Press, 2016).
2. David Harvey, *The Enigma of Capital, and the Crises of Capitalism* (New York: Oxford University Press, 2011); David McNally, *Global Slump: The Economics and Politics of Crisis and Resistance* (Halifax: Fernwood, 2011); Paul Mason, *Meltdown: The End of the Age of Greed* (New York and London: Verso, 2010); Wolfgang Streeck, *Buying Time. The Delayed Crisis of Democratic Capitalism* (New York and London: Verso, 2014).
3. John Bellamy Foster, Brett Clark and Richard York, *The Ecological Rift: Capitalism's War on the Earth* (New York: Monthly Review Press, 2011); Naomi Klein, *This Changes Everything: Capitalism vs. the Climate* (London: Penguin Books, 2014); Andreas Malm, *Fossil Capital: The Rise of Steam Power and the Roots of Global Warming* (New York and London: Verso, 2016); *The Progress of this Storm: Nature and Society in a Warming World* (New York and London: Verso, 2018); Jason W. Moore, *Capitalism in the Web of Life* (New York and London: Verso, 2015).
4. Thomas Piketty, *Capital in the Twenty-First Century* (Cambridge: Belknap Press, 2014).
5. Joyce Oldham Appleby, *The Relentless Revolution: A History of Capitalism* (New York, W.W. Norton & Company, 2010); Sven Beckert, *Empire of Cotton: A Global History* (New York: Alfred A. Knopf, 2014); Henry Heller, *The Birth of Capitalism: A Twenty-First-Century Perspective* (Halifax: Fernwood, 2011); Jürgen Kocka, *Capitalism: A Short History* (Princeton: Princeton University Press, 2016); Jürgen Kocka and Marcel van der Linden, *Capitalism: The Reemergence of a Historical Concept* (London: Bloomsbury, 2016); Larry Neal and Jeffrey G. Williamson, *The Cambridge History of Capitalism* (Cambridge, Cambridge University Press, 2014).

6. See, for instance, Edward Baptist, *The Half Has Never Been Told: Slavery and the Making of American Capitalism* (New York: Basic Books, 2014); "Toward a Political Economy of Slave Labor: Hands, Whipping-Machines, and Modern Power," in *Slavery's Capitalism: A New History of American Economic Development*, ed. Sven Beckert and Seth Rockman (Philadelphia: University of Pennsylvania Press, 2016); Svan Beckert and Christine Desan, *American Capitalism: New Histories* (New York, Columbia University Press, 2018); Joshua Clark Davis, *From Head Shops to Whole Foods: The Rise and Fall of Activist Entrepreneurs* (New York: Columbia University Press, 2017); Louis Hyman, *Debtor Nation: The History of America Red Ink* (Princeton: Princeton University Press, 2011); Steven H. Jaffe and Jessica Lautin, *Capital of Capital: Money, Banking, and Power in New York City* (New York: Columbia University Press, 2014); Julia C. Ott, *When Wall Street Met Main Street: The Quest for an Investors' Democracy* (Cambridge, Harvard University Press, 2014); Joshua D. Rothman, *Flush Times and Fever Dreams: A Story of Capitalism and Slavery in the Age of Jackson* (Athens: University of Georgia Press, 2012); Calvin Schermerhorn, *The Business of Slavery and the Rise of American Capitalism, 1815–1860* (New Haven: Yale University Press, 2015). For a critique of the "new history of capitalism" and of its analysis of slavery, see Charles Post, "Slavery and the New History of Capitalism," Catalyst 1, no. 1 (2017): 173–192.
7. Ellen Meiksins Wood, *The Origin of Capitalism: A Longer View* (London: Verso Books, 2002), 11–12, 28.
8. Larry Neal, "Introduction," in *The Cambridge History of Capitalism*, ed. Larry Neal and Jeffrey G. Williamson (Cambridge: Cambridge University Press, 2014), 2.
9. Ibid., 6.
10. Kocka, *Capitalism*, viii.
11. Ibid., 23–24.
12. Heller, *The Birth of Capitalism*, 9–11.
13. Ibid., 10.
14. Appleby, *The Relentless Revolution*, 21.
15. Ibid., 12. Brenner and Wood have also often insisted that mature trade networks were a necessity but an insufficient condition for a capitalist transition. See, for instance, Wood, *The Origin of Capitalism*, 175.
16. Appleby, *The Relentless Revolution*, 12.
17. Ibid., 10–11, 21, 26.
18. Presenting capitalism as a "cultural system" and getting her theoretical inspiration from Weber's work, Appleby (*The Relentless Revolution*, 3, 7, 17) approaches the issue by focusing on the evolution of "values, habits, and modes of reasoning". According to her, breakthroughs paving the way to a capitalist society were due to "inventors" and "determined and

disciplined pathbreakers" that showed sufficient will to "get out of the straightjacket of custom" and "to resist the siren call to return to the habitual order of things". Here, Appleby seems to fall back into a narrative focused on the elimination of obstacles.

19. The phrases "political Marxism" and "*Capital*-centric Marxism" are used interchangeably throughout this volume.
20. Adam Smith, *The Wealth of Nations* (New York: Bantham, 2003). For a summary of Smith's account, see Robert Brenner, "Bourgeois Revolution and Transition to Capitalism," in *The First Modern Society: Essays in English History in Honour of Lawrence Stone*, ed. A.L. Beier, David Cannadine and James M. Rosenheim (Cambridge: Cambridge University Press,1989), 280–281; Robert J. Holton, *The Transition from Feudalism to Capitalism* (Houndmills, Macmillan, 1985), 35.
21. Smith, *The Wealth of Nations*, 350.
22. Max Weber, *General Economic History* (New Brunswick: Transaction Books, 1981), 275–278.
23. Max Weber, *The Protestant Ethic and the Spirit of Capitalism* (Los Angeles: Roxbury, 2002).
24. Ira J. Cohen, "Max Weber on Modern Western Capitalism," in *General Economic History*, by Max Weber (New Brunswick: Transaction Books, 1981), XXV–XXVI; Holton, *The Transition*, 126–127.
25. Cohen, "Max Weber," XLI–XLII; Randall Collins, "Weber's Last Theory of Capitalism: a Systematization," *American Sociological Review* 45, no. 6 (1981), 933.
26. Ellen Meiksins Wood, *Democracy against Capitalism: Renewing Historical Materialism* (New York: Cambridge University Press, 1995), 158–163.
27. Collins, "Weber's Last Theory of Capitalism," 930; Wood, *Democracy against Capitalism*, 172–173.
28. Stephen Kalberg, "Introduction," in *The Protestant Ethic and the Spirit of Capitalism*, by Max Weber (Los Angeles: Roxbury, 2002), LXI. See also Wood, *Democracy against Capitalism*, 172–173.
29. Max Weber, "The Separation of the Worker from the Means of Production, the Spread of Officialdom, and Organizational Discipline in the Factory," in *Max Weber: Readings and Commentary on Modernity*, ed. Stephen Kalberg (Malden: Blackwell, 2005), 136; Holton, *The Transition*, 139–140; Wood, *Democracy against Capitalism*, 164–165.
30. Weber, "The Separation of the Worker," 131.
31. For a detailed summary of Marx's first narrative of the emergence of capitalism, see Brenner, "Bourgeois Revolution," 276–278.
32. For discussions of this evolution of Marx's thought, see Brenner, "Bourgeois Revolution", and Wood, *The Origin of Capitalism*, 35–37.
33. Karl Marx, *Grundrisse* (London: Penguin Books, 1993), 506.
34. Karl Marx, *Capital, Volume 3* (London: Penguin Books, 1991), 730–732.

35. Ibid., 444.
36. Ibid., 444–445.
37. Ibid., 449–450.
38. Ibid., 926.
39. Marx, *Grundrisse*, 493; Brenner, "Bourgeois Revolution," 285–288.
40. Marx, *Capital, Volume 3*, 926.
41. Brenner, "Bourgeois Revolution," 288–291.
42. Karl Marx, *Capital, Volume 1* (London: Penguin Books, 1990), 874; emphasis added.
43. Ibid., 932.
44. Ibid., 874–875.
45. Ibid., 908.
46. See Leon Trotsky, "Three Concepts of the Russian Revolution," in *Stalin: An Appraisal of the Man and his Influence*, ed. Charles Malamuth (New York: Harper & Brothers, 1941); and Neil Davidson, *How Revolutionary Were the Bourgeois Revolutions?* (Chicago: Haymarket Books, 2012), Chapters 11–14.
47. M.N. Pokrovsky, *Brief History of Russia, Volume II* (New York: International Publishers, 1933).
48. Maurice Dobb, *Studies in the Development of Capitalism* (New York: International Publishers, 1946), in particular Chapters I–IV.
49. Our assessment of the strengths and weaknesses of Dobb's account of the transition is based on Robert Brenner, "Dobb on the Transition from Feudalism to Capitalism," *Cambridge Journal of Economics* 2 (1978): 121–140 and Wood, *The Origin of Capitalism*, 37–43.
50. Paul Sweezy, "A Critique," in *The Transition from Feudalism to Capitalism*, ed. Rodney Hilton (London: New Left Books, 1976).
51. The entire debate is collected in Rodney Hilton, ed., *The Transition from Feudalism to Capitalism* (London: New Left Books, 1976).
52. Henri Pirenne, *Medieval Cities: Their Origins and the Revival of Trade* (Princeton: Princeton University Press, 1956 [1927]).
53. Paul Sweezy, "A Critique" and "A Rejoinder," in *The Transition from Feudalism to Capitalism*, ed. Rodney Hilton (London: New Left Books, 1976).
54. Rodney Hilton, "Comment," in *The Transition from Feudalism to Capitalism*, ed. Rodney Hilton (London: New Left Books, 1976).
55. A similar conception of household producers as "capitalists in embryo" awaiting their liberation from non-market constraints can be found in Karl Kautsky, *The Agrarian Question* (London: Swan Books, 1988 [1899]), and V.I. Lenin, "The Development of Capitalism in Russia," in *Lenin's Collected Works* (Moscow: Progress Publishers, 1964 [1898]).
56. Lawrence Stone, *The Crisis of the Aristocracy, 1558–1641* (New York: Oxford University Press, 1965).

57. George C. Comninel, *Rethinking the French Revolution: Marxism and the Revisionist Challenge* (London: Verso, 1991), and Xavier Lafrance, "Citizens and Wage-Laborers: Capitalism and the Making of a Working Class in France" (PhD diss., York University, 2013).
58. Robert P. Brenner, "Agrarian Class Structure and Economic Development in Pre-Industrial Europe," in *The Brenner Debate: Agrarian Class Structure and Economic Development in Pre-Industrial Europe*, ed. T.H. Aston and C.H.E. Philpin (New York: Cambridge University Press, 1985). Our assessment of the "Brenner Debate" is shaped by Wood, *The Origin of Capitalism*, 50–61.
59. Douglas North and Robert P. Thomas, *The Rise of the Western World: A New Economic History* (New York: Cambridge University Press, 1973).
60. M.M. Postan, "Medieval Agrarian Society in its Prime: England," in *Cambridge Economic History of Europe from the Decline of the Roman Empire*, Volume 1, *Agrarian Life of the Middle Ages*, ed. M.M. Postan (New York: Cambridge University Press, 1966).
61. Emmanuel Le Roy Ladurie, *The Peasants of Languedoc* (Champaign: University of Illinois Press, 1974).
62. The implications of Brenner's argument for a Marxism that rejects notions of "necessary stages of history" marked by a necessary sequence of modes of production (primitive communism-slavery-feudalism-capitalism-socialism) are drawn out by Daniel Bensaïd, *Marx for Our Times: Adventures and Misadventures of a Critique* (London: Verso, 2002), Part I.
63. Emmanuel Le Roy Ladurie, "A Reply to Robert Brenner," in *The Brenner Debate*, ed. T.H. Aston and C.H.E. Philpin (New York: Cambridge University Press, 1985).
64. Guy Bois, "Against the Neo-Malthussian Orthodoxy," in *The Brenner Debate.*
65. Rodney Hilton, "A Crisis of Feudalism," in *The Brenner Debate.*
66. Robert P. Brenner, "Agrarian Roots of European Capitalism," in *The Brenner Debate*, 246–253.
67. Ibid., 242–253.
68. Wood, *The Origin of Capitalism*, 55.
69. Heidi Gerstenberger, "The Bourgeois State Form Revisited," in *Open Marxism*, Volume I: *Dialectics and History*, ed. Werner Bonefeld et al. (London: Pluto Press, 1992) and *Impersonal Power: History and Theory of the Bourgeois State* (Chicago: Haymarket Books, 2009).
70. For a defense of this notion, see Charles Post, "Capital-Centric Marxism' and the Capitalist State," *Verso Books Blog*, 2015, http://www.versobooks.com/blogs/2345-charles-post-the-separation-of-the-economic-and-the-political-under-capitalism-capital-centric-marxism-and-the-capitalist-state.

71. Immanuel Wallerstein, *The Modern World System:* Volume I: *Capitalist Agriculture and the Origins of the European World-Economy in the Sixteenth Century* (New York: Academic Press, 1974).
72. W.W. Rostow, *Stages of Economic Growth: A Non-Communist Manifesto* (New York, Cambridge University Press, 1960).
73. Andre Gunder Frank, *Capitalism and Underdevelopment in Latin America* (New York: Monthly Review Press, 1967), 9.
74. Arghiri Emmanuel, *Unequal Exchange: A Study of the Imperialism of Trade* (New York: Monthly Review Press, 1972).
75. Robert P. Brenner, "The Origins of Capitalism: A Critique of Neo-Smithian Marxism," *New Left Review* I, no. 104 (1977): 27–92.
76. Adam Smith, *An Inquiry into the Nature and Causes of the Wealth of Nations* (New York: Modern Library, 1937 [1776]), Book I.
77. John Hatcher and Mark Bailey, *Modelling the Middle Ages: The History and Theory of England's Economic Development* (Oxford: Oxford University Press, 2001).
78. S.H. Rigby, *English Society in the Later Middle Ages: Class, Status and Gender* (Basingstoke and London: Macmillan, 1995).
79. Spencer Dimmock, *The Origin of Capitalism in England, 1400–1600* (Leiden: Brill, 2014), 34–48.
80. S.R. Epstein, *Freedom and Growth: The Rise of States and Markets in Europe, 1300–1750* (London and New York: Routledge, 2000).
81. H.R. French and R.W. Hoyle, *The Character of English Rural Society: Earls Colne, 1550–1750* (Manchester and New York: Manchester University Press, 2007).
82. Jane Whittle, *The Development of Agrarian Capitalism: Land and Labor in Norfolk, 1440–1580* (Oxford: Clarendon Press, 2000), 305–313.
83. Wood, *The Origin of* Capitalism, 6–8.
84. Dimmock, *The Origin of Capitalism in England*, 2014, 118–120.
85. For a discussion and critique of the "canonical" version of historical materialism, see Vivek Chibber, "What is Living and What is Dead in the Marxist Theory of History?" *Historical Materialism* 19, no. 2 (2011): 60–91. An important essay by Arthur Prinz ("Background and Ulterior Motive of Marx's Preface of 1859," *Journal of the History of Ideas* 30, (1969): 437–450) raises serious questions about the scientific status of the 1859 preface to *A Contribution to the Critique of Political Economy*—the key text cited by those who argue that Marx believed that the transhistorical development of the productive forces was the driving force of historical development. After carefully reviewing the strictures Prussian and other German state censors placed on the publication of critical and radical materials, Prinz concludes that key passages of the 1859 Preface may have been written to *elude* censorship rather than to elaborate Marx's concept of history.

86. Chris Harman ("From Feudalism to Capitalism," *International Socialism Journal* 2, no. 45 (1989): 35–87; "The Rise of Capitalism," *International Socialism Journal* 2, no. 102 (2004); "The Origins of Capitalism," *International Socialism Journal* 2, no. 111 (2006)) and Alex Callinicos (*Making History: Agency, Structure and Change in Social Theory* (Chicago: Haymarket Books, 2009 [1987])) initially rejected historical arguments based on the "primacy of the productive forces" but embraced it in Alex Callinicos, *Theories and Narratives: Reflections on the Philosophy of History* (Durham: University of North Carolina Press, 1995).
87. Harman, "From Feudalism to Capitalism."
88. Harman, "The Rise of Capitalism" and "The Origins of Capitalism."
89. Robert P. Brenner, "The Origins of Capitalism," *International Socialism Journal* 2, no. 102 (2006).
90. Harman and other "productive forces" Marxists claim that Brenner argues that all forms of social labor before capitalism experienced technological *stagnation*. This is a caricature of Brenner's position. Brenner and other "political Marxists" have consistently argued that the development of the productivity of labor through new tools and methods is *highly episodic* before capitalism and often has a "once and for all" character because of the ability of pre-capitalist dominant and producing classes to reproduce themselves without successful market competition. Only under capitalism do we see the *systematic* development of the forces of production under the "whip" of market competition—the operation of the law of value.
91. Chibber ("What is Living") makes this point.
92. Brenner, "The Origins of Capitalism."
93. Alex Anievas and Kerem Nisancioglu, *How The West Came to Rule: The Geopolitical Origins of Capitalism* (London: Pluto Press, 2015).
94. Leon Trotsky, *The History of the Russian Revolution* (London: Victor Gallancz, 1932), Chapter 1.
95. Our criticisms of Anievas and Nisancioglu are based upon Spencer Dimmock, "The Eastern Origins of Capitalism?" *Historical Materialism Blog*, 2016, http://www.historicalmaterialism.org/blog/eastern-origins-capitalism; Sebastian Rioux, "Mind the (Theoretical) Gap: On the Poverty of International Relations Theorising of Uneven and Combined Development," *Global Society* 29, no. 4 (2015); and Charles Post, "The Use and Misuse of Uneven and Combined Development: A Critique of Aneivas and Niscancioglu, *How The West Came To Rule: The Geopolitical Origins Of Capitalism*," *Historical Materialism* (forthcoming).
96. Sam Ashman ("Capitalism, Uneven and Combined Development and the Transhistoric," *Cambridge Review of International Affairs* 22, no. 1 (2009): 29–46) makes this point in her critique of earlier attempts to universalize the "law of uneven and combined development".

97. Wood, *Democracy against Capitalism.*
98. Ibid., 26.
99. Robert P. Brenner, "Property and Progress: Where Adam Smith Went Wrong," in *Marxist History-Writing for the Twenty-First Century*, ed. Chris Wickham (Oxford: Oxford University Press, 2007), 58.
100. Anievas and Nisancioglu (*How the West Came to Rule*, 24) made this critique.
101. Wood, *Democracy against Capitalism*, 23–28, 49–75.
102. Benno Teschke, *The Myth of 1648: Class, Geopolitics, and the Making of Modern International Relations* (London, Verso Books, 2003).
103. Robert P. Brenner, "The Social Basis of Economic Development," in *Analytical Marxism*, ed. John Roemer (Cambridge: Cambridge University Press, 1986), 31–32.
104. Wood, *Democracy against Capitalism*, Chapter 1.
105. Karl Polanyi, *The Great Transformation* (Boston: 2001, Beacon Press, 2001).
106. See, for instance, Anievas and Nisancioglu, *How the West Came to Rule*, 29–30 and "What's at Stake in the Transition Debate? Rethinking the Origins of Capitalism and the 'Rise of the West'," *Millennium: Journal of international Studies* 42, no. 1 (2013): 78–102.
107. Shaikh, *Capitalism*, 726.

CHAPTER 2

Expropriation and the Political Origins of Agrarian Capitalism in England

Spencer Dimmock

> Who will not be contented with pulling down houses of husbandry, so that he may stuff his bags full of money? Who cares about offending and breaking the laws when he has plenty of money to stop the execution of them.[1]

In feudal societies, the vast majority of the population are peasants engaged in agriculture (husbandry) who possess lands which furnish them with their means of production and subsistence. In capitalist societies, the vast majority of the population are landless wage workers compelled to seek employment from capital-owning entrepreneurs, on whom they are thereby dependent for their income. In order, therefore, to understand the transition from feudalism to capitalism, the fundamental task is to explain how the workers become landless and dependent in this way. The case of England has been central in debates on capitalist origins because it is widely acknowledged that England was the first country to both generate capitalist transformations in agrarian organization and production from the late fifteenth century *and* sustain them through to the first

S. Dimmock (✉)
Swansea University, Swansea, UK

X. Lafrance, C. Post (eds.), *Case Studies in the Origins of Capitalism*, Marx, Engels, and Marxisms,
https://doi.org/10.1007/978-3-319-95657-2_2

modern industrial revolution in the eighteenth century. And, given that England was an economic backwater in terms of comparative levels of commercialization in the late medieval period, the transition to agrarian and then industrial capitalism there appears all the more intriguing.

Looming large in the history of capitalism in England is the role of forced expropriation from the second half of the fifteenth century in rendering the English peasantry landless and reluctant subsequent generations entirely dependent upon waged employment. Forced expropriation was achieved either through direct, violent eviction by lords and their farmers, lawyers and merchants or through intimidation and disruption of the viability of peasant production to the same end. In recent years, this aspect of England's transition has been pushed to the margins of mainstream historical research, and innocuous, painless forms of market-centered causation are usually cited instead. In fact, according to one historian, 'there is no evidence for widespread evictions' in England.[2] While forced expropriation may or may not have accounted for the majority of cases in which peasants found themselves landless, I nevertheless argue for its fundamental role in coloring all aspects of the transformation in England. To that end, I introduce some initial findings of new research on nearly 600 well-known cases of illegal eviction and depopulating enclosure that were uncovered by a royal commission in 1517. In conjunction with this evidence, I foreground the often enraged commentaries of contemporaries (such as that of John Hales in the opening quote of this chapter and below) on the world-historical changes they were witnessing.

Social and political divisions *within* peasantries, aristocracies and state-monarchy executive bodies are as important for historical causation as those fundamentally opposed class interests that exist *between* the main classes.[3] The significance of this horizontal element within the operation of social property relations is not sufficiently recognized, and this has resulted in striking misinterpretations of the political Marxist perspective.[4] So I emphasize here conflicting and unifying relationships *within* the English ruling class and discuss the impact of these relationships on the origins of feudalism and capitalism in England. At the same time, I highlight more generally the distinguishing features of English feudal social property relations (in both origin and development) and their role in the emergence of English capitalism.

The Origin and Development of English Feudal Social Property Relations

It is central to Robert Brenner's thesis that the origin of the dramatic divergence of economic, social and political developments in European polities in the fifteenth and sixteenth centuries can be traced back to the origin and establishment of specific feudal social property relations in these polities in the tenth and eleventh centuries.[5] In contrast to continental polities, the English monarchy and aristocracy emerged in the eleventh century comparatively unified, cohesive and interdependent within a highly politically integrated state, and this distinctiveness has key implications for England's transition to capitalism. Because England was the first to develop sustained capitalist social property relations and related Smithian or modern capitalist economic growth directly out of feudal social property relations during the medieval phase of European history, clarification of the nature of these origins (*circa* 880–1080) and developments through to the feudal crisis in the late thirteenth century and beyond is essential.[6]

After centuries of struggle between and within monarchies, aristocracies and peasantries, feudal social property relations became established by the end of the eleventh century across Europe. What distinguishes these new *feudal* societies that developed from the ninth century across this region from the peasant societies of the post-Roman, early medieval period (*circa* 400–900) is the fragmentation of productive units from large tribute-rendering or rent-paying territories or estates into manors which were held by a consequently much enlarged and militarized class of knights. Autonomous peasants of the early medieval period who owned their own lands were entirely expropriated and became indistinguishable from rent-paying "free" and unfree peasants and slaves who were the vast majority of people in Europe. All were increasingly subjected to much greater controls within manors, and obligations of the unfree to labor for the lord and other dues, fines and taxes in produce or money were introduced or substantially increased. Slaves became peasants with particularly onerous obligations to their lords.[7] The consequences of this transformation in social property relations were a greater intensity and extension of agricultural production and organization, a proliferation of markets and towns, urban and industrial expansion, overseas trade expansion, a rapidly rising population and a multiplication of new rural settlements.

While feudal social property relations in all polities had their variations, there were a number of salient differences between their origin and establishment in England and the continent as a whole. The continent experienced not only the fragmentation of estates but the privatization of the previously extensive public or royal power that had been imposed during the construction of the Carolingian Empire during the eighth century. Aristocrats accumulated territories and developed their own private administrations and judiciaries which therefore excluded royal power. They built castles to augment or at least to protect these territories and peasants from incursions by other aristocrats and bands of warriors. Very often the knights or castellans charged by their aristocratic patrons with holding these castles appropriated them and developed them as their own manorial bases. So the process of fragmentation continued.[8]

In England "great estates" were fragmented into smaller manors as they were on the continent. But crucially, the fate of royal power took the opposite course to the continent. Between the 880s and 950, the armies of the West Saxon (Wessex) kings re-conquered Scandinavian kingdoms in "English" territory that had been formed by invading Viking settlers. During the re-conquest, Carolingian forms of royal administration and institutions such as shires and hundreds were introduced *at the same time as they were declining on the continent*. By 950, England had more or less become a centralized state with national (royal) institutions throughout.[9] As a result, the English monarchy and aristocracy were now comparatively very strong and wealthy in relation to the rest of the population: "England had … moved from being the post-Roman province with the least peasant subjection, in 700, to the land where peasant subjection was the completest and most totalizing in the whole of Europe, by as early as 900 in much of the country, and by the eleventh century at the latest elsewhere".[10] However, the extent of royal authority in England ensured that the aristocracy was comparatively less privileged in relation to the monarch than its continental counterparts. The local powers of the greatest magnates were limited. Their estates lay scattered through the shires as they were accumulated piecemeal through royal grants. Treason laws developed by the Carolingians were interpreted more harshly by English rulers. Aristocratic oaths of allegiance were only allowed to the king, private warfare was outlawed, the only mints were royal mints, the only castles in pre-conquest England were royal castles, and there were no private courts administering high justice.[11]

A crucial outcome of the unification of the English state through the re-conquest of English territory was the development of central assemblies from the tenth century and their interconnection with the provincial and local royal institutions of shire and hundred. Councils summoned by the king met frequently and were truly national councils drawing on a broad sweep of landowners in addition to the greater aristocracy. These "witans" drew men from distant parts of the realm, discussed the realm's business and saw the generation of laws to cover the whole realm. There were no provincial or private rivals to these royal assemblies.[12] In addition, a national taxation system was instituted by Æthelred in the 990s, something not achieved on the continent before 1200.[13]

So above all, it is endogenous developments in the centuries before the Norman Conquest that determined English distinctiveness in the centuries to come. And yet the Conquest did impose significant changes which were also unique to England. Initially, it reinforced the unrivalled power of the English monarchy over its aristocracy. All of the English landed estates were essentially appropriated by the king. He then through his own unrivalled powers of patronage enfeoffed them to his new conquering aristocracy. Thus, due to this tenurial revolution, Norman aristocrats became potentially even less autonomous from the crown than their English predecessors had been. And yet with regard to the *vertical* social property relationship between lords and peasants, the lords' own demesnes (home farms either supplying the household or producing marketable produce) in these estates were expanded further at the expense of the free peasantry, thus augmenting the relatively large demesnes that English lords possessed throughout the medieval period. Dramatic reductions in the numbers of free peasants occurred as a result of the Conquest and further labor customs were introduced. Apart from many regions in the North which saw the values of estates reduced by 1086, because of the severe loss of population due to widespread violent retribution against resistance there, the evidence records very large hikes in manorial rents in addition to extortionate royal taxation.[14]

There were important continuities and developments in the Anglo-Saxon and Norman institutions and social and economic organization in the centuries to come. Central assemblies across Europe which had an advisory function for the monarch developed into forms of representative assemblies between the eleventh century and 1300. But none of them compare in their organization and ability to restrain royal power with the English parliament which was formed by the latter date.[15] The subjection of everyone in England to nonexempted taxation from the early thirteenth century was reciprocated with an even greater desire than hitherto for "politicized debate" on how the money was to be spent. Maddicott argues that, paradoxically, it was the strength of the English monarchy which generated this institutionalized restraint on its powers. It was the relatively unprivileged nature of the English aristocracy by comparison with its continental counterparts that unified a broad opposition to arbitrary kingship.[16] By the 1270s, knights were being elected as members of parliament through the shire system by local freemen of status, a representative body therefore without comparison elsewhere in Europe.[17] The institution was also a useful tool through which the crown could rule, and it was another example of the interdependence and cohesion between the broad English ruling elite and the monarchy.

The relatively harsh controls on the English peasantry also continued and were intensified at the same time as peasants on the continent were winning charters of liberty from their lords. Henry II's legal reforms in the decades around 1200 enforced a sharp distinction between free and unfree peasants by allowing only freemen access to the royal courts and common law. Some historians from different perspectives and in different ways have sought to equate these reforms with peasant liberation.[18] In fact, they represent one of the key periods for the *depression* of the status of the English peasantry. They seem to have codified the outcomes of class conflicts between lords and peasants in previous decades.[19]

Across Europe, developments from the establishment of feudal social property relations led to feudal crisis. Predatory extraction of peasant surpluses by monarchies and lords for the purpose of warfare and display, and peasant overpopulation and underemployment, led to a 60 percent reduction in labor productivity in England by 1300.[20] The cumulative reduction in peasant discretionary expenditure led to stagnant local urban economies and a reduction in lordship income from their estates. Widespread famine c. 1315–22, the Black Death in 1348–49 and subsequent plagues in the 1360s were exacerbated and bit deeply due to generations of malnourishment. By the late fourteenth century, the English population was reduced by 50 percent and showed no signs of rising from that nadir for at least a century.

The Origin of English Capitalist Social Property Relations

The social and political power wielded by English lords over the peasantry by virtue of their comparative cohesion, interdependency with the monarchy and the political integration of the state did not protect their incomes from effects of the dramatic loss of population in the wake of these disasters.

Initially, the lords aimed to maintain rents and serfdom controls at pre-Black Death levels at further expense to the peasantry. The crown supported them and its own landowning interests by capping wages by statute. Many peasants moved to manors where the least harsh conditions prevailed as the sharp decline in their numbers gave them increased bargaining power and forced lords to compete for tenants. Peasants also tried to mitigate the depredations of arbitrary private lordship by seeking legal channels in order to prove that their lands were originally held from the crown. Finally, following an unprecedented series of royal poll taxes between 1377 and 1381, they resorted to one of the most famous national rebellions in medieval Europe in which they aimed to remove lordship altogether. This ambition was not fulfilled, but the threat of rebellion and ongoing resistance ensured that by the 1440s the dues and controls which characterized serfdom had largely disappeared across England.

For English lords, the loss of these controls and the ability to arbitrarily increase income through them was a fundamental blow. However, English lords retained possession of very large demesnes compared to those known on the continent at between 25 and 30 percent of the best manorial land. They also clearly retained the social and political power to avoid the stagnation of their rental income by preventing the previously unfree or customary lands of the peasants becoming the equivalent of hereditary freeholds. This was something the lords suffered in parts of France, forcing them to seek their reproduction through venal office in the developing monarch-dominated state. Because of the massive reduction in demand for surplus produce from the demesnes, the reduced availability and therefore hike in the price of labor to work them and also the liability of these demesnes to royal taxation, the lords were compelled to offer them as leaseholds to the highest bidders (mostly between 1380 and 1420) and to turn hereditary villein or unfree tenures into "copyholds". However, although the latter no longer carried the taint of servility, the new copyholds still favored the lords in the important respect that they were temporary tenancies for either a set period of time or for a succession of lives, usually three, at which point the holding would be subject to the highest bidder, similar to the leaseholds. Rents and entry fines for these tenures rose from the late fifteenth century and were increasingly beyond the reach of ordinary peasants during the sixteenth century.

The ability of lords to make these changes in their ongoing struggle for the peasants' surplus proved to be significant for the transformation to capitalist social property relations in England. The vast majority of people who took up the demesne leases were from the upper strata of the peasantry. This was an unprecedented development. Leading lords had previously leased their demesnes in the twelfth century when conditions were similarly not conducive to direct management, but during that earlier phase, the lessees were crucially lesser lords, not peasants. The new lessees of the fifteenth century had typically only previously held thirty acres and were now often holding between three and five hundred.[21] These leases proved to be desirable, despite the wide availability of land in the first half of the fifteenth century and the good return the lords received from them. During the fifteenth century, these enterprises expanded as other adjacent peasant holdings were attached, and they became increasingly specialized and entirely market-dependent in the sense that the farmers running them paid competitive market rents for them and increasingly relinquished other means of subsistence. Relatively large farms were also created outside of the demesnes through accumulations of copyholds and other traditional peasant holdings.

Crucial for the transformation was the mutual relationship that developed between the upper strata of the peasantry who took up the demesnes and the lords. These new "yeomen" had now moved into the lords' sphere of operations and this gave them common interests. Thus emerged the first two elements of an agrarian capitalist social structure in England. The latter took the form of a triad: commercial landlord, capitalist farmer and landless laborer. From the activities of the first two elements the third would increasingly represent the majority of the people in England as these enterprises expanded and more and more peasants were removed from their holdings.[22]

Having leased their demesnes, many lords were increasingly active in the second half of the fifteenth century radically reorganizing their estates. Typically, they created compact estates for the purpose of developing sheep runs for wool and hunting parks for recreation and display. The wool supplied the symbiotic growth of the nascent English cloth industry which had been stimulated by the growth of the Antwerp Entrepot during the upturn in the European economy. Lords commissioned detailed surveys of their lordships in the decades around 1500, and their administrators and lawyers were tasked with drawing every possible form of income from their estates. Reorganization also meant the eviction of peasants, and it is in these decades that most of the explicit evidence of forced depopulation by the nobility and gentry appears.[23] Evictions of peasants had begun fifty years earlier however as the outcome of ongoing lord-peasant class struggles.

Historians have long argued over the means in which peasants were removed from the land in England, so paving the way for capitalism. Currently, the emphasis is often placed on accumulations by the peasants themselves or on the polarization of landholding through winners and losers on a free land market. A related argument has been derived from a political Marxist perspective. George C. Comninel also assumes that engrossment and enclosure were carried out by "largely legal means", although he acknowledges that the law could be oppressive. His thesis points to the large amount of freehold land in England subject to the common law of the state rather than private jurisdiction, a legacy of the unique penetration and continuity of royal jurisdiction within English feudal social property relations. English lords and other freeholders could, in the absence of customary restrictions, improve and extend their already extensive freehold lands for commercial purposes, thus making it increasingly difficult for small customary peasants with increasingly fewer resources to compete.[24] Some historians recognize that evictions and enclosure formed a significant strand of rural conflict in this period but argue that the large-scale clearances did not form the majority of cases because it would only be possible for the most powerful lords to achieve them. Lords had other options than removing peasants through violence or its threat which could work to the same disruptive effect, such as overstocking common lands and fencing the demesne to prevent common grazing or encouraging (or turning a blind eye to) their farmers' disruption of the traditional agrarian routine. It has been suggested that when lords were involved they were usually just clearing up the remnants of "sickly villages".[25]

My own view is that forced eviction for the purpose of privatizing enclosure should be treated as fundamental to the transition in England, whether evictions were violent and direct or slightly less direct. In conjunction with lords' continued possession of large demesnes and controls over customary tenures, this phenomenon is what clearly marks out the experiences of the English people from the rest of the continent in the fifteenth and sixteenth centuries. It cannot be proven which form of dispossession or expropriation was statistically the most significant. Nevertheless, large-scale forced enclosure by powerful lords and their farmers would have focused the minds of other lords and peasants across Midland, Southern and Eastern England at least in this period. People would have been shocked at the news of forced evictions of whole villages nearby, and it shocked the state into actions aimed to halt and reverse the dramatic changes. In the thirteenth century, wealthier peasants had also made significant accumulations over their lifetimes, but these were always later divided among offspring. In this new context, some peasants chose to consolidate and pass on their accumulations, perhaps recognizing their vulnerability as traditional open fields, common lands and customs were threatened. Clearance of the remnants of the population and the destruction of churches sounded the death knell of villages. There would be no possibility of repopulation at a later date as it happened to villages on the continent. So the lords clearing the 'remnants' had extremely serious implications for the future of rural life in England. English lords calculated that it was more in their interests as well as within their powers to follow an increasingly radical path which (although initially unintentional) would end the lord-peasant class relationship altogether and be altogether more lucrative.

My response to Comninel's thesis is that it is not the amount of *freehold* land in England and its relationship with the common law stemming from English feudal social property relations that is significant for the origin of capitalism in England but the relative amount of *property* the lords controlled in its various forms. This had less to do with the penetration of royal jurisdiction and more to do with the ability of lords to accumulate and control it at the expense of peasants. Aside from the maintenance of controls over customary tenures, the much greater amount of property the lords possessed in hand compared to their continental counterparts was significant for the origin of capitalism because when it was leased at market rates, it had a revolutionary effect on the nature of as much as 20–30 percent of property-holding in England within a few decades and with immediate implications for the fate of property outside of the demesnes. It is also debatable as to what extent the monarchy (as opposed to the lords) was responsible for the continuity of freeholds in England. As we have seen earlier, the number of peasant freeholders was dramatically reduced by the Norman Conquest (which Comninel incorrectly assumes to essentially mark the beginning of feudal social property relations in England). And Comninel's contention that the monarchy's legal reforms in the decades around 1200 were responsible for liberating a large section of the peasantry from manorial lordship by asserting the right of all freemen to seek justice through the common law in royal courts is also misleading. Whether peasants were able to maintain themselves as freemen and freeholders in the first place depended on the outcomes of local class struggles with lords, and in the second place it depended on whether freemen had written proof of their status (something which was unlikely in an age of unwritten custom). Freemen bore the brunt of these reforms, and many had their status depressed into villeinage as a consequence. Paradoxically, lords themselves were responsible for creating large numbers of peasant freeholds during the thirteenth century, which Comninel acknowledges. In a period of increasingly intense demographic pressure, many peasants were given the carrot of freehold in return for extending the lords' estates by means of assarting into more marginal territory.

Some political Marxists have taken on board criticism of the idea stemming from Brenner's thesis that the comparative "strength" of lords in different polities is a key factor in accounting for capitalist or noncapitalist paths. For example, Colin Mooers questions how was it that English lords did not have the power to prevent the decline of serfdom in England, and yet they did have the power to remove peasants off the land?[26] Hence Comninel has pointed to the determinative effect of distinctive forms of legal institution in England as a result of the unique origin and development of feudal social property relations in that country. Others have sought to "re-historicize" what they interpret as Brenner's overly structuralist account.[27] My response is that first, the substantial evidence for direct illegal forced eviction of peasants' holdings by free or copyhold tenure is not accounted for. In other words, the law was ignored, and successfully so, because its execution was clearly dependent on social and political power. And second, what is being missed is the significance of the co-opting of the English yeomanry into the ruling class through the leasing of the large demesnes (and often the manorial court as well) which enhanced their status and rendered them suitable for local manorial and royal office holding. Mooers's juxtaposition of the decline of serfdom with the eviction of peasants is misleading because during and after the decline of serfdom social property relations underwent a process of fundamental change thanks to the development of a new mutual relationship between the lords and their yeomen lessees. During the fifteenth century, English lords enhanced their class power at the expense of the peasantry and, *as a result*, the latter's "Golden Age" ended abruptly with widespread evictions and increasing entry fines. So when Brenner talks about comparative 'strength' in relation to political communities in different polities it should not, and need not, be regarded as something structurally determined, abstract, or de-historicized, which is the charge against him. That comparative "strength" (social and political power) is measured in political communities' involvement in political and legal institutions, class alliances, related social networks and in property, and it had to be constantly maintained through struggle, both individual and collective.

In reorganizing their estates in the second half of the fifteenth and early sixteenth centuries, lords eventually came across opposition from the monarchy and state officials. The state only seriously intervened, however, with a statute against depopulating enclosure in 1515, supported by a royal inquisition in 1517. This intervention was led by Thomas Wolsey who as Lord Chancellor was the leading state official in England. An earlier statute was instituted in 1488 in Henry VII's reign after petitions and speeches from inside and outside of parliament expressed fear of the breakup of the body politic or commonwealth of the country as a result of widespread evictions of peasants. John Rous, a chantry priest of Warwick, wrote *The History of the Realm of England* (*circa* 1485–91) in which he recounted that he had petitioned several parliaments from as early as 1459 in order to remedy what for him was not only a moral outrage but disastrous for the country. He wrote of "enemies of the commonwealth" and "murderers of the poor" who were "collecting together a great part of this realm, towns and hamlets, from which they have ignominiously and violently driven out the inhabitants". He listed fifty-eight villages in Warwickshire that were "either destroyed or shrunken" as a result. Now, "instead of buyers and sellers in cities and market towns there are swarms of beggars, driven out by the destroyers of villages from their houses and lands":

> And, in these days, the number of the common folk is much reduced with the destruction of villages, hamlets and houses, and countless unhappy men and women. For men who are turned out with their families ... do not attend any longer to the procreation of children, but all their care is on how they are to live. Many do so by begging, and many, driven by necessity, resort to theft and robbery, and their wives and daughters exist by harlotry, and most of their days are spent in idleness. Those who resort to theft are finally hanged, and those who resort to idleness and begging live miserably ...[28]

John Russell, the Lord Chancellor in 1483, concurred in a speech he gave to parliament that year. He spoke of the "common and public body of the realm" falling into decay "and we see daily it does by enclosures and imparking, by driving away tenants and pulling down of their holdings".[29]

The resulting statute of 1488 was neither heeded nor enforced as it required the enclosing lords and their farmers to report themselves.[30] Moreover, in order to enforce and administer his broader ambitions and consolidate his personal monarchy in the aftermath of the dynastic struggles of the previous thirty years, Henry VII recruited and raised the ambitions of many "lesser men" in the gentry from modest social backgrounds. These would be more beholden to him than the traditional governing aristocracy. So professional administrators and lawyers were drafted into royal government partly at the latter's expense. However, in contrast to their pretenses to "good governance" and equality before the law, the landowning and office-holding ambitions of these "new men" enthusiastically fed the general mood of accumulation and enclosure at all levels and increased its impetus and ruthlessness. In this way, the law in the form of practicing lawyers, if not the written law, was on the side of enclosure.[31]

The particular targets of the inquisition that began in May 1517 were "diverse of our liege lords, not having before their eyes either god or the advantage or interest of our realm or the defence of the same". At the end of each submitted county inquiry (where that part of the return is complete), it was written that the enclosures were "a pernicious example to others and that there are delinquents lingering in neighbouring parts waiting to do the same".[32] The inquisition therefore sought both to convict those who had enclosed illegally and to serve as a warning to others. It aimed to cover the whole of England except the Northern border counties, although its remit could not include cases before 1488. Groups of commissioners made up of leading lawyers, churchmen and gentry were allocated for particular regions on a county-by-county basis. Local juries, made up of those deemed worthy, and clerks were assembled in each county to hear and administer the evidence from local people with knowledge of the events going back more than thirty years. They had until September or October to do so. All of the evidence for individual cases derived from local knowledge then had to be sharply summarized and drawn up in Latin into short abstracts by clerks for the legitimate presentation to the common law judges and lawyers of the royal courts at Westminster.

The conception, ambition and potential for such a project are testament to the centralized and interconnected nature of royal power and royal institutions which had characterized England for centuries. *It was as unique in sixteenth-century Europe as Domesday Book was in the eleventh century*. While Domesday Book records the final establishment of the feudal order in England, the 1517 inquisition reflects a momentous and epochal rupture in that order and represents the first serious remedial action taken. Politics and the royal court were turbulent in 1516, and many leading peers were punished for retaining military followers. On 2 May 1516, a year after the statute against depopulating enclosure and exactly a year before the inquisition, Wolsey delivered a speech before the king and several leading nobility warning of his intention to impose "indifferent justice" on all offenders, whether lord or peasant, before the common law.[33] Previous statutes had declared this ambition but Wolsey meant it, and to this end he went through the trouble of generating the royal prerogative courts beyond the common law courts and the grip of the gentry and aristocracy's lawyers. The court of requests, for example, was designed as a potential avenue for the poor to gain a voice beyond the usual channels. Wolsey's timing for the speech may also have been influenced by the blatant bias shown by the gentry and the legal profession in dealing with cases of enclosure brought against them by villagers, stemming from his enforcement of the statute of 1515.[34] Of the same mind was Sir Thomas More, another leading light in government circles who worked loyally for Wolsey. At the same time as Wolsey gave his speech on indifferent justice, More was writing *Utopia* (published in December 1516) in which he (albeit indirectly) described what was happening:

> [O]ne covetous and insatiable cormorant and very plague of its native country may compass about and enclose many thousands of acres of ground together within one pale or hedge, the husbandmen are thrust out of their own, or else either by deception or fraud or by violent oppression they are put besides it, or by wrongs and injuries they are so wearied that they are compelled to sell all. By one means, therefore, or by other, either by hook or crook, they must needs depart away, poor, silly, wretched souls, men, women, husbands, wives, fatherless children, widows, woeful mothers with their young babes, and their whole household small in substance and much in number, as husbandry requires many hands.[35]

Over a hundred years ago, one historian discovered 1361 cases of illegal depopulating enclosure in England which were uncovered by the inquisition in 1517. These were unearthed in surviving central court records alone although were not made available.[36] 582 cases from the circuit of counties in the midlands survive in the summary abstract form in which they were submitted in 1517 and have been published.[37] The latter source is far from complete and may only represent a minority of cases in that region. Numerous membranes from the rolls are missing, many other cases have been found from court evidence that do not appear in the source, cases that went to court before the inquisition were not included and cases before September 1488 were immune from prosecution. A case involving the Earl of Shrewsbury is instructive. Partly because of the latter's relative absence from the published record of the 1517 inquisition, Bernard concludes that the earl's lax estate management style in this period was indicative of a "paternalist nirvana".[38] However, meticulous research into unpublished evidence from the Westminster courts reveals that in 1494 the same earl evicted and enclosed the whole village of Bittesby in Leicestershire. This evidence records that "sixty people ... left their homes in tears and were rendered workless; in short, they were reduced, as is believed, to extreme poverty and their lives were brought to an end".[39]

John Hales was a leading commissioner of another important inquisition in 1548. With first-hand experience of investigating illegal depopulation and enclosure, and as someone who had listened to evidence from local peasants, he concluded that most of the cases occurred before the remit cutoff date of 1488. Hales also spoke frankly about the difficulty of executing the law in the face of the social power and resources of the accused:

> Some [offenders] found the means to have their servants sworn in the juries to the intent to hazard their souls to save their greediness. And as I have learned since, it is not possible in any of the shires where we were, to form a jury without them, such is the multitude of retainers and hangers-on ... Some poor men were threatened to be put from their holdings if they presented [evidence to the jury], some also as I further learned have no certainty of their holdings which were let by copyhold tenure for lives or years, because they at no time nor in nothing should offend their landlords, but do and say whatsoever they will command them. As it pleases my landlord so shall it be ... Some were also indicted because they presented the truth ...[40]

Hales's testimony in 1549 could equally apply to difficulties executing the law in earlier decades. Gunn has assembled detailed evidence of social networks which clearly reveals that during Henry VII's reign (1485–1509), "some [jury] panels were as packed as any in Henry VII's dreams". In other surviving evidence from Wolsey's royal prerogative court of requests, peasants from Ascot in Oxfordshire complained that they had been evicted as a reprisal for giving evidence before the commissioners in that county during another inquisition in 1526.[41]

Aside from these difficulties, what we can say is that 70 of the 582 cases in this sample in 1517 involved the alleged eviction of at least 20 people. The majority of these cases involved many more and as many as 120 in one village. These dramatic events often ended with the entire destruction of the village and even the church. However, many of the "minor" cases often affected the same village and so were cumulatively serious, in addition to what had already transpired before 1488. Often we find that after an initial shock in a particular village, where a number of households were violently removed together in one day, this was followed by a more piecemeal forced removal of one or two households which became cumulatively significant over time. Sometimes we find concerted actions by gentry owners in a particular village evicting households on the same day, and yet they appear in the record as separate, minor cases. Individual gentry can also be identified in separate cases either evicting households in a single village over a number of years or carrying out evictions in a series of villages within a short period of time.

The evidence from 1517 is limited to what was recorded and what has survived, and what has survived may be simply the result of its use as a practical reference by John Hales during the later inquisition of 1548 in which he was in charge of the Midland circuit. And yet, even on its own, this evidence reveals one of the worst atrocities on English soil (outside of warfare and rebellion). Most evictions were carried out during the winter when there was neither work available nor shelter necessary for survival. Frequently, the clerks tasked with summarizing the evidence provided insights into the fate of the peasants after detailing the property involved and the numbers of people affected. Typically, their elaborations include the phrases "it is to be lamented", the evicted went away "in tears seeking bread and work", or they "wandered as vagrants" or were "made wretched", or "led a miserable way of life and ended their lives thus", or it is assumed that they "probably perished". These heavily abbreviated lines often end with the further abbreviation "*etc.*" in lieu of extended peasant testimonies. Many clerks do not elaborate at all and the language used (as well, no doubt, as the level of evidence they were willing to provide) varies from clerk to clerk and from county to county. These short lines are therefore pregnant with what must have been pages of testimony drawn from local peasants and artisans who recounted something that had happened either very recently or within living memory and were in fear of it happening to them.

The most vigorous illegal enclosers were a cross section of the English ruling class in the late fifteenth century and early Tudor period. In terms of social and economic status, they ranged from aristocratic peers and bishops, down through to the lesser barons, abbots and priors, greater and lesser gentry and finally to local yeomen who with their demesne leases of hundreds of acres increasingly dominated the landholding of their local parishes. In terms of political and official status, they ranged from the king's closest confidants, members of the broader royal privy council and royal household, down through the various royal commissioners and tax collectors, provincial administrators (aristocratic sheriffs and justices of the peace), leading lawyers, county assize court judges, metropolitan and provincial mayors and recorders, and urban and rural officials. Indeed, even some of Wolsey's most trusted commissioners in 1517 were enclosers.[42]

The interconnections and interdependence among this enclosing ruling class at all levels is also striking, and this is testament to the political integration of the English state and its tax, administrative and judicial institutions. Networks linked aristocrats at the king's side with village officialdom. In addition to serving the crown in royal household capacities, central government and warfare, leading gentry and peers also served the crown by administering its rapidly expanding personal royal estates as receivers and surveyors. Lesser gentry served the greater gentry and aristocratic peers as administrators on their estates, as their deputies in the administration of the crown estates and as military retainers. Yeomen served greater and lesser gentry on their estates as local manorial bailiffs while also leasing their demesnes. Yeomen were now co-opted into the bottom rungs of a broad ruling class who relied on them "as honest men" to keep the peace. Local cohesion was formed through retinues of gentry and yeomen who were interconnected through land holding as feoffees and will executors and through shared membership of the new oligarchies in both town and village. Problems and resistance to enclosure on the ground would have reverberated through these networks to those at the top. In this way, massive social power stood at the back of enclosers at all levels. These interconnections were also powerfully influenced and reinforced by networks of ambitious lawyers and the inns of court in London who represented the interests of the aristocracy and gentry in legal disputes and as leading administrators for which they were also retained and often salaried on a permanent basis.[43]

The remarkable interrelatedness of the broad English ruling class as both a legacy of specific feudal social property relations and the co-opting of the yeomanry provided a formidable obstacle to peasants aiming either to defend themselves at law or through physical resistance. But as we have seen, leading officials in the state intervened on their behalf. The extent to which the inquisition was successful rested on the ability of the nobility to resist the allegations against it by using the institutions (with which it was very familiar) and its interdependent relationship with the king to its own advantage.

Cases were easily thrown out or postponed indefinitely based on technicalities. In many cases, lawyers managed to gain a reduction in the stated number of people who had been evicted or the number of houses destroyed.[44] Increasingly, because of the massive workload generated by the commission, cases were sent back to county assize courts where lords had even greater influence. Because of legally induced delays and serious time lapses between the offence (if admitted) and the beginning of proceedings against offenders, lawyers were able to argue that to revert back to the *status quo ante* would cause more harm to the local economy and the inhabitants than if left entirely alone. It is typical for proceedings to continue until the 1540s and indeed well beyond in some cases. Offenders were sometimes requested to rebuild what they had destroyed. Commissioners or their deputies recorded that they had satisfied themselves in person that the work had been done. But evidence that the villages in question were deserted soon after makes such statements appear highly dubious.[45] Evidence from a later inquisition is also informative. On John Hales's advice, the offenders in 1548 were granted a general pardon in exchange for returning their enclosures to their previous state. However:

> Some of the rich men, as soon as they had the pardon, returned to their old vomit. They began immediately to enclose, to take away the poor men's commons, and were more greedy than ever they were before. They thought, and some said, that the commission was but a storm for a time and soon would pass over, as a great many hope it will also do now.[46]

The illegal evictions had generated facts on the ground and this evidence is indicative of the problems experienced by a commission endeavoring to reverse the changes. Evidence from an economic study which has consolidated past and new data (in addition to that presented in this chapter) suggests that capitalist social property relations and new related economic patterns were locking in by the middle of the sixteenth century. Although the population began to rise again from the late fifteenth century, and rapidly from 1540, there was no decline in labor productivity in England from that point.[47] Meanwhile, the continent became locked in another Malthusian cycle in which labor productivity suffered as the population rose and the downward economic spiral returned with its social and political implications.

In addition to the influence enclosers brought to bear on legal proceedings in the courts is the influence they had on the monarch himself. Many were the king's household men, his closest confidants. Others, "[i]n consideration of good and loyal service", were pardoned serious illegal enclosing activities, not only for past offences but for any which they may undertake in the future.[48] Aristocrats in England all paid taxes, were part-time administrators and household men for the crown, and headed the king's armies. The English king could allow Wolsey and More the space to uphold statute, but ultimately he was forced to show favor in order to raise taxes, run the country and execute his militaristic foreign policy.

Peasants may have lost in the courts despite Wolsey's efforts, but resistance came in the thirty years or so after the 1517 commission in the form of further royal commissions as we have seen, the acting head of state himself, rebellion across Midland, Southern and Eastern England, and evangelicals (Protestants) like John Hales and other authors of similar mind. In the aftermath of the dissolution of the monasteries in the 1530s (which led to a more intense reorganization and accumulation of estates), the language of commonwealth and "body politic" and vociferous anti-enclosure rhetoric and legislation continued.[49] Like the rebels in the major rebellions of 1536–7 and 1548–9, evangelicals advocated a return to the *status quo ante*, (although without the monasteries). The Duke of Somerset who led the government of Henry VIII's child heir in 1547 set himself on the side of the dispossessed in this respect. It has been persuasively argued that this position against enclosure was one of the ways aspects of Protestantism found sympathy from peasants during the early period of the Reformation.[50] The inquisition into depopulating enclosure which Somerset commissioned in 1548, and in which John Hales was assigned to the Midland counties, aimed to redress peasant grievances against enclosers and hikes in copyhold rents and fines, but it could not prevent one of the most important peasant rebellions in English history. The gentry were entirely mistrusted and peasants in some areas set up camps and carried out local administration of the laws themselves. But what was initially a peaceful, deliberately law-abiding rebellion was aggravated through aristocratic incompetence and eventually put down violently. Thousands died fighting to recreate the time before the enclosures and raised rents, and Somerset was toppled by the enclosers in the state's leading council. They blamed him and men like Hales for stirring up the rebellion. Writing during or immediately after the rebellion, Robert Crowley, a clergyman, took the view from below:

> If I should demand of the poor man of the countryside which thing he thinks was the cause of sedition, I know his answer. He would tell me that the great farmers, the graziers, the rich butchers, the men of law, the knights, the lords, and I cannot tell who; men that have no name because they are doers in all things that any gain hangs upon … Men that would have all in their own hands; men that would leave nothing for others; men that would be alone on the earth; men that are never satisfied. Cormorants, greedy gulls, yes, men that would eat up men, women and children are the causes of sedition. They take our houses over our heads, they buy our grounds out of our hands, they raise our rents, they levy great (yes, unreasonable) fines, they enclose our commons! No custom, no law or statute can keep them from oppressing us in such a way, that we know not which way to turn to live. Very need constrains us to stand up against them! In the countryside we cannot stay, or we must be their slaves and labour until our hearts burst, and then they must have all. And to go to the cities we have no hope, for there we hear these insatiable beasts have all in their hands.[51]

One of the reasons so little is known of the widespread anti-enclosure nature of the 1548–9 rebellions is that the gentry destroyed all known records of it and complaints that led to it in what McCulloch has described as "a deliberate communal act of forgetting". An alternative version centering on just one "traitor" in Norfolk was soon contrived for subsequent generations of school children as "Kett's Rebellion". Only recent meticulous research which has pieced together evidence from 'backward glances in later cases' in conjunction with evidence from a myriad of other fragmented sources is now beginning to bring the true scale of the crisis to light.[52] The same undoubtedly applies to earlier resistance to enclosure both within and outside of the law.

Conclusion

This discussion has sought to emphasize, firstly, the relationship between the origin and establishment of feudalism and the origin of agrarian capitalism in England, and secondly, the role of expropriation in the latter.

A centralized state and strong interdependent monarchy and aristocracy had already formed before the Norman Conquest, and increasingly, a very broad and interconnected ruling class developed with the common law and parliament which placed a strong burden of consent on monarchical rule by the end of the thirteenth century. This interdependency also ensured the continuity of the lords' social and political power over the peasantry even when subjected to the decline of serfdom after the Black Death, not only at the manorial level with implications for the maintenance of its extensive demesnes and controls on peasant tenures but at the official judicial and governmental level, given the high level of political integration of the aristocracy and gentry in state and other institutions. The co-opting and integration of yeomen into the bottom rungs of the ruling elite during the fifteenth century through the leasing of the demesnes and related office holding aided the latter's obstruction of state interference into its business interests and enhanced its social and political power which enabled it to overcome peasant and state resistance to the (initially unintended) capitalist transformation of agriculture. As the initially blurred lines of the agrarian capitalist triad sharpened through the sixteenth and seventeenth centuries, commercial landlords, large tenant farmers and rural wage laborers became entirely market-dependent for their income for which they now had to compete. These market imperatives led to Smithian growth by the middle of the sixteenth century because the farmers were forced to invest, accumulate and innovate in order to improve labor productivity. The vertical class and horizontal political struggles that brought these market imperatives into being would continue to both challenge and maintain them in the following centuries.

Notes

1. John Hales, "The defense of John Hales against certain slanders and false reports made of him," in *A Discourse of the Common Weal of this Realm of England*, ed. Elizabeth Lamond (Cambridge: Cambridge University Press, 1929), lxiv. Hales was a royal commissioner in 1548 tasked with recording cases of illegal forced depopulation in the English Midlands. His "defense" was written in 1549. All quotes from original sources have either been translated from Latin or modernized.
2. Jane Whittle, "Land and People," in *A Social History of England, 1500–1750*, ed. Keith Wrightson (Cambridge: Cambridge University Press, 2017), 157.

3. Robert Brenner, "Property and Progress: Where Adam Smith Went Wrong," in *Marxist History-Writing for the Twenty-First Century*, ed. Chris Wickham (Oxford: Oxford University Press, 2007), 58.
4. Spencer Dimmock, *The Origin of Capitalism in England, 1400–1600* (Leiden: Brill, 2014), Part I. By "social property relations" I refer to a three-way dialectical relationship encompassing the direct producers and the environment (raw materials, ecology), the "vertical" exploitative social relation *between* the main classes and the "horizontal" social relation *within* the main classes.
5. Robert Brenner, "The Agrarian Roots of European Capitalism," in *The Brenner Debate: Agrarian Class Structure and Economic Development in Pre-Industrial Europe*, ed. T. H. Aston and C. H. E. Philpin (Cambridge: Cambridge University Press, 1985), 215.
6. "Smithian growth" refers to an economic pattern in which labor productivity and population rise simultaneously. This contrasts with economic patterns characteristic of feudal social property relations (or their "recharged absolutist form"), in which labor productivity declines in the wake of rises in population. Sustained Smithian growth is achieved by market-dependent entrepreneurs specializing production in response to changing commodity prices. Surpluses are accumulated and systematically invested in technological innovations in order to increase both overall (GDP) productivity and labor (GDP per head) productivity and thereby profits. It can be equated with "modern economic growth" although the latter is sometimes reserved for the industrial revolution phase of capitalism.
7. Chris Wickham, *The Inheritance of Rome: a History of Europe from 400 to 1000* (London: Allen Lane, 2009), 467–471, 529–551; Christopher Dyer, *Making a Living in the Middle Ages: The People of Britain, 850–1520* (New Haven: Yale University Press, 2002), 26–36.
8. Wickham, *Inheritance of Rome*, 375–551.
9. J. R. Maddicott, *The Origins of the English Parliament, 924–1327* (Oxford: Oxford University Press, 2010), 2–3; Pauline Stafford, *A Political and Social History of England in the Tenth and Eleventh Centuries* (London: Edward Arnold, 1989); Wickham, *Inheritance of Rome*, 453–471.
10. Wickham, *Inheritance of Rome*, 469–470.
11. Maddicott, *English Parliament*, 381–382.
12. Maddicott, *English Parliament*, 393.
13. Wickham, *Inheritance of Rome*, 464.
14. For a useful recent synthesis, see Stephen Baxter, "Lordship and Labour," in *A Social History of England, 900–1200*, ed. Julia Crick (Cambridge: Cambridge University Press, 2011), 98–114.
15. John Watts, *The Making of Polities: Europe, 1300–1500* (Cambridge: Cambridge University Press, 2009), 126–127.

16. Maddicott, *English Parliament*, 393, 431–440, 451.
17. Maddicott, *English Parliament*, 387–389, 394–440.
18. B. M. S. Campbell, "The Agrarian Problem in the Early Fourteenth Century," *Past and Present* 188, no. 1 (August 2005): 45, 54–55; George C. Comninel, "English Feudalism and the Origins of Capitalism," *The Journal of Peasant Studies* 27, no. 4 (July 2000): 29–30, 44–45.
19. Baxter, "Lordship and Labour," 110–112.
20. Campbell, "Agrarian Problem", 62–65.
21. Christopher Dyer, *An Age of Transition? Economy and Society in England in the Later Middle Ages* (Oxford: Oxford University Press, 2005), 197.
22. Dimmock, *Origin of Capitalism*, 105–127.
23. Christine Carpenter, *Locality and Polity: A Study of Warwickshire Landed Society, 1401–1499* (Cambridge: Cambridge University Press, 1992), Part I; Steven Gunn, *Henry VII's New Men & the Making of Tudor England* (Oxford: Oxford University Press, 2016), 201–284.
24. Comninel, "English Feudalism," 38–39, 46–47.
25. Dyer, *Age of Transition*, 66–85; B. M. S. Campbell, "The Land," in *A Social History of England, 1200–1500*, ed. Rosemary Horrox and W. M. Ormrod (Cambridge: Cambridge University Press, 2006), 207–208.
26. Cited in Comninel, "English Feudalism," 44–45, and in Samuel Knafo and Benno Teschke, "The Rules of Reproduction of Capitalism: An Historicist Critique," University of Sussex Working Paper, no. 12 (2017): 12.
27. Knafo and Teschke, "Rules of Reproduction".
28. A. R. Myers, ed., *English Historical Documents, Volume IV, 1327–1485* (London: Eyre and Spottiswoode, 1969), 1014–1016.
29. Myers, *English Historical Documents*, 1016–1017.
30. Maurice Beresford, *The Lost Villages of England* (Stroud: Sutton Publishing Limited, 1998), 102–106, 118.
31. Gunn, *New Men*; Ives, *Common Lawyers.*
32. I. S. Leadam, *The Domesday of Inclosures, 1517–18* (London: Longmans, Green & Co., 1897), 81, 242.
33. G. W. Bernard, *The Power of the Early Tudor Nobility: A Study of the Fourth and Fifth Earls of Shrewsbury* (Brighton: The Harvester Press, 1985), 20–21.
34. Dyer, *Age of Transition*, 68–70.
35. Thomas More, *Utopia* (London: J. M. Dent & Sons Ltd, 1985), 26.
36. Edwin F. Gay, "The Inquisitions of Depopulation in 1517 and the Domesday of Inclosures," *Transactions of the Royal Historical Society* 14 (1900), 238–240.
37. Leadam, *Domesday of Inclosures.*
38. Bernard, *Early Tudor Nobility*, 144–145.
39. Parker, "Enclosure in Leicestershire," 36–38.

40. Hales, "Defence," lix.
41. Gunn, *New Men*, 150; Leadam, *Domesday of Inclosures* 343, no. 1.
42. Gunn, *New Men*, 201–284.
43. Gunn, *New Men*, 113–200; Ives, *Common Lawyers*; Andy Wood, *The 1549 Rebellions and the Making of Early Modern England* (Cambridge: Cambridge University Press, 2007), 16–17, 48, 53.
44. Eric Kerridge, "The Returns of the Inquisitions of Depopulation," *English Historical Review* 70, no. 1 (April 1955). Kerridge's still influential article acts as a defense for the accused.
45. L. A. Parker, "Enclosure in Leicestershire, 1485–1607" (PhD diss., University of London, 1948), 193–194.
46. Hales, "Defence," lxi–lxii.
47. Steven Broadberry, B. M. S Campbell, Alexander Klein, Mark Overton and Bas Van Leeuwen, *British Economic Growth, 1270–1870* (Cambridge: Cambridge University Press, 2015), 128–129, 209–213.
48. Leadam, *Domesday of Inclosures*, 424–427.
49. R. H. Tawney, *The Agrarian Problem in the Sixteenth Century* (London: Longmans, Green & Co., 1912), 313–409.
50. Ethan H. Shagan, *Popular Politics and the English Reformation* (Cambridge: Cambridge University Press, 2003), 270–304.
51. Robert Crowley, "The Way to Wealth," in *The Select Works of Robert Crowley*, ed. J. M. Cooper (London: N. Trübner & Co, 1872), 132–133.
52. Anthony Fletcher and Diarmaid MacCulloch, *Tudor Rebellions, Sixth Edition* (Routledge: London and New York, 2016), 70–75; Amanda Jones, "Commotion Time: The English Risings of 1549" (PhD diss., University of Warwick, 2003).

CHAPTER 3

"Compelled to Sell All": Proletarianization, Agrarian Capitalism and the Industrial Revolution

Michael Andrew Žmolek

> "… your sheep that were wont to be so meek and tame, and so small eaters, now, as I heard say, be become so great devourers and so wild, that they eat up, and swallow the very men themselves … the husbandmen be thrust out of their own … so wearied, that they be compelled to sell all …"
> —Sir Thomas More, *Utopia* (1516)[1]

It has been shown in the previous chapter by Spencer Dimmock that by the sixteenth century, English agriculture had undergone a transformation to a capitalist pattern of development, distinguished, first, by the way in which the various economic agents had become subject to a state of *market dependence*. The mass expulsion of peasants from tenures which allowed them to engage in production for self-subsistence simultaneously brought about a transformation of the domestic market, as food and other necessities for survival increasingly had to be obtained through markets. New markets were thereby called into being and producers responded to the

M. A. Žmolek (✉)
University of Iowa, Iowa City, IA, USA

X. Lafrance, C. Post (eds.), *Case Studies in the Origins of Capitalism*, Marx, Engels, and Marxisms,
https://doi.org/10.1007/978-3-319-95657-2_3

rise in consumer demand. England and Wales, and later Scotland, witnessed the rise of the first integrated domestic market characterized by regional specialization and *mass* proletarianization. Second, economic agents were increasingly subject to *market imperatives*, driven by competition, which compelled them to specialize, to innovate and to maximize their output. In a capitalist economy, the way in which both the direct producers and the appropriators of their surplus become subject to market imperatives amounts to a system-wide transformation of survival strategies. Wood uses the term market imperatives in an effort to counter "the tendency to take capitalism for granted by simply explaining the *obstacles* which prevented [commercial cities in Italy and Flanders, for example] from reaching maturity".[2] Too often, the emergence of industrial capitalism has been explained in terms of what "fetters" or obstacles to its development—guilds, monopolies, sinecures and so on—were removed. But what truly marks the industrial revolution is what was *new*, not simply in terms of how industrialization yielded an unprecedented variety of mechanical and organizational innovations but more importantly in how new survival strategies profoundly restructured class and social property relations.

The transition to capitalist industry was fiercely resisted, however, by artisans pursuing survival strategies rooted in a pre-capitalist economic logic. This posed a limit to the degree to which market imperatives could operate freely in manufacturing and would therefore require that the class of expropriators gain effective control of the state in order, on the one hand, to apply wholesale changes to the legal system, and on the other hand, to apply the coercive powers of the state to suppress the resistance through force. Meanwhile, Merchant employers were compelled to seek out cheap labor beyond the purview of the guilds. In the context of the enclosure movement and the increasing market dependence of agrarian producers, agrarian capitalism was creating conditions propitious for this marriage of convenience between merchant employers putting out materials to rural cottage dwellers to work on. In the seventeenth century, Peasants engaging in various manufacturing activities as by-employments was not a new phenomenon in Western Europe. What was new was the scale of the expansion of such "cottage industries".

It is not difficult to see why many have interpreted the expansion of rural manufactures across Western Europe as a "stage" of "proto-industrialization" preceding and leading in the direction of industrial capitalism. Several factors which anticipated and would later be key to the development of industrial capitalism expanded during this period: the development of a semi-proletarian workforce trained in manufacturing skills, an increasing degree of market dependence as well as an increasing consumerism. The process was far from uniform, however. As often as not, regions which experienced "proto-industrialization" failed to proceed on to full-scale industrialization, thus rendering the "proto-" prefix moot.

Jan de Vries paints a picture of a gradual and more-or-less simultaneous transformation in the organization and the location of domestic manufacturing across the whole of Western Europe.[3] Describing this as an "industrious revolution", de Vries suggests that from the mid-seventeenth century and bound up with the agricultural depression lasting well into the eighteenth century, a dual transformation took place, consisting of:

> … the reduction of leisure time as the marginal utility of money income rose, and the reallocation of labor from goods and services for direct consumption to marketed goods that is, a new strategy for the maximization of household utility. We see it among peasant households concentrating their labor in marketed food production, in cottar households directing underemployed labor to protoindustrial production, in the more extensive market-oriented labor of women and children, and finally, in the pace or intensity of work.[4]

This general intensification of labor in and increasing market-orientation of domestic manufacturing was part of a consumer revolution as well:

> The peasant who bought a pair of shoes or cotton calicoes in the market ceased making their equivalents himself. He not only entered the market to buy, he also entered the market to sell because a portion of his household's labor was diverted from self-provision of crafts to market production of food. When thousands of households shift their production and consumption habits in this way, the economy benefits from trade creation and specialization. The economy becomes more productive even though no technological advances have been introduced.[5]

Bound up with the process of increasing market dependence was the doubling of the population of major cities, the increasing emphasis upon raising livestock and fodder and of course the expansion of rural manufacturing. Since de Vries does not provide such detail as a country-by-country breakdown of the degree of market dependence, to say nothing of regional data, one is left with the impression that de Vries is conflating both the Dutch and the English experiences as the two economies which advanced furthest in the direction of market dependence, and then generalizing this experience across Western Europe. And yet, de Vries finds that England enjoyed an "uncanny ability to establish a position in an industry enjoying dynamically growing demand".[6] What then explains the English difference?

In his discussion of "The So-Called Primitive Accumulation", Marx identifies the "expropriation of the agricultural producer, of the peasant, from the soil [as] the basis of the whole process". While this process takes different forms in different countries, Marx wrote, in "England alone … has it the classic form".[7] Often waxing poetic in words bristling with moral outrage and peppered with sarcasm, Marx's sweeping account of the "forcible expropriation of the people from the soil" in the form of the enclosures movement and the "genesis of the industrial capitalist" is compressed in terms of its time frame, leaving much to unpack. It remains one of Marx's most widely debated writings. It is here that Marx delves into English history to begin to get at the way in which the separation of the direct producers from the means of production in land was key to the emergence of capitalism, setting much of the context for both the Transition Debate[8] and the Brenner Debate.[9] There can be no doubt that the separation of the direct producers, the English peasantry, from the land, rendering them market dependent and thus available to serve as proletarian wage laborers, whether in agriculture or manufacturing, is central to the transition to capitalism. But as we shall argue, proletarianization is not the *sine qua non* of capitalist social relations, as proletarianized labor forces have existed in many pre-capitalist economies.

From at least the thirteenth century, ore extraction operations in Europe attracted large numbers of property-less or "proletarian" workers. Did this mean that these operations were "capitalist"? Several factors suggest otherwise. The great mine-owning families were monopolists. Rather than operating in the context of free market competition, they enjoyed crown charters granting exclusive access to markets and even guaranteed sales. "Mining communities," writes Langton, "had a very strong influence over their terms and conditions of work through 'miner's freedom', which derived from the impossibility of supervising and the difficulty of even monitoring their use of the means of production … They were not archetypal proletarians. In their own eyes, each was a craftsman".[10] Whether it was collier serfdom, practiced in Scotland from 1606 to 1799 or the practice of "binding" which prevailed in the Northeast of England, labor relations were governed by normative or customary rules and expectations. Groups of colliers were organized under a contractor whose role was similar to the master of the urban craft workshop. In the absence of market imperatives, there was little pressure to revolutionize the production process in order to increase the efficiency of labor. In the Midlands, the "little butty" system gave way to the "big butty" system, where the contracting foreman no longer worked alongside his workmen. Like the factor who "put out" yarn and looms in the putting out system, the "big butty" was in a position to extract more labor from the workers, but the relationship remained a formal subsumption of labor to capital. Thus, (semi-) proletarian workforces existed long before the full commodification of labor found its logical expression in the modern factory.

Brenner's "most important historical insight",[11] according to Wood, lies in explicating how the long transition to market dependence, for both direct producers and their exploiters, took place long before the real subsumption of labor to capital. What is involved is a society in which not only the direct producers have become market dependent but one in which both they and the appropriators of their surplus become subject to market imperatives is a system-wide transformation of survival strategies. Understood in this way, the concept of market imperatives serves as a useful short-hand for describing how, under capitalism, the decision-making processes of both producers and appropriators become locked-in, as it were, to new patterns of survival strategies and the near impossibility of turning back. The emphasis is on the fact that these survival strategies are *new*; they simply did not exist under the old manorial system of agriculture or the monopoly system of the guilds. The task that remains is to show how the development of this *agrarian capitalism* made the first Industrial Revolution possible, or in other words, how these market imperatives which had taken hold of English agriculture also converted the social property relations of English manufacturing to a capitalist logic.

The present chapter is an attempt to present, in very broad terms, the transition from agrarian to industrial capitalism, as explored in greater depth in *Rethinking the Industrial Revolution*.[12] Although the development of the domestic market and the deepening of market dependence took hold of the whole of English society, the capitalist transformation of agriculture through enclosures generally *preceded* the capitalist transformation of manufacturing. This is because the former is mainly about the subsumption of land to capital or the commodification of land, not labor. The tenant farmers who led this transformation did not absolutely require wage labor in order to specialize, innovate and accumulate in response to market imperatives, even though a rural semi-proletariat performing unskilled labor tasks emerges from this process. Industrialization, by contrast, was primarily about the subsumption of labor to capital or its full commodification. Since most jobs in agriculture and mining required relatively little skill, treating labor in these sectors as abstract labor could be carried off with relatively less resistance. Craft production, on the other hand, had long rested on the transmission of the requisite and refined skills in secret from one generation of artisans to the next. It is our argument, then, that so long as artisans themselves were in control of the labor process, this made it possible for them to offer a sustained campaign of resistance to the commodification of labor power in general, and so long as employers had not achieved the real subsumption of labor to capital, market imperatives could not fully come into play. In the context of a competitive market economy, innovation was increasingly rewarded. In one line of manufacturing after another, the customary mode of producing which artisans had long practiced lacked the competitive sufficiency to compete with innovations in labor organization and machinery in the capitalist industry.

Agrarian Capitalism, Manufacturing and Queen Betty's Reforms

The emergence of and long evolution of agrarian capitalism did have a number of profound effects on manufacturing in England. Unlike subsistence producers on open fields, agrarian capitalist tenant farmers working the new enclosed farms were compelled to specialize in single crops in order to maximize output and, increasingly, to find other, innovative ways to maximize yields. Failure to maximize output could spell the loss of the leasehold agreement. The result was a steady improvement in agricultural productivity, which meant falling grain prices, which in turn meant cheaper food for urban laboring craftsmen. The trading element within the guilds could now pay lower nominal wages and claim a greater share of the return on the sale of guild products. Increasing stratification within manufacturing created new social pressures, prompting the state to intervene in at least three ways: (1) by reinforcing customary modes of regulating labor such as the apprenticeship system, (2) by shielding the expanding numbers of landless poor from destitution and (3) by seeking means of providing employment to the poor. As the pressures of market competition continued to build, however, appeals to custom steadily gave way to cries to open up trade in general to free competition, resulting in episodes of open social conflict in which the state ultimately came down on the side against the demands of the artisans.

Over the course of the fifteenth century, the English guilds would undergo a process of internal stratification. Guild masters involved directly in trade sought legislation to suppress wages, raised entrance fees and raised the cost of attaining the status of master. Wealthier masters took to wearing "livery", robes and regalia reflecting their higher social status. Meanwhile, journeymen sought greater independence and began forming their own dues-paying associations of "yeomen" which represented their increasingly specialized interest and which disbursed relief funds in times of distress.[13] While stratification within guilds was common across Western Europe in the aftermath of the plague, it was more pronounced in England. Unwin has argued that the English guilds were the first in Europe to decline in terms of their regulatory powers, specifically the enforcement of apprenticeship rules, with the decline starting as early as the sixteenth century. More recent work suggests this decline actually took place in the early eighteenth century, with the pessimists citing the fall of wages as a factor, while the optimists see the expansion of the domestic market and of new opportunities of employment outside the purview of company regulations as the cause.[14] There were dozens of guild companies in England, each serving a multiplicity of different functions. "A company's forms and procedures were endlessly reshaped and rewritten by the immediate concerns of its members in a rapidly changing metropolitan context".[15] While the general trend from the sixteenth to the eighteenth centuries was one of decline, each guild had its own unique history and so the pace or stages of decline could vary greatly. A common denominator which could explain England's precociousness with regard to the early decline of the guilds' powers is the way in which falling grain prices facilitated this process of stratification. The ending of the Wars of the Roses and the subsequent greater stability which accompanied the founding of the Tudor dynasty enabled the domestic market to expand. Town-based craft guilds now faced new competition from similar products made in other towns. This promoted regional specialization while at the same time weakening the producing element within the guilds relative to the traders or merchants, who stood to benefit from the new opportunities which the expansion of new markets afforded.

The wealth and rank of the liverymen set them apart from the "commonalty". In order to maintain this disparity, they assumed control of the guild elections and established internal courts which excluded lesser masters. Incorporation allowed the livery companies to buy and sell property, including land, making speculative ventures possible. A wave of amalgamations ensued, with greater guilds absorbing lesser guilds. The twelve Great Companies of London set out an Order of Precedence in 1516, at the head of which was the Company of Mercers (merchant traders, usually in textiles). For the first time, those seeking to join could bypass the mandatory period of apprenticeship for training in the craft by buying their way in. Unsurprisingly, the associations of yeomen protested these changes, first by petitioning Parliament and then, in 1517, it was the apprentices who led the "Evil May Day" riots against the influx of foreigners, whom they blamed for stealing their jobs.[16] The growing social distance between the livery and the rank-and-file within the craft guilds expressed itself in two additional ways. The first was the appearance of ever larger operations, some employing hundreds of workers in horizontally integrated textile works. The second was the "putting out" of textile operations to one-time peasants, now mostly landless cottagers living in the countryside, where the by-laws of the guilds held no sway. By the first half of the sixteenth century, landlords sought more land but were content to turn peasants out onto the roads, while in the towns, apprentices and journeymen faced falling wages and harsher conditions.

The potential for serious labor unrest was but one of many crises which Elizabeth I inherited upon her accession to the throne in 1558. With characteristic deftness, "Queen Betty" handled the crisis by seeking to balance contending interests. Where Edward VI had declared it illegal for craft confederacies to enforce secret oaths or attempt to fix wages, Elizabeth's Statute of Artificers and Apprentices of 1563 sought to calm journeymen's fears that a growing tide of rural laborers seeking urban employment would dilute their wages by upholding the rule of seven years' apprenticeship in the sixty-one registered trades to which the Statute applied. Checking the exodus of agrarian laborers would also check their wages, keeping tenant farmers and landlords happy. The least-paid journeymen benefited the most from the new law, but better-paid journeymen lost ground while masters gained. Masters also benefited from the law's recognition of the guild's rights of search and seizure in the event of interlopers attempting to set up shop within their area of jurisdiction. In return for sanctioning such monopoly practices, masters agreed not to interfere in the operations of company merchants.[17] "Queen Betty's Law", as it came to be affectionately known among craftsmen, could be seen as an attempt to modernize English manufactures by applying, for the first time, a uniform national code. Yet, paradoxically, it also enshrined in statute law the fundamental tenets of the medieval era by-laws of the many companies: apprenticeship, rights of search and seizure and monopolistic control of production within a given urban center in the interest of maintaining a high quality, and thus also a high price, for the product. Likewise, the right to control the "mysteries" of the trade remained squarely in the hands of the master, whose job it was to initiate his men (and some women) in the requisite skills which, in order to prevent interloping, were kept secret. This was arguably the most important aspect, because it meant that it was the workers themselves, the direct producers, who maintained control over the labor process and they now had an act under statute law to back them up.

Domestic laborers in the suburbs and countryside also enjoyed direct control over the labor process, even if they merely rented the spinning wheels, looms or knitting frames which they worked in their cottages. But they were in no position to achieve what the urban craftsmen had: legal recognition of their ancient rights and privileges, an achievement which reflected the power of their collective solidarity. The primary means by which merchant capital would achieve a formal subsumption of labor in the suburbs and the countryside would be in the form of the putting-out system, through which merchant employers could achieve absolute increases in labor output, even if they had not yet seized direct control of the labor process to enable them to achieve relative increases in labor output. Since it enabled merchant employers to pay lower wages, to recruit and dismiss laborers at will and to indirectly the control the pace and volume of production, the expansion of putting-out operations made it possible for merchant employers to both evade and at the same time undermine the by-laws and collective solidarity of the artisan guilds. Yet both guild production and cottage "industry" remained noncapitalist. So long as the labor process was controlled by the workers themselves, it remained impossible to effect increases in labor productivity on a regular and sustained basis. Achieving this "improvement" would require some way of "enclosing" labor, and the form which this would take would be the factory, whose arrival would be resisted by artisans and domestic workers alike. As a concession to the guild as a non-capitalist form of labor organization, the Statute of Artificers and Apprentices likely slowed the degradation of the status of the journeymen, yet that decline continued. By the late seventeenth century, writes Wilson, "there were 'illegal men' in all occupations".[18] It may seem paradoxical to suggest that Queen Betty's Law slowed the decline of the English guilds when the English guilds were the first in Europe to decline. But we would suggest that the answer to this riddle lies in the unique development of English agrarian capitalism, which was generating the forces to undermine the guilds, such as falling grain prices and wages, the dispossession of peasants who were compelled to take up cottage manufacturing activities and both rapid population growth and rapid urbanization, stimulating rapidly expanding demand for manufactures beyond which the guilds were in a position to meet.

Elizabeth had dealt with the urban employed, but what about the "problem of the poor"? As part of a religiously inspired campaign of promoting the "common weal", charities and local experiments with putting the able-bodied poor to work in "workhouses", notably in Puritan towns, date from the later sixteenth century. Edward VI had converted the palace of Bridewell into an institution for putting the idle poor to work in 1552. The Parliament took the next steps in 1572 and 1576, setting up Overseers of the Poor to collect contributions locally for the upkeep of the aged and infirm poor and calling for houses of industry or "bridewells" where the able-bodied poor would be put to work to be set up in each county.[19] As with the crafts, the Elizabethan Poor Laws of 1597 and 1601 brought a national framework to the regulation of poverty, although their administration remained a local affair. As part of the system of poor law administration, the "corporations for the poor" were highly ambitious, purporting to offer education and medical assistance in addition to "plentiful living" for those poor set to work on the premises.[20] The employers, as sponsors, were also to benefit in the form of profits. By the middle of the seventeenth century, however, it became clear that workhouses could not compete with private enterprises producing the same wares. They lost money instead. The Society for the Promotion of Christian Knowledge took charge of the movement for most of the eighteenth century, but they continued to lose money and the movement lost steam.[21] Why then did workhouses continue to be built and on an ever-increasing scale? The answer to this question will provide us with a clue to the emergence of the factory.

The Defeat of Copyholders and Radicals and the Emergence of Capitalist Factories

The period between the Civil Wars and the mid-eighteenth century saw the virtual completion of the conversion of the mass of the British population to a state of market dependency. So far, we have discussed three types of proletarian or semi-proletarian workers. Colliers may represent the earliest proletarianized workforce in the modern age. In the mines, they generally maintained control over the labor process, over which they continued to exercise a significant measure of customary control. Urban craft workers or artisans had always been dependent upon the market for the realization of the return on the products. Their guilds, whose origins stretched back through the middle ages, had by now been largely overtaken by merchants or amalgamated into larger companies. From the seventeenth century, they set up "friendly societies" in an effort to maintain both mutual security and solidarity. With the control *over* markets, which they had enjoyed in the form of chartered companies with monopoly rights, effectively lost, they continued to exert control *behind* the market by seeking to enforce apprenticeship rules, by asserting their customary rights of search and seizure—in the face of an increasing lack of support for such customary rights on the part of officials and the courts, as well as increasingly successful efforts by employers to flaunt such rules—and finally, by maintaining the control over the labor process. It would be precisely control over the labor process, however, which would-be industrialists sought to extinguish, just as the enclosure movement had extinguished customary control over agrarian labor on the open fields. Colliers, artisans and cottagers, all were market-dependent. But where the emerging market in land leases had unleashed competitive market pressures which over time made agrarian production on open fields non-viable because farming on enclosed fields allowed tenant farmers and landowners to transform production so as to increase productivity on a constant basis, the general form by which a similar result could be induced from manufacturing, namely the factory, would not emerge until the eighteenth century.

In 1600, England's principle export, by far, was wool, and Holland, where unfinished English cloths were dyed and finished, the principal export destination. Between 1614 and 1617, an ill-fated scheme led by Sir William Cokayne to open dyeing and finishing works in England to try and break this dependence on Holland soon collapsed due to insufficient preparation in setting up dyeing and finishing works in England and training the workers in the requisite skills. The "Cokayne crisis" precipitated a wave of hundreds of bankruptcies and was blamed for the severe export slump which followed, ameliorated only by the recent introduction of Norwich's lighter and cheaper "new draperies". The deeper causes of the crisis were external, having to do with currency manipulations in the Baltic. The economic disruption of the Thirty Years War would prolong the economic crisis. Facing unemployment or reduced wages, droves of journeymen took to the highways in search of better employment. Journeymen and small masters complained about the loss of control over their own companies, but their principal grievance was the flaunting of apprenticeship rules. High grain prices during this period amounted to a reversal of the situation in the late fifteenth century, when high prices for wool had encouraged the enclosure of marginal lands for sheep runs. Now there was an intensified incentive to enclose arable land, which meant even more peasants were extruded from the manorial system with a large share of them become cottagers whose best option was to turn to domestic production, primarily spinning and weaving wool, to earn an income. It also meant that there were greater numbers of property-less workers seeking entry into the registered trades, adding to the pressures on existing journeymen and small masters.

The upheavals of the 1640s would only magnify these pressures. The distress of the urban artisans played a significant role in the Civil Wars. Cromwell's New Model Army drew its members largely from the ranks of London's skilled artisans. The radical movement which staged a municipal revolution and took over London's Common Council in 1641–1642 was made up of an alliance of artisans, shopkeepers and the new merchants who, as interlopers, posed a threat to the monopoly privileges of the old, chartered merchant companies.[22] The Levellers' demand for universal male suffrage was undoubtedly informed by the experience of artisans who, having lost a large measure of democratic control within their own companies, now demanded a say in the affairs of state. For Cromwell and his generals, the temporary alliance with the radicals was a mere matter of expediency driven by the need to raise an army. Once victory over Royalist forces was attained, the radicals were crushed.

The urban radicals enjoyed a tacit alliance with rural copyholders. The first order of business of Parliament after the Restoration of Charles II in 1660 was to confirm acts of Parliament passed in 1646 and 1656 abolishing the Court of Wards, the institution charged with overseeing the collection of feudal dues. Effectively, all land in England was converted to the status of freehold tenure. A campaign to win property rights for tenants who were copyholders was defeated. This removed all legal impediments preventing lords from enclosing 'their' lands or from expelling copyholders. Where Tudor and Stuart monarchies had previously made less than strenuous efforts to fine enclosers, henceforth: "encouragement of agricultural improvements was a major object of government policy; attempts to prevent enclosure were abandoned".[23] As much as the abolition of the Court of Wards may serve as a major milestone in English history, such sweeping legislation alone could not transform local government and property relations across the realm overnight. With only about a quarter of the land in England enclosed, resistance to further enclosures in the name of custom would persist for another century and more.

The Glorious Revolution of 1688–1689 restored unity to England's ruling landed elite after decades of schism over religion and the threat of Stuart absolutism. With these questions settled and the Dutch *Stadtholder* on the throne of England, the government could now get down to the business of reform. The Act of Settlement set out a new line of succession and would endure the attempts by the Young and Old Pretenders, respectively, to reclaim the throne for the Stuart line. A financial revolution aimed at raising funds for William's wars on the continent in the cause of checking French expansion would result in the creation of a permanent national debt overseen by the new Bank of England, founded in 1694. And the policies of "free trade" which had been most vigorously pursued by Cromwell would be continued, in particular the Navigation Acts, which restricted other countries from having access to England's colonial markets. From the 1650s to the 1670s, England had fought three wars with Holland in order to secure England's place as the predominant maritime power. It was now England's turn to experience a kind of "golden age".

Understood in terms of class, the English Civil Wars and the Glorious Revolution yielded a state clearly dominated by the landed classes, or what one might call an agrarian capitalist state. The crushing defeat of both the artisan-based radicals and the copyholders had eliminated the most obvious sources of resistance to this dominance and to the emerging (agrarian) capitalist system. While the crown was no mere figurehead and the arrangement between crown and Parliament was one of nearly co-equal powers, Parliament controlled the purse strings. The king could continue to direct foreign policy, but the Parliament would now set about the business of facilitating the development of agrarian capitalism, and concomitantly, the expansion of market imperatives. "Free trade" was the order of the day, and this slogan was championed above all by the new merchants, the would-be interlopers who sought entry into protected trades by attacking the monopolies and privileged status of the older merchant companies. The medieval principle of paying a high price to ensure high quality was effectively overthrown in this period as it gave way to the principle of seeing who could meet expanding demand at the best price. In this environment, efforts by guilds and companies of journeymen to regulate their trades and exclude would-be interlopers became increasingly untenable. The withdrawal of direct state regulation of trade and production enabled a growing institutional separation between political and economic institutions. Where direct producers, whether urban or rural, actively resisted the loss of long-cherished rights and privileges, the coercive powers of the state would be brought to bear to ensure the triumph of "free trade".

The period between the 1690s and the 1720s was a curiously "happy" time inasmuch as lordly estates expanding rapidly as a free market in land allowed for the increasingly concentrated ownership of land. At the same time, however, new overseas markets meant that even as rural producers were being dispossessed of access to land and converted into cottagers, ever larger numbers of them obliged to turn to the market to sustain themselves and their families on domestic handicraft production. This "turn to the market" by peasants, beginning in the thirteenth and fourteenth centuries, was driven "by necessity rather than by choice … under conditions where peasants had no other options",[24] and "was not a picture of wealth, but of scarcely controlled poverty".[25] Whether the wholesale conversion to capitalism could have been completed in the absence of the ability of rural producers to sustain themselves through such by-employments as they lost access to the means of subsistence, combined with the Poor Laws serving as a kind of early welfare buffering the impacts of market exposure and unemployment, remains an open question.

The eighteenth century began with an unprecedented proliferation of noble titles alongside an unprecedented concentration of landed property by engrossment into huge estates, this accompanied of course by an unprecedented building boom in palatial country houses. Throughout the century, Parliament and thus the state would be in the hands of a class of landlords. Membership in this class was increasingly fluid as the market in landed estates made available the opportunity for merchants and other urban climbers to buy their way into the gentry by purchasing a country estate, furthering the transformation of England's elite from aristocracy to oligarchy. The period of high prices for grain having ended around 1660, the early eighteenth century was characterized by low grain prices and thus low wages but rising real incomes. Whether this was a period of agrarian depression depended upon to which segment of which class one belonged. For the old Tory squire falling into insurmountable debt in his struggle to keep from falling behind the new wealth, and for copyholders facing the loss of landholdings, it was a time of bitter realities. For engrossing lords, investing merchants and successful "yeomen" tenant farmers, rising rates of agrarian productivity translated into rising rents and rising profits. What was truly unprecedented was the way in which, perhaps for the first time in agrarian history, rents *rose* even as the price of grain fell.[26] Where historically the response to a price fall had been to decrease investments in or even withdraw land from production, the response of landlords and tenant farmers in early eighteenth-century Britain was to rapidly increase investments. The period is marked by a surge of new literature promoting new methods of agricultural "improvement", as well as the appearance of mechanical devices such as Tull's seed drill in 1702, designed to further enhance the productivity of the soil. England became a net exporter of grain, with exports peaking in 1844, when the price of grain hit its lowest mark of the century.

It was the success of English farmers in constantly increasing the output of yield per acre which explains how it was possible for rents to rise and investments in improving the land to increase even as prices continued to fall from the combined effects of slow demand and the overproduction of grain. English agriculture had now begun to achieve self-sustaining growth, a process which Adam Smith would later identify as the key to making it possible for the "wealth of nations" to be expanded indefinitely, breaking with long-standing mercantilist assumptions. The self-sustaining nature of the new economic relationships centered upon improved farming can be characterized by several "feedback loops". Engrossment and investment led to higher yields, producing higher profits and rents and making further such investments possible. Higher output meant more fodder and this meant more animals could be retained, which in turn meant a greater supply of manure, better fertilization and higher output; and so on.[27] Low grain prices had a stimulating effect on the economy as a whole. Britons began to enjoy an ever-widening variety of foreign commodities, from coffee and tea to Indian prints and Chinese porcelains.

Low prices stimulated an export boom, and while exports no doubt made this surge of imports possible, what was of "vital significance", according to A.H. John, was the "demand released by increased agricultural productivity".[28]

If the folly of the South Sea Bubble may serve as testament to the economic exuberance of the period, it could equally be said to have found its expression in the long period of Whig hegemony characterized by "Old Corruption" in the form of the systematic dispensation of political patronage, led most notably by Sir Robert Walpole. The astonishingly rapid decline of the Tory party after the Jacobite rising of 1715 effectively meant that Great Britain would be governed by what amounted to a single party state throughout most of the rest of the eighteenth century. Whig governments would pursue the elaboration of new legislation which would become known as the "Bloody Code", an unprecedented expansion of capital offences for even the most trivial of infractions. If the foundation of the Code was the Riot Act of 1715, which criminalized long-standing habits of protest which had enjoyed a significant measure of legitimacy under customary law, the cornerstone was the Waltham Black Act of 1723, which made such offences as poaching or steeling deer, firing a weapon indoors, or committing arson, punishable by death. While not initially enforced widely, the Black Act established the precedent for a succession of acts passed over the course of the next century which expanded the list of capital offences to over 300. In this way, Britain's landed elites sought to curtail virtually any conceivable transgression of their property rights.

In 1723, the Parliament also passed the Workhouse Test Act. Through this Act, Parliament largely divested itself of the task of administering the poor law system by buttressing the authority of local officials, who were now empowered to deny poor relief to any able-bodied person who refused the "test" of whether he or she was able to perform labor in a workhouse. To the local Justice of the Peace, this would have a salutary effect, in that denying relief to a certain portion of claimants would go a long way toward redressing the complaints of rate payers. Abandoning the pretense that workhouses could turn a profit, the expense of their maintenance could be justified by the lowering of the rates collected. Having worked out this formula, whereby the workhouse was now seen as an intentional deterrent against idleness, nearly every town in England had soon constructed its own. The new formula effectively demanded that conditions in the workhouse be made as unappealing as possible.

Both the workhouse and the putting-out system operated outside the purview of the craft guilds. The workhouse differed from the putting-out system, however, in two important respects. First, the tasks were set by the overseers, whereas rural cottagers, like urban craftsmen, continued to enjoy control over the labor process, setting their own hours and typically observing "Saint Monday". Second, workhouses brought large numbers of laborers together under one roof. It is not difficult to see then how the workhouse conditioned the arrival of the factory. Indeed, the earliest factories closely resembled the workhouse in the way they provided schooling and dormitories for the pauper children they employed as apprentices. Local authorities surely welcomed any employer willing to set up a for-profit operation offering employment and a modicum of skills training. Only the urban craftsmen had grounds to object, but by the eighteenth century their appeals to ancient custom and even to Queen Betty's Law were losing favor in the courts.

It is suggestive to note that in 1724, just one year after the passage of the Workhouse Test Act, the world's first modern factory, the Old Silk Mill at Derby, became fully operational as a producer of high quality *organzine* silk thread with the aid of machinery driven by an external power source—in this case, a water wheel.[29] Its multi-story brick design set the model for the factories to come. Its workforce would be made up largely of pauper apprentices and young women. England's earliest modern factories were bedeviled by a host of challenges: ice and weather damaging buildings or halting waterwheels, irregularity of supply in raw materials and the disorderly behavior of workers, to name but a few. Between the 1730s and 1770s, dozens of smaller factories for spinning tram, lower quality silk thread, would appear. During the same period, the first experiment in establish a handful of factories for spinning cotton thread were set using the machine invented by John Wyatt and Lewis Paul. While it has been suggested that it was the machine itself which proved unworkable, problems of labor discipline, poor management and the lack of a carding machine to keep pace with the bobbin-based spinning machine were likely to blame as well. There is also the question of timing. Wyatt and Paul's factories were first set up in the 1740s, the decade in which grain prices reached their lowest point. The 1750s brought sharp rises in grain prices, which prompted protests over food prices and sharpened conflict between employers and their workers. A very poor harvest in 1757 prompted armed uprisings in Lancashire, prompting authorities in

Manchester to put the city under armed guard and to arm the citizenry of Liverpool. In light of the dearer cost of bread, artisan organizations quickly re-emerged from obscurity to demand higher piece rates, higher wages and enforcement of apprenticeship rules.[30] In the context of rising wages and increased labor militancy, employers now had a powerful incentive to turn to machinery as a means to cut labor costs. Recent data presents a stark contrast between Britain, where wages climbed steadily from 1525 onwards, and the rest of Europe, where real wages *fell* moderately but steadily, in the two centuries between 1625 and 1825, with the exception again being the Northern Netherlands, where wages rose alongside those in Britain until the late seventeenth century, after which they flatlined.[31] In Britain, the rate at which wages rose slowed in the early eighteenth century but accelerated again rapidly after 1750, especially in Northern England.

Despite Toynbee's red-letter date of 1760 to mark the onset of the Industrial Revolution, the dominant changes in the British economy of the latter half of the eighteenth century were parliamentary enclosures or, even more dramatic, the wholesale conversion of the Scottish Lowlands to "improved" farming. From 1750 onwards, Britain saw a steady recovery of grain prices and a significant rise in the rate of population growth. The state now began to intervene directly in local disputes over enclosure by passing a series of enclosure bills. Many enclosure bills were simply making official enclosing which had already been carried out. By the 1790s, the vast majority of arable land in England, Wales and across the Scottish Lowlands had been enclosed. The British peasant was a thing of the past; those who remained in the rural villages were typically cottagers who had at least been afforded a garden and who worked as wage laborers on enclosed farms or who span yarn or wove cloth under the domestic system. Cottagers generally continued to enjoy access to the wastes and commons around the fields for collecting firewood (*firebote*), grazing their animals (*pannage*), fishing in the local pond (*piscary*) and so on. These customary rights ensuring access to such necessities (*estovers*) enhanced the ability of cottagers to enjoy a modestly comfortable livelihood over the course of the seventeenth and eighteenth centuries, particularly during the long period of low grain prices. The significant expansion of outdoor relief, by providing a safety net, added a degree of security to the life of this rural semi-proletariat. Thus, even as the Industrial Revolution began, agrarian capitalism had generated a class of semi- or fully proletarian rural cottage workers who, for a time, could earn wages sufficient enough to enjoy a decent standard of living. Weavers' wages peaked in the 1790s, but this was the same decade in which the Parliament's attention turned to the wastes and commons surrounding the villages. The enclosure bills to follow would curtail access to the commons and make "trespass" a punishable offence. This same decade would see several very poor harvests, war with France and a political crisis prompted by the re-emergence of radicalism in the aftermath of the French Revolution, a crisis which would carry on well into the succeeding century.

The onset of the Industrial Revolution involved a reorganization of the labor process along capitalist lines. Multiple examples of such a capitalist reorganization of labor in the absence of any introduction of machinery can be cited, such as in the button-making workshops of John Taylor or the Great Manufactory of Matthew Boulton, but the potteries of Josiah Wedgwood serve as the classic example. In his so-called "proto-factories", Wedgwood, starting in 1765, took not only the division of labor but also the regulation of production to levels of detail anticipating Taylorism. Deploying mechanical technology no more advanced than the spinning wheel and the trundle cart, Wedgwood sought to make of his men "such machines ... as cannot err",[32] by training his laborers in minute tasks organized in assembly-line fashion. Obsessed with market trends, Wedgwood assumed personal command of the entire labor process. This enabled him to organize production *and to innovate* in direct response to market signals. This man who had once served as an apprentice in a pottery workshop organized along customary lines took some of the greatest strides toward breaking entirely with custom.

For factory owners who did employ machinery, it offered two remarkable advantages. First of all, men like Richard Arkwright or Jedediah Strutt did not suffer the need, as Wedgwood did, to carefully train their workers in newly defined skill sets. By literally replacing the hands of the worker with a tool that works the product, the worker became an appendage to the machine. "De-skilling" was implied from the outset. Secondly, whether Thomas Highs or Richard Arkwright was the true inventor of the water frame, it was Arkwright who first demonstrated another key advantage afforded by machinery: the ease with which the machine-driven factory, once proven successful, could be reduplicated. Arkwright was the first to pioneer the establishment of a factory *system*, building nearly one new mill per annum between 1767 and 1784.[33]

What unifies Wedgwood and Arkwright was the economic environment in which they were operating. By the latter half of the eighteenth century, the peasant class in England had virtually ceased to exist. The overwhelming majority of the population was now, in one way or another, dependent upon the market for their subsistence and self-reproduction. Where merchants had long been 'putting out' materials to domestic workers residing outside the reach of companies of urban artisans seeking to enforce customary rights of apprenticeship and search, the increasingly competitive marketplace would reward the employer who seized control of the labor process and reorganized it such a way as to respond more efficiently to market imperatives.

The arrival of the factory did not, however, spell the end of the role of custom in manufacturing. The period between 1750 and 1850 was characterized by an extraordinary series of conflicts, at the heart of which was a struggle for control of the labor process.[34] The French Revolution of 1789 and its aftermath greatly politicized this struggle by putting all "combinations" of workers in Britain under suspicion of harboring revolutionary or Jacobin designs. Yet a number of major events preceded and anticipated this sharpening divide. The trade depression which Britain suffered during the American Revolutionary War sparked an early episode of machine breaking, in particular the ransacking and destruction of over a dozen textile mills in Lancashire 1779 by a crowd of thousands of aggrieved workers, most notably Arkwright's Birkacre Mill near Chorley, which was burned to the ground. One year later, after weeks of unprecedented upheaval in London during the so-called Gordon Riots, or what Nicholson has dubbed the Great Liberty Riot, the state's response by way of sending in the Red Coats to apply excessive military force, killing hundreds, produced the stark realization on the part of the surviving protestors, among whom London's skilled artisans were no doubt prominent, that the state was no longer willing to observe long-standing customary expectations regarding the legitimacy of protest.[35]

Peace with the Americans in 1783 brought an end to the trade depression but also stimulated a new wave of enclosing and factory building. After Britain declared war on France in 1792, radical political organizations like the London Corresponding Society were driven into secrecy. Seven years later, the Combination Acts of 1799 and 1800 drove urban craft associations underground for the next quarter century. The machine-breaking disturbances in the Midlands led by the Luddites between 1811 and 1815 were met with the "invasion of Middle Britain"[36] by a force of some 14,400 soldiers in April and May of 1812. Napoleon's final defeat at Waterloo, bringing the Napoleonic Wars to an end in 1815, brought no end to the strife, as the Peterloo Massacre of 1819 would testify.

The politicization of economic struggles likely served to hasten the dismantling of remaining labor laws recognizing the legitimacy of customary modes of organizing production. Most notable was the final repeal of the Statute of Artificers and Apprentices in 1814. Remarkably, however, as E.P. Thompson demonstrated, the role of custom now came to the fore as appeals in defense of custom by the "working class" of England reached extraordinary heights, even in some cases inventing new customs to defend.[37] However, just as the final abolition of the Court of Wards in 1600 had deprived copyholders of a legal recourse which could provide some protection against the subsumption of land to capital, the final repeal of Queen Betty's law in 1814 deprived artisans of a legal framework which had shielded them from the advance of the real subsumption of labor to capital.

Conclusion

So long as they still maintained direct control over the labor process, artisans would not submit to the real subordination of their labor to capital without a struggle. Moreover, it was the struggle of artisans to defend their respectability as sturdy, independent craftsmen which informed political conflicts from the English Civil Wars to Luddism and Chartism. It stands to reason that artisans specifically should seek to reproduce themselves *as* artisans by defending the laws and customs which defined their economic agency and that this struggle would last so long as significant numbers of artisans remained a part of the economy. This does not mean, however, that customary workshops were immune to innovation. Many artisan workshops adopted the spinning jenny upon its advent, and in Yorkshire's West Riding, there were even efforts to establish "company mills", factories employing artisans working spinning jennies. For relatively brief periods of time in different lines of manufacturing, artisanal production may have managed to compete favorably with production undertaken in capitalist factories or proto-factories. But in an increasingly unregulated economy where the market rewards innovation, employers would eventually find that older modes of producing would lack the competitive sufficiency to keep them in the game. Pre-capitalist methods of production regulated by custom, rather than serving as "fetters" to the emergence of an already-existing capitalism, were *superseded* by the production methods of capitalism *as they were invented or discovered.*

Lest all of this smack of teleology, let us add that the artisan-led resistance to the real subsumption of labor to capital in England was strong enough and effective enough to necessitate the application of the coercive powers of the state, both military and legislative. We have already mentioned the military interventions of 1780, 1812 and 1819, as well as coercive legislation in the form of the "Bloody Code" and the Combination Acts of 1799–1800. In the aftermath of the violent suppression of the Swing Riots of 1830–1831, the reform of the Old Poor Law in 1834 tightened restrictions on poor relief by ending most relief out-of-doors and for the able-bodied, making service in the workhouse mandatory. As it was by now well-known among the poor that workhouse conditions were intentionally made intolerable, no person in his or her right mind would voluntarily choose to go. The terror of the workhouse now served to corral market-dependent workers into seeking out and accepting any form of employment, even where conditions were only marginally better than in the workhouse. Under such conditions, the appearance of workers "choosing" to accept menial work at minimal wages without being forced back to work at the point of a bayonet could be interpreted as a simple exchange of labor for wages in a free marketplace, the coercive powers of the state now receding into the background.

Notes

1. Sir Thomas More, "Pasturage destroying Husbandry," in *English Prose. Vol I: Fourteenth to Sixteenth Century*, ed. Henry Craik (London: Macmillan & Co. Ltd., 1893). From *Utopia*, Book I.
2. Ellen Meiksins Wood, "From Opportunity to Imperative," *Monthly Review* 46, no. 3 (1994): 30.
3. Jan de Vries, *The Economy of Europe in an Age of Crisis, 1600–1750* (Cambridge University Press, 1996), 84.
4. Jan de Vries, "The Industrial Revolution and the Industrious Revolution," *The Journal of Economic History* 54, no. 2 (1994): 257.
5. de Vries, *Economy of Europe*, 181.
6. de Vries, *Economy of Europe*, 105.
7. Karl Marx, *Capital: A Critique of Political Economy*, Vol. 1, eds. Friedrich Engels and Ernest Untermann (New York: The Modern Library, 1906), 787.
8. Paul Sweezy et al., *The Transition from Feudalism to Capitalism* (London: Verso, 1978).
9. Trevor Aston and Charles Philpin, eds., *The Brenner Debate* (Cambridge University Press, 1985).

10. John Langton, "Proletarianization in the Industrial Revolution," *Transactions of the Institute of British Geographers* NS 25, no. 1 (2000): 36.
11. Ellen Meiksins Wood, *The Ellen Meiksins Wood Reader*, ed. Larry Patriquin (Chicago: Haymarket Books, 2012), 52.
12. Michael Andrew Žmolek, *Rethinking the Industrial Revolution* (Leiden: Brill, 2013).
13. George Unwin, *Industrial Organization in the Sixteenth and Seventeenth Centuries* (London: Frank Cass; Oxford: Clarendon Press, 1963), 51.
14. Giorgio Riello, "The Shaping of a Family Trade," in *Guilds, Society & Economy in London, 1450–1800*, ed. Ian Anders Gadd and Patrick Wallis (London: Centre for Metropolitan History and Institute of Historical Research in association with Guildhall Library/Corporation of London, 2002), 144–145; citing George Unwin, *The Gilds and Companies of London* (London: Methuen, 1908).
15. Ian Anders Gadd and Patrick Wallis, eds., *Guilds, Society & Economy in London 1450–1800*, (London: Centre for Metropolitan History, University of London, in association with Guildhall Library/Corporation of London, 2002), p. 5.
16. John Duncan Mackie, *The Early Tudors, 1485–1558* (Oxford University Press, 1952).
17. Unwin, *Industrial Organization*, 12.
18. Charles Wilson, *England's Apprenticeship 1603–1763*, 2nd edn (London and New York: Longman, 1984), 177.
19. Joanna Innes "Prisons for the Poor," in *Labour, Law and Crime: An Historical Perspective*, ed. Francis Snyder and Douglas Hay (London: Tavistock Publications, 1987).
20. Paul Slack, *The English Poor Law 1531–1782* (Houndsmills, Basingstoke, Hampshire and London: Macmillan Education, 1990), 24.
21. Wilson, *England's Apprenticeship*, 394.
22. Robert Brenner, *Merchants and Revolution* (Princeton University Press, 1993), 395.
23. Christopher Hill, *The Century of Revolution 1603–1714* (New York; London: W.W. Norton, 1961), 127–128.
24. Robert Brenner, "Property and Progress," in *Marxist History-writing for the Twenty-first Century*, ed. Chris Wickham (Oxford University Press/ British Academy, 2007), 80.
25. B.H. Slicher van Bath, "The Rise of Intensive Husbandry in the Low Countries," in *Britain and the Netherlands*, ed. J. Bromley and E.H. Kossman (London: Chatto & Windus, 1960), 15.
26. Wilson, *England's Apprenticeship*, 248.
27. Cf. Žmolek, *Rethinking*, 192–198, where five such feedback loops are identified.

28. A.H. John, "Agricultural Productivity and Economic Growth in England, 1700–1760," *Journal of Economic History* 25, no. 1 (1965): 24.
29. Žmolek, *Rethinking*, 368–379.
30. Alfred Powell Wadsworth and Julia De Lacy Mann, *The Cotton Trade and Industrial Lancashire 1600–1780* (Manchester University Press, 1965), 359–362.
31. R.C. Allen, "Why the industrial revolution was British," *Economic History Review* 64, no. 2 (2011): 360–361; esp. Fig. 1.
32. Neil McKendrick, "Josiah Wedgwood and Factory Discipline," *The Historical Journal* 4, no. 1 (1961): 34; quoting a letter penned by Wedgwood dated 9 October 1769.
33. Cf. Žmolek *Rethinking*, 436, Table 8.1.
34. Žmolek, *Rethinking*, Part Three: Custom's Last Stand seeks to provide a narrative theorizing this struggle.
35. Cf. John Nicholson, *The great liberty riot of 1780* (London: BM Bozo, 1985).
36. Kirkpatrick Sale, *Rebels Against the Future* (Reading, MA: Addison-Wesley Publishing Company, 1996), 126–149.
37. Cf. E.P. Thompson, *The Making of the English Working Class* (London: Penguin, 1991).

CHAPTER 4

Peasant Farming in Eighteenth- and Nineteenth-Century France and the Transition to Capitalism Under Charles de Gaulle

Stephen Miller

Since the 1990s, Philip Hoffman, Jean-Marc Moriceau, and Gilles Postel-Vinay have revised the economic history of France. Whereas previous generations of historians had documented centuries of slow growth and crises, the revisionists argue that the tenant farmers of the Paris Basin made a number of improvements, which augmented productivity and land rents at the end of the seventeenth, and over the course of the eighteenth, centuries. Market demand, they argue, provided the stimulus for rural development. According to Moriceau, "The Parisian attraction favored a type of agriculture precociously engaged in capitalism. From all parts, it incited [farmers] to transform … the feudal organization … it diffused an air of modernity in the nearby countryside."[1]

The assumption underlying this thesis is that once the towns beckoned, lords and peasants—spellbound, as if their inner nature were suddenly

S. Miller (✉)
University of Alabama at Birmingham, Birmingham, AL, USA

X. Lafrance, C. Post (eds.), *Case Studies in the Origins of Capitalism*, Marx, Engels, and Marxisms,
https://doi.org/10.1007/978-3-319-95657-2_4

released—abandoned concerns about seigneurial authority and rights, and about community resources and subsistence, and focused on the opportunity to specialize in products with market value. I argue, in contrast, that the peasants, as a legacy of the conflicts of the feudal period, possessed land, which, though typically inadequate to assure their subsistence, constituted the core of their strategies for supporting their households and communities. The peasants deployed however much family labor was needed to assure their existence. To them, labor was embedded in households and communities and did not represent a cost. It was sensible to make use of this labor rather than dissipate resources for the equipment to do the same work. To be precise, the peasants did not face the constraints of capitalist agriculturalists, obliged by price competition, to reduce the costs of labor relative to the returns of their harvests. The market did not force the peasants to constantly raise the monetary value of their time. Moreover, because peasant families increased drudgery, even as its remuneration declined, so as to retain their plots, the landed classes (ecclesiastics, nobles, and other well-off townspeople) exploited rural inhabitants anxious to gain the income needed to assure the livelihood of their households. The landed classes consequently did not invest in labor-saving improvements. These rational tendencies stifled development in the modern sense of growing production relative to the work-time of the inhabitants.

Non-capitalist tendencies persisted, I argue, all the way until the administration of Charles de Gaulle intervened in rural society to establish economically viable farms, discourage the use of low-cost rural labor, and oblige growers to take out loans with the purpose of financing the latest inputs. These policies compelled farmers to work for money to service debts rather than for subsistence. Farmers then had to compete with one another and finance up-to-date implements in order to match the prices of competitors and stay afloat. Xavier Lafrance shows, in his chapter in this book, that the French state succeeded in triggering a capitalist transformation of manufacturing from the 1860s and over subsequent decades. Yet, the industrial growth, which ensued, was slowed down by non-capitalist tendencies in the countryside. I argue, in the same vein, that it took the generalization of the capitalist compulsion to enhance the cash value of labor hours in rural areas for the economy to develop rapidly after the late 1950s.

This definition of development, as expanding output relative to a population's labor, comes from Robert Brenner's understanding of Marx's

Capital. The idea is that businesses are subordinate to capitalist laws compelling each one to extend capital so as to preserve it and, by this extension, bring about accumulation. Specifically, they must reinvest a portion of profits to match improvements and prices achieved by competitors or perish economically. Price competition forces capitalists to produce "relative surplus." In other words, they must not only extract additional work from employees but also upgrade their organization and technology so as to reduce expenditures on personnel, which generally represent the largest recurrent costs of an enterprise. These capitalist laws build up the productive power of capitalist societies relative to their manual effort.[2]

Spencer Dimmock and Mike Zmolek, in their chapters in this book, explain the transformations that lay behind the steady rise in labor productivity in English agriculture over the course of the early modern period. The key to this development was the transformation of peasant communities into individual free laborers, whose costs were calculable and persistently had to diminish on account of the price competition of the tenant farmers. Marx called this transformation primitive accumulation, or the dispossession of the rural population. It was absolutely crucial to his argument, because members of peasant villages, in possession of the means to reproduce themselves, do not have to find work and so do not form proletarian labor power abstracted from the community of human existence and made into a cost on the balance sheet of businesses. Marx devoted the entire eighth part of *Capital* to this issue.[3]

Peasant Labor and Growth in Eighteenth-Century France

From this premise, I argue that capitalism did not determine the evolution of the French economy. If one looks at the period from the Middle Ages through the 1840s, one notices that the peasantry made available landless workhands and paupers, but not labor as an abstract cost. The peasants won de facto rights over the greater part of the land by the 1200s, but did not fully control their livelihood, because they faced a lordly class ingrained in the political and social fabric of the kingdom. The lords came to accept the legality of the peasants' plots over the following two centuries, at the same time as they updated seigneurial inventories. Duties that had fallen into abeyance were discovered in the implications of customs, others were invented and added to the tangle of levies, and a seigneurial burden accumulated on the peasants. These also had to pay tax collectors and vendors of essential goods and often had to sell produce when prices were lowest in order to make ends meet. After a long period of growth, from the end of the 1400s until the 1670s and 1680s, the peasants faced mounting difficulties, as the subdivision of their plots among offspring left them with parcels inadequate for their subsistence. They faced debts and foreclosures, and the nobles ended up with estates as large as 300 hectares in the Paris Basin during a period of stagnation which lasted into the eighteenth century.[4]

These estates did not represent the outcome of primitive accumulation so much as solutions by default, when peasants abandoned the land in a time of crisis.[5] What is more, when prices rose again in the second half of the eighteenth century—when the revisionists allege that productivity on the large farms surged ahead—the landed estates shed peasant plots.[6] Every carefully researched measurement of property from about 1730 or 1740 through the 1800s shows that the nobles lost ground, and the bourgeoisie found itself on the defensive, as peasants racked up debts to acquire land. The extent of peasant property varied from one region to another and overall amounted to 30 percent or 40 percent of the total at the end of the eighteenth century.[7]

By means of an examination of Lyonnais, Poitou, Berry, and the Paris Basin, I show in what follows that the peasants succeeded in extending their share of the soil by exploiting their household labor. They had many family members relative to the size of their landholdings. Rather than cast off this labor, and make the land yield income relative to the time spent working it, they used the members to raise the overall output in labor-intensive lines in which their superabundant capacity for work gave them a competitive advantage.

In Lyonnais, where the population grew in the eighteenth century into one of the densest concentrations in the realm, peasants possessed progressively more land in farms of fewer than five, often fewer than two, hectares. Many of these resulted from indefatigable work converting woods and stony soils into vineyards with the aim of complementing holdings in rye and wheat for bread, hemp for cloth, and oats for animals. Vineyards did not require outlays on cattle, fertilizer, plows, or carts and brought in two-and-a-half to five times more income per hectare than did grains. In contrast to grain farming and its dead seasons, viticulture filled the calendar year with hewing, layering to multiply the base of the vines, plowings with hoes, putting in stakes for vine shoots, preparing vessels and basins, harvesting, fermenting, pressing, and many other tasks, which permitted households to put their labor to use generating income for their subsistence. The Lyonnais countryside buzzed with tiny vineyards spread around the arable fields of the landed classes.[8]

The peasants of Poitou possessed anywhere from 2 percent of the land around Poitiers to 25 percent in areas of the Vendée and 70 percent in remote areas of the eastern part of the province. They had a much greater percent of the land in hemp and vines. Hemp required much labor soaking the stems, grinding the dried ones a month later, cleaning and combing, spinning, and then putting the hanks on winders for making cloth. Artisans typically worked a quarter of the year in rural workshops, the rest on their parcels of land. They planted turnips after the hemp to bring nutrients to the topsoil and prepare it for rye. This crop, which predominated on the peasants' fields, did not fetch as high a price as did wheat but did better on land lacking fertilizer and helped assure their subsistence.[9]

Cereals covered at least 70, and usually 80–90, percent of Poitevin fields, especially those of the landed classes. They took up the main part of the peasants' work. Even so, fodder crops, for commercial cattle, began to appear on the farms of peasants and sharecroppers in the wooded countryside with small irregular-shaped fields and many hedges and copses in western Poitou. The smallholders developed rotations of buckwheat to renew the soil, and then broom, gorse bush, vetches, and sainfoin, along with barley and oats, after the wheat harvest. The gorse bush on the heaths fixed lime and phosphorous in these acidic soils naturally deficient in nutrients. Peasants left the broom and gorse on paths to be saturated by rain and animal droppings and trampled by cattle and people. They obtained excellent fertilizer in this way and had fodder to rear about one draft animal per two hectares, a proportion superior to that obtained on the commercial cereal domains and open fields of northern France.[10]

This husbandry required the peasants to till plots for several years, abandon them, and then clear the unplanted land. The peasants used hoes to divide the broom and gorse and to plow several times with the aim of breaking up the roots and taking out the weeds. The hoes required more drudgery than did plows but ventilated and weeded the soil better and reduced outlays on equipment. The land preparation required the toil of both sexes and all ages. It appeared as time wasted to urban critics but, to the peasants, represented a means of applying otherwise idle hands to activities that generated the resources needed to sustain a dense population.[11]

The peasants of Berry, in central France, reared oxen. Horses worked more rapidly but cost more to buy and maintain. Since the peasants did not face competitive pressure to maximize the market value of their time, they saw the horses as needless expenses. They reserved the best land for subsistence crops rather than fodder, and their oxen did not produce optimal amounts of fertilizer. Yet, the peasants still had more manure for their fields than the landed classes of Berry had for their commercial cereal domains, which comprised extensive sheep grazing, fallow, and few bovines. The peasants intensively applied household labor farming peas, broad beans, and turnips, which renewed the soil and raised yields. Fallow receded from their plots long before it did from the large domains. The peasants of Berry laid out gardens and vineyards and farmed hemp to make household clothing and maybe have a few surplus garments to sell. They used spades and hoes, which required more labor than did plows, but could be made with wood from the forests, and did not necessitate expenditures on replacements and maintenance. The peasants saved instead for new parcels to assure their livelihood.[12]

The population of the Paris Basin grew 31 percent in the eighteenth century, making the region the second most densely inhabited of the realm. It is known for farms as large as 300 hectares in certain areas. Yet peasant plots, mostly smaller than 2 hectares, existed in nearly every parish and covered anywhere from 5 percent to 45 percent of the farmland. These plots expanded at the expense of the large farms in the eighteenth and nineteenth centuries, as the peasants took on debts to buy land in the hopes of attaining self-sufficiency and security in old age.[13]

The expansion of peasant agriculture depended on the unpaid work of family members in labor-intensive lines such as market gardening in the parishes bordering Paris to the northeast. Peasants gardened with spades and sickles, even though these did not accomplish much work relative to the labor expended, because more efficient implements would not have increased output but would have depleted household income. Peasants of the Paris Basin also created vineyards, which, like the gardens, generated more income per hectare than did wheat fields. They had far fewer prairies and woods than did the landed classes, but nearly all of the regional vineyards.[14]

Peasants and the Large Estates

In short, the economic vitality of early modern France came from peasant ingenuity. Yet, this growth came at constant or even falling returns to each additional hour of peasant labor. It turned, moreover, to the benefit of the landed classes. To understand why, one must recognize that the rural inhabitants put in much of the additional time working with the intention of obtaining the land, food, and jobs on offer from their social betters. The peasants' drudgery thus contributed to increases in the price of land and bread relative to the remuneration of labor. Most peasants did not have the surpluses to speculate on grain markets. They more commonly used the income from market gardening, cloth production, and viticulture to purchase part of their subsistence and additional parcels of land at a time of rising prices. While no one actually starved, the population's malnutrition is well documented.[15]

In Lyonnais, only one-third of the vintners owned the two hectares necessary to support a family. The rest obtained the needed income by laboring on the arable fields of the landed classes. The growing population, and its reliance on labor markets for income and grain markets for food, drove up the price of the staple crop, rye, faster than the agricultural wages. Growth came to halt as a result of the saturation of vineyards in the region of Lyon. Wine prices rose over the course of the eighteenth century, as consumption recovered from the crisis of the end of the seventeenth century. But output eventually surpassed demand, as urban residents sacrificed wine purchases to necessities in years of high prices. Grape harvests expanded excessively, drove down prices from 1776 to 1785, and plunged the peasants into precariousness.[16]

After 1770, rising land rents and rural poverty diminished the market for non-essential goods and provoked a downturn in artisanal activity affecting all the households of Poitou reliant on ancillary income from hemp. While the price of grain and other staples rose, that of wine and flax fell on account of all of the vineyards and hemp fields carved out of the hillsides and poor lands, where cereals did not grow. The vintners of northern Poitou saw the value of their plots decline in the 1780s. Livestock sales increased briskly in the fairs of western Poitou from 1758 to 1776 but then faced a brutal recession. The peasants did not have sufficient land, beyond their parcels in rye, for the fodder to sustain animal fattening and had to sell amid falling prices for non-essential goods like cattle.

The after-death inventories, measured against Poitevin grain prices, show a 20 percent decline in fortunes over the course of the eighteenth century and a particularly sharp decline among day laborers and tenants without much land. As the number of indigents swelled in western Poitou, the trend toward population growth reversed in the 1780s.[17]

The peasants, in a word, struggled to wring subsistence from their plots. Very few had the land and livestock to avoid reliance on wages, on taking up sharecropping domains to combine with their own inadequate holdings, or even on leasing whole units of production to provide for their families. Rural communities harbored growing numbers of poor laborers. Yet, these laborers remained embedded in the community and thus were only amenable to the customary practice of pinning country-dwellers down to the soil by means of overlapping forms of seigneurial rights, tenancy, and remunerated work. The landed classes, in this way, took additional profits from the peasants' drudgery but did not calculate it as a cost, face competitive pressure to reduce it, or accumulate surpluses. The landed classes had no thought of expropriating the peasants and turning their labor into a commodity.

The rental agreements—drawn up for the benefit of the merchants, office holders, and nobles of Lyonnais, Poitou, and Berry—contained traditional, quasi feudal, arrangements for seigneurial dues and for services carting goods to market or to the landowner's table in the towns. They generally bound the tenants to the soil in unpayable debts. Leases spelled out traditional methods and restricted the lands for seeding through binding rotations of grains and fallows so as to prevent soil exhaustion. The landed classes did not worry about meager harvests, which increased the value of their grain reserves. Besides, customary rotations assured the availability of the crops liable to seigneurial dues at harvest time. As the eighteenth century wore on, the leases obliged the tenants to cede progressively more of the harvests. The proprietors thus had little reason to invest in livestock, stables, fodder crops, and other forms of labor-saving improvements.[18]

These extractive feudal-like relations also prevailed in the Paris Basin, where revisionists purport to show development. Moriceau and Postel-Vinay argue that tenant farmers, motivated by the profit available on the urban market, grouped together compact farms and thereby gained the flexibility to plant artificial prairies and fodder crops and slightly reduce the fallow land. The value of the fodder increased, thanks to all of the horses used in Paris, and brought wealth into the countryside. With larger farms and additional horses, the tenant farmers economized on the labor of shepherds, plowmen, and carters. Yields rose slightly, as they applied fertilizer to all of their fields by using the droppings of penned-up sheep and especially the manure of the horses in Paris. Improvements of this sort, Hoffman calculates, increased total factor productivity or production minus its costs.[19]

If one unpacks this research, one notices that the large farms presented by Moriceau reached their maximum extent of about 200 hectares in 1675–1699 but then contracted to 160–170 in 1775–1799. This sequence resulted more likely from the vagaries of the peasant economy than from the consolidation of cost-effective farms. Landlords were stuck with properties in the crisis of the seventeenth century—as the peasants no longer made ends meet amid falling prices—but then sold parcels to peasants willing to take on debts, deploy additional labor, and wring more income from the land, as prices rose in the eighteenth century.[20]

This scenario makes sense when one notices that the typical tenant, overseeing the large farms of the Paris Basin, did not amass surpluses. Gérard Béaur has gone over the evidence and has pointed out that, in contrast to the habit of capitalists to accumulate cash reserves, the tenant studied by Moriceau and Postel-Vinay used up his profits in a fierce quest for land. The tenant undertook risks, depleted revenues, even went into debt, and sterilized investment so as to secure landholdings for the children. He adhered to a traditional economic logic of assuring social respectability for his sons.[21]

Indeed, the research of Moriceau and Postel-Vinay shows little evidence that the tenant farmers invested to cut costs. It shows that a minimum of 26.3 percent and usually about 30 percent of their arable fields remained fallow. Moriceau and Postel-Vinay document nitrogen-restoring fodder crops on 31.8 percent of the arable land of one farm but, on average, a maximum of only 4.3 across the Paris Basin. Nearly 40 percent of tenant farmers left no mention of artificial prairies in their after-death inventories.[22] The enduring expanse of fallow, along with this negligible presence of fodder crops, demonstrates that the tenants did not put into practice the interconnected undertakings intrinsic to early modern agricultural revolutions. Specifically, the tenants did not replace fallow with nitrogen-restoring fodder crops, build stables, rear draft animals, amass manure fertilizer, and expand the arable surface for the purpose of cutting costs and accruing surpluses.[23] Given the evidence from Berry and Poitou, it is likely that the slight reduction in fallow, and increased acreage of fodder crops, recorded by Moriceau and Postel-Vinay, resulted from the efforts of peasants to use the supplementary work of family members to eke more income out of the land.

Peasant creativity, in labor-intensive farming, no doubt accounts for the yields documented by Moriceau and Postel-Vinay.[24] The proliferation of smallholders, and their need for income, permitted farm managers to profit from the peasants' expertise, discussed earlier, in weeding, renewing the soil, augmenting fertilizer, and raising yields. Tenant farmers thus wrung extra labor from the peasantry, in intensive hoeing and tilling, to obtain added output for the Paris market. Increased drudgery, rather than investments and labor-saving improvements, accounts for the high yields on the estates run by the tenant farmers. Having gone over Moriceau's evidence, Jean-Michel Chevet shows that it does not demonstrate the consolidation of landholdings. He shows, above all, that Moriceau's evidence does not prove the addition of horsepower and improved plowing. The tenant farmers used more laborers, not fewer, in the herding of sheep and the harvesting of oats and hay for the horse-feed market in Paris. Chevet's research suggests, in short, that the tenant farmers controlled the work of communities and thus did not calculate and curtail the labor costs through investment in improved husbandry.[25]

These extractive feudal-like relations also explain the rising total factor productivity calculated by Hoffman. Estimating the cost of labor in early modern France remains elusive, for most work was not remunerated with a wage, and no one made any effort to use it sparingly. The peasants valued labor differently than did the market, because it allowed them to retain their family plots. Households employed labor at odd intervals and in conditions uneconomical for employers. The true marginal cost of household labor did not match the recorded wage. For other inputs as well, Hoffman had to use hardy arbitration, supposing the same costs for farms in different regions, thus allowing a margin of error. The prices of most of these inputs remained constant. The cost of renting land, however, varied and represented Hoffman's principal measure. Land rents, however, reflected the bargaining power inherent in the relations between landlords and lessees and could thus lead to deceptive conclusions for a period like 1750–1789 when they rose rapidly relative to other prices.[26]

One would be wise not to discount the bargaining power of the landed classes given all the empirical studies that indicate seigneurial relations rather than monetary rents determined by productivity. In the eighteenth century, as the rural population and grain prices increased, landlords had the leverage to take extra work from rural households and make rents more lucrative. They added stipulations of a feudal character to leases with the aim of extracting produce and money. Peasants of the Paris Basin often gave the landlord seigneurial dues, fruit from gardens, and chickens or other animals on Christmas Day. The clauses in leases indicated debts obliging the tenants to submit to all sorts of burdens, such as unpaid carting services, hardly distinguishable from the medieval corvée.[27]

The tenant farmers of the Paris Basin resembled seigneurial stewards more than they did rural capitalists. They threw their weight around in the lord's name, hired local laborers, collected dues, and stored grain for charity, wages, and other means of influence. They often held the peasantry in debt and benefited from the lord's tax privileges. Landlords and their stewards, in a word, did not exhibit the economic behavior suggestive of the capitalist requirement to reduce expenditures on personnel.[28] As result, output per farmer did not increase in France over the course of the early modern period and fell to less than half of the rate of agricultural labor productivity in England by the end of the eighteenth century.[29]

The continued existence of the rural community, in which the rural labor of France was rooted, made possible the revolts of the Revolution against the foregoing forms of exploitation. The peasants banded together in innumerable uprisings, which resulted in the definitive abolition of feudalism in 1793. They laid hold of property belonging to the king and émigrés and cleared and cultivated lands held on a communal basis. They had hesitated to farm this land prior to 1789 for fear that the lords would assert feudal claims to it and foist burdens on the cultivators. For decades after 1789, peasants purchased church and émigré properties acquired by speculators for the purpose of reselling them to land-hungry rural inhabitants. The peasants' portion of the land varied from region to region but probably increased from about 30 percent or 40 percent of the national total to about 50 percent after the Revolution.[30]

The Agricultural Revolution in Modern France

The countryside hardly evolved in the first half of the nineteenth century. Rural households perfected the resourceful methods used since the 1740s, clearing land, cultivating nitrogen-restoring plants on fallow fields, tending vineyards, growing maize, potatoes, rye, and other labor-intensive high-yield subsistence crops, marketing produce and livestock, churning out cloths, and accruing debts to finance land acquisitions. The purchase of plots improved the peasants' standard of living and allowed offspring to create households.[31]

The number of farms declined slightly toward the end of the nineteenth century, as low-priced cloth from industrial districts made it more difficult for micro-proprietors to scrape by with supplemental income from rural workshops. The disappearance of these small farms did not benefit the large specialized growers so much as the mass of households with 5–10 hectares. These households improved rotations, tilled nitrogen-restoring crops, planted oats as fodder, augmented the output of grasses, expanded the number of horses, used heavier plows, enhanced yields in many parts of the country, and replaced inferior grains with wheat. They made the foregoing improvements with household labor and the income it yielded. The formation of the Crédit agricole, and the provision of low interest loans after 1900, did not finance improvements so much as help the peasants to acquire land and enlarge their holdings. Thus, in the years prior to World War I, the peasants became more entrenched in the rural landscape than ever before, while national levels of agricultural productivity remained close to the bottom of Western European nations, far behind Denmark, Belgium, the Netherlands, Germany, and Great Britain. The agrarian sector did not support the urbanization, which did take place, and a quarter of France's food had to be imported from foreign countries.[32]

In 1945, subsistence agriculture—with a little budgeting for taxes, rice, oil, coffee and sugar, as well as meat for the holidays—remained common to about four million farms, all unique yet analogous, in villages of fewer than 2000 inhabitants comprising about 45 percent of the national population. Farmers continued to gather around the typical fire and table at which they ate the products of the farm from a pot much like they had in the Middle Ages. Some households baked their own bread. Others traded grain for it at the local bakery. All over France, aside from the arable fields in the Paris Basin and vineyards in Languedoc, livestock ate the fodder grown on the fields and excreted manure back to them. Peasants had the skills of wheelwrights; knew metalwork; and repaired tools, wagons, and carts. If they purchased a machine, it was to fend off disruptions, such as vanishing casual labor, and to preserve their way of life. Money had marginal value, used only to buy a tool, save and purchase land, or pay off siblings at the time of inheritance.[33]

On the farms belonging to townspeople in many parts of France, sharecropping remained a servile bond obliging indebted cultivators to perform services for the master. Ninety percent of leases, accounting for about forty percent of the agricultural land, lasted no longer than nine years and gave the tenants little incentive to invest in roads, deep plowings, wells, drainage, or the application of lime. Propositions went before the legislature in 1848 and 1889 to have the surplus value of capital divided equally among the proprietors, farm managers, and workers. But the rentier class in control of the legislatures defended the inviolable principle of property, written in the Declaration of the Rights of Man. Landlords extolled the abundant rural population and the law of supply and demand, which allowed them to employ wives and children at low wages, sometimes paid to the male head of the family's plot of land.[34] For this reason, the large specialized growers, proprietors in the Paris Basin and viticulture enterprises in Languedoc, remained underdeveloped relative to other capitalist farmers of Western Europe.

Remarkably, the countryside did not change much in the decade following World War II. The General Confederation of Agriculture (CGA) aimed to modernize husbandry by leaving non-farming landlords, discussed in the preceding paragraph, aside and offering the actual cultivators low-cost loans to realize the plans of state administrators. But the former farm unions of the Vichy period denounced the CGA as an artificial politicized organization, and rural areas voted for the Popular Republican Movement (MRP) and other conservatives. Pierre Pflimlin of the MRP, a partisan of the National Federation of Unions of Farmers (FNSEA), became Minister of Agriculture at the end of 1947 and defended the unity of the peasantry, tradition, and regionalism as beneficial to the national identity.[35]

Agricultural rhythms accelerated but did not undergo transformation. The total wheat harvest did not reach the 1907 level until 1954. Most farmers relied on horses and oxen rather than tractors. They relied on human labor at harvest time to squeeze in the bales, transport the millstones, thresh, and do other tasks. Machines such as the combine harvester remained marginal. The FNSEA organized big protests in 1956 and obtained the indexing of agricultural prices to those of industry. Large landowners obtained guaranteed profits, and the countryside seemed set to follow the accustomed course with much non-specialized subsistence farming and average yields less than half of those attained in Belgium.[36]

But then, after the late 1950s, wheat yields and plot sizes tripled, the number of agricultural properties declined four times over, and farmers fell from 30 percent to 4 percent of the national population. The number of tractors mounted from 140,000 in 1950, to 558,000 in 1958, and nearly 1,000,000 in 1963. The number of combine harvesters rose from 37,900 in 1958 to 102,000 in 1965, and abruptly eliminated the seasonal laborers. Growers used more than five times as much fertilizer in 1978 as they had in 1946. The number of lawn-tractors, moto-mowers, balers, and mechanical seed drills rose by the same proportions. Productivity grew 8 percent a year in agriculture between 1963 and 1967 whereas it grew at 5 percent in the rest of the economy. Labor productivity doubled from 1949 to 1963, rising at an annual rate equal to industry of 7 percent, whereas, prior to 1938 it rose about 2 percent a year. The building of new homes, or the remodeling of old ones, doubled in rural areas in the 1960s. The farmers' buying power grew every year from 1965 to 1973, as their lifestyle aligned with the rest of the country.[37]

Nearly all of the agricultural implements were manufactured domestically, and metallurgical and machine industries grew rapidly. Farmers furnished raw material for food-processing, one of the principal industries of France. Factories for meat, sweets, biscuits/cookies, flour, dairy, and other products generated about 15 percent of industrial output by the end of the twentieth century.[38]

Previously, farmers had avoided changes liable to threaten the security of subsistence farming. What wrenched them from their accustomed life were the policies of De Gaulle's ministers, eager to turn agriculture into a surplus-generating export industry. Georges Pompidou, the adviser of the Prime Minister Michel Debré, pointed to Europe and the goal of having the common market offer remunerative outlets for agriculture. Administrators found a constituency among the associations representing the farmers of small and medium-sized holding, often from poorer regions. Previously, the large growers at the head of the FNSEA had gotten their poorer brethren to go along with the program of price supports and traditional farming. A substantial proportion of farmers recoiled before the prospect of exiting subsistence agriculture and becoming market dependent. But by the late 1950s, new leaders, seeing the benefits of changes elsewhere in Europe, made many rural inhabitants impatient with the conservative leadership of the wealthiest landowners and convinced them to embrace the idea of organizing, with the aid of the state, to carry through an agricultural revolution. The government then suppressed price indexes at the end of 1958. The price equilibrium subsequently came from exports, which grew 22 percent a year within the European common market.[39]

In this way, the farmers turned agriculture into one of the leading industries of France. Their success depended on state programs to structure the land market, which left to itself, over previous centuries, had handed down an uneconomic division of the territory. Legislation of 1960 and 1962 prevented rentiers from hoarding farmland or operating it with hired labor and peasants from dividing it into unviable plots. The laws offered lifetime annuities to farmers over 65 to cede their holdings to growers with a plan for market production. The state established a fund to preempt sales and group plots together in ways suitable for farmers committed to investing in the latest implements and using solely the labor of a couple. By dint of this legislation, the government took nearly one-third of the national territory and put it in the hands of enterprising farmers.[40]

The most transformative policy was to charge the Crédit Agricole with opening branches across the towns of rural France and offering 30-year loans at 3 percent interest. To obtain these funds, growers had to have a minimum farm size, and half of them were excluded in some parts of the country, eventually forced by market imperatives to leave agriculture. As farmers took out loans to acquire the latest implements and achieve maximum yields, others had to follow suit or succumb to competitive pricing and go under. Rural debts, in this way, grew 14-fold from 1960 to 1973.[41]

State subsidies to purchase tractors and fuel permitted farmers to plow fields in a matter of days rather than weeks as in the past. But to get the full value from the investment, growers bid up land prices by purchasing and renting additional fields. The tractor led them to cut down obstructive orchards, make new openings in buildings, level and widen pathways, and dispense with horses and oxen. Its adoption forced the reconversion of the artisan, blacksmith, and farrier trades. Farmers had to buy new tools and attachments to enhance the tractor's versatility, new fertilizers to augment yields, and special seed-strains to resist disease. One innovation required a slew of others, which in turn required new trips to the Crédit Agricole. Farmers had to join cooperatives to assure the sale of wheat as soon as it was harvested and thus raise the revenue needed to service the debts.[42]

These changes augmented output 1.5–2 percent annually after the mid-1960s, whereas, demand grew only 0.5 percent. To maintain the equivalent of industrial salaries, farmers had to grow nearly six times more wheat in 1982 than they had in 1952. They had to take out additional loans and make investments in order to augment yields and avoid poverty. Buying and maintaining machines; paying insurance; and purchasing seed, fertilizer, and pesticide required capital at the start of each yearly cycle. The expenses mounted from a quarter of sales in 1959 to a half at the end of the century. Households had to practice minute accounting to service their debts and stay afloat. In this way, while the spectacular gains in productivity augmented the rural standard of living, and turned France into the world's fourth leading exporter of agricultural commodities, the bulk of the revenue went in payments to the banks.[43]

Conclusion

Under the Old Regime, the peasants' tendency—to increase drudgery and diminish consumption with the aim of retaining subsistence plots and assuring their presence in rural communities—augmented output but not labor productivity. Most of the land belonged to the ecclesiastics, nobles, and bourgeoisie and consisted of an uneconomic patchwork of parcels and estates. These proprietors enforced exploitative sharecropping and tenancy agreements, seigneurial rights, and debts and thus prevented the peasants from making their households more secure.

While peasant agriculture did not offer a path toward development, village solidarity made possible the anti-seigneurial revolts of the Revolution and the abolition of feudalism in 1793. The peasants thus extended their landholdings and supported their households and communities well into the twentieth century. France became a country of modern industry between the 1890s and 1920s. Yet the rural population, despite the urban demand, did not specialize, as today's consensus of economic historians would suppose, in the crops and livestock offering the highest exchange value. Rather, the cultivators, even in the decade following World War II, continued to use the income from sales to acquire land, diversify their crop mixes, reduce drudgery, and assure their existence among fellow villagers. Large landowners continued to take advantage of the rural population in the traditional way, renting land at extortionist prices and paying little for the labor of peasant families.

The economy of France thus developed late in comparison to its neighbors. Rapid development only took hold at the end of the 1950s, when the government pursued policies to make people farm for the market and improve the productivity of their labor. Gaullist administrators reorganized the agrarian landscape to facilitate the use of the latest techniques and technologies.

Rural development proceeded above all by way of indebtedness. To obtain land through the state, farmers had to have a plan for market production and take out loans to purchase the latest inputs. Agriculturalists thus ceased to farm for local use and instead competed with others, who had also made this leap, so as to maintain or expand their share of the market. Farmers had to make their time productive by mechanizing as many tasks as possible. This transformation amounted to an agricultural revolution. Industrialization took off in the 1960s and early 1970s thanks to rising productivity in agriculture, its demand for machines, its materials to be processed, the workers it shed, and the costs of production it controlled thanks to the output of low-cost staples.

Notes

1. Jean-Marc Moriceau, *Les Fermiers de l'Ile de France: l'ascension d'un patronat agricole (XVe–XVIIIe siècle)* (Paris: Librairie Arthème Fayard, 1994), 72. Other major revisionist works are Jean-Marc Moriceau and Gilles Postel-Vinay, *Ferme, entreprise, famille: Grande exploitation et changements agricoles: les Chartier (XVIIe-XIXe siècles)* (Paris: Éditions de l'EHESS, 1994); Jean-Marc Moriceau, "Au rendez-vous de la « Révolution agricole » dans la France du XVIIIe siècle. À propos des régions de grande culture," *Annales. Histoire, Sciences Sociales* 49, no. 1 (1994); Philip Hoffman, *Growth in a Traditional Society: The French Countryside, 1450–1815* (Princeton: Princeton University Press, 1996).
2. Robert Brenner, "Agrarian class structure and economic development in pre-industrial Europe," in *The Brenner Debate: Agrarian Class Structure and Economic Development in Pre-Industrial Europe*, ed. T. H. Aston and C. H. E. Philpin (Cambridge: Cambridge University Press, 1985).
3. Karl Marx, *Capital*, trans. Ben Fowkes (London: Penguin, 1990).
4. Marc Bloch, *French Rural History: An Essay on its Basic Characteristics*, trans. Janet Sondheimer (Berkeley: University of California Press, 1966), 128–134, 140–143, 217, 233; Jean Meuvret, "*Le problème des subsistances à l'époque Louis XIV* (Paris: Éditions de l'EHESS, 1987), 75–76, 86, 88–89; Jean Jacquart, La rente foncière, indice conjoncturel?" *Revue historique* 514 (1975), 362–365, 373–375; Guy Fourquin, "Le temps de la croissance" and "Au seuil du XIVe siècle," in *Histoire de la France rurale* t. 1. *La formation des campagnes françaises des origines à 1340*, ed. Georges Duby and Armand Wallon (Paris: Seuil, 1975), 423, 542–544, 548, 550, 552, 563, 637, 645–647.
5. Meuvret, *Le problème*, 88–89.
6. For these revisionist accounts, see below pp. 11–13.

7. Gérard Béaur, *Le marché foncier à la veille de la Révolution: les mouvements de propriété beaucerons dans les régions de Maintenon et de Janville de 1761 à 1790* (Paris: Éditions de l'EHESS, 1984), 270, 336, 339; Omer Tulippe, *L'habitat rural en Seine-et-Oise: Essai de géographie du peuplement* (Paris: Sirey, 1934), 110, 161–163, 241, 318–319; Edward Berenson, *Populist Religion and Left-Wing Politics in France, 1830–1852* (Princeton, NJ: Princeton University Press, 1984), 9–10, 18, 20, 22–23; Thomas Brennan, "Peasants and Debt in Eighteenth-Century Champagne," *Journal of Interdisciplinary History* 37, no. 2 (2006): 183, 186, 189–190, 193, 197–198; Philippe Jarnoux, *Les bourgeois et la terre: Fortunes et strategies foncières à Rennes au XVIIIe siècle* (Rennes: Presses Universitaires de Rennes, 1996), 268; Ernest Labrousse, "The Evolution of Peasant Society in France from the Eighteenth Century to the Present," in *French Society and Culture since the Old Regime*, ed. Evelyn Acomb and Marvin Brown (New York: Holt, Rinehart and Winston, 1966), 48–51; Bernard Bodinier, Éric Teyssier, and François Antoine, *« L'événement le plus important de la Révolution »: la vente des biens nationaux (1789–1867) en France et dans les territories annexes* (Paris: CTHS, 2000), 368; Georges Lefebvre, *Les paysans du Nord pendant la révolution française* (Paris: F. Rieder et cie, 1924), 47–50, 57; Roger Price, "The Onset of Labour Shortage in Nineteenth-Century French Agriculture," *The Economic History Review* 28, no. 2 (1975): 271; George Grantham, "Scale and Organization in French Farming, 1840 to 1880," in *European Peasants and their Markets*, ed. E.L. Jones and W.N. Parker (Princeton: Princeton University Press, 1975), 292–306.
8. Gérard Berger, *Le Pays de Saint-Bonnet-le-Château (Haut-Forez), de 1775 à 1975: Flux et reflux d'une société* (Saint-Etienne: Centre d'histoire régionale, 1985), 183–184; François Tomas, "Alleux et parcellaire à Sury-le-Comtal (Forez): Un essai de reconstitution du cadastre ancien," *Cahiers d'histoire* 12, no. 4 (1967): 409–410; Jean Pierre Gutton, *La société et les pauvres: L'exemple de la généralité de Lyon, 1534–1789* (Paris: Société d'édition "Les Belles Lettres," 1971), 172; Joseph Jomand, *Chaponost en Lyonnais* (Lyon: E. Vitte, 1966), 230, 291–292, 447, 507–508; Edouard Brenot, *Documents pour servir l'histoire de Grigny-en Lyonnais des origines à 1789* (Lyon: L'imprimerie des Beaux-Arts J. Tixier & Fils S.A, 1980), 235; Jacques Dupâquier, *Histoire de la population française* (Paris: PUF, 1995), 76; Serge Bianchi, *La terre et les paysans en France et en Grande Bretagne: Du début du XVIIe à la fin du XVIIIe siècle* (Paris: Armand Colin 1999), 53.
9. Jacques Peret, *Les paysans de Gâtine poitevine au XVIIIe siècle* (La Crèche: Geste Editions, 1998), 43–44, 98; Dominique Guillemet, Nicole Pellegrin, and Jacques Peret, *Le Haut Poitou au XVIIIe siècle* (Poitiers: CNDP, 1981), 11, 14–15; Louis Merle, *La métairie et l'évolution agraire de la*

Gâtine poitevine de la fin du Moyen Age à la Révolution (Paris: S.E.V.P.E.N.,1958), 40–41, 64; Philippe Bossis, "Le milieu paysan aux confins de l'Anjou, du Poitou et de la Bretagne, 1771–1789," *Etudes rurales* 47 (1972): 132–133, 135–136; Jean Elie, "Note sur l'économie agricole en Haut-Poitou au XVIIIe siècle. La Chapelle Moulière: Un exemple ou un cas particulier?" *Revue historique du Centre-Ouest* 2 (2003): 238; Jack Pichon, "La taille tarifée dans quatre paroisses du Haut-Poitou: Approche statistique d'un essai de répartition équitable de l'impôt au xviiie siècle," *Revue historique du Centre Ouest* 3 (2004): 149, 152, 154; Nicole Pellegrin, "Ruralité et modernité du textile en Haut-Poitou au XVIIIe siècle: La leçon des inventaires après-décès," in *Congrès national des Sociétés savantes, Lyon, Section d'histoire moderne et contemporaine* (Paris: CTHS, 1987), 380–381; Bernard Martin, *La vie en Poitou dans la seconde moitié du XVIIIe siècle: Mazeuil, paroisse du Mirebalais* (Maulévrier: Hérault 1988), 64.

10. André Benoist, *Paysans du Sud-Deux-Sèvres, XVIIe-XVIIIe siècle: La terre, les traditions, les hommes* (La Crèche: Geste 2005), 120, 184–185, 294–295; Idem., "Vie paysanne et protestantisme en « Moyen-Poitou » du XVIe siècle à la Révolution," *Annales de Bretagne et des pays de l'Ouest* 92, no. 2 (1985): 163–165, 167; Philippe Bossis, "La foire aux bestiaux en Vendée au XVIIIe siècle: Une restructuration du monde rural," *Études rurales* 78, no.1 (1980): 143; Charles Tilly, *The Vendée* (Cambridge, MA: Harvard University Press, 1964), 33; Alain Gérard, *Pourquoi la Vendée?* (Paris: Armand Colin, 1990), 42–44.
11. Annie Antoine, "Systèmes agraires de la France de l'Ouest: Une rationalité méconnue?" *Histoire économie et société* 18, no. 1 (1999): 121, 124–126, 128–129, 131.
12. François-P Gay, *La champagne du Berry: Essai sur la formation d'un paysage agraire et l'évolution d'une société rurale* (Bourges: Tardy, 1967), 159–160, 162–163, 169, 184–185, 308.
13. I. V. Loutchisky, "Régime Agraire et populations agricoles dans les environs de Paris à la veille de la Révolution," *Revue d'histoire moderne* 8, no. 7 (1933): 121, 123, 134; Jean Jacquart, *La crise rurale en Ile-de-France 1550–1670* (Paris: Librairie Armand Colin, 1974), 104–105, 107, 117; Pierre Brunet, *Structure agraire et économie rurale des plateau tertiaires entre la Seine et l'Oise* (Caen: Société d'impressions Caron, 1960), 284; Michel Vovelle, *Ville et campagne au 18e siècle: Chartres et la Beauce* (Paris: Éditions sociales, 1980), 85, 217, 202; Dupâquier, *Histoire*, 76; Idem., *La propriété et l'exploitation foncières à la fin de l'Ancien Régime dans la Gâtinais septentrional* (Paris: PUF, 1956), 145–146, 214, 255; Tulippe, *L'habitat*, 110; Béaur, *Le marché*, 128; Idem., "Investissement foncier, épargne et cycle de vie dans le pays chartrain au XVIIIe siècle," *Histoire & mesure* 6, no. 3–4 (1991): 285, 287.

14. Jean-Jacques Peru, "L'évolution de l'outillage aratoire dans trios communautés au nord-est de Paris (1600–1850)," in *Jardinages en région parisienne du XVIIe au XXe siècle*, ed. Jean-René Trochet and Jean-Jacques Péru (Paris: Créaphis, 2003), 68–69, 71; Roger Dion, *Histoire de la vigne et du vin en France des origines au XIXe siècle* (Paris: Imprimerie Sévin et Cie, 1959), 32, 466–467; Ernest Labrousse, *La crise de l'économie française à la fin de l'Ancien Régime et au début de la Révolution* (Paris: PUF, 1944) 554, 558; Micheline Baulant, "Groupes mobiles dans une société sédentaire : La société rurale autour de Meaux au xviie et xviiie siècle," in *Les Marginaux et les exclus dans l'histoire* (Paris: Union générale d'éditions, 1979), 96.
15. Maurice Aymard, "Autoconsommation et marchés : Chayanov, Labrousse ou Le Roy Ladurie?" in *La Terre et les Hommes : France et Grande-Bretagne XVIIe–XVIIIe siècle*, ed. Gérard Béaur (Paris: Hachette Litteratures, 1988), 235; Cynthia Bouton, *The Flour War: Gender, Class, and Community in Late Ancien Régime French Society* (University Park, Pa.: Pennsylvania State University Press, 1993), 57–59; Ernest Labrousse, *Esquisse du mouvement des prix et des revenues en France au XVIIIe siècle* (Paris: reedition Éditions des Archives Contemporaines, 1984), 362, 437–440, 509, 599, 612, 616.
16. Georges Durand, *Vin vigne et vignerons en lyonnais et Beaujolais* (Paris: Éditions de l'EHESS, 1979), 41–42, 291–292, 507–508; Gutton, *La société*, 71.
17. Joseph Dehergne, *Le Bas Poitou à la veille de la Révolution* (Paris: Centre national de la recherche scientifique, 1963), 23, 28, 54, 70; Peret, *Les paysans*, 47, 157; Martin, *La vie en Poitou*, 71–72; Bossis, "Le milieu paysan," 136; Gérard, *Pourquoi la Vendée?*, 55.
18. Henri Couturier, *La préparation des états généraux de 1789 en Poitou, principalement d'après les cahiers des paroisses et des corporations: Étude d'histoire du droit* (Poitiers: Société française d'imprimerie et de librairie, 1909), 74–76; Pierre Massé, *Varennes et ses maîtres: Un domaine rural, de l'Ancien Régime à la Monarchie de juillet (1778–1842)* (Paris: S.E.V.P.E.N., 1956), 24, 28; M. L. Autexier, *Les droits féodaux et les droits seigneuriaux en Poitou de 1559 à 1799* (Fontenay-le-Comte: P. & O. Lussaud frères imprimeurs, 1947), 85, 147–148; Jacques Peret, *Seigneurs et seigneuries en Gâtine poitevine: La duché de la Meilleraye XVIIe–XVIII siècles* (Poitiers: Au siège de la Société, 1976), 101, 132–133, 194, 225; Pierre-Yannick Legal, "Paysans Bas-Poitevins entre plaine, bocage, Gatine et marais (1730–1750)," *Recherches vendéennes* 2 (1995): 331–332, 348–349; François Tomas, "Problèmes de démographie historique : Le Forez au XVIIIe siècle," *Cahiers d'histoire* 13 (1968): 395; Josette Garnier, *Bourgeoisie et propriété immobilière en Forez aux XVIIe et XVIIIe siècles* (Saint-Etienne:

Centre d'études foréziennes, 1982), 363, 381; Louis Vignon, *Annales d'un village de France, Charly-Vernaison en Lyonnais* (Vernaison: Vignon, 1978), 451–452; Serge Dontenwill, "La mise en valeur des terres en Roannais Brionnais au dernier siècle de l'Ancien Régime (1670–1789)," in *Les contrats agraires de l'Antiquité à nos jours. Actes du colloque de Caen (10–13 septembre 1997*, ed. Anne Varet-Vitu, Mathieu Arnoux, and Gérard Béaur (Rennes: Association d'histoire des sociétés Rurales, 2003), 123, 127; J-P Surrault, *L'Indre: Le Bas-Berry de la préhistoire à nos jours* (Saint-Jean-d'Angély: Bordessoules, 1990), 197; Ernest Menault, *Histoire de l'agriculture en Berry: La condition paysanne du Ve au XVIIIe siècle* (Mayenne: Royer, 1991), 118; Dehergne, *Le Bas Poitou*, 28, 117–118, 177–178; Guillemet, Pellegrin, and Peret, *Le Haut Poitou*, 12, 14; Elie, "Note sur l'économie," 236; Gay, *La champagne du Berry*, 276.

19. Moriceau and Postel-Vinay, *Ferme,* 191–195, 197–198, 204–206, 209–212; Moriceau, "Au rendez-vous," 33–34, 38, 50–51, 53, 58; Moriceau, *Les Fermiers*, 640–643, 659–660, 779; Hoffman, *Growth in a Traditional Society*, 82, 102, 133, 144–146, 150–151.
20. Moriceau *Les Fermiers*, 631; Jacquart, "La rente," 362–365, 373–375.
21. Gérard Béaur, "Les Chartier et le mystère de la révolution agricole," *Histoire et mesure* 11, no. 3–4 (1996): 381–383, 385.
22. Moriceau and Postel-Vinay, *Ferme,* 191–195; Moriceau, "Au rendez-vous," 50–51.
23. George Grantham, "The Diffusion of the New Husbandry in Northern France, 1815–1840," *The Journal of Economic History* 38, no. 2 (1978): 332–323. For the agricultural revolution in early modern Europe, see the chapters of Dimmock and Zmolek in this book.
24. Moriceau and Postel-Vinay, *Ferme,* 210–212; Moriceau, "Au rendez-vous," 33–34.
25. Jean-Michel Chevet, "Production et productivité: Un modèle de développement économique des campagnes de la région parisienne aux xviiie et xixe siècles," *Histoire & mesure* 9, no. 1–2 (1994): 118–119, 123–127, 136, 138–139; Béaur, "Les Chartier," 374.
26. George Grantham, "The French Agricultural Productivity Paradox: Measuring the Unmeasurable," *Historical Methods* 33, no. 1 (2000): 38–39; Gérard Béaur, *Histoire agraire de la France au XVIIIe siècle: Inerties et changements dans les campagnes françaises entre 1715 et 1815* (Paris: SEDES, 2000), 59.
27. Raymonde Lejosne, "Champarts autours d'Étampes," *89 en Essonne* 2 (1989): 61–62; Marc Venard, *Bourgeois et paysans au XVIIe siècle : Recherches sur le rôle des bourgeois parisiens dans la vie agricole au Sud de Paris au XVIIe siècle* (Paris: S.E.V.P.E.N. 1957), 72–73, 83; Jacquart, "La rente," 359, 362–363; Loutchisky, "Régime Agraire," 141–142; Aymard, "Autoconsommation et marches," 222, 225.

28. Emile Mireaux, *Une province française au temps du grand roi : La Brie* (Paris: Hachette, 1958), 112–113, 117–118, 120–121; Anatoli Ado, *Paysans en Révolution : Terre, pouvoir et jacquerie 1789–1794*, trans. Serge Aberdam (Paris: Société des Études Robespierristes, 1996), 57–58; Jean Jacquart, *La crise rurale*, 272–274, 317, 757–758; Bouton, *The Flour War*, 44–45. George C. Comninel provides a good analysis of this non-capitalist commercial agriculture of the Paris Basin. *Rethinking the French Revolution: Marxism and the Revisionist Challenge* (London: Verso, 1987), 183–193.
29. Robert Allen, "Economic Structure and Agricultural Productivity in Europe, 1300–1800," *European Review of Economic History* 4, no. 1 (2000): 20; Gregory Clarke, "Agriculture in the Industrial Revolution, 1700–1860," in *The British Industrial Revolution*, ed. Joel Mokyr (Boulder, CO: Westview Press, 1999), 211.
30. Jean Nicolas, *La rébellion française: mouvements populaires et conscience sociale 1661–1789* (Paris: Éditions du Seuil, 2002), 76–77; Stephen Miller, *State and Society in Eighteenth Century France: A Study of Political Power and Social Revolution in Languedoc* (Washington, DC: The Catholic University of America Press, 2008), 193–194.
31. Annie Moulin, *Peasantry and Society in France since 1789* (Cambridge: Cambridge University Press, 1991), 3, 49, 60, 93, 109, 114, 142, 144–145; Berenson, *Populist*, 6–7, 9–10, 22.
32. Edward Berenson, "Politics and the French Peasantry: The Debate Continues," *Social History* 12 (1987): 219–229; Jean-Pierre Jessenne, *Les campagnes françaises: entre mythe et histoire (XVIIIe-XXIe siècle)* (Paris: Armand Colin, 2006), 202, 212, 215; Peter Amann, *The Corncribs of Buzet: Modernizing Agriculture in the French Southwest* (Princeton, N.J.: Princeton University Press, 1990), 177–178, 186, 196–197, 201, 216; Hugh Clout, *The Land of France 1815–1914* (London: George Allen & Unwin, 1983), 49–50, 79, 80–83, 100, 102, 148, 150–152; Scott Haine, *The History of France* (Westport, Conn.: Greenwood Press, 2000), 150.
33. Pierre Barral, "Le secteur agricole dans la France industrialisée, 1950–1974," in *Histoire économique et sociale de la France,* vol. IV, *L'ère industrielle et la société d'aujourd'hui (siècle 1880–1980): années 1950–1980, le Second XXe siècle. Vers quells horizons?*, ed. Fernand Braudel and Ernest Labrousse (Paris: PUF, 1982), 1427–1428; Laurence Duboys Fresney and Henri Mendras, *La seconde Révolution française : 1965–1984* (Paris: Gallimard, 1988), 28, 30–31.
34. Michel Augé-Laribé, *La politique agricole de la France de 1880 á 1940* (Paris: PUF, 1950), 93–94, 97–98; Arthur Conte, *Les paysans de France de l'an 1000 à l'an 2000* (Saint-Amand-Montrond: Librairie Plon, 2001), 222; Amann, *The Corncribs*, 196–197, 203, 207–208.

35. Pierre Miquel, *La France et ses paysans: une histoire du monde rural au XXe Siècle* (Paris: Éditions de l'Archipel, nouvelle édition revue et augmentée 2004, 2001), 187, 189, 191, 205–206, 223–225.
36. Fresney and Mendras, *La seconde Révolution*, 29–30.
37. Barral, "Le secteur agricole," 1429–1430, 1459; Jessenne, *Les campagnes françaises*, 225–228, 233–234, 239; Moulin, *Peasantry*, 170–171, 181–182, 194.
38. Barral, "Le secteur agricole," 1429; Miquel, *La France*, 226, 235–236, 259–260.
39. Geneviève Gavignaud-Fontaine, *La Révolution rurale dans la France contemporaine XVIIIe- XXe siècle* (Paris: Éditions L'Harmattan 1996), 143–144; Gordon Wright, *Rural Revolution in France: The Peasantry in the Twentieth Century* (Stanford: Stanford University Press, 1964), 154, 157, 170–171; Jessenne, *Les campagnes françaises*, 230.
40. Amann, *The Corncribs*, 206, 208, 211; Miquel, *La France*, 192, 237–238, 240–241, 243–244, 249.
41. Moulin, *Peasantry*, 168–169, 171, 174–176, 182; Fresney and Mendras, *La seconde Révolution*, 30; Gavignaud-Fontaine, *La Révolution rurale*, 144, 150.
42. Jessenne, *Les campagnes françaises*, 228; Michael Bess, *The Light-Green Society: Ecology and Technological Modernity in France, 1960–2000* (Chicago: University of Chicago Press, 2003), 43–44; Barral, "Le secteur agricole," 1433–1434.
43. José Bové, François Dufour, and Gilles Luneau, *The World is not for Sale: Farmers against Junk Food* (London: Verso, 2001), 44–45; Moulin, *Peasantry*, 171, 173, 182; Amann, *The Corncribs*, 230; Gavignaud-Fontaine, *La Révolution rurale*, 148, 150.

CHAPTER 5

The Transition to Industrial Capitalism in Nineteenth-Century France

Xavier Lafrance

This chapter addresses the issue of the rise of capitalism in France, contending that it first emerged in the country's industrial sector from the 1860s and over the following decades. Two of the main and partially interrelated historiographical debates that pertain to the issues of industrial development and capitalism in France both have their own "revisionist" strand. The first of these debates concerns the nature of the French Revolution (Was it capitalist or not?), while the second has to do with nineteenth-century France's economic development (Was it rapid or sluggish?).

Within the first of these debates, the Marxist "social interpretation" of the Revolution, which can be traced to the early twentieth-century work of Jean Jaurès,[1] was dominant until the 1960s. Its leading exponents, George Lefebvre, Albert Mathiez, and Albert Soboul, present the Revolution as the act of a bourgeoisie liberating itself from the shackle of feudalism, thus allowing capitalism to fully blossom in France.[2] Beginning with Alfred Cobban in the 1950s, and continuing with influential figures such as François Furet from the early 1970s, a revisionist current of

X. Lafrance (✉)
University of Québec in Montréal, Montréal, QC, Canada

X. Lafrance, C. Post (eds.), *Case Studies in the Origins of Capitalism*, Marx, Engels, and Marxisms,
https://doi.org/10.1007/978-3-319-95657-2_5

historians stressed that the French bourgeois that led the Revolution were not capitalists but rather landowners, state officials or lawyers.[3] Rejecting class analysis, revisionists asserted that the Revolution was not capitalist in nature and actually consolidated small peasant property as well as the position of conservative landowning elites. While some Marxists clung to the classical version of the social interpretation,[4] others fell back on a "consequentialist" perspective that maintained that, notwithstanding the capitalist motives of revolutionary agents, the Revolution had established a new political, legal and social context that would subsequently be conducive to capitalism.[5] In spite of the considerable influence achieved by revisionists, this perception of the Revolution as a gateway to mature industrial capitalism had been widespread among historians—including influential social historians of the French working class[6]—and is probably accepted as a truism by a majority of social scientists today.

The pace and form of capitalist industrialization in post-revolutionary France—the second historiographical debate mentioned earlier—has however been the object of extensive arguments among economic historians. During the post-war years, what François Crouzet named the "retardation-stagnation" thesis was dominant.[7] Perhaps best exemplified by David Landes's 1949 article on French entrepreneurship and industrial growth in nineteenth-century France, this thesis focused on cultural factors and maintained that French businessmen were conservative entrepreneurs that lacked the drive and initiative necessary for a rapid and sustained process of industrialization.[8] From the 1960s, a revisionist perspective began to challenge this prevailing orthodoxy as some historians stressed that the growth of French per capita national income had actually been quite respectable over the nineteenth century, compared to Britain. In 1964, Maurice Lévy-Leboyer was the first to stress that France and Britain had in any case followed distinct paths of industrialization[9]—a line of argument taken over by several historians subsequently, most famously by Patrick O'brien and Caglar Keyder in the anglophone world.[10] Departing from the British paradigm of mechanized mass production of standardized merchandises, French industrialization was based on the labor-intensive production of quality and luxury goods. This path was followed not because of French cultural idiosyncrasies, but rather because of objective factors, such as Napoleonic military defeats, the country's relative lack of coal resources, or its specific demographic patterns. As Crouzet explains, a "moderate" version of this revisionist strand came to prevail over recent decades and remains dominant today.[11]

Against the latter revisionist strand (within the debate on nineteenth century French economic growth), I argue in this chapter that French industrialization was significantly slower and weaker than Britain's over most of the nineteenth century. This was because, as revisionist economic historians working on this issue are right to stress, France followed a path of economic development that differed from Britain's. But departing from the revisionist thesis, I stress that France's industrialization was actually sluggish because, for most of the nineteenth century, *it was not capitalist in nature.*

While retaining a (alternative) Marxist class conception of the Revolution,[12] and departing on this latter point from revisionist historians of the French Revolution, I agree that 1789 did not pave the way to capitalism. Until around the 1860s, French industrial entrepreneurs did not evolve in capitalist competitive markets that would have compelled them to systematically maximize their profits in order to survive by steadily investing in productivity enhancing mechanization and by taking control of labor processes. While some merchants and industrialists did seize new opportunities, and were inspired by English mechanical production, they were not coerced by market imperatives to act as capitalists. Members of the French ruling class were still largely acting as rentiers, always keeping an eye on lucrative state positions and seeking a "proprietary"—as opposed to a capitalist—kind of wealth.[13]

Capitalism did not develop endogenously in France but resulted from decisive state interventions. As is explained later, these interventions initiated a capitalist transition in the industrial sector under the Second Empire and the Third republic. Geopolitical and economic competitive pressure exercised by Britain had however led French state officials to envisage liberal economic reforms much earlier—a point to which we now turn.

The False Start of the Old Regime

Robert Brenner has showed the deeply different ways in which France and England came out of the fourteenth-century crisis of European feudalism.[14] In England, the "economic" rents that were implemented imposed market imperatives on tenants that propelled a unique pattern of sustained economic development. In France, by contrast, landlords reacted to decreasing revenues by consolidating their extra-economic mode of appropriation under the aegis of an absolutist state. As explained by Stephen Miller in his chapter in this book and elsewhere,[15] the upshot was that both agrarian and artisan labor productivity remained stagnant, and probably declined, in Old Regime France. The economic advantage that England built over France was translated in a military superiority that became increasingly manifest over the eighteenth century.

As a consequence, the need to reform the economy of the kingdom was felt with soaring urgency among sections of French political elites. Already from the 1720s, memoirs and pamphlets were published that put emphasis on the constant innovations and improvements that explained English agrarian superiority.[16] These reflections were taken over and systematized around mid-eighteenth century by the Physiocrats who were seeking to emulate English agrarian capitalism in order to restore the dominant geopolitical standing of the French crown.[17] From the late 1740s, a group of liberal state servants aiming to reform not only the agrarian but also the industrial economy of the kingdom had assembled under the intellectual influence of Vincent de Gournay and began to lodge themselves in the corridors of power, all the way up to the royal council. Over the 1760s, followers of Gournay were instrumental in the adoption of different liberal measures such as the liberalization of grain trade or the lifting of the prohibition of printed calico. These policies, however, often produced widespread discontent and many were withdrawn.[18] The influence of liberal reformers within the state apparatus reached its zenith with Anne Robert Jacques Turgot's tenure as controller general from 1774 to 1776. Turgot's most controversial edict enacted the abolition of artisan guilds. The edict was once more rapidly retracted after it had ignited growing insubordination among artisans and strong dissatisfaction among large sections of French elites (including a large proportion of merchants). Jacques Necker, Turgot's successor, pursued policies informed by a much milder liberalism.

All in all, the balance sheet of liberal reforms seems rather thin in retrospect. This is not very surprising, considering that the liberal ideology that was promoted by Gournay and Turgot, and others had revolutionary implications in a society that had, as its basic units, not atomized individuals connected by market exchange but rather *corps* interwoven under the crown's authority.[19] The liberalism of French reformers not only endangered specific privileges but also threatened to erode the very "substance of privilege … and [to] gnaw at the corporatist heart of the *ancient regime*".[20]

A substantial proportion of French merchants were opposed to Gournay's liberalism, and many remained attached to state and guild regulations that ensured the quality and reputation of manufactured goods. Moreover, even when contesting specific regulations, merchants did not call for the dissolution of *corps* and of privileges. On the contrary, the freedom that they demanded subscribed to the existing system of privileges and was actualized through it. Within the context of the old regime, freedom was the privilege to freely organize as a body—as a *corps intermédiaire*—with the concurrence of the crown.[21] This was the institutional terrain on which French merchants operated—a world apart from the competitive market imperatives that propelled British capitalist enterprises. Consequently, assessing the activities of French textile merchants, "nowhere can we find traces of even rudimentary entrepreneurial calculation; no breakdown for material, labor, storage or unit cost were made".[22]

The French state's attempts to stimulate the kingdom's economy, either via liberal reforms or by granting diverse forms of privileges, brought disappointing results and no radical transformation of agrarian or industrial production. As Crouzet puts it, the expansion of the French economy over the eighteenth century "took place in a framework that, in its organizational aspects and in terms of methods, remained very much traditional … On the eve of the Revolution, the French economy was not fundamentally different than what it had been under Louis XIV: it only produced more".[23] In the industrial sector, the ability of British enterprises to mobilize technological innovations was much greater than in France. On the eve of the Revolution, in its cotton trade, England had 260 spindles per 1000 inhabitants against 2 in France. There were 900 spinning jennies in France against 20,000 in Britain and no more than a dozen mule-jennies in the former country against 9000 in the latter. Eight French establishments were using Arkwright's water frame compared with 200 in England. There were ten times more steam engines in use in Britain than there were in France, where only a few dozen could be found. Finally, the proportion of iron produced in blast furnace using coke reached 30–40 percent in Britain while it stagnated at 2 percent in France.[24]

The relative frailness of the French economy was most spectacularly and painfully revealed by the impact of the Anglo-French commercial treaty of 1786, the immediate effects of which were nothing short of "catastrophic" for the French industrial economy.[25] Cotton production collapsed in Haute-Normandy, and other industries such as metal, pottery and paper production were also harshly hit. Moreover, French exports to Britain (mostly wine and some luxury goods) grew by 75 percent as a result of the treaty, and until 1789, British exports to France rose by 360 percent over the same period.[26] Clearly, the first attempts of the French state to emulate the capitalist mode of development of its British rival had failed. The Revolution of 1789 did not change this situation; in ways, it actually consolidated it.

The French Revolution as a Moment of Labor Emancipation

Abolishing privileges and provincial particularism, the Revolution built a unified, judicially and administratively leveled, national territory. Internal custom barriers vanished and weights and measures were officially standardized. In 1791, the D'Allarde decree abolished trade corporations, while the Le Chapelier decree prohibited both workers and merchant-manufacturers associations or coalitions. The same year, the Goudard decree abolished state-backed fabrication rules and suppressed the royal inspectors that enforced them. These transformations form much of the stuff of the "consequentialist" reading of the Revolution. They also inform the related "artisan capitalism" thesis put forth by William H. Sewell and others.[27] According to Sewell, the decrees of 1791 brought "absolute private property" to France. He maintains that "property [of the means of production] was no longer, as under the Old Regime, to be subject to manifold public regulations bringing its use into harmony with preestablished public order", and that the elimination of guilds granted employers "the 'natural and inalienable and sacred right' to dispose of their property as they wished".[28] Sewell suggests that the disappearance of guilds and public regulations paved the way to a capitalist restructuring of artisan production in France.

Against Sewell's account, I argue that we cannot assume that employers and master artisans were capitalists in waiting that responded to market opportunities by becoming profit-maximizers as soon as the removal of public or corporate hindrances would allow them to. For capitalists to arise, we need social property relations that compel employers, through market competitive imperatives, to maximize profits in order to reproduce themselves. Contrary to Sewell's belief, the French Revolution actually consolidated non-capitalist social property relations—and the normative regulations of production that they entailed—in both towns and the countryside.

The Revolution opened the state as an instrument of enrichment for larger layers of the ruling class. While the venality of offices was formally eliminated, not much had changed in practice.[29] Lucrative and status-enhancing state functions were more than ever sought-after, making the state a persistent hub of surplus appropriation. The post-revolutionary ruling class continued to overwhelmingly favor "proprietary", or rentier (as opposed to capitalist), wealth and revenues such as land and urban property, state bonds, annuities or interests on private loans. Non-capitalist forms of surplus appropriation still largely prevailed in post-revolutionary France.

In parallel, social relations of production also retained a non-capitalist form. There is a wide historiographical agreement that the Revolution had the effect of safeguarding traditional small autarchic peasant tenure. As Stephen Miller explained in the previous chapter, this situation prevailed throughout the nineteenth century and into the twentieth. A less well-known fact is that the French Revolution also represented a moment of labor emancipation and actually perpetuated, and even expanded, the normative regulation of artisanal and industrial work.

It is first worth noting that the "moral economy", or *bon droit* of artisan and industrial France was not simply hanging by the thread of guilds. Many trades actually never established guilds, but nevertheless maintained normative regulations, often under the supervision of municipal governments and through an intricate network of high and low courts, parliaments, *bureau de marque*, police offices, as well as popular mobilizations. At a distance from, but often in tense dialogue with, guilds, one could find what Sonenscher has named "bazaar economies"—spaces where normative regulations of economic activities prevailed.[30] Even in areas were the state had formally authorized artisanal production outside the jurisdiction of guilds, such as in the Parisian *faubourg Saint-Antoine*, popular *bon droit* and artisan regulations remained strong.[31]

Moreover, the abolition of guilds "was not, as is usually thought, an outgrowth of the commitment of the revolutionary bourgeoisie to the principle of economic freedom".[32] An analysis of *cahiers de doléances* and of the process leading to the eradication of guilds clearly shows that it stemmed from resistance from below exercised by journeymen and masters who were not in charge of guilds.[33] Relying on, and promoting, their *bon droit*, while borrowing and appropriating from Enlightenment philosophers, French workers had long been organizing and struggling against the subordination imposed by guild masters, over the century leading to the Revolution.[34]

These popular struggles intensified with the coming of the Revolution, as assemblies sprouted, demonstrations multiplied and numerous petitions were signed. Workers interpreted the Revolution as a complete overthrow of the old labor regime. They were vividly aware of the emancipatory potential of the abolition of privileges by the Constituent Assembly on the night of August 4 and were determined to apply this revolutionary rupture in the field of labor relations by rejecting subordination to their employers.[35] This intention materialized rapidly as rapidly growing numbers of workers overtly and unilaterally overlooked oppressive guild rules, left their masters and ignored the consequences. Well before their formal abolition in 1791, guilds had been de facto disintegrating.[36]

As Alain Cottereau explains, all of the upheavals brought forth by the Revolution, from the abolition of privileges to the abolition of guilds, through the Declaration of the Rights of Man and of the Citizens, "were intensively lived as an effective worker's emancipation, as a triumph of old moral struggles, and as the consecration of an effective capacity to fairly negotiate with employers. These were not only formal civil rights, but indeed new real possibilities, massively used".[37] A vast majority of workers were freed from subordination from their employers. Already before the Revolution, *louage d'ouvrage* and *louage de service* had existed as distinct forms of employment. The former was a type of contract that guaranteed that workers could retain their autonomy in the face of their employers and that they could organize their labor as they saw fit, granted customary *usages* were respected. As for the second type of contract, it was closer to a relation of domesticity and implied submission to a master's directives. The rights conquered by workers in the wake of the Revolution materialized through an immediate and widespread expansion of workers that entered *louage d'ouvrage* contract. Toward the end of the Second Empire, still about 90 percent of French workers performed labor under the aegis of this type of contract.[38]

Tough often characterized as liberal, the Civil Code, which had been in preparation since 1793 and was finally promulgated in 1804, actually safeguarded these new emancipatory rights. There is no space here to deal with this issue in detail, but a few points should be made.[39] The Code did recognize the difference between *louage d'ouvrage* and *louage de service* and how the former ruled out any form of subordination of employees to employers. Accordingly, the jurist Charles Renouard insisted in 1854 that the Civil Code "clearly established that the renting of one's labor is not an alienation of the capacity to work, and that this faculty, inherent to human activity, remains the property of the worker".[40]

If workers were now formally, and effectively, freed from the subordination that had been enforced by guilds, this did not imply that they were thrown on unregulated labor markets—on the contrary. While article 1134 of the Civil Code mentions that "contracts freely established have force of law to those who established them"—an excerpt often cited as proof of the Code's liberal character—article 1135 immediately specifies that "contracts compel not only to what they express, but also to every follow-up that equity, usage or the law pose as an obligation according to its nature".[41] Equity and usage were components of a *bon droit* that was administered and enforced underneath and in spite of a spreading elite liberal discourse by a set of local and regional institutions.

Municipal government played an important role in this, setting tariffs at which workers were paid or overseeing and mediating negotiations that set those in different trades. In 1790, the Constituent Assembly established *justices de paix*, proximity courts that offered a simplified, rapid and free form of justice. Favoring a conciliatory approach, justices of the peace dealt with a vast range of day-to-day disputes, but also specifically intervened in conflicts pertaining to labor relations and commercial exchanges.[42] They arbitrated hundreds of thousands of legal conflicts in 1791, and between 2 and 4 million over the 80 years that followed.[43] These figures give an indication of the new roles of citizens in the administration of their community life and signaled a durable institutionalization of *bon droit* in the realm of labor relations in post-revolutionary France.

First appearing in 1806 in Lyon as an outgrowth of eighteenth-century and revolutionary struggles and demands, *conseils de prud'hommes* were conceived as industrial justices of the peace. They also had a crucial function of economic and labor regulation. Elected within trade communities, the council's officials pronounced judgments and provided conciliatory advice on all aspects of labor relations. Doing this, they systematically refused to grant arbitrary powers to employers and to let unfettered market competition set wages and working conditions.[44] *Prud'hommes* ensured that artisan and industrial production was conducted according to local and trade usages and cracked down on every attempt by employer to unilaterally encroach on those.[45] In this, municipal and regional political authorities often backed them. For instance, rejecting factory rules unilaterally set by employers, Roubaix's mayor issued a decree in 1837 that explained that such unilateral rules "injure distributive justice and natural equity, since they concede to masters rights it refuses to workers".[46]

In such a context, the subsumption of labor by capital was not possible. As shown by Mike Zmolek is his contribution to this book, normative regulation of artisan and industrial trades eroded rapidly in Britain as the country underwent a transition to industrial capitalism. As a result, employers were increasingly able to control the labor process and to impose new divisions of labor and time discipline.[47] In this, and as capitalist industrialization unfolded, employers were backed by the state, which was strengthening the judiciary repression and control of the labor force. Until the mid-1870s, the *Law of Master and Servant* ensured that employees remained legally, and practically, subordinated to their employers.

In France, as we saw, workers had emancipated themselves from this kind of subordination, were free to leave their employers as they willed and faced them as equals. Moreover, the forms of capitalist management that were spreading in Britain remained absence in France for decades after the Revolution. French factories and workshops collected workers together but did not implement the kind of capitalist division of labor that was emerging and spreading in Britain. Workers remained in control of their labor and preserved a relationship of employment with factory owners that remained largely similar to the one that artisan and output workers had with merchants. Rather than acting as wage-laborers, they rented a spot in a mill, buying raw material and selling back final products to the owner.[48] Accordingly, discipline was weak and hierarchical supervisory structures almost completely absent.[49]

Until approximately the last third of the nineteenth century, for French merchants and industrialists, "to organize work was not economically relevant ... In the end, the idea of organizing work was not even envisaged".[50] As noted by Michelle Perrot, French factory owners "did not have during this period a true productivity policy".[51] Lefebvre explains this lack of concern for the organization of production by French employers by a lack of "sufficient competition to be forced to pay great attention to production costs".[52] The absence of capitalist market competition explains the relatively slow process of industrialization that took place in France over the first half of the nineteenth century.

The Absence of Capitalist Market Imperatives and Opportunity-Driven Industrialization in Post-Revolutionary France

All economic historians, including revisionists, agree that nineteenth-century France's absolute gross domestic product (GDP) growth was sluggish compared with Britain's. Economic and industrial growth did take place in France over the decades following the Revolution. This growth, however, was largely labor-intensive—it relied on the exploitation of large reserves of cheap labor in the countryside. Accordingly, labor productivity growth remained relatively slow in France, compared to Britain. As Craft indicates, the French industrial output per worker was only equal to 51.1 percent of the output in Britain in 1855–1864.[53]

This productivity gap was associated with the much slower mechanization of production that took place in France over the first half of the nineteenth century. The number of power looms in use in the French textile industries, for instance, went from 5000 in 1834 up to 31,000 in 1846 and to 85,000 in 1875.[54] Much of the additional looms taken into account in 1875, however, were actually introduced after 1860 and as a consequence of the capitalist transformation of French industry that is discussed in the next section. In any case, as impressive as this evolution may appear, it was outshined by British figures. The combined number of power looms in England and Scotland went from 55,500 in 1829 up to 100,000 in 1833 and up again to 250,000 in 1857.[55]

The magnitude of horsepower produced by steam engines was also much smaller in France than it was in capitalist Britain. In 1830, 3000 steam engines could be found in France, producing a total of 15,000 horsepower, while Britain numbered 15,000, having an overall capacity of 220,000 horsepower.[56] In 1840, France, with a population of 35 million, possessed steam engines producing 34,000 horsepower, while Britain, with a population of 19 million, comprised steam engines producing 350,000 horsepower. In 1850, these figures had respectively increased to 67,000 horsepower (again, mostly as a result of railroad development) against 544,000 in Britain, and France had by then fallen behind Prussia.[57] While this gap was reduced during the last decades of the century, in 1870, the quantity of horsepower per industrial employee in France was equal to only 21 percent of that amount in Britain.[58]

Such technological gaps cannot be explained away, as revisionist economists would have it, simply by pointing to "distinct paths of industrialization" related to different endowments of natural resources, workforce, capital or technology. Hobsbawm has noted that "the supremacy of French science" over this period fueled a vibrant technological inventiveness, which was simply not mobilized in industrial production as systematically as it was in Britain.[59] He also notes that France was in possession of large capital reserves and that, together with London, Paris was the great financial capital of Europe.[60] It is true that the French banking system remained archaic for decades following the Revolution. Investment banking and modern deposit banking did not emerge until the Second Empire and, even then, remained embryonic if compared to British equivalents.[61] Yet, the lacuna of French financial institutions was much more a reflection than a cause of the relatively slow industrialization of France.

An important factor behind the relative slowness of French industrialization was the absence of a mass internal consumer market in France—which was itself a consequence of the absence of agrarian capitalism in this country. But, as always, we should not assume that growing market opportunities would, on their own, naturally have led merchants, factory owners or artisan producers to act as capitalists and to engage in cost-cutting and profit maximizing practices. Beyond their depth, we must also consider the nature of markets. Only when facing the imperatives stemming from *competitive* markets are businesses compelled to act in a capitalist fashion. Markets become capitalists precisely when they no longer simply offer opportunities but become coercive structures. In a capitalist economy, markets themselves become social property relations—meaning that the capitalists' ongoing access to the means of production now depends on their ability to beat competitors. Facing price competition, and losing the capacity to control market conditions, capital owners must follow "rules of reproduction" that compel them to direct the labor process, to maximize profits, and to invest a constant part of their revenues so as to continuously cut costs through the usage of "state of the art" technologies. Yet, the emergence of competitive, or capitalist, markets is a rare historical occurrence.[62] Until approximately the last third of the nineteenth century, such competitive markets remained absent in France.

Besides the aforementioned persistence of customary regulations—which acted as alternatives to market competition as means of coordination of social relations of production—two main factors explain the absence of competitive markets in post-revolutionary France. The first of these factors was the disintegrated character of the French economic space. While the Revolution and Napoleonic era abolished commercial barriers and internal tariffs, the absence of adequate transport infrastructures implied that the French national economic space remained importantly fragmented. Until the last decades of the nineteenth century, the country remained "constituted of a series of local and regional markets grouped around one or two country towns; such markets had only loose connections with each other and a national market scarcely existed".[63] French merchant-industrialists made much of their profits in circulation by acting as mediators between these disconnected economic spaces. Consequently, until the 1860s, "the logic of an ongoing decompartmentalization of circulation, of a levelling of costs and prices did not exist in the attitudes of the vast majority of merchants, or even in the declarations of their representatives. Above all, as years passed, nothing indicated an evolution toward a less 'imperfect' market, nor a will to reduce the number of filters through which supply and demand were at play".[64]

The second factor that explains the lack of capitalist market imperatives in post-revolutionary France was the strong economic protectionism adopted and renewed by the state until the Anglo-French commercial treaty of 1860. Following the end of the Napoleonic Wars and of the Continental Blockade, in 1816 and 1817, the new regime adopted tariff schedules that were uniformly high and often prohibitive and included outright prohibition of cotton products importations as well as tariffs of 50 percent on iron, which were hiked up to 120 percent in 1822.[65] As a consequence, British industrial competition was strongly refracted or almost completely muffled for most industrial branches.

Because of the combined effects of fragmentation of markets, of protection from British capitalist competition and of customary regulations of social relations of production, French industrial firms were not compelled to *systematically* mechanize production and to improve labor processes so as to beat competition and remain afloat. Consequently, the mechanization of French industrial production that took place in France, until the last decade Second Empire, was fuelled by market *opportunities* rather than by market compulsion. Assessing the development of textile production—the most important French industrial sector at the time—at the turn of the nineteenth century and during the decades that followed the Revolution, Reddy stresses "just how weak the force of competition" remained in France and explains that firms were not evolving on "price-forming markets" and were consequently not compelled to engage in "cost-conscious management".[66] At the same time, the "twenty-fold advantage in productivity", and the attendant profit boosting potential that English machines provided to their owners did not escape French merchant-industrialists.[67]

In 1786–1789, under the Anglo-French commercial treaty, French textile firms had responded to English competition largely by ending production. After 1816, insulated from English competition, they could now seize market opportunities and invest in mechanization. In this much safer context, "if one could just get a set of the new spinning machines into operation, one was *assured* a handsome profit".[68] A clear indicator that French industrialization was driven by market opportunity rather than by capitalist market compulsion is the fact that, when demand contracted and opportunities evaporated—as was the case during the slumps of 1811–1812, of 1814 and again from 1827 to 1831—textile firms tended to put production on hold or to move out of the market altogether.[69] In sharp contrast, evolving in a capitalist context, English manufacturers were compelled by price competition over the same period to respond to economic slumps by stepping up their investment "to seek every means possible to reduce the costs of production. This was done chiefly by speeding-up machinery and by adding power-loom weaving to spinning".[70] In England, contrary to France, the market was a coercive force—not simply an opportunity.

The end of this slow-moving mode of industrialization called for state interventions to impose a new market discipline and to give capital the power to subsume labor. Such interventions decisively began under the Second Empire.

The State-Led Capitalist Transformation of French Industry

The capitalist restructuring of the French industrial sector was initiated under the Second Empire and the Third Republic. While state interventions established its prerequisites from the 1850s, this restructuring really began from the 1860s and unfolded over the following decades. During this period, the European geopolitical balance of power was transformed, as new unified nation-states emerged and new European powers—most importantly Germany—underwent rapid processes of capitalist industrialization, while British development continued apace. In order to maintain its position as a major power, France had to adapt to this new international context.

While less prone to impose a capitalist restructuring of agriculture that would upset the peasantry that had formed to linchpin of successive regimes since the Revolution,[71] the French state felt strong pressure to modernize and develop the country's industrial sector so as to support its geopolitical standing. Not all sectors of French elites agreed with this project, however, and many were still attached to their ideal of a rural and non-industrialized France. Conflicts over the need to imitate English capitalism raged outside and within the state well into the Third Republic and passed the turn of the twentieth century.

In the wake of the 1851 coup that made the president an emperor, Napoleon III was able to override this resistance and to introduce structural economic changes. In spite of its ostensibly democratic (but in fact tightly controlled) electoral processes, the Second Empire imposed a personalized dictatorship that was largely freed of parliamentary control that monarchs had had to concede after the Restoration.[72] Sharply breaking with July monarchy policies on economic issues, the new regime was the first to give a clear priority to industrial growth. Under the influence of liberal Saint-Simonian high-ranking servants, economic advisors and bankers—who were all fascinated and greatly inspired by the British experience—the Emperor made his priorities clear right from 1852. For him, "the nation's greatness depended—no less than on military victory—on the success of an 'industrial revolution', in the broadest sense, that would hoist France to the level already reached by England".[73] The economic welfare that would ensue would eliminate unemployment, increase popular consumption and empower France geopolitically—all of which would contribute to stabilize the regime.

The new regime rapidly acted in order to reform the French financial sector, which had retained a conservative rentier attitude in the 1840s. The Emperor supported the creation of the Pereire brothers' Crédit Mobilier in the early 1850s. This arrival of the new financial institution was widely resisted by the conservative *Haute Banque* concentrated in Paris, but the latter was eventually forced to modernize its lending practices. This modernization, however, remained significantly limited, and the French finance continued to secure most of its profits out of speculative activities (increasingly related to railroad building in these years) and interests on state loans, rather than out of productive investment in the country's industrial sector.[74] Yet, if the involvement of French finance in the industrial sector remained peripheral, it was less out of sheer conservatism (though this remained a factor) than because of the fact that domestic demand for capital was still relatively weak. In addition to reforming finance, the regime needed to create a context in which firms would be compelled to invest.

Napoleon III and his advisors were well aware that the key for the "industrial revolution" that they wished to launch was to incite price competition that would force industrial firms to modernize their installations and activities. A first crucial element to incite this competition was to develop transport and communication networks. An 1842 law had launched the formation of a national railway network, but its construction was slow and France lagged behind several European countries. The Emperor's entourage understood that granting concessions to private companies that built and exploited railway lines was not enough—resolute state action was needed to actually mobilize the capital invested in these developments. The government granted 99 years concessions to companies and authorized them to emit bonds (an initiative already taken by the Second Republic). It also guaranteed the payment of 4 percent interests on these bonds and on loans contracted by railway companies to finance their investments. Once the initial network was completed toward the late 1850s, the government actively intervened to direct the Bank of France to support the building of branch lines and continued to back interest payment.[75]

These efforts rapidly paid-off. Counting 1931 km in 1850, France's railway network expanded to 4100 km in 1860 and again to 17,400 km, before reaching 23,600 km in 1880. Rail transport quickly increased in parallel, going from 100 million tons per kilometer in 1845 up to 5057 million tons in 1870. Already by 1869, all the main routes of the present-day network had been built and France had caught up or surpassed most of its neighbors.[76] In parallel, during the 1850s, the French state developed a national electric telegraph network that was made available to the public by the mid-1850s and became widely used, including by private industrial firms.[77]

The rapid development of modern transport and communication infrastructures by the Second Empire came together with a profound transformation of commercial and marketing practices. Increasingly, product circulation was rationalized and the number of commercial intermediaries significantly decreased. Contacts between producers and consumers became much more direct and constant, as the former began to display systematic efforts to reach the latter. The co-dependence of industry and commerce also significantly intensified, as production began to systematically follow the impulsion of orders that could now be placed on a daily basis and swiftly shipped. The new figure of the commercial commissioner embodied these transformations. Establishing themselves in all branches, commissioner houses developed a mode of distribution that allowed consumers to simultaneously have access to similar products made by different French as well as foreign firms. This induced a price competition that was also facilitated by the emergence of *grands magasins*, which made their influence felt in Paris and in other larger cities especially strongly from the 1860s and 1870s.[78]

The development of railways in the 1860s led to the emergence of a national market that became an increasingly implacable economic reality as its unification reached completion by the late 1870s. This was the end of the internal compartmentalization of the French economic space. The multitude of local and regional economies that had endured into the nineteenth century were now being integrated to, and subsumed under, a national market. The important inter-regional price disparities that had persisted in post-revolutionary France were consequently rapidly eroding. The ensuing price competition caused the disappearance of guaranteed incomes attached to regional monopolies, and whole regional industries were in some cases wiped out as a result. This leads Caron to suggest that the formation of a unified national market was as important a factor as the intensification of international competition in causing the economic transformation of France during the Second Empire and beyond.[79] Modern transport infrastructures were in fact also a vector of the foreign competition that began to seriously impact French firms in the wake of the signature of commercial treaties by the French state.

The government of Napoleon III signed a commercial treaty with Britain in 1860 with diplomatic intents—France wanted to stabilize a geopolitical alliance with its powerful neighbor. Modernizing the economy was another central goal of the government. The intent was to impose a change of context so that "the most highly protected French industries would be forced to equip themselves to world standards on pain of losing their home market, and thus their whole basis for existence".[80] While the emperor was opposed to complete free trade, he had been convinced by his Saint-Simonian entourage of the need to liberalize international trade in order to stimulate economic development. The vast majority of French industrialists, however, were pungently opposed to any questioning of the prevailing and long-standing protectionist policy. Their strong lobbying organizations, their capacity to mobilize the support of their workers on this issue and their numerous powerful allies within the state had allowed them to impose and to reproduce a protectionist orthodoxy since the fall of the First Empire.

Napoleon III and his entourage advanced with caution. Already in 1853, duties on iron and coal were reduced to support the construction of railroads. Other duties reductions followed and, in 1856, a bill to replace prohibitions on textile imports with moderate duties was put forth before being repelled by the strong opposition it incited within the *corps législatif* and among industrialist circles.[81] In spite of this rejection, the emperor announced that international trade would be liberalized within five years and proceeded to circumvent legislative power. Following secret negotiations with Britain led by Michel Chevalier, Napoleon used his constitutional power to sign international treaties. The commercial treaty of 1860 that resulted—denounced as a "*coup d'État douanier*" by industrialists and members of the legislative assembly—did not impose free trade. While Britain would not enforce any tariffs on trade (thus sticking the free trade posture that it had already adopted), the treaty stipulated that French tariffs could not exceed 30 percent (25 percent from 1864). Separate conventions were subsequently negotiated, also in 1860, to fix duties for specific sectors. In order to avoid the economic debacle that followed the trade treaty in 1786 and to appease industrialists, the government put in place a commission of enquiry to guide the negotiation of these conventions. It also offered low interest loans to support the modernizing efforts of French firms.[82]

The Anglo-French treaty of 1860 served as a template for some 14 others signed by France with European countries in the years that followed. While a movement toward higher duties began in the early 1880s and continued in the early 1890s, France became exposed to an international economic competition that never fully receded from the 1860s until the interwar period in the twentieth century. Indeed, the Méline law of 1892 introduced tariffs that were remarkably moderate (especially for industrial products) compared to those of the first half of the nineteenth century. In the new context of a unified national market exposed to international competition, French industrial firms were compelled to seize control over labor process in order to survive.

These efforts were facilitated by important judicial transformations as sectors of the French state sought, from the second half of the 1860s, to invalidate the power of proximity justice courts that prevented the subsumption of labor by capital. In 1866, a ruling made by the *Cour de cassation*—France's highest court of justice—invalidated a previous ruling made by a *prud'hommes* council and was widely publicized. Against the council, the high court had confirmed that an employer could retain two weeks' pay from a worker who had entered the workshop with her clogs, in violation of rules established unilaterally by her employers.[83] Similar decisions granting arbitrary powers to employers were issued under the Third Republic during the 1870s. These rulings often brought public outrage and members of the *Chambre des députés* proposed bills seeking to overturn some of them. These attempts, however, were systematically blocked by the Senate, which sided with the *Cour de cassation*. Parallel to these developments, the publication of treatises by liberal jurists from the 1880s launched a profound revision of legal doctrines pertaining to labor relations.[84] All of this had the effect of consolidating the arbitrary power of employers. Crucially, these judicial transformations also had the effect of increasingly prohibiting the adoption of tariffs fixing the workers' wages. They also sparked a crisis among *prud'hommes*, which caused many to resign in protest, while others bent under the pressure coming from above.

As gains made by French workers in the wake of the 1789 Revolution were increasingly imperiled, employers moved forward to assert their control over production in parallel. The inquiry launched as part of the 1860 commercial treaty revealed that managerial style had not really changed since a previous similar enquiry into import prohibition conducted in 1834. But things changed rapidly from the 1860s and over the following decades. While textile employers had unsuccessfully attempted to interfere with the work process once or twice since 1820, attempts to impose labor management become routine in the emerging capitalist context of the last decades of the nineteenth century.[85] From the last decade of the Second Empire, and even more evidently during the 1870s and 1880s, industrial labor began to be divided and rationalized so as to sustain the maximization of profits, while factory and workshop owners developed hierarchical structures, enforced internal factory rules, and hired growing numbers of foremen to direct and discipline workers.[86]

The age-old merchant model, in which individual or teams of workers bought raw material, rented access to factory facilities (and sometimes to tools as well), and sold their products to mill owners, gave way to new hiring practices in which workers were directly engaged by employers as wage-laborers.[87] With the rise of this new employer-employee relationship, industrial workers began to sell their *labor-power*[88]; a transformation that paved the way to the capitalist alienation of labor that *louage d'ouvrage* contracts had until then prevented. This subsumption and speed-up of labor also began to spread into smaller craft production. While these transformations were highly contested by French workers, who increasingly resorted to strike and street protests to defend their *bon droit*, new forms of time discipline were internalized and overtime became normal practice from the 1890s.[89]

In addition to seeking direct control over the labor process, incipient capitalist employers began to transform industrial production by mechanizing it at a much more rapid pace. From the 1860s, and for a period of two or three decades, France did not fare very well economically. It was soon surpassed by Germany and several other European countries were also rapidly catching up with the newly formed Republic. By the 1870s, France's trade balance had become negative. As price competition strongly intensified, profits fell and the number of bankruptcy rates increased sharply.[90] Comparatively, France was hit especially hard by the depression of the last third of the nineteenth century. Rates of industrial growth decelerated, going from 2.5 percent per year from 1815 to 1854 down to 1.6 percent per year from the turn of the 1860s to the turn of the 1890s.[91]

Yet, in spite, or in fact *because*, of this tighter price competition, in a depressed economic context characterized by falling profits and decreasing market opportunities, French industrial firms did not diminish but actually *intensified* investments aimed at mechanizing their facilities. This, probably more than anything else, was a clear signal of the capitalist transformation of France's industrial sector: whereas firms had previously paused their activities in times of economic slowdown, they now systematically invested to cope with tighter markets. The last third of the nineteenth century brought a clear epochal break as French firms adopted a "capitalistic" style of industrial development in which the capital factor was increasingly replacing the labor factor.[92] The overall share of investments in the country's GDP went from 12.1 percent in the 1850s, up to 13 percent from 1875 to 1889, before reaching 14.2 percent from 1905 to 1913. Moreover, the share of industrial investments in total investments reached 38 percent from 1905 to 1913, up from 13 percent from the mid-1840s to the mid-1850.[93] Accordingly, the average annual growth of horsepower in use in industry accelerated and went from 9500 from 1839 to 1869, up to 32,800 from 1871 to 1894, before reaching 73,350 from 1883 to 1903 and 141,800 from 1903 to 1913.[94]

Clearly, exposed to foreign as well as domestic competition in a leveled national economic space where customary regulations of production and of labor markets were being rolled back, French firms had been forced to adapt. New social property relations had imposed new rules of reproduction: cost cutting and profit maximization had become a matter of economic survival for industrial firms. In the wake of the trade treaty signed with Britain and subsequent ones, French cotton producers had to abandon cottage handweaving. The production of cotton and of woolen goods was rapidly mechanized and the use self-acting mules soon became the norm. Even the silk industry mechanized, in an effort to penetrate entry-level markets for cheaper goods.[95] Already from the 1850s, the government's decision to reduce dues on imported iron goods had also compelled rapidly growing number of iron producing firms to use coke-fired blast furnaces. During the 1860s, this technology had become quasi-universal across France and productivity-enhancing innovations became frequent and spread rapidly.[96] Overall, incapacity to adopt top-of-the-art technologies became crippling in a rising number of industrial sectors.

Because of the extraordinary persistence of a mass peasantry in France described by Stephen Miller in the previous chapter, France lacked the mass internal consumer market that would have allowed the country to experience a process of capitalist industrialization as impressive as the one that occurred in Germany over the last decades of the nineteenth century. This factor also explains why small artisan production remained so important in France well into the twentieth century. Yet, from the end of the nineteenth century, a clear tendency could be witnessed in France that led to the gradual concentration of production in larger factories, as industrial growth became more diversified and new capital-intensive sectors emerged. The upshot of this capitalist transformation of French industry was that labor productivity growth reached 2.4 percent per year over the 1890s—twice the rate of the rest of the nineteenth century.[97] This allowed France to experience rapid economic growth from the mid-1890s to World War I that was on par or higher than the growth of leading capitalist countries.

Conclusion

Against the revisionist perspective on modern French economic growth summarized in the introduction, this chapter has shown how the absence of capitalist social property relations explains why French industrialization lagged far behind Britain's during the eighteenth century and most of the nineteenth century. It also explained how the French Revolution of 1789, far from announcing the rapid rise of capitalism, actually consolidated non-capitalist social property relations and reinforced and developed the customary rights of French workers.

One could say that, for half a century, post-Revolutionary France sat on fence between capitalism and socialism. Rapid capitalist industrialization in Britain had long been frightening French elites, but it also inspired some French merchants-industrialists to seize market opportunities and to use English machinery, albeit on a much smaller scale. This was a development that prefigured future capitalist transformations. It prefigured, but in no way ensured these transformations. Indeed, a socialist alternative also gained traction. While French entrepreneurs were not *compelled* to use new technologies until the last third of the nineteenth century, French workers had made gains in the wake of the 1789 Revolution that served as the basis on which they built a strong labor movement over the 1830s and 1840s. This movement demanded a "democratic and social republic". Workers wanted a democratic republic that would transform a state that was still and increasingly used by the ruling class as a nexus of surplus appropriation. They also wanted a social republic, one that would consolidate and develop the customary rights that had been enhanced following 1789. The revolution of 1848 offered an opportunity to bring about this democratic socialism.[98]

It was the repression of this socialist ideal with the crushing of the 1848 revolution and, decisively, of the Paris Commune, that finally settled the matter. In the closing decades of the nineteenth century, France underwent fundamental transformations of its class structures that ensured that it would enter World War I as an industrial capitalist power.

Notes

1. Jean Jaurès, *Histoire socialiste de la Révolution française* (Paris: Les Édition sociales, 2014–2015 [1901–1908]).
2. George Lefebvre, *The Coming of the French Revolution* (Princeton: Princeton University Press, 2015 [1947]); Albert Mathiez, *La Révolution française* (Paris: Armand Colin, 1964); Albert Soboul, *La Révolution Française* (Paris: Presses universitaires de France, 1975).
3. Alfred Cobban, *The Social Interpretation of the French Revolution* (Cambridge: Cambridge University Press, 1964); François Furet, *Penser la Révolution française* (Paris: Gallimard, 1978).
4. See, for instance, Henry Heller, *The Bourgeois Revolution in France 1789–1815* (New York: Berghahn, 2006).
5. See, for instance, Neil Davidson, *How Revolutionary Were the Bourgeois Revolutions?* (Chicago: Haymarket Books, 2012).
6. See, for instance, William H. Sewell, *Work and Revolution in France: The Language of Labor from the Old Regime to 1848* (Cambridge: Cambridge University Press, 1980).
7. François Crouzet, "The Historiography of French Economic Growth in the Nineteenth Century," *The Economic History Review* 56, no. 2 (2003): 215.
8. David S. Landes, "French Entrepreneurship and Industrial Growth in the Nineteenth Century," *The Journal of Economic History* 9, no. 1 (1949): 45–61.

9. Maurice Lévy-Leboyer, *Les banques européennes et l'industrialisation internationale dans la première moitié du XIXe siècle* (Paris: Presses Universitaires de France, 1964).
10. Patrick O'brien and Caglar Keyder, *Economic Growth in Britain and France 1789–1919* (New York: Routledge, 2012 [1978]).
11. Crouzet, "The Historiography of French Economic Growth," 215.
12. Developed in George C. Comninel, *Rethinking the French Revolution: Marxism and the Revisionist Challenge* (London, Verso, 1987); and Ellen Meiksins Wood, *The Pristine Culture of Capitalism: A Historical Essay on Old Regimes and Modern States* (London and New York: Verso, 1991) and *Liberty and Property: A Social History of Western Political Thought from Renaissance to Enlightment* (New York: Verso, 2012).
13. On the notion of proprietary wealth and its form in Old Regime France, see George V. Taylor, "Noncapitalist Wealth and the Origins of the French Revolution," *The American Historical Review* 72, no. 2 (1967): 469–496.
14. Robert Brenner, "Agrarian Class Structure and Economic Development in Pre-Industrial Europe 1985" and "Agrarian Roots of European Capitalism," in *The Brenner Debate: Agrarian Class Structure and Economic Development in Pre-Industrial Europe*, ed. T.H. Aston and C.H.E. Philpin (New York: Cambridge University Press, 1985).
15. Stephen Miller, "The Economy of France in the Eighteenth and Nineteenth Centuries: Market Opportunity and Labor Productivity in Languedoc," *Rural History* 20, no. 1 (2009): 1–30.
16. François Crouzet, *De la supériorité de l'Angleterre sur la France: l'économique et l'imaginaire, XVIIe–XXe siècles* (Paris: Librairie académique Perrin, 1985), 112.
17. David McNally, *Political Economy and the Rise of Capitalism: A Reinterpretation* (Berkeley: University of California Press, 1988), 90–131.
18. For a presentation of the reform attempts of Gournay and his supporters, see Pierre Deyon and Philippe Guignet, "The royal manufactures and economic and technological progress in France before the industrial revolution," *Journal of European Economic History* 9 (1980): 611–632; P.M. Jones, *Reform and Revolution in France. The Politics of Transition, 1774–1791* (Cambridge: Cambridge University Press, 1995).
19. Philippe Minard, *La fortune du colbertisme: État et industrie dans la France des Lumières* (Paris: Fayard, 1998), 318.
20. Jones, *Reform and Revolution in France*, 111.
21. This very important point is made by Minard, *La fortune du colbertisme*, 117. See also Deyon and Guignet, "The royal manufactures," 626.
22. William M. Reddy, *The Rise of Market Culture: The Textile Trade and French Society, 1750–1900* (Cambridge: Cambridge University Press, 1984) 22.

23. François Crouzet, "Angleterre et France au XVIIIe siècle: essai d'analyse comparée de deux croissances économiques," *Annales, Économies, Sociétés, Civilisations* 21, no. 2 (1966): 271–272, my translation.
24. Jean-Charles Asselain, *Histoire économique de la France du XVIIIe siècle à nos jours, tome 1: De l'Ancien Régime à la Première Guerre mondiale* (Paris: Éditions du Seuil, 1984), 98; Francis Démier, *La France du XIXe siècle, 1814–1914* (Paris: Éditions du Seuil, 2000), 40; David Parker, *Class and State in Early Modern France: The Road to Modernity?* (New York: Routledge, 1996), 214; Reddy, *The Rise of Market Culture*, 53.
25. Asselain, *Histoire économique*, 107.
26. Guy Lemarchand, *L'économie en France de 1770 à 1830. De la crise de l'Ancien Régime à la Révolution industrielle* (Paris: Armand Collin, 2008), 112.
27. Sewell, *Work and Revolution*, 1980; see also, for instance, Christopher H. Johnson, "The Revolution of 1830 in French Economic History," in *1830 in France*, ed. John M. Merriman (New York: New Viewpoints, 1975); Robert J. Bezucha, "The French Revolution of 1848 and the Social History of Work," *Theory and Society* 12, no. 4 (1983): 469–484.
28. Sewell, *Work and Revolution*, 114–115, 135, 139–140.
29. Adeline Daumard, "Caractères de la société bourgeoise," in *Histoire économique et sociale de la France. Tome 3*, ed. Fernand Braudel and Ernest Labrousse (Paris: Presses universitaires de France, 1993), 832–833, 837.
30. Alain Cottereau, "Review of "Work and Wages: Natural Law, Politics and the Eighteenth-Century French Trades" by Michael Sonenscher," *Le Mouvement social*, no. 165 (1993): 113; Michael Sonenscher, *Work and Wages: Natural Law, Politics and the Eighteenth-Century French Trades* (Cambridge: Cambridge University Press, 1989): 5, 28–29, 30, 33, 280.
31. Alain Thillay, *Le faubourg Saint-Antoine et ses «faux ouvriers». La liberté du travail à Paris aux XVIIe et XVIIIe siècles* (Seyssel: Champ Vallon, 2002).
32. Vardi, quoted in Cissie Fairchilds, "Three Views on the Guilds," *French Historical Studies* 15, no. 4 (1988): 691.
33. Liana Vardi, "The Abolition of the Guilds during the French Revolution," *French Historical Studies* 15, no. 4 (1988): 708, 712.
34. Samuel Guicheteau, *Les ouvriers en France 1700–1835* (Paris: Armand Colin, 2014), 62, 99–105.
35. Ibid., 131.
36. Vardi, "The Abolition of the Guilds," 712.
37. Alain Cottereau, "Sens du juste et usages du droit du travail: une évolution contrastée entre la France et la Grande-Bretagne au XIXe siècle," *Revue d'histoire du XIXe siècle*, no. 33 (2006): 104, my translation.
38. Alain Cottereau, "Droit et bon droit. Un droit des ouvriers instauré, puis évincé par le droit du travail (France, XIXe siècle)," *Annales. Histoire, Sciences Sociales* 57, no. 6 (2002): 1530, 1546; "Sens du juste," 113–114.

39. See Cottereau, "Droit et bon droit" and "Sens du juste"; and Sonenscher, *Work and Wages*, 367 for a longer discussion of the Civil Code and how it prevented unequal relationships between employers and employees.
40. Quoted in Cottereau, "Droit et bon droit," 1553, my translation.
41. Cottereau, "Droit et bon droit," 1553.
42. Guicheteau, *Les ouvriers en France*, 173.
43. Cottereau, "Droit et bon droit," 1545.
44. Cottereau, "Justice et injustice ordinaire sur les lieux de travail d'après les audiences prud'homales (1806–1866)," *Le Mouvement social*, no. 144 (1987): 25–59; Delsalle, 1987.
45. Cottereau, "Droit et bon droit," 1547–1549; 2011, p. 10; Paul Delsalle, "Tisserands et fabricants chez les prud'hommes dans la région de Lille-Roubaix-Tourcoing (1810–1848)," *Le Mouvement social*, no. 141 (1987): 69.
46. Cottereau, "Droit et bon droit," 1549–1550.
47. Pollard, *The Genesis of Modern Management. A Study of the Industrial Revolution in Great Britain* (London: Edward Arnold, 1965).
48. Philippe Lefebvre, *L'invention de la grande entreprise: Travail, hiérarchie, marché (France, fin XVIIIe-Début XXe siècle)* (Paris: Presses universitaires de Frances, 2003), 65.
49. Lefebvre, *L'invention de la grande entreprise*, 16; François Jarrige and Cécile Chalmin, "L'émergence du contremaître. L'ambivalence d'une autorité en construction dans l'industrie textile française (1800–1860)," *Le Mouvement social*, no. 224 (2008): 47–60.
50. Lefebvre, *L'invention de la grande entreprise*, 65, my translation.
51. Michelle Perrot, *Les ouvriers en grève, France 1871–1890* (Paris: Mouton, 1974), 275, my translation.
52. Lefebvre, *L'invention de la grande entreprise*, 131, my translation.
53. N.F.R. Crafts, "Economic Growth in France and Britain, 1830–1910: A Review of the Evidence," *The Journal of Economic History* 44, no. 1 (1984): 64–66.
54. Albert Broder, *L'économie française au XIXe siècle* (Paris: Ophrys, 1993), 67; Alain Beltran and Pascal Griset, *La croissance économique de la France: 1815–1914* (Paris: Armand Colin, 1994), 96.
55. Richard L. Hills, *Power from Steam: A History of the Stationary Steam Engine* (Cambridge: Cambridge University Press, 1989), 117.
56. Lemarchand, *L'économie en France*, 256.
57. Beltran and Griset, *La croissance économique*, 96; Broder, *L'économie française*, 67.
58. Crafts, "Economic Growth in France and Britain," 65.
59. Eric Hobsbawm, *The Age of Revolution, 1789–1848* (New York: Vintage Books, 1996), 177.

60. Ibid., p. 117.
61. Asselain, *Histoire économique*, 135.
62. Ellen Meiksins Wood, "The Question of Market Dependence," *Journal of Agrarian Change* 2, no. 1 (2002): 50–87.
63. Tom Kemp, *Economic Forces in French History. An Essay on the Development of the French Economy* (London: Dobson, 1971), 118.
64. Jean-Pierre Hirsch, *Les deux rêves du commerce. Entreprise et institution dans la région lilloise (1780–1860)* (Paris: Éditions de l'École des hautes études en sciences sociales, 1991), 392; my translation.
65. Asselain, *Histoire économique*, 136.
66. Reddy, *The Rise of Market Culture*, 74, 100.
67. Ibid., 83.
68. Reddy, *The Rise of Market Culture*, 74, my emphasis; see also Claude Fohlen, *L'industrie textile au temps du second empire* (Paris: Librairie Plon, 1956), 91.
69. It is my contention that this is the conclusion that should be drawn from a close reading of the work of Reddy (*The Rise of Market Culture*, 77) and of Charles Engrand ("Les industries lilloises et la crise économique de 1826 à 1832," *Revue du Nord* 63, no. 248 (1981): 233–251) on this issue—even though both authors come to a somewhat different conclusion.
70. Frances Collier, *The family economy of the working classes in the cotton industry, 1784–1833* (Manchester: Manchester University Press, 1964), 12.
71. Kemp, *Economic Forces in French History*, 228.
72. Alain Plessis, *The Rise and Fall of the Second Empire, 1852–1871* (Cambridge: Cambridge University Press, 1985), 15–18.
73. Ibid., 62.
74. Kemp, *Economic Forces in French History*, 168; Plessis, *The Rise and Fall*, 78, 82.
75. Éric Anceau, *Napoléon III* (Paris: Tallandier, 2012), 352.
76. Pierre Léon, "La conquête de l'espace national," in *Histoire économique et sociale de la France. Tome 3*, ed. Fernand Braudel and Ernest Labrousse (Paris: Presses universitaires de France, 1993), 264–265, 293–295.
77. Anceau, *Napoléon III*, 351.
78. Fohlen, *L'industrie textile*, 149–157; Léon, "Conquête," 285–290.
79. François Caron, *Histoire économique de la France: XIXe–XXe siècle* (Paris: Armand Colin, 1999) 120.
80. Kemp, *Economic Forces in French History*, 174.
81. Anceau, *Napoléon III*, 377.
82. Anceau, *Napoléon III*, 379; Kemp, *Economic Forces in French History*, 175–176.
83. Cottereau, "Droit et bon droit," 1555.

84. Cottereau, "Droit et bon droit," 1521, 1524–1525; Philippe Lefebvre, "Subordination et « révolutions » du travail et du droit du travail (1776–2010)," *Entreprises et histoire*, no. 57 (2009): 45–78.
85. Reddy, *The Rise of Market Culture*, 237, 241.
86. Beltran and Griset, *La croissance économique*, 120–121; Lefebvre, *L'invention de la grande entreprise*.
87. Lefebvre, *L'invention de la grande entreprise*, 160–161.
88. Reddy, *The Rise of Market Culture*, 251.
89. Jérôme Bourdieu and Bénédicte Reynaud, "Discipline d'atelier et externalités dans la réduction du travail au XIXe siècle," in *La France et le temps de travail (1814–2004)*, ed. Patrick Fridenson and Bénédicte Reynaud (Paris: Odile Jacob, 2004); Perrot, *Les ouvriers en* grève.
90. Caron, *Histoire économique de la France*, 121–122; Patrick Verley, *Nouvelle histoire économique de la France contemporaine* (Paris: La Découverte, 1993), 56.
91. Asselain, 1984, p. 130.
92. Caron, *Histoire économique de la France*, 115, 123, 129; Broder, *L'économie française*, 59.
93. Asselain, 1988, p. 1232; Caron quoted in Broder, *L'économie française*, 216–217.
94. Caron, *Histoire économique de la France*, 120, 123.
95. Caron, *Histoire économique de la France*, 129–136.
96. Louis Bergeron, *Les capitalistes en France (1780–1914)* (Paris: Gallimard, 1978), 73–74; Bertrand Gille, *La sidérurgie française au XIXe siècle* (Genève: Librairie Droz, 1968), 69.
97. Oliver Marchand and Claude Thélot, *Deux siècles de travail en France* (Paris: INSEE, 1991) 143–144.
98. I will address the issue of the formation of the French working-class in a non-capitalist context in an upcoming book, to be published as part of Brill's Historical Materialism Series, that will also present and develop the arguments presented in this chapter.

CHAPTER 6

The Transition to Capitalism in Catalonia

Javier Moreno Zacarés

Introduction

In the eighteenth century, Catalonia witnessed the rise of a powerful commercial agriculture and a dynamic textile industry that was described by contemporaries as "a little England in the heart of Spain".[1] A pattern of development without parallel in the Mediterranean Basin, the dynamism of this economic formation allowed Catalonia to prevail over competing industrial regions and consolidate itself as the undisputed industrial powerhouse of Spain by the early decades of the nineteenth century.[2] By the latter decades of that century, the region concentrated the practical totality of Spain's cotton industry and approached the levels of cotton yarn production of France or Germany.[3]

Buried in the footnotes of his famous essay on the English origins of capitalism, Robert Brenner left the passing remark that Catalonia had experienced an agrarian transition to capitalism in parallel to England.[4] For Brenner, Catalonia's economic divergence harked all the way back to the early sixteenth century, when the abolition of serfdom would have set in motion a long-term process of agrarian growth built upon an English-style pattern of large-scale farming. Brenner's view, however, was founded

J. Moreno Zacarés (✉)
University of Warwick, Coventry, UK

X. Lafrance, C. Post (eds.), *Case Studies in the Origins of Capitalism*, Marx, Engels, and Marxisms,
https://doi.org/10.1007/978-3-319-95657-2_6

upon a number of empirical inaccuracies that were soon pointed out by Jaume Torras, who noted that agrarian growth of the sort identified by Brenner would only arrive much later and was driven by small family farms rather than English-style *engrossed* farms.[5] Such decisive rebuttal brought to an end the 'Brenner Debate' in Catalan historiography even before it began elsewhere.

In a 2001 article, Robert Brenner departed from his original focus on large-scale commercial farming as the singular source of capitalist mutation when he identified another early agrarian transition in the market dependent family farms of the Netherlands. Brenner's work on the Dutch transition prompted a schism with Ellen Meiksins Wood, who came to reject the usefulness of the concept of market dependence to track the genesis of capitalist development, and instead proposed a theorization of the origins of capitalism that focused on the emergence of "*market imperatives*", highlighting the creative agency of social actors in the process of transition.[6]

This chapter seeks to pick up where the Brenner-Wood debate left off and extend the discussion to the Catalan case. Building upon Wood's analysis, it will be argued that the Catalan experience illustrates how structural criteria, such as "market dependence", remain insufficient to explain the capitalist breakthrough: in this case at least, the transition was sealed by localized socio-cultural struggles around production and labor. Building on this perspective, the chapter proposes a reformulation of the problem of the origins of capitalism around the social construction of capitalist imperatives.

The chapter is divided into two parts. The first part is dedicated to theoretical issues around the origins of capitalism and is split into two sections. The first section addresses the Brenner-Wood debate on the Netherlands and unpacks the limitations of the concept of "market dependence". The second section explores some useful theoretical avenues to better capture the agency and subjectivity of the social actors involved in the process of transition. The second part of the chapter delves into the Catalan case to illustrate these theoretical points. It is divided into three sections. The first section addresses the limitations of Brenner's account of a Catalan agrarian transition and the revisions of Brenner's account by Catalan historians. Overall, it is argued that pre-capitalist social property relations persisted in agriculture throughout the period of transition. The second section examines why in recent decades the specialist literature has increasingly linked the region's economic take-off to the spread of domestic forms of manufacture or "proto-industry". The third section explores the origins of this proto-industrial dynamism, tracing it to socio-cultural struggles to revolutionize the organization and orientation of production in the region's hinterlands, focusing on the localities of Terrassa, Igualada, Manresa, and Sabadell.

Political Marxism Beyond Market Dependence

The Ambiguity of Market Dependence

One of the strongest criticisms raised by Robert Brenner's against preceding theories of the origin of capitalism focused on a widespread tendency to assume that capitalism had emerged out of an outgrowth of market exchange.[7] In Brenner's view, this focus failed to draw a clear distinction between pre-capitalist and capitalist markets. The result was a blurring of the historical specificity of capitalism and a muddying of the question of a "transition" altogether (since instances of market exchange can be traced back to time immemorial). To avoid this transhistorical slippage, political Marxist theory draws an important distinction between age-old *market opportunities*, which constitute mere conjunctures for profit-making via market exchange, and specifically capitalist *market imperatives*, which refer to the pressures to systematically improve the productivity of labor. The Brenner Thesis identified the historical emergence of such imperatives in the English peasantry's dependence on commercial leases for access to the land, their most basic means of subsistence. This associated capitalist social relations with contexts of *market dependence*: the necessity to engage in market exchange in order to reproduce one's social position, be it through profit-making or the sale of labor power.[8]

However, the conflation of market dependence with market imperatives resulted in some problematic ambiguities that surfaced during the Brenner-Wood Debate.[9] The source of the dispute was Brenner's claim that, for reasons different and in parallel to England, the agricultural producers of the northern Netherlands experienced an early capitalist transition in the 1600s. The starting point was an environmental degradation of the countryside, which forced Dutch peasants to depend upon the market for grain. This generated a context of market dependence for their most basic need to realize their subsistence: food. In response, they were forced to produce commodities for exchange, focusing on cattle breeding and dairy farming for export. Eventually, with the help of urban finance and land reclamations, their market dependence would set in motion a train of specialization, investment, and productive improvement along similar lines to England.

Ellen Meiksins Wood parted ways with Brenner on this issue. She asserted that Brenner had relapsed into the kind of reasoning he once criticized: that an outgrowth of market relations detonated by "objective economic forces" (in this case, environmental degradation) was sufficient to account for a capitalist mutation. In this process, much like the proponents of commercialization that preceded him, he had forgotten to elucidate whether the market had truly become an imperative or not. In her revision of the case, she reached the conclusion that the Dutch peasantry, though indeed market dependent for access to their means of subsistence (i.e. food, clothing), continued to reproduce their grip over the means of production (i.e. land) via pre-capitalist economic dynamics.

Her argument, which injected a dose of theoretical clarity into the often muddled discussions around pre-capitalist markets, can be summarized in the following four points[10]: (1) The success of Dutch agriculture was based on the military and commercial prowess of its Republic and its merchants. As is usual of pre-capitalist trade, extra-economic institutions, such as monopolistic guilds and companies, ensured the realization of profits in advance, usually through the cornering markets or by exploiting a navy with superior transport capacities. In short, *profits were made in circulation by politically constituted means* and not in production by a need to relentlessly and systematically develop the productive forces. (2) *Market dependence in grain was not forcing an intensification of the productive process.* The comparatively low prices of Baltic wheat and the pre-capitalist commercial sophistication of the Dutch Republic was enough to realize profits along the age-old practice of arbitrage: buying cheap and selling dear in different markets. (3) *Specialization*, which for Brenner is a crucial index of capitalist development, *has long existed in pre-capitalist economies without being driven by an impulse toward economic efficiency.* A quick example would be the massive conversion of arable fields into pastoral lands in late medieval Castile to exploit the opportunities of a lucrative wool market abroad.[11] (4) In order to spot the emergence of capitalist rationalities, much more telling than the upward surge in an economic cycle is *the reaction of economic actors when this cycle is exhausted.* Only this allows us to track the existence of self-sustaining capitalist imperatives. In the Netherlands, investment in the production process soared when conditions for profit were good, but when agrarian prices collapsed across Europe in the mid-seventeenth century, they retreated from productive innovation altogether, a dynamic which Wood identifies as typical of pre-capitalist societies. By contrast, English agriculture had crossed a point of no return and displayed a new kind of price sensitivity. In the face of downturn, peasants reliant on the market for their access to the land could not simply withdraw from production, so they kept innovating their production methods to maximize profits. Failure to compete meant dispossession and the prospect of waged labor, migration, or starvation.

Market dependence might seem like an appropriate index of capitalist production when comparing serfdom and capitalist farming, but this indicator runs into problems when dealing with the whole spectrum of commercial agricultures in between, including pre-capitalist social formations capable of a considerable market dynamism, like the Dutch or, as we shall see, the Catalan. This folds back on a criticism recurrently levelled against the Brenner Thesis: that it rests on a static portrayal of pre-capitalist agricultures that exaggerates the degree of self-subsistence of the pre-capitalist peasantry.[12] The reality is that pre-industrial Europe witnessed the emergence of highly commercial and pluriactive peasantries that often specialized in production for the market and purchased their staples instead. These producers were not blasted into the market by outright dispossession, but rather by a need to complement their incomes for subsistence; they were *semi-proletarians*. Like this, "by the end of the sixteenth century few parts of Europe remained autarkic 'less developed economies' engaging in subsistence production. Instead, Europe was turning into a differentiated patchwork of inter-dependent regions".[13]

The most important contribution of Wood's intervention was the recognition that market dependence is far from a sufficient condition to determine the emergence of capitalist imperatives. If market dependent actors seize profitable opportunities with a more or less guaranteed return, then we can hardly speak of self-sustaining imperatives. To bridge dependence and imperatives, she argued, there needs to be a *competitive market* for the transmission of capitalist pressures. Though what this looks like can vary, she sketched a number of "irreducible conditions" for such competitive qualities to emerge: (1) the absence of politically constituted monopolies, like those secured by guild forms of production or colonial trading systems; (2) the potential for price competition between suppliers responding to the same conditions; (3) the reasonable access of supply and demand to one another so that price/cost pressures generate a need for cost-effective production; and (4) the existence of a common standard to measure value, whether monetary or some other compelling social average of labor costs.[14]

The Social Construction of Market Imperatives

Wood's work turns our attention to the forms of political change that allowed capitalist dynamics to appear by "levelling the playing field" of the market, such as the erosion of corporative structures or the unification of disjointed markets, what she referred to as the "separation of economic and the political". Her approach echoes of Karl Polanyi's notion of "disembedding", according to which the capitalist market was distilled from the removal of "non-economic" institutions (i.e. kinship, communal, religious, political) that had previously arrested the emergence of economic competition. However, one problem arises from this formulation: while the disembedding of the market may act as a structural precondition for the emergence of capitalist competition, there is no reason to assume that this will cause pre-capitalist dynamics to automatically wither away. If anything, given the unprecedented nature of capitalist rationalities, we should assume that pre-capitalist dynamics tend to perpetuate themselves out of a certain cultural inertia unless challenged by a new economic culture, a process bound to prompt a clash between old and new subjectivities. In short, if we are not to relapse into an analysis that privileges "objective economic forces", we ought to sharpen the focus upon the creative agency and subjectivity of the social actors enmeshed in the process of transition. The problem is that Wood left little indications as to how to integrate the role of *social construction* in the analysis of capitalist transitions.

In the blind alleys of history, we find an eighteenth-century case that illustrates why the social construction of capitalist imperatives cannot be taken for granted. The case of the smallholders of Galicia, in Spain's northwest corner, reveals an example of market dependent producers that ignored corporate regulations and yet did not set in motion a train of capitalist development.[15] In a pattern similar to Catalonia, the shrinkage of land plots below subsistence levels in this region forced the peasantry to resort to the market for their social reproduction. Many turned to selling their labor power in putting-out networks of cloth production for their export to Castilian markets, facing competition from other regional suppliers. The dispersed nature of their industry allowed them to avoid guild regulations altogether; the realm of production was "disembedded" from corporate oversight and no one prevented them from innovating or accumulating more intensely. The region displayed a considerable advance at first, and was compared by the Enlightenment thinker Pedro Rodríguez de Campomanes (1723–1802) as a worthy competitor of Catalonia's proto-industrial prowess. However, the atomization of production in pluriactive peasant households discouraged commercial middlemen and the dealers of the final product from intervening in the production process. In the meantime, peasant producers reproduced inefficient methods that had become culturally entrenched: an insistence to bleach the yarn on the middle of the production process rather than the finished piece relegated Galician cloths to the bottom range of quality. Sealed from competitive stimuli, capitalist rationalities failed to take hold and Galicia's proto-industrial producers were eventually outpaced by the might of English and Catalan textiles in the early nineteenth century.

Ahead of exploring the Catalan case in greater detail, a comparison between Galician and Catalan proto-industrial experiences would suggest that despite striking similarities across their manufacturing districts the latter would execute a successful capitalist breakthrough contingent upon localized social conflicts and accompanied by a change in the consciousness of proto-industrial producers. Three theoretical insights on how to accommodate subjectivity in the formation of market imperatives can be derived from this experience:

(1) The transformation of market competition into capitalist imperatives depends, in the final analysis, *upon a mutation in the consciousness of market actors.* Neither the pressures to socially reproduce one's means of subsistence via market exchange (market dependence) nor the emergence of market competition can warrant the appearance of capitalist accumulation, especially in historical periods in which it may have seemed unintuitive to systematically compete by intensifying the process of production. To be sure, the appearance of capitalist production requires a series of enabling contextual conditions; however the emergence of a capitalist class depends upon a recognition of the challenges of capitalist competition and upon the capacity and willingness to rise up to them. In the Catalan case, this process is observable and can be clearly historicized.

(2) Rather than as law-like forces that automatically subordinate everything to their orbit, capitalist imperatives should be thought of as *a collective representation of all the actions reproducing the pressures to intensify the production process.* Through these lenses, subjectivity assumes a much more pressing role in the process of transition, for it is only through an active socialization of the logic of permanent productive improvement that capitalist dynamics can take hold. As we shall see, in Catalonia this process is most revolutionary in the changing understandings of proto-industrial production and labor.

(3) This process of social construction is bound to be *mediated by successive waves of social and cultural conflict.* Capitalist imperatives are the crystallization of a permanently renegotiated socio-political relation, one that is built upon the layering of past struggles that gradually left their imprint upon economic norms and regulations. This allows us to identify much more clearly the creative agencies driving the appearance and spread of capitalist dynamics. In the case of Catalonia, the spark of capitalist transformation were localized struggles over the subordination of labor that were gradually and unevenly replicated across a number of localities.

The Catalan Transition to Capitalism

An Agrarian Transition?

> … the only real alternative to the 'classical English' landlord-large tenant-wage labour form of capitalist agriculture seems to have been an *equally capitalist system* based on large-scale owner-cultivators also generally using wage labour. The latter was the structure which in fact emerged in Catalonia at the end of the fifteenth century out of the previous period of agrarian struggle.[16]

In the footnotes of his famous 1976 essay, Robert Brenner claimed that Catalonia had experienced an agrarian capitalist transition that ran in parallel with that of England. What caught Brenner's attention was the agrarian class structure that emerged from the peasant revolts of the late fifteenth century, the *Remença Wars,* which culminated in the abolition of serfdom in the region. For Brenner, the subsequent introduction of freehold leases would have been the source of "a concomitant increase in agricultural productivity in this era" that would allow the region to become "one of the few areas to escape the 'general economic crisis of the seventeenth century', and, like England, to avoid demographic catastrophe while achieving continued economic development".[17] However, Brenner's account soon met the powerful rebuttal of Jaume Torras, who pointed out that "the signs of the rise which Brenner detects in England at the end of the sixteenth century are nowhere to be found in Catalonia", as it would take at least until the late seventeenth century for food crises and wild fluctuations in agricultural prices to stabilize.[18] And even then, the agricultural advance of the region would not be spearheaded by English-style engrossed farms, but by family farms focused on commercial viticulture that rarely employed waged labor.

Brenner was right to identify a radical change in the agrarian class structure of Catalonia after the conclusion of the Remença War in 1495, but the change was different to what he assumed. Freehold tenure spread in the form of *emphyteutic* leases, through which peasant families leased lands from their lords in perpetuity. Title holders could pass on their land leases to their offspring, transfer them to third parties, or sublease them to tenants of their own.[19] The lords claimed a nominal rent, fixed at the time of lease, and could not evict their tenants unless they failed to cultivate all the land. As time went by, peasant families, by marriage, inheritance, or purchase, began concentrating land leases beyond their capacity to cultivate them. At which point, they began to sublease parts of their estate to sharecroppers of their own in order to keep their family lands. This process of fragmentation was called *eixamenament* (to "swarm" or to "hive-off"), and by 1700 most of those families who held the original leases from the lords were no longer cultivating the land themselves; a wealthy class between the landlords and the directly cultivating tenants had emerged.[20] The new middling class of landowners were usually professionals (lawyers, shopkeepers, etc.) with a greater commercial sensibility than their lords, who had their agrarian rents fixed to the terms of a preceding age. This class would seek to profit from the soaring of the price of wines and spirits on the back of the French-Dutch Wars of the late seventeenth century.[21] Adding clauses to their sharecropping leases, landowners began to force their tenants to cultivate vines, claiming shares of their yield as rent so they could turn them into wines and spirits for export.[22] These contracts, known as *rabassa morta* leases, attracted considerable internal migration to the coastal districts, where they were used to extend arable lands into forested areas. This set in motion a train of agrarian specialization that continued into the coming century, giving rise to an export-driven agriculture that had to be supplemented with massive grain imports from the Baltic area as the peasantry started purchasing their staples on the market.[23] From the 1720s, the diffusion of grain supply networks inland can be mapped on to the spread of viticulture. By the 1780s, a regional grain market with synchronized price movements had come into existence.[24]

In light of this atomized commercial agriculture, it is not surprising that Catalan agrarian historians have long dismissed Brenner's work for reifying the English agrarian experience as the sole benchmark for agrarian economic development.[25] Brenner's work has only recently been reappraised and redeployed for the Catalan case by Julie Marfany, who has reclaimed his notion of market dependence to explain the commercial transformation of the Catalan peasantry in the eighteenth century, a pattern of development which she identifies as a "transition to agrarian capitalism". For Marfany, the impulse of the transition came from commercial viticulture because it submerged peasant households in commercial dynamics that, transcending simple forms of "market involvement", turned the market into a compulsive force in their social reproduction.[26]

Through the fragmentation of sharecropping and its extension of arable lands, *rabassa morta* leases allowed many peasants to access the property ladder, but this process also carried its own contradiction. Land ownership was a fundamental requirement for marriage, the expansion of the supply of property facilitated household formation, something of particular importance in a region with strong primogeniture traditions, where the eldest son inherited the whole estate of his father. And as sharecropping facilitated access to property to disinherited sons, it also facilitated marriage and procreation.[27] Thus, with the diffusion of *rabassa morta* leases came a 56 percent increase in population between 1718 and 1787.[28] As demographic pressure built in this context of impartible inheritance, leases became smaller and shrank beneath subsistence levels (under 5 or 6 ha.), forcing peasant households to complement their incomes with waged labor.[29]

This also made peasants increasingly reliant upon the sale of their labor power. By the turn of the nineteenth century, there was a vast semi-proletariat and a growing landless proletariat that had fallen off the property ladder altogether. Agriculture could not absorb this market dependent population: in a landscape of family farms, only the larger farms would occasionally hire workers for harvests or for the maintenance of buildings.[30] Instead, many households turned to the textile industries, where they found greater wages and stable employment. This often meant women and children performing weaving and spinning tasks in peasant households for local clothiers, or migration to Barcelona, where a flourishing cotton industry absorbed a large number of workers from the countryside.[31]

Marfany's market dependence thesis bears a lot of resemblance to Brenner's later work on the Netherlands, in which he arguably transcended his initial focus on English-style farms by identifying an agrarian transition in a context of commercial smallholders. However, the problems that Wood identified in Brenner's analysis extends here to Marfany's account: despite a high degree of commercialization, an analysis of market imperatives would suggest that agrarian production remained insulated from capitalist competition in this period for at least three reasons:

(1) *The long-term nature of sharecropping leases insulated cultivators from competitive pressures to renew their access to the means of production.* Traditionally, emphyteutic leases were in perpetuity, something that buffered cultivators from the competitive pressures derived from constant rent inflation. From 1765 there was a gradual increase in contracts with a defined temporal duration.[32] Yet, it remained common for a sharecropping lease to span over 40–50 years, something that rendered cultivators fairly insulated from competition to renew their access to the land. In any case, the spread of agreements with a defined duration was an extremely protracted process. In many areas, clauses limiting the duration of leases did not become frequent until the middle of the nineteenth century. To be sure, this does not mean that sharecropping rendered peasants immune to the vicissitudes of the market: cultivators still bore the risks of a bad harvest, as the costs could render them unable to cultivate the land and open the door to their eviction. However, their insulation from the prospect of constantly rising rents is highly significant, particularly as this pressure was the driver of "improvement" in England.

(2) *Sharecropping leases restricted the power of landowners to impose a systematic intensification of the production process "from the outside".* Originally, sharecropping contracts merely stipulated that the vine ought to be cultivated "following the norms and custom of the good peasant", something that tied productive methods to customary norms and eschewed the possibility of productive change.

This clause did not completely preclude change, as it condensed unwritten rules that were mutable; however, a change in convention often required an amount of bargaining and conflict that could span over generations.[33] Admittedly, this started to change from the 1760s, when landowners began to engage in localized strategies to bend the juridical nature of their emphyteutic leases in order to turn them into *aparcería* contracts, a similar sharecropping agreement that increased the obligations of tenants. This translated into an erosion of custom accompanied by a gradual increase in specifications regarding how the productive process should be carried out.[34] Nevertheless, the long duration of sharecropping leases continued to slow down the pace of change: sharecropping arrangements prevented landowners from intervening in the production methods of their tenants once the contracts were in force. To demand changes in the production process, landowners had to wait until the expiry of the contract in order to engrave new clauses into them, rendering them unable to match the fluctuations of the market.

(3) In the context of this architecture of tenure, *the limits of the Mediterranean environment discouraged competitive investment in production*. At the time, only vast irrigation systems unaffordable to atomized peasants could bring substantive productive change, and credit for agrarian ventures of this scale seems to have been unavailable.[35]

The Proto-industrial Path to Capitalism

Brenner's work on Catalonia was inspired by that of Marxist historian Pierre Vilar,[36] who in a classic three-volume study ascribed the impetus of the Catalan transition to capitalism in the demographic and agrarian shifts arising from the integration of peasant production into the circuits of a rising Atlantic economy. However, he saw the turning point of this process in "the transformation of commercial capital into industrial capital—the only decisive factor in the birth of a new society in Catalonia and of uneven development at the heart of the Iberian Peninsula", a topic he reserved for an uncompleted fourth volume to his study.[37]

The task of accommodating the role of industry into the story of the Catalan transition passed on to Vilar's immediate followers, who in the

1970s shifted the locus of capitalist development to the calico-printing manufactures of Barcelona.[38] Focusing on the stamping of colorful designs upon imported cotton and linen yarns, the calico-printing industry developed out of private initiatives between the 1720s and 1740s and reached its zenith in the 1780s.[39] Unlike traditional forms of production, which were segmented into separate trades, the printing industry was characterized by its bypass of guild structures and its vertical integration of the different stages of the production process (weaving, dyeing, printing, etc.) in relatively large concerns that at their peak could employ between 50–185 workers.[40]

This paradigm faced important challenges during the 1980s, particularly as new lines of research cast doubt on the continuity between Barcelona's manufactures of the eighteenth century and the region's subsequent pattern of industrial development in the nineteenth century. It emerged that the trend of vertical integration of the cotton industry was reversed in the 1780s, when the printing manufactures were supplanted by smaller units of production dispersed across the region.[41] These were instances of "proto-industry": forms of manufacturing reliant upon domestic forms of labor (usually in peasant households, although not only) that were geared toward production for export in extra-regional markets. The intense competition and growth radiating from this sector at the turn of the nineteenth century has convinced a growing number of historians that the region found its path to capitalism, or at least a bridge into capitalist industrialization, via its proto-industrial experience.[42]

The study of the Catalan proto-industrial experience was pioneered by none other than Brenner's most staunch critic: Jaume Torras.[43] In his critique of the Brenner Thesis, Torras had charged against what he saw as an excessively narrow definition of capitalism that gave rise to a "unilinear and strictly endogenous" account of the transition. These concerns would resurface in his subsequent embrace of "proto-industrialization", a concept that he believed transcended the sterile dichotomy between "internalist" and "externalist" approaches in the Transition Debate, as the idea of proto-industry showed how "internal" changes in peasant production were deeply intertwined with "external" commercial factors in the transition to capitalism.[44] The problem with Torras' holistic view is that, in drawing a causal equivalence between the "conjuncture" and the "critical juncture", it delivers a narrative of the transition that eschews the primacy of agency and contingency in the process of capitalist change.

There is no doubt that Catalan capitalism emerged in the context of a broader trading system and that it could have not done so without it. Indeed, the take-off of the textile industry across the region would be unintelligible without the rise of commercial viticulture: crucial inputs such as ready spun yarn or raw cotton were the returns of *eau-de-vie* and wine exports.[45] To this we should add the abolition of customs between the realms of Aragon and Castile after the War of Succession (1714), a political development that gave Catalan producers access to the Madrid market, where the bulk of their proto-industrial output was sold in the eighteenth century.[46]

However, equally true is that capitalism did not emerge *because* of this commercial context. Viticulture stimulated textile manufacturing in other regions of Spain, like Andalusia, where vines were cultivated on much larger plots to produce wines of a higher added value. Yet this region only saw the emergence of a handful of cotton manufactures and a pocket of rural industry in the foothills of Málaga that decayed at the turn of the nineteenth century.[47] The proto-industrial center in Béjar (Salamanca) counted with units of production capable of higher output and was exempt from the 8 percent sales tax that Catalan producers faced in the Madrid market. Yet, despite such notable competitive advantage, they were outpaced by the Catalans all the same.[48] It is noteworthy that the Catalan proto-industrial sector did have one a priori structural advantage: *compactness*, a cluster formation that facilitated the emergence of an elastic labor market with industry-specific skills and the diffusion of technological advances by word of mouth.[49] However, even then, the capacity to unlock this structural potential would hinge upon a prior erosion of the guild system and upon changes in economic attitudes.

Socio-cultural Struggle and Capitalist Breakthrough

In the seventeenth century, as the influx of precious metals from the Americas inflated production costs, many textile guilds from Barcelona relocated to the countryside and focused on the production of woollens for rural markets.[50] The industry flourished in the central highlands of Catalonia, where producers navigated the long crisis of the seventeenth century via a process of hierarchical differentiation.[51] The clothiers (*paraires*), the section of the guild in charge of finishing the textiles and of organizing the whole production process, pushed for the relaxation of corporative regulations in order to centralize production and cut costs at the expense of the weavers' wages and employment. These efforts had uneven geographical results. In the steep areas of the north, rural industry remained confined to its traditional role of producing for local consumption. The middle areas experienced considerable growth and became regional suppliers, some of which eventually moved on to produce medium quality cloths that were marketed outside of Catalonia. But in the Southern areas of rural manufacturing, by the mid-eighteenth century, a string of interconnected towns had formed a dense cluster of proto-industry where higher quality cloths were produced for extra-regional export, the vast majority to the Madrid market. To achieve this, the first stages of production (weaving, spinning) were "put out" to nearby peasant households, and the resulting yarns were then processed (cutting, dyeing, etc.) in workshops by specialists. This last zone would be the incubator of capitalist relations of production.

The capitalist transformation of this proto-industrial sector was contingent upon the success of the clothier class in their assault on medieval structures of production. Dissolving the politically constituted institutions that regulated surplus extraction at the expense of competition, in a number of localities across the region, the clothiers would attempt to subordinate the production process to their command in order to restyle the textile industry along competitive lines. Driving this process was an explicit desire to increase their responsiveness to market signals, as they realized that their success depended on their capacity to mount a flexible response to changing fashions in consumer markets.[52]

It appears that these strategies were first successful in the town of Terrassa.[53] Military occupation during the War of Spanish Succession plunged the Catalan textile sector into crisis, and in the midst of chaos, corporative regulations unravelled: production evaded quality controls and weavers were drafted outside of the guilds. With the arrival of peace, the guild order was re-established in different local settlements. However, the woollens guild of Terrassa emerged out of this process with a radical twist: the new ordinances of 1724 excluded the weavers from the corporation and blasted them into an unregulated labor market. Clothiers kept some guild coverage for themselves to restrict further access into the trade and avoid competition, but by 1742 the salaries of weavers were no longer fixed and fluctuated across firms within the same town. This allowed weaving (and later spinning) practices to be outsourced to peasant households in putting-out networks, the radius of which quickly expanded to the nearby hills and towns. Clothiers also began to break out of the local monopolies by "importing" skilled specialists from outside of the town, determining their obligations without legal constraint.

Terrassa's revolutionary turn did not go unnoticed. The clothiers of nearby towns quickly maneuvered to replicate its model by different means. In Igualada, a proto-industrial town on the road to Madrid, wool clothiers spoke of the "exalted" firms of Terrassa as a source of inspiration, remarking that they bypassed the authority of master weavers by putting "youths [directly] at the disposal of the manufacturer, achieving like this their famous reputation".[54] Here they would resort to wearing down their own woollens guild through legal battles and by mobilizing their influence in local government. By the 1750s, corporative regulations were no longer being enforced and journeymen were employed circumventing traditional labor regulations. In the town of Manresa, the transformation occurred in the silk industry rather than in the woollens.[55] There wealthy clothiers captured guild institutions and used their regulations to dispossess and subordinate fellow artisans. With the pretext of quality control infractions, they started imposing heavy disciplinary fines on hired guild masters, confiscating their raw materials and forcing them into a condition of financial dependence. Within a few decades, the number of independent artisans sharply declined: in 1746, the number of craftsmen owning their means of production amounted to 53.8 percent of the local workforce. By 1765 this figure had halved to 25.4 percent, and by 1788 it had gone down to a mere 11.7 percent.

Yet capitalist production did not spontaneously emerge from the erosion of corporative regulations; it was actively crafted. The struggle over proto-industrial social property relations was simultaneously a process of social construction that shaped a new understanding of production and labor. We see this normativity in the ways in which the clothiers legitimized their unorthodox practices by comparing themselves to the prestigious managers of the realm's Colbert-style manufactures. In the midst of legal battles with the weavers in 1762, a group of clothiers from Igualada who openly styled themselves as "manufacturers" (*fabricants*) made the following case (quoted in Marfany 2012, 75):

> In all the factories of the kingdom … there is a director, who rules, governs and orders everything necessary for the factory … Without any interference in the running of these concerns from any dependent individuals within them, such as the weavers, and what a Director is to the royal factories, so is a manufacturer in his own manufacturing concern, since he takes an interest in the quality of the cloths in order to sell them well afterwards, and obtains the necessary credit without which no enterprise can survive.[56]

The weavers' response is an attestation of just how contested these new ideas were:

> The clothiers who style themselves manufacturers are no such thing, rather, they practice one of the four crafts involved in the manufacture of a cloth [apart from weaving] these are the clothier, dyer and cropper ... and although it would be more fitting to describe the weaver as a cloth manufacturer than the clothier, there is no reason for one to dominate the other, and raise himself up to be a master, for each is only master of the work that falls to him.

The spread of capitalist development across the region hinged upon the outcome and sequence of socio-cultural struggles of this sort.[57] In the town of Sabadell, in the vicinity of Terrassa, the advance of capitalist production was temporarily stalled by the balance of forces. The weavers succeeded in resisting the assault of the clothiers in the 1760s, who lamented being "deprived of the choice to have their cloth manufactured by the workers they deemed most skillful". However, a renewed cycle of struggle in the latter decades of the century tipped the balance in their favor and the power of guilds was gradually chipped away, resulting in production doubling in size. By contrast, attempts to emulate Terrassa's practices would altogether fail in the towns of Esparreguera and Olesa, resulting in the eventual subsumption of their peasant weavers under Terrassa's orbit.

At first, Barcelona witnessed an alternative passage out of medieval industry in this period. As early as 1721—even before Terrassa's turn—the wool clothiers of the city had tried and failed in their attempt to centralize production and subordinate weavers into commodified workers.[58] Instead, the city would see the development of a powerful calico-printing cotton industry out of private initiatives to emulate the realm's "royal manufactures".[59] As James Thomson has argued, rather than a reflection of their own internal dynamism, the organizational form of Barcelona's manufactures (i.e. relatively large size, vertical integration, side-lining of guilds) arose out of attempts to align themselves with the dominant trends in absolutist political economy in order to tap into political favor (e.g. tailored tariffs, monopolistic privileges, etc.).[60] But these protected firms would come to feel the pressures of competition in labor, yarn, and cloth markets radiating from smaller proto-industrial competitors. With the influx of raw cotton from the United States from the mid-1770s, a large number of "unregulated" spinning and printing workshops proliferated in

Barcelona, manufacturing high-quality cheap cotton textiles outside of the corporatist shell of the large printers.[61] The large printers also came up against the adoption of cotton manufacturing by a number of centers in the countryside. An industrial survey in 1784 reported the use of American cotton in the towns of Reus, Capellades, Igualada, Manresa, Olot, Mataró, Agramunt, and Seu d'Urgell.[62]

The diffusion of capitalist production was facilitated by changes in the economic attitudes of state officials from the 1760s. During the reign of Charles III (1759–1788), Spanish mercantilism acquired a "liberal" bent that took inspiration from British commercial policy and physiocratic theories.[63] At the same time, Catalonia's *Junta de Comercio*, the regional chamber of commerce, became increasingly favorable toward the practices of the proto-industrial sector given their commercial success. The changing mentalities of policy makers had a direct impact on textile production. The royal ordinances of 1769 allowed firms across the region to concentrate all stages in the production process and to hire as many weavers as they pleased, "choosing them at their discretion and commanding them at will".[64] Between 1778 and 1789, a series of decrees eroded the power of the guilds, allowing all textile producers to vary cloth types and alter production processes. In 1789, the *Junta de Comercio* declared the freedom of enterprise in the city's textile industry while charging against "the damage and inconveniences that guild ordinances cause to the progress of the arts and crafts".[65] That being said, it remains extremely noteworthy that the clothiers of Terrassa, Igualada, and Manresa did not wait for the enactment of these regulations to revolutionize their production processes.

The interventions of the *Junta* would also be decisive in consolidating the advance of proto-industrialization and in securing the transmission of capitalist pressures. When the large printers of Barcelona came up against the dynamism of smaller competitors in the 1780s, the potentates of the sector pooled their resources into the Royal Spinning Company of Barcelona and demanded the monopoly over cotton spinning in the city, a distinctly pre-capitalist strategy that would have insulated them from competition. However, the *Junta* rejected the proposal worried that this measure would strangle the dynamism of proto-industrial producers. Without politically constituted privileges, the manufactures of Barcelona were soon overtaken by their smaller proto-industrial competitors. After some time attempting to take their putting-out operations elsewhere in the countryside, the dominance of the large printers in cotton manufacturing was liquidated between 1785 and 1790.

The center of gravity of the Catalan textile industry shifted to the countryside; "cotton manufacturing ceased to be fundamentally Barcelonese and became Catalan".[66] The supersession of the calico-printing manufactures by proto-industrial units of production was accompanied by clear symptoms of capitalist development.[67] Rapid industrial expansion saturated the market and prompted the first crisis of overproduction between 1786 and 1789. After a sharp contraction of demand, production rebounded with vigor: the levels of cotton import of 1785 were matched again in 1789, and their total doubled one year later.

Expansion continued until 1792, when the advent of the French Revolutionary and Napoleonic Wars (1792–1815) and the independence of the Latin American colonies (1810–1833) plunged the country into a long depression that rolled back the industrial advances of the eighteenth century in most regions. However, Catalonia's proto-industrial sector would successfully weather the crisis and overtake the role of other regions in the provision of the domestic market. It is highly remarkable that this process occurred without the effective aid of protective tariffs: though the state continued to officially pursue a protectionist policy, the contraband of foreign imports was rife on the ground. Even as English textiles flooded the market, Catalan firms managed to resist the onslaught and secure 34 percent of share in the Spanish cotton cloth market between 1792 and 1827.[68] Rather than divesting in the face of retreating market opportunities, the proto-industrial firms of Catalonia poised themselves strategically to face the conjuncture. After switching to cotton, the manufacturers of Manresa opted for intensifying production and introduced water-powered technology with great success: by 1830, out of the 40 concerns using water-power in the region, 11 were located in Manresa alone.[69] Manresa was the center of the broader Bages district, an industrious area which in this period came to outstrip Barcelona itself. By contrast, the centers of Sabadell and Terrassa opted for deepening their specialization in wool and upgrading the quality of their product.[70] In stark contrast, the remainder of Barcelona's printing manufactures were obliterated by the crisis, reducing the city's textile industry to an underlying layer of small workshops; the "discontinuity with the eighteenth century calico-printing industry was nearly total".[71]

The resurgence of Barcelona would come with the arrival of steam power in 1833, only then would the city's textile workforce recover the numbers of the 1790s.[72] The new technology required large sums of fixed capital investment and the import of coal by sea, making industry flock to Barcelona's old merchant families for the provision of finance and inputs. Production became fully mechanized and concentrated in large steam mills that exploited economies of scale, crushing the preceding wave of proto-industrial capitalism by the 1850s. However, even then the transformation of Barcelona into the "factory of Spain" would owe much to the effervescence of its proto-industrial hinterlands. The new factory proletariat drafted its armies from the ranks of proto-industrial skilled workers accustomed to working outside of the guild system, and many of the proto-industrial manufacturers put out of business assumed managerial roles in the new factories.[73]

Conclusion

As Wood pointed out in her dispute with Brenner over the Dutch transition, the pressures forcing social actors to engage in market exchange to fulfill their social reproduction (*market dependence*) cannot explain the emergence of drives to permanently improve the productivity of labor when producing for the market (*capitalist imperatives*). Catalan sharecroppers were blasted onto the market by a combination of impartible inheritance and the progressive fragmentation of land leases. However, the architecture of tenure insulated their commercial agriculture from competition and prevented capitalist imperative to take hold. The situation was different in the textile proto-industry where many of these semi-proletarianized households sold their labor power to complement their incomes. This sector would incubate a capitalist breakthrough that was contingent on the success of socio-cultural struggles to subordinate production and labor to the vicissitudes of competition. Through this process, Catalan proto-industry broke out of corporatist regulations and carved out a firm position in the Madrid market without the protection of politically constituted privileges.

Rather than making profits in circulation (the age-old practice of buying cheap and selling dear), or relying upon politically constituted means to corner their markets (ensuring their profits in advance), Catalan proto-industry derived its prowess from competitive production practices. The erosion of politically constituted means of surplus extraction (i.e. the local monopolies of the guild system) and the commodification of labor allowed capitalist entrepreneurs to qualitatively transform age-old systems of production, but these factors alone did not ensure a capitalist mutation. In Barcelona, the erosion of the guild system culminated in an alternative passage out of feudal industry: the calico-printing manufactures. Catalonia's proto-industrial road to capitalism was cemented by a process of social construction that actively crafted a new culture of production and labor based on the principles of competition.

To be sure, the claim here is not that capitalism emerged out of the will of a handful of entrepreneurs. The circumstances of the capitalist breakthrough were shaped by long-term developments and contextual pre-conditions that laid out a structural context without which capitalist change could have not occurred. However, the dilemma cannot be to draw an equivalence between the broader conjuncture and the specific critical juncture when establishing out the causal determinants of the transition, as structural pre-conditions did not ensure the eventual success of Catalan proto-industry. In the final analysis, the weight of such a historical shift fell on the shoulders of everyday people making their own history, even if not under conditions of their own making.

Notes

1. Sydney Pollard, *Peaceful Conquest: The Industrialization of Europe 1760-1970* (Oxford: Oxford University Press, 1981).
2. James Thomson, "Explaining the 'take-off' of the Catalan Cotton Industry," *Economic History Review* 4, no. LVIII (2005): 701–735.
3. Jaume Torras, "Small Towns, Craft Guilds and Proto-Industry in Spain," *Jahrbuch Für Wirtschaftsgeschichte / Economic History Yearbook* 39, no. 2 (1998): 253–265.
4. Robert Brenner, "Agrarian Class Structure and Economic Development in Pre-Industrial Europe," *Past & Present* 70 (1976): 63–64.
5. Jaume Torras, "Class Struggle in Catalonia: A Note on Brenner," *Review (Fernand Braudel Center)* 4, no. 2 (1980): 253–265.
6. Ellen Meiksins Wood, "The Question of Market Dependence," *Journal of Agrarian Change* 2, no. 1 (2002): 50–87.
7. Robert Brenner, "The Origins of Capitalist Development: A Critique of Neo-Smithian Marxism," *New Left Review* I, no. 104 (1977): 25–92.
8. Ellen Meiksins Wood, *The Origin of Capitalism: A Longer View* (London: Verso, 2002), 2–3.
9. Robert P. Brenner, "The Low Countries in the Transition to Capitalism," *Journal of Agrarian Change* 1, no. 2 (2001): 169–241; Wood, "The Question of Market Dependence"; Charles Post, "Comments on the Brenner–Wood Exchange on the Low Countries," *Journal of Agrarian Change* 2, no. 1 (2002): 88–95.

10. Wood, "The Question of Market Dependence," 52–59; 69–70.
11. Perry Anderson, *Lineages of the Absolutist State* (London: Verso, 2013), 66.
12. Julie Marfany, *Land, Proto-Industry and Population in Catalonia c.1680–1829: An Alternative Transition to Capitalism?* (Farnham: Ashgate, 2012), 7.
13. Sheilagh Ogilvie, "Social Institutions and Proto-Industrialization," in *European Proto-Industrialization* (Cambridge: Cambridge University Press, 1996), 23.
14. Wood, "The Question of Market Dependence," 68.
15. Torras, "Small Towns, Craft Guilds," 81–82.
16. Brenner, "Agrarian Class Structure," 63, emphasis added.
17. Ibid., 66.
18. Torras, "Class Struggle in Catalonia," 255–259.
19. Marfany, *Land, Proto-Industry and Population*, 26–31.
20. In the meantime, the Catalan aristocracy had evacuated the countryside to focus on the scramble for public office. The high nobility relocated to Castile, where many of their lines became extinct as they blended with those of the local aristocracy. The resident nobility became dominated by a lower gentry drafted from an urban patriciate (*ciutadans honrats*) that would perform tax farming functions in Catalonia's self-governing institutions until their abolition after the War of Spanish Succession (after, tax collecting functions would pass on to Castilian-style *corregidores* that were overwhelmingly drafted from the ranks of the Castilian military). See Pere Molas Ribalta, "Noblesa Absentista i Retòrica Catalana," *Butlletí de La Societat Catalana d'Estudis Històrics*, no. 12 (2001): 27–41; Miquel Pérez Latre, "Nobleses i Generalitat: La Classe Dirigent i l'exercici Del Poder Des de Les Institucions (Segles Xvi–Xvii)," *Acta Artis: Estudis d'Art Modern* 3 (2015): 27–39.
21. Jaume Torras, "Especialización agricola e industria rural en Cataluña en el siglo XVIII," *Agricultura, industria y actividades urbanas en la España moderna* 2, no. 3 (1984): 113–127.
22. Belén Moreno Claverías, "La rabassa morta y la defensa de su carácter enfiteútico," 2013, http://webfacil.tinet.org/usuaris/turesplu/Belen_Moreno_20130906110309.pdf.
23. Josep María Oliva Melgar, "Los intercambios en la Cataluña del siglo XVIII," *Manuscrits*, no. 11 (1993): 199.
24. Ramón Garrabou, "Sobre la formació del mercat català en el segle XVIII. Una primera aproximació a base dels preus dels grans a Tàrrega (1732–1811)," *Recerques: Història, economia i cultura*, no. 1 (1970): 83–121.
25. Ramón Garrabou, Jordi Planas, and Enric Saguer, *Un capitalisme impossible?: La gestió de la propietat agrària a la Catalunya contemporània* (Barcelona: Eumo, 2001), 225.

26. Marfany, *Land, Proto-Industry and Population*, 5–9; 44–49; 175–178; 183–185.
27. See Marfany, 93–121. Paradoxically, testators had the legal freedom to allocate 75 percent of their testaments at will, and the children (eldest included) were only legally entitled to the remaining 25 percent. Yet the strength of primogeniture traditions was such that the allocation 75–80 percent of the parents' property to the eldest son was virtually universal. The legal transfer of property was settled upon the marriage of the heir.
28. Llorenç Ferrer i Alòs, "Agricultura i agricultors," in *Pierre Vilar i la Història de Catalunya*, ed. Joaquim Albareda et al. (Barcelona: Base, 2006), 109.
29. Marfany, *Land, Proto-Industry and Population*, 33–41; 141–143.
30. Ramón Garrabou, Jordi Planas, and Enric Saguer, "Sharecropping and the Management of Large Rural Estates in Contemporary Catalonia," *Journal of Peasant Studies* 28, no. 3 (2001): 94–95.
31. Josep Fontana, *Cambio económico y actitudes políticas en la España del siglo XIX* (Barcelona: Crítica, 1975), 73.
32. Moreno Claverías, "La rabassa morta".
33. Garrabou, Planas, and Saguer, "Sharecropping and the Management," 100.
34. Although this brought some instances of increased relative surplus extraction (e.g. indications on the use of fertilizer), landowners mostly acquired new capacities to increase the rate of exploitation through distinctively pre-capitalist means. These usually involved (1) an extension of absolute surplus extracted (e.g. by claiming greater shares of the yield or by specifying distances between rows of vines in order to prevent tenants from growing wheat for themselves) or (2) a relapse on "extra-economic" means of exploitation (e.g. tenants were forced to perform periodic labor dues). Overall, Catalan agriculture continued to bear a greater resemblance with feudal agrarian practices than with competitive capitalist agriculture. For more details, see Marfany, *Land, Proto-Industry and Population*, 52; Moreno Claverías, "La rabassa morta".
35. Garrabou, Planas, and Saguer, "Sharecropping and the Management," 96.
36. Pierre Vilar, *La Catalogne dans l'Espagne moderne. Vol. 1, 2, 3* (Paris: Flammarion, 1992). The perspective underpinning Vilar's monolithic work on Catalonia was inspired by his intervention in the early stages of the transition debate, during the famous dispute between Maurice Dobb and Paul Sweezy. Although Dobb had argued that feudalism unravelled when market dynamics creeped into the countryside, and Sweezy stressed that the impetus of change came from the external shocks of urban-based long-distance trade, Vilar reformulated the antimony between these "endogenous" and "exogenous" factors as a problem of finding the right synthesis between the two, himself emphasizing the rise of the Atlantic economy.

See Pierre Vilar, "Problems of the Formation of Capitalism," *Past & Present* 10, no. 1 (1956): 15–38. For a discussion of Vilar's intervention in the Dobb-Sweezy debate, see Francesc Valls Junyent, "Indústria i industrials," in *Pierre Vilar i la Història de Catalunya*, ed. Joaquim Albareda et al. (Barcelona: Base, 2006).

37. Vilar quoted in Valls Junyent, "Indústria i industrials".
38. See Ramon Grau and Marina Lopez, "Empresari i capitalista a la manufactura catalana del segle XVIII. Introduccio a l'estudi de fabriques d'indianes," *Recerques: història, economia, cultura* 4 (1974); Fontana, *Cambio económico.*
39. James Thomson, *A Distinctive Industrialization: Cotton in Barcelona 1728–1832* (Cambridge: Cambridge University Press, 1992), 50–89, 230.
40. Thomson, 230.
41. Álex Sánchez, "La era de la manufactura algodonera en Barcelona, 1736–1839," *Estudios de historia social*, no. 48–49 (1989): 65–113; Thomson, *A Distinctive Industrialization: Cotton in Barcelona 1728–1832*; Thomson, "Explaining the 'take-off' of the Catalan Cotton Industry"; James Thomson, "Consideracions sobre la indústria cotonera i la seva evolució a Barcelona, 1730–1840," in *La industria de les indianes a Barcelona, 1730–1850*, ed. Álex Sánchez, 17 (Barcelona: Ajuntament de Barcelona, 2012), 317–330.
42. Llorenç Ferrer i Alòs, *Els Orígens de La Industrialització a La Catalunya Central* (Barcelona: Rafael Dalmau, 1986); Josep M. Benaul, "Los orígenes de la empresa textil lanera en Sabadell y Terrassa en el siglo XVIII," *Revista de Historia Industrial* 1 (1992): 32–62; Albert García Balañà, *La fabricació de la fábrica: Treball i política a la Catalunya cotonera (1784–1874)* (Barcelona: L'Abadia de Montserrat, 2004); Marfany, *Land, Proto-Industry and Population in Catalonia c.1680–1829: An Alternative Transition to Capitalism?*; Thomson, "Consideracions sobre la indústria cotonera i la seva evolució a Barcelona, 1730–1840".
43. Torras, "Especialización agricola e industria rural en Cataluña en el siglo XVIII"; Jaume Torras, "La 'protoindustrialización': balance de una peripecia historiográfica," *Areas: Revista internacional de ciencias sociales* 10 (1989): 83–88; Jaume Torras, "From Craft to Class: Cloth Manufacturing in a Catalan Town," in *The Workplace before the Factory: Artisans and Proletarians 1500–1800*, ed. Thomas Max Safley and Leonard Ronsenband (Ithaca: Cornell University Press, 1993); Torras, "Small Towns, Craft Guilds and Proto-Industry in Spain"; Jaume Torras, *Fabricants sense fábrica: els Torelló, d'Igualada (1691–1794)* (Vic: Eumo, 2007).
44. Torras, "La 'protoindustrialización': balance de una peripecia historiográfica".

45. Francesc Valls Junyent, *La Catalunya atlàntica: Aiguardent i teixits a l'arrencada industrial catalana* (Barcelona: Eumo, 2003), 27–34.
46. Torras, *Fabricants sense fàbrica*, 103–121.
47. Josep M. Benaul, "La industria en vísperas de la industrialización, 1750–1813. Manufactura tradicional e industria moderna," in *Atlas de la Industrialización en España*, ed. Jordi Nadal (Barcelona: Crítica, 2003), 25–56.
48. See Rosa Ros, *La Industria Textil Lanera de Béjar (1680–1850)* (Valladolid: Junta de Castilla y León, 1999). Béjar underwent a process of transformation similar to that of Terrassa in the first decades of the eighteenth century. However, as explained, a "guild reaction" from 1765 eschewed these advances.
49. Torras, "Small Towns, Craft Guilds," 87.
50. Torras, *Fabricants sense fàbrica*, 49; Thomson, *A Distinctive Industrialization*, 34–49.
51. Benaul, "Los orígenes de la empresa," 32–62.
52. Benaul: 40–44; Torras, *Fabricants sense fàbrica*, 147–157.
53. Benaul, "Los orígenes de la empresa," 40–44.
54. See Torras, "From Craft to Class".
55. Ferrer i Alòs, *Els Orígens*, 20–25.
56. Quoted in Marfany, *Land, Proto-Industry and Population*, 75. The clothiers of Sabadell raised similar arguments, citing the example of Barcelona's cotton manufactures, where "owners rule absolutely and do not depend in any way from the weavers or the other employees". See Benaul, "Los orígenes de la empresa," 45.
57. Benaul, "Los orígenes de la empresa," 40–45.
58. Pere Molas Ribalta, *Los Gremios Barceloneses Del Siglo XVIII* (Madrid: Confederación Española de Cajas de Ahorros, 1970), 386.
59. The calico industry emerged in the age of Philip V (1700–1746), a period marked by the founding of Colbertian state manufactures. Although Barcelona's calico industry was left to the private sector (no cotton manufactures were ever founded by the state), private investment always depended on remarkable opportunities for import-substitution. The bulk of their sales were geared at the heavily protected Spanish market and supplemented by exports to the captive colonial markets. See Thomson, "Explaining the 'take-off'," 703–716; Oliva Melgar, "Los intercambios".
60. Thomson, "Consideracions sobre la indústria cotonera," 703–716.
61. Thomson, *A Distinctive Industrialization*, 185.
62. Thomson, "Explaining the 'take-off'," 722.
63. Ibid., 716–718.
64. Torras, *Fabricants sense fàbrica*, 147; Molas Ribalta, *Los Gremios Barceloneses*, 388.

65. Belén Moreno Claverías, "El aprendiz de gremio en la Barcelona del siglo XVIII," *Revista Internacional de Ciencias Sociales* 34, no. Gremios y corporaciones laborales en la transición del feudalismo al capitalismo (2015): 709.
66. Sánchez, "La era de la manufactura," 99.
67. Thomson, *A Distinctive Industrialization*; Thomson, "Explaining the 'take-off'," 725.
68. James Thomson, "Olot, Barcelona and Ávila and the Introduction of the Arkwright Technology to Catalonia," *Revista de Historia Económica* 21, no. 2 (2003): 302.
69. Ferrer i Alòs, *Els Orígens*, 302.
70. Benaul, "Los orígenes de la empresa".
71. Thomson, *A Distinctive Industrialization: Cotton*, 294–301.
72. Thomson, "Consideracions sobre la indústria cotonera," 322–328.
73. Marfany, *Land, Proto-Industry and Population*, 82–83; García Balañà, *La fabricació de la fábrica*, 331–337.

CHAPTER 7

The American Road to Capitalism

Charles Post

A historical paradox marks the English colonization in the Americas. The British colonial empire was unique among the European empires of the seventeenth and eighteenth centuries. Continental European colonization of the New World was driven by the dynamics of absolutist-feudal states,[1] in particular their need to raise revenues without bankrupting non-capitalist agriculture, and was organized by merchants with royal monopolies on colonial trade. English colonization of the Americas was driven by the unique development of capitalist agriculture in England. English capitalist-tenant farmers, whose productive specialization required them to purchase consumer goods, became a mass market for new products like tobacco, coffee, sugar and tea. Those who took up the trade in these goods were not "royal merchants" who dominated English trade prior to the seventeenth century but the "new" merchants who operated in a competitive market. The new merchants, not traditional royal monopolists, organized the process of English colonial settlement in the Caribbean (Barbados, Jamaica) and the East Coast of North America. Despite the

C. Post (✉)
Graduate Center and Borough of Manhattan Community College,
City University of New York, New York, NY, USA

X. Lafrance, C. Post (eds.), *Case Studies in the Origins of Capitalism*, Marx, Engels, and Marxisms,
https://doi.org/10.1007/978-3-319-95657-2_7

specifically capitalist impulse behind English colonialism, however, they *were unable to reproduce agrarian capitalist social property relations in their mainland colonies.*

The key to this paradox was the inability of British merchants and landlords and their allies among local colonial elites to establish an *effective social monopoly of landed property.* The British state granted legal title to large tracts of North America to aspiring colonial landlords and merchants. However, the Imperial government and their colonial allies were unable to enforce these claims outside of limited areas near the Atlantic coast.[2] Vast geographic distances and the relatively small size of the British military precluded the direct colonial rule that marked the seventeenth-century English colonization of Northern Ireland. British troops only arrived in North America in 1754 and were stationed along the frontier to fend off attacks from the French and Native Americans.[3] Britain ruled its North American possessions indirectly, relying on the domestic merchants, landowners and planters who dominated the elected colonial assemblies. While the local ruling class sought to enforce legal claims on land in the interior, they were forced to rely on colonial militias, composed primarily of independent farmers and artisans who resisted the commodification of landed property. The existence of unoccupied lands, available at little or no cost other than the labor required to clear the land and begin the production of food and handicrafts, made the establishment of capitalist social property relations impossible.

This chapter seeks to explain how a commercial but *non-capitalist society* became the capitalist US by the end of the Civil War. The first section analyzes the dynamics of the two dominant non-capitalist social property relations in the colonial period—independent household production in the North and plantation slavery in the South. The extensive growth of these forms of social labor laid the basis for a national economy linked together by colonial merchants in the coastal cities, creating the conditions for conflicts with Britain that ended in US independence. The post-revolutionary struggles of independent household producers and the resulting Constitutional Settlement of 1787 created a state in North America with the capacity to impose a social monopoly of land through public land sales.

The development of land markets had radically different effects in the North and South. On the one hand, plantation slavery gained a new lease on life as tobacco planters shifted to growing cotton for the capitalist industry in Britain. The result was the continuation of *extensive growth*—the geographic expansion of the cotton economy involved more slaves and more land with only *episodic* technical innovation. On the other hand, Northern farmers found themselves compelled to compete in the market place in order to pay taxes and debts accrued to purchase and maintain their possession of landed property. *Intensive development*—the increased output per capita as the result of productive specialization, technical innovation and accumulation—marked the geographic expansion of Northern agriculture. While the South remained the least industrialized region of the Antebellum US, Northern family farms provided an expanding market for both capital and consumer goods, fueling the growth of industry and manufacture in the two decades before the Civil War. The transformation of Northern family farming from "safety-first" independent household production to "market-dependent" petty-capitalist agriculture marked the emergence of capitalism in the US and set the stage for the political conflicts that culminated in the Civil War, which consolidated capitalism in the US.

The Non-capitalist Colonial Economy and Society

Plantation Slavery

In the 1620s, English settlers in Virginia began cultivating tobacco as a profitable export crop.[4] Native Americans were quickly pushed into the interior and the initial English settlers grabbed land to grow tobacco. The large plantations in the fertile Tidewater regions became the center of tobacco production. Tobacco exports grew over 18-fold between 1628 and 1669, from 500,000 to 9,026,000 pounds annually.[5] The only limit on tobacco cultivation was the availability of labor. With plentiful land beyond the emerging Tidewater plantation districts available for occupation at little or no cost, legally free wage labor was effectively precluded.[6] Unable to enslave the Native Americans, English tobacco planters initially brought indentured servants from England and other parts of Europe to labor on their plantations in the Chesapeake.[7] Drawn primarily from the ranks of displaced peasants in England and Ireland, indentured servants agreed to sell their capacity to work for a period of 5–7 years in return for passage to the Americas. Upon arrival in Maryland and Virginia, the planters would purchase the servants' contracts (terms of indenture). The servants' person and capacity to labor became the property of their masters for the duration of their terms of indenture. If they survived 5–7 years of strenuous labor and an inhospitable disease environment, the servants became "freemen," collected "freedom dues" (small amounts of cash, work animals, tools and weapons) and moved to unsettled lands to become self-sufficient farmers in the interior.[8]

By the late seventeenth century, struggles between planters and servants and former servants led to the replacement of European servants with African slaves.[9] Faced with falling tobacco prices, planters in the 1660s and 1670s sought to reduce labor costs. Individual planters reduced food rations, increased punishments for insubordination and extended servants' terms of indenture. The planter-dominated Virginia assembly imposed poll taxes on newly freed servants and granted legal title to large swathes of land on the frontier to large landowners. Former servants, after 1660, "found it increasingly difficult to locate workable land that was not already claimed."[10] To survive, more and more former servants labored for wages. Growing tensions between the planters and their servants and the armed ex-servants grew through the 1660s and 1670s.[11] The conclusion of a peace treaty between the assembly and Native Americans in 1676 effectively closed off much of the frontier to the former servant, sparking Bacon's Rebellion—the largest revolt in North America before the American Revolution. In the wake of Bacon's Rebellion, African slaves displaced indentured servitude on the tobacco plantations.[12]

While the land and slaves of planters in French, Spanish and Portuguese colonies were protected from seizure for unpaid debt, British merchants imposed colonial land laws on the Southern planters that allowed their expropriation for credit defaults.[13] As a result, planters in the British colonies were compelled to "sell to survive." It is this market *compulsion* that explains many of what appear to be "capitalist" characteristics of plantation slavery: the close supervision of the slaves' labor, the accumulation of more slaves and land, the collateralization of slaves and land to finance expansion and the search for new techniques that could boost labor productivity.

But slavery, despite the planters' market dependence, did not duplicate the workings of capitalism with wage labor. The relationship of master and slave, *unlike* the relationship of capitalist and wage worker, *set up barriers* to planters effectively cutting costs in the ways that capitalists do—through the relatively continuous introduction of labor-saving technological changes and productive specialization.[14] Under slavery, the non-producers did not purchase the *labor power*—ability to work for fixed periods of time—of the direct producers. Instead, the planters purchased *the laborers* as a form of *fixed capital*—a constant element of the production process. If planters introduced cost-cutting techniques that saved labor, they would not be able, like their capitalist counterparts, to simply lay off workers because they needed to recoup their initial investments in the slaves as "means of production in human form." They would be stuck with continuing ownership of the laborer(s), having to maintain them around until they could find *purchasers*. Like other non-capitalist forms of social labor, slavery did allow *episodic* improvements in productivity. However, innovation under slavery had a "once and for all" character, taking place when new crops were introduced or plantation agriculture moved to a new frontier.[15]

Tobacco planters in seventeenth- and eighteenth-century Virginia and Maryland created coordinated labor processes that maximized the use of human labor.[16] Tobacco plantations were organized around the task system, where the ten or more slaves on the plantation were broken into groups of two to three using hoes and other hand tools and assigned daily work quotas that overseers would ensure were met. Planters increased the volume of production, from 9 million pounds of tobacco annually in 1669 to over 100 million pounds in the 1770s,[17] through intensifying work and moving production to more fertile land.

The master-slave social property relation also produced the tendency of New World slave owners to make their plantations self-sufficient in food and other productive inputs. In order for masters to realize their investments in slaves, the slaves must be compelled to work year round. Agriculture is not well suited to providing year round, continuous work because of sharp discontinuities between the time human labor is required to plant, harvest and cultivate crops (labor time) and the time required for natural-biological processes to bring crops to maturity (production time).[18] Especially "after the crop was hung in the tobacco house," in the late fall, "masters had to manufacture new work for their slaves if they expected them to continue to labor."[19] The slaveholders were able to organize the growing of corn and the raising of hogs, allowing most of the slaves' basic food ration (ground corn and pork) to be produced directly on the plantation rather than purchased. The slaves were also granted garden plots which they tilled during their "free" time, growing vegetables and root crops and keeping chickens and ducks.[20]

Independent Household Production

To facilitate colonial settlement in the Northern colonies, imperial authorities made land grants either to settlers creating townships (New England) or to large mercantile companies that sold land to large landowners (Mid-Atlantic). Despite growing social inequality among rural households and the steady increase in the sales of grain, timber and meat to Northern cities and towns and in the plantations of the Caribbean, Northern farmers were *non-capitalist* independent household producers whose possession of landed property did not depend upon successful commodity production.[21]

Northern colonial rural households' capacity to engage in independent household production was rooted in the inability of colonial landowners to enforce their legal claims to landed property beyond the densely settled coastal areas. Most settlers, illegally occupied ("squatted") on lands owned by private owners, later purchased title at below market prices. As a result, rural households were able to establish, maintain and expand their landholdings without extensive commodity production.[22] This was evident in the countryside surrounding Philadelphia—the largest urban market in colonial North America. From the 1690s, the Pennsylvania assembly attempted to promote an "orderly settlement" of Southeastern Pennsylvania through the sale of large tracts of land to private landholders, who were expected to resell or lease land to actual settlers. However, "indiscriminate location" and squatting remained widespread. Squatters organized land occupations to resist attempts to force settlers to either purchase land or pay rents during the mid-eighteenth century. In 1765, the Penn family and their allies ceased all attempts to enforce legal title to lands in the hinterland of Philadelphia, and adopted the "application system," which gave those occupying land legal title ("warrants") at low prices.[23]

The economic survival of Northern rural households *was not conditioned upon the profitable sale of agricultural goods.* The absence of market-based prices or rents for land, high taxes or debts that must be paid in cash with interest allowed Northern independent landowning farmers to engage in "safety-first" agriculture where they marketed only physical surpluses. Even in the Philadelphia region, most farmers grew a mix of wheat, rye, oats, barley, buckwheat, fruit and potatoes for household consumption; flax and hemp for household manufacture of clothing and rope; and turnips, grasses, legumes and corn to feed cows, oxen, swine and other livestock which they and their neighbors consumed.[24] At most, the better-off family farmers in Southeastern Pennsylvania marketed no more than 40–50% of their total output, well below the 60% that most agrarian historians believe indicates a high degree of market dependence.[25] Freedom from the compulsion to produce for the market to maintain land ownership allowed the emergence of dense webs of kinship and communal relations that structured "neighborly exchange" of goods and labor among households—marked by the extension of "credit" for labor and produce that went on for years and never accrued interest.

The long-settled regions in the Northern colonies, like most of early modern Western Europe outside of England, displayed tendencies toward the parcellization of landholdings and social differentiation of rural households.[26] Growing population, partible inheritance (the division of the family landholdings among all male heirs) and the technical stagnation inherent in independent household production led to a division and subdivision of landholdings from one generation to another. This parcellization of landholdings created some plots too small to support a rural household.[27] As in pre-industrial Western Europe, land parcellization and rising land prices produced inequalities in landholdings among rural households. Landless populations appeared by the early to mid-eighteenth century as the worst-off rural households sold their meager landholdings to their better-off neighbors.[28] Unlike social differentiation under capitalist production, the growing inequality among independent producers was clearly limited. In the 1740s, after nearly a century of continuous occupation, the richest 5% of landowners in a Massachusetts town owned no more than 15% of the land, and the best-off 10% owned no more than a quarter of land.[29] Growing social differentiation of rural households did not lead to a consolidation of landholdings. As in pre-industrial Western Europe, large landholdings in New England were broken into miniscule plots scattered through the fields.[30]

The American Revolution and Constitutional Settlement

Over the course of the seventeenth and eighteenth centuries, the British colonies on the North American mainland developed a distinctive, commercial, but non-capitalist, economy. The close political and economic ties between the original colonial merchants and landowners and the British state "did not prevent the colonial economy from developing less on the strength of the British domestic market than on the growing interdependence of colonial settlements."[31] Northern farmers produced and sold large surpluses of grains and meat to the Northern ports of Boston, New York and Philadelphia and to the growing sugar plantations of the Caribbean. Southern plantations, while generally self-sufficient in food, sold tobacco in the Caribbean, the Northern colonies and Britain.[32]

At the center of the independent colonial North American economy, binding together rural independent household production and plantation slavery was a class of colonial merchants. These merchants first emerged as junior partners of British merchants, who held a monopoly on trade and credit with Britain's colonial empire under the Navigation Acts. Colonial American merchants acted as agents of British merchants in the "triangular trade," organizing the import of British manufactures to North America and the Caribbean and the export of tobacco to Britain.[33] As Northern independent household producers began to produce surpluses of food for sale, New York, Philadelphia and Boston merchants gathered rural surpluses from hundreds of small traders and shopkeepers scattered across the Northern countryside, consolidated them and shipped them to other parts of colonial North America and the Caribbean.[34]

The development of a commercial, non-capitalist colonial economy laid the foundation for the settler colonists' bid for independence under the leadership of the merchants. Even before independence, colonial merchants in the North and planters in the South were able to exercise political power through elected assemblies in all of the colonies.[35] British imperial attempts to impose new taxes, restrict trade and ban the expansion of settlement into the interior after 1763 allowed the merchants to forge an alliance of all free people in colonial North America. Under their leadership, a coalition of slaveholding planters, independent farmers, urban artisans and wage workers, land speculators and back country traders successfully ended British colonial rule.

The Revolutionary War of 1776–1783 disrupted agricultural production in the Northern US. State governments purchased food, cloth and other supplies from Northern farm households at inflated prices to support the war effort. As a result, farmers began to devote more and more family labor to the production of commodities. Unable to produce the variety of goods previously manufactured in their self-sufficient communities, rural households borrowed from local storekeepers to purchase US manufactures during the war and British manufactures after the war. These debts became particularly burdensome after 1783, as the newly independent Northern state government raised land taxes to fund the enormous public debt accrued during the war. The growth of debts and taxes forced Northern households to market larger and larger portions of both their subsistence and surplus output in order to maintain their landed property in the 1780s, setting the stage for class conflicts that produced a very different type of state—one committed to and capable of enforcing legal claims on landed property in the countryside.[36]

The end of the war opened a period of intense social conflict among the classes that had made the American Revolution. The colonial merchants and land speculators sought to create state institutions that could secure the public debt and reestablish US commercial credit in the Atlantic economy, enforce legal claims to land on the frontier and allow landowners to profit from the sale of these lands. Arrayed against the merchants and speculators were the vast majority of Northern and Southern independent household producers who feared a strong central state capable of imposing taxes and collecting debts and slave-owning planters who wanted to exclude all other social classes from interfering with the master-slave relation of production.

During the first decade of independence, the merchants and land speculators were unable to craft a state that would establish their political dominance. Under the Articles of Confederation, the US state was decentralized and the national Congress lacked the independent capacity to levy taxes. The Confederation was incapable of either securing the public debt or maintaining a peacetime standing army.[37] Their experience with regular British troops during the American Revolution deepened long-standing hostility to a standing army among farmers and artisans. The planters successfully relied on militias made up of non-slave-holding white farmers to control the slave populations and had no interest in strengthening the central state with a standing army. Despite attempts by the political representatives of the merchants to force Congress to maintain and expand the standing army—including an abortive military conspiracy in 1783—the standing army was effectively disbanded after the revolutionary war.[38] By 1789, the US army consisted of a total of 718 men—mostly stationed on the frontier. The tiny army was incapable of either effectively expropriating Native Americans or preventing thousands of squatters from "pouring into the Ohio Valley, threatening to deter purchase of federal land by speculators and settlers."[39]

Shay's Rebellion of 1786, the first revolt of Northern farmers against the burdens of debts and taxes that threatened to make their possession of landed property dependent upon successful market competition, initiated a political realignment among the dominant classes in the US. As armed farmers and artisans closed down courts attempting to expropriate farms for the failure to pay debts and taxes in the fall of 1786, "the local militia sided with Shay's Rebellion initially, and it took several months before the revolt was quashed."[40] Planters, frightened by Massachusetts militia's difficulty in suppressing Shay's Rebellion, joined the merchants in demanding a more centralized state. The Constitutional Settlement of 1787 contained a series of concessions to planters—most importantly preventing any other social classes represented in the federal government from interfering with the master-slave relationship in the South. However, the new federal state created in 1787–1789 generated a national judiciary, a corps of tax collectors, centralized control of the state militias and built a standing army capable of enforcing the legal claims of landowners and creditors.[41] By 1794, the regular US army had grown from 718 to 3818 troops and the president had the power to mobilize reorganized state militias.

The new state institutions allowed merchants and land speculators to defeat independent household producers in the cycle of class struggles of the 1780s and 1790s. Independent farmers fought tax collectors, merchant-creditors and land speculators over the conditions of their economic survival in a series of armed confrontations across the Northern countryside. Faced with a merchant class backed by a standing army, the independent farmers were defeated. The new US ruling class demonstrated its military capacity to impose taxes and secure landed property in crushing both the Whiskey Rebellion of 1794 and the smaller Fries Rebellion in 1799.[42] The consolidation of the federal state, backed by a standing army capable of enforcing the claims of merchants and speculators, set the stage in the early nineteenth century for the establishment of the public land system in the US—where millions of acres expropriated from the indigenous populations were sold at public auction to the highest bidder. While the effective commodification of landed property allowed plantation slavery to survive and expand, it transformed Northern agriculture from independent household to petty-capitalist production—creating the conditions for the emergence of capitalism in the US.

The Antebellum Origins of US Capitalism

Plantation Slavery

Falling tobacco prices after the American Revolution led some Tidewater planters to break up their plantations, sell surplus slaves and produce grains on smaller farms, fueling political speculation that slavery was dying a "natural death" in North America. However, the massive expansion of British capitalist textile production and the elimination of technical obstacles to cultivating new strains of cotton gave slavery a new lease on life. The transition from tobacco to cotton allowed a twofold but "once and for all" transformation in the plantation labor process. First, cotton cultivation made possible the introduction of gang labor on Southern cotton plantations, giving the masters greater control over the tempo and organization of their slaves' labor, and allowed a growing scale of production. In cotton planting, the slaves were divided into five gangs, each responsible for a specific aspect of soil preparation and seed placement. During cultivation, the nurturing of the cotton plants while they grew to maturity, the hoe gang and the plow gang would work in close coordination chopping weeds and stirring the soil. The detailed division of labor broke down during the harvest, as undifferentiated groups of slaves would pick the cotton by hand.[43]

Second, the growth of cotton production opened the way for the introduction of the horse- or mule-drawn "sweeper" plow (replacing the hand hoe) and of the "Petit Gulf" cotton hybrid in the 1820s and 1830s. The introduction of new cotton hybrids has been credited with the nearly 2.3% annualized annual growth in labor productivity in the cotton harvest in the 60 years before the Civil War.[44] While a number of cotton hybrids were introduced before the Civil War, only the "Petit Gulf" strain produced a significant increase in output per slave during the cotton harvest.[45] After these innovations, labor-saving technical innovation stagnated. Further increases in output were the consequences of the diffusion of new hybrids and horse-drawn plows from the Southwestern frontier to older regions of cotton cultivation, the movement of production to more fertile soils and the intensification of the slaves' labor through the close supervision of work gangs.[46]

The continuity of the master-slave social property relation also recreated the conditions for *plantation self-sufficiency*. In cotton production, the harvest season (late October through November) was the peak of labor time, when slaves would work 11 hours per day, 7 days per week. A lengthy slack season followed, ending with renewed planting in the early spring. Corn, a major source of food for both slaves and plantation livestock, had a complementary crop cycle to cotton. The planters organized the production of corn, with the slaves working in gangs utilizing the same tools (plows and hoes) they wielded in cotton production. The planters also organized the raising of hogs, which were allowed to forage in the woodlands surrounding most plantations before being confined to pens to fatten on corn for several weeks prior to slaughter. Together cotton and corn production kept the slaves working some 280–290 days per year, some 3000 hours per year—a 60 hour week, 50 weeks per year.[47]

In addition to the planters' organization of corn and pork production, which supplied most of the rations slaves received from their masters, most planters granted garden plots of approximately one acre to each slave household in the cotton South. On their own time (usually evenings, Saturday afternoons and Sundays), the slaves organized their own independent production of cabbage, collards, turnips, sweet potatoes and other vegetables. Usually, one slave household was able to grow enough vegetables in its garden to feed the household and provide a surplus for exchange with other slaves and for sale of plantation. Slaves in the cotton South also raised the majority of chickens and other fowl and engaged in hunting and fishing to supplement their diets. Slaves also produced a wide variety of handicrafts, including baskets, brooms, horse collars and bows both for household consumption and for sale.[48]

Together, plantation slavery's relatively unchanging labor process and the tendency toward self-sufficiency in food stuffs produced a very shallow social division of labor in the cotton South. The masters' ownership of the slave as "means of production in human form" and the resulting inability to "expel labor" from the production process created a highly episodic process of labor-saving technical innovation and a fixed and inflexible ratio of labor to land and tools. The relatively unchanging tools and implements used on the slave plantations of the US South, along with the attempts of planters to produce hoes and plows on the plantation, severely limited demand for capital goods. The masters' need to keep the slaves employed continuously throughout the year impelled the planters to put the slaves to work growing corn and raising hogs, making the cotton plantations generally "self-sufficient" in food. Plantation self-sufficiency severely limited the purchase of consumption goods to simple clothing and shoes for the slaves. In sum, plantation slavery produced a limited home market for industrial capitalist production of capital and consumer goods, making the South the least industrialized region of the Antebellum US and potentially short-circuiting the development of capitalist agriculture and industry in regions it dominated.[49]

The cotton plantations of the Antebellum South met the growing demand for raw cotton on the part of industrialists in Britain and the Northern US through extensive growth—*geographic expansion*. The center of slave cotton production shifted Southwesterly through the early nineteenth century, from coastal South Carolina and Georgia in 1815, to Western Georgia and Southern Mississippi and Alabama in 1830, to Northern Mississippi and Alabama and Louisiana and Texas in 1850.[50] Between 1840 and 1860, the production of cotton in the US rose 173%, from approximately 834 million pounds to 2.3 billion pounds. At the same time, cotton acreage grew 167%, from approximately 4.5 million acres to 12 million acres and the number of slaves producing cotton grew 87.5%, from approximately 1.2 million to 2.25 million.[51] Put simply, the addition of more slaves and more land, combined with the intensification of the slaves' labor and increased yields per acre resulting from the cultivation of more fertile soils, were the basis for expanding cotton production in the Antebellum period. The regular introduction of labor-saving techniques was incompatible with the master-slave social property relations, necessitating this pattern of *extensive* growth.

Petty-Capitalist Agriculture in the North

The defeat of the small producers in the Northeast in the last two decades of the eighteenth century, while sealing the fate of independent household production in the original area of colonial settlement, did not spell the end of this social property form in the Northern US. In the Ohio Valley and Great Plains, independent production developed as Native Americans were forcibly "removed" and white settlers took initial possession of land in most areas at little or no cost. Although federal land law promoted the transfer of the massive "public domain" into the hands of private landholders, "squatters" were often able to defend their landholding against the claims of land speculators and investors before the 1830s. Nearly two-thirds of all farmers in Illinois were "squatters" in 1828, and in some communities 40% of all farmers were still "squatters" in 1840. "Claims clubs" of settlers on public lands without legal title successfully "warned off" urban land companies and later arriving farmers and secured land for a minority of settlers at federal minimum prices. Generally, land speculators did not attempt to bid on "squatters" lands, instead buying up the huge tracks of unoccupied lands in sparsely settled regions at federal land auctions.[52]

At least temporarily secure in their possession of land without recourse to production for the market, the "yeomanry" of the Middle West were able to reestablish crucial elements of independent household production in the early nineteenth century. Through the 1830s, the bulk of rural households and communities in the Ohio Valley and Great Plains appears to be self-sufficient in food and many handicraft items. Farmers grew a wide variety of goods for consumption by their families and neighbors and marketed only about 30% of their total output in the 1820s and 1830s.[53] Secure in their basic foodstuffs, many households also engaged in extensive craft production of tools, implements, utensils and clothing for local consumption. Locally produced "general use" implements and the inexpensive oxen, although less efficient than manufactured tools or horses, fit into the logic of "self-sufficient" household production.[54] The spread of transportation facilities (roads and canals) facilitated the circulation of rural "surpluses" as commodities bound for urban markets but did not change the rural households and communities' relationship to their land and their ability to produce the majority of their subsistence as use values before 1840.[55]

The outcome of the class conflicts of the 1780s and 1790s severely delimited the Midwestern farmers' autonomy from commodity production. Most importantly, the federal laws administering the distribution of the vast "public domain" stretching Westward from the Appalachian mountains promoted land speculation and raised the cost of landed property to the vast majority of farmers who settled the Midwest. Conceived between 1796 and 1820, Antebellum federal land policy provided for the survey and auction sale of public land after all Native American and foreign claims on the public domain were settled through wars of conquest and treaties. The federal government set minimum prices and acreage to be purchased, but put no restrictions on the maximum size of purchase, allowing the operation of "market mechanisms" to set the price obtained at public auction.[56]

The system of public auction of government lands promoted successive waves of land speculation in the West during the Antebellum period.[57] The speculative expansion and crisis of the 1830s and early 1840s radically transformed the class relations of Northern agriculture. Land, railroad and canal companies were able to appropriate much of the best located and most fertile lands, forcing prospective settlers to purchase land from them at prices well above the federal minimum. Land speculators' operations were so effective that in Iowa, a relatively sparsely settled "frontier" region in the decade before the Civil War, 78.1% of farmers had purchased their land from speculators in 1850 and 85.7% had obtained land from speculators in 1860.[58]

Land speculation increased the costs of "farm building"—the costs of establishing a viable farm—in the 1840s and 1850s. In the 1830s, the cost of developing an 80-acre farm in Illinois, including clearing and fencing the land, buying implements and livestock and constructing housing, ranged between $500 and $600.[59] By the 1850s, the purchase price of land in Illinois, available primarily from land companies, ranged from three to ten dollars per acre, making the land costs alone between $240 and $800 for an 80-acre farm. By 1860, 80 acres of land in Illinois had risen to $1345. These prices were usually greater than the cash resources of most perspective settlers, who also had to make considerable investments in fencing, seed, livestock, housing, farm implements and, on the prairies, expensive soil preparation ("sod busting") and drainage. As a result, the great majority of farmers seeking fertile and well-located land in the Midwest during the 1840s and 1850s had to borrow money to purchase land and capital equipment.[60] The burden of these debts ensured that farmers would specialize, innovate and accumulate in order to pay mortgages (and taxes) and prevent the loss of their land. In sum, the creations of a social monopoly of land in the 1830s made successful commodity production a necessary condition for the acquisition, maintenance and expansion of landed property, establishing agrarian petty capitalism throughout the Northern countryside in the two decades before the Civil War.

The development of petty-capitalist production in the Ohio valley and Great Plains in the two decades before the Civil War spawned an "agricultural revolution"—the growth of the size and proportion of output produced as commodities, increasing specialization in cash crops, rising labor productivity with the introductions of new seeds, fertilizers and improved implements and machinery and growing social inequalities among rural households. While Antebellum farmers in the "old Northwest," like thoroughly commercial farmers today, continued to produce elements of their own subsistence (meat, dairy, eggs, vegetables and some hand tools), they radically reoriented their productive activity during the 1840s and 1850s. By 1860, Northwestern farmers were selling approximately 60% of their total yield.[61]

Market-dependent farmers were compelled to specialize in cash crop production best adapted to their soil types[62] and to reduce household manufacture of items for family and community consumption. Between 1840 and 1860, per capita household output of such goods as cloth, tools, implements, fencing, packed or processed meat and grain (flour) and the like in the Northern US fell from $1.34 to $.36, a drop of 73%. While independent household craft production fell most rapidly in the Northeast, from $1.16 per capita in 1840 to $.28 per capita in 1860, a drop of 76%, it also declined consistently in the Northwest, from $1.11 per capita in 1840 to $.39 per capita in 1860, a drop of 65%.[63] Goods that had been produced in rural households for immediate consumption were being purchased on the marketplace in the 1840s and 1850s. In the case of meat packing and farm implements' production, their separation from farm households led to the industrialization of their labor processes and their relocation in the urban centers of Chicago and Cincinnati.[64]

Cash crop specialization under the impact of the "market imperative" allowed for a very rapid and continuous rise in labor productivity in agriculture from the 1840s and 1850s. While economists and historians debate the precise rate of growth of labor productivity (estimates range from 2.0% to 2.6% per annum for wheat and from 1.5% to 2.15% for corn for the period from 1840–1860 to 1900–1910), there is a general consensus that the rate of growth of productivity in Northern US agriculture matched or surpassed other branches of production. The introduction of superior implements and machinery accounted for approximately 50% of the improvements in rural labor productivity, the rest resulting from improved fertilizers, seeds and methods of crop rotation.[65] Technical innovation in Antebellum Northern agriculture tended to be concentrated in the soil preparation-planting and harvesting phases of grain growing, which required the greatest and most intensive labor. Before 1840, cast iron plows pulled by oxen prepared the soil, and seeds were hand-broadcast in planting, which worked poorly on the hard prairie soils that came under cultivation in the late 1830s and 1840s. Pressures to lower costs in the two decades before the Civil War led to the rapid diffusion of the horse-drawn "self-scouring" John Deere steel plow and a variety of seed drills that together improved soil and labor productivity.[66]

Perhaps the most dramatic improvements in rural labor productivity came with the mechanization of grain harvesting. Prior to the introduction of the mass-produced McCormick mechanical reaper, the main tool for harvesting wheat and other grains was the wheat cradle, a hand tool. With a cradle, one person could reap 2–3 acres per day, with additional labor being expended raking and gathering the cut wheat. The horse-drawn, mechanical reaper combined the tasks of reaping and raking, increasing the acreage a single person could harvest to 12 acres per day, an increase in labor productivity of approximately 75%. Along with the reaper, the mechanical thresher, which separated the wheat from the chaff, also radically reduced the amount of labor needed to prepare grain for the market. The thresher's cost was usually well beyond the means of all but the most wealthy commercial farmers, promoting the development of independent "specialists" who traveled throughout the Midwest preparing grain for milling.[67]

The pace and pattern of industrial development in the US was directly linked to the transformation of Northern family farming in the 20 years before the Civil War. The impact of the transformation of the rural class structure on industrialization in the 1840s and 1850s can be seen directly in the growth of an "agro-industrial" complex in the US industry. The industries producing farm machinery, tools and supplies and processing agricultural raw materials (meat packing, leather tanning, canning, flour milling, baking, etc.) were at the center of the US Industrial Revolution. Farm implement and machine production alone made up 19.4% of all machine production in 1860, rising to 25.5% in 1870.[68] Further, these industries experienced important developments in their labor processes (e.g., mechanization of flour milling, the development of the first "disassembly" line in meat packing and the use of standardized parts in the construction of reapers) and stimulated technical transformations in other crucial industries.[69] For example, the formation of the "agro-industrial complex" spurred technological innovation in the Antebellum iron industry. Specialized industrial producers (who needed lower-quality and less versatile iron) replaced rural blacksmiths and farmers (who needed high-quality and versatile iron to produce a wide variety of products) as the main consumers of iron, providing the impetus for the centralization of iron production and the use of coal, rather than charcoal, in the smelting process.[70]

The Social Origins and Consequences of the US Civil War

The roots of the catastrophic political crisis that culminated in the US Civil War are found in the contradictions between the social and political conditions of the continued development of capitalist manufacturing and plantation slavery after 1840. The development of industrial capitalism in the US rested on *the continuous expansion of agrarian petty capitalism*—household production subject to "market coercion" that compelled producers to specialize, innovate and accumulate, providing a mass home market for industrial capitalist production. The expansion of plantation slavery—*the necessary form of the expanded reproduction of this form of social labor*—was incompatible with the development of capitalist production in the regions it dominated. In sum, the social and economic contradictions between the development of capitalism and slavery after 1840 produced the growing radicalization of Northern and Southern public opinion, the marginalization of the advocates of sectional compromise and the collapse of the nationally organized Whig and Democratic Parties.

Before the 1840s, the social dominance of merchant capitalists—land and transportation infrastructure speculators, merchants and bankers—allowed the stability of the nationally organized Whig and Democratic Parties and the marginalization of debates on the social character of the geographic expansion of commodity production across the North American continent. The transformation of the US economy after c.1840—the dominance of agrarian petty capitalism—marginalized merchant capitalists politically and socially and opened the way for the political polarization that ended in Civil War.

The growing radicalization of Northern public opinion in the late 1840s and 1850s, manifested in the defections of Whig and Democratic farmers, manufacturers, artisans and urban professionals to the Free Soil and Republican Parties,[71] which championed the *containment* of plantation slavery within the South, *corresponding to the social position* of manufacturers and commercial farmers in the North. The parallel radicalization of the planters[72] organized in the Democratic Party was manifested in their refusal to countenance any restriction on the expansion of slavery, their advocacy of US expansion into the Caribbean and Central America and their championing of the demand for a Congressional slave code for the Western territories. The planters' embrace of "slave soil" politics flowed from the *social requirements* of the reproduction of their form of social labor. Just as the future development of capitalism in the North required reserving the Western territories for capitalist producers, the future of plantation slavery depended upon securing, either within the US state or through an independent state of their own, the legal-political conditions for the spread of slavery to new territories.

The changing matrix of social relations of production and exchange doomed the forces of sectional compromise—the Democratic land speculators and the Whig merchants—to irrelevance in the political crisis of the 1840s and 1850s. The attempts of both Northern Democrats and Conservative Whigs (and later Americans and Constitutional Unionists) to avoid the question of the social character of geographic expansion reflected the "lived experience" of merchant capital's *structural indifference* to the social relations of commodity production. The inability of either the Northern Democrats or the Conservative Whigs to impose enduring compromises on the question of slavery expansion after 1850[73] was the unavoidable consequence of the subordination of merchant to industrial capital in the US economy, which made the expansion of slavery and capitalism irreconcilable.

Ultimately, the victory of the Republican-led Union Army in the Civil War secured the conditions for the dominance and expansion of capitalism in the US. The most important was the abolition of slavery, a measure forced upon the Republican manufacturers by military contingency and the struggle of the slaves themselves.[74] Although the class struggles in the reconstruction period did not result in the emergence of either capitalist plantation agriculture or the formation of a black petty-capitalist farmer class, the non-capitalist form that did replace slavery, sharecropping, did not pose an obstacle to the development of capitalism outside of the cotton South. While sharecropping did pose definite limits to the transformation of the labor process, it did not have plantation slavery's geographically imperialist tendencies, which had posed an obstacle to the Western expansion of petty-capitalist production. Sharecropping also eliminated plantation "self-sufficiency," making the direct producers more dependent on commodity circulation for their reproduction and deepening the social division of labor in the South.[75]

The war also produced a more centralized and interventionist capitalist state. The creation of a national currency and banking system, the liberalization of immigration, the erection of protective tariffs, the expansion of the military and civilian officialdom of the federal state, the establishment of national (rather than state) citizenship and voting rights and the passage of the Homestead Act and railroad land grants spurred the development of capitalism in the Gilded Age. The passage of the Homestead Act of 1862 did not provide the rural small holders with their long hoped for utopia of free land to the tiller and an end to land speculation and engrossment. The portions of the public domain reserved for free settlement tended to be of the worst soil quality and distant from the railroads. The railroads, on the other hand, were given, under the provisions of the Homestead and corollary land-grant acts, large alternating blocks of the public domain along their routes, while the federal government reserved the other blocks of land for sale at public auction. This plundering of the public domain through huge land grants to railroads and mining companies, and the sale of government land at public auction, provided a tremendous lever for the commodification of the land and created a permanent obstacle to "natural economy."[76]

Notes

1. Robert P. Brenner, *Merchants and Revolution: Commercial Change, Political Conflict, and London's Overseas Traders, 1550–1653* (Princeton, NJ: Princeton University Press, 1993), Part I; Robin Blackburn, *The Making of New World Slavery: From the Baroque to the Modern* (London: Verso, 1997), Part I; Ellen Meiksins Wood, *Empire of Capital* (London: Verso Books, 2003), 37–43, 61–88.
2. Percy Bidwell and John I. Falconer, *History of Agriculture in the Northern United States, 1620–1860*, Volume I (Washington, DC: Carnegie Institution, 1925), Chapter 5; Cecil Lewis Gray, *History of Agriculture in the Southern United States to 1860*, volume I (Washington, DC: The Carnegie Institution, 1933), Chapter VXII.
3. Russel F. Weigly, *History of the United States Army* (Bloomington, IN: University of Indiana Press, 1984), Chapter 2.
4. Gray, *Southern Agriculture* I, 21–22; Edmund S. Morgan, *American Slavery, American Freedom: The Ordeal of Colonial Virginia* (New York: W&W Norton, 1975), 110–115.
5. Gray, *Southern Agriculture* I, 213.
6. Evsey D. Domar, "The Causes of Slavery and Serfdom: A Hypothesis," *Journal of Economic History* 30 (1970): 18–32; Russell R. Menard, "From Servants to Slaves: The Transformation of the Chesapeake Labor System," *Journal of Southern Studies* 16 (1977): 335–390; Morgan, *American Slavery*, Chapter 5.
7. David W. Galenson, *White Servitude in Colonial America: An Economic Analysis* (New York: Cambridge University Press, 1981).

8. Morgan, *American Slavery*, Chapters 6–8.
9. Ibid., Book III.
10. Ibid., 220, 223.
11. Ibid., 246–247.
12. Barbara J. Fields, "Slavery, Race and Ideology in the USA," *New Left Review* I, no. 181 (1990): 95–118.
13. Claire Priest, "Creating an American Property Law," *Harvard Law Review* 120, no. 2 (2006): 385–459.
14. The following paragraphs draw upon Marx's discussion of capitalist social property relations in *Capital* I (Harmondsworth: Penguin Books, 1976) and discussions of slave social property relations in Dale W. Tomich, *Slavery in the Circuit of Sugar: Martinique in the World Economy, 1830–1848* (Baltimore: The Johns Hopkins University Press, 1990), Chapter 4.
15. Robert P. Brenner, "The Origins of Capitalist Development: A Critique of Neo-Smithian Marxism," *New Left Review* I, no. 104 (1977): 36–37.
16. Ira Berlin, *Many Thousands Gone: The First Two Centuries of Slavery in North America* (Cambridge, MA: Harvard University Press, 1998),118–119; Gray, *Southern Agriculture* II, 215–217, 545–546; Alan Kulikoff, *Tobacco and Slaves: The Development of Southern Culture in the Chesapeake, 1680–1800* (Chapel Hill, NC: University of North Carolina Press, 1986), 324–325, 384–386, 408–412.
17. Gray, *Southern Agriculture* I, 213–214.
18. Susan A. Mann, *Agrarian Capitalism in Theory and Practice* (Chapel Hill, NC: University of North Carolina Press, 1990), Chapter 2.
19. Kulikoff, *Tobacco and Slaves*, 412.
20. Kulikoff, *Tobacco and Slaves*, 337–340, 392–393, 411–413.
21. Bidwell and Falconer, *Northern Agriculture*, 49–62, 115–117, 126–133; Phillip J. Greven, *Four Generations: Population, Land and Family in Colonial Andover, Massachusetts* (Ithaca, NY: Cornell University Press, 1970).
22. Henretta, "Families and Farms," in *American Capitalism*; Gregory H. Nobles, "Breaking into the Backcountry: New Approaches to the Early American Frontier, 1750–1800," *William and Mary Quarterly* 3, no. 46 (1989): 647–650, 654–661.
23. Lemon, *Poor Man's Country*, 49–61.
24. Lemon, *Poor Man's Country*, 150–176.
25. Clarence H. Danhof, *Changes in Agriculture: The Northern United States, 1820–1860* (Cambridge, MA: Cambridge University Press, 1969).
26. Robert P. Brenner, "Agrarian Class Structure and Economic Development in Pre-Industrial Europe" and "Agrarian Roots of European Capitalism," in *The Brenner Debate*, ed. T.H. Aston and C.H.E. Philpin (New York: Cambridge University Press, 1985), 54–63, 284–319.
27. Greven, *Four Generations*; Lemon, *Poor Man's Country*, 74–92.

28. Bidwell and Falconer, *Northern Agriculture*, 54–59; Greven, *Four Generations*, Part III.
29. Kenneth Lockridge, *A New England Town: The First Hundred Years* (New York: W.W. Norton, 1970), 141–142.
30. Brenner, "Agrarian Roots," 305.
31. Wood, *Empire of Capital*, 107.
32. Margi Mayer and Margaret A. Fay, "The Formation of the American Nation State," *Kapitalistate* 6 (1977): 41–84.
33. Brenner, *Merchants and Revolution*, Chapter XII; Kulikoff, *Tobacco and Slaves*, 122–131; Gray, *Southern Agriculture* I, Chapter XVII; Eric Williams, *Capitalism and Slavery* (Chapel Hill, NC: University of North Carolina Press, 1944).
34. Cathy Matson, *Merchants & Empire: Trading in Colonial North America* (Baltimore: The Johns Hopkins University Press, 1998).
35. Mayer and Fay, "Formation," 53–55.
36. Henretta, "The War for Independence," in *American Capitalism*, 231–241; David P. Szatmary, *Shays' Rebellion: The Making of An Agrarian Insurrection* (Amherst, MA: University of Massachusetts Press, 1980), 19–23.
37. Lawrence D. Cress, *Citizens in Arms: The Army and the Militia in American Society to the War of 1812* (Chapel Hill, NC: University of North Carolina Press, 1982), Chapter 2; Weigly, *History of the Army*, 75–84.
38. Richard H. Kohn, *The Federalists and the Creation of the Military Establishment in America, 1783–1802* (New York: The Free Press, 1975), Chapters 2–4.
39. Kohn, *The Federalists*, 55.
40. Cress, *Citizens in Arms*, 95–96.
41. Robert W. Coakley, *The Role of Federal Military Forces in Domestic Disorder, 1789–1878* (Washington, DC: Center of Military History-US Army, 1988), Chapter 1; Cress, *Citizens in Arms*, Chapter 6.
42. Coakley, *Federal Military*, Chapters 2–3; Cress, *Citizens in Arms*, 69–77, 101–103.
43. Robert W. Fogel and Stanley L. Engerman, *Time on the Cross: The Economics of American Negro Slavery* (Boston; Houghton Mifflin, 1974), 203–204.
44. Alan L. Olmstead and Paul W. Rhode, *Creating Abundance: Biological Innovation and American Agricultural Development* (New York: Cambridge University Press, 2008), Chapter 4.
45. Olmstead and Rhode, *Creating Abundance*, Table 4.2, 117–118. This table lists three hybrids other than Petit Gulf introduced before the Civil War: Cluster/Dixon (1843), Semicluster/Peerless (1847) and Eastern Big Boil/Truitt (1857). The former two were characterized as "difficult, trash" to pick. Only Eastern Big Boll/Truitt, introduced on the eve of the War, was characterized as "easier" to pick.

46. For a discussion of differential soil productivity in the Antebellum South, see James D. Foust and Dale E. Swan, "Productivity and Profitability of Antebellum Slave Labor: A Micro-Approach," *Agricultural History* 44, no. 1 (1970): 44–45; Franklee Gilbert Whartenby, "Land and Labor Productivity in United States Cotton Production, 1800–1840" (PhD diss., University of Chicago, 1963), Chapters II, V.
47. Ralph V. Anderson and Robert E. Gallman, "Slaves as Fixed-Capital: Slave Labor and Southern Economic Development," *Journal of American History* 64, no. 1 (1977): 29–32; Sam Bowers Hilliard, *Hog Meat and Hoecake: Food Supply in the Old South, 1840–1860* (Carbondale, IL: Southern Illinois University Press, 1972), 95–102.
48. John Campbell, "As 'A Kind of Freeman?': Slaves' Market-Related Activities in the South Carolina Up Country, 1800–1860," in *Cultivation and Culture: Labor and the Shaping of Slave Life in the Americas*, ed. I. Berlin and P.D. Morgan (Charlottesville, VA: University of Virginia Press, 1993), 245–246; Hilliard, *Hog Meat*, 172–185; Joseph P. Reidy, *From Slavery to Agrarian Capitalism in the Cotton Plantation South: Central Georgia, 1800–1880* (Chapel Hill, NC: University of North Carolina Press, 1992), 60–61, 67–70.
49. William N. Parker, "Slavery and Southern Economic Development," *Agricultural History* 44, no. 1 (1970): 115–125; Stephen F. Hahn, *The Roots of Southern Populism: Yeoman Farmers and the Transformation of the Georgia Upcountry, 1850–1890* (New York: Oxford University Press, 1983), Part I.
50. Paul W. Gates, *The Farmers' Age: Agriculture 1815–1860* (New York: Holt, Rinehart & Winston, 1960), 7–8, 10–11; Gray, *Southern Agriculture* II, 893–907.
51. Matthew B. Hammond, *The Cotton Industry, An Essay in American Economic History*, Part I, *The Cotton Culture and Cotton Trade* (New York: Macmillan, 1897), 59–61, 74, Appendix I.
52. Alan G. Bogue, "The Iowa Claims Clubs: Symbol and Substance," *Mississippi Valley Historical Review* 45, no. 1 (1958): 231–253; Robert P. Swierenga, *Pioneers and Profits: Land Speculation on the Iowa Frontier* (Ames, IA: University of Iowa Press, 1968), 11–17, 214–215.
53. Clarence Danhof, "The Farm Enterprise: The Northern United States, 1820–1860s," *Research in Economic History* 4 (1979): 129–133.
54. Danhof, *Changes in Agriculture*, 142.
55. Jeremy Attack and Fred Bateman, *To Their Own Soil Agriculture in the Antebellum North* (Aimes, IA: University of Iowa Press, 1987), 202–207; Gates, *Farmers Age*, 48–50.
56. Gates, *Farmers Age*, 54–57, 67–69, 71–75; John Opie, *The Law of the Land: Two Hundred Years of American Farmland Policy* (Lincoln, NB: University of Nebraska Press 1991), Chapters 1–35.

57. The following is upon A.H. Cole, "Cyclical and Seasonal Variations in the Sale of Public Lands, 1816–1860," in *The Public Lands: Studies in the History of the Public Domain*, ed. Vernon Carstensen (Madison, WI: University of Wisconsin Press, 1963); Opie, *Law of the Land*, Chapters 4–5.
58. Swierenga, *Pioneers and Profit*, 48–50, 100–123.
59. Allen G. Bogue, *From Prairies to Corn Belt: Farming on the Illinois and Iowa Prairies in the 19th Century* (Chicago: University of Chicago Press, 1963), 169–170.
60. Atack and Bateman, *To Their Own Soil*, Chapter 8; Bogue, *Prairies to Corn Belt*, Chapter IV; Danhof, *Changes in Agriculture*, Chapters 4 and 5; Jonathan Levy, "The Mortgage Worked the Harvest: The Fat of Landed Independence in Nineteenth-Century America," in *Capitalism Takes Command: The Social Transformation of Nineteenth-Century America*, ed. M. Zakim and G.J. Kornblith (Chicago: University of Chicago Press, 2012); Swierenga, *Prioners and Profit*, 107–123, 215–216.
61. Atack and Bateman, *To Their Own Soil*, 202–204, 208–253.
62. Atack and Bateman, *To Their Own Soil*, Chapters 9–10; Clark, *Roots of Rural Capitalism*, 295–309; Danhof, *Changes in Agriculture*, 144–153.
63. Rolla M. Tyron, *Household Manufactures in the United States, 1640–1860* (Chicago: University of Chicago Press, 1917), 308–309; Atack and Bateman, *To Their Own Soil*, 205.
64. Mary Beth Pudup, "From Farm to Factory: Structuring and Location of the US Farm Machinery Industry," *Economic Geography* 53, no. 3 (1987): 203–222.
65. Atack and Bateman, *To Their Own Soil*, 188–194; Danhof, *Changes in Agriculture*, 251–277.
66. Danhof, *Changes in Agriculture*, 142–144, 189–203, 206–217; Gates, *Farmers' Age*, 280–282.
67. Atack and Bateman, *To Their Own Soil*, 194–200; Danhof, *Changes in Agriculture*, 221–249.
68. Computed from *Manufactures of the United States in 1860: Compiled from the Original Returns of the Eight Census* (Washington DC 1865), clxxvii, ccxvi; *Ninth Census, 1870 Volume III: The Statistics of Wealth and Industry in the United States* (Washington 1872), 588–589, 614–615.
69. For a more detailed discussion of the "agro-industrial complex," see Pudup, "From Farm to Factory".
70. Louis C. Hunter, "The Influence of the Market Upon Technique in the Iron Industry in Western Pennsylvania up to 1860," *Journal of Economic and Business History* I (1929): 241–281.

71. Sven Beckert, *The Monied Metropolis: New York City and the Consolidation of the American Bourgeoisie, 1850–1896* (New York: Cambridge University Press, 1993), 89–97; Frederick J. Blue, *The Free Soilers: Third Party Politics, 1848–1854* (Chicago: University of Chicago Press, 1973).
72. William L. Barney, *The Road to Secession: A New Perspective on the Old South* (New York: Praeger, 1972)
73. Beckert, *Monied Metropolis*, 78–93, Chapter 3; Philip Foner, *Business and Slavery: The New York Merchants and the Irrepressible Conflict* (Chapel Hill, NC: University of North Carolina Press, 1941).
74. Bruce Levine, *The Fall of the House of Dixie: The Civil War and the Social Revolution That Transformed the South* (New York: Random House, 2012).
75. Roger L. Ransom and Richard Sutch, *One Kind of Freedom: The Economic Consequences of Emancipation* (New York: Cambridge University Press, 1977); Jonathan M. Weiner, "Class Structure and Economic Development in the American South, 1865–1955," *American Historical Review* 84, no. 4 (1979): 970–992.
76. Eric Foner, *Reconstruction: America's Unfinished Revolution* (New York: Harper & Row, 1988), Chapter 1; Paul W. Gates, "The Homestead Act in an Incongruous Land System," *American Historical Review* 41, no. 4 (1936): 652–681.

CHAPTER 8

Colonialism, Racism, and the Transition to Capitalism in Canada

Jessica Evans

Perhaps the most enduring bourgeois myth about capitalism concerns its, ostensibly, necessary relationship to liberal politics, understood as a politically disinterested state providing the framework for equal individuals to act freely in the pursuit of their own rational interests. This characteristic trait of capitalism is allegedly the quality which distinguishes it from previous historical modes of production, wherein hierarchical relationships were coded in an inequitable division of political power and coercive capacity. The reason for this, of course, is that capitalism's market compulsion requires people to engage in waged labor to survive (and it is in a manipulation of the wage that surplus is extracted). Accordingly, people "voluntarily" enter contracts, through which they are then exploited. This contrasts to earlier modes of production where relations of political coercion were necessary to compel labor.[1]

When removed from the realm of abstraction, this account of capitalism is clearly incompatible with empirical evidence. In the first instance, wage labor was only ever assumed a "rational" endeavor to be voluntarily undertaken, following the violence of the enclosures.[2] More importantly,

J. Evans (✉)
York University, Toronto, ON, Canada

X. Lafrance, C. Post (eds.), *Case Studies in the Origins of Capitalism*, Marx, Engels, and Marxisms,
https://doi.org/10.1007/978-3-319-95657-2_8

however, capitalism has been bound into myriad forms of politically coercive, unequal, and exploitative relations including those of colonialism, armed incursion, discrimination on the basis of gender, age, sexuality, ethnicity, race, ability, and so forth. At the forefront of efforts to demystify capitalism's pretensions to greater equality have been scholars working in the Marxist tradition. However, within the broad array of Marxist critical social science, there has been a considerable debate around Political Marxism's relationship to this demystification. More specifically, detractors claim that the analysis advanced by Political Marxists (PM) is one which accepts the liberal myth of equality. This contribution is an intervention in this debate. I argue that the analytical tools of PM are capable of analyzing unequal subjectivities under capitalism. Indeed, I will show how, through an analysis of social property relations in the transition to capitalism in Canada, such inequality in subjectivity was materially productive of the settler colonial state.

Throughout this chapter, I will argue that a PM approach reveals that variability in political forms is not only compatible with, but an inevitable product of, the capitalist mode of production. The expansion of capitalist social relations was a deliberate, politically mediated response to the tensions and contradictions presented in the context of British industrialization.[3] Resolving these contradictions, the British sought to politically direct an extension of "the market" to temperate regions, of which Canada was one. The way that "Canada" responded to this politically directed expansion of the market was through politically directed development, vis-à-vis a national organization of state power. I will show that the emergence of capitalism in Canada was bound up with transformations in settler colonial social property relations following a reconfiguration of Britain's structures of empire and that these changes were intimately connected to the production of racialized subjectivities.

In the next section, I address, at a broad theoretical level, the issue of legal subjectivities under capitalism, specifically, whether or not, abstractly, a "liberal" subject is "necessary". Following this I trace out the historical trajectory of capitalism's initial global spread, from the culmination of Britain's capitalist transition to the globally uneven spread of capitalist social relations. I then turn to the case study proper, showing how Canada's racial-colonial relations coincided with an emergent global economy driven by British market imperatives. I subsequently turn to the consolidation of the provinces under the Act of Union and argue that the creation of racialized and illiberal legal subjectivities vis-à-vis indigenous peoples was central to a strategy of development in the emergent world economy subjected to market pressures. Finally, I show how the directed transformation of Canadian social property relations in the nineteenth century was underpinned by, and reproduced, these illiberal and racialized subjectivities, as a means to a capitalist transformation of agricultural production.

Does Capitalism Universalize the "Liberal" Subject?

One of the most recent versions of the critique of PM can be found in an impressive historical volume by Alexander Anievas and Kerem Nisancioglu: *How the West Came to Rule: the Geopolitical Origins of Capitalism*.[4] According to the authors, Robert Brenner's account of the transition to capitalism[5] is limited by its focus on too narrow an event—the freeing of labor—in too local a context—rural England. The result of this narrow focus is that Brenner's subsequent understanding of what capitalism is becomes wholly dependent on an assumed universalization of the liberal political subject, "free" from political coercion and engaged in "free" waged labor. Indeed, it is argued that because Brenner understood the transition to capitalism to have been an endogenously driven development, he cannot account for political inequality within capitalism: "by framing capitalism's emergence as separate from histories of colonialism, slavery and imperialism, Brenner (is said to) 'freeze' capitalism in history".[6] Irrespective of some contentious formulations of the relationship between, for example, race and capitalism within the PM cannon,[7] I will argue that a "race" neutral capitalism does not follow logically from the premises of PM.

To argue that PM does not necessitate the universalization of a single (liberal) subject form, it is necessary to more fully develop the relationship between social property relations and subject formation. In brief, the form and content of subjectivity are not determined by the mode of production, per se, but are determined by the complex outcome of social, political, economic, and property relations. These relations are historically grounded and specific, such that there can never really be a singular subject form under capitalism, but rather, that form is always being adapted to unique environments. The particular developments in England that led to a formally "free" and juridically "equal" political subject were contingent to empirical changes to the rules of (social) reproduction between feudalism and capitalism. In *German Thought in International Relations*, Robbie Shilliam explores the uneven and combined processes of subject formation, drawing on the concept of social property relations.[8] According to Shilliam, the privatization of land had the effect of removing it from a social relation of rights and obligations, which had previously socialized the reproduction of serfs. As land became private, so too did the conditions of social reproduction, such that economic and political authority became disentangled. The result was an official separation of political and economic authority so that neutral market mechanisms rather than personalized political power dictated the distribution of socio-economic power through access to land and other means of production. This separation allowed for a levelling out of political subjectivity, even while the sources and distribution of socio-economic power remained fundamentally uneven.[9]

In England, the transition to agrarian capitalism extracted the individual from corporate institutions which had defined rights, privilege, ability, and obligation.[10] Thus emerged the atomized individual, detached from both communal forms of extra-economic coercion, but also detached from collective systems of social reproduction. While, substantively, political and economic relations remained intertwined, formally the two were disentangled. It became possible to posit a realm in which the price of land moved freely without attachment to political privilege, making ownership over the means of (re)production, theoretically, open to all. Political subjectivity could then be posited on a universal plane of rights and obligations to an "economically disinterested" and neutral state.[11] The "individual" thus existed in relation to an "impersonal" sovereign—the state. Hence the transition to agrarian capitalism in England brought with it the rise of what Shilliam has termed the "impersonal individual".

Social Property Relations, the Externalization of Capitalist Social Relations, and Settler Colonization

If the establishment of the liberal political subject in England was the specific outcome of the historical and spatial contingencies of social class and property relations, the impact of its consolidation was nevertheless far reaching. However, I must be clear that the impact of this consolidated subject was not, as has often been assumed of Marxist analyses, found in its functioning as a modular template to be endlessly imposed and replicated. Rather, the consolidation of the liberal subject in England precipitated a general recession peaking in the 1840s, which became crucial to global economic relations henceforth.[12] The consequence of this crisis was that capitalist England sought to reformulate the form and content of its empire, generating a transformation in colonial relations and the rise of the first globally competitive world market.

In short, the production of the liberal subject realized the full subsumption of labor to capital, allowing for a massive transformation in productive capacity through the industrial revolution and therefore generating greater pools of the reserve army of labor. The intensification of agricultural production, at the same time, gave rise to an overaccumulation of capital which was unable to find outlets for productive investment in England, at the same time domestic markets were being saturated.[13] Policy makers at this time sought the promotion of free trade and the repeal of the Corn Laws in 1846 in order to "fix" the problem of rising poverty, population, and social unrest that accompanied overaccumulation.[14] However, a turn to free trade was not in itself enough. The Colonial Reformers, including Edward Gibbon Wakefield and Charles Buller argued that free trade would only temporarily forestall and shift the problem of market gluts for both labor and capital. Free trade would, for Wakefield and Buller, create a competitive market which would serve to drive down wages and reduce employment such that gluts would be a recurrent problem.[15]

As a complement to free trade, a program of systemic emigration and foreign market development was deemed necessary. The solution was through the program of systematic colonization (today known as settler colonization) in which mass emigration was to enable an extension of the "field of employment" for capital and labor. The settler colony would absorb surplus labor, industrial commodities, and investment capital and, in turn, would begin to produce agricultural commodities for domestic English consumption.[16] The Colonial Reformers, then, saw in capitalism the inherent tendency to produce an oversupply of labor and capital and sought to remedy this with a new form of colonization.

Throughout the 1840s, Canada was increasingly drawn into a global market based on staples production, predominantly in grains. As Canada and other settler states gained independence, and British capital was funnelled abroad, there emerged perhaps the first globally competitive world market. This marked a dramatic shift from the system of imperial preference and trade predicated on Ricardian comparative advantage. "This was a new form of capitalist development: whereas the European metropoles had fostered proto-industry and colonial trade through mercantilist policies, the settler states at once *defined national territories and established fully commercial—and integrated—sectors of production*".[17] The US, having achieved its own independence from Britain nearly a century prior to the British Dominions, had long since developed a robust national basis for wheat production, and with the opening of trade in the 1840s, the US had a significant competitive advantage.[18] The condition of competitive market production, centered on the Atlantic and Western Europe, was itself a conduit for the massive expansion in Western agricultural production, consumption, infrastructural construction, and wealth generation. It was in this competitive pitch to develop a national, autonomous, and colonial settler economy that Canada was compelled to transform its own structures of production.

If economies were increasingly characterized as "national", we need to recognize that this socio-economic organization was presupposed by some form of collective identification. Indeed, Shilliam has argued that the absence of such a collective identification in France made it near impossible for the state to impose taxation or engage in the kind of heavy borrowing necessary to make quantitative leaps in productivity. Thus, Canada, predicated on mass indigenous displacement and a patchwork of immigrants from diverse ethnic, religious, territorial, and class backgrounds, was particularly disadvantaged in the forging of this "collective" identification which could legitimize and reproduce the conditions necessary for production of competitive staples. I argue throughout the remainder of this chapter that it was through the production of the idea of "racial whiteness" that this shared identity came to be forged—binding together diverse settlers, with unequal and politically mediated access to land, and setting themselves apart from dispossessed indigenous peoples.

Contact, Conquest, and Settlement in British North America

Turning now to the Canadian case, I want to first begin with an examination of European settlement in the sixteenth century. This is important, as Anievas and Nisancioglu suggest that colonialism and the Spanish conquests beginning in 1492 were, in fact, central to capitalism's development and the structuration of settler-indigenous relations along racially defined lines. I, in contrast, am arguing that these processes do not happen in the settler colonial Atlantic until the nineteenth century reorganization of social property relations under competitive pressures from the global economy.[19] This is precisely because racialized subjectivities were not a vestige of premodern practice, but were instead constitutive of capitalist social relations in the settler colony. Thus, contra Anievas and Nisancioglu, the colonialism of the fifteenth century must be distinguished as categorically different than that of the nineteenth century, and this distinction pivots on the goals of the colonial endeavor (i.e. mercantile plunder or capitalist settlement and production).

While European contact with today's North America has a lengthy history, it was toward the middle of the sixteenth century that new salting and curing techniques were developed which necessitated the procurement of timber from coastal shores. From the need for timber began a gradual inland movement of Europeans from North American shores (in today's Canadian east coast). Such incursions increasingly brought European fishers into contact with indigenous peoples, leading to the discovery of the fur trade as a valuable corollary to cod fishing. The French fur trade was heavily reliant on indigenous peoples for almost the entirety of the operation—everything from hunting, trapping, and preparing the furs to the customs and skills involved in the negotiation of trade. Furthermore, intermarriage was often a strategy deployed in order to insinuate settlers into indigenous societies, for the purposes of security and access to cultural resources.[20] As such, the French relationship with indigenous peoples as it settled territories and built forts for the conduct of a fur trade necessitated the maintenance of indigenous peoples' physical and cultural existence. "The main goal of the early Imperial presence was resource extraction through the fur-trade, an economic activity that absolutely depended on Native people's labor and knowledge ...".[21]

While, no doubt, violent and oppressive asymmetrical power relations existed throughout this period, they were not marked by a systematic attempt to eliminate indigenous peoples and their practices, nor were they characterized by attempts to radically alter the nature of indigenous social forms. Rather, it was precisely these differences in material and cultural systems that created the conditions for an exploitative relationship: "... the boundaries between who should be considered "European" and who should be considered "Native" (and by what means) have not always been clear".[22] The point at which these blurred lines become solidified is the transition *from merchant trade to competitive capitalist markets* (instigated by English industrialization), which transformed the social organization of colonialism. This transformed colonialism eliminated the centrality of the trading post and instead configured production and consumption both at home and abroad to suit the needs of metropolitan capital. The indigenous middlemen and security forces, once integral to colonial mercantile networks, were thus rendered obsolete.[23]

The distinction between mercantilist and capitalist colonialism has been explored by Maia Pal who, through an international analysis of legal regimes of territoriality, argued that the objectives and conditions of empire have been historically variable. It was not until the late eighteenth century, that the politics of empire became attached to attempts to develop jurisdiction over indigenous populations *on the basis of the colonizers' own legal (as well as intellectual, moral, and productive) systems.*[24] And it was only in the nineteenth century that this became attached to the project of transforming the existing productive relations of indigenous peoples; in other words, at this point that capitalism becomes intertwined with the colonial endeavor.

The distinctiveness of this colonial relationship can be captured through an examination of the 1763 Royal Proclamation, which, until the establishment of the Indian Act in 1876, governed the legal relationship between European and indigenous peoples. The Royal Proclamation emerged from a context within which the contest for territory among the American, French, and British had been recently settled through a series of treaties, largely in favor of the British in what is now Canada. This victory, while legitimating sovereign claims to the land among imperial forces, did not legitimize or normalize such claims in the eyes of indigenous peoples, nor did it automatically establish bonds of loyalty between British and indigenous populations. One of the primary means through which this was to be achieved was through a demonstration of the Crown's good intentions, notably by limiting English intrusion on indigenous lands.[25] Additionally, the conditions of the Proclamation served as a buffer against American expansionism, which remained an ever present threat. Indigenous peoples occupying lands along the boundaries between the provinces and America could be relied on to defend their own lands from intrusion and thereby reduce the costs of military expenditure.[26] The Royal Proclamation, in other words, spoke to geopolitical and socioeconomic concerns that were not subject to a competitive profit motive.

Among the main provisions of the Royal Proclamation were stipulations over the means through which indigenous land could come under the auspices of the Crown and/or British subjects. The public purchase of lands by the Crown became the only sanctioned means of acquisition, while the settlement of land directly by British subjects or the private purchase of land was prohibited.[27] Indigenous peoples were, under these provisions, ostensibly entitled to the undisturbed possession of any lands that had not been ceded to or purchased by the Crown.[28] These early articulations of an "Indian Policy" had as their goal—at least rhetorically—the protection of indigenous peoples in the hopes of maintaining established trade relationships and military alliances, while fostering new connections with those indigenous peoples who had previously been under French colonial rule. The Royal Proclamation established and recognized a nation-to-nation relationship with indigenous peoples, signaling that forcible subordination to the settler colonial "sovereign" had not yet been established.[29] Indeed, the administrative tools for dealing with indigenous peoples were diplomatic channels through the British Imperial Indian Department, rather than a sovereign right to command.[30] This trajectory is consonant with Patrick Wolfe's assertion that racialization emerges in the transition from mercantile colonialism to global practices conditioned by capitalist industrialization in Britain.[31]

Under a policy of colonial mercantilism, then, there seemed to be a more fluid and flexible understanding of the indigenous populations of North America. The fixing of racial difference through legal code and its deployment in the process of capitalist production, I will argue, resulted from the settler's need to foment a national identity in the aftermath of Confederation, which importantly was bound into the international development of competitive agricultural commodity markets which relied upon the settler state's ability to enforce a monopoly over the rights of access to land. As Eva Mackey has argued, it was at the moment that territorial boundaries began to assume an institutionalized form (such as property, reserves, land surveys, etc.) that the boundaries of so-called "race" and culture began to harden.[32]

From Raw Commodity Export to the Beginnings of Domestic Production Structures

By the early decades of the nineteenth century, permanent European settlements had been established in today's Canada. Simultaneous with the collapse of the fur trade in Lower Canada was the rise of the timber trade in both Upper and Lower Canada. Unlike the fur trade, the barons of the timber trade were operating productive enterprises within Canada, such as sawmills and logging camps. Timber enterprises required large quantities of labor and generated the nucleus of a domestic market through the development of forward and backward linkages related to ancillary production activities.[33] Nevertheless, the land on which timber magnates reaped exceptional profits were governed by politically constituted rights, primarily associated with the absolutist regime in France.[34] As such, timber, while generating distinctive geopolitical interests, was not itself conducive to a transformation of production relations. However, these shifts *did* have the important consequence of generating a class of merchants whose interests were not automatically aligned with those of Britain, but instead sought their fortunes within the colony.

For the emerging financial and merchant classes, the problems of imperial rule were generally linked to trade regulations which restrained the local elite's accumulation of wealth. The Navigation Acts, for example, restricted the shipment of goods to or from the colony on non-British ships, while further colonial regulations restricted the manufacture of clothing (1768) in Canada, and trade with the US and West Indies (1784).[35] These conditions, when combined with the effects of the British Corn Laws on trade with Britain itself, effectively denied growth opportunities for Canadian merchants. Early on, William Lyon Mackenzie pushed for colonial reform, and eventually, independence. The Colonial Advocate, a Reform newspaper edited by Mackenzie, in 1824 decried British dependence:

> We earnestly desire to see established, throughout Upper and Lower Canada, New-Brunswick, and Nova Scotia, efficient societies for the improvement of arts and manufactures. We would like to see the manufacturer not quite four thousand miles from the farmer … Our foreign commerce, confined and shackled as it is, and it has been, is entirely in the hands of the British capitalists: our lumber trade is merely encouraged to support British worn-out shipping. We are inundated, glutted with British manufactures …[36]

By 1837, Mackenzie was demanding outright independence: "Until Independence is won, trade and industry will be dormant, houses and lands will be unsaleable, merchants will be embarrassed, and farmers and mechanics harassed and troubled …".[37]

This burgeoning anti-imperial sentiment coincided with the British project of radically reconceptualizing the structure of its empire and the nature of its relations with colonial dependencies.[38] The solution was found in the promotion of colonial agricultural production to provide much needed food exports and, in turn, form a consumer market for British manufactures. This, in turn, relied on a reconfiguration of jurisdictional claims by the colonial authority. As Pal argues, the British in the nineteenth century practiced a form of extraterritoriality where empire was created through the granting of semi-sovereign status, generating the tools necessary to modernize local legal systems that could protect the interests of capital.[39] Put another way, the necessity of "extending the field of employment" for English capital meant that colonialism was transformed from a purely extractive endeavor to a productive project. Rather than relying on the indigenous inhabitants to independently procure and move valuable raw commodities, the new colonialism instead required either (a) their elimination or (b) their social transformation so as to render the land productive for excess English capital. Ellen Wood, indeed, accounts for precisely this qualitative difference in the political economy of empire, through the lens of PM, when she notes that British imperialism, instead of seeking profit from plunder and colonial trade, sought to promote commodity production itself in the colonies.[40] The problem for Anievas and Nisancioglu in their critique of PM is that they homogenize colonialism as a transhistorical practice, projecting onto previous forms of colonial conduct the intent of specifically capitalist colonial relations.

Obstacles to Agricultural Production and Public Finance in the Canadas Prior to the Act of Union

In the immediate aftermath of colonial and trade reform, pre-existing property and productive relations imposed significant constraints on the capacity for local agriculture to respond to competitive imperatives. As was argued by Frantz Gheller, a significant problem in transforming production relations was the fiscal and administrative weakness of the respective governments of the provinces. Emaciated public finance and politically fragmented authority made the concerted redirection of productive activities to respond to market imperatives nearly impossible. Although each of the provinces was marked by different sets of social property relations and production structures, both Upper and Lower Canada experienced obstacles to centralized public financial administration which mitigated attempts to intensify the production of agricultural commodity exports.[41]

Indeed, Charles Post finds similar problems plaguing the Thirteen Colonies, noting that despite being driven by the imperatives of British capitalism, colonists were "*unable to reproduce the agrarian capitalist social-property relations* … [owing to] the inability of British merchants and landlords and their allies among local colonial elites to establish and *effective social monopoly of landed property*".[42] Similar to the Canadian case, Post attributes this colonial problem to the existence of the frontier. The frontier made land widely available to Europeans for little labor beyond that necessary to clear and till. When coupled with colonial and local administrative weakness, it was nearly impossible to effectively police settler squatting.[43] In the Northern colonies, squatters were even effective at organizing "claims clubs" to resist landowners' pressures to assert title or force squatters to purchase the land they occupied.[44] These problems of administrative weakness in the face of an expansive and unmanageable frontier in the Canadas underpinned colonial social property relations and stymied efforts to organize production on a national scale.

In Lower Canada, the nature of the French Absolutist state as a colonial power with its own distinct class composition and internal reproductive conditions was such that it did not have an expropriated mass of peasants to commit to colonial emigration and settlement.[45] Additionally, France's internal elite reproduction had been predicated on the appropriation of taxation, including duties and other benefits reaped through personal privilege in access to the rewards of the colonial carrying trade.[46] In this sense, the French colonial state had both an internal interest in fostering and maintaining colonial ventures of a mercantile nature, such as the fur and timber trade, and in reproducing feudal-type property relations in the colony via the seigneurial system. In French Lower Canada, lands did not produce sufficient rents, but were instead the source of the landholders' power to secure the profits of "politically constituted unequal exchange".[47] In New France, the colonial settlement's social property relations and ensuing strategies of elite reproduction did not allow for a taxable population base.

In Upper Canada, despite being colonized by the British, the creation of a centralized state with the powers of taxation to foster a plan of socio-economic development was not possible. Land was obtained through the dispossession and *exclusion* of indigenous peoples from the imperial polity. As a result, land was plentiful and its distribution was not subjected to market imperatives. Rather land was subjected in the first instance to a clientelist system of distribution in which privilege and status were the main avenues to property. As a result, waged labor was scarce, with most of the elite profiting from speculative activities and tenant-settlers preferring to erect a family farm model, providing the bulk of the labor themselves.[48]

In large, land was distributed or occupied through two dominant mechanisms. In the first instance, the establishment of Land Boards in the final decades of the eighteenth century facilitated a clientelistic pattern of land distribution. Initially intended to abate the illegal occupation of indigenous lands under the Royal Proclamation (which threatened Britain's military alliances with indigenous peoples against the US), the Land Boards came to be a means of advancing the position and holdings of land speculators throughout the province.[49] The Land Boards were to receive petitions for land and examine the loyalty of the applicant to the British Empire. Upon approval, a location ticket for a 200-acre lot, valid for one year would be issued.[50] Many of these lots were awarded on the basis of militaristic loyalty and relations of political patronage. For those without the political relations necessary to apply to the Land Boards, the other major means of land access was squatting. Squatting, according to Clarke, was a dominant practice in the Upper Canadas throughout the latter half of the eighteenth century owing to the cumbersome and corrupt formal channels of land acquisition. Many such squatters, having emigrated with the dream of pioneer farming, were able to make "improvements" to the land, erecting buildings and tilling the earth. However, at this time, these improvements were geared only toward self-sufficiency and did not constitute a means to capitalizing agricultural production.

Until the middle of the nineteenth century, many people accessed land through political channels, or informal squatting. Where rents were paid, they were paid in kind (often as a percentage of crop yield), and as such there existed little incentive to improve the efficiency of agricultural production. Market imperatives had yet to fully yield their effect, and consequently, there existed little opportunity or incentive to organize and centralize policies of taxation.[51] Thus, when there was an attempt to erect British legal and institutional models in the Canadas, it occurred in a drastically different environment. This, I argue, is the point at which we see the uneven and combined development of social property relations; the institutional innovations of Britain (which were predicated on specific arrangements of social property relations) were combined with and adapted to Canada's very different social property relations, themselves refracted though the more recent dynamics of settler colonization.

Confederation and the Turn to Nationalism

If the British strategies of accumulation through the mid nineteenth century required a refashioning of Empire, one which doled out aspects of sovereignty to its imperial possessions, while maintaining fundamental loyalty or compliance to the project of Empire, the granting of responsible government to Canada faced at least one central obstacle. This was the relative position of financial and demographic power of the French in Lower Canada. The French of Lower Canada had greater population, less debt and greater access to financial resources, owing to their collection of customs revenue, than Upper Canada. The granting of political autonomy to the provinces would have posed the potential problem of allowing the French to gain ascendency and thus develop a national project unsympathetic to that of Empire.[52] The geopolitical conflict resulting from contending systems of social property relations was therefore played out within the provinces and resulted in Britain's imposition of its own administrative fiscal structures as a means to subordinate the French population. This came about, largely, through the Act of Union in 1841.

The constitution of the Assembly under the Act of Union was intended to avoid creating deep rifts that could crystallize and politicize into unmanageable party factions. However, in the process, as Ryerson has argued, a bi-national coalition of anti-imperial reformists emerged. These reformers sought responsible government and rejected colonial control, and indeed, it was on the basis of anti-imperial and anti-American sentiment that English and French Canada could find some common ideological and historical ground. This rejection of colonial control was brought together by of the second part of the British strategy of colonial reconfiguration—free trade. The repeal of the Corn Laws in 1846 began, in many ways, the long path to self-government and later Confederation. Thrown out of the system of imperial preference, and still dealing with a commercial mercantile economy, the occupants of the provinces found themselves increasingly under threat. In 1854, replacing the system of imperial preferences, a series of treaties of reciprocity were concluded with the US. The Canadian elites hoped these treaties would allow the provinces to continue to conduct their affairs as they had previously, focusing primarily on commercial policy. With the onset of the American Civil War, however, the treaties were effectively rendered useless, and by 1865, notice had been given for the formal cancellation of the pacts.[53] The provinces were once more faced with the task of developing a competitive national economy in the "bracing atmosphere" of the free market.[54]

The existing merchant and emerging financial classes of the Canadas could find common ground precisely because their business interests were increasingly conditioned by the necessity of modernizing state structures and tearing down restrictive and dependent colonial structures. Of course, because the architecture of Union had been intentionally unequal, a strategic element of incorporation was necessary to solidify a common and stable domestic base of colonial rejection premised on capitalist development.[55] Endogenous development was to produce and supply for global competitive agricultural markets, requiring a dismantling of some of the most pernicious of colonial trade regulations. In turn, agricultural development was to rely on infrastructure and immigration. Debt being an ongoing issue, it was determined that the revenue to service infrastructural debt would be found in the sale of Crown lands to create a Sinking Fund, a strategy that would increasingly transform the conditions stipulated under the Royal Proclamation, and thus the relations of political subjectivity that existed between settler and indigenous populations.[56]

In the lead-up to the Act of Union, a central means to shore up administrative capacity, build state revenue, and ensure the continued subordination of the French element to British interests was the 1837 Public Lands Disposal Act. The Act abolished the practice of free grants, and sought to make the distribution of Crown Lands subject to a transparent and administratively robust process. Public auctions were to be the primary means of land disposal, followed by the possibility of private sales.[57] These conditions were renewed in 1839 and again in the Land Act of 1841 under Lord Sydenham who would become one of the main administrative reformers of the Dominion. Under the Act, which would last until 1853, Crown Reserves were sold at a cost of 8s. per acre, through the Canada Company, a price that required many to turn to money-lenders for credit.[58]

While the sale of Crown Lands to generate revenue was a central motivation behind the Act, there remained a tension between the bald fact of selling land for revenue (potentially to speculators) and the need to ensure land would be used for developmental objectives. Thus, reflecting Wakefield's emphasis on governmental intervention in the distribution of land to promote development, agents of the Crown Lands Department were given discretion to facilitate the purchase of lands by squatters who had contributed to its improvement.[59]

The sale of Crown Lands to generate government revenue marked the beginnings of market dependency, as criteria for squatters' and settlers' eventual title to land rested on "improvement" requiring capital investment. These conditions then led to a cash and credit dependency which would, eventually, stimulate market dependency (either through the sale of labor or of agricultural commodities) to fulfill obligations to money-lenders and to ensure their consummation of land titles.[60] At the same time, these criteria provided the contours of racialized exclusion by distinguishing between deserving and underserving land occupancy, on the basis of physical and technical improvements. The language to justify and explain the systematical dispossession of the indigenous people of their land was beginning to take shape.

In the 1850s, legislation was passed to create Indian reservations and established settlers' sovereign monopoly over the majority of land within the United Provinces by parceling marginal pieces of land for indigenous peoples. Following this, the 1857 Gradual Civilization Act allowed for reserve lands to be further fractured and converted into freehold plots to be alienated by those wishing to enfranchise and give up their "Indian" status.[61] It was at this point, then, that the settler state began to build up its public coffers through a demarcation of indigenous peoples, predicated on racial difference. Whiteness became the mark of all the "Indian" was not (made explicit in the 1876 Indian Act, and Gradual Enfranchisement Act of 1869), and this was intimately bound with the transformation of property relations. To renounce a collective right to the land was to transition from "Indian" status into "whiteness" (albeit in a subordinate position). It was on these general premises that the French and English Canadian elites would find common ground. This is not to say, of course, that the Anglo-French rift was paved over during this time—indeed it persists to this day. However, in order to pursue the common goal of settler capitalist development, a common national goal was identified. This entailed the rationalization and centralization of state administrative apparatuses, independent policy making, and infrastructural development to stimulate and aid the settlement and development of agricultural regions. The extant social property relations in the provinces had created a crisis in state financial capacity. In the context of a dismantled system of colonial preference, and the pressures of competitive agricultural commodity production, the English and French merchants and landowners came together to adapt political and fiscal structures from the British state to local exigencies. Importantly, such adaptations required the mass displacement of indigenous populations without their subsequent proletarianization. It was precisely because settler colonization entailed the imposition of alien sovereignty that indigenous peoples (the embodied denial of that alien sovereignty) were subjected to racially defined and hierarchicalized conditions of political subjectivity.

White Canada, Indigenous Elimination, and the Transition to Capitalism

As much as the policies around enfranchisement and land holding were central to the settler state's attempt to nationalize the agricultural economy, in practice, these policies were less successful than hoped. Indeed, very few indigenous peoples were interested in acquiring the electoral rights and freehold tenure promised by enfranchisement, and this lack of participation meant ongoing fiscal obligation by the federal government to indigenous peoples, as well as the task of managing conflict between indigenous practices and agrarian, pastoral, and infrastructural projects.[62] Indian Commissioner Edgar Dewdney, at the time, suggested that the bureaucratic response could be nothing less than "sheer compulsion".[63] As a result, recourse to increasingly draconian legal policies were enacted in order to enforce moral regulation on the reserve and encourage enfranchisement. The 1876 Indian Act, to be sure, contained a number of such policies, as there was a clear acknowledgement for the need to apply coercive pressure in order to maintain the integrity of the reserve system. However, subsequent amendments to the Act ratcheted up the severity and scope of the role of the penal system in the management of indigenous peoples, casting those on the reserve as inherently contra-legal, furthering the codified divide between the citizen-subject and the racialized ward of state. Indeed, as Sherry Gavigan has argued, the application of criminal law to the indigenous populations on reserves was less about "criminalizing" such peoples and more about racializing them.[64] Through policies such as the pass system, the prohibition of hunting, fishing, dance rituals, and the potlatch, fears that indigenous mobility posed a threat to agricultural, pastoral, and rail interests were muted. In the process, indigenous identity was constructed as outside of legality, contrary to the interests of the nation, and racially "barbaric". The racial justifications for indigenous land theft and segregation provided the institutional and ideological means to bind together a "nation" capable of pursuing capitalist agricultural development.

It was on this basis, of racialized exclusions, that the ground was set for Canada's capitalist transformation. Having asserted a sovereign monopoly over land, centralized and rationalized state fiscal resources, and (temporarily) resolved the internal manifestations of geopolitical conflict, Canada was positioned to advance a project of mass settlement, infrastructural development and increasingly subject new farmers to the exigencies of competitive production. Thus, in 1872, the Canadian state was able to implement the Land's Act, whereby the public monopoly of land could then be transformed into a public, and concerted, program of settlement which imposed upon farmers the condition of agricultural improvement. The Land Act granted plots of land to settlers for a CAD 10 administration fee and the requirement that at least six months of every year, for three years, must be spent cultivating the land. Only after this period would settlers obtain a deed.[65] This public settlement scheme served as the stimulus for Canada's transition to capitalism in that it, firstly, inhibited the development of a class of large landowners, as the public ceiling on the price of land ensured a wider distribution of plots. Additionally, the price ceiling would prevent a return to subsistence-based agriculture, and clientelist or feudal forms of property relations. Secondly, the dominance of agrarian capitalist household production meant that the dominant class interests reflected at the state level were those of merchants in Montreal and Toronto whose reproduction relied on a protected economy. This collusion of regional class interests was in large part responsible for the passing of the National Policy of 1876 under the MacDonald government.[66] The combination of public land transfers and their attendant requirements for cultivation, along with the small-scale and diversified ownership of land on the prairies created the conditions under which small-scale, owner operated agricultural production predominated.[67]

Under the National Policy, a high tariff, massive immigration and rail development were prioritized. The tariff made the production of wheat both necessary and capital intensive, thereby stimulating technological transformation in farming practices. On the one hand, the tariff meant that state revenue would have to rely on commodity exports, which at the time were centered on wheat.[68] At the same time, the cost of Canadian-produced farm implements was higher than imports. Producing competitive wheat exports, then, became a central struggle for farmers who were faced with two options: either manipulate the variable component of their costs—that is, labor—or revolutionize the production process through a rise in the organic composition of capital. Because land was widely available through the homesteading process, inhibiting the development of a landless working class, the latter option dominated.[69] Thus, distinct regional class groups came together in support of a nationwide policy, which was rooted in the (often forgotten) institutional and legal exclusion of indigenous peoples based on racial constructs of inferiority, barbarity, and so forth. Through the National Policy, the Canadian government was then able to pursue a policy of infrastructural development, immigration recruitment, as well as control and direct the internal movement of settlers.

Conclusion

The above account has shown how social property relations, following the transition to capitalism in England, generated both colonial and racial forms of subjectivity which were crucial in the global and local reproduction of capitalist social relations in the so-called West. In the first instance, colonialism was *the* mechanism through which English capitalism was able to transform the *global* economy, precipitating the rise of competitive, nationally organized economies. Additionally, the ability for settler colonial economies, such as Canada, to respond to these new economic imperatives required a revolution in property and administrative configurations along the model of the English state.

I have argued that the administrative and subject forms that emerged with English capitalism were the distinct outcome of spatially and historically contingent social property relations. When these models were abstracted from their histories and transposed onto a radically different terrain of social property relations, myriad substitutions were required. Importantly, the condition of subject equality and politically and fiscally centralized state legitimacy was impossible without a cohesive monopoly on national territories. This entailed *both* the amalgamation of French and British settlers under a common political subjectivity *and* the expropriation of land from and subsequent political exclusion of the sovereign indigenous peoples of the territories. Without religion, history, cultural practice, or language to bind the French and English in a common project—a construction of fraternity—the concept of "racial whiteness" came to define the national Canadian subject, where "whiteness" was the qualifying condition of citizen equality, freedom, and rationality.

Notes

1. Ellen Meiksins Wood, *The Origins of Capitalism: A Longer View* (London: Verso, 2002), 6.
2. Ibid., 54.
3. Benno Teschke, *The Myth of 1648* (London: Verso, 2003), 365; Radhika Desai, "Introduction: Nationalisms and their Understandings in Historical Perspective," *Third World Quarterly* 29, no. 3 (2008): 405.

4. Alexander Anievas and Kerem Nisancioglu, *How the West Came to Rule: The Geopolitical Origins of Capitalism* (London: Pluto Press, 2015).
5. Robert Brenner, "The Agrarian Roots of European Capitalism," *Past and Present* 97, (1982): 16–113.
6. Anievas and Nisancioglu, *How the West Came to Rule*, 23.
7. Ellen Meiksins Wood, "Class, Race, and Capitalism," *Political Power and Social Theory*, (2015): 276.
8. Robbie Shilliam, *German Thought and International Relations: The Rise and Fall of a Liberal Project* (New York: Palgrave Macmillan, 2009).
9. Ibid.
10. Ellen Meiksins Wood, *The Ellen Meiksins Wood Reader*, ed. Larry Patriquin (Boston: Brill, 2012), 189.
11. Robbie Shilliam, "The Atlantic as a Vector of Uneven and Combined Development," *Cambridge Review of International Affairs* 22, no. 1 (2009).
12. John R. Davis, "The British Sonderweg: The Peculiarities of British Free Trade, 1845–1880," *Diplomacy and Statecraft* 8, no. 3 (1997): 69; Eric Hobsbawm, *Industry and empire: from 1750 to the present day* (London: Penguin Books, 1999), 142; Phillip McMichael, *Settlers and the Agrarian Question: Foundations of Capitalism in Colonial Australia* (Cambridge: Cambridge University Press, 1984), 179.
13. Eric Hobsbawm. *Industry and empire: from 1750 to the present day* (London: Penguin Books, 1999), 176; Philip McMichael, *Settlers and the Agrarian Question: Foundations of Capitalism in Colonial Australia* (Cambridge: Cambridge University Press, 1984), 175.
14. Andrew Michael Zmolek. *Rethinking the Industrial Revolution: Five Centuries of Transition from Agrarian to Industrial Capitalism in England* (Boston: Brill, 2013), 777; Jeffrey G. Williamson, "The Impact of the Corn Laws Just Prior to Repeal," *Explorations in Economic History* 27, (1990), 125.
15. Bernard Semmel, *The Rise of Free Trade Imperialism: Classical Political Economy, the Empire of Free Trade and Imperialism: 1750–1850* (Cambridge: Cambridge University Press, 1970), 169.
16. Edward Gibbon Wakefield, *A view of the art of colonization* (Gloucestershire: Clarendon Press, 1914), 12–13.
17. Harriet Friedman and Phillip McMichael, "Agriculture and the State System: The Rise and Decline of National Agricultures, 1870 to the Present," *Sociologia Ruralis* 29, no. 2 (1989): 101.
18. James Belich, *Replenishing the Earth: The Settler Revolution and the Rise of the Anglo-World, 1783–1939* (Oxford: Oxford University Press, 2009), 449.
19. Anievas and Nisancioglu, *How the West Came to Rule*.

20. Bonita Lawrence, "Gender, Race, and the Regulation of Native Identity in Canada and the United States: an Overview," *Hypatia* 18, no. 2 (2003): 8.
21. Eva Mackey, *The House of Difference: Cultural Politics and National Identity in Canada* (London: Routledge, 1999), 38.
22. Lawrence, "Gender, Race, and the Regulation," 8.
23. Patrick Wolfe, *Traces of History: Elementary Structures of Race* (London: Verso, 2016), 8.
24. Maia Pal, "The Politics of Extraterritoriality: A Historical Sociology of Public International Law" (PhD diss., University of Sussex, 2012), 157.
25. Brian Slattery, "The Hidden Constitution: Aboriginal Rights in Canada," *The American Journal of Comparative Law* 32, no. 2 (1984): 368.
26. Mackey, *The House of Difference*, 40.
27. Slattery, "The Hidden Constitution," 369.
28. Ibid., 370.
29. Lawrence, "Gender, Race, and the Regulation," 6.
30. Ibid., 7.
31. Wolfe, *Traces of History*.
32. Mackey, *The House of Difference*, 41.
33. Stanley Ryerson, *Unequal Union: Roots of Crisis in the Canadas, 1815–1873* (Toronto: Progress Books, 1983), 37.
34. Frantz Gheller, "Geopolitics, State-Formation and Economic Development in Quebec and Ontario" (PhD diss., York University, 2015), 119.
35. Ryerson, *Unequal Union*, 106.
36. As quoted in Ryerson, *Unequal Union*, 91.
37. Ryerson, *Unequal Union*, 108; This process of domestic, non-capitalist merchant elite formation to promote the ends of independence from colonial rule were also present in the US, as Charles Post has previously noted of the Northern colonies (*The American Road to Capitalism: Studies in Class-Structure, Economic Development and Political Conflict, 1620–1877* (Chicago: Haymarket Books, 2011), 186), suggesting that there is particular dynamic trajectory of settler colonial class and property relations that should be understood as modifying the nature of capitalist transformations. Indeed, that the US and Canada (along with settler colonial Argentina, Australia, New Zealand, and South Africa) formed their states through articulations of white nationalism is telling, the path to capitalism in these spaces, marked by distinct colonial forms, requires the very type of social analysis which PM provides.
38. David Farr, *The Colonial Office and Canada, 1867–1887* (Toronto: University of Toronto Press, 1955), 3–5.
39. Maia Pal, "'My Capitalism is Bigger than Yours': Histories of Legal Sovereignty and U&CD's Delusions," *Historical Materialism* (Forthcoming).
40. Ellen Meiksins Wood, *The Empire of Capital* (London: Verso, 2003), 74.

41. Gheller, "Geopolitics, State-Formation and Economic Development."
42. Post, *The American Road to Capitalism*, 172.
43. Ibid., 173.
44. Ibid., 181.
45. Gheller, "Geopolitics, State-Formation and Economic Development," 110.
46. Shilliam, *German Thought in International Relations*, 38–40.
47. Gheller, "Geopolitics, State-Formation and Economic Development," 110.
48. Ibid., 170.
49. John Clarke, *Land, Power, and Economics on the Frontier of Upper Canada* (Montreal: McGill-Queen's Press, 2001), 104,
50. Ibid., 101.
51. Gheller, "Geopolitics, State-Formation and Economic Development," 187.
52. Ryerson, *Unequal Union*, 141.
53. Frank Scott, "Political Nationalism and Confederation," *The Canadian Journal of Economics and Political Science* 8, no. 3 (1942): 386.
54. Donald Creighton, "Economic Nationalism and Confederation," *Report of the Annual Meeting of the Canadian Historical Association* 1, no. 1 (1942): 46–50.
55. Ryerson, *Unequal Union*, 169.
56. Michael Piva, "Government Finance and the Development of the Canadian State," in *Colonial Leviathan: State Formation in mid-19th C Canada*, ed. Allan Greer and Ian Radforth (Toronto: University of Toronto Press, 1992), 259.
57. Michelle Vosburgh, "Agents of Progress: The Role of Crown Land Agents and Surveyors in the Distribution of Crown Lands in Upper Canada, 1837–1870" (PhD diss., McMaster University, 2004), 34.
58. Lillian Gates, *The Land Policies of Upper Canada* (Toronto: University of Toronto Press, 1968), 267.
59. Vosburgh, "Agents of Progress," 35; "The Crown Lands Department, the Government, and the Settlers of McNab Township, Canada West," *Ontario History* 100, no. 1 (2008): 82.
60. Daniel Bilak, "The Law of the Land: Rural Debt and Private Land Transfer in Upper Canada, 1841–1867," *Social History* XX, no. 39 (1987): 180.
61. Lawrence, "Gender, Race, and the Regulation," 7.
62. Marion Boswell, *'Civilizing' the Indian: Government Administration of Indians, 1876–1896* (Ottawa: University of Ottawa Press, 1970), 97.
63. Cited in J.R. Miller, "Owen Glendower, Hotspur, and Canadian Indian Policy," *Ethnohistory* 37, no. 4 (1990): 389.

64. Shelley Gavigan, *Hunger, Horses, and Government Men: Criminal Law on the Aboriginal Plains, 1870–1905* (Vancouver: The University of British Columbia Press, 2012), 25.
65. Jeremy Adelman, *Frontier Development: Land, Labour, and Capital in Argentina and Canada, 1890 1914* (Gloucestershire: Clarendon Press, 1994), 23.
66. Jessica Evans, "Rejecting the Staples Thesis and Recentring Migration: A Comparative Analysis of 'Late Development' in Canada and Argentina," in *Historical Sociology and World History: Uneven and Combined Development over the Longue Durée*, ed. Alexander Anievas and Kamran Matin (London: Rowman & Littlefield, 2016), 140–141.
67. Adelman, *Frontier Development*, 24–49.
68. Carl Solberg, *The Prairies and the Pampas: Agrarian Policy in Canada and Argentina, 1880–1930* (Stanford: Stanford University Press, 1987), 55–58.
69. Evans, "Rejecting the Staples Thesis," 141.

CHAPTER 9

The Peasantry and Tenancy-Market Dependence: Rural Capitalism in Meiji-Era Japan

Mark Cohen

Introduction

The history of Japanese capitalism traces a path that few other countries have managed to follow. A century and a half ago, Japan was a backwards agrarian economy, reeling under the trade and diplomatic pressure of the Western imperial powers; today it stands among the richest capitalist economies. Scholars of development have offered accounts of how the Japanese "developmental state" was able to superintend the country's postwar "economic miracle."[1] Yet few would deny that the miraculous growth that began in the 1950s was built on an existing social foundation; capitalist industrial development had already begun in *pre*war Japan. This earlier development, starting in the 1880s, was modest compared to what came later, but in the late-nineteenth-century context, it is no less an exceptional historical event. Within the wide perspective of this volume, the significance of Japan's economic trajectory in the Meiji Era (1868–1912)

M. Cohen (✉)
Chinese University of Hong Kong, Shatin, China

X. Lafrance, C. Post (eds.), *Case Studies in the Origins of Capitalism*, Marx, Engels, and Marxisms,
https://doi.org/10.1007/978-3-319-95657-2_9

is that it made the epochal transition from the oscillations of the pre-capitalist economy to the tumultuous but persistent growth of capitalism. This chapter will offer an analysis of Japan's transition, focused on the rural sector. This focus, aside from following the lead of Brenner's seminal account of England,[2] is based on the contentious claim that the rural Japanese economy did, crucially, undergo a transition to capitalism following the Meiji Restoration of 1868.

The contentiousness of this claim lies in its opposition to the two, main, competing accounts of Meiji-era Japanese economic history. These two alternative positions—which will be surveyed below—can be concisely stated as arguing that no such transition occurred, either because rural social relations remained semi-feudal well into the twentieth century or because the rural economy had already been essentially commercialized for generations. The former—long the dominant interpretation among Japanese Marxists—insists that the beginnings of Japanese industrialization were nurtured by state policy within a hothouse of subsidized capital formation, cheap and strictly policed labor, and a captive market of government purchases. Industrial capitalism in Japan was thus built on top of an essentially non-capitalist social foundation in the countryside. The latter minimizes the transformation that occurred following 1868, based on the argument that the feudal regime's nominal restrictions on peasants' involvement in markets for land, labor, and various products including cash crops and handicrafts had, since the eighteenth century at the latest, lost most of their force. Peasants, long used to adapting their economic strategies to market opportunities, unsurprisingly jumped at the chances for new income opened up by foreign trade and the government's reforms.

In this chapter, I argue that neither of these accounts can capture and explain the beginning of capitalist development in late-nineteenth-century Japan. The rural commercialization of the preceding period was not—and showed no signs of—a transition to capitalism. Yet, at the same time, the dynamism of the rural sector—in both agriculture and small-scale industry—after 1868 belies an image of a stagnant, pre-capitalist agrarian economy. Instead, the Meiji state—seeking to solidify the fiscal and social base for its political projects, above all military modernization—ended up transforming the structure of relations linking landlords and tenants. The wealthy rural commoners who had occupied positions of patronage within the communal institutions of the feudal countryside were "freed" to wield the economic power of their property. The effectiveness of this economic power was given substance because the cultivating majority—most of whom needed to rent at least some land to support themselves—were "freed" from the protective norms of what had previously been legally autonomous village communities.

As a case of the transition to capitalism, Japan is significant not only because of the country's historical position but also for its key theoretical lessons. The central question that must be addressed in making sense of Japan's economic history is how and under what circumstances peasants—cultivating households that plant a mix of staple and cash crops, using predominately family labor—can come to participate in the characteristic dynamics of capitalist development. Such producers—the majority in Japan until the 1920s—are not dependent on the *labor* market to obtain the means of their subsistence. Instead, in Meiji-era Japan but not before, peasants were subjected to the discipline of competitive production through relations of debt and tenancy. Analytical difficulties arise because neither indebtedness nor the fall from owning into renting were new and unique phenomena—though of course the same could be said about agricultural wage labor in early modern Europe. It is this apparent continuity in the organization of cultivation that has drawn the attention of most scholars of the agrarian economy of prewar Japan. The argument advanced here is that this apparent continuity of patterns conceals a change in their character.

The next two sections will consider and criticize the dominant interpretations of continuity in the rural economy. The historical evidence can neither support the claim that the Meiji-era rural economy followed pre-capitalist lines of development nor that the Tokugawa-era economy was already experiencing the beginnings of modern economic growth. The following section, with these points setting up the baseline that a structural transformation took place, shows how a reconfiguration of rural property relations was set in motion following the Meiji Restoration.

Uneven Development and Political Mediation

For the generation of Japanese radicals who confronted the authoritarian and militaristic state of the interwar period, the essential theoretical and political question seemed to be what it was about Japanese capitalism that made possible such an *incompletely bourgeois* society and political system, and the positions advanced in debates surrounding this question came to constitute the frame for academic historical research in the decades following the Second World War.[3] The answer to this question—on this point nearly all the participants agreed—was deeply bound up with how one understood the timing and process of the transition to capitalism in Japan. What were the conditions of the key classes—feudal nobility, peasantry, and bourgeoisie—in the late Tokugawa period? What role did they each play in the Meiji Restoration? What pattern of class relations emerged following that event?

In the interpretation that emerged as dominant among historians after the war, the fundamental anomaly of Japanese history was that so much of the superstructure of feudal rule up to 1868 was so rapidly dismantled by a regime lacking both bourgeois leadership and the impetus of a mass revolutionary movement.[4] The explanation for this anomaly is found, according to these accounts, in two points, one about the internal trends of social development within Tokugawa-era Japan and the other concerning the international environment of the mid-nineteenth century. Internally, the development of merchant capital during the Tokugawa era began to increasingly undercut the foundations of feudal rule in the countryside, which had been premised on subsistence-oriented smallholder peasant farming. Nonetheless, the feudal regime remained strong enough to prevent the emergence of an autonomous bourgeoisie that could have posed a social and political threat, and in this sense, in the mid-nineteenth century, the first shoots of Japanese capitalism remained too "immature" for a proper bourgeois revolution. However, on the external side, the exposure of Japan to the rising force of global capitalism and imperialism placed the feudal ruling class—or at least some members of it—in the position of needing to carry out certain aspects of such a revolution, in order to confront the threat of geopolitical subordination. To a considerable extent, they achieved this result, though, unsurprisingly given their social origin, they sought to minimize the social and economic upheaval that accompanied the unavoidable transformations.

Yet, according to the scholars who developed this account, Japan's anomalous revolution also brought with it fateful consequences. Meiji-era Japan was diagnosed as having an economic structure and political institutions that were hybrids of capitalist and feudal elements.[5] Industrialization began, but it relied on the state stepping in to take an exceptionally direct role in the accumulation and to some extent the direction of industrial capital, in lieu of the underdeveloped bourgeoisie. The funding for industrial capital formation was funneled from the agrarian sector by high rates of taxation and rent, but there was no revolution in the scale or technology of cultivation. The income of labor, in both agriculture and industry, remained extremely low, which on the one hand made elites wary of extending democratic rights and on the other constrained the domestic consumer market, thereby encouraging an imperial alliance between capital, landlords, and the state.[6]

This paradigm constituted a quasi-orthodoxy in Japanese historiography for several decades. It has since been dethroned. The most sustained and effective criticism of it came from empirical historical research that often set itself up as opposing the overtly Marxist stance of the old orthodoxy. The next section will summarize and assess this research. Yet, at the same time, significant doubts can be raised against this framework from the perspective of the accounts of capitalism's origins and development advanced by Brenner and scholars following him.

First, the view advanced of the Meiji Restoration by this perspective is framed by a contrast with the ideal type of a bourgeois revolution. However, it has become increasingly clear that the classic image of a "rising" bourgeoisie emerging to lead a mass movement to thoroughly dismantle the institutions of feudal rule and replace them with those of capitalism describes *no* actual modern revolution. Thus, from a comparative perspective, it reveals relatively little that the first few generations of leaders of the Meiji state came predominately from samurai backgrounds, or that the state took reactionary stances toward peasant unrest. Similarly, the slowness and ultimate incompleteness with which civil rights and electoral representation were established can hardly be seen as evidence of a distinctively incomplete capitalist transition in Japan.

Second, and more centrally for the question of the dynamics of Japanese economic development, the claim made by the classic Marxist accounts was that capitalist accumulation was initially made possible *merely* by the redirection of the agricultural surplus, which was extracted by essentially similar means as under the feudal regime. Industrial capitalism was established in growing, state-sheltered islands within a stagnant agrarian sea. Peasants were gradually pulled into the capitalist economy, but the relationship between capitalism and agriculture remained an "external" one.[7] However, on a theoretical level, the *feasibility* of this path of industrialization is open to doubt, for analogous reasons to those advanced by Brenner against the idea of early modern European cities as natural capitalist enclaves.[8] If the social property relations in rural Japan remained basically pre-capitalist, what was the mechanism drawing peasants progressively into market exchange?

It is on this doubt that the empirical evidence collected by revisionist economic historians over several decades weighs in most decisively.[9] The agrarian sector was not an internally stagnant source of surplus but instead grew at a rate that kept pace with the economy as a whole into the 1910s. This growth was not driven solely by expanded area under production or intensified labor but also the increased productivity of a stable or slowly shrinking labor force. In a wider theoretical lens, it should not be surprising that the beginning of industrialization in Japan was supported by dynamism in agriculture.[10] Yet, the stylized fact underlying influential theories of Japanese development was precisely the supposed puzzle of the absence of such agricultural growth. It turns out that what needs to be explained is the engine of the Meiji-era rural economy. The revisionists, for their part, have their own preferred story, but it too is flawed, as laid out in the next section.

The Continuity of Commercialization and Capitalism?

On a theoretical level, the argument of the economic historians who so thoroughly documented the dynamism of rural areas diagnosed as "semi-feudal" by earlier research was that if there were no overt *restraints* put on the economic activity of peasant cultivators, then they could have been expected to pursue the opportunities for income that presented themselves in a growing market economy. Yet, they saw no reason to restrict this logic to only the period that followed the Meiji Restoration. Indeed, the revisionist account of Meiji-era growth went hand-in-hand with a reassessment of the Tokugawa-era economy.[11] The result was a narrative of Japanese economic history since the seventeenth century that disagreed with the existing orthodoxy on nearly every point.

According to this view, feudal institutions had over the course of the Tokugawa era increasingly become a thin shell covering a highly commercialized, dynamic economy. Whatever the nominally restrictive laws proclaimed by the feudal authorities, peasants were in practice free—and willing—to pursue the economic opportunities that presented themselves. By the mid-nineteenth century, the major constraint it faced was its limited exposure to the opportunities available in international trade.[12] The forced opening of Japan did compel elites to come to terms with the world market, but in practice, what they did was merely to strip away the remaining feudal trappings and embrace the market economy that had been growing underneath. The Restoration was thus the culmination of a long-term process rather than a major break. Even before the Meiji state's reforms, "peasants' property rights in land approximated those of a fee-simple title by the end of the Tokugawa period," and so they "were readily converted to the modern private-property system" following the Meiji Restoration.[13] Economically, the rural economic growth that supported industrialization in the Meiji era was merely the continuation of the trend of rural commercialization that was apparent from the eighteenth century onward.[14] The trend accelerated after the opening of the ports because this led to an immense expansion of market opportunities, most notably in rural textile industries that employed imported technology (such as the new cotton spinning mills) or were oriented to export (such as the explosion of the raw silk industry).[15] Overall, in this view Meiji-era economic development was remarkably ordinary: broad-based in terms of both geography and sectors, beginning with labor-intensive production but gradually intensifying the use of capital, and not exceptionally focused on investment or government spending rather than household consumption.

However, this image of continuous development is strained both theoretically and empirically. It rests on a slippage between the flexibility displayed by peasants in their struggle to eke out subsistence in difficult circumstances and the continual adjustment of economic activity that generates self-sustaining growth. Peasant households whose members take up part-time cottage industry can be said to be responding to the "incentives" generated by market conditions, but their willingness to adjust labor patterns in this way does not imply that they will steadily expand the productivity of that labor in either handicrafts or cultivation. What happened in rural Japan during the Tokugawa era was that peasants became more involved with commerce and industry only as part of a redistribution of people and economic activity *away* from the established cities. The urbanization rate began to *fall* in western Japan (home to the commercial and industrial center of Osaka) after the early eighteenth century and nationwide through most of the nineteenth century.[16] Thus, rural commercialization did not translate into structural change in the economy, with agriculture steadily representing an estimated 61% of output throughout the latter half of the Tokugawa era.[17]

The Meiji era brought with it both a marked acceleration of growth and, more broadly, a new trajectory of development. From 1874 to 1913, the economy as a whole grew over 60% in real terms, per capita—an average annual rate of 1.2%—and the structural shift toward industry began in earnest.[18] This latter trend was not merely a reversal of what came before, with industry and the urban economy expanding at the expense of rural areas. Nor was the growth exclusively centered on new export industries or those that benefited from imported technology, as would be implied by the explanation that the opening of the country to world markets was the decisive change. Most importantly, despite a gradual flow of labor into other activities, output of the staple grain rice increased by over 1% per year through the 1910s.[19]

Thus, the revisionists' insistence on a continuity of commercial growth obscures a decisive shift in the rate and dynamics of economic change. Prior to the Meiji Restoration, the gradual movement of existing industry from established towns into the hinterland intensified peasant labor to make up for reduced land availability without altering the aggregate structure of the economy. The trajectory of economic development in the Meiji era was fundamentally different. Steadily increasing productivity in staple agriculture freed labor and other resources for a surge in other economic sectors, in both rural and urban areas. *Many* of the industries that most benefited from this growth process were those linked with the newly opened opportunities of the world market, but it was not *only* such sectors that saw a transition to intensive growth. It remains, then, to identify the mechanisms that drove the emergence of capitalist development in Japan; the next section turns to this question.

Taxation and the Economic Power of Landlords

The upshot of the previous two sections is that neither of the prominent paradigms of research on the economic development of rural Japan up to the early twentieth century offer convincing explanations of the mechanisms of that development. The classic arguments of Japanese Marxists overstated the "semi-feudal" character of Meiji-era agriculture, and the economic historians who have developed revisionist narratives of steady commercialization have to excessively downplay the acceleration of growth following the Meiji Restoration. In other words, neither can account for the *transition* from the de-urbanizing, macro-economically stationary commercialization of the Tokugawa era to the broad-based, multisectoral dynamism of the Meiji era.

As a starting point, it is important to note that this transition was not the result of an intentionally radical program of economic transformation adopted by Meiji-era political elites. As emphasized equally by scholars advancing both major interpretations, the Meiji Restoration of 1868 was by no means a "bourgeois" revolution in terms of leadership, support, or goals. Instead, it was the product of a movement led by subordinate members of the feudal elite, which first overthrew the feudal overlord of the Tokugawa shogunate and then abolished the hereditary rule of magnate lords over feudal domains on which the old regime had been based.[20] The crisis that created the opening for this movement was the combination of typical fiscal pressures on a pre-capitalist state and the acute threat represented by the capitalist imperial powers.[21] By 1868, the Western states had imposed on Japan the opening of several "treaty ports," with restricted tariffs and extraterritorial legal rights for foreign merchants. Improving on the manifest inability of the old regime to muster an effective response to this geopolitical threat—either in terms of pursuing coherent national policy or of mobilizing fiscal resources—was central to the new government's claim of legitimacy to other members of the elite. The priorities of the leaders of the Meiji state were, accordingly, to secure first their administrative control of the country and second the stable fiscal base needed to finance military modernization aimed at improving Japan's geopolitical position. Social and economic policies—including the dismantling of village autonomy that will be central to the analysis below—were crafted in pursuit of these primary goals.

Not only was transformation as such not a goal of the state, the appearance of continuity was further reinforced by the fact that there was only gradual change to the patterns of who produced what, and how, in the rural economy. Cultivation was carried out on a very small scale, and rented land was used most often to match the labor available within a peasant household. Wage labor constituted a limited share of the agricultural workforce. Moreover, the number of these family farmers was stubbornly constant all the way to the middle of the twentieth century. The contractual terms of tenancy likewise displayed remarkable continuity. Rent was usually set and collected in kind, even after taxes—which continued to fall heavily on agricultural land—began to be paid in cash in the 1870s. The level of rent was also extremely high, leaving the tenant farmer little more (or less) than a subsistence income, and thus in the Meiji era, there was little greater scope for capital accumulation by farmers themselves than there had been earlier.[22] Thus, on all of these grounds, it might seem that whatever one's judgment of the economic tendencies of agriculture prior to the Meiji Restoration, similar tendencies were likely to continue afterwards.

However, these continuities concealed a very important shift in the relations between landlords and their tenants, based on a fundamental change in the character of landlords' ownership of property. The Meiji state in the 1870s took up, as the feudal rulers had not, the role of recognizing, guaranteeing, and enforcing the ownership of land by individuals. Previously, the regulation of landownership was the responsibility and prerogative of the villages themselves.[23] The members of each village were by no means equal, in terms of either status or wealth. A few prominent households were employers, lenders, and landlords—and in some cases merchant-brokers—to their poorer neighbors. The village, as a community, enforced expectations that tenants and debtors would work diligently to pay their obligations to the patron families. Yet, this enforcement of the interests of the patrons was built fundamentally on the consent of the village residents as a whole. Landlords had access to no *independent* force to threaten recalcitrant debtors and tenants, either held personally by them or to which they could appeal outside the village.[24]

The feudal rulers, prior to the Meiji Restoration, had little interest in acting as arbiters of property rights within villages. The political problem to which the Tokugawa-era political system offered a solution was the instability of relations within the ruling class, which had produced decades of rebellion and civil war in the sixteenth century. Central to the solution that resulted in the long "Pax Tokugawa" was the pruning and institutional and spatial concentration of the warrior nobility. Instead of being scattered across the countryside on fiefs, samurai in each domain were pulled into the "castle town" that was the seat of their liege-lord's rule. Internal to the villages, it was this policy of "separating warriors and peasants" that left social and economic inequalities in the villages, while denying landlord families—often claiming status as descended from or formerly affiliated to rural samurai—the freedom to hold coercive capacity on their own. On the other side, rather than being controlled by individual samurai, the villages were governed by the administrations of, in effect, small-scale absolutist states with populations from a few tens of thousand to several hundred thousand. This government was, moreover, relatively hands-off—decrees and tax demands were handed down to the villages as units, which were largely responsible for maintaining order and distributing and collecting taxes internally.[25]

This was a cheap and, from the evidence of over two centuries without a major armed rebellion, remarkably stable method of rule. It also proved a system with space for enrichment for a few well-placed members of the rural population. Their role was to act as patrons and intermediaries for their poorer neighbors. When a peasant family had a bad year and was unable to cover its share of the tax burden, it could borrow from a better-off family, with the sanction of the village community as a whole. From the perspective of the community, this procedure threw the struggling family a lifeline—desirable because it forestalled the reduction in the number of households across which the annual tax burden was distributed—while enforcing the expectation that each household needed to be responsible for its proportionate contribution to taxes. Such loans were secured with a fraction of the borrowing family's land, and if—not uncommonly—the borrower was unable to muster the extra income to repay the principal of the loan in addition to the new burden of interest, the debt relationship typically transformed directly into one of tenancy.[26]

These tenancy relations continued to be regulated and enforced by the village community. Officially, the feudal rulers did not recognize the right of peasants to "permanently alienate" their land, but in practice they just stayed out of transactions and relations within each village.[27] Yet, this situation also represented a key constraint on the landlords' side. As just mentioned, village members as a collectivity shared a strong interest in the continued viability of each member household so as to maintain the distribution of the tax burden. Landlords' efforts at rent collection needed to accommodate this interest. The way this manifested itself was not in the nominal rate of rent—often stated as a volume of rice that made up two-thirds or more of a normal harvest, though this included the rice that would be paid as taxes.[28] Instead, its effect could be seen in the amount of *actual* rent collected each year, which was usually reduced by adjustments granted by the landlord and by simple non-payment. Table 9.1 presents examples of the range and average payment rates—the actual volume of rice collected over the formal rent level—from the record-books of Tokugawa-era landlords studied by historians. As will be seen shortly, these wide fluctuations, averaging around two-thirds and three-quarters, would not persist into the Meiji period.

Table 9.1 Examples of rent collection in the Tokugawa era[29]

Modern-day prefecture	*Time period*	*Payment rate range*	*Average*
Hyogo	1758/'72/'81/'84	70.1%–80.3%	74.3%
Yamagata	1817–1841	5.3%–97.8%	69.0%
Niigata	1825–1861	21.8%–86.0%	60.9%
Okayama	1856–1867	62.7%–88.6%	79.4%

Put in another way, political and economic relations remained fused together in the villages of Tokugawa-era Japan, because of each village's collective responsibility for the payment of feudal dues to the warrior nobility. The significance of the Meiji state's Land Tax Reform, carried out over several years beginning in 1873, was that it broke this fusion and ended up offering landlords the independent enforcement mechanism they had previously lacked. The state's interest in reform was of course strictly fiscal—political elites wanted to secure a stable cash income, instead of the fluctuating payments in kind that the new regime inherited from the old and to regularize tax policies and the collection apparatus nationally to replace the patchwork feudal system.[30] To achieve this, the basis for tax assessment was switched from the village harvest to the cash value of individual households' landholdings. To determine each taxpayer's annual obligation, prefectural officials in cooperation with local representatives surveyed land value and ownership, issuing deeds for each plot, which would subsequently be the marker both of tax responsibility and basically unlimited property rights.[31]

In principle, the interests of landlords, owner-cultivators, and tenants could coincide with respect to the land tax reform. Because valuations were generally based on benchmark estimates of yield for each prefecture, county, and village, all rural residents who owned any land whatsoever—a category that included most tenants—would prefer to push down land value assessments. In some regions, notably in Okayama and Niigata prefectures, landlords organized campaigns to resist the government's attempts to impose a valuation standard that met expected revenue targets. However, the governments' fiscal demands eventually prevailed, and a major reason was the latent class conflict between landlords and tenants. In Okayama, there was distinct reluctance by landlords to overtly mobilize the mass of the peasantry, for fear that it would turn against them.[32] In Niigata, tax reform officials themselves made the argument to oppositional landlords that they should accept the government's assessment because any increase could simply be passed on to their tenants in the form of higher rents. After all, if tenants objected, they could simply be evicted, "and since the tenants do not know any trade other than farming, after a year away from cultivation, by the second or third year, unable to stand their hunger and thirst, when they once again entreat the landlord, the increase in rent will go according as the landlord wills."[33]

Indeed, this rather blunt official advice leads to a further point: the Meiji state explicitly renounced any desire or authority to intervene in what it saw as private transactions of sale, debt, or tenancy. The government made no provision for customary rights of tenants, and most often landlords were awarded unilateral ownership.[34] More generally, the new government liquidated the regulatory authority of the village community and refused to legally recognize the norms regarding tenancy and rent that it had previously enforced.[35] In 1875, local officials asked for Tokyo's opinion on tenants' customary rights and received an unequivocal response that "perpetual" tenancy had no legal basis and that once officials had determined who owned the land, "increases or decreases in rental payments should be determined by private settlement between landlords and tenants."[36] A significant number of disputes regarding the latter point arose in the late 1870s in response to a national reduction in the land tax rate issued by the government; tenants demanded that landlords pass on at least part of the savings to them in the form of lower rent. In one lawsuit filed in Kōchi prefecture in 1877, the Supreme Court initially ruled that half of the reduction should be passed on to tenants but after a second hearing reversed itself, setting the firm precedent that tax law had no bearing on the private contracts setting rent levels.[37] Thus, the administrative and judicial arms of the state established clearly the principle that landlords' control of the land was complete and tenants' access to it was strictly conditional on landlords' contractual agreement. Tenants could and did protest against "landlords strongly asserting their interests as land owners," for instance, by "dispossessing tenants of their customary rights or arbitrarily increasing rents."[38] However, the state was now firmly standing behind the landlords, and when poor peasants resorted to more violent means of resistance against their creditors and landlords, it proved itself ready and able to quickly put down the rebellions.[39]

The effect of landlords' consolidated property rights manifested in their efforts to collect rent. The basic format of rent collection remained the same—a fixed nominal rate against which reductions were offered based on harvest conditions—but the large and variable reductions seen in the Tokugawa era shrank and stabilized from the 1880s onward. In account books studied by historians and periodic surveys of tenancy conditions carried out by the government, the ratio between contractual rent and collected payments settled at a predictable level of 90% or more. Table 9.2 presents examples from individual landlords' records analyzed by historians. A nationwide survey—based on county-level reports of prevailing yields and contractual and actually paid rental rates for 1908 to 1912—shows an average of 92% of the contractual rent being paid on middle-grade rice paddy.[40] Moreover, this was not driven by any easing up on the

Table 9.2 Examples of rent collection after the land tax reform[42]

Prefecture	*Time period*	*Payment rate range*	*Average*
Okayama	1879–1887	56.0%–99.8%	90.0%
Okayama	1884–1914	45.8%–98.4%	87.0%
Okayama	1907–1920	81.5%–94.8%	89.3%
Shiga	1895–1918	58.5%–100.0%	87.0%
Shizuoka	1905–1915	61.5%–94.5%	86.4% (paddy)
		94.5%–100.0%	98.0% (dry)

contractual rents being imposed by landlords. Through the Meiji period, rent levels kept pace with—or even slightly outpaced—the steady increase in the productivity of land.[41]

The significance of this stabilization of rent collection was that it decisively reoriented the pressures facing cultivators. The village community had previously disciplined cultivators according to prevalent norms for diligent cultivation, but beyond this point, landlords were expected to accommodate the subsistence needs of tenants. This was why they had to accept such inconsistent levels of rent payment. However, by the 1880s, the situation was quite different. Tenants' access to land came to depend on their success in meeting the prevailing levels of agricultural productivity. Rent was the price of this access, determined by how much income, socially, it should be possible to extract from a plot of land. Peasant cultivators who needed to rent land to operate a viable farm were thus dependent on this rental market, and this brought with it the imperative for increased productivity that follows from market dependence.

This change in the balance of power between landlords and tenants was accompanied by an overall expansion of tenancy and increased concentration of land in the hands of landlords. The process by which land came to be cultivated by tenants was not fundamentally different from what it had been in the Tokugawa era. On the one hand, the vast majority of the new land brought under cultivation was tenanted; the area of irrigated paddy increased by 216,000 hectares (8%) between 1880 and 1910.[43] On the other, peasants lost ownership of plots of land pledged as collateral to loans on which they defaulted, with a notable acceleration during the deflationary episode of the early 1880s.[44] The result of this process was not the proliferation of farmers whose *only* access to land was through tenancy, let alone of landless farm laborers—though the number of the former if not the latter certainly increased—but instead the deepening of a pattern in which the plurality of cultivators combined some land ownership with tenancy. In 1912, including pure tenants, over half of cultivating households owned less than half a hectare, but the median cultivator worked between one-half and one hectare. Even if most cultivators owned some land and just over half of the land, by area, was cultivated by its owners, over two-thirds of cultivators rented at least some land.[45]

Thus, a vast majority of cultivators faced the pressure of rent that was rising to capture the steady growth in the prevailing productivity of land. This pressure forced cultivators to adopt strategies to maximize the income earned by household members. First, the traditional pattern by which more land or agricultural output was simply soaked up by a growing rural population was broken. Despite continued expansion of arable land and accelerated population growth *overall*, the number of cultivating households and the agricultural labor force ceased growth completely and even began to edge downward in Japan's three main islands.[46] Second, peasants needed to pursue what opportunities they could find to make their labor more lucrative. On the one hand, this meant the more intensive deployment of the labor of household members, which created the pool of workers essential to the rural-led industrialization of the Meiji era. On the other hand, cultivators adopted improved techniques that yielded a steady increase in labor productivity.

The suite of techniques that drove the productivity increases of the period, which has come to be known as the "Meiji agricultural methods" (*Meiji nōhō*), was based on refinements of practices that had made their appearance in a much more limited way in the Tokugawa era.[47] Its key elements were improved seeds; more careful nursing, transplanting, and weeding; the use of controlled irrigation to enable deep plowing with animal power as well as double-cropping; and ever-intensifying application of fertilizer.[48] This trajectory of development was adapted to the small scale of Japanese agriculture, and it relied more on increasing current inputs than on adding more fixed capital. Indeed, the pathways through which the rural population pursued increased income in the Meiji era *paralleled* those followed by earlier generations needing to intensify their labor to increase the income they could squeeze from a given plot of land to compensate for increasing population-land ratios. What set Meiji-era agriculture apart from its Tokugawa-era past—or from other cases like France as seen in Miller's chapter in this volume or eighteenth-century China as shown by Brenner and Isett[49]—was that the fitful development of new techniques became a steady stream driving increased productivity not only of the land but also per worker.[50] This new trajectory of rising productivity was in turn essential in supporting structural change in the overall economy.

There was one additional piece of the puzzle. As much as peasant cultivators were pressed to find new ways of improving their productivity, the truth is that their economic conditions (including the rent and taxes they had to pay) did not leave them with the financial leeway to undertake the upfront investment needed to innovate production techniques themselves.[51] Instead, the Meiji-era growth dynamic relied on there being a steady stream of improvements that smallholders could adopt incrementally. Opportunities for off-farm employment likewise depended on ongoing capital investment that peasants obviously could not make themselves. On both sides, landlords played a central role. In agriculture, it was especially the smaller or medium-scale landlords who cultivated some portion of their holding directly who were also the farmers with the resources to experiment through trial-and-error in the selection of crops, techniques, and seeds, and it was their activity that drove the impressive improvements in productivity seen in the era.[52] Landlords were also important investors and entrepreneurs in the industries that expanded rapidly beginning in the 1880s, including textiles and finance.[53]

The significance of this is that it represents the other pole of the transformation of rural property relations set in motion by the Land Tax Reform. Not only did peasants lose the backing of village institutions for their access to land but landlords were freed simultaneously of the *privileges* and *burdens* that came with their positions in these institutions. The Meiji era was one of immense opportunities for the growth of wealth—for those landlords and merchants who were willing and able to take them. Many did, but far from all, and it was not only peasant cultivators who found themselves pressured to sell their land or losing it to foreclosure. Many large landlords built their estates with land acquired from *other landlords* in addition to from smallholder peasants.[54] Thus, in sum, following the Meiji Restoration, the character of landownership and of tenancy had changed so as to bring to bear the imperatives and dynamics of capitalism on both owners and cultivators.

Conclusion

This chapter has adopted the theoretical framing of Brenner's account of the transition to capitalism to intervene in long-standing debates over the beginning of economic development in Japan—in particular in Japanese agriculture—in the late nineteenth and early twentieth centuries. The mid-century orthodox interpretation saw Meiji-era Japan as a hybrid social formation: capitalist industrialization built on top of a fundamentally "semi-feudal" agrarian structure, resulting in various instabilities and imbalances that it fell to the state to manage. This characterization became the target of criticism by revisionist economic historians, who offered instead a picture of a thoroughly "normal" beginning to Japanese industrialization that was basically continuous with the commercialization of the Tokugawa era. I have argued that as a *descriptive account* of the economic dynamics of Meiji-era Japan, the revisionists are far closer to the truth, but their claim of "continuous commercialization" fails to account for the immense shift in the trends of economic growth and development after the 1870s. My contention instead is that the Meiji state's policies involved with dismantling the system of feudal domains and instituting a new, direct land tax fundamentally altered the balance of power, in rural areas, between those who owned land and those who produced their livelihoods by working it. Cultivators became dependent on markets—above all, a competitive rental market—for their survival, while for the first time the state provided the political framework to enforce the economic power of property owners. The result was an increase in the economic risk faced by the rural poor but also the imposition of pressure to continually improve productivity in cultivation and other rural economic activities.

What the earlier Marxist accounts surely got right was to insist on the decisive importance of the new, post-Restoration relationship between landlords and the state. However, I characterize this relationship in a very different way. Landlords constituted the social base for the Meiji state in the sense that they were a crucial—and initially leading—node in the capital accumulation without which political elites' program was impossible. In terms of political institutions, substantial landowners constituted a large share of the electorate for the Diet beginning in 1890, setting them up as the main negotiating partners for state elites in securing increased tax revenue. In contrast, the image presented by earlier Marxist accounts—typically under the headings of "semi-feudal" tenancy and "parasitic" landlordism—centered on landlords' supposed "extra-economic" authority, based on village social institutions and the political power of the state.[55] Indeed, according to this theory, the "landlord system" in Japanese agriculture represented a distinct mode of production, for which state power "became the indispensable intermediary joining" it with developing industrial capitalism.[56] However, as argued above, this view belies the dynamics of capital accumulation and intensive growth *in the rural sector itself*. It is simply not the case that there was a "stagnation" in agriculture that could only be explained by the persistence of a distinctive, non-capitalist agrarian structure.

The explanation for the growth dynamics of agriculture, and the rural sector more broadly, can be found in the transformation of rural social property relations following the Meiji Restoration. In the Tokugawa era, landlords who formerly had often at least been on the edges of the knightly class were "disarmed" and thereby prevented from directly exerting coercive power over the peasantry in the manner of pre-capitalist elites. In this respect, their economic wealth could be said to have been "separated" from political power. Yet, what was missing, from the perspective of the "separation of the economic and the political" that is so essential to capitalist social property relations,[57] was a political framework to enforce their "strictly economic" rights to their property. Instead, the peasantry continued to defend its claim to subsistence from the land, enforced by communal institutions, and so the landlords had to settle for, as it were, vicariously relying on the coercive power of the feudal rulers in their position as intermediaries between lords and peasants. The Meiji state thus in effect needed only to finish the second half of the job, which it did through the disestablishment of the peasant community's legal authority over the land as part of the land tax reform.

The resulting growth did build on existing economic patterns, but it is a mistake to see Meiji-era development as a mere continuation of previous trends of commercialization. This point is linked to the nature of capitalist growth. At the risk of repeating a claim made repeatedly in this volume, the rules of reproduction generated by capitalist social property relations tend to lead, on aggregate, to the consistent rising of productivity despite periodic booms and recessions. Precisely how productivity increases will come about—producing what goods, with what kind of technology—depends on the circumstances of effective demand and the availability of factors of production. Thus, *given* a capitalist economy, it is not incorrect to say that Japan's economic growth and industrialization depended substantially on opportunities presented by the interaction of previously developed commercial patterns, demographic and ecological conditions, and the world market. Yet the confluence of conditions like the three just listed do not, in themselves, cause sustained growth. Instead, it was only within the compulsion of market dependence in capitalism that they became the *means* of development. Market dependence compels people throughout the economy to seek out what opportunities they can find, and in addition to newly opened possibilities, these can just as easily come from avenues that were overlooked or not fully exploited before, as with the growth in rice productivity in Meiji-era Japan. It is this multifariousness of growth in capitalism that generates self-sustaining development, rather than discrete but limited bursts of expansion to take advantage of particular shifts in economic conditions. The rural commercialization of the Tokugawa era was an example of the latter.

At the same time, if the theoretical argument is accepted that market dependence is a crucial structural feature that makes for capitalism's distinctive dynamics, it is important to not place excessive emphasis on any one *institutional form* of such dependence. In other words, a lesson of Japan's Meiji-era experience is that it is possible for direct producers to become subject to the competitive imperatives of capitalism through dependence on different markets, and in different ways, than in the more well-known capitalist transitions. The logic of the relationship between tenant and landlord can end up being quite close to that between capitalist and wage laborer, even if the direction of payment is ostensibly reversed. Just as capitalist employers hire (and will continue to employ) wage workers only insofar as the workers produce commodities with sufficient productivity to give to the owners the market rate of return on their property in capital, so do tenants who lack customary rights to subsistence need to be sufficiently productive to earn for landlords the market rate of return on their property in land. That various conditions led landlords to lease their land in small plots to peasant households, rather than in large tracts to tenant farmers who hired wage labor, does not change the essential character of the relations.

Finally, I should note one gap in this chapter's analysis, which points to an important avenue of research not just on the case of Japan but within the wider project influenced by Brenner's work. Here, I have skirted around what, for the earlier "debates on Japanese capitalism," was the essential question—the link between capitalism and Japan's authoritarian and imperialist state. These were originally, after all, disagreements over *political strategy* among Japanese radicals: the thesis of the incompleteness of Japan's transition to capitalism was presented as a diagnosis of the political situation.[58] By challenging the supposed survival of non-capitalist relations in agriculture that allegedly required a unique kind of state mediation between that sector and nascent industrial capitalism, my argument casts doubt on this diagnosis. Yet this was only the *answer* offered by the earlier accounts, and I have not in this chapter presented an alternative response to the original question. Prewar Japan's authoritarianism was perhaps less of an anomaly that Japanese radicals seemed to think; the premise that capitalism naturally tends toward liberal democracy is unsupported by the historical record.[59] Nonetheless, the theory of capitalist social property relations that has done so much to clarify our understanding of the transition to capitalism, as seen in the studies in this volume, has room to develop toward giving an account of how the transition then reverberates on state institutions, especially in the militaristic and imperialistic world environment of the eighteenth, nineteenth, and early twentieth centuries.

Notes

1. Chalmers Johnson, *MITI and the Japanese Miracle: The Growth of Industrial Policy, 1925–1975* (Tokyo: Charles E. Tuttle Co., 1982).
2. Robert Brenner, "The Agrarian Roots of Modern Capitalism," in *The Brenner Debate*, ed. T. H. Aston and C. H. E. Philpin (Cambridge: Cambridge University Press, 1985).
3. For a summary in English of these debates, see Germaine A. Hoston, *Marxism and the Crisis of Development in Prewar Japan* (Princeton: Princeton University Press, 1986).
4. Kōhachirō Takahashi, "Nihon No Tochiseido-Shi Ni Okeru Meiji Ishin No Ichi," in *Sekai No Naka No Meiji Ishin*, ed. Akira Tanaka (Tokyo: Yoshikawakōbunkan, 2001); Shigeki Tōyama, "Meiji Ishin," in *Tōyama Shigeki Chosakushū Vol. 1* (Tokyo: Iwanami Shoten, 1991). Note that to ensure consistency, in citations Japanese names will be given in the Western order.
5. Masanori Nakamura, "Nihon Jinushiseishi Kenkyū Josetsu: Senzen Nihon Shihonshugi To Kisei Jinushisei To No Kenren Wo Megutte," *Hitotsubashi Daigaku Kenkyū Nenpō, Keizaigaku Kenkyū* 12 (1968).
6. English-language representatives of this line of argument include Jamie C. Allinson and Alexander Anievas, "The Uneven and Combined Development of the Meiji Restoration: A Passive Revolutionary Road to Capitalist Modernity," *Capital & Class* 34, no. 3 (2010); Jon Halliday, *A Political History of Japanese Capitalism* (New York: Pantheon Books, 1975); Barrington Jr. Moore, *Social Origins of Dictatorship and Democracy: Lord and Peasant in the Making of the Modern World* (Boston: Beacon Press, 1966); E. H. Norman, "Japan's Emergence as a Modern State," in *Origins of the Modern Japanese State*, ed. John W. Dower (New York: Pantheon Books, 1975); Ellen Kay Trimberger, *Revolution from Above: Military Bureaucrats and Development in Japan, Turkey, Egypt, and Peru* (New Brunswick, NJ: Transaction Books, 1978).

7. In the words of one scholar, who in other ways pushes back against the "seminar faction" interpretation, the agricultural sector did eventually come to be "subsumed" in the capitalist economy, but "the process of subordinating agriculture to capital did not take the form of capital directly grasping agricultural production but instead ... an indirect form ... 'an external solution.'" Sumiaki Iwamoto, "Kindai-Teki Tochi Shoyū To Kiseijinushi-Teki Tochi Shoyū: Kindai No Giron O Megutte," *Nōgyō Keizai Kenkyū* 50, no. 3: 139.
8. Robert Brenner, "The Origins of Capitalist Development: A Critique of Neo-Smithian Marxism," *New Left Review* I, no. 104 (1977).
9. Penelope Francks, *Rural Economic Development in Japan* (London: Routledge, 2006); Yujiro Hayami and Saburo Yamada, eds., *The Agricultural Development of Japan: A Century's Perspective* (Tokyo: University of Tokyo Press, 1991).
10. Massoud Karshenas, *Industrialization and Agricultural Surplus: A Comparative Study of Economic Development in Asia* (Oxford: Oxford University Press, 1995).
11. Susan B. Hanley and Kozo Yamamura, *Economic and Demographic Change in Preindustrial Japan, 1600–1868* (Princeton: Princeton University Press, 1977).
12. Kozo Yamamura, "Pre-Industrial Landholding Patterns in Japan and England," in *Japan: A Comparative View*, ed. A. M. Craig (Princeton: Princeton University Press, 1979), 320.
13. Yujiro Hayami and Vernon W. Ruttan, "Toward a Theory of Induced Institutional Innovation," in *Can Economic Growth Be Sustained? The Collective Papers of Vernon W. Ruttan and Yujiro Hayami*, ed. Keijiro Otsuka and C. Ford Runge (Oxford: Oxford University Press, 2011), 227.
14. Francks, *Rural Economic Development in Japan*.
15. Osamu Saitō and Masayuki Tanimoto, "The Transformation of Traditional Industries," in *The Economic History of Japan: 1600–1990, Volume 1: Emergence of Economic Society in Japan, 1600–1859*, ed. Akira Hayami, Osamu Saitō, and Ronald P. Toby (Oxford: Oxford University Press, 2004).
16. Osamu Saito and Masanori Takashima, "Population, Urbanisation and Farm Output in Early Modern Japan, 1600—1874: A Review of Data and Benchmark Estimates," *RCESR Discussion Paper Series* no. DP15-3 (Tokyo: The Research Center for Economic and Social Risks, Institute of Economic Research, Hitotsubashi University, 2015): 10.
17. Osamu Saito, "Japan," in *A History of the Global Economy: From 1500 to the Present*, ed. Joerg Baten (Cambridge: Cambridge University Press, 2016), 173.
18. Ibid.

19. Hayami and Yamada, *The Agricultural Development of Japan*, Table A-1.
20. Mark Cohen, "The Political Process of the Revolutionary Samurai: A Comparative Reconsideration of Japan's Meiji Restoration," *Theory and Society* 43, no. 2 (2014).
21. Mark Cohen, "Historical Sociology's Puzzle of the Missing Transitions: A Case Study of Early Modern Japan," *American Sociological Review* 80, no. 3 (2015).
22. Munekazu Kurauchi, "Senzenki Kosakuryō No Dōkō To Keizaiteki Seikaku," *Ningen To Shakai* 7 (1996).
23. Yutaka Arimoto, "Kaihatsu Keizaigaku Kara Mita Jichi Sonraku Ron," *Rekishigaku Kenkyū* 40 (2006); Kunio Niwa, *Tochi Mondai No Kigen: Mura To Shizen To Meiji Ishin* (Tokyo: Heibonsha, 1989).
24. Thomas C. Smith, *The Agrarian Origins of Modern Japan* (Stanford: Stanford University Press, 1959).
25. John Whitney Hall, "Foundations of the Modern Japanese Daimyo," in *Studies in the Institutional History of Early Modern Japan*, ed. John Whitney Hall and Marius B. Jansen (Princeton: Princeton University Press, 1968); Naohiro Asao, "The Sixteenth-Century Unification," in *Cambridge History of Japan, Volume 4: Early Modern Japan*, ed. John Whitney Hall (Cambridge: Cambridge University Press, 1991); Osamu Wakita, "The Emergence of the State in Sixteenth-Century Japan: From Oda to Tokugawa," *Journal of Japanese Studies* 8, no. 2 (1982).
26. Edward E. Pratt, *Japan's Protoindustrial Elite: The Economic Foundations of the Gōnō* (Cambridge, MA: Harvard University Press, 1999); Yutaka Arimoto, "Kosakuryō Genmen Kankō To Torihiki Hiyō," *Nōgyōshi Kenkyū* 39 (2005).
27. Masaki Nakabayashi, "Torihiki No Tōchi To Shoshijō No Chikujitekina Kakudai," in *Nihon Keizai No Nagai Kindaika: Tōchi To Shijō, Soshite Soshiki, 1600–1970*, ed. Masaki Nakabayashi (Nagoya, Japan: Nagoya Daigaku Shuppankai, 2013), 23–24.
28. For instance, as seen in what is now Niigata prefecture, Kiyoshi Nakayama, *Kyodai Jinushi Keiei No Shiteki Kōzō* (Tokyo: Iwata Shoin, 2001), 51–56.
29. Sources: Hyogo: Hiroki Ikeda, *Kinsei Nihon No Ōjinushi Keisei Kenkyū* (Tokyo: Kokusho Kankokai, 2008), 22; Yamagata: Hideki Abe, *Kinsei Shonai Jinushi No Seisei* (Tokyo: Nihon Keizai Hyoronsha, 1994), 165; Okayma: Nakayama, *Kyodai Jinushi Keiei No Shiteki Kōzō*, 84–85 (Niigata); Ōta, *Nihon Jinushisei Seiritsu Katei No Kenkyū*, 362.
30. W. G. Beasley, "Meiji Political Institutions," in *The Cambridge History of Japan, Volume 5: The Nineteenth Century*, ed. Marius B. Jansen (Cambridge: Cambridge University Press, 1989), 639.
31. On the process of assessing land values, see Haruki Okuda, *Meiji Kokka To Kindaiteki Tochi Shoyū* (Tokyo: Dōseisha, 2007). The back of the docu-

ment included the following statement: "The Japanese citizen who holds this deed has the right to freely employ or hold this land, as well as the right to sell, transfer, mortgage, or pawn it." Quoted in Takeo Ono, *Meiji Zenki Tochi Seido Shiron* (Tokyo: Yūhikaku, 1948), 220.

32. Ken'ichi Ōta, *Nihon Jinushisei Seiritsu Katei No Kenkyū: Kinki-Gata Jinushi Keiei No Bunseki* (Okayama-shi: Fukutake Shoten, 1981), 306. This was not an unfounded fear, based on the example of anti-tax protests in the late Tokugawa era; see Stephen Vlastos, *Peasant Protests and Uprisings in Tokugawa Japan* (Berkeley: University of California Press, 1986), 140–141.
33. Quoted in Nakayama, *Kyodai Jinushi Keiei No Shiteki Kōzō*, 379.
34. Ono, *Meiji Zenki Tochi Seido Shiron.*
35. Niwa, *Tochi Mondai No Kigen*, 221.
36. Quoted in Munekazu Kurauchi, "Chiso Kaisei To Jinushisei," *Ningen To Shakai* 1 (1990): 24.
37. Ono, *Meiji Zenki Tochi Seido Shiron*, 206.
38. Ibid., 295.
39. Roger W. Bowen, *Rebellion and Democracy in Meiji Japan* (Berkeley: University of California Press, 1980).
40. Nōchi Seido Shiryō Shūsei Hensan Iinkai, *Nōchi Seido Shiryō Shūsei Vol. 1: Kosaku Kankō Ni Kansuru Shiryō* (Tokyo: Ochanomizu Shobo, 1970), 21–23.
41. Kurauchi, "Senzenki Kosakuryō No Dōkō To Keizaiteki Seikaku."
42. Sources: Okayama 1879–1887: Ōta, *Nihon Jinushisei Seiritsu Katei No Kenkyū*, 362; Okayama 1884–1914: Kaichirō Ōishi, ed. *Kindai Nihon Ni Okeru Jinushi Keiei No Tenkai: Okayama-Ken Ushimado-Chō Nishihattori-Ke No Kenkyū* (Tōkyō: Ochanomizu Shobō, 1985), 221–228; Okayama 1907–1920: Masao Arimoto, "Kyodai Jinushi No Shokakki To 'Saiseisan Kidō': Okayama Ken Kojima-Gun Nozaki-Ke No Bunseki," *Tochi Seido Shigaku* 12, no. 4 (1970): 40–41; Shiga: Takemaro Mori, "Kinki Chihō Ni Okeru Jinushi Keiei No Tenkai," *Shisō* 20 (1979): 82; Shizuoka: Masao Tsutsui, "Nihon Teikoku Shugi Seiritsu-Ki Ni Okeru Nōson Shihai Taisei: Shizuoka-Ken Harasato-Mura No Jirei O Chūshin Ni," *Tochi Seido Shigaku* 27, no. 1 (1984): 20.
43. Hayami and Yamada, *The Agricultural Development of Japan*, 253.
44. Toshio Furushima, *Shihonsei Seisan No Hatten To Jinushisei* (Tōkyō: Ochanomizu Shobō, 1963), 500.
45. Nōshōmu Daijin Kanbō Tōkeika, *Nōshōmu Tōkeihyō, No. 25* (Tokyo: Nōshōmushō, 1914), 1–5.
46. Mataji Umemura, *Long-Term Economic Statistics of Japan, Vol. 2: Labor* (Tokyo: Tōyō Keizai Shinpōsha, 1988), 216–225.

47. Shunsaku Shōji, *Kingendai Nihon No Nōson: Nōsei No Genten Wo Saguru* (Tokyo: Yoshikawa Kōbunkan, 2003), 38–39.
48. Masami Ōba, "'Meiji Nōhō' No Dōnyū Katei," in *Zenji Nisshi: Kaidai*, ed. Toyohara Kenkyūkai (Tokyo: Nōgyō Sōgō Kenkyūjo, 1976); Penelope Francks, *Technology and Agricultural Development in Pre-War Japan* (New Haven: Yale University Press, 1983), 160–170.
49. Robert Brenner and Christopher Isett, "England's Divergence from China's Yangtze Delta: Property Relations, Microeconomics, and Patterns of Development," *Journal of Asian Studies* 62, no. 2 (2002).
50. Consider the following estimates, from Hayami and Yamada, *The Agricultural Development of Japan*. Between 1880 and 1910, the value of livestock as an input in agriculture increased 46%, of feed by 76%, and of fertilizer by 97%, while investment in machinery and implements lagged, growing only 27% in the same period (Table A-8). In terms of productivity, the increase was 45% per area of arable land, 78% per worker, and 28% per estimated work hour (Tables A-1, A-5, and A-6).
51. This is illustrated dramatically by the typical household budgets revealed by survey reports in the early twentieth century; see Mankichi Saitō, *Jitchi Keizai Nōgyō Shishin: Nihon Nōgyō No Keizaiteki Hensen* (Tōkyō: Nō-sangyoson Bunka Kyōkai, 1975).
52. Ann Waswo, *Japanese Landlords: The Decline of a Rural Elite* (Berkeley: University of California Press, 1977), 38–42.
53. Kozo Yamamura, *A Study of Samurai Income and Entrepreneurship: Quantitative Analyses of Economic and Social Aspects of the Samurai in Tokugawa and Meiji Japan* (Cambridge, MA: Harvard University Press, 1974); Naofumi Nakamura, *Chihō Kara No Sangyō Kakumei* (Nagoya, Japan: Nagoya Daigaku Shuppankai, 2010); Pratt, *Japan's Protoindustrial Elite*.
54. Furushima, *Shihonsei Seisan No Hatten To Jinushisei*, 196–198; Nakayama, *Kyodai Jinushi Keiei No Shiteki Kōzō*, 418–449; Ōta, *Nihon Jinushisei Seiritsu Katei No Kenkyū*, 352–324.
55. Yukiteru Ōguri, "Nihon Jinushi-Sei No Tenkai Ni Kansuru Jakkan No Ronten," *Nōgyōshi Kenkyū* 31–32 (1998).
56. Nakamura, "Nihon Jinushiseishi Kenkyū Josetsu," 238.
57. Ellen Meiksins Wood, "The Separation of the Economic and the Political in Capitalism," *New Left Review* I, no. 127 (1981).
58. Hoston, *Marxism and the Crisis of Development in Prewar Japan*.
59. As Vivek Chibber argues in his confrontation with not-unrelated currents in Indian historiography; see Vivek Chibber, *Postcolonial Theory and the Specter of Capital* (London: Verso, 2013).

CHAPTER 10

Rural Property Relations and the Regional Dynamics of Brazilian Capitalism

Chris Carlson

Brazilian economist Edmar Bacha once referred to his country as "Belindia"—a mixture between a small, wealthy country like Belgium and a large, poor country like India, all rolled into one.[1] This metaphor might seem like an exaggeration, but it is not totally inaccurate. In many ways, Brazil is an amalgamation of two or more very different societies co-existing within the same country. The social and economic structures vary significantly from one region to the next, especially between the northern and southern regions, and this has had major consequences for the country's historical development.

In some ways, Brazil's development process is comparable to the United States, loosely divided along North-South lines. However, in Brazil it is the Southeast that became the wealthier, more industrialized part of the country. The Northeast has remained poor and underdeveloped to this day. Much of the Northeast still maintains a social structure heavily shaped by its history of slavery and plantation agriculture, whereas much of the Southeast came to be characterized by smallholder agriculture, and rapid industrialization by the early twentieth century. The result is that Brazil's

C. Carlson (✉)
Graduate Center of the City University of New York, New York, NY, USA

X. Lafrance, C. Post (eds.), *Case Studies in the Origins of Capitalism*, Marx, Engels, and Marxisms,
https://doi.org/10.1007/978-3-319-95657-2_10

Northeast region is today, with a population of nearly 60 million people, the largest concentration of mass poverty in the Western Hemisphere. Meanwhile, Brazil's Southeast is by far the wealthiest and most industrialized region in Latin America.

These very stark regional differences have often been overlooked when discussing the development of capitalism in Brazil. Scholars have tended to view capitalism as having arrived in Brazil as a result of colonialism and Brazil's insertion into the world economy. Others see it as the result of the transition from slavery to wage labor in the nineteenth and the proletarianization of the peasantry in the twentieth century. In either case, the transition is seen as having occurred, uniformly across Brazil in a similar fashion.

In this chapter, I argue that there are significant differences in how and when capitalism emerged in the various regions of Brazil, and these differences are key to understanding the vast divergence in development outcomes. In the Southeast, the transition occurred in a manner similar to the Northern United States, with an expanding frontier of family farms where access to land was mediated by market mechanisms.[2] This led to capitalist property relations, with producers subject to market discipline and a dynamic of specialization, innovation, and accumulation.[3] In the Northeast, wealthy and powerful elites appropriated land outside of market mechanisms, leaving them free to allow their land to be underutilized or sit completely idle. These differences have had enormous consequences for the development trajectory of each region.

This chapter provides an account of the development of rural property relations in the Southeast and Northeast regions of Brazil. I argue that the key difference between these two regions was the predominant forms of land appropriation that came to characterize the rural economy by the early twentieth century. This led to a very different rural productive logic in each region, which greatly impacted their subsequent trajectories in terms of industrialization. After a brief review of the debate on the origins of capitalism in Brazil, I attempt to show that an account based on the development of rural property relations allows the most complete understanding of the stark regional differences that continue to characterize Brazil to this day.

The Origins of Capitalism in Brazil

The question of how and when capitalism first emerged in Brazil was at the center of debate among Brazilian scholars in the twentieth century, especially between Marxists and other leftists concerned with the country's relative underdevelopment. To these intellectuals, the question was crucial not only for understanding the roots of Brazil's economic "backwardness", but also for developing adequate political strategies to transform the economy and set it on the path to greater prosperity. Depending on their view of how far capitalism had advanced within the country, scholars often came to very different conclusions about what the key causes and potential solutions were for the country's major social problems.

One of the earliest contributions to this debate came out of the Brazilian Communist Party (PCB) in the 1940s and 1950s. The "feudal current", mostly members of the PCB, argued that the dominance of "feudalism" or "semi-feudalism" in the Brazilian countryside was the root cause of underdevelopment.[4] The predominance of large estates and their use of various forms of non-capitalist labor relations was evidence the vestiges of feudalism inherited from the days of colonialism were still present. Portugal purportedly exported its feudal system to the colonies, and this system persevered well into the twentieth century, as extra-economic forms of control over labor kept workers tied to the large estates in situations of virtual servitude.

This understanding of the problem led these scholars to the conclusion that a thorough land reform was needed in order to "uproot and destroy, in our agriculture, the feudal type of relations of production …".[5] It was the pre-capitalist relations in agriculture that were the fundamental limiting factor on the country's economic development, as they greatly constrained the purchasing power of the rural masses and, thereby, prevented the expansion of a domestic market to fuel industrialization. Dividing up the large estates and eradicating the backward labor regimes would allow for a capitalist transformation of the countryside, and the Communists called for an alliance with the "national bourgeoisie" to challenge the landed classes and assist in ushering in capitalist relations. This view lost credibility, however, when in 1964 the bourgeoisie and landed classes united against the workers and peasants behind a repressive military coup d'état.

In response to the feudal current, another perspective arose that was influential on the Brazilian left for much the rest of the twentieth century. From this perspective, Brazil's agricultural sector was not "feudal" or "semi-feudal" as others had claimed, but rather had been capitalist from the moment Brazil became incorporated into the colonial mercantile system and began exporting goods on the world market.[6] Any seemingly pre-capitalist characteristics in the countryside were argued to instead be capitalist, or at least functional to capital accumulation in the cities, and therefore not a barrier to industrialization.[7] This view overlapped with the emerging dependency perspective, which sought to explain underdevelopment as the product of imperialism and integration into the capitalist world economy, and not on a pre-capitalist history in Brazil.[8]

From the dependency view, it was the workings of capitalism itself that progressively underdeveloped the countries of the periphery, as the global economy siphoned off wealth from poor countries to the rich countries, and relegated poor countries to the periphery of the international division of labor. The large rural estates and various forms of tenancy that earlier scholars had pointed to were not seen as representing vestiges of feudalism, but rather had been capitalist since the colonial period due to their involvement in commodity production for the market and their incorporation into the international division of labor. Therefore, from this point of view, there was no need to usher in capitalist relations or seek capitalist transformation in the countryside. Rather, global capitalism was the primary barrier to development, and, therefore, socialism was the only likely solution.[9]

Along these same lines were those who criticized the nature of the Brazilian bourgeoisie and questioned whether Brazil had really experienced a "bourgeois revolution" that would lead to full-fledged capitalist development. From this view, Brazilian social relations had long been capitalist, yet there had been a partial transition out of "mercantile" or capitalism, and thus Brazil's bourgeoisie remained "dependent" on foreign capital and unwilling to lead the fight for democracy and development.[10] The incomplete industrialization process was not due to the persistence of backward social relations in the countryside, as the feudal current had claimed, but rather was the product of the dependence on and collaboration with multinational corporations that were progressively penetrating Brazil's domestic market in the second half of the twentieth century.[11] In other words, the crux of the problem still had to do with Brazil's international trade relations and position in the world economy, not the persistence of pre-capitalist relations of production.

Subsequent studies on the social relations in agriculture, however, at least partially challenged these dependency interpretations, and provided support to certain aspects of the feudal thesis. Various scholars showed that, in fact, pre-capitalist or non-capitalist labor relations had persisted in agriculture until well beyond the end of slavery and that the transition to wage labor on the large estates was a fairly recent phenomenon.[12] After the abolition of slavery in the late nineteenth century, various forms of labor tenancy, sharecropping, and debt peonage were used by landlords to keep workers tied to the large estates in both northern and southern Brazil, and this persisted until well into the twentieth century in most places. This did not mean that social relations in the countryside had been "feudal", as the feudal current claimed, but it did support the notion that there had been an incomplete development of capitalist relations in rural zones. In the Northeast, the transition to wage labor in agriculture did not occur until the 1960s and 1970s and has still not fully occurred in some places.[13]

This relatively late transition to wage labor has led many contemporary scholars to view the 1960s and 1970s as the beginning of capitalist agriculture in Brazil. As traditional sharecropping and labor tenancy regimes were slowly phased out, there was a certain modernization in terms of the technology and methods of production used on the large estates, and agriculture throughout the country became increasingly capitalized in the second half of the twentieth century. This has come to be seen by many as evidence that capitalist relations finally penetrated the Brazilian countryside around this time, as the traditional landholdings transitioned to capitalistic enterprises characterized by modern forms of labor relations, and a certain rationalization of production began to occur.[14]

Indeed, today there is little debate on the nature of productive relations in the Brazilian countryside. It is generally assumed among scholars that agriculture is fully governed by capitalist dynamics and that capitalist modernization is now running its course. In fact, many now see agricultural modernization as part of the problem in rural areas, as it expels workers from the land and reduces employment in agriculture, thus worsening urban unemployment and poverty.[15] Therefore, the focus of many scholars has shifted more to the *distribution* of land, rather than the specific social relations or productive logic on the land. Extreme land concentration is seen as the primary cause of poverty, as it concentrates wealth, while at the same time condemning the vast majority of the rural population to precarious conditions. The obvious solution, therefore, is land reform and the widespread redistribution of land to the landless masses.

What none of these various interpretations can account for, however, are the vast regional differences within Brazil and the fact that some regions did, in fact, develop highly productive, modernized agriculture from relatively early on, while other regions remained stagnant and undercapitalized throughout the twentieth century. In the Southeast, for example, a clear process of capitalist development in agriculture was set in motion in the early twentieth century, long before the decline of labor tenancy and the generalization of wage labor in the countryside. Meanwhile, in much of northern Brazil, modernization has been much more drawn-out and episodic, even after the transition to capitalist labor relations in the second half of the twentieth century.

In other words, the changes in labor relations in agriculture cannot explain the very different dynamics that developed in agriculture at different times and in different places in Brazil. Although the feudal current was correct to point to the persistence of certain non-capitalist productive relations in the countryside, this does not explain why certain regions of the country became much more dynamic than others from relatively early on, despite the relative absence of capitalist labor relations. Likewise, the dependency-inspired approaches that focus on the international division of labor and Brazil's position in the capitalist world economy cannot explain why these factors affected the country so unevenly from one region to the next. Indeed, both the coffee economy of the Southeast and the sugar economy of the Northeast were heavily integrated into the world economy as primary exporters. Yet, one experienced rapid development in the twentieth century, while the other did not. This stark regional divergence simply cannot be adequately explained within the framework of dependency theory, or by a focus on changes in rural labor regimes.

A much more lucid account of the development of capitalism in Brazil can be had by looking at the historical development of rural *property relations* in the various regions of the country. Despite similarities in terms of labor regimes and integration into the world economy, the property relations in agriculture—the specific relationships between rural producers and their land—developed quite differently from one region of Brazil to the next, and this can go a long way toward explaining the differences in each region's process of modernization. Starting in the late nineteenth century, important changes began to occur in and around the coffee economy of São Paulo, leading to a dynamic agricultural sector that would drive a process of industrialization and development in the Southeast. Meanwhile, throughout much of the Northeast, the rural property relations changed very little during the twentieth century, even as the labor regimes and capital intensity of agriculture were significantly altered. This led to a much more conservative process of modernization in the Northeast and has greatly hindered its economic development to this day.

The key to understanding these differences is in the predominant forms of land appropriation that came to characterize each region by the late nineteenth and early twentieth centuries. Along the coffee frontier in the Southeast, certain changes began to emerge in how agricultural land was being acquired, leading to new property relations fundamentally distinct from much the rest of the country. These distinct property relations, in turn, resulted in very different production strategies among rural producers, and, thereby, a very different overall productive logic in the rural economy. In the Northeast, on the other hand, land appropriation remained dominated by wealthy elites and landlords who were not market-dependent, and therefore a similar transformation in property relations never occurred, leaving the agricultural sector to continue under a logic of low productivity and lack of investment. In the next section, I briefly trace the history of land appropriation in Brazil and attempt to show how the development of distinct rural property relations in the Northeast and Southeast led to key differences in the rural productive logic of each region and, thereby, their overall economic development.

Rural Property Relations in Brazil

The colonial system of land appropriation in Brazil was, in many ways, a product of the feudal system in Portugal. For the first three centuries after the arrival of the Portuguese, land in Brazil was distributed by the crown and its agents and was largely appropriated outside of any market mechanisms. The colony was divided into hereditary fiefs known as *capitanias* under the control of Portuguese nobles, and land within each *capitania* was distributed to potential settlers by land grants known as *sesmarias*, a system devised to distribute land in Portugal after the Black Death. Though the feudal system was never really transported to Brazil, vast swaths of land in Brazil were granted through the *sesmaria* system to anyone who possessed the necessary capital to invest in its cultivation, usually with unclear dimensions or boundaries dividing one land grant from another.[16]

Immediately, this system created a particular type of property relations that was not conducive to economic development. Despite the crown's intent to encourage intensive cultivation, the predominant way in which land was appropriated had the opposite effect. Because nobles and land grantees received the land at little cost to themselves, they were under little pressure to use the land effectively by making investments in its cultivation or maximizing output. Instead, they tended to utilize only a small portion of the land granted to them, leaving large areas uncultivated and virtually abandoned. This became a problem that the crown would deal with throughout the colonial period and to which a good solution would never be found. Even when threatened with the revocation of their land grants, grantees often made no attempt to increase investment.[17]

Instead of investing in intensive agriculture, many grantees channeled their profits into less risky, more profitable endeavors such as colonial trade or other urban businesses in the coastal cities. Much of their unused land in the countryside was eventually reverted back to the crown and became known as the *terras devolutas*, or "returned lands". This was the beginning of a pattern of land use and investment that would continue in various forms until well beyond the colonial period. Large landholders would seldom use their land effectively, while those without land grants would engage in other forms of non-market land appropriation, such as squatting on unused portions of the *sesmarias* or occupying the *terras devolutas* without any title to the land. These various types of informal land appropriation, known as *posse*, became a common way of acquiring land for both large and small landholdings, and led to production strategies very similar to the *sesmarias.*

Throughout the colonial period, those with capital to invest in slaves and sugar mills typically occupied the coastal areas and river valleys and set up production for export to European markets. Meanwhile, cattle ranchers slowly occupied vast areas of the interior, using the land very extensively and without clear boundaries or titles to the land. Those without capital to invest generally cleared their own plots of land on the margins of the large sugar and cattle plantations and engaged in subsistence production. Over time, this created the *latifundia-minifundia* agrarian structure so common throughout Latin America, characterized by large-scale plantation production occupying the vast majority of the land, and smallholder subsistence production squeezed into the interstices.

This situation would go largely unchanged until after independence in 1822, when local authorities did away with the *sesmaria* system and made various attempts to control the informal appropriation of land. The 1850 Land Law, for example, created an institutional framework for land markets and the buying and selling of land. Instead of distributing land via land grants, all public land was now to be sold in public auctions, and all irregular land being held as *posses* or *sesmarias* would have to be surveyed and registered with the Brazilian state to assure its legitimacy. However, while the 1850 law allowed for land to be legally bought and sold on the market for the first time, the newly formed Brazilian state did not have the institutional capacity to enforce it, and, therefore, informal occupation continued to be the primary form of land appropriation for many years to come.[18]

It was not until the end of the nineteenth century that this would begin to change, as the decreasing availability of vacant, well-located land meant market purchases were slowly becoming the predominant form of land appropriation in many regions. However, the lack of land titles and clear boundaries meant creditors were hesitant to loan money for the purchase of land, and laws dating from the colonial period made foreclosure against landowners difficult and expensive.[19] This meant that only those with considerable resources such as urban merchants and large landowners were generally able to acquire land on the market, as smallholders could seldom use land as collateral to obtain mortgages. This not only worsened the concentration of land in the hands of the elite, but it also perpetuated a kind of property relations similar to that of the colonial period.

Though by this time land appropriation was increasingly taking place via the market, the fact that this process was dominated by wealthy elites ended up recreating a relationship to the land in which low-intensity, low-investment productive strategies were still very much the norm. Large landowners and urban merchants engaged in various economic activities in the cities generally had a certain amount of wealth, and thus their economic survival seldom depended on maximizing the output of their landholdings. Land was purchased as a speculative investment, or as a source of income that could be channeled into other economic activities, without requiring major investments in intensive cultivation. In other words, even though much of the elite were purchasing land on the market by the late nineteenth century, they were still under little market pressure to maximize the output of their land, and production strategies that channeled investment away from productivity continued much like before.

By the end of the nineteenth century, a highly concentrated, plantation-based agrarian structure was well established up and down the eastern coast of the country, both in the sugar-producing Northeast and in the coffee-producing Southeast. With the decline and eventual abolition of slavery, large landowners increasingly secured laborers for their plantations through various forms of labor tenancy and sharecropping, and most former slaves remained on the plantations as tenants known as *moradores*. Yet, there were still massive amounts of high-quality frontier land in the interior of the country that had not been claimed or occupied by settlers, especially along the expanding coffee frontier in the Southeast. This left open the possibility for new forms of land appropriation to emerge, and, indeed, many smallholders in the Southeast began to acquire land of their own around the turn of the century. It was here that, for the first time, capitalist property relations emerged in the Brazilian countryside.

The Transition to Capitalism in the Southeast

Although Southeast Brazil would eventually become the center of Brazilian capitalism in the twentieth century, this was far from obvious at the end of the nineteenth century. The rural property relations were initially very similar to much the rest of the country, as land appropriation had taken place through the *sesmaria* system until well into the nineteenth century. Many of the first landholdings in and around São Paulo were granted to wealthy merchants and government officials speculating in land, and these were then subdivided and sold off to planters as the plantation economy expanded into the frontier zones of the state.[20] The booming coffee economy of the late nineteenth century led to a process of frontier expansion and meant that money could be made through land deals in which speculators would acquire title to land in the interior and then sell to those looking to establish coffee plantations. Informal *posse* of land was also common throughout the region, and powerful landowners often determined how land was to be appropriated by virtue of their control over the process of legitimating claims.[21]

While plantation owners in the expanding coffee economy often purchased land from speculators, it was usually sold for relatively low prices that did not reflect its quality or potential productivity. Land markets were fairly undeveloped until well into the nineteenth century, as land was abundant and generally not considered to be a valuable commodity. Indeed, lenders would seldom accept land as collateral for loans, instead using slaves and the debts of tenant laborers as mortgage security on plantations.[22] This meant that even when planters were indebted to lenders, there was little to compel them to use their land intensively, and they often left large tracts of their holdings entirely uncultivated or under extensive cattle grazing.

Much like the sugar and cocoa plantations in other parts of Brazil, coffee plantations in the Southeast seldom specialized production, but rather used various parts of their land for the production of various goods such as staple foods, cattle, cotton for clothing, and sugar cane. Little effort was made to maximize output or preserve the fertility of the land, as planters could simply move on to new lands when the soil became exhausted.[23] Instead of investing profits back into improving the productivity of their plantations, coffee planters tended to channel investment into acquiring more land, or into commerce, banking, and real estate in the cities.[24] In other words, the coffee economy of the Southeast region began with much the same logic as the plantation economies in other regions of Brazil, characterized by extensive production strategies, concentrated landownership, and the channeling of investment away from productivity.

What eventually brought change to this system were the growing labor needs of the plantation economy as the coffee frontier expanded westward. As the supply of slave and tenant laborers became ever scarcer over the course of the nineteenth century, it became clear to many planters that something needed to be done to provide the needed labor to keep their plantations operating. Internal traffic of slaves from northeastern Brazil had provided a partial solution after the end of the African slave trade in the mid-nineteenth century. Yet, by the second half of the century, the promotion of immigrant labor was increasingly seen as the only viable solution to the labor shortages, and many plantation owners began experimenting with various schemes to attract immigrants from Europe.[25] These efforts would eventually lead to a major influx of immigrants to Southeast Brazil and would have unforeseen consequences with respect to rural property relations.

Coffee planters sought the aid of the state to facilitate the immigration process, and the government of São Paulo began subsidizing the transportation costs of European immigrants who would sign labor contracts with the coffee plantations. The labor contracts usually included some kind of payment for the worker to tend a section of coffee groves on the plantation, along with housing and a subsistence plot for the family to grow subsistence crops. As time went on, planters and state authorities realized they would not be able to attract enough labor from Europe without offering better working conditions, and thus labor contracts became more generous, and conditions on the plantations slowly improved. By the 1870s, immigration into São Paulo was undergoing a sustained expansion, with the large majority of the immigrants coming from Italy in the first few decades and tens of thousands of Spanish and Portuguese immigrants contributing to a second wave in the early twentieth century.

State authorities had somewhat contradictory motives for promoting European immigration. On the one hand, the state needed to supply the dominant plantation economy with labor, and immigrant labor was seen as the only feasible way to do that. However, on the other hand, it was viewed to be in the state's interests to facilitate the settlement of the vast territory of the interior and to establish European-style smallholder agriculture, which was seen as more productive than plantation agriculture. This presented a dilemma for state authorities, for if immigrants could acquire their own land in São Paulo, then they would not work on the coffee plantations and thus would not provide a solution to the labor problem. Indeed, planters were pushing for laws to make it difficult for immigrants to acquire frontier land so that they would be forced to work for them.[26] Yet, most European immigrants were looking to go places where they could acquire land of their own, and, therefore, it would be difficult to attract them to Brazil without at least offering them this possibility.

In the end, the state tried to do both things, continuing to subsidize the immigration of those who would work on the plantations while also offering plots of land to colonists in various immigrant "colonies" around the state. But eventually state policy would become subordinated to the needs of the dominant plantation economy, and the state-sponsored colonization schemes were molded to serve the interests of planters. Immigrant colonies ended up being few and far between and were mostly located near large plantations with the purpose of serving as a reserve labor source to supply seasonal workers to coffee plantations. In addition, colony plots were sold at prices that most immigrants could not afford upon arriving to Brazil.[27] In other words, both the state and coffee planters initially tried to make it difficult for immigrants to acquire land, so that they would be forced to work on the plantations.

However, despite the various efforts to prevent it, many immigrants began acquiring land in São Paulo's frontier zones by the early twentieth century. The more generous labor contracts and improved working conditions that were necessary to attract waves of immigrants to work on São Paulo's plantations were also what eventually gave many plantation workers the possibility to acquire land of their own. After working on the coffee plantations for a few years to save up money, wave after wave of immigrant laborers began to move off the plantations and purchase land of their own on the frontier, only to be replaced by a new wave of immigrants coming into the country to work on the plantations. As one state authority reported in 1904:

> ... the coffee planter is constantly searching for laborers to replace those who, after a few years, having finished the last harvest and calculated their gains, go off in search of realizing the most natural and just aspiration of a rural worker: to possess, for himself and his family, a place where the plowing and sowing are for only his own benefit.[28]

A few years later another would report:

> The end of the harvest results in a general relocation of the agricultural workers. The *colonos* are truly nomadic ... It is no exaggeration to say that a third of all families employed in coffee cultivation move [off the plantations] each year ...[29]

It was this dynamic of plantation laborers saving up money and then moving off the plantations to buy land of their own that led to new patterns of land appropriation in Brazil's Southeast. The high demand for land from immigrant laborers meant that land began to be treated as a valuable commodity to be divided up and sold off. As a rapid increase in market sales began to take hold, land on the frontier would no longer be appropriated according to the prerogatives of powerful landowners and merchants, but rather would begin to be sold piecemeal on a competitive market. This appears to have happened through two separate processes. First, private landowners began to divide up and sell off excess or unused portions of their plantations, often with help from the state. Then, soon after, new entrepreneurs in the form of colonization companies began to buy up frontier land, divide it into plots, and sell it off to settlers.

After 1910, dozens of Brazilian and foreign-owned firms began operating in the western and northwestern parts of São Paulo state, founding new municipalities, and dividing up lands along the edges of the advancing railroad lines. One of the first of these companies was the San Paulo Land & Lumber Company, a firm of British and Brazilian investors that started with the purchase of 15,600 hectares in 1912. By 1922, advertisements in local newspapers were reporting that the company had sold more than 2000 plots of land of between 10 and 500 hectares to immigrants from Spain, Portugal, Italy, Germany, and Austria.[30] Various Japanese firms were also involved in colonization efforts, doing everything from transporting families from Japan, to purchasing state lands and dividing them into plots, and then selling those plots to the incoming families.[31] Railroad companies also got involved, selling off plots along the railway lines as they expanded out into the frontier.

This new pattern of land appropriation via competitive market sales led to fundamentally new property relations in the frontier zones of central and western São Paulo. The high demand for land from waves of immigrants caused land to experience a "fantastic jump" in prices, as its cost began to reflect the land's fertility and potential output.[32] In addition, land sold to immigrant smallholders was typically purchased through mortgages paid over a period of several years. This created a relationship of market dependence between landholders and their land where the ability to maintain possession of the land depended on their ability to continually produce a competitive level of output and sell that output on the market. Thus, in order to pay for their land, producers were forced to specialize production for the market and to channel investment back into the productivity of the land to remain competitive and assure their economic survival.

The same pattern of colonization that began in western São Paulo would characterize the process of frontier expansion throughout Southeast Brazil during much of the twentieth century. Companies such as the *Companhia de Terras Norte do Paraná* and the *Companhia Viação São Paulo-Mato Grosso* carried the colonization activities over into the bordering states of Paraná and Mato Grosso. The incessant dividing up of land into plots to be sold to smallholders transformed vast areas of these southeastern states from uncultivated backlands and extensive cattle ranching to flourishing centers of smallholder agriculture. Meanwhile, the development of this parallel economy based on smallholder agriculture began to weaken the dominance of the old plantation economy and would eventually lead to much larger transformations in and around the state of São Paulo.

As the countryside became increasingly dominated by independent farmers compelled by market forces to specialize production and maximize productivity, this led to rising agricultural productivity and a major expansion in the production of various agricultural goods for the market, such as grains, cotton, fruit, and livestock. This supplied many of the agricultural inputs for a budding industrial sector in the cities, while also creating an ever-growing demand for industrial goods from this new class of rural consumers that were increasingly purchasing their subsistence needs and farm inputs on the market. Indeed, it is argued that it was the development of this new class of agricultural producers in the countryside that was the basis for the rapid industrialization of São Paulo in the first decades of the twentieth century, as new industries emerged to meet the demand of this growing domestic market.[33]

New business opportunities created by the changing rural economy also led to important shifts in the investment decisions of much of São Paulo's traditional elite. For example, as the coffee frontier expanded ever westward, one group of prominent coffee planters began to shift their investment toward transportation infrastructure, founding a major railroad company, the *Companhia Paulista de Estradas de Ferro*, to transport coffee to the coastal ports. Then, as the dynamics of the land market began to change with the influx of immigration, the same investors founded a colonization company, the *Companhia de Agricultura, Imigração e Colonização*, to divide up large landholdings into small plots and sell them off to immigrant smallholders, often along the lines of their growing railroad network.[34] Several years later, when the burgeoning smallholder economy once again presented new opportunities, the same investors got involved in farm mechanization and agricultural infrastructure projects directed toward this new class of rural producers.

Indeed, the industries leading the growth in the first decades of the twentieth century were, in large part, those sectors associated with the burgeoning small and medium-sized producers. Industries such as cotton textiles and food processing expanded rapidly and began to rival coffee's predominant position as the state's economy became increasingly integrated and diversified. The number of cotton mills more than doubled between 1900 and 1915, and the value of total industrial input also nearly doubled in the same time period.[35] With the development of consumer goods industries—such as textiles, beer, soft drinks, shoes, hats, and furniture—a capital goods industry began to develop by the 1920s to supply these local industries with production-related inputs.[36] By 1940, the state of São Paulo possessed the largest agglomeration of manufacturing capacity in all of Latin America, and, in contrast to plantation economies throughout the rest of the continent, the manufacturing sector quickly eclipsed other sectors, including coffee, in the first decades of the twentieth century.

In other words, the emergence of capitalist property relations in the rural areas of São Paulo led to the transformation of the local economy from one almost entirely dependent on a single agricultural export—coffee—to a highly diversified and industrialized economy in the first half of the twentieth century. Rising agricultural productivity led to rising income per capita in the countryside, fueling demand for industrial goods and spurring the rapid growth of other sectors of the economy. This resulted in a sustained process of industrialization largely centered around the state of São Paulo, and one that would remain concentrated in this region for much the rest of the twentieth century. By the end of the century, the state of São Paulo had an economy that was, all by itself, the second largest economy in all of South America, with among the highest standards of living of any Latin American country.

This contrasts greatly with much the rest of Brazil, and especially the Northeast region, which remained one of the poorest areas in Latin America throughout the twentieth century. Whereas the state of São Paulo eventually came to account for more than a third of Brazil's total GDP, and over 40 percent of all industry, the nine states that make up Brazil's Northeast altogether only accounted for about 15 percent of GDP and around 10 percent of the nation's industry, despite a significantly larger total population.[37] As will be explained in the next section, this is largely due to the fact that the rural property relations in the Northeast underwent a very distinct evolution from that of Southeast Brazil, with enormous consequences for the region's overall development process.

An Incomplete Transition in the Northeast

Unlike in the Southeast, in Northeast Brazil there was little need to import immigrant labor after the decline of slavery in the second half of the nineteenth century. Without a rapidly expanding frontier of plantation agriculture, most landowners were able to secure labor locally through various tenancy arrangements, and they began to sell off their slaves to coffee planters in the Southeast when they were no longer needed. Natural population growth, together with concentrated landownership in the hands of the elite, meant that there was by this time enough of a landless population so that landowners could secure laborers by offering them access to plots of land on their plantations in exchange for labor, and this led to the eventual replacement of slaves by labor tenants known as *moradores.*

Moreover, by the turn of the century, most of the best land in the Northeast had already been claimed, and little public land remained for the taking. This meant that there was less chance that immigrants would be able to acquire land of their own and become independent farmers.[38] Any newcomers to the region would likely be forced to work for the sugar planters or cattle ranchers, and, unlike in São Paulo, they would have less hope of eventually escaping that fate by moving off the plantations onto their own land.[39] For this reason—and probably for reasons related to the tropical climate—there would be no significant waves of immigrants to the Northeast around the turn of the century and thus no impetus for dynamic land markets and the related changes in property relations that occurred in the Southeast.

Instead, land appropriation in the Northeast remained dominated by elites like urban businessmen, merchants, and large landowners throughout this period and well into the twentieth century. As the sugar industry transitioned from the more primitive sugar mills powered by animal and water power (*engenhos*), to more modern steam-driven plants (*usinas*) around the turn of the century, there was also a transition to ever-larger productive units as the *usinas* absorbed many of the *engenhos* in their immediate orbit. This occurred through a process in which plantation owners and urban investors took advantage of government incentives and cheap credit to establish modern sugar plants throughout the countryside and then acquire massive amounts of the surrounding farmland once occupied by the *engenhos*.[40]

In the drier interior, where sugar production was not feasible, massive cattle ranches and cotton farms operating on the basis of sharecropping solidified their control over the vast majority of the land. Though most of this land was originally acquired through colonial land grants, by the end of the nineteenth century, wealthy elites from the cities were also buying up large tracts of land in the interior. This was not to be used for intensive agriculture, but rather as investments used as a hedge against inflation and to store wealth accumulated in other economic activities. Often times these large tracts of land remained virtually abandoned or were used very extensively as free-range cattle ranches, with little investment in improvements or the intensification of production.

In places that were not being used for large-scale commercial agriculture, smallholders managed to obtain a small portion of the land. Landless peasants would often squat on unused or marginal land, using it for subsistence crops like beans and corn. Their access to credit was limited, since they had generally squatted on land to which they had no title and could not prove ownership. Even when peasants did formally purchase land, banks would seldom accept their small plots as collateral for loans and generally preferred to only lend to large landholders. This meant that smallholders in the Northeast seldom acquired land through market mechanisms like mortgages or long-term rental agreements in which their possession of the land depended on their ability to maintain a competitive level of output. As a result, there was little to force them into market specialization and capital accumulation as occurred among smallholders in the Southeast by the early twentieth century. Instead, in the Northeast smallholders generally adopted low-risk production strategies that prioritized subsistence over market production and invested little in raising productivity.[41]

The continuation of these various types of land appropriation throughout the twentieth century perpetuated and recreated property relations that allowed for a continuation of a low-productivity logic of production. Unlike agricultural producers in the Southeast, who were compelled by market forces to continually maximize productivity, in the Northeast landholders were generally under little market pressure to maximize productivity and therefore did not systematically channel investment back into improvements. This was especially the case among the large landowners who occupied the vast majority of the land. As members of the economic and political elite, these landowners seldom depended on increasing the productivity of the land to assure their economic survival. They had wealth from a range of business activities and had privileged access to state resources and loans, meaning they could channel their profits away from agriculture into consumption or commerce, with little risk of losing their landholdings. Land was used as a basis to expand their wealth, by channeling profits and credits into other investment opportunities, while leaving vast areas of fertile land under low-intensity production.

Indeed, technology in sugar production in the Northeast changed little for centuries before the emergence of the *usinas* around the turn of the century. The adoption of new technology took place only when the state began to provide major incentives at the end of the nineteenth century. Even then, the agricultural side of production changed very little. Planters seldom made investments in improvements such as irrigation, fertilizers, or new crop varieties that would improve the productivity of their land. The same variety of sugar cane planted by the Portuguese in the sixteenth century was still widely grown three centuries later, even though improved varieties and technologies were well known in other parts of the world.[42] Resistance to new varieties continued well into the twentieth century, while mechanization in soil preparation, harvesting, and irrigation was only sporadically adopted. Growth in total output was seldom the result of improving the productivity of land or laborers, but rather took place through the expansion of internal frontiers, for example, the expansion of cultivation onto unused lands on the plantations.[43]

By the mid-twentieth century, large landowners were beginning to adopt certain modern technologies. Yet they were still far from maximizing the productivity of their land. This led to what scholars have termed the "conservative modernization" or "pseudo-modernization" of plantation agriculture. Certain improvements were adopted on large farms, yet the low-intensity production strategies often continued relatively unchanged. In sugar production, the use of fertilizers and pesticides greatly increased in the second half of the twentieth century, yet soil preparation remained primitive, and planting and harvesting continued to be manual in most places. Yields slowly increased, but remained significantly lower than those of the sugar plantations of São Paulo, where technology was constantly updated and mechanization was more widespread. Likewise, in cattle ranching, vaccines and planted pastures were increasingly adopted by the 1970s and 1980s. Yet the total output per hectare increased only slightly, while vast areas of fertile land apt for more intensive, higher-value crops remained under extensive cattle grazing.[44]

This same logic of production has continued into the twenty-first century. Despite the rise and fall of various elite groups over the years, the vast majority of the land still remains in the hands of the old elite, and most of the major sugar mills continue to be controlled by descendants of prominent landholding families. These elite groups have wide-ranging economic empires, yet they are well known for leaving large portions of their landholdings virtually unused or under low-productivity activities. In 2010, the national land reform agency reported that between 75 and 85 percent of all large landowners' land in the Northeast was considered "unproductive".[45] This meant that the vast majority of the large landowners' land did not meet even the minimum level of productivity or land use requirements as determined by federal law. By contrast, only 33 percent of large landholdings in the state of São Paulo were considered "unproductive", and this is despite the fact that productivity requirements are much more stringent for the Southeast region.

Among smallholders in the Northeast, the overall logic of production has also continued much as before, even though their situation was slowly eroded in the second half of the twentieth century. Demographic growth and the continual subdivision of small farms resulted in decreasing plot sizes for most small farmers, eventually rendering them inadequate for subsistence purposes. This meant that most smallholders were forced to find other forms of income outside of agriculture in order to supplement farm income, and most began selling an ever-greater portion of their production on the market. Nevertheless, smallholders' land generally remained under traditional methods of production, with little investment in modern technologies or improvements.[46] Although state policies have greatly increased the availability of credit among small farmers, most have continued to prefer low-input, low-risk production methods rather than take on the necessary debts for investment in modern inputs and more intensive production.[47] Thus, even though small farms are generally more productive than large farms, they have also remained locked into a logic of low productivity.

In other words, the specific property relations that developed historically in the Northeast have caused both small and large producers to engage in production strategies that involve low investment in productivity and, therefore, have cut short the process of capital accumulation in agriculture. This is linked to the various ways in which land has been appropriated in this region, outside the constraints of competitive land markets and market competition, which has freed producers from the pressure to systematically invest in new technologies and increase productivity. This has translated to low productivity in the agricultural sector as a whole, greatly limiting income growth among the rural masses and inhibiting the growth of other sectors of the economy, such as industry.

As a result, the industrial sector in the Northeast has long been far smaller and less dynamic than its counterpart in Southeast Brazil, and many scholars agree that this has its roots in the particular social structure and productive logic that resulted from the underlying agrarian economy. Highly concentrated land ownership translated into high levels of inequality and, therefore, a relatively small group of potential consumers with significant purchasing power.[48] Meanwhile, low agricultural productivity led to low wages in rural zones, which also put downward pressure on wages in urban zones. This resulted in a rather narrow local market for industrial goods in the Northeast, despite a relatively large population, and, therefore, less investment in local production of industrial goods.

Those industries that did emerge in the Northeast have been almost entirely concentrated in low-tech, labor-intensive production, mostly of low-value, non-durable goods like textiles and food processing. Few of the more modern, high-tech, non-durable, or capital goods industries that are common in the Southeast region have never gained much traction in the northeastern states. This is also due to the general characteristics of the local market in the Northeast and the lack of economies of scale for higher-value industrial goods. Meanwhile, weak demand for industrial goods has led to oligopolistic market structures in which only a few firms dominate the market in each sector. This often results in a kind of "peaceful collusion" between industrial firms in the Northeast, and a lack of competitive pressures, which only further reduces the dynamism of the industrial sector and curtails industrial growth.[49]

The end result is that the Northeast remains vastly less industrialized than the southern regions of Brazil, and its economy remains far less diversified, still very dependent on the production of primary goods like sugar, cotton, and cattle. Total manufacturing output in the Northeast today is less than one-fifth of what it is in the Southeast region, and only about one-fourth in per capita terms. Whereas changes in rural property relations in the Southeast spurred high-productivity agriculture and rapid industrial growth in the first decades of the twentieth century, the perpetuation of certain property relations in the Northeast impeded productivity growth in agriculture and thereby cut short the industrialization process. This was the primary factor at the root of the development differences that began to appear on a regional level in Brazil around the turn of the twentieth century and which have continued to this day.

Conclusion

The Brazilian case provides strong support for a property relations-centered account of the development of capitalism. Other frameworks that focus on the international division of labor, or on the changing labor regimes, cannot adequately explain the drastically different outcomes that characterized the various regions of the country in the twentieth century. Both Northeast and Southeast Brazil were similarly integrated into the international division of labor as exporters of primary goods, yet one region experienced economic development and rapid industrialization, while the other did not. And while the transition toward proletarianized labor differed in various ways from one region to the next, these differences do not explain the regions' different economic paths, as the particular logic of production in agriculture in each region remained relatively constant throughout the twentieth century, despite the changing labor regimes.

A more important variable for examining the regional dynamics of Brazilian capitalism are the property relations that came to characterize agriculture in each region. It was these relations—the specific relationships between landholders and the land—that largely determined the particular investment and reproduction strategies of agricultural producers in each place, and, thereby, the overall productive logic of the rural economy. These relationships were greatly influenced by the predominant forms of land appropriation that were carried out in each region, which by the twentieth century were fundamentally different in the Southeast and the Northeast. Capitalist property relations first emerged in the state of São Paulo when land appropriation became dominated by smallholder farmers and competitive land markets, and this then spread throughout much of the Southeast and beyond. Meanwhile, in much of the northern part of the country, such a transition never took place, and land appropriation continued to be dominated by wealthy elites and subsistence smallholders not subject to the same constraints as producers in the Southeast. This fundamental difference set the two regions on very different economic paths, and would result in the creation of two very different societies within the same country.

Notes

1. Edmar Lisboa Bacha, "El economist y el rey de Belindia: una fabula para tecnócratas," *Cuadernos De Economía* 11, no. 33 (1974): 60–64.
2. Charles Post, *The American Road to Capitalism: studies in class-structure, economic development, and political conflict, 1620–1877* (Leiden, The Netherlands: Brill, 2011).
3. For a discussion of capitalist property relations, see Robert Brenner, "Agrarian class structure and economic development in pre-industrial Europe," *Past & Present* 70, no. 1 (1976): 30–75, or Ellen Wood, *The Origin of Capitalism: A Longer View*. (London: Verso, 2002).
4. Nelson Werneck Sodré, *Formação da sociedade Brasileira* (Rio de Janeiro: José Olympio, 1944).
5. Alberto Passos Guimarães, *Quatro séculos de latifúndio* (Rio de Janeiro: Paz e Terra, 1964), 32.
6. Caio Prado Jr., *A revolução brasileira* (São Paulo: Brasiliense, 1966).
7. Francisco Oliveira, "Economia brasileira: critica a razão dualista," *Estudos CEBRAP* 2 (1972).
8. André Gunder Frank, *Capitalism and Development in Latin America* (New York: Monthly Review, 1967).
9. Theotônio dos Santos, *Socialismo o fascismo: el Nuevo charácter de dependencia y el dilema latinoamericano* (Buenos Aires: Periferia, 1973).
10. Florestan Fernandes, *Estrutura de classes e subdesenvolvimento* (Rio de Janeiro: Zahar, 1968).

11. Fernando Henrique Cardoso and Enzo Faletto. *Dependencia e desenvolvimento na América latina: ensaio de interpretação sociológica* (Rio de Janeiro: Zahar, 1970); Peter B. Evans, *Dependent development: the alliance of multinational, state, and local capital in Brazil* (Princeton: Princeton University Press, 1979).
12. Octávio Ianni, *A classe operária vai ao campo* (São Paulo: Caderno CEBRAP, 1976); Juarez Rubens Brandão Lopes, *Do latifundio a empresa: unidade e diversidade do capitalismo no campo* (Rio de Janeiro: Centro Edelstein de Pesquisas Sociais, 2008).
13. Thomas D. Rogers, *The Deepest Wounds: A Labor and Environmental History of Sugar in Northeast Brazil* (Chapel Hill: University of North Carolina Press, 2010).
14. Lopes, *Do latifúndio a empresa*; Anthony W. Pereira, *The end of the peasantry: the rural labor movement in northeast Brazil, 1961–1988* (Pittsburgh: University of Pittsburgh Press, 1997)
15. Antonio Canuto, "Agronegócio: a modernização conservadora que gera exclusão pela produtividade," *Revista NERA*, ano 7, no. 5 (2004).
16. Though the land system was similar, other features of the feudal system, such as independent taxation by regional lords, were less common.
17. Fragmon Carlos Borges, "Origens históricas da propriedade da Terra," in *A questão agrária no Brasil*, ed. João Pedro Stédile (São Paulo: Expressão Popular, 2011), 259–281.
18. Bernardo Pinheiro Mueller, "The economic history, political economy and frontier settlement of land in Brazil" (PhD diss., University of Illinois, 1994), 62–69.
19. Mary Ann Mahony, "The world cacao made: Society, politics, and history in southern Bahia, Brazil, 1822–1919" (PhD diss., Yale University, 1996), 359–413.
20. Warren Dean, *Rio Claro: A Brazilian Plantation System, 1820–1920* (Stanford University Press, 1976), 11–16.
21. Mauricio A. Font, *Coffee and Transformation in São Paulo, Brazil* (Lanham, Md: Lexington Books, 2010), 23.
22. Dean, *Rio Claro*, 34.
23. Ibid., 25.
24. Ibid., 192.
25. Dean, *Rio Claro*, 90; Thomas Holloway, "The coffee colono in São Paulo, Brazil: migration and mobility, 1880–1930", in *Land and Labour in Latin America*, ed. Kenneth Duncan and Ian Rutledge (Cambridge University Press, 1977).
26. Warren Dean, "Latifundia and Land Policy in Nineteenth-Century Brazil," *The Hispanic American Historical Review* 51, no. 4 (1971): 614.

27. Secretary of Agriculture Annual Report, 1901, 130, Arquivo Público do Estado de São Paulo, São Paulo.
28. Secretary of Agriculture, 1904, 133–134.
29. Sergio Silva, *Expansão cafeeira e origens da indústria no Brasil* (São Paulo: Alfa-Omega 1976), 54.
30. Pierre Monbeig, *Pioneiros e fazendeiros de São Paulo* (São Paulo: Editora Hucitec, 1984), 202.
31. Secretary of Agriculture, 1914, 147.
32. Silva, *Expansão*, 72.
33. Font, *Coffee and Transformation*, 89–121.
34. Monbeig, *Pioneiros e fazendeiros*, 238.
35. Warren Dean, *The Industrialization of São Paulo: 1880–1945* (Austin: University of Texas Press, 1969), 83.
36. Mauricio A. Font, *Coffee, Contention, and Change in the Making of Modern Brazil* (Cambridge, MA: Basil Blackwell, 1990), 98–101.
37. Brazilian Institute of Geography and Statistics (IBGE), *Contas Regionais Do Brasil 2005–2009*, https://ww2.ibge.gov.br.
38. Teresa Sales, *Agreste, Agrestes: trasformações recentes na agricultura nordestina* (Rio de Janeiro: Paz e Terra, 1982), 71.
39. Peter L. Eisenberg, *The sugar industry in Pernambuco: modernization without change 1840–1910* (Berkeley: University of California Press, 1974), 233.
40. Gadiel Perruci, *A republica das usinas: um estudo de historia social e económica do Nordeste, 1889–1930* (Rio de Janeiro: Paz e Terra, 1978), 123–127.
41. World Bank, *Brazil—Rural development issues and options in Northeast Brazil* (Washington, DC: World Bank, 1975), vi-ix.
42. Maria da Guia Santos-Gareis, "Senhores de engenho e inovação tecnológica; Caso do Nordeste Brasileiro," *Iberoamericana* III, no. 11 (2003): 21–39.
43. Rogers, *The deepest wounds*, 99–124.
44. Ana Maria de Souza Mello Bicalho and Scott William Hoefle, "Urban Capital and Pseudo-modernization of Agriculture in the Rural Hinterland of Northeast Brazil," *Yearbook (Conference of Latin Americanist Geographers)* 15, (1989): 35–48.
45. National Institute of Colonization and Agrarian Reform (INCRA), National System of Rural Cadaster, 2010, https://sncr.serpro.gov.br.
46. Sales, *Agreste, Agrestes*, 180; Anália Carmem Silva de Almeida, Rinaldo Luiz Caraciolo Ferreira, Mércia Virgínia Ferreira dos Santos, José Antônio Aleixo da Silva, Mário Andrade Lira, "Caracterização de produtores e propriedades rurais em três municípios do estado de Pernambuco," *Revista Caatinga* 19, no. 2 (2006): 323–332.

47. World Bank, *Brazil*, 52–60.
48. Luciano Coutinho and João Carlos Ferraz, *Estudo da competitividade brasileira* (Campinas: Papirus, 1994).
49. Carlos António Brandão, "O processo de subdesenvolvimento, as desigualdades espaciais e o 'jogo das escalas'," in *Desigualdades regionais*, ed. Secretaria do Planejamento (Salvador: SEI, Governo da Bahia, 2004).

CHAPTER 11

The Political Economy of the Transition to Capitalism in the Ottoman Empire and Turkey: Towards a New Interpretation

Eren Duzgun

If there is one argument in the field of Turkish Studies that unites different currents more than any other, it is that the Ottoman Empire, and its primary heir, Turkey, transitioned to capitalism during the late nineteenth and early twentieth centuries. Drawing on Political Marxism, this chapter provides a theoretical critique of this framework and offers a new periodization of the transition to capitalism in Turkey. In contrast to the conventional interpretation, I argue that there was no transition to capitalism in Turkey until the 1950s, and that the late Ottoman Empire (1839–1918) and early Turkish Republic (1923–1945) pursued a non-capitalist path to modernity. While the transition to capitalism began in the 1950s, capitalist development was limited and protracted. In addition, the period after the 1950s witnessed the rise of a new capitalist class in provincial Anatolian towns. Disgruntled by their systematic exclusion from the state-generated economic rents, commercial groups of Anatolian towns organized themselves in and through the Islamic "National View" Movement (NVM).

E. Duzgun (✉)
Leiden University, Leiden, Netherlands

X. Lafrance, C. Post (eds.), *Case Studies in the Origins of Capitalism*, Marx, Engels, and Marxisms,
https://doi.org/10.1007/978-3-319-95657-2_11

The movement, *pace* its conventional interpretations, neither supported a "petty bourgeois" or statist capitalism, nor was it simply an Islamic critique of the developing market society. Instead, the movement envisioned a novel political space as the foundation of a capitalist industrialization strategy unencumbered by earlier Republican policies. Although the NVM was unable to take control of the state, its conservative capitalist heritage was appropriated by the Justice and Development Party, which has led to an unprecedented consolidation and deepening of capitalist social relations in Turkey since the beginning of the new millennium.

Market Dependence: The "Politics" and the "International" of Capitalism

Different theoretical starting points usually inform different conceptions of capitalism, which in turn provide competing answers to the problem as to how, where and when capitalism emerged and expanded. The debate on the spatial and temporal origins of capitalism continues; however, much that has been written about the origin of capitalism is consistently hamstrung by two methodological problems. First, many theories of the development of capitalism assume rather than explain capitalism's origins. The presence of trade, wage labor and private property are taken to be the necessary precursors of capitalism. The problem is, as Ellen Wood famously put it, this tends to presume the prior existence of capitalism (in some embryonic form) in order to explain its emergence. Capitalism clearly increases the volume of production, commerce and the size of a commodifiable workforce. However, they collapse capitalism's consequences and causes.

Second, the simple equation of capitalism to wage labor or trade fails to capture the historically and spatially changing dynamics of the transition to capitalism. Identifying capitalism with wage labor, for example, tends to obscure the fact that under certain socio-legal and international circumstances non-wage forms (such as commodity production based on non-waged family labor) "can and have permitted a more or less direct transition to capitalism" without widespread dispossession of the workforce.[1] As such, the problem with conventional accounts is not only the circularity of their argument, but their recurrent tendency to posit certain societies as ideal types and judging other societies based on the extent to which they conform to or diverge from a pre-given and static norm of capitalism.

Read together, we need a concept of capitalism that *both* avoids circular explanations of capitalism's origins *and* captures the international and historical conditions of the transition to capitalism. Political Marxism (PM) is able to provide precisely such a specific and dynamic conception of capitalism by drawing attention to the "political" and the "international" aspects of the transition to capitalism. PM contends that the transitions to capitalism cannot be understood as the quantitative extension of any "economic" phenomena, but are best understood in terms of socially and temporally varying ways of organizing human relations and the institutions that produce the historically specific forms of "market dependence".[2] Put differently, the transitions to capitalism did not follow a universal pattern, but all transitions, in principle, presuppose a *strategic political intervention* into the conditions of access to land and the elimination of non-market survival strategies.[3] By focusing on the political/legal/institutional moment of the origin of capitalism, PM diverts our attention from the transhistorical development of commerce, wealth or wage labor. It argues that only when people are compelled to depend on the market for their means of subsistence, they are *systematically* forced to alter the conditions of production, increase "the ratio of unpaid labor to paid" and to shape the space and scale of production according to the requirements of profitability and competitiveness. As such, capitalism as market dependence does not *presume* capitalism existence, but *explains* capitalism's rise through the interventions into the political and institutional structure governing social reproduction.

What is more, PM emphasizes the "international," accommodating the socio-temporally changing and internationally determined conditions of capitalist transitions. PM insists that there can be no single path to capitalism because of the changing inter-societal context and variations in social reactions from "below". For "once breakthroughs to ongoing capitalist economic development took place in various regions these irrevocably transformed the conditions and the character of the analogous processes, which were to occur subsequently elsewhere".[4] While market dependence signifies the minimum socio-legal prerequisites of the existence of capitalist social relations, their forms vary. Depending on past socio-institutional legacies and the timing and international context of capitalist transition, the mechanisms that ensure market dependence take different forms. As a consequence, PM neither sets up pre-given norms for the transition to capitalism, nor does it treat subsequent transitions as counter models to privileged ideal types. In sum, PM has a potential to save "modernity" from the straitjacket of ever-present and static conceptions of capitalism, providing an understanding of the social content, tempo and *multi-linearity* of world historical development.

"Petty Commodity Production" Route to Capitalism?: The Late Ottoman Empire and Early Republican Turkey (1850–1950)

In the conventional historical sociological analysis of the late Ottoman Empire and early Republican Turkey, capitalism is almost unanimously presumed to be there starting from the nineteenth century, based on the intensification of commercial relations with capitalist Europe. Capitalism, albeit in a "peripheral" or "underdeveloped" form, is assumed to have developed merely by virtue of the commercial ties linking the Empire to the capitalist "world-system". For example, a large group of scholars who have written extensively on Turkey from World-Systems Theory (WST) and Dependency Theory perspectives have especially employed this conception. While some of these scholars presume a direct and necessary relation between the rise of large commercial farms and the rise of capitalism,[5] more nuanced works shift their focus from big farms to "petty commodity production". Their argument is that alongside the emergence of large landholdings cultivated by sharecropping peasants, the dominant institution in agriculture remained small family farms; this implies that the vast majority of agricultural producers, who used to be subsistence farmers, turned into "petty commodity producers" in the course of the nineteenth century. Petty commodity producers, instead of a commercially oriented landed elite, became the main catalyst of the rise of capitalism in the late Ottoman Empire and early Republican Turkey.[6] The character of petty commodity production, so goes the argument, was initially shaped both by the dominance of "merchant capital" that preferred to "expand its area of operation within existing social relations" and "the redistributive pre-capitalist concerns of the Porte", which together "conditioned and influenced the pattern of installation of commodity production" in the form of peasant households.[7] Likewise, in the early Republican period, the state actively promoted the further enrichment of the petty commodity producers (as well as big landlords), which not only fostered the production of crops necessary to industrialization but also created a stable base for the deepening of the internal market.[8] Thus, from the mid-nineteenth century to the mid-twentieth century, partly driven by world market conditions and partly by state support programs, the level of "marketization" increased on middle holdings, ultimately leading to the consolidation of "an autonomously functioning economy" ruled by market imperatives or the "law of value".[9]

In short, a form of capitalism based on "petty commodity production" seems to have taken root from the nineteenth century onwards. Clearly, depending on the larger socio-institutional context of social reproduction, the existence of small producers may not necessarily preclude the development of market dependence among agricultural producers.[10] For this, however, two conditions must be present. First, the reproduction of productive units organized as small family farms must increasingly depend upon commodity production. This requires the increasing elimination of non-market access to land and the promotion of policies that would enable the peasantry to increasingly shift the majority of their labor time from subsistence-first agriculture to commodity production (through, e.g., provision of credit, stabilization of food supply, building of irrigation networks, transport facilities, etc.). Second, in a context of labor scarcity, peasant production in sharecropping arrangements provides large landowners with a low-cost option for securing harvest labor. And indeed, when the sharecropping unit is relatively big and the land/labor ratio is relatively high, one can expect fairly continuous involvement in commodity production. Despite extensive participation in the market, however, for sharecropping to be considered a capitalist form of social labor, the landlord and sharecropper, in principle, must be able and willing to organize the labor process according to the dictates of market competition. This, in turn, requires available land in a given area to be held under the monopoly of the landlord class. For it is ultimately the landlord class' monopoly on land and the resultant closure of access to free or inexpensive land that would force the sharecropper to be more willing to cooperate with the landlord, to increasingly specialize and fully engage in commodity production. Unless these conditions apply, and especially if land clearance is a viable option for the sharecropper, higher yields that could be produced by increased utilization of labor-saving tools and techniques would not only benefit the sharecropping landlord but would also help sharecroppers pay off their debts and become "independent" peasants again. With no monopoly over land and no access to an alternative labor market, the sharecropping landlord would be more likely to choose not to invest in the means of production that could otherwise cause him to lose his only source of labor. As such, sharecropping put definite limits on the transformation of the labor process, deterring the introduction of labor-saving techniques and the capitalist reorganization of production.

Therefore, for petty commodity production and sharecropping to be considered (proto)capitalist forms of social labor, we need to be able to show that the social reproduction of agricultural units must increasingly depend on their willingness and ability to commodify their means of life. How successful were the Ottoman Empire and Early Republican Turkey at reorienting the peasant strategy of production for subsistence towards that of production of commodities? As mentioned earlier, peasant smallholdings prevailed in most areas of the Empire as the basic unit of taxation and seem to have remained remarkably stable during the commercial boom and bust of the latter nineteenth century. According to one estimate, for example, of all cultivable land in 1859, 82 percent entailed smallholdings, with the average farm size somewhere between 6 and 8 hectares and roughly the same proportions applied in 1900.[11] In Anatolia the "majority of private plots were less than 5 hectares" and "even such small plots were likely to be fragmented into tiny parcels of land in a number of different places around the village".[12] In Western Anatolia, which was one of the most commercially oriented areas of the empire, the average size of a peasant landholding varied from 1.2 to 8 hectares.[13] Given the size of their land and the low levels of productivity, most peasants were extremely vulnerable to unfavorable weather conditions and taxation, which also rendered usury and peasant indebtedness a widespread and chronic phenomenon. Whatever was left after the tax collector and the usurer had taken their shares was hardly enough for subsistence. "The small producers frequently had to struggle to survive from one year to the next", with no prospect of "capital improvements in land and implements".[14]

If access to land had been mediated through the market and had cheap credit been sufficiently provided, the combined pressure of taxes and debt might have generated a capitalist growth dynamic in the Ottoman countryside by compelling and enabling a richer stratum of the peasantry to break the cycle of indebtedness, improve productivity, market ever larger portions of their subsistence and to eventually oust the less competitive producers from the land. And in fact, especially during 1850–1873 (and then 1896–1908), a high world market demand for agricultural goods, together with the establishment of modern means of transport, encouraged peasants to extend production and participate in the market. Population growth, the sedentarization of tribes, the settlement of immigrants and the availability of cultivable land also contributed to the expansion of agricultural output, especially for grains, tobacco, raisins and cotton.[15] How much of these grains were marketed? Despite the relative absence of reliable data especially for the period before 1900, Issawi estimates that in the Ottoman Empire "even during the 1863 cotton boom, by far the greater part of the land was planted to wheat, barley and other grains, which were mostly consumed on the farm".[16] Quataert similarly notes that although "enormous changes over time occurred in the agrarian sector", in 1900 most cultivators still "possessed small landholdings, engaging in a host of tasks, with their crops and animal products mainly dedicated to self-consumption".[17]

Implied here is the persistence of the peasants' "subsistence logic". Perhaps more importantly, however, we need to be aware that in a given year and place "peasants may have any proportion of subsistence to cash crop production, including complete specialization" and still this may not indicate the existence of "petty commodity production". That is to say, the transition from "peasant production" to "petty commodity production" cannot be grasped in quantitative terms only, but depends on qualitative changes in the rules of accessing the factors of production.[18] After all, it is not commodity production per se, but the socio-legal mobilization of land, labor and credit that forces, enables and permits peasant family units to produce competitively, reorganize production and accumulate land in the face of their less competitive neighbors. With this qualification in mind, we need to recall that even in the most market-oriented areas, such as Western Anatolia, "uncultivated marginal lands were always available for purchase from the state at nominal prices or in return for regular payments of tithe for ten years".[19] Furthermore, although some significant attempts were made by the state to extend low-interest credit to induce market production, these were far from satisfactory, as most of the agricultural support targeting the land-hungry and technologically backward peasantry was siphoned off by bureaucrats, local notables and big landlords.[20] Considering their relatively uninhibited access to marginal lands and lack of credit, peasants were neither under compulsion nor willing to devote the majority of their labor time to commodity production and reorganizing their labor process according to the dictates of market competition. Despite their participation in the market, "basic subsistence considerations [remained] paramount and accordingly most decisions betray[ed] risk-avoiding behavior".[21] In other words, small family farmers, already distressed by their subsistence, chose not to subject their generational security to the uncertainties of the market. Instead they were "ready to exert and be content with very low levels of consumption which made it easier for them to retain their holdings" in the face of the tax collector and the usurer.[22] Even when peasants were encouraged by high cash-crop prices, their involvement in the market was sporadic. Tobacco production, for example, which became especially popular among small producers during the last quarter of the nineteenth century, was carried out by peasants who were "only marginally" involved in and "were able to withdraw from the market".[23]

Relatedly, with no monopoly over land and no access to an alternative labor market, commercial landlords did not develop any systematic interest in supervising and improving the labor process. Large estates, producing mainly cotton and cultivated almost exclusively by sharecropping peasants, experienced no systematic improvements in the means of production (which would otherwise help sharecroppers pay off their debts, thereby causing the landlord to lose their only source of labor supply). Sharecropping peasants were overburdened by taxes, rents, debt and even labor services in some parts of the empire, yet, regardless of the size of the landholding, they began and completed the production cycle themselves. In the absence of a transformation of social relations and institutions that would set free alternate sources of credit and food supply, sharecropping peasants were inherently unwilling/unable to avoid subsistence farming, respond to fluctuating market conditions and transform the conditions of production and incapable of reinvesting in land. Consequently, the engrossment of commercial landholdings, which occurred partly as a response to rising world market prices (especially of cotton) and often to the detriment of small peasant holdings, did not lead to a qualitative transformation in the prevalent forms of exploitation.

In short, no continuous, systematic and regular commodification of subsistence took place in the Ottoman countryside. Neither agricultural households nor large estates became enterprises "whose relations to outsiders progressively take the forms of buying, selling and competition".[24] How much of this picture changed during the early Republican period (1923–1950)? Approaching the 1920s, land ownership was so concentrated in the Anatolian countryside that, according to one estimate, 87 percent of the rural population occupied only 35 percent of the cultivable land, and 8 percent were totally landless.[25] Regardless of regional differences, the overwhelming majority of the land-hungry population was heavily indebted to the landlord class, thus subject to relations of usury and involved in sharecropping to be able to meet their subsistence needs.[26] "Middle farmers", who were able to produce for their subsistence as well as for the market, were a "very thin" strata of the rural population.[27] Peasant indebtedness and (near) landlessness was the major source of labor supply for sharecropping landowners. The latter remained as "absentee" landlord and were disinterested in production and in investing in land.[28]

By enhancing the status of private property, the first Republican constitution (in 1924) facilitated the legal consolidation of large estates. Landlords obtained full legal title over their lands. Also, through the 1920s, the state reduced agricultural taxes, distributed some state-owned lands to the landless and injected substantial loans into the agricultural sector with the hope that the small landholdings would increase production for the market and reduce their extreme dependence on the big landlords and usurers.[29] Yet, neither the constitution nor the new civil code (in 1926) took any measures to prevent the morcellization of land. Ottoman laws prescribing partible inheritance remained in full force and effect.[30] More importantly, "the greatest difficulties were encountered in applying the rules relating to land"; consequently, arable land continued to be created and transferred without official registration.[31] This means that there was no political attempt to establish landlord/merchant monopoly over land. Marginal lands of little or no cost continued to be readily available.[32] Furthermore, the state's attempts at breaking the relations of usury bore no fruit in the countryside: land distribution was too limited to generate a qualitative impact on the peasantry[33] and the plots distributed to a limited number of cultivators were "far less than was required to maintain a family".[34] Likewise, most of the state-provided credit was used up by landholders with large holdings,[35] and even when the peasantry obtained some access to these funds, most of them had to use these monies to pay off a portion of their debts, instead of investing the money in equipment, fertilizer and irrigation.[36] Throughout the 1920s, partly driven by increases in population and partly thanks to the improvements in security and transportation, peasants extended and divided the area under cultivation, yet remained unable or unwilling to develop a capitalist logic of social reproduction.[37] Furthermore, given that there was no alternative source of labor supply and that the land was expandable and divisible by the peasantry, sharecropping landlords did not develop any systematic interest in supervising and improving the labor process on large estates. On average 90–95 percent of the land within big estates was left uncultivated.[38] Relatedly, sharecropping arrangements on big estates were governed by the same logic of reproduction that prevailed on small peasant holdings.[39]

If anything, these socio-economic patterns deteriorated during and after the Great Depression: Anatolian peasants gave up product specialization, reverted to subsistence farming, fell into further debt and increasingly became sharecroppers.[40] Price and credit support programs remained far from changing the adverse terms of trade impacting the peasantry.[41] Likewise, state support did not amount to a structural transformation of the power of big landlords and commercial agents. The sharecropping landlord and big merchants made huge profits thanks to state credit and price support programs,[42] which were, in turn, spent on luxury consumption, rather than invested in production.[43] Furthermore, these production, investment and consumption patterns inherently inimical to capitalism were further solidified during the Second World War under the impact of military mobilization and the forced levy on agricultural produce.[44]

The flip side of the non-development of capitalism in the Turkish countryside was the persistence of chronic labor shortages in industrial towns.[45] Given the chronic shortages in labor supply, "extremely high" turnover rates prevailed in both state and private factories: workers often quit their jobs simply because they could easily return if they chose, which rendered totally ineffective employers' control over labor which could have been otherwise exercised through recruitment practices. Relatedly, in a context where workers could easily exit and re-enter the labor market, the deskilling of labor and the scientific management of the labor process were most likely to backfire, hence countering the interests of factory management. There was, therefore, no willingness or compulsion to supervise the labor process. Even in industries approved for state support, there was no increase in the level of productivity[46]; "workers were not fired even after they were fined for absenteeism at various times"; and there was no well-defined wage policy in place, no clear and accessible system of remuneration that would reward more productive workers and in some factories not even proper bookkeeping.[47]

The implication is that although Turkey experienced an industrial "boom" based on massive import suppression during the interwar period, the emerging industries existed only thanks to government support and tariff protection.[48] Given the protection of business and the unavailability of a permanent workforce, industrialists were neither able nor willing to intensify their control over the labor process (despite the enactment of highly authoritarian labor regulations and penal laws). In other words, they were neither allowed nor compelled to transform "labor power" into "labor", systematically increase the "organic composition of capital" and reduce the "socially necessary labor time" involved in appropriating "surplus value". In such conditions no industrialist could transform into a "capitalist", that is, a "supervisor and director of the [labor] process, as a mere function, as it were endowed with consciousness and will, of the capital engaged in the process of valorizing itself".[49]

In short, during the first hundred years of modernization in Turkey, neither land nor factory was organized on the basis of market imperatives. Private property developed, so did the accumulation of private wealth, yet neither of these presupposed capitalist property and capitalist accumulation within itself as a developmental tendency. Quite the contrary, for capitalist property to develop, the dominant relations and institutions of private property would have to undergo a radical transformation.

The Transition to Capitalism: Farmers, Oligopolists and the State

The 1950s witnessed the beginning of structural transformation in the Turkish countryside with peasants slowly turning into petty commodity producers, that is, farmers whose relation to the means of subsistence was increasingly determined by their capability to maintain landholdings with recourse to commodity production. Three factors were important in enabling this structural transformation. First, after more than a hundred years of modernization, Turkey finally found the (geo)political breathing space in which capitalist property relations could be established without the imminent threat of foreign intervention. While the growing US recognition of Turkey's geopolitical importance in the newly emerging bipolar world assured Turkey against foreign military pressure (especially that of Soviets), it also allowed considerable leeway for the state to initiate structural transformation in agriculture without being much concerned about the masses that would be dislocated as a result of this transformation.

Second, if the emergence of a bipolar world order laid the (geo)political foundations for capitalist development in Turkey, foreign economic assistance and favorable state policies indirectly galvanized the process of transition during the 1950s by undermining sharecropping relations and encouraging petty commodity production as the new norm in agriculture. Throughout the 1950s the peasantry was freed from most wartime taxes and gained access to state-provided cheap and long-term agricultural credits (which were made possible by the Marshall aid in the first place).

Favorable credit conditions gave peasants the opportunity to buy/rent agricultural machinery and draft animals without incurring too much debt. In this respect, the intensification of credit relations between the state and the peasantry not only increased peasant production and relative living standards but also protected them against relations of debt and usury. Combined with the state provision of floor prices, distribution of state-owned land and infrastructural investment, most landless peasants ultimately broke the cycle of debt-sharecropping: the number of owner-occupied farms increased by 30 percent between 1952 and 1963, while landlessness declined from 16 percent to 10 percent of the rural population between 1950 and 1960.[50] As smallholdings reached an economically feasible size and peasants were provided credit and price support, they became consumers as well as suppliers of the domestic market for the first time in Republican history.[51] This increasing market orientation was further supported by US food aid, which contributed to the peasants gradually losing their ability to revert to subsistence production and their increasing specialization in cash-crop production.

Third, during the early 1950s, mechanization, good weather and world market conditions, government price/credit support and population increase enabled the rapid opening up of previously uncultivated lands (including meadows and pastures). While the area under cultivation increased by 67 percent over the decade,[52] however, the extensive limits of profitable cultivation began to be tested from 1956 onwards.[53] For, continuing to produce on lands of poorer quality or inferior location lowered yields and depleted investment funds. Producers, with little pressure to produce competitively, expanded agricultural frontier as much as possible, while yields remained almost stagnant.[54] The result was repeated foreign exchange crises in the latter half of the 1950s which foreshadowed the increasing inability to import tractors and the end of the expansion of the agricultural frontier.[55] This decade-long expansion and eventual closure of cultivable land, combined with the state's implementation of a stricter land registration system,[56] had an important implication on the structure of agrarian relations, which made the 1950s a prelude to the intensive capitalist development that was to take place in the following decades. That is, "with the frontier reached in the 1950s, agricultural growth became almost exclusively dependent on increased yields (real GDP per hectare) through intensification of cultivation",[57] which eventually made the peasantry increasingly market-dependent for their production and consumption. From this angle, it is no wonder that during the 1960s and

1970s agricultural productivity and yields increased, in line with increases in the use of industrial tools and products in agriculture.[58] Combined with low agricultural taxes and provision of floor prices to agricultural producers, rural settlements rose as important centers of consumption for domestic industries such as agricultural machinery, textiles, processed food, consumer durables and cars.[59] Furthermore, given the peasantry's increasing inability to meet the new standards of subsistence without recourse to the market, it is not surprising that the 1950s witnessed the first permanent mass migrations from the countryside to the towns. Chronic labor shortages, which haunted the earlier attempts at industrialization, thus began to be overcome with the continuous flow of a permanent labor force. The emergence of a stronger labor (and consumer) market, in turn, significantly contributed to the smooth transformation of sharecropping landlords into capitalist entrepreneurs. With the structural makeover of labor markets and alluring prospects for productive activity (both in agriculture and manufacturing), the sharecropping landlords finally began to find it feasible and profitable to reorganize the labor process by driving off sharecroppers and improving their holdings.

Despite the transition to capitalism in the countryside, however, market society in Turkey remained far from being consolidated until the end of the 1990s. The main "culprit" for this was the industrialists. Through import substitution policies, Turkey underwent a spectacular industrial expansion between 1962 and 1979, and manufacturing for the first time surpassed agriculture in terms of its contribution to total growth.[60] The private sector received generous support and protection from the state. Behind high tariff walls, the state provided tax rebates, scarce foreign currencies and various subsidy schemes to the manufacturing bourgeoisie so that they could import capital and intermediate goods to produce consumer products. However, since the state had no power to sanction cooperation and no control over the allocation of public funds, the state support could not be conditioned to manufacturers' ability to compete in international markets and earn foreign exchange (as was the case in successful late-late industrializers like South Korea). The state plans to restructure existing tax, credit, subsidy and investment regimes with a view to the expanded reproduction of capital was criticized and eventually rejected by industrialists and their representatives in the parliament for violating "freedom of property" and "democratic rights".[61] As such, state promotion of industrialization, by and large, boiled down to mere distribution of fiscal privileges and favors with almost no gain that could have been accrued from increases in productivity and competition. Tariffs and quotas led to "overprotection" and the "building of excess capacity" in many industries. For "allocations of foreign exchange … were based solely on considerations of capacity".[62] "Any firm by receiving a percentage of the total exchange allocation was automatically guaranteed a share of the domestic market".[63] No wonder only 17.9 percent of the total subsidies received by firms between 1968 and 1980 was invested in accordance with developmental directives.[64] Industrialists generated almost no foreign exchange, while benefiting from "substantial access to foreign markets for their investment and raw material needs".[65] Most industrial profits were thus made by "manipulating" state intervention.[66]

Big industrialists were the main beneficiaries of import quotas and subsidies.[67] Unsurprisingly, large industrialists, at least until the late 1970s, "across the board" fiercely opposed and systematically undermined government initiatives to devalue the lira, selectively expose the private sector to international competition and so on.[68] Relatedly, they supported Turkey's integration with the European Economic Community mainly because of the prospect of cheaper imports and additional foreign funds, while remaining adamant that the integration should not bring about the lira's devaluation.[69] In short, oligopolistic manufacturers, formed in the domestic market thanks to state support and protection, were inherently inimical to further capitalist development: "it was perfectly rational for the industrialists to use their economic power to choke off further industrialization, rather than promoting the deepening of industrial capital".[70] Big industrialists represented an "infant" capitalist class whose very presence became an impediment to the further development of capitalism in Turkey. What is more interesting, however, is that the blueprint for a capitalism "proper", based on "the expanded reproduction of capital and the extraction of relative surplus value", was being cooked elsewhere. A discussion of the rise of "Islamic capitalism" is in order.

Capitalism of the Oppressed: Re-interpreting the National View Movement

Coming to the end of the 1970s, a new bourgeois class, mainly based in Anatolian towns, comprised of small and medium-sized enterprises (SMEs) and in close connection with certain Islamic Sufi sects, was in the making. Let me begin by contesting an all-too-common conception about this new bourgeois class whose political demands were organized in the so-called "National View Movement". The conventional interpretation holds that the Anatolian bourgeoisie of the 1970s was essentially a protectionist, inward-looking and non-competitive group of entrepreneurs in favor of a pseudo-etatist industrialization strategy. The National View's conception of development "combined a shopkeeper ideology with demands for state interventionism in large industry, thus guaranteeing that the transition to monopoly capitalism should occur without the destruction of small business".[71] The new bourgeois class was disturbed by the expansion of modern capitalist industries concentrated in big cities in Western Turkey and threatened by the looming threat of international competition due to the state's plans to form a customs union with the European Economic Community (EEC).[72] In this respect, so the argument goes, the new bourgeois class was the mirror image of Turkish Industry and Business Association (TUSIAD), the business association formed by big, mainly Istanbul-based secular capitalists that supported an outward-looking industrial strategy, including Turkey's integration with the EEC.[73] To be able to preserve their small-sized and technologically backward enterprises in the face of domestic and international competition, they translated "the discontent of the small town traditional petty bourgeoisie into a platform of Islamic revivalism ... [in lieu of] the nostalgic image of community lost through uncontrolled capitalism".[74] They needed and demanded greater state protection and larger shares of bank credits, hence their constant emphasis on Islamic "justice", conservative values, rejection of the West, the dislike of Kemalism and so on.

Clearly there is a kernel of truth in the conventional interpretation: the Anatolian bourgeoisie reacted against the Istanbul-based industrial monopolies and the state's "unjust" credit policies favoring big business. They also fiercely rejected "Western" values and showed great dismay towards Kemalism, while remaining fearful of the possibility of abolition of quotas and tariffs between Turkey and the EEC. What is fundamentally misleading, however, is the assumption that the Anatolian bourgeoisie was merely an inward-looking class of entrepreneurs trying to defend "petty bourgeois" interests against competition from big domestic and foreign industrialists.

The size of an industrial firm is far from being a clear indicator of its investment and productive patterns, nor does its owners' demand for *economic openness* necessarily equate with support for *structural economic reform*. By way of example, the TUSIAD, the presumably most free-trade oriented interest association of large industrialists, actually had a completely ambivalent stance towards economic reform throughout the 1970s and early 1980s. TUSIAD members, almost all of whom were oligopolists, were completely protected from foreign competition and had exclusive access to an easy subsidy regime. It is true that things began to change after 1978 when the foreign exchange and debt crisis reached its tipping point. Cleavages in the existing power bloc eventually deepened, and TUSIAD became increasingly and vocally critical of Import Substitution Industrialization (ISI) policies, charging the government, trade unions and other industrialists with sacrificing the country's future for their short-term gains.[75] For all this change in discourse, however, TUSIAD's "long-term commitment to the outward oriented measures was doubtful".[76] TUSIAD conceded some limited reform measures as long as "they resulted in infusion of foreign exchange (thus imports of their inputs) into the economy", yet once foreign exchange became easily accessible after the 1980 military coup (more on this below), they reverted to their old stance of criticizing the government for continuing with reform measures at their expense. During the 1980s, TUSIAD would by and large (though not entirely) remain as the association of non-competitive, protectionist and inward-looking industrialists, opposing (yet no longer able to completely derail) the economic restructuring begun in 1980.[77]

The "National View", and the two political parties established as its offspring, the National Order Party (NOP, 1969–1971) and the National Salvation Party (NSP, 1973–1980), developed as a reaction to the dominance of big industrialists.[78] Small firms were almost completely excluded from state-generated credit and subsidy circles, although they produced 25 percent of total industrial production and 88.3 percent of the total manufacture of footwear, apparel and textiles (which were three of the few industrial sectors showing strong export potential).[79] Furthermore, although Anatolian industrialists were much less dependent on foreign imports for their production and consumption, their share of public (manufacturing) investment remained much lower than their counterparts based in Istanbul and Izmir.[80] Despite being subjected to various politico-economic exclusions, however, the Anatolian bourgeoisie largely operated outside centrally supervised industrial relations, thereby having access to a non-unionized (hence cheaper) workforce. Also, their willingness to export to the relatively less competitive markets in the Middle East was improving especially after the rise in oil prices in the 1970s. Given these constraints and opportunities, it was perhaps a fairly foreseeable phenomenon that the Anatolian industrialists were calling for a fairer distribution of state support and an end to inter-regional discrepancies. What needs to be emphasized, however, is that this disgruntled "petty bourgeoisie" believed that the answer to these ills lied not in less, but more capitalism.

Necmettin Erbakan, a mechanical engineer trained in West Germany, was the intellectual father of the National View and the leader of the NOP and NSP. Erbakan argued that industrialization was much less a matter of "planning" and "engineering" than of transforming the obstructive "structure" of the general order.[81] The key to this transformation was neither "statism" per se nor "liberalism".[82] Statism and liberalism have both been tried in Turkey, yet they benefited either only bureaucrats or a small minority of businessmen. These two groups, together with their foreign partners, squandered the scarce resources of a poor country by establishing low productivity and non-competitive industries.[83] Moreover, both statism and liberalism came to promote a "materialistic" lifestyle and education by slavishly mimicking the West (*taklitçilik*), which resulted in "interest-based exploitation" of the masses (*sömürücü faizcilik*) and their drift towards anarchism and communism.[84] In this view, the economic system is thus led by a "Masonic", "Zionist" and "Comprador" minority that heavily taxed and borrowed from the people, but did not offer any payback by creating jobs and "real" investment. As such, Turkish industrialization was marked by a "vegetative growth" (*nebati inkişaf*), which structurally inhibited an overwhelming majority of the people from participating as manufacturers, and even when people became workers, their wages were not based on "strong money", thereby rapidly eroding under inflation.[85]

Thus, without a wholesale transformation of existing political organization (*teşkilat*), rules and legislation (*mevzuat*), and mentality (*zihniyet*), no plan could deliver expected economic outcomes in Turkey.[86] "Real industrialization" was then not only about "economic" planning, but required the transition to a "horizontal statism" (*ufki devletçilik*) and moralism (*maneviyatçılık*) that together would promote the development of an "intensive" (*yoğun*) private sector. To accomplish this goal, Erbakan proposed a number of politico-cultural measures: the presidency and prime ministry will be combined in a presidential system and the president will be directly elected by the people (instead of by parliament).[87] Ministries dealing with economic issues will be combined and reorganized in line with the requirements of rapid industrialization and export growth.[88] "Communists" and "freemasons" will be removed from state service.[89] State economic enterprises, unless they have a "leading" function in the economy, will operate in the same way private enterprises do, and those with "leading" functions will be privatized once they complete their tasks.[90] The credit system will be overhauled in such ways that the allocation of credit will be commensurate with the level of productivity of industrial undertakings.[91] The interest rate system will be abolished. Taxes will be imposed on wealth, not on profits. Banks will be directly involved in production and share profits with industrialists by establishing joint productive ventures. With interest rates replaced by "profit-sharing", bank operations will not only facilitate production but also decrease the cost of borrowing and inflation, thereby increasing export competitiveness.[92] The state will lead and induce the deepening and spread of private industrial investment with the condition that production will be made contingent on "satisfactory profit" and "world market prices".[93] However, this does not mean that Turkey should completely give up economic protectionism. Rather, protection has to be selective: for example "as opposed to struggling with the EEC to be able to sell some parsley … we should sell our agricultural and manufactured goods to Muslim states [and] build their industries [and] their roads".[94] Instead of being Europe's "servant", we should lower tariffs with our neighbors in the Middle East and Africa. "We should be men and … sell our products to the markets that we can control".[95]

Erbakan's conception of "social justice" (*içtimai adalet*) is more or less a natural outcome of the order prescribed above, according to which social justice is seen by and large as a derivation of the political transformation that would spread the fruits of increased competition, productivity, currency stability and an improved investment climate. In other words, social justice cannot be maintained through minor social fixes to existing "masonic" "liberal" capitalism,[96] and in fact, any attempt to do so is doomed to failure, for they would lead in the long run to nothing, but higher inflation, higher unemployment, higher taxes on the poor and, thereby, communism.[97] Social justice, therefore, requires a radical departure from the existing economic order towards the establishment of a productivity-based system that would create jobs for the unemployed, cut waste, increase opportunities of enrichment for hardworking people while enabling workers to earn better pay and even get a share of profits (*kârdan hisse*).[98] Needless to say, all this depends on disciplining not only the rich but also the workers and small farmers. Small farmers "should be able to sell their produce at its real value",[99] unions will operate independently of "political" influences, and workers and employers will treat each other like brothers who cooperate and work for the common goal.[100]

This new conception of social justice, alongside Erbakan's proposal to shift power from parliament towards the top of the state and the executive, and the strategic reordering of state support and credit in ways to subordinate production to the dictates of market competition, while short of a comprehensive economic plan, provided the outlines of a novel project of capitalist development. From this angle, the National View Movement, taken as a whole, offered a totally fresh foundation for capitalist development in Turkey. It sought to unburden "modernization" from its Republican yoke, which it saw responsible for causing "anarchy" and creating a corrupted capitalism. By linking social and economic rights to productivity increases, it aimed to subordinate the poor ever more powerfully to the dictates of capitalist competition. The moral improvement and material welfare of the poor was imagined as a direct derivation of their subordination to the discipline of capitalist accumulation. Erbakan's attack on "interest-based exploitation" was just the flip side of his attempt to deepen capitalist property relations. Regardless of Erbakan's intentions, however, the National View did not muster enough power to materialize its societal vision until the 2000s. Although the NVM's call for a productive and just order found a strong resonance among the urban poor (especially the non-unionized workers and unemployed) from the 1970s to the end of the 1990s, the political parties associated with the NVM either acted only as minor partners in coalition governments or were prevented by the status quo powers from taking control of the state. The National Views' societal vision would have to wait till the 2000s to be realized.

Consolidation of Capitalism: The Rise of the Justice and Development Party

In many ways, the 1980 military takeover represented a watershed in Turkish political economy. While the coup decisively suspended the constitution, shut down political parties and unions, lowered the wages and brutally repressed the left, it also took measures to "discipline" the bourgeois class. The coup introduced several institutional and legal changes designed to overcome potential political clashes within the state and restrict the influence of societal groups over economic policy making. The sustainability of these legal and institutional changes in the post-coup period, however, was dependent on the formation of a coalition whose interests rested on the expansion and deepening of capitalist social relations.

Turgut Özal, the first prime minister of the post-coup period, through funds provided by international financial institutions and foreign governments, designed new incentives (subsidies, credits, foreign exchange allocations and tax exemptions) to reinforce and deepen the pro-reform groups within the business community. The most consistent support for Özal's export drive came from the companies that, "frequently in conflict with TUSIAD, lobbied for the maintenance and increase of incentives presented to exporters".[101] Among these, the most prominent were Turkish construction companies and industrialists (predominantly textile and to a lesser extent iron and steel manufacturers) operating in or producing for the expanding Middle Eastern markets, where "a company's religious affiliation mattered a great deal to potential customers".[102] No wonder most TUSIAD members remained suspicious of Özal during the 1980s, criticizing him for frequent devaluations (hence rising prices for their imports), import liberalization (hence increasing foreign competition) and the government's support for "exporters" over the "investing industrialists".[103] This is not to deny that the policies encouraging export-led growth initiated a protracted transformation within the group of big industrialists: some import substitution holding companies (especially Sabancı and Koç Holdings), facing increasing competition for the domestic market and encouraged by generous export subsidies and lower wages, began to take an outward orientation from the mid-1980s. Yet, it is equally true that given their immense resources and political links, the bulk of export subsidies were still received by large holding companies with almost no export potential.[104] In other words, in spite of the emergence of a number of strongly export-oriented sectors in competitive industries with smaller producers (especially textiles and ready-wear), most export support policies benefited non-competitive and monopolistic actors, who did not have to export to survive. As a result, "various forms of incentives, such as tax rebates, preferential credits and grants, ended up becoming 'giveaways', pure and simple".[105] "Rent-oriented networks" which appear to have no economic rationale continued to be "the norm with respect to the Turkish incentive regime".[106]

The things got even worse when the state liberalized the capital account in 1989 to finance its deficits, which in fact provided big business with a golden opportunity for turning potential losses into profits. After the opening of the capital account in 1989, the holding banks became the central benefactors of state borrowing practices. Lured by high interest rates, these banks, almost all of which were parts of holding companies with industrial bases, made profits by purchasing government securities and exploiting the difference between the exchange rate and the interest rate. That is, they first obtained funds on international markets as credit denominated in dollars, converted this into Turkish lira and then lent to the government at high interest rates. It does not require great foresight to predict that an increasingly high proportion of profits were obtained in the financial activities associated with the holding of government securities. With holding companies enjoying oligopolistic markets and financial rents, there was eventually only little need for reinvestment, which is an indicator of the degree of stagnation of investment levels throughout the 1990s. The point is that throughout the 1980s and 1990s the social reproduction of the big bourgeoisie, in spite of their rhetorical support for structural reforms, remained by and large dependent on the state's systematic transfer of monopoly and financial rents. This created a vicious rent-debt cycle, which ultimately prevented the completion of the capitalist restructuring process begun in 1980. As the state's attempt at strategically leading capitalist development degenerated into the mere distribution of tax revenues, the restructuring of productive capacity of the economy via the deepening of capitalist social relations was undermined.

All this would change with the overhaul of the power bloc in 2002. In 2000–2001, two major economic crises erupted in Turkey, and unsurprisingly the elections held the following year completely crushed the political parties of the 1990s, pushing big businesses to the margins of future power arrangements. While none of the center-right parties managed to enter parliament, the National View Movement with a brand new party, Justice and Development Party, and with a brand new leader, Recep Tayyip Erdoğan, secured 34 percent of the votes and 66 percent of the seats in parliament. The heirs of the NVM thus seized the government in 2002. Once the 2001 crisis subsided, what replaced technocrats, therefore, was not a fragmented political structure susceptible to reproducing the old political economy, but a single-party government with organic links to a new capitalist bourgeois class. In the decade to follow, Islamists would breathe new life into capitalism.

The Justice and Development Party (JDP) signals the rise of a distinct project of capitalist modernity. A new bourgeois class, previously excluded from the official credit channels and political privileges enjoyed by the old bourgeois class, has emerged with a politically/religiously distinct project of capitalist transformation. Its previous exclusion from state-generated rents forced it to envision (at least initially) a society in which economic competitiveness, underlined by a specific politico-religious subjectivity, would be the ultimate basis for the allocation of resources. The new bourgeois class became the supporter of structural reforms, thereby helping to consolidate the reform process and ensure its irreversibility. In turn, the JDP provided various incentives to the Islamic bourgeoisie, reversing their unfavorable treatment in public contracts and privatization bids, thereby leading to their further enrichment and internationalization. With the JDP and Islamic bourgeoisie converging on an anti-monopolist agenda, the big bourgeoisie was to make strategic compromises to the Islamic bourgeoisie concerning the political and institutional structure of the economy. Forced by the new configuration of political power, and encouraged by prospects for economic expansion under a single-party government and European Union membership (at least until 2010), the big bourgeoisie seem to have ceded its resistance to reform.

On the whole, such a restructuring signaled the reorganization of Turkish economy based on increasing productivity and competitiveness in the international markets. Implied here is a departure from the previous pattern of accumulation based on the redistribution of profits through the state towards a mode of accumulation based on production through increasing international competitiveness and labor productivity. This is a historically specific political economy, which, despite the extensive use of political power for personal economic advantage, is premised on the ability of public and private powers to achieve material reproduction through the world market and on the capacity to reproduce the fiction of self-regulating markets. This is a fully capitalist modernity underlined by the consolidation of capitalist social relations.

Notes

1. Robert Brenner, "The origins of capitalist development," *New Left Review*, no. 104 (1977): 52.
2. Ellen Meiksins Wood, "The question of market dependence," *Journal of Agrarian Change* 2, no. 1 (2002): 50–87.
3. Robert Brenner, "Agrarian Class Structures and Economic Development in pre-industrial Europe," in *The Brenner Debate*, ed. Trevor Aston and C.H.E Philpin (Cambridge: Cambridge University Press, 1985), 20.
4. Robert Brenner, "The agrarian roots of European capitalism," in *The Brenner Debate*, ed. Trevor Aston and C.H.E Philpin (Cambridge: Cambridge University Press, 1985), 322.

5. Reşat Kasaba, *The Ottoman Empire and the World-Economy* (Albany: State University of New York Press, 1988); Berch Berberoglu, *Turkey in Crisis* (London: Zed Books, 1982).
6. Çağlar Keyder, *State and Class in Turkey* (London: Verso, 1987); Şevket Pamuk, *The Ottoman Empire and European capitalism* (Cambridge: Cambridge University Press, 1987).
7. Çağlar Keyder, *The Definition of a Peripheral Economy: Turkey* (Cambridge: Cambridge University Press, 1981), 1, 3; Keyder *State and Class*, 43–44.
8. Keyder, *State*, 129.
9. Ibid., 128.
10. Harriet Friedmann, "Household Production and the National Economy," *Journal of Peasant Studies* 7, no. 2 (1980): 158–184.
11. Pamuk, *The Ottoman*, 91.
12. Roger Owen, *The Middle East in the World Economy* (New York: Methuen, 1981), 208.
13. Charles Issawi, *The Economic History of Turkey, 1800–1914* (Chicago: University of Chicago Press, 1980), 203; Pamuk, *The Ottoman*, 100.
14. Pamuk, *The Ottoman*, 89.
15. Donald Quataert, "The Age of Reforms," in *An Economic and Social History of the Ottoman Empire, Vol. 2*, ed. Suraiya Faroqhi, Bruce McGowan, Donald Quataert, Sevket Pamuk and Halil Inalcik (Cambridge: Cambridge University Press, 1994), 844, 847.
16. Issawi, *The Economic History*, 200.
17. Donald Quataert, *The Ottoman Empire, 1700–1922* (Cambridge: Cambridge University Press, 2005), 130–131.
18. Friedmann, "Household," 167.
19. Pamuk, *The Ottoman*, 87.
20. Quataert, "The Age," 871–872.
21. Çağlar Keyder, "The cycle of sharecropping and the consolidation of small peasant ownership in Turkey," *Journal of Peasant Studies* 10, no. 2 (1983): 136.
22. Pamuk, *The Ottoman*, 101.
23. Mustafa Koç, "Persistence of Small Commodity Production in Agriculture" (PhD diss., University of Toronto, 1988), 65–71.
24. Friedmann, "Household Production," 163.
25. Feroz Ahmad, *Modern Türkiye'nin Oluşumu* (Istanbul: Kaynak, 2002), 43.
26. Oya Silier, *Türkiye'de Tarımsal Yapının Gelişimi* (Istanbul: Boğaziçi Üniversitesi Yayinlari, 1981), 15.
27. Silier, *Türkiye'de*, 14.
28. Ibid., 15–16.
29. Zvi Hershlag, *Turkey: The Challenge of Growth* (Leiden: Brill, 1968), 49.

30. Yahya Tezel, *Cumhuriyet Döneminin İktisadi Tarihi* (Istanbul: Tarih Vakfi, 1986), 340–341.
31. Vakur Versan, "The Kemalist reform of Turkish law," in *Ataturk and the Modernization of Turkey*, ed. Jan Landau (Leiden: Brill, 1984), 250.
32. Keyder, *Peripheral*, 24.
33. Tezel, *Cumhuriyet*, 345.
34. Zvi Hershlag, *Introduction to the Modern Economic History of the Middle East* (Leiden: Brill, 1975), 172.
35. Silier, *Türkiye'de*, 44–45.
36. Hershlag, *Turkey*, 113.
37. Hershlag, *Turkey*, 112; Tezel, *Cumhuriyet*, 340–341.
38. Silier, *Türkiye'de*, 16.
39. Ilhan Tekeli and Selim Ilkin, "Devletçilik Dönemi Tarım Politikaları," in *Türkiye'de Tarımsal Yapılar*, ed. Şevket Pamuk and Zafer Toprak (Ankara: Yurt Yayınları, 1988), 40, 89.
40. Elif Akçetin, "Anatolian peasants in the Great Depression," *New Perspectives on Turkey*, no. 23 (2000): 93–98.
41. Roger Owen and Şevket Pamuk, *A History of Middle East Economies in the Twentieth Century* (Cambridge: Tauris, 1999), 22.
42. Silier, *Türkiye'de*, 88.
43. Tezel, *Cumhuriyet*, 439.
44. Keyder, "Cycle," 140.
45. Hershlag, *Turkey*, 106.
46. Ibid., 106.
47. Görkem Akgöz, "Many voices of a Turkish state factory" (PhD diss., University of Amsterdam, 2012): 65–71.
48. Hershlag, *Introduction*, 190.
49. Karl Marx, *Capital, Vol. 1* (London: Penguin, 1990), 1022.
50. Keyder, *State*, 131.
51. Çağlar Keyder, "Türk Tarımında Küçük Meta Üretiminin Yerleşmesi," in *Turkiye'de Tarimsal Yapilar*, ed. Şevket Pamuk and Zafer Toprak (Ankara: Yurt Yayinlari, 1988), 164.
52. Feroz Ahmad, *The Turkish Experiment in Democracy, 1950–1975* (London: Hurst & Co Publishers, 1977), 135.
53. Bent Hansen, *Egypt and Turkey: The Political Economy of Poverty, Equity and Growth* (New York: Oxford University Press, 1991), 260, 341–344.
54. Owen and Pamuk, *A History*, 107–108.
55. Hansen, *Egypt and Turkey*, 344, 439.
56. Erik Jan Zurcher, *Turkey: A Modern History* (London: I.B. Tauris, 2004), 227.
57. Hansen, *Egypt and Turkey*, 357.

58. William Hale, *The Political and Economic Development of Modern Turkey* (New York: St. Martin's Press, 1981), 178.
59. Zülküf Aydın, *The Political Economy of Turkey* (London: Pluto Press 2005): 154–155.
60. Hansen, *Egypt and Turkey*, 357.
61. Vedat Milor, "A Comparative Study of Planning and Economic Development in Turkey.and France" (PhD diss., University of California, Berkeley 1989), 240.
62. Henri J. Barkey, *The State and the Industrialization Crisis in Turkey* (Boulder: Westview Press, 1990), 91–92.
63. Hale, *The Political*, 202.
64. Milor, "A Comparative," 255–256.
65. Ali Tekin, "Turkey's Aborted Attempt at Export-Led Growth Strategy," *Middle Eastern Studies* 42, no. 1 (2006): 139.
66. Tekin, "Turkey's," 133.
67. Barkey, *The State*, 118.
68. Ibid., 119.
69. Tekin, "Turkey's," 140, 145–146.
70. Milor, "A Comparative," 233.
71. Çağlar Keyder, "The Political Economy of Turkish Democracy," *New Left Review*, no. 115 (1979): 35.
72. Ahmad, *The Turkish*, 382.
73. Yildiz Atasoy, *Turkey, Islamists and Democracy* (New York: I. B. Tauris, 2005), 119.
74. Keyder, "The Political," 35.
75. Barkey, *The State*, 117; Ali Tekin, "The Political Economy of Foreign Trade Policy Reforms" (PhD diss., University of Pittsburgh, 1997), 239.
76. Tekin, "The Political," 220–221.
77. Ibid., 249–250.
78. Jacob Landau, *Politics and Islam* (Salt Lake: University of Utah, 1976), 21.
79. Atasoy, *Turkey*, 119; Tekin, "Turkey's Aborted," 153.
80. Barkey, *The State*, 132–133.
81. Necmettin Erbakan, *Erbakan Külliyati Vol. 2* (Istanbul: MGV Yayinlari, 2013), 404.
82. Necmettin Erbakan, *Erbakan Külliyati Vol. 5* (Istanbul: MGV Yayinlari, 2013), 63.
83. Erbakan, *Külliyati Vol. 5*, 50.
84. Erbakan, *Külliyati Vol. 2*, 403; Erbakan, *Külliyati Vol. 5*, 268.
85. Erbakan, *Külliyati Vol. 5*, 51, 62; Necmettin Erbakan, *Erbakan Külliyati Vol.1* (Istanbul: MGV Yayinlari, 2013), 105.
86. Erbakan, *Külliyati Vol. 5*, 53–55.

87. Erbakan, *Külliyati Vol. 1*, 59.
88. Erbakan, *Külliyati Vol. 1*, 60; Erbakan, *Külliyati Vol. 2*, 402.
89. Erbakan, *Külliyati Vol. 2*, 402.
90. Necmettin Erbakan, *Erbakan Külliyati Vol. 3* (Istanbul: MGV Yayinlari, 2013), 127.
91. Erbakan, *Külliyati Vol. 2*, 403.
92. Erbakan, *Külliyati Vol. 1*, 105–106.
93. Erbakan, *Külliyati Vol. 5*, 63.
94. Erbakan quoted in Atasoy, *Turkey*, 128.
95. Erbakan, *Külliyati Vol. 5*, 70–71.
96. Ibid., 52.
97. Erbakan, *Külliyati Vol. 1*, 102.
98. Ibid., 105.
99. Landau, *Politics*, 17.
100. Erbakan, *Külliyati Vol. 1*, 104–106.
101. Sadik Ünay, *The Political Economy of Development and Planning in Turkey* (New York: Nova, 2006), 74.
102. Barkey, *The State*, 178.
103. Tekin, "The Political," 249.
104. Jesse Biddle and Vedat Milor, "Institutional Influences on Economic Policy in Turkey," *World Bank PSD Occasional Paper*, no. 3 (1995): 6.
105. Biddle and Milor, "Institutional," 57.
106. Ibid., 6.

CHAPTER 12

Uncertainty, Contingency, and Late Development in Taiwan

Christopher Isett

Introduction

Taiwan is a striking example of the successful transition to capitalism and breakthrough to self-sustaining growth. The case is notable, first of all, because, over the course of world economic history, the domestic conditions required to underpin economic development have emerged only rarely and with difficulty, given that pre-capitalist social property relations constitute the point of departure. Outside of this capitalist core, and the white settler colonies that represented extensions of it, examples of the transition from pre-capitalism to capitalist development in what might be loosely termed the "Third World" are scarce, with Taiwan constituting a major exception, along with its counterparts in East Asia.

What makes the Taiwanese example all the more remarkable, however, is how difficult it has generally been for later developers to follow a path of dynamic development even in places where they have experienced a

I wish to express gratitude to the editors, Stephen Miller, Perry Anderson, and most of all Robert Brenner.

C. Isett (✉)
University of Minnesota, Minneapolis, MN, USA

X. Lafrance, C. Post (eds.), *Case Studies in the Origins of Capitalism*, Marx, Engels, and Marxisms,
https://doi.org/10.1007/978-3-319-95657-2_12

transition to capitalist social property relations. The earlier developers at the core of the global economy, including the US, Western Europe, Japan, and the settler colonies, wielding as they did advanced technologies making for low costs of production, posed too great a competitive threat. As a rule, in order to underwrite self-sustaining growth, the ruling class and state of the later developer had to implement economic policies and erect a complex of institutions ("organized capitalism") explicitly aimed at overcoming withering international competition.

Taiwan thus witnessed not only the emergence of a rather pure form of capitalist social property relations but also, on that foundation, the rise of a new capitalist ruling class and state capable of organizing an economy unusually well-equipped for producing competitively on the world market. As a result, Taiwan was able to sustain one of the most spectacular trajectories of economic development ever, with rates of growth of GDP, of investment, of labor productivity, and of wages as rapid as any other in world history. In this chapter, I will spell out the inherently contradictory historical processes required to enable capitalism to arise in the presence of pre-capitalist social economies, show how processes take place in Taiwan, and why Taiwan was able to move beyond establishing capitalism to undertake a spectacular and rarely matched path of later development.

Uncertainty and Contingency in the Transition to Capitalism

In his account of the transition from feudalism to capitalism, Robert Brenner argues that the process by which capitalist development takes place, when it does occur, is marked by fundamental paradox or problem, which explains its difficulty and rarity. On the one hand, the onset of self-sustaining growth requires the emergence of a set of (capitalist) social property relations in the presence of which the direct producers, in order to ensure their survival, have no choice but to adopt the set of individual economic strategies, or rules for reproduction, required to bring about economic growth in the aggregate. On the other hand, the general form of (pre-capitalist) social property relations that has prevailed in virtually every agrarian economy since the rise of settled agriculture has enabled and obliged all individual economic agents to adopt rules for reproduction that run counter to the needs of overall development so long as those social property relations remain in place.[1]

It has also impelled the main social classes, both lords and peasants, to act collectively in their own interest not to bring in capitalist social property relations, but, on the contrary to strengthen, in one way or another, the prevailing pre-capitalist social property relations, generally at the expense of the opposing class. So long as pre-capitalist social property relations continue to obtain, the direct producers and the exploiters as individuals will adopt pre-capitalist rules for reproduction making for pre-capitalist developmental patterns, while the political communities of direct producers and exploiters organized collectively to pursue their class interests will have as their goal to sustain those social property relations in ways favorable to themselves at the expense of the other. The upshot is that a transition from pre-capitalism to capitalist development will only take place as an exception to the rule—as an unintended consequence of actions of pre-capitalist individuals and collectivities pursuing pre-capitalist rules for reproduction in aid of pre-capitalist goals.

Whereas the appearance and development of capitalism might seem to open the way for emulation, especially by states seeking to self-strengthen in response to external threats, we cannot expect them to do so out of political necessity for the same reasons that we cannot expect pre-capitalist elites or producers to adopt capitalist rules for reproduction out of their economic interest. The heads of the non-capitalist state, under threat from rival states, may wish to compel political elites and peasants to adopt rules for reproduction that would lead to self-sustaining, capitalist growth, yet both classes constitute a significant barrier to any such project insofar as they will resist any threat to their reproduction. Elites predictably respond to such efforts at the top-down imposition of capitalism by drawing upon their control of the bureaucracy of the pre-capitalist state, and their authority over local communities, to block reforms. Similarly, peasants mobilize their political communities to resist efforts to diminish control over the means of subsistence and to subject their reproduction to the market's discipline.[2] For these reasons, the transition to capitalism, both initially *and for late comers*, can generally occur only as an unintended consequence of the pre-capitalist ruling class *seeking to sustain their position by pre-capitalist means.*

In this chapter I argue that a convergence of developments on postwar Taiwan provided a singular opportunity for Kuomintang (KMT) leadership to impose capitalist rules for reproduction on economic elites and workers alike, even after decades of failed attempts to induce self-sustaining growth on the mainland. Separated from their economic base on the mainland (no longer embedded in the mainland's social property relations), and wholly reliant for their survival on the party leadership's command over the military and state, the national representatives and party members who followed Chiang Kaishek into exile on Taiwan implemented land reform for the first time in the party's history. The party leadership could do so only because the state bureaucracy had no vested interest in preserving the island's social property relations as these functioned in 1945 and because it had every interest in eradicating Taiwan's landlord class since it constituted the only viable native political opposition to Chiang and his large entourage.

Nonetheless, even with the political field cleared of political opposition, and market discipline imposed upon firms, the island's fledging entrepreneurs were caught in a bind. Now under competitive constraints, but without sufficient home demand to supports costly investments in plant and machinery, their success depended upon their ability to exploit markets overseas. Given their lack of competitiveness, however, their success depended first on whether foreign markets, in particular in the US, would allow the types and intensity of state intervention needed to aid Taiwan's export drive. Second, it depended on the capacity and willingness of the advanced capitalist countries to sustain damage to their own manufacturing sectors while continuing to export capital and equipment overseas. These were political questions and as such they lay beyond Taiwan's control. As it turns out, two international developments were key in this regard. First, the Cold War invested US foreign policy makers in Taiwan's industrialization, insofar as the containment of the Soviet and China required a politically stable and economically productive alliance. Second, the postwar boom centered in the US, Japan, and Western Europe created propitious conditions. The investment boom propelled wage growth and demand to new heights, while the accompanying inter-capitalist competition pushed technology and capital overseas.

The Cold War

In 1950 both the Nationalists on Taiwan and foreign policy makers in Washington faced profound strategic challenges. Both responded by subordinating questions of economy to security.[3] Holding uncontested military and economic power, the US held sway over postwar rule-making bodies such as the International Monetary Fund (IMF), World Bank, and General Agreement on Tariffs and Trade (GATT), which it wielded to bring capitalist national competitors in line with its political and economic vision. At the height of World War II, planners were preoccupied by the problem of postwar recovery. Viewed in light of the failure to adjust to 1918, and in keeping with ideological commitment to free commerce and private enterprise, Washington sought a global order to guarantee the free movement of goods and capital.[4] Policy makers were drawn increasingly from business and financial circles that desired an end to the statist and anti-democratic practices. They anticipated a global Open Door order, secured with low tariffs and currency convertibility.[5] When postwar recovery proved stubborn in strategic Europe and Japan, and a general leftward political drift gathered speed in both zones, however, Washington adopted a more pragmatic approach to the methods of economic dirigisme. Allies exploited their weaknesses to secure terms of economic engagement with the US that were amenable to their emerging statist approaches to recovery, growth, and trade expansion. In search of geostrategic advantage over the USSR, the US abandoned ideological purity and accepted, in the words of one scholar, "dictators and cartels in the name of democracy and free trade."[6]

Whereas the first significant test of America's wartime economic vision for the world came in Europe (especially in Great Britain and Germany), Taiwan benefited more directly from developments in Japan. With US hopes in the Chinese Civil War floundering, Tokyo became the epicenter of America's effort to consolidate an Asian front against communism. But this hinged upon Japan's economic recovery. With only emergency aid from Washington, an untenable "dollar gap" opened to cover the importation of basics and requisite capital goods. Three years after the war's end, Japan's industrial output was still less than half that of 1934–1936 levels. Head of the US State Department's Policy Planning Staff, the author of US containment George Kennan feared a permanent left government in Tokyo. Newly anointed Secretary of State Dean Acheson dispatched Detroit banker Joseph Dodge, who arrived in early 1949 fresh from putting to rest Germany's currency crisis.[7] His nine-point prescription for Japan's economic recovery included a "super-balanced" budget, price and wage freezes, tax enforcement, and restrictions on lending. But, it also included policies designed to encourage exports, most radically the fixing of the Yen-Dollar rate at an export-friendly 360 to 1.

The effect was immediate and unsettling. Employers cut costs, reduced their workforce, and got unions to agree to tie wages to productivity. Yet, lending restrictions designed to tame inflation hit key upstream enterprises, including the slowing down of energy output to a trickle. Downstream firms were at a loss to locate inputs and failed to take advantage of improved export conditions. The economic panic of 1949 ended only with the outbreak of the Korean War. As the US turned to Japanese firms to ease military procurements, Tokyo's Ministry of International Trade and Industry pressured manufacturers to link up, re-combine, and rationalize. It pushed the city banks to lend to targeted industries and experimented with tariffs and rebates to protect and promote exporters. Despite US warnings that Japan would do best to leverage its comparative advantage in low-tech, labor-intensive manufacturing, by the end of the Korean war, Japan Inc.'s key market and government arrangements were in place: a national economic policy; private firms allied in *keiretsu*; firm-friendly city banks; overlending; the use of interest rates, tariffs, and rebates to guide investment; a cheap *yen*; and policy designed to develop across the full spectrum of industry.[8]

Despite its strong distaste for dirigisme, Washington quickly accommodated to state interventions that brought regional stability and longer-term predictability to its alliances. Washington not only accepted a reversal in its trading fortunes and net capital outflows but also the flouting of its economic prescriptions and recommendations.[9] In so doing, it recognized two realities. First, the struggle against communism was going to be "a long-pull," and the US recognized that it stood alone in its capacity to coordinate that struggle.[10] Second, the durability of its alliance system hinged upon a widening world-system of capital accumulation of which American firms were only one part. For the sake of victory over communism, the US would make the world safe for capital regardless of nationality.[11] The result was a recognition of the particularities of local economic problems and threats. Policy bureaucrats in agencies such as United States Agency for International Development (USAID) accepted and even promoted deviations from principle, confident that allies would eventually warm to America's superior way. On Taiwan, economic policy makers, soon headed by Chiang Kaishek's son Chiang Ching-kuo, took note of these developments.

After some equivocation, the US finally drew the exiled KMT on Taiwan under its military umbrella in 1950. Sitting astride shipping lanes that tied Japan to key markets in Southeast Asia, the Pentagon had long recognized Taiwan's military value.[12] But the rank incompetence of Chiang Kaishek, and the KMT leadership generally, caused the State Department pause. Early KMT actions on the island did not inspire confidence. Rough treatment of the local population by Chiang's appointed governor sparked a three-month rebellion, during which some 30,000 Taiwanese perished. The mismanagement of the Bank of Taiwan pushed inflation above 1000 percent. The KMT degraded manufacturing capacity by stripping factories of machines and shipped parts to Shanghai. The party's long-standing economic thinking won no acolytes in Washington either. On the mainland, the KMT used state banks and large public enterprises in steel, mining, machinery, armaments, and communications to control markets, impose monopoly prices, and most importantly to compel the political and financial allegiance of business leaders.[13] On Taiwan, the KMT nationalized Japanese property, industry, and banks. It imposed monopolies on key exports and even contemplated the nationalization of all agricultural production.

Whereas Washington conditioned the renewal of aid on the Nationalist's rejection of central planning, and its promise to respect private enterprise, the KMT refused fully to relinquish control over the economy. In its view, the threatening international conditions and domestic political stability required powerful administrative instruments and methods. While relinquishing to US demands on certain fronts such as land reform, the party adopted strategic controls in industry. It took advantage of US-recommended import-substitution programs to build up domestic manufacturing, providing space to grow for selected private enterprises, and used the scarcity of foreign exchange to justify tightening controls over trade and savings.

Taiwan's fledgling economic bureaucracy was assisted in this regard by US advisors on the ground. Coming from the State Department's Aid program, as noted these men took a less orthodox approach to the economy. Washington had dispatched them to Taiwan to support regional strategic goals that, after 1950, hinged on the political viability of Chiang and the KMT regime. Finding Taiwanese firms too timid and poorly equipped to forge industrialization, the American staff recommended unorthodox state interventions.[14] Across the 1950s, with the assistance of the Council on US Aid (CUSA), the size and reach of Taiwan's economic bureaucracy grew. It nationalized and then subordinated finance to the interests of manufacturing, stabilized prices with strict monetary policy, and moderated the effects of foreign trade on the domestic market. It used tariffs, import and exchange rate controls, as well as its supervision of foreign dollar reserves to guide industrial behavior. It prioritized exports early, to earn much needed foreign exchange, and it assisted with the importation and dissemination to firms of technology needed to export. Finally, the state invested through public enterprises in the manufacture of capital and intermediary goods, power generation, and transportation.[15] As the state adjusted policy in the late 1950s to prioritize exports, it relied more than ever on these bureaucratic controls to guide firm behavior, to mollify risks, and to maintain the party's command.

Despite the KMT's ongoing and systematic interventions in the market, US aid accounted for two-fifths of capital formation when it ended in 1965. Thereafter, Washington did little to tame Taiwan's growing trade surplus. It even encouraged US private investment that added more value-added imports from Taiwan to the American ledger. Indeed, America's growing trade deficits signaled to Taiwan's manufacturers that the US remained both a dependable market and source for invaluable technology and know-how to its allies. Guaranteed access to the US market and capital, and protected by its own economic bureaucracy, Taiwanese manufacturing looked to exploit niches in the global division of labor.

During the Cold War, Washington ceded economic sovereignty to its allies in return for geopolitical advantage. So long as states committed to the fundamentals of capitalist accumulation, US administrations suffered illiberal policies that accelerated growth and added to America's trade imbalance. America in the 1950s and 1960s could afford to be generous: the size of its economy meant it remained confident in the attraction and superiority of its economic model. America's grand strategy for the Cold War, drafted under Truman, sought to bind by alliance the industrial zones in Western Europe and Northeast Asia. The durability of these arrangements rested on an end to class war through policies that promoted sustained economic growth via constant and rapid technological upgrading.[16] Of course, the coincidence of US geostrategic interests in Asia with Taiwan's export-led path to industrialization grew from American interests in defending its economic way of life. The upshot, as Perry Anderson shows, was a radical amendment to America's commitment to its early Open Door policy: "The US state would henceforward act," Anderson concludes of the Cold War, "not primarily as a projection of the concerns of US capital, but as a guardian of the general interest of all capitals, sacrificing—where necessary, and for as long as needed—national gain for international advantage, in the confidence of ultimate pay-off."[17] Thus, in the midst of what it considered an ideological fight to the death, Washington accepted economically dirigiste departures when these served to contain the communist threat to bourgeois property worldwide.

But industrialization—especially at the pace achieved on Taiwan—required more than the building up of the economic bureaucracy and statist intervention. First, Taiwan needed overseas inputs and markets that would allow firms to accumulate at rates well beyond what the domestic market allowed. Second, growth required the breaking of traditional patterns of investment and the subjugation of capital to the rigors of market prices. Neither outcome was guaranteed, and each rested upon distinct and contingent political developments. We now turn to the first of these two requirements.

The Postwar Boom and Taiwan's Investment Expansion

The Nationalist's development strategy before the war hinged on the exploitation of the mainland's vast albeit poor market and its substantial reserves of raw materials. With the party's removal to Taiwan, the regime was left with no choice but to look offshore for both, while the need for dollars to fund defense only added pressure. The KMT benefited enormously therefore from the economic boom that ran from 1950 to the early 1970s. Centered in the advanced capitalist countries, it generated unprecedented demand for technology-rich consumer goods and outward flows of capital. At its center was the US. Having contracted significantly in the 1930s, its economy grew 6.5 percent in the first half of the next decade. The manufacturing sector was the greatest beneficiary. Already at the "frontier" of innovation, the war widened the technological gap between the US and its rivals.[18] In 1945, America's economic hegemony was expressed in its technological lead, vast trade surpluses, and global demand for dollars. America accounted for 40 percent of global GDP, half of global manufacturing, and provisioned one-third of the world's industrial exports.[19] Meanwhile, world GDP grew five percent annually, more than double the pace of the expansion of 1873 to 1913, while global trade grew nearly twice as fast, quintupling between 1948 and 1971.[20] While America's rate of growth halved following peace, and stayed at around 2.5 percent for the duration of the 1960s, wages grew. The capacity of the US to act as importer of first and last resort remained therefore robust and, even as it weakened, America continued to offer growth as its banks and manufacturers responded to intensifying competition at home by sending technology overseas.[21]

The US economy also reaped enormous advantages from international arrangements that Washington had mostly designed and over which it maintained command. The US also brought clarity to trading rules through agreements that benefited allies, while the global need for dollars, established at Bretton Woods, permitted deep and long-run deficits. The US used these to finance its military expenditures, foreign aid deliveries, Foreign Direct Investment (FDI) outflows, and most importantly run trade deficits far greater and for far longer than its economic performance would otherwise have allowed. The combined effect prolonged and sped the economic expansion of others.[22]

On Taiwan, the KMT leveraged these conditions, to piece together policy mixes that favored the export of manufactures.[23] The key agencies that guided policy were ad hoc creations of the late 1940s, originally intended to confront emergency conditions that arose from the KMT's defeat, rebellion, hyperinflation, the administration of aid, and the foreign exchange crisis. The party strengthened bureaucratic command and control capacity to address each problem as it appeared. In rapid succession, it formed and dissolved agencies, rotated personnel, and adjusted policy as required. The National Resource Council, established on the mainland, was replaced by the Taiwan Production Board (TPB) in 1949. The TPB's writ was quickly broadened from managing former Japanese properties to coordinating economic and financial matters across all levels of the bureaucracy. The Economic Stabilization Board (ESB)—formed in 1951 from an ad hoc group charged with bringing prices under control through the better coordination of trade, monetary supply, and fiscal matters—absorbed the functions of the TPB in 1953. The ESB also took control of the Industrial Financing Committee, a small working group that had managed US dollars reserve, and broadened its purview with the needs of the economy. It soon became the brain trust for industrial policy, which it administered by assigning foreign exchange, controlling imports, and targeting export assistance.

Like the TPB before it, the ESB was a coordinating office. It contained five groups corresponding to key areas of the economy and operated between and above the regular ministries. It included the Industrial Development Commission, which managed early manufacturing policy in addition to developing the first five-year economic plan. With the end of inflation, the party leadership disbanded the ESB in 1958. Some of its tasks went to the ministries, but the job of policy formulation and economic coordination was kept separate. These moved first to the Joint Commission on Industrial Development within the Council for US Aid—an organization created with US assistance in 1948—and then to the Council for International Economic Cooperation and Development, created in 1963 in anticipation of the end to US aid. By the time the CIECD was formed, the coordinating agencies had aggregated significant powers over the economic bureaucracy.[24]

The rapid reshuffling of organizations served several goals. First, it preserved the central leadership's command of the bureaucracy, allowing for the removal and transfer of key personnel. Second, it allowed flexibility in the face of rapidly changing international and domestic conditions. Third, the recruitment and rotation of staff created a large stable of expert technocrats who could assure continuity of vision and purpose. By assigning individuals multiple positions simultaneously, and by rotating technocrats through different responsibilities, the party leadership secured command of the economy's heights while preventing bureaucratic turf wars that might otherwise interfere with policy coordination.[25] At the center of the mix was Chiang Ching-kuo, whose first-hand experience with Leninist party control in the USSR informed his understanding of political control. Steadily, he built his political base first in the security apparatus and then over economic policy making.[26]

In the 1950s the KMT had few good economic choices. On the one hand, the leadership understood it could not afford the mistakes of the past. On the other, a combination of problems portended economic collapse: hardline anti-inflationary lending policies discouraged the upgrading needed to export; import-substitution policies, intended to protect poorly capitalized firms, fueled overproduction and deflation; insufficient government revenue, and the cost of a vast army inherited from the civil war, threatened to bust the budget; and the island's reliance on imported raw materials rendered the import bill unsustainable. To break the vicious cycle, the bureaucracy bundled incentives and protections in ways to force local manufacturers to export. Tax rebates and offsetting were extended to all imports assembled into exports. The cost of dollars to exporters was discounted. The government allowed firms to retain a portion of their foreign exchange earnings that went to the generation of exports. Multiple exchange rates shaped costs to improve export competitiveness and, when it was introduced in 1960, the unified exchange rate was set at a level that cheapened Taiwan's goods abroad. Meanwhile, the party commanded state-owned upstream enterprises to adjust output to meet demand for intermediary inputs, ensuring that precious dollars went to essential intermediary goods. Far from ending protections and price adjustments, the state honed them.[27]

The total volume of exported goods picked up, growing 6.4 percent annually across the 1950s and then 21.8 percent across the 1960s. By 1960 industrial products accounted for 23.3 percent of exports, up from only 9 percent. By 1964 they topped two-fifths of the export share and three-quarters by the end of the decade.[28] Manufacturing's share of GDP swelled as a result. It surpassed 25 percent in 1962 and hit 39 percent in 1989, at which time manufactured goods accounted for 84 percent of exports. As exports grew on the back of Organisation for Economic Co-operation and Development (OECD) wage growth, expectations of further demand expansion induced more investment and greater risk taking.

Whereas the long-run achievements of Taiwanese manufacturers rested upon their capacity to adjust continually to changing international prices, that flexibility can hardly explain their initial venture into the global market. In the absence of technology and knowledge, export hopes were moot. The pervasive uncertainty and the risk of going head-to-head against established multinationals in their own markets dampened any enthusiasm for investment in the export sector. There was no reason in the early days for entrepreneurs to assume that statist interventions would work to their benefit. Not only were government systems of support entirely untried, there was no way for Taiwan's firms to know whether the state could continue to match their needs once they committed to exporting. By the mid-1950s, the interest of the Taiwanese bourgeoisie lay not in exporting, but in the import-substitution policies that fostered their appearance and secured their revenues in the first place.

The dilemma faced by the heads of Taiwanese manufacturing firms was clear: US and Japanese advantages in their own markets reached below leading edge industries to much older ones. This was especially true in the case of Japan, Taiwan's chief trade competitor in labor-intensive manufacturing. Deep inventories of technology compensated for its relatively higher wages. The investment boom that commenced in Japan in 1950, and was the basis of its own export-led growth, led first in those industries most appropriate to Taiwan's conditions—textiles and electronics. As it turned out, however, the contours of the postwar recovery in the OECD countries proved exceedingly opportune for Taiwan. In addition to driving the demand that Taiwan's manufacturers needed and heeded, the intensified global competition within the OECD bloc pressured its firms to look to low-wage countries like Taiwan to reduce their bill. The ancillary cheapening of global shipping, and the wartime revolution in telecommunications, supported such developments.

The entry of low-cost Japanese and German competitors forced US firms overseas first.[29] They consequently moved the more labor-intensive parts of their production chains to low-wage countries such as Taiwan, leaving capital-intensive processes at home. But, just as US firms shifted overseas, Japanese firms followed. They set up shop in Taiwan and South Korea and were aided in these efforts by Japan's Import-Export Bank, which among other things wished to see firms prolong their product and profit cycles while upgrading production at home.[30] Japanese textile firms Toyobo, Kanebo, and Unitika were among the first to invest on Taiwan, initially to bypass US import limits on Japanese textiles. Electronics firms seeking the same advantages followed.[31] While Japanese firms outsourced those parts of the manufacturing process from the bottom rung of the industrial ladder, these were not without technical complexity. As the pace of accumulation accelerated, moreover, Japanese multinationals found themselves facing intensifying wage pressures at home. They responded by shedding still technology-richer processing. US textile and electronics firms refused to stand idle. They responded to the new round of price pressure from Japan in kind by recruiting still more Taiwanese subsidiaries of their own.[32] Firms such as RCA set up plants to assemble US-manufactured capital-intensive components into final goods for re-export as well as the manufacture of intermediary inputs suitable for assembly back home. As the bottom line of Japanese and US firms benefited by prolonging commodity life cycles, Taiwanese companies acquired valuable technology and experience.

The benefits of these investments to Taiwan manufacturing were greater than the scale of capital flows suggests. First, although multinational investment tended to employ fewer workers, because of their greater reliance on machines, this equipment brought with it the very know-how needed to access the OECD market. Moreover, while these investments tended to produce goods that carried the higher-per-unit value needed to justify shipping, the embodied technology had not topped out at the time of investment.[33] Finally, because market conditions demanded up-to-date machinery, and because the life cycle of consumer products was shortening, early investments made to capitalize on cheap labor called forth regular upgrading at shortening intervals.[34]

Second, though FDI to Taiwan was a small share of all investment, its contribution to both exports and manufacturing employment was greater on a dollar basis than local or overseas Chinese investment. Across the 1950s and 1960s, FDI accounted for 4 to 5 percent of capital formation, but 11 percent of manufacturing investment, one-fifth of export share, 16 percent of manufacturing employment.[35] The disproportionate effect was due to its concentration in exports back to the OECD bloc, where highly competitive markets featured rapid product obsolescence and technological innovation. Between 1966 and 1971, the ratio of fixed assets to employees in foreign-owned firms and subsidiaries on Taiwan rose fastest, especially after passing so-called Lewis threshold in the mid-1960s. Thereafter, growing domestic incomes spurred more domestic savings, which augmented capital formation. Still, by the mid-1970s export sales in leading edge manufacturing such as electronics and tool making, where FDI was concentrated, employed per dollar three times as many industrial workers as domestic sales.[36] Most importantly, as subsidiaries and joint ventures connected with local suppliers, Taiwan's small and medium enterprises acquired often by linking up the economies of scale necessary to afford upgrading on their own. To force FDI upgrading, the state required ever higher local content for foreign plants. As a share of all purchases of machinery and equipment, FDI domestic acquisitions reached two-fifths in 1987.[37]

In 1950 Taiwan's leading firms were stuck. They lacked the technology needed to enter foreign markets and the dollar earnings to acquire it and were unable to compete in foreign markets on the basis of cheap labor alone. Assistance came in two main forms. First, multinationals that needed to cut costs in the face of heightened competition set up shop on the island. Attracted initially by cheap labor, they found that in order to maintain market share they had no choice but to offshore technology-richer and richer processes, link up with domestic suppliers, and assist in their partners' upgrading. Second, had the state not faced head on the inflationary threat of the expansionary adjustments to the exchange rate, and the compounding effects of the investment boom entailed in the rapid upgrading of manufacturing, the gains from exports would have undoubtedly disappeared under the pressure of rising wages and rising costs. All things equal, Taiwan's astounding levels of capital formation should have driven prices to levels that squeezed private corporate profits and investment and slowed the expansion.

Yet across three decades, private and public capital formation rose as a share of GDP, reaching their highest annual levels at times of greatest depressed global demand. This was achieved by the state's pushing of prices in directions they would otherwise not have gone. The turn to exports was, therefore, accompanied not by the lessening but by the enhancing and more sophisticated targeting of bureaucratic systems of command and control. The state's early adoption of the strategic targeting of firms for loans and other forms of support, its invitation to foreign firms to invest in the export sector, and its parsimonious control of money supply brought a new discipline to public and private firms, while signaling to the private sector its intention to favor exporters.[38] While these developments followed upon and most certainly consolidated Taiwan's transition to capitalism and its rapid industrialization, they were not its cause. To understand how market discipline was brought to bear on producers and workers alike—to explain the adoption of capitalist rules for reproduction—we must return to the political terrain and the formation of a native bourgeoisie.

Party and State in Taiwan's Transition to Industrial Capitalism

Taiwan's transition to capitalism, which began in the mid-1950s, required the presence of a special kind of state. In the first instance, what was needed was a state capable of both recognizing the need to enforce the adoption of capitalist rules of production in the economy and overcoming resistance from elites and producers alike. In the second instance, with capitalist social property relations in place, the state had to remain sufficiently autonomous of social classes in order to insist on firms adopting accumulation strategies commensurate with requirements of growth via exports. In other words, the state had subsequently to resist capture by either social elites or workers. On Taiwan, this meant that KMT state had to be prepared to and capable of eradicating the local landlord and merchant classes, the chief beneficiaries of Japanese rule, who remained wedded to pre-capitalist accumulation strategies, and replace them with a competitively constrained bourgeoisie.

In the early 1900s, Japan streamlined the island's property rights by abrogating claims of those landlords who lived in the mainland and enhancing the claims of those on the island. It pushed a green revolution with investments in irrigation, new strains of rice and sugarcane, and chemical fertilizers that greatly enhanced yields and total farm output. It transformed cane processing and promoted the export of rice and sugar to the homeland. Though the greatest profits went to Japanese businesses, native landlords and merchants benefited significantly from the rise in trade and rent.[39] Their sons received education and entered the colonial administration or even sojourned in Japan. The end of colonial rule in 1945 opened the way for native Taiwanese merchants and landlords, who had benefited greatly from the colonial order, to capture the state and use its power to enhance their economic position. Similar to the landed elites of Latin America, they would have directed the state to lower tariffs and cheapen food exports, to reduce or eliminate taxes on their income, to attack tenant security and enable rent squeezing, to invest in infrastructure that lowered the cost of food exports, and to counter depressed prices and earnings with price supports.

Most importantly, wanting to trap cheap labor on the land, landlords resisted any progressive laws including land reform that protected worker's rights or aided smallholders at a cost to them. Such policies would undoubtedly have protected the incomes of landlords and merchants, while strengthening the island's comparative advantage in cheap farm produce, but would do so at the expense of manufacturing. Without aggressive and consistent state assistance in the forms of cheap loans and tariffs, Taiwanese manufacturers would remain undercapitalized. Unable to compete internationally, off farm employment would not materialize, farm wages would stagnate (or even decline in the face of population increase), and there would be ever-less incentive to cut farming costs. So long as farming remained under the direct management of smallholders and tenants without means, moreover, the surest way for individual families to combat costs was by exploiting cheap household labor rather than upgrading of equipment. In other words, given the structures imposed by landlords and merchants on the countryside, micro-economic behavior would be inconsistent with the needs of capitalist or modern economic development.

But this course was blocked by the KMT, which in the key years between 1949 and 1952 transformed itself from a party in defeat and disarray into a disciplined and cohesive organization. In the closing months of the Chinese Civil War, the destruction of party records and loss of members bled the party of what little organizational capacity it had. As Chiang Kaishek departed permanently to Taiwan, he reflected on the causes of his defeat and blamed the party itself. The party failed to enforce discipline, it was paralyzed by factionalism, it did not adequately understand social conditions, and it had no capacity for mobilizing society. In short, Chiang concluded that the KMT had ceased to act as a revolutionary vanguard organization.[40] Within weeks of settling in Taipei, with the assistance of his Soviet-trained son Chiang Ching-kuo, he forced through reforms that produced a party that looked remarkably like the Chinese Communist Party in its structure and organizational functions.[41]

As head of the party, Chiang outlined the direction of reform, but entrusted his son to secure control. Together they picked men to draw up reform plans and then oversaw the formation and work of the Central Reform Committee (CRC). They packed it with relatively young yet highly educated and very loyal party members. To assure control over its agenda, the CRC was placed under the authority of a working group of 25 steered by Chiang senior. For the next two years, the working group reorganized the party from top to bottom. Many members were required to reapply. Some 30,000 new party cells were formed, operating at all levels of administration, the military, the state, and bureaucracy. The central party conducted intensive ideological work to rebuild morale and purpose, building a cadre school and establishing the Anti-Communist Youth Corps. When completed in 1952, the factions that had plagued the party since the 1920s were broken. No doubt the threat of invasion by communist forces steeled party cohesion, but the reforms gave it organizational structure, numbers, and new purpose. One of every 14 people on the island was now a party member.[42]

Simultaneously, Chiang asserted personal charge over the state. He turned control of the security apparatus, military, and youth groups over to his son, who headed the Central Standing Committee of the party.[43] The 1948 Temporary Provisions (martial law) gave extraordinary powers to the president's office as well as the Executive Yuan, which the president constitutionally headed. Chiang ended presidential term limits and bypassed all legal checks on his authority in the name of the "national emergency." By informal and formal mechanisms, he captured the national law-making body or Legislative Yuan. He stuffed it with uncompetitive seats occupied by mainlanders representing their pre-1948 constituencies and procedurally he moved its legislative authority into the Executive Yuan. He placed the bureaucracy under the control of the Executive Yuan and then administered it through a small cabinet of ministerial heads, the provincial governor, generals, and key economic advisors. He handpicked men to fill these positions. Finally, the KMT's Policy Coordination Committee, facilitated by the KMT dominated Control Yuan, disciplined party members and assured policy implementation.[44]

In the name of national security, Chiang took economic policy making out of the ministries and placed it in ad hoc agencies, liberating economic management of the territorial and career interests of bureaucrats. He was assisted in this by the early installment on Taiwan of the American-Chinese jointly run CUSA. Initially managing the dispensation of American aid, CUSA quickly acquired status as a hothouse for economic policy, training technocratic engineers and economists who subsequently cycled through the Cabinet, the chief economic ministries, and public enterprises. Though the guiding agency of the economy would change names and membership (CUSA became the Council for International Economic Cooperation and Development in 1963, the Economic Planning Council in 1973, and the Council for Economic Planning and Development in 1977), it remained an autonomous advisory agency with ministerial status that spoke directly to the president and the Executive Yuan. Staffed by men chosen by the president, not only did its opinions carry great weight, these agencies intervened directly in the management and administration of everything from import controls and technology imports to emergency fund requests from firms. Because each member of the body had experience working in leadership roles across multiple agencies, including the Economic Affairs and Finance ministries and the Central Bank, they possessed both expertise and a vision.[45]

In short order, therefore, Chiang, his son, and a small group of loyalists succeeded in deepening party control over state and society, while transforming the bureaucracy into cohesive, disciplined, and highly functioning administrative instrument effectively free of legislative oversight. The economy's commanding heights were run by a focused cohort of party members and nationalists, supported by a growing number of talented technocrats, entirely dedicated to the idea of China's national reconstruction. However, it remained to be seen whether the re-energized emergency state, fully in place in 1955, could impose its will on the native population and, more to the point, whether those classes whose economic behavior and interests ran counter to the requirements of export-driven industrialization would continue to hinder industrialization.

The placation of Taiwanese society began brutally. The party's suppression of an island-wide revolt left 30,000 dead. The imposition of martial law eviscerated constitutional liberties. With public security turned over to the Garrison Command, the police, secret service, and judiciary had free rein to harass and imprison political opponents. Social control was extended in corporatist fashion over civic groups, trade and industrial organizations, and both labor and farmer unions.[46] Yet, by far the most transformative actions were those resulting in the removal of native colonial merchant and landlord classes. The merchant class was euthanized early, when the KMT took total control of trade in 1945. This began with the establishment of state monopolies in all exports and quickened with the implementation of strict import limits and import-export licensing, and the forced remittance of foreign exchange earnings.[47] These programs were intended to remedy the balance of payments crises, brought on by the sudden surge of imports needed to support an additional two million mainlanders, and to assure the allocation of precious dollar reserves to strategic necessities such as food, fuel, and machinery. But the effect was to eliminate the traditional merchant class and bring trading practices in line with state priorities.

With the state in control of trade, and the general population subdued, only landlords remained as a viable native social opposition. While the US demanded land reform as a condition of aid, the KMT was uncharacteristically enthusiastic. The party's legislative representatives had doggedly resisted land reform before 1949. Many held wealth in land in the mainland. The party's retreat to Taiwan, however, cut those ties, while rendering representatives who fled to Taiwan dependent for their livelihood upon the power of the state to tax and administer the local economy. Without any allegiance to Taiwan's landlords, and unencumbered of an oppositional elite within the state, the KMT leadership passed a land reform law as radical in its results as that carried out simultaneously on the mainland. A 1947 reduction of rent by 40 percent, designed to pressure landlords to cash out, was followed in 1950 by a three-hectare limit on land holdings that ended landlordism. Despite compensation in government bonds and stock in public enterprises, landlords failed to make the transition to commerce or manufacturing.[48] The combined effect of land reform and trade controls was the termination of existing pattern of investment and accumulation, which had done nothing to promote industrialization in the past and to force those with savings to find alternative strategies.

The state did not stand still, however. The economic bureaucracy focused single-mindedly on manufacturing, at the expense of agriculture and services, out of conviction that this was the surest way to protect national sovereignty and pave the way to greater autonomy in international affairs. Benefiting from improvements to agricultural production under Japanese rule, and utilizing many of the same schemes to extract savings from farming households, the KMT squeezed the countryside. In taxes, forced rice sales, and price fixing, the state took about one-quarter of total farm output. It invested in public enterprises, infrastructure, and private loans.[49] Because one did not exist, the KMT created a bourgeoisie and then assured its profitability. It recruited the journalist Wu Sanlian to run a large textile manufacturing plant in Tainan and the lumberyard owner Y. C. Wang to manage newly established Formosa Plastics. The state provided capital, machines, raw materials, and a market, while protecting investments behind tariff walls and import controls.[50] Through a variety of measures, the state compelled former tenants to deepen their dependency upon the market for inputs and earnings, and agricultural productivity grew first in absolute and then in relative terms. In search of cash, farm households shed labor to local labor-intensive manufacturing, at first seasonally but soon permanently. The labor force was thus increasingly separated from farming and tied to the urban markets.

The transition to capitalism was now complete. Denied the ability to profit through rents and arbitrage trading, capital was left with no choice but to accrue by way of specialization, cost cutting, and switching lines. When the limits of domestic demand were reached in the mid-1950s, and firms confronted a crisis of overproduction and falling profits, the economic bureaucracy contrived to drive manufacturers into the global market. It undid some protections, created new ones, directed small firms to combine, reduced the cost of exporting, and required cost cutting. Disciplined by the existential threat of the People's Republic of China (PRC), relieved of the need to answer to entrenched domestic class interests, and in possession of a disciplined cadre of administrators, the party leadership had acquired remarkable freedom of movement, which lasted well into the 1970s. It wielded this new-found power and autonomy to keep the field clear of structural obstacles to growth, while avoiding the pitfalls of rent-seeking predatory practices and the dissipation of scarce resources on uneconomic projects that would have otherwise followed.[51]

Conclusion

In 1962 Alexander Gerschenkron pointed to the entangled nature of non-development.[52] He argued that risk is great in undeveloped countries because labor is stuck in low-productivity activities; private savings are diffused and flow to rent-seeking activities; it favors unproductive military needs; high costs, poor infrastructure, and the absence of basic industries hamper markets; the available knowledge and skill sets are unsuited to the needs of the modern economy; and to the extent that the state has an industrial policy, this favors the military. Cascading and intertwining bottlenecks from feeble demand and high risk combine to inhibit specialization, undermine efficiencies, preclude rationalization, and lock capital in unproductive agriculture. But Gerschenkron assigns no cause, other than the unsatisfactory state of "backwardness" itself. Brenner's breakthrough was to show that these entangled barriers to growth are the result of general patterns of behavior that find their structural basis in the existing social property relations.

To this we must add the fact that even when latecomers adopt capitalist rules for reproduction, they must still overcome the significant barriers to entry that have been raised by the world's leading capitalist economies, on the basis of past and ongoing successes. The leading economies benefit from their proximity and ease of access to knowledgeable suppliers, skilled and flexible labor, tool and machine builders, experienced distributers and wholesalers, specialized financial institutions, and the most up-to-date infrastructure. In other words, they benefit from a state of generalized market interdependency. Consequently, while providing a model for latecomers to emulate, the success of that model poses a threat to those that wish to follow. It is little wonder that, with leaders setting the terms, the developmental state takes on the task of lowering uncertainty at home. Yet, there is no reason to expect the condition of underdevelopment to elicit a remedy. Just as Brenner spotlights the politically contingent nature of capitalism's first appearance in England, so it is necessary to recognize Taiwan's highly contingent and political road to capitalist development.

With the arrival of the Cold War, America's strategic needs trumped national business interests. As Washington took on the task of protecting US business by protecting global capital, it acquiesced to its allies' departures from liberal economic principles. The trade and budget deficits that followed were the cost of fighting communism. It focused its attention on gradually easing the global flow of goods and capital while encouraging recovery and capitalist expansion through the formation of regional and global production chains that paralleled and undergirded its alliance system. The postwar revival of capitalist accumulation, driven by extraordinarily high rates of investment, set in motion dynamics propitious to Taiwan's export growth.[53] The OECD's postwar expansion via trade grew consumer demand but also intensified manufacturing competition, producing both the pull for imports and the outflow of capital and know-how to produce them overseas at lower cost.

For Third World nations to take advantage of these developments, however, required the appearance of an extraordinary set of domestic social conditions.[54] Nothing about the KMT before 1949 suggests it could produce them. Yet, its retreat to Taiwan freed the party from class interests that were otherwise detrimental to capitalist expansion via industrialization. It bound the survival of those who fled to the island, to the party, and state. Shocked into reform and separated from its base, the party achieved remarkable cohesion and autonomy. In swift succession, it ended traditional investment strategies of native landlords and merchants; it created a domestic bourgeoisie; and it subordinated accumulation strategies to the requirements of the most advanced markets in Japan, the US, and Europe. With American permission, and under the guidance of powerful coordinating agencies within the state, the KMT shaped relative prices to countermand Taiwan's prevailing conditions.

Disciplined by external threats, which it could best confront by building up manufacturing, and by its American guardian, which required growth on the basis of private capital in exchange for security, the KMT found that to contradict the requirements of capital accumulation would undermine sovereignty and governance. The authoritarian party was subject henceforth to the same disciplining forces that shaped the export sector: its actions could not ignore the disciplining force of competition. By the late 1950s, in other words, state power rested on the prosperity of an economy governed by the requirements of private profitability.

Notes

1. Robert Brenner, "The Agrarian Roots of European Capitalism," *Past and Present* 97 (1982): 12–113; Spencer Dimmock, *The Origin of Capitalism in England, 1400–1600* (Leiden: Brill, 2014).
2. Theda Skocpol, *States and Revolution: A Comparative Analysis of France, Russia, and China.* (Cambridge: Cambridge University Press, 1979); Barrington Moore, *The Social Origins of Dictatorship and Democracy: Lord and Peasant in the Making of the Modern World* (Boston: Beacon Press, 1966).
3. Robert Baldwin, Tain-Jy Chen and Douglass Nelson, *Political Economy of US-Taiwan Trade* (Ann Arbor: University of Michigan Press, 1995).

4. Odd Westad, *The Global Cold War: Third World Interventions and the Making of Our Times* (Cambridge: Cambridge University Press, 2005).
5. Perry Anderson, *American Foreign Policy and its Thinkers* (London: Verso Press, 2013).
6. David Engerman, "Ideology and the Origins of the Cold War, 1917–1962," in *The Cambridge History of the Cold War: Volume One, Origins*, ed. Melvyn Leffler and Odd Arne Westad (Cambridge: Cambridge University Press, 2010), 33.
7. Ronald L. McGlothlen, *Controlling the Waves: Dean Acheson and U.S. Foreign Policy in Asia* (New York: W.W. Norton, 1993), 39.
8. Chalmers Johnson, *MITI and the Japanese Miracle* (Stanford: Stanford University Press, 1982), 198–200.
9. Johnson, *MITI*.
10. Westad, *Global Cold War*.
11. Anderson, *American Foreign Policy*.
12. McGlothlen, *Controlling*, 90, 134.
13. Denis Fred Simon, "External Incorporation and Internal Reform," in *Contending Approaches to the Political Economy of Taiwan*, ed. Edwin Winckler and Susan Greenhalgh (Armonk: ME Sharpe, 1988), 141.
14. Nick Cullather, "'Fuel for the Good Dragon': The United States and Industrial Policy in Taiwan, 1950–1965," *Diplomatic History* 20, no. 1 (1996): 9–13.
15. Robert Wade, *Governing the Market: Economic Theory and the Role of Government in East Asian Industrialization* (Princeton: Princeton University Press, 1990).
16. Charles Maier, "The World Economy and the Cold War in the middle of the Twentieth Century," in *The Cambridge History of the Cold War: Volume One, Origins*, ed. Melvyn Leffler and Odd Arne Westad (Cambridge: Cambridge University Press, 48–49).
17. Anderson, *American Foreign Policy*, 55.
18. Philip Armstrong, Andrew Glyn and John Harrison, *Capitalism Since 1945* (Oxford: Basil Blackwell, 1991).
19. Robert Baldwin and Douglass Nelson, "The Political Economy of U. S.-Taiwanese Trade and Other International Economic Relations," in *Trade and Protectionism*, ed. Takatoshi Ito and Anne O. Krueger (Chicago: University of Chicago Press, 1993), 307– 7.
20. Angus Maddison, *The Contours of the World Economy, 1-2030 A.D: Essays in Macro Economic History* (Oxford: Oxford University Press, 2007), 71–72; Eric Hobsbawm, *The Age of Extremes: The Short Twentieth Century, 1914–1990* (New York: Vintage Press, 1994), 88.
21. Robert Brenner, *The Economics of Global Turbulence* (London: Verso Press, 2006); Robert Castley, *Korea's Economic Miracle: The Crucial Role of Japan* (New York: St. Martin's Press, 1997).

22. Barry Eichengreen, *Exorbitant Privilege: The Rise and Fall of the Dollar and the Future of the International Monetary System* (Oxford: Oxford University Press, 2011); Baldwin, *U.S. Taiwan Trade.*
23. Baldwin, *U.S. Taiwan Trade.*
24. Chien-Kuo Pang, *The State and Economic Transformation: The Taiwan Case* (London: Garland, 1992), 49–54.
25. Vivek Chibber, "Bureaucratic Rationality and the Developmental State," *American Journal of Sociology* 107, no. 4 (2002): 951–989.
26. Edwin A. Winckler, 1988. "Elite Political Struggle 1945–1985," in *Contending Approaches to the Political Economy of Taiwan, ed.* Edwin Winckler and Susan Greenhalgh (Armonk: Sharpe, 1988), 151–171.
27. Ching-yuan Lin, *Industrialization in Taiwan, 1946–1972* (New York: Praeger, 1973), 83–98.
28. Shirley Kuo and John Fei, "Causes and Roles of Export Expansion in the Republic of China," in *Foreign Trade and Investment: Economic Development in the Newly industrializing Asian Countries*, ed. Walter Galenson (Madison: University of Wisconsin Press, 1985), 45–84.
29. Brenner, *Turbulence.*
30. Robert Steven, *Japan's New Imperialism* (Armonk: M.E. Sharpe, 1990).
31. Steven, *New Imperialism*, 69–71.
32. Jordan Schreiber, *U.S. Corporate Investment in Taiwan* (New York: The Dunellen Company, 1970); Steven, *New Imperialism.*
33. Schreiber, *Corporate Investment.*
34. Anant Negandhi, *Management and Economic Development: The Case of Taiwan* (The Hague: Martinus Nijhoff, 1973); Gustav Ranis and Chi Schive, "Direct Foreign Investment in Taiwan's Development," in *Foreign Trade and Investment: Economic Development in the Newly industrializing Asian Countries*, ed. Walter Galenson (Madison: University of Wisconsin Press, 1985), 122; Chi Schive, *The Foreign Factor: The Multinational Corporation's Contribution to the Economic Modernization of the Republic of China* (Stanford: Hoover Institution Press, 1990).
35. Ranis and Schive, *Foreign Investment*, 95, 100.
36. Ibid., 97, 110.
37. Chich-Heng Kuo, *International Capital Movements and the Developing World: The Case of Taiwan* (New York: Praeger, 1991), 63.
38. Lin, *Industrialization.*
39. Chih-ming Ka, *Japanese Colonialism in Taiwan: Land Tenure, Development, and Dependency* (New York: M. E. Sharpe, 1998).
40. Fuming Xu, *Zhongguo guomindang de gaizao, 1950–1952* (Taipei: Zhongzheng shuju, 1986); Bruce Dickson, "The Lessons of Defeat: The Reorganization of the Kuomintang on Taiwan, 1950–1952," *The China Quarterly* 133 (1993): 56–84. Chiang Kaishek reflected: "The failure of

our anti-communist military strategy on the mainland was not because of any supposed communist superiority or strength, nor its capacity to defeat our Nationalist Revolutionary Army. Our defeat had everything to do with the party's leadership of the National Revolution: the collapse of party organization, the neglect of discipline, the collapse of spirit" (quoted in Xu, *Zhongguo*, 46).

41. Edwin A. Winkler, "Elite Political Struggle 1945–1985," in *Contending Approaches to the Political Economy of Taiwan*, ed. Edwin A. Winkler and Susan Greenhalgh (Armonk: M.E. Sharpe, 1988).
42. Hung-mao Tien, *The Great Transition: Political and Social Change in the Republic of China* (Stanford: Hoover Institution Press, 1989).
43. Winkler, "Elite Political Struggle."
44. Shelley Rigger, *Politics in Taiwan* (London: Routledge, 1999).
45. Pang, *Economic Transformation.*
46. Yunjie Li, *Taiwan gonghui zhengce de zhengshi jingji fenxi* (Taipei: Juliuyuan shugongsi, 1992), 52–59; Ming-sho Ho, "The Rise and Fall of Leninist Control in Taiwan's Industry," *The China Quarterly* 189 (2007): 162–179.
47. Lin, *Industrialization*, 47–48.
48. Thomas Gold, *State and Society in the Taiwan Miracle* (Armonk; M.E. Sharpe, 1986).
49. Christopher Isett and Steven Miller, *The Social History of Agriculture: From the Origins to the Current Crisis* (New York: Rowman and Littlefield, 2016), 267–281.
50. Gold, *State and Society.*
51. Chibber, *Bureaucratic Rationality.*
52. Alexander Gerschenkron, 1962. *Economic Backwardness in Historical Perspective* (Cambridge: Harvard University Press, 1962).
53. Armstrong et al., *Capitalism*; Brenner, *Turbulence.*
54. Evans, *Embedded.*

CHAPTER 13

Rethinking the Rules of Reproduction and the Transition to Capitalism: Reading Federici and Brenner Together

Nicole Leach

This chapter takes a slightly different direction from those that proceed and follow. While this chapter presents an application and extension of political Marxism, it does so from a critical perspective, using Marxist feminism to challenge political Marxism and simultaneously using political Marxism to challenge Marxist feminism. The point behind engaging these two fields is to trouble the question of patriarchal capitalism's arrival. Motivating this engagement is the hypothesis that there is something specific in the transition to capitalism that ruptured previous forms of political economic organization, *as well as*, previous gender regimes. I suggest the resulting dynamic that was then set in motion as that of an internal relation between gender and class oppression; as opposed to separate capitalist and patriarchal systems that intersect and interact.

Within this understanding, class exploitation and gender oppression are considered co-constitutive elements of capitalist social property relations. To explore this assertion, two troubling tendencies plaguing Marxist and

N. Leach (✉)
York University, Toronto, ON, Canada

X. Lafrance, C. Post (eds.), *Case Studies in the Origins of Capitalism*, Marx, Engels, and Marxisms,
https://doi.org/10.1007/978-3-319-95657-2_13

Marxist feminist theorizing must be addressed. First, the legacy of dual systems theorizing within Marxist feminism is challenged for its ahistorical assumptions regarding patriarchal capitalism's arrival. When the distinctive qualities of capitalist social property relations are taken for granted, room is left for the argument that patriarchy's historical existence explains its contemporary manifestation, that is, its manifestation as a distinct and closed system that interacts and intersects with capitalist social property relations, but that is ultimately separate or external to them. The analysis forwarded within this chapter seeks to provide a rebuke to this troubling theoretical practice by defending the argument, advanced by Marxist feminists such as Federici,[1] that capitalism has been a gendered social relation from the moment of its birth. Federici investigates the structural components that allow and facilitate the continuation of exploitative gender relations without having to rely on ahistorical or functionalist answers and argues that the transition period was punctuated at each moment by a transformation in the organization of social reproduction and oppressive gender relations.

The second tendency that this chapter tackles is the lack of historical specificity within Federici's Marxist feminist reading of the transition. Throughout her attack on these ahistorical hypotheses regarding patriarchy's historical transcendence, she simultaneously relies on an overly expansive geographic and temporal reading of the transition to capitalism that lacks a robust historical specificity—the kind of historical specificity that is necessary for fully challenging these ahistorical feminist theses. This is critically challenged by turning to political Marxism's specific methodological approach, conceptualization of capitalism and economic development, and privileging of class struggle and agency, which provide a welcomed challenge to previous transition models that place higher emphasis on market relations over social relations as well as redressing Federici's lack of historical specificity.

While political Marxism uniquely provides much needed historical nuance to Federici's lack of historical specificity and dual systems theory's ahistoricity, political Marxism continues to reproduce the common Marxist failure to produce a strong and substantive gender analysis. If the ahistoricity of dual systems analysis is to be effectively challenged using a political Marxist methodology, then those strains within political Marxism that cede room to a dual systems approach to the study of capitalist exploitation and women's oppression must simultaneously be critically revisited.

For example, Wood's structural separation of sexism and class exploitation,

> The point, though, is that if capital derives advantages from racism or sexism, it is not because of any structural tendency in capitalism toward racial inequality or gender oppression, but on the contrary because they disguise the structural realities of the capitalist system and because they divide the working class. At any rate, capitalist exploitation can in principle be conducted without any consideration for colour, race, creed, gender, any dependence upon extra-economic inequality or difference.[2]

This structural separation is a result of the analytical separation of social production and social reproduction that recognizes class as an economic relation and gender oppression as a political relation. This analytical fragmenting is called into question by a social reproduction feminist analysis which views social production and reproduction as comprised of differentiated, yet internally related, moments within a social whole.

By marrying this social reproduction feminist analysis to political Marxism's historically specific account of the development of capitalist social relations, it is possible to advance an alternative methodology that focuses on the co-constitutive relationship of gender and class relations as an original and foundational component of capitalist social property relations. This chapter proceeds under the belief that a revised political Marxism has the potential to set up a non-teleological and historically specific account of the origins of gendered capitalist social property relations. Bringing together the best aspects of Federici, a broader social reproduction feminist cannon, and political Marxism allows this potential to be realized.

Reflections on Federici

How to account for the continued oppression of women under capitalism, especially given that capitalism is often problematically described as taking a genderblind approach to exploitation? This was the question bubbling underneath the surface of the 1970s feminist domestic labor debates and it is a question and a debate that still confronts socialist feminism today. The various approaches to addressing this question and resulting positions expressed throughout the debates provided much productive and useful theorizing regarding the avenues of exploitation, processes of oppression, and the social relations surrounding women's unpaid labor. The focus of the domestic labor debate centered on how to understand the coexistence of capitalism and patriarchy in its current configuration and not on the origins of patriarchal capitalism. While a historical materialist analysis was present at times, and made certain contributions to these debates, the existence of capitalism was often taken for granted.

On the other hand, mainstream Marxist and liberal historiographies of the transition to capitalism have proceeded by and large with little to no consideration of the role of patriarchy, gender oppression, or gendered divisions of labor on the origins and development of capitalism. Neither the commercialization model,[3] world systems theory,[4] neo-Malthusian demographic models,[5] nor political Marxism[6] advances a strong feminist analysis within their methodological approaches to questioning the gendered origins of capitalist social relations. Even the neo-Malthusian demographic models, with their central focus on demographics and population, evade serious discussions of social reproduction or gender constructions.

Against this backdrop, Federici explicitly revisits the transition as a means to investigate the structural components that facilitate the continuation of exploitative gender relations without having to rely on ahistorical or functionalist answers.[7] *Caliban and the Witch* presents an immensely important step forward in addressing the lacuna in socialist feminist theorizing that allows for the origins of patriarchal capitalism to be taken for granted and Federici challenges ahistorical hypotheses that use patriarchy's historic existence as justification for its continued conceptualization as an autonomous system. As well, the all too familiar dismissal of a gender analysis within Marxist transition debates is challenged by Federici's extensive discussions of how the loss of the commons was never a gender neutral process. She includes an analysis of how the witch hunts were a specific part of the processes of primitive accumulation and significantly contributed to a specifically capitalist gendered division of labor. Federici returns to this crucial period to contemplate and discover the ways in which capitalism, from its moment of birth, required the suppression and oppression of women to develop, take form, and advance. Through her analysis of the differential effects of the loss of the commons, the patriarchy of the wage, the disciplining of women's bodies, and the creation of new and insidious ways of policing women's bodies, Federici chronicles how gender oppression was a part of, rather than apart from, the development of capitalist social relations. However, while her work is highly influential, it is not immune to criticism. To borrow Teschke's words, Federici's take on the transition is "brilliant but not unproblematic."[8]

Although Federici moves beyond an "add gender and stir analysis," she does not go far enough in challenging these Marxist takes on the transition, and there remains a certain slipping back into the common feminist problem of relying on Marxist interpretations of production relations while pairing them with feminist interpretations of gender relations.[9] Federici avoids this problematic tendency better than most; however, she continues to rely heavily on certain Marxist methodologies to provide the majority of her explanation about the contours of the transition period and is insufficiently critical of the ways in which these transition models impede a historically specific analysis of the transition. Specifically, Federici relies heavily on a combination of world systems theory's and the commercialization model to inform her feminist re-evaluation of primitive accumulation. This theoretical mixture which inspires Federici's conceptual apparatus and methodology lacks a certain historical specificity and, in turn, advances an overly expansive understanding of primitive accumulation that fails to provide a non-teleological view of the transition. In this regard, Federici's appropriation of their methodological leanings means a simultaneous appropriation of their lack of historical specificity produces a similarly extended temporal and geographical reach that relies on geographically and temporarily eclectic evidentiary supports.

Despite this reliance on transition theories that arguably contain elements of a teleological view of capitalism's arrival and development, Federici claims to support a non-teleological view of capitalism's arrival, and is even careful in her usage of the term transition,

> the concept of 'transition,' then, helps us to think of a prolonged process of change and of societies in which capitalist accumulation coexisted with political formations not yet predominantly capitalistic. The term, however, suggests a gradual, linear historical development, whereas the period it names was among the bloodiest and most discontinuous in world history ... I use the term primarily in a temporal sense.[10]

However, this aspiration for a non-teleological, non-linear approach is not consistently pursued. The generalized overview of the temporal period that marks the transition within Federici's analysis is overly expansive and is applied to the whole of Europe (at times even including the Americas). Federici's conceptualization of the initiation and development of capitalism is primarily present within her expanded discussion of primitive accumulation which is deciphered through reviewing the amalgamated histories of Italy, Germany, France, England, America, and across a four-century time frame.

It is difficult to get a full sense of what exactly constitutes capitalism in *Caliban and the Witch*. When it is directly addressed, capitalism is discussed as a counter-revolution or as "the response of the feudal lords, the patrician merchants, the bishops and popes, to a centuries-long social conflict that, in the end, shook their power, and truly gave 'all the world a big jolt'. Capitalism was the counter-revolution that destroyed the possibilities that had emerged from the anti-feudal struggle."[11] The principle way that capitalism is described is in reference to the separation of producers from the lands, and from their direct means of reproduction, through processes of primitive accumulation.[12] Throughout her discussion of feudal class relations, Federici highlights feudal lords' and exploiters' need for the use of direct force to exact authority and exploitation; this is reminiscent of Brenner's discussion of politically constituted versus economic compulsion; however, it is not clear if this is held as a defining characteristic.[13] Federici focuses attention on the role that the commutation of labor services into monetarized payments in eroding serfdom and leading to a process of "proletarianization", but a full articulation of the connection between commutation of labor services and of the end of serfdom as either part of a process or as constituting the transition to capitalism is missing.[14] Implicitly from these discussions, capitalism's emergence corresponds with the end of serfdom, the separation of the producer from their means of reproduction, as well as the extension and expansion of the market and the commercialization of everyday life.

This vague definition of capitalist social relations, however, relies on a generous and selective reading of the text and glosses over many issues. If the end of serfdom is held as a defining feature of the transition and of capitalism, then this reduces capitalism's definition to its reliance on wage labor. This invites a number of problematic economistic readings of capitalism that Federici would no doubt challenge. In addition, this definition would again stretch the temporal timeline of the transition and further contribute to a teleological reading of the transition period,

> [if] feudalism is defined in terms of the lord-serf relations, post-fourteenth-century—not to speak of post seventeenth-century—French society cannot qualify as feudal. More specifically, if feudalism is defined by serfdom and if capitalism is defined by wage-labour—both non-existent in early modern France—then the four centuries between the late fourteenth century and 1789 could only qualify as a long period of transition.[15]

Tethering capitalism's definition to the extension and expansion of the market is equally problematic as it reduces capitalism to a market relation as opposed to a set of social relations. This is the central subject of Brenner's critique of the commercialization model and it assumes a teleological trajectory of capitalism's arrival.[16]

Federici's discussion of capitalism lacks an abstract theory that lays out the theoretical and concrete parameters around the constitutive aspects of capitalism that allow theorists to identify and distinguish capitalism from other modes of production. While an abstract definition such as this contains a large degree of risk of abstract formalism, proceeding without a clear conceptualization of capitalism's distinct form is also problematic. As Wood makes clear,

> Of course, there is no single capitalism. But neither can we proceed with a conception of capitalism so vague and minimal that it doesn't give us any solid grounds for distinguishing capitalist societies, in all their diversity, from any other social form. If the concept of capitalism is to have any meaning at all, it has to be fairly precise in identifying the common operating principles ... We have to be able to identify the common 'laws of motion' or, better still, the 'rules for reproduction', that make all these cases capitalist.[17]

The lack of historical specificity and constant temporal and geographic shifting in Federici's narrative betray her commitment to a non-determinist and non-teleological approach to the transition. It both muddies her conceptualization of capitalism's distinct character and in turn expands conceptualizations of primitive accumulation to such an extent that it becomes all encompassing. This all-encompassing narrative presents a picture of a singular connected process, as evident in Federici's discussion of the violence that accompanied capitalism's arrival where North American colonization, Eastern Europe's second serfdom, Western European enclosures, and the witch hunts are all referenced within the same breath.[18] This collapsing of multiple processes and locations into a singular narrative of the transition presents a picture of capitalism's arrival as inevitable, as following a certain historical logic, and it hesitates in distinguishing between historical precursors and historical prerequisites. One could allow a generous reading is applied to Federici's expansive inclusion that suggests these vast breadths of geographical locales are evoked to show that capitalism, even in different forms, is inseparably bound with women's oppression. However, the problem with presenting them simultaneously and without critical reflection is that it fails to specify capitalism's origins, calling the larger argument into question. And this is exactly what political Marxists, in various iterations, have done.[19]

In this account, primitive accumulation becomes an all-inclusive singular process whose particular deployments are connected as the functional requirements for the violent, forceful imposition of capitalist production relations. Federici states that the transition was a violent rupture in the social relations of work and reproduction and not a gradual linear process but, by not spelling out a historically specific account of the transition, her conceptualization of primitive accumulation is asserted rather than demonstrated. Federici states that "to describe the social and economic restructuring that the European ruling class initiated in response to its accumulation crisis … [it] is a useful concept, for it connects the 'feudal reaction' with the development of a capitalist economy, and it identifies the *historical* and *logical* conditions for the development of the capitalist system".[20] But this does not explain how capitalism took hold, why this specific "feudal reaction" resulted in capitalist social relations, or what precisely constitutes capitalist social relations. That it is retrospectively intelligible that primitive accumulation was a necessary element is not an explanation of the emergence of a set of specifically gendered capitalist social relations.

This overly inclusive categorization of primitive accumulation, according to Blank, is an inherited shortcoming of the Marxist theory of the transition to which Federici applies her feminist view point: "betraying the influence of Marxian world systems theory, Federici regards the transition as a centuries long process encompassing not only the entirety of Europe but the New World as well, and entailing not only enclosures, land privatization and the witch hunts, but also colonialism, the second serfdom and slavery."[21] The lack of clarity within Federici's conceptualization of primitive accumulation is especially troubling as it is central to her project to acknowledge that "primitive accumulation, then, was not simply an accumulation and concentration of exploitable workers and capital. It was *also an accumulation of differences and divisions within the working class*, whereby hierarchies built upon gender, as well as 'race' and age, became constitutive of class rule and the formation of the modern proletariat."[22] This insistence that understanding the co-constitutive nature of capitalism and patriarchy requires a renewed analysis of primitive accumulation to understand the specifically gendered aspects and the war for control of social reproduction and of women's bodies makes *Caliban and the Witch* so powerful, which is why her overly eclectic inclusion of evidentiary supports is so problematic.

Federici's analysis of primitive accumulation is undercut by the lack of attention to the results of these processes in their historical contexts—their impact on the corresponding structure of social property relations. These differences in outcomes are substantively important to how capitalism, or how patriarchal capitalism, is understood. This problem is highlighted in Brenner's critique of the neo-Malthusian demographic model, specifically, his crucial criticism that the same demographic patterns produced opposing results, calling into question the explanatory efficacy of this model.[23]

This is a crucial lesson that can be aptly applied to Federici's analysis of the role of eco-demographic crisis following the Black Death. The social struggles and oscillation of class power following the crisis that spread throughout Europe provide important contextual background on the dynamics of the transition. For example, she discusses the social struggles over serfdom that proceeded, the impact that the eco-demographic crisis had in the lead up to the enclosures, and uniquely important to Federici, the panic produced around social reproduction, and the need to harness and control reproductive capacities through this period.[24]

While the eco-demographic crisis hit hard across Europe, tallying all results and reactions together under one banner is unhelpful and conceals more than it reveals about women's exploitation through the transition. As Brenner demonstrated in his challenge to the neo-Malthusian model, differentiating the English and French trajectories of long-term economic, social, and political development is important for analyzing this transition period. Although the eco-demographic crisis was not unique to the English example, the reactions to these crises were not universal across these jurisdictions. As Teschke, another prominent political Marxist, explains,

> it is important here to realize that these two regions [England and France] not only emerged differently from the fourteenth-century crisis, but that they already entered into it with diverging class constellations ... pre-crisis France experienced a gradual decline of the lords' capacity for surplus extraction, since they were caught between peasant resistance and royal support for petty peasant property. When eco-demographic crisis struck the French countryside in the fourteenth century, the seigneurial reaction failed due to the persistence of these two factors ... peasants managed to consolidate their de facto property rights over their smallholdings, diminishing noble rights of direct extra-economic coercion.[25]

Teschke further remarks that the result of these differing constellations of class forces prior to and through the crisis resulted in differing outcomes in terms of processes of enclosure, access to land, and continuation or rupture in existing social property relations. In other words, the experience in the English countryside was decisively different than the experience of the French nobility and peasantry,

> [in France] the result was the entrenchment of petty peasant property, now taxed by an increasingly centrally organized absolutist state revolving around the court, the centre of intrigue, faction, sinecure, and inter-noble rivalry … the general crisis accelerated the transformation of a feudal, lord-peasant rent regime into an absolutist, king peasant tax regime.[26]

Federici relies on the eco-demographic crisis and its connection with the processes of primitive accumulation and the subsequent development of capitalist social relations for the social context producing a newly entrenched focus on the populousness of the nation, the uptake of ideologies aimed at controlling women's bodies and reproductive labor in particular. However, while making these connections, evidentiary support is drawn from across almost the whole of Europe. Where Teschke and Brenner chart different reactions to the eco-demographic crisis, based on different class constellations that resulted in differing outcomes of class struggle, Federici amalgamates multiple histories into one movement.

If political Marxists are believed, and the reactions to the eco-demographic crisis including the enclosure initiatives played out differently in England than in France—with only England leading to the instantiation of capitalist social property relations—then what happens to Federici's analysis of the patriarchy of the wage that relies on both the English and French examples as explanatory evidence? The power of Federici's intervention is cut short when these processes, which are presented as uniformly instituted across various locations and periods, are shown not to be universal in their timing and application across jurisdictions. If the point is to trouble the ways in which patriarchy is assumed to have naturally progressed through time in a historic fashion, then it is necessary to replace these theorizations with a historically specific account of the transition of specific social property relations that does not assume a universal progression across jurisdictions from one epoch to the next.

This call for historically specific accounts of the transitions, which does not rely on a single universal progression, must include an examination of the role of the witch hunts and attacks on women's control over their bodies and reproductive capacities. Federici is correct in arguing for rooting these processes in an analysis of primitive accumulation; however, further research is required to tease out the full ramifications and complexities of this argument. As Teschke's intervention makes clear, this further research needs to account for the different contexts surrounding the eco-demographic crisis in England and on the European continent, where countries both entered and exited the crisis differently. This suggests a need to distinguish the transition to agrarian capitalist social property relations in England following the crisis from the further development and entrenchment of an Absolutist state in France, and in turn, to distinguish between the role and impact of the witch hunts in each jurisdiction. Federici's connection between the enclosures and the witch hunts as processes of primitive accumulation constitutively tying the subjugation of women and the imposition of capitalist social relations is theoretically and historically supportable, but only within specific historical contexts. This hypothesis falls short when applied to the continent broadly, and particularly France where the eco-demographic crisis resulted in the entrenchment of peasant property and the consolidation of an Absolutist State. New investigations are needed to question the role and impact of the witch hunts in this specific historical context.

Federici's assertion that the crisis augmented the ideological importance given to a country's populousness as a signal of power and source of strength needs to be further questioned to consider the applicability of this assertion to specific jurisdictions and contexts. This means examining the connection of the importance of populousness and predominant accumulation strategies which crucially entails paying specific attention to the differences between English and French social property relations. On the one hand, the introduction of capitalist social property relations in England imposed a focus on productivity growth and technological advancement as centrally important to profit accumulation strategies. On the other, continued reliance on territorial expansion, absolute surplus extraction, and extra-economic coercion as central elements of accumulation and value extraction was dominant in pre-capitalist, Absolutist France.[27] Social reproductions' connection to society's rules of reproduction, as impacted by specific social property relations, are complicated and require further investigation that is not present within *Caliban and the Witch* but that political Marxism is potentially in a position to provide.

This is not to argue that an analysis of the witch hunts needs to take a back seat to an analysis of production relations. Rather, the point that is being made is that the constellations of class forces, of class struggle, and of historically specific social and production relations on the ground substantially matter to the organization of social reproduction and vice versa. Without situating the witch hunts within specific social-historical contexts, uniformity is being assumed and not investigated. This means that the ways in which the subversion of women's autonomy over their bodies, control over reproductive capacities, and exploitative relations of social reproduction are not being properly integrated into feminist historical materialist investigations of the transition.

Reflections on Political Marxism[28]

Political Marxism's prioritization of historical specificity, agency, and rules of reproduction provide a potential solution to the ahistoricity present within dual systems theory and the geographic and temporal overexpansion of Federici's analysis of primitive accumulation. Political Marxism's methodological approach has much to offer the investigation of the witch hunts, primitive accumulation, and transformation in processes of exploitation centered on women's bodies and especially their reproductive capacities in its social-historical specific contexts. However, in order for political Marxism's methodological approach to be effective, a critical appraisal is necessary in order to address those aspects of political Marxism that cedes room to a dual systems approach to the study of capitalist exploitation and women's oppression. Specifically, we need to challenge the claim of some within the political Marxist canon that capitalism is indifferent to gender or any other "extra-economic inequality or difference".[29]

These types of assertions, that capitalism does not contain any structural tendency toward racial inequality or gender oppression, are premised on a limited conceptualization of social reproduction. Even at an abstract level, social reproduction feminists, such as Lise Vogel, question the efficacy of Marxist conceptions of capitalist social relations that do not question the availability, renewal, and replacement of labor power.[30] Vogel, in particular, suggests that the social organization of certain processes of social reproduction constitutes a "material precondition for the social construction of gender differences" under capitalism that are central to, and not separate from, capitalist accumulation processes.[31] It is thus necessary to challenge the methodological choices within political

Marxism which accept and proceed from a limited conceptualization of class structure that relies on one-sided definitions of social reproduction, compounded by an unnecessary economistic focus on labor performed at the site of production.

In asserting that Brenner and subsequently political Marxism unnecessarily limit their focus to that of labor performed at the point of production, I am referencing Brenner's particular definition of class structure. As class struggle and class power play such a central role in Brenner's analysis of the transition to capitalism, the evacuation of gender contained in this principle definition is unsatisfactory. Brenner defines class structure as containing

> two analytically distinct, but historically unified aspects. First, the relations of the direct producers to one another to their tools and to the land in the immediate process of production—what has been called the 'labour process' or the 'social forces of production'. Second, the inherently conflictive relations of property—always guaranteed directly or indirectly, in the last analysis, by force—by which an unpaid-for part of the product is extracted from the direct producers by a class of non-producers—which might be called the 'property relationship' or the 'surplus extraction relationship.'[32]

Within this definition of class structure, there is a fixation on labor performed at the point of production that excludes a full consideration of the complexity of labor that is not directly mediated by the market, but which still shapes and is shaped by capitalist social relations.[33] Furthermore, considering that of primary importance to political Marxism's methodology is the insistence that capitalism is a social property relation and not merely a market relation; this is a troubling approach to conceptualizing labor as it relies on an unnecessarily economistic reading of the social. In effect, Brenner's definition reduces capitalist social relations to only those exploitative relations within the direct work site. Moreover, this definition effectively renders a discussion of social reproduction mute, as nowhere in this definition is there an eye toward the problem of how laborers come to be present at this direct site of production. How labor power is renewed, ensured, raised, and repaired is rendered outside of this constrained definition of class structure.

Naming only that labor that is present in the immediate process of production as definitional to class structure is not merely an analytical move, it is also a coded means of limiting the field of inquiry to that labor deemed productive of surplus value. Unpaid social reproductive labor, in particular, is rendered external to this type of class analysis. This is both unnecessary and unacceptable; Rioux agrees: "value-producing labor, social reproductionists argue, while central to 'the ways people co-operate to provide for their daily and future needs', is a necessary yet insufficient condition of historical analysis."[34] Limiting analysis in this way does not allow for a full discussion of a society's rules of reproduction to be fully considered, a condition that political Marxism names as fundamental in understanding what differentiates feudal and capitalist social production relations. In narrowly defining class structure in this way, rules of reproduction are likewise able to be assigned a production-centered and economistic definition limited to the economic imperative to sell one's labor power on the market, without reference or acknowledgement to how that labor power comes to be available.

Social reproduction feminism and feminist theorists like Federici who focus attention on social reproduction examine both the ways that capitalism exploits workers and how capitalism is simultaneously gendered challenge this limited purview of Marxist scholars and theories, like Brenner and political Marxism, who fail to understand the internally related and complex ways that social production and social reproduction are related. Within political Marxism, and mainstream Marxism generally, social reproduction is often defined one-dimensionally. Brenner and Laslett argue that, for many Marxists, social reproduction is narrowly conceptualized as the social nature of procreation (or demographics generally) or "in its most common usage, within Marxist theory, social reproduction refers to the perpetuation of modes of production and the structures of class inequality inscribed within them."[35] Even more problematically, social reproduction is used by many Marxists as merely a synonym for consumption. Social reproduction feminism, on the other hand, has the potential to add much needed nuance to this conversation. Moving beyond these limited definitions, Brenner and Laslett understand social reproduction as

> the activities and attitudes, behaviours and emotions, responsibilities and relationships directly involved in the maintenance of life on a daily basis, and intergenerationally … Social reproduction can thus be seen to include various kinds of work—mental, manual, and emotional—aimed at providing the historically and socially, as well as biologically, defined care necessary to maintain existing life and to reproduce the next generation.[36]

Similarly, Bakker and Gill articulate that social reproduction

> refers to both biological reproduction of the species (and indeed its ecological framework) and ongoing reproduction of the commodity labor power. In addition social reproduction involves institutions, processes and social relations associated with the *creation and maintenance* of communities—and upon which, ultimately, all production and exchange rests.[37]

Political Marxism's rules for reproduction often get trapped in a narrowly economistic frame, perhaps as a result of engaging on the terrain of the commercialization model, when criticizing that model's focus on the market as opportunity. When the market, or the immediate process of production, is held as the focal point of analysis, the question of how labor power comes to be available on the market or at the immediate process of production is either glossed over or mechanically assumed. For Brenner, this mechanical assumption creeps in via his continued reliance on a Malthusian two-phase population cycle to account for the social reproduction of labor power. In Brenner's own words,

> Population growth, in the face of stagnant technique, led in the up-phase of the cycle to increased returns to land relative to labour, increased food prices relative to manufactures, and declining output per person ... Ultimately, over-population was self-correcting, eventuating in a reversal of the demographic trend ... This two-phase cyclical pattern prevailed in the economy of most of Europe in the later medieval period (1100–1450), and continued to predominate over large parts of it into the early modern period (1450–1700). My intention was not to deny the existence of these two-phase cycles; it was to expose the limitations of the neo-Malthusian cum Ricardian models advanced by the demographic interpreters in actually *explaining* the long-term patterns of income distribution.[38]

This continued reliance on a neo-Malthusian two-phase population thesis problematically limits Brenner's ability to include a fully realized conceptualization of social reproduction and facilitates a continued exclusion of a thorough gender analysis within his theorizing. The Malthusian two-phase population thesis, even if primarily relied upon for its descriptive abilities, allows for the continued dehistoricization of population growth and renewal and limits social reproduction to a crude demographics analysis. Rather than applying his social property relations analysis to explain the influence and contradictions imposed by different processes of social reproduction that underscore processes of social production, Brenner instead succumbs to neo-Malthusian's demographic determinism and conceptualizes demographic fluctuations as objective factors mechanically resulting from the contradictions between certain natural processes. Malthus relies on a series of natural laws to explain what enables, arrests, and limits population growth; political and social relations are strictly excluded from his explanation.[39] There is no room within Malthus' theory for accounting for the social or political relations surrounding population dynamics; his is the opposite of an historical materialist account. Relying on Malthus' descriptive abilities, while acknowledging the methodological failures within the Malthusian and neo-Malthusian models, undermines claims of a robust historical materialist analysis and goes against a central claim that political Marxism holds as a point of privilege—their choice to explain historical relations rather than assume them.

It is crucial for political Marxism that social property relations be examined and not assumed, thus it is unacceptable that social reproduction is not accorded the same consideration. Social reproduction feminists remind Marxists that it was Marx himself who argued that "when viewed, therefore, as a connected whole, and as flowing on with incessant renewal, every social process of production is, at the same time, a process of reproduction."[40] Brenner and later political Marxists criticize the commercialization model for viewing capitalism as a market relation as opposed to a set of social property relations. However, if this critique is going to hold, then political Marxism needs to recognize the social reproduction of people as part of social property relations. This is necessary because, as social reproduction feminists argue, "social reproduction involves institutions, processes and social relations associated with the *creation and maintenance* of communities—and upon which, ultimately, all production and exchange rests."[41]

The problem with accepting Malthus' population thesis, even if only in its descriptive character and abandoning its descriptive validity once applied to capitalism, is that it leads to ignoring the real historical movements that produce the narrative that Malthus describes. It means accepting a reified and naturalized version of social reproduction, which, in turn, means there is no longer a need to question the social relations, social processes, or social struggles surrounding social reproduction. Accepting the neo-Malthusian thesis, Brenner reiterates that "over-population leads, therefore, to a compensatory demographic drop-off, resulting in a reversal of the land/labour ratio and a new onset of demographic growth—the two-phase, self-correcting cycle. There is no reason to challenge the logic of this model."[42] However, social reproduction feminism does implicitly challenge the logic of this model. In particular, Federici's discussion of the Black Death and the resulting eco-demographic crisis, while not immune to criticism, challenges this blanket assumption and illuminates the importance of questioning the social and political consequences of demographic fluctuations. This is not because demographics play a determining role in economic growth, as the neo-Malthusians argue, but because the social conditions of labor power renewal and the organization of social reproduction are sites of struggle with real consequences on class power, class mobilization, and survival strategies.

Restricting Malthus' population thesis to being descriptively valid under feudal social and demographic relations does not improve this situation. Brenner supports Ladurie's claim that "'Malthus came too late': ironically, Malthus' model was correct not for the emergent industrial economy he was analysing, but for the stagnant backward society from which this had arisen."[43] Severing ties with Malthus' thesis post transition does not compel Brenner to provide a new fully formed analysis of population dynamics, let alone of social reproduction. Rather, Brenner points to the need to recognize a different disequilibrium than that of the two-phase hypothesis—"between the conflicting needs of conflicting social classes, not just between population and resources."[44] The new production possibilities introduced through capitalism's ascension are used to explain the new redundancy of Malthus' population thesis, as the arithmetic relation of resource production no longer applies. Rather than population pressures resulting in demographic crisis, as Malthus' theory describes, under the capitalist mode of production, increasing labor productivity through technological improvement lifts these pressures.[45]

Within this articulation of changing population dynamics, Brenner assumes that improved agricultural production and technology ushered in by the dynamics of the new system of social property relations made sustained demographic growth possible, as was witnessed within the early phases of capitalist development.[46] Thus the production dynamics created through the introduction of capitalist social property relations did not need to rely on Malthus' population thesis to explain demographic growth. However, this is an insufficient to produce a full view of social reproduction. The implication is that, without a food shortage or the imperative of scarcity, generational reproduction will expand unfettered assumes that, in the wake of enclosures, proletarianization, pauperization, and resistance to the implementation of capitalist social property relations, unchecked population growth continued merely because of the technical possibilities of increasing yields. Such an economistic reductionist understanding of social reproduction is insufficient.

In the *Grundrisse*, Marx argues, contra Malthus, that population growth is not a natural phenomenon or a law of nature.[47] Instead Marx specifically acknowledges population as historically and socially organized.[48] Brenner's hypothesis that increased productive capacities nullify the population pressures that motivate Malthus' theory does not live up to the historicizing and socializing of reproduction that Marx advocates in the *Grundrisse*. Brenner's approach to explain away the conditions of demographic reproduction, assumes exactly that which still needs to be proven: "economic needs or desires cannot explain their own satisfaction, nor can opportunities account for the capacity to take advantage of them."[49] Just as political Marxists do not consider the availability of linen, thread, and sewing machines as adequate variables of analysis in explaining the production of a certain quantity of coats, and reject quantitative views of capitalism that ignore capitalism's qualitative particularities,[50] the same methodology needs to be more fully applied to analyses of social reproduction.

While the Marx of the *Grundrisse* advocates a historical materialist analysis of population patterns, an unfortunate turn is taken within *Capital: Volume 1*, where Marx articulates his law of population in the capitalist mode of production which falls back onto a naturalized understanding of social reproduction to explain generational renewal. This law states that "the maintenance and reproduction of the working class remains a necessary condition for the reproduction of capital. But the capitalist may safely leave this to the worker's drive for self-preservation and promulgation."[51] The problem, as Federici names it, is "why procreation should be a fact of nature rather than a social, historically determined activity, invested by diverse interests and power relations, is a question Marx did not ask."[52] Political Marxism has also allowed this question to linger.

This assumed replacement of labor power unhelpfully cuts short theorizing the fullness of capitalist social property relations. It is a reversal of Marx's thinking within the *Grundrisse* that chastises Malthus for depoliticizing and dehistoricizing population and overpopulation, and a return to the sort of biological reductionism that most Marxists would reject as an ahistorical and depoliticized ways of theorizing. Federici succinctly articulates that

> [Marx] argued that capitalist development proceeds irrespective of population numbers because by virtue of the increasing productivity of labor, the labor that capital exploits constantly diminishes in relation to 'constant' capital (that is, the capital investment in machinery and other production assets), with the consequent determination of a 'surplus population'. But this dynamic, which Marx defines as the 'law of population' typical of the capitalist mode of production' could only prevail if procreation were a purely biological process, or an activity responding to economic change.[53]

Marx's capitalist law of population returns theorizing around social reproduction to a similarly limited and stifling scope as that of Malthus and the neo-Malthusians. And for political Marxism to accept this naturalized law is to again repeat the cardinal sin—assuming exactly that which needs to be explained. Instead, returning to social reproduction this time as an internal relation, and not an external variable, presents an opportunity for political Marxism to address this methodological and theoretical oversight, and this can be accomplished through a sincere but critical engagement with Federici's writings on the transition and with the wider literature of social reproduction feminism.

Even considering the criticism levied earlier, it is clear from reading *Caliban and the Witch* that mainstream Marxism has ignored a substantial swath of data in their various accounts of the transition. Federici is not the first feminist to say as much; however, the sheer amount of information that Federici uncovers, and her direct engagement with Marxist accounts of the transition, clearly demonstrates that this information does not lie outside the grasp of Marxist inquiry; Marxists have so far just failed to reach for it. This willful ignorance on the part of Marxism, and political Marxism, to take into consideration the wealth of information about the social struggles of women that are undoubtedly connected to the transition is compounded by a failure to challenge Marx's original scarcity of theorizing on the oppression of women. A major contribution to Marxist and Marxist feminist theorizing is Lise Vogel's *Marxism and the Oppression of Women*.[54] Within this provocative text, Vogel moves beyond the common feminist practice of trying to make Marx's economic or definitional categories overlay onto feminist concepts and conceptualizations and instead returns to Marx's methodology. As Ferguson and McNally observe, "instead of trying to graft a theory of women's oppression onto Marx's political economy of capitalism, Vogel extends the conceptual reach of Marx's method and analysis to be able to account for women's oppression under capitalism."[55] The substantial breakthrough that Vogel realizes through this methodological extension is the importance and significance of a non-reductionist or economistic theorization of social reproduction.

Federici introduces compelling historical evidence for returning to the transition period to question why, throughout this politically, economically, and socially tumultuous time, a war on women—over control of their labor, their bodies, their reproductive capacities—was persued viciously. Throughout this period there is a marked change in the gendered division of labor that is not solely reducible to the more stringent division of labor introduced by capitalist production relations. There is a marked change in the ideological construction of gender norms that is not reducible to a new bourgeois or protestant work ethic being evoked. There is a marked change in the disciplining and policing of women's bodies and reproductive capacities that cannot be explained by neo-Malthusian population theories or by Marx's capitalist law of population. The problem with Malthus' population thesis, with Marx's law of capitalist population, and with continuing to assume rather than explain the arrival of labor power on the market, is that biological generational reproduction is a socially organized activity based on specific biological differences. It cannot be explained by biologically reductionist or naturalized formula, nor is it a functional output of economic needs or conditions. And given the centrality within processes of primitive accumulation of separating workers from their means of production and means of social reproduction, social reproduction cannot be left "to the worker's drive for self-preservation and promulgation."[56] Unfortunately for capital, "birth, childbearing, and lactation are specific biological tasks; the body is biologically (in this sense naturally) reproduced, not capitalistically. However, the organisation of this biologic activity is also historically and socially conditioned."[57] Flowing from this acknowledgement,

> the social organization of biological difference constitutes a 'material precondition for the social construction of gender differences.' It is not biology per se that dictates women's oppression; but rather, capital's dependence upon biological processes specific to women—pregnancy, childbirth, lactation—to secure the reproduction of the working class. It is this that induces capital and its state to control and regulate female reproduction and which impels them to induce a male-dominant gender-order.[58]

Vogel's theoretical contribution assists in locating the intimate relationship between capitalism and the oppression of women as something engrained in the logic of capitalist exploitation, not merely a vestige of status relations left over from earlier epochs or as the product of an ahistorical, ever present, unchanging, patriarchal system. Ferguson notes that "in insisting biology matters, proponents of the [social reproduction feminism] perspective effectively suggest that the type of laboring body (e.g., the concrete particularity of bodies) is critically significant to underwriting the experience of gender in a capitalist world."[59] Rather, it is the struggle over social reproductions (from above and below), including all the contradictions that this generates and entails, and the social property relations involved in and reproduced through these activities, which establishes and reproduces the dominant gender order. This indicates that, rather than a separate system with separate logics, with attachment to a different kind of accumulation strategy, gender discrimination is part of the internal workings of capitalist social property relations.

Conclusion

This chapter began by positing the general hypothesis that there is something specific in transitions to capitalism that rupture previous forms of political economic organization, *as well as* previous gender regimes, and that the resulting dynamic that is then set in motion is that of an internal relation between gender and class oppression—not separate capitalist and patriarchal systems that intersect and interact. Despite disagreements with Federici's analysis, her provocative inquiry in *Caliban and the Witch* demands that Marxists take into consideration the dramatic changes that took place through and following the transition to capitalism. All of the historical moments that Federici punctuates still require an explanation: changes in reproductive policy adopted by the state, new forms of surveillance of women's bodies, and new narratives within public discourse that equated a country's prosperity with populousness. Similarly, the critique levied at political Marxism for lacking a thorough feminist analysis and excluding a full consideration of social reproduction does not invalidate political Marxism. Political Marxism's insistence on questioning rather than assuming capitalism's arrival and on approaching capitalism as a social property relation is centrally important to this hypothesis. This does, however, signal that something crucial is lacking in both accounts and further theorizing and historical research are still required. The motivation for putting these fields in conversation is that their shortcomings are complimentary and moving forward entails working with the best aspects of each to create a research program that is able to strengthen the hypothesis guiding this chapter.

This research program needs to follow the lead of social reproduction feminists who challenge those who relegate these questions to the periphery and insist on maintaining a dual systems analysis of capitalist production relations and patriarchal power relations. At an abstract level, Vogel's intervention clearly demonstrates that there is a material bases for the (re) construction of gender difference and women's oppression that cannot be externalized or separated from capitalist social property relations.[60] At a concrete level, Federici categorizes the various ways that gender difference and women's oppression have been central to the instantiation of capitalism, to the specifically gendered impacts of primitive accumulation and loss of the commons, to the war over women's bodies and control over their reproductive capacities.

This research program must incorporate political Marxism's "conception of capitalism as a specific social form, with a distinctive social structure and distinctive social relations of production, which compel economic agents to behave in specific ways and generate specific laws of motion."[61] However, this conception of capitalism as a specific social form must abandon its commitment to an economistic reading of the social. This means that political Marxism needs to challenge its narrow one-dimensional view of social reproduction that limits their conceptualization of "rules of reproduction" to an economistic frame.[62] Engaging with Federici's analysis and with the larger social reproduction feminism canon means that "if 'rules of reproduction' are to be sufficiently comprehensive, they must recognize the mutually constituted nature of relations of exploitation, on the one hand, and gender relations on the other."[63]

This research program needs a new theory that learns from both Federici's and political Marxism's readings of primitive accumulation in order to fine tune historical specificity without neglecting necessary and constitutive elements. Federici amalgamates an overly expansive temporal and geographic history to demonstrate the gendered nature of primitive accumulation and processes of dispossession. While questioning this jurisdictional jumping is necessary, an explanation is still needed to understand why and how these processes are taking similar forms across varying fields, the difference between forms across jurisdictions, and the specific socio-historic contexts that are producing these dynamics. Levien's comparative analysis of the gendered impacts of land dispossession corroborates Federici's analysis that there is something specifically gendered at play in processes of primitive accumulation that are necessary to understanding the transition and to conceptualizing capitalism in general.[64] These connections need to be further explored.

Marxist feminists cannot rely on generalized sweeping statements about patriarchy's historic existence as determining its existence contemporarily. Nor can political Marxists rely on Marx's capitalist law of population to account for the availability and renewal of labor power. It is time that Marxist feminists and political Marxists stopped relying on these assumptions and seek to explore that which needs to be explained.

Notes

1. Silvia Federici, *Caliban and the Witch: Women, the Body and Primitive Accumulation* (New York: Autonomedia, 2004).
2. Ellen Meiksins Wood, *Democracy Against Capitalism: Renewing Historical Materialism* (Cambridge University Press, 1995), 267.
3. Paul Sweezy, "Paul Sweezy: A Critique," in *The Transition from Feudalism to Capitalism*, ed. Rodney Hilton (London: Verso, 1978), 33–68.
4. Andre Gunder Frank, *Capitalism and Underdevelopment in Latin America* (New York: Monthly Review Press, 1967).
5. Emmanuel Le Roy Ladurie, *The Peasants of Languedoc*, trans. John Day (Chicago: University of Illinois Press, 1976); M.M Postan, *Essays on Medieval Agriculture and General Problems of the Medieval Economy* (Cambridge: Cambridge University Press, 1973).
6. Robert Brenner, "Agrarian Class Structure and Economic Development in Pre-Industrial Europe," in *The Brenner Debate: Agrarian Class Structure and Economic Development in Pre-Industrial Europe*, ed. Trevor Henry Aston and C.H.E. Philpin (Cambridge: Cambridge University Press, 1985), 10–63; Benno Teschke, *The Myth of 1648: Class, Geopolitics, and the Making of Modern International Relations* (London: Verso, 2003); Ellen Meiksins Wood, *The Origin of Capitalism: A Longer View* (London: Verso, 2002).
7. Federici, *Caliban and the Witch*, 5.
8. Teschke, *The Myth of 1648*, 158.
9. Heidi Hartmann, "The Unhappy Marriage of Marxism and Feminism: Toward a More Progressive Union," in *Feminist Theory Reader: Local and Global Perspectives*, ed. Carole McCann and Kim Seung-Kyung (New York: Routledge, 2003), 206–221; Iris Marion Young, "Socialist Feminism and the Limits of Dual Systems Theory," *Socialist Review* 50, no. 5 (1980): 169–188.
10. Federici, *Caliban and the Witch*, 62.
11. Ibid., 21.

12. Ibid., 63–65.
13. Ibid., 24.
14. Ibid., 28–29.
15. Teschke, *The Myth of 1648*, 157.
16. Brenner, "Agrarian Class Structure and Economic Development in Pre-Industrial Europe."
17. Ellen Meiksins Wood, "Class, Race, and Capitalism," How does Race Relate to Class? A Debate (2009), 9, http://advancethestruggle.files.wordpress.com/2009/06/how_does_race_relate_to_class-2.pdf.
18. Federici, *Caliban and the Witch*, 64.
19. Brenner, "Agrarian Class Structure and Economic Development in Pre-Industrial Europe"; Xavier Lafrance, "Citizens and Wage-Labourers: Capitalism and the Formation of a Working Class in France" (PhD thesis, York University, 2013); Charles Post, *The American Road to Capitalism: Studies in Class-Structure, Economic Development and Political Conflict, 1620–1877* (Leiden: Brill, 2011); Teschke, *The Myth of 1648*.
20. Federici, *Caliban and the Witch*, 63.
21. Gary Blank, "Marxism, Gender and 'the Transition': A Comparative Review of Federici and Seccombe," *Analize* 2, no. 16 (2014), 3.
22. Federici, *Caliban and the Witch*, 63–64.
23. Brenner, "Agrarian Class Structure and Economic Development in Pre-Industrial Europe," 21.
24. Federici, *Caliban and the Witch*, 44.
25. Teschke, *The Myth of 1648*, 168.
26. Ibid., 169.
27. Robert Brenner, "The Origins of Capitalist Development: A Critique of Neo-Smithian Marxism," *New Left Review* 104 (1977), 30.
28. This section draws heavily on the argument developed in Nicole Leach, "Transitions to Capitalism: Social-Reproduction Feminism Encounters Political Marxism," *Historical Materialism* 24, no. 2 (2016): 111–137.
29. Wood, *Democracy Against Capitalism*, 267.
30. Lise Vogel, *Marxism and the Oppression of Women: Toward a Unitary Theory* (Chicago: Haymarket Books, 2014).
31. Vogel, *Marxism and the Oppression of Women*, 147.
32. Brenner, "Agrarian Class Structure and Economic Development in Pre-Industrial Europe," 11.
33. For an extended conversation on social reproduction feminism's troubling of Marxist conceptions of labor, see Isabella Bakker and Stephen Gill, eds., *Power, Production and Social Reproduction: Human In/Security in the Global Political Economy* (New York: Palgrave Macmillan, 2003); Sue Ferguson, "Canadian Contributions to Social Reproduction Feminism, Race and Embodied Labor," *Race, Gender & Class* 15, no. 1/2 (2008):

42–57; Leach, "Transitions to Capitalism: Social-Reproduction Feminism Encounters Political Marxism."
34. Sebastien Rioux, "Embodied Contradictions: Capitalism, Social Reproduction and Body Formation," *Women's Studies International Forum* 48 (2015), 197.
35. Barbara Laslett and Johanna Brenner, "Gender and Social Reproduction: Historical Perspectives," *Annual Review of Sociology* 15 (1989), 383.
36. Laslett and Brenner, *Gender and Social Reproduction*, 382–383.
37. Isabella Bakker and Stephen Gill, "Ontology, Method, and Hypotheses," in *Power, Production and Social Reproduction: Human In/Security in the Global Political Economy*, ed. Isabella Bakker and Stephen Gill (New York: Palgrave Macmillan, 2003), 17–18.
38. Robert Brenner, "The Agrarian Roots of European Capitalism," in *The Brenner Debate: Agrarian Class Structure and Economic Development in Pre-Industrial Europe*, ed. Trevor Henry Aston and C.H.E. Philpin (Cambridge: Cambridge University Press, 1985), 217.
39. Thomas Malthus, *An Essay on the Principle of Population and A Summary View of the Principle of Population* (New York: Penguin Books, 1982), 76–92.
40. Karl Marx, *Capital: A Critique of Political Economy*, vol. 1 (London: Penguin Books, 1990), 711.
41. Bakker and Gill, "Ontology, Method, and Hypotheses," 17–18.
42. Brenner, "The Agrarian Roots of European Capitalism," 223.
43. Quoted in Brenner, "Agrarian Class Structure and Economic Development in Pre-Industrial Europe," 14.
44. Brenner, "The Agrarian Roots of European Capitalism," 268.
45. Ibid., 225.
46. Ibid., 217.
47. Karl Marx, *Grundrisse: Foundations of the Critique of Political Economy (Rough Draft)* (New York: Penguin Books, 1973), 605.
48. Marx, *Grundrisse*, 606.
49. Brenner, "The Agrarian Roots of European Capitalism," 282.
50. Brenner, "The Origins of Capitalist Development," 29.
51. Marx, *Capital*, 718.
52. Federici, *Caliban and the Witch*, 91.
53. Ibid.
54. Vogel, *Marxism and the Oppression of Women.*
55. Sue Ferguson and David McNally, "Capital, Labour-Power, and Gender-Relations: Introduction to the Historical Materialism Edition of Marxism and the Oppression of Women," in *Marxism and the Oppression of Women: Toward a Unitary Theory*, by Lise Vogel (Chicago: Haymarket Books, 2014), XXIII.

56. Marx, *Capital*, 718.
57. Leach, "Transitions to Capitalism," 126.
58. Ferguson and McNally, "Capital, Labour-Power, and Gender-Relations," XXIX.
59. Ferguson, "Canadian Contributions to Social Reproduction Feminism, Race and Embodied Labor," 50.
60. Vogel, *Marxism and the Oppression of Women*, 147.
61. Wood, *The Origin of Capitalism*, 31.
62. Leach, "Transitions to Capitalism," 131–132.
63. Gary Blank, "Gender, Production, and 'the Transition to Capitalism': Assessing the Historical Basis for a Unitary Materialist Theory," *New Proposals* 4, no. 2 (2011), 14.
64. Michael Levien, "Gender and Land Dispossession: A Comparative Analysis," *The Journal of Peasant Studies* 44, no. 6 (2017): 1111–1134.

CHAPTER 14

Conclusion

Xavier Lafrance and Charles Post

The case studies in the origins of capitalism presented in this book highlight the profound variations in the processes that lead to the emergence of capitalism in different countries and regions. Everywhere it appeared capitalism implied a radical transformation of social property relations forcing both the class of appropriators and the direct producers to competitively reproduce themselves on the market. But the path to these new class relations was never the same and often varied widely.

The pace of capitalist restructuring fluctuated from on case to the other. Whereas in England, the diffusion of agrarian capitalism took place over centuries, the process was generally much faster in succeeding cases. Likewise, as Michael Zmolek demonstrates, English industrial capitalism emerged long after the capitalist transformation of social property relations in the countryside and only after a protracted process of state repression of manufacturing workers that led to the subsumption of labor by capital. Subsequent cases see more temporally proximate agrarian and

X. Lafrance (✉)
University of Québec in Montréal, Montréal, QC, Canada

C. Post
Graduate Center and Borough of Manhattan Community College,
City University of New York, New York, NY, USA

X. Lafrance, C. Post (eds.), *Case Studies in the Origins of Capitalism*, Marx, Engels, and Marxisms,
https://doi.org/10.1007/978-3-319-95657-2_14

industrial capitalist transitions. At least in the case of France, and also perhaps Catalonia, industrial capitalism emerges several decades before any conclusive capitalist transformation of the countryside.

While English agrarian capitalism gave rise to the classical triad of aristocratic landholders, capitalist tenant farmers, and agricultural wage-laborers, similar patterns were absent in the subsequent transitions examined here. In the US, Canada or Japan, for instance, it was individual family units facing new market imperatives that were at the heart of the transformation of agriculture. This transformation took place on much smaller holdings and did not involve the relatively rapid and massive dispossession of the peasantry that had occurred in England. These variations necessarily had a direct impact on the rhythms of proletarianization in different societies.

The role, as well as the form, of the state involved in the transitions discussed here was also diverse. While it played an active role in shaping the transition, the English state was radically transformed by the rise of capitalism. On the European Continent, as is shown by the French case, it was absolutist states that—at first reluctantly—initiated the transition. In North America (US and Canada), the state form was different, and its institutional consolidation was necessary before new social property relations could be imposed. States also played distinctive, yet decisive roles in Japan, Brazil, Turkey or Taiwan. State leaders implemented strategies that sometimes implied sharp regional developmental strategies, as capitalist transitions were at first (and sometimes for a protracted period) bounded to specific areas of a given country, as exemplified by the Brazilian and Canadian cases.

Many other variations among our cases could be identified and explored—so many that we do not have the space to discuss them here. What is clear, however, is that once capitalism emerged in England, it never surfaced again in the same way in any other region of the globe. Once we break with the idea that capitalism is simply the logical conclusion of a universal trend toward commercial expansion, important differences between cases should come as no surprise. As has been stressed throughout this book, a capitalist transition implies a reconfiguration of social property relations—that is, a radical transformation of social power and of the legal, political and cultural institutions and relations that allow a class exploitation where both producers and exploiters become market dependent for their reproduction. Such a process of reconfiguration will always be unique, for different reasons. First, a given country or region will approach the transition with a specific socio-legal and political history. The distinct evolution of the balances of power within the ruling class and between classes is also a crucial factor to consider. Ruling class strategies and successes in implementing capitalist reforms will vary according to the resistance from both elites and direct producers. As Nicole Leach's and Jessica Evans's chapters in this book make clear, a consideration of capitalist restructuring strategies, and of the resistances they meet, remain incomplete in the absence of a broader consideration of the impact of gender and racial relations. Moreover, these strategies and their consequences will be different given the geopolitical pressures faced by rulers and the given historical point in the development of the international system at which the transition is attempted. To conclude this volume, we discuss the impact of the evolution of international relations on the global spread of capitalism, before identifying topics for further research.

The International System, Imperialism and the Transitions to Capitalism

Some have argued that political Marxism adopts a reductionist "internalist" perspective on the transition to capitalism that focuses narrowly on domestic class relations, leaving out any serious consideration of "the international".[1] This seems to us to be a groundless accusation. Different "political Marxists" have considered the international dimension of the origins and global dissemination of capitalism.[2] Doing so, as Benno Teschke has argued, our interest is not simply to compare national cases, but also to situate these cases in "the great international arch of the regionally differentiated transition to capitalism".[3] We recognize that capitalist transitions (and the evolution of social property regimes in general) never simply take place "internally" and in isolation from one another—"national" or regional transitions to capitalism are always a co-constituted phenomenon.

It follows that the opposition between an "internalist" perspective and one that takes into consideration "international determinations" is off the mark. The point is to integrate to an analysis of geopolitical competition as a dimension of the social reproduction of the ruling classes and of the ways specific social property relations of a given polity determine how it will be inserted into the inter-state system and react to its imperatives.[4] If we do not take into account the mediating role of social property relations, our consideration of the impact of the "international" remains abstract. At the same time, we also need to appreciate the ways in which the emergence of new social property regimes within states can modify the working logic of the international system as a whole. This is certainly the theoretical perspective that informed the cases studies of this book.

Building on Brenner's work, Dimmock's chapter clearly indicates that the process through which the kingdom of Wessex re-conquered the Scandinavian kingdoms of England from the 880s to 950, as well as the Norman conquest of the eleventh century, shaped specific social property relations that preceded the emergence of agrarian capitalism. The development of the new capitalist state that emerged in England was also directly influenced by its insertion into the early modern European state system. Stuart kings attempted to emulate the absolutist evolution of their continental rivals—especially France. This, however, threatened the class interests of the English aristocracy who were reliant on an economic mode of surplus appropriation by the seventeenth century. In the aftermath of the revolutionary period, the English ruling class extinguished absolutist aspirations and consolidated new property and state forms. The economic mode of exploitation concomitant to agrarian capitalism made it possible for England to move beyond the personal appropriation of state power as a strategy of ruling class reproduction that persisted on the Continent. This de-patrimonialization of the state paved the way to a process of rationalization that amounted to the development of the first modern public administration in Britain in the century that followed the "Glorious Revolution" of 1688.[5]

Britain now possessed a much more productive economy, but also state and administrative institutions that could more efficiently canalize surpluses toward military ventures. This greater economic and administrative power also made it easier to borrow on European financial markets at significantly lower interest rates. Britain mobilized its military, administrative and financial advantages to face continental absolutist "state-classes" that continued to rely on geopolitical accumulation (territorial expansion) to reproduce themselves—the so-called "Westphalian" European state system "was still dominated by the logic of predation".[6] The emerging British "military superpower" adapted by developing a "dual foreign policy strategy". The latter involved, first, "active power-balancing versus its rivals on the continent", without direct military intervention, but through highly malleable diplomatic interferences and alliances, as well as constant financial subsidies to different states with the intent of countering any incipient hegemon. On the other hand, and outside of Europe, Britain pursued a "blue water" strategy of uninhibited colonial expansion and military control of trade routes.[7]

This dual foreign policy exposed continental powers to extraordinary geopolitical pressures that threatened the reproduction of the politically constituted modes of appropriation of European ruling classes. As explained in Xavier Lafrance's chapter in this book, already in the middle of the eighteenth century, and especially in the wake of France's costly defeat to Britain during the Seven Year's War, a part of French elites were compelled to seriously consider the need to emulate the British economic model. The capitalist restructuring of social property relations, however, implied transformations that threatened the structures of appropriations that allowed European ruling classes to reproduce themselves and could incite dangerous social resistance from below. It follows that capitalist transitions did not emerge endogenously or spontaneously on the European continent—capitalism was transposed there through the geopolitical pressure exercised by Britain.[8]

Once *industrial* capitalism was consolidated in Britain over the second third of the nineteenth century, it became increasingly evident for continental ruling classes, which had clung to states as means of extra-economic appropriation and reproduction, that their survival depended on a capitalist restructuring of their respective society. The result was the state-led imposition of capitalist transitions "from above" in the mid-nineteenth century in Western and Central Europe and Japan. In her famous *States and Social Revolutions*, Theda Skocpol demonstrated how the Japanese state successfully adapted to intensified geopolitical competition by modernizing its administrative structures and its economy, while the tsarist regime's attempt to concentrate and to direct economic resources toward industrial development was stalled by a stagnant rural economy and eventually ended in a revolutionary collapse in the geopolitically extreme context of World War I.[9] What Skocpol fails to specify, however, is that Japan's successful industrialization (and its subsequent geopolitical achievements) had been dependent on a parallel (or even slightly earlier) transition to agrarian capitalism, as Mark Cohen demonstrates in his chapter in this book.

The international state system, fueled by *geopolitical competition*, thus acted as the conveyer belt of the first wave of the global propagation of capitalism to continental Europe and Japan. The *capitalist transformation of imperialism* promoted the spread of capitalism to what we today call the "Global South".

Over the sixteenth and seventeenth centuries, various European powers engaged in the "discoveries" and plunders of the New World, the rise of the African slave trade, and the conquest of colonies and development of slave plantations in the Americas, the Caribbean and in South and South-East Asia. For World System and Dependency theorists, colonization and slavery were the decisive factors in the emergence of Western European capitalism. Theoretically, this perspective falls back on the commercialization model and its theory of the "primitive accumulation" of a critical mass of wealth as a sufficient condition to explain the emergence of capitalism. Empirically, this perspective is challenged by the fact that Spain and Portugal, the dominant early colonizers of the America, directed the massive wealth that they extracted from their colonies not to agricultural or industrial production, but the purchase of state offices and feudal estates. Only England, a relatively late colonial power, converted the wealth appropriated from colonies and derived from slave plantations into capital that fuelled the process of industrialization. England's uniquely capitalist social property relations alone allowed this transformation.[10] The development of European—and subsequently of Atlantic commercial networks and colonial ventures—were necessary, but not sufficient conditions for the emergence and development of English capitalism.

Yet, if colonialism did not, and could not, on its own, cause the transition to capitalism, the emergence of English capitalism did lead to the development of a new form of colonialism.[11] *Capitalist* imperialism became an important vector of subsequent transitions to capitalism. Still enmeshed in a non-capitalist international system, England continued to rely on age-old strategies of colonial expansion (outside of Europe), control of trade routes and cornering of markets in order to grab foreign wealth. The development of capitalism actually intensified these old imperial practices and fueled the development of slavery plantations. But capitalism also led to the development of a new and distinct colonial logic. Agrarian capitalism produced a growing surplus population that had been expelled from the land, compelled the English state to create White settler colonies to a greater extent than other European powers. More importantly, the new form of colonial ventures privileged by the English state involved the outward projection of capitalist social property relations into the colonies. England first used this new imperial strategy in Ireland, were the capitalist transformation of social property relation was used as adjunct to the use of military power to subjugate the Irish population. By integrating the Irish economy into its metropolitan orbit, England was able to reinforce its imperial control over its colony.[12]

English imperial attempts to export capitalist social property relations faced many obstacles before the mid-nineteenth century. In India, stable non-capitalist political and economic institutions led colonial agents to rely on extra-economic forms of exploitation, inserting themselves at the apex of already existing class structures. In North America, by contrast, it was the extensive availability of land after the expropriation of indigenous populations and the inability of colonial state institutions to monopolize access land that led to the failure of the capitalist imperial strategy.

After the mid-nineteenth century, consolidation of capitalism in the contemporary Global North—Britain, Western and Central Europe, the US, Canada and Japan—capitalist imperialism was much more successful in imposing capitalist social property relations in the rest of the world. This process proceeded in an uneven and combined manner. Initially, the new imperialism produced capitalist "enclaves" of raw material production (mining and plantation agriculture) in the midst of non-capitalist household production.[13] By the late twentieth century global imperialism had compelled most ruling classes in the Global South to adapt capitalist social property relations. The role of Western European, and especially US, imperialism in these transformations is highlighted in Eren Duzgun's chapter on Turkey and Chris Isett's chapter on Taiwan.

An Agenda for Further Research

The case studies gathered in this volume reflect the current state of research on the comparative origins of capitalism from a "*Capital*-centric" Marxist perspective. Not surprisingly, there remain major gaps in our research project. Hopefully, this volume inspires scholars to fill these lacunae.

The first arena for future research is the consolidation of capitalism in what becomes the Global North in the mid-nineteenth century. While the contributions of Cohen, Evans, Lafrance and Post detail how the pressures of political-military competition compelled the transformation of social property relations in Japan, Canada, France and the US, the process still remains unstudied for what become central capitalist powers—Germany and Italy in Continental Europe, and the White settler colonies of Australia and New Zealand in south Asia. Equally important, we need a detailed study of how capitalist transformation was successfully resisted in Russia, whose state remained Feudal-Absolutist and whose agriculture remained non-capitalist until at least 1917.

The second area is the uneven and combined expansion of capitalism to what is today the Global South. Unfortunately, promising research on the origins of capitalism in South Africa in the late 1970s[14] was short-circuited as many of the most important scholars embraced post-structuralism, post-modernism and other forms of "discourse" analysis. The chapters of Duzgun, Carlson and Issett on Turkey, Brazil and Taiwan provide an excellent alternative to this dead-end. Hopefully, their work can be duplicated for the spread of capitalism to other parts of Africa, Asia and Latin America.

Finally, "*Capital*-Centric" Marxism needs to grapple with the relationship of race and gender to capitalist social property relations. Our perspective is widely viewed as being incapable of explaining the origins and persistence of racial oppression.[15] One formulation by Ellen Meiksins Wood, in particular, has lent credence to such claims:

> At the very least, class equality means something different and requires different conditions from sexual or racial equality. In particular, the abolition of class inequality would by definition mean the end of capitalism. But is the same necessarily true about the abolition of sexual or racial inequality? Sexual and racial equality … are not in principle incompatible with capitalism. The disappearance of class inequalities, on the other hand, is by definition incompatible with capitalism. At the same time, although class exploitation is constitutive of capitalism as sexual or racial inequalities are not, capitalism subjects all social relations to its requirements. It can co-opt and reinforce inequalities and oppressions that it did not create and adapt them to the interests of class exploitation.[16]

Wood's formulation is problematic theoretically and methodologically. She confuses the theoretical and historical ***preconditions*** of capitalist social property relations with the ***spontaneous results***—the ***unintended consequences*** of the reproduction of these social property relations.[17] Nicole Leach's chapter in this book begins to address the "gender" blindness of "political" Marxism by integrating the insights of social reproduction theorists. Jessica Evans's chapter on Canada also points to how a "*Capital*-centric" Marxist approach to the transformation of social property relations can account for the changing forms of racialization and racial subordination. Others have attempted to begin to address race through the lens of theories of real capitalist accumulation and competition.[18] However, much further historical research will be required to consolidate a consistent "political" Marxist account of race and gender.

Notes

1. Alex Anievas and Kerem Nisancioglu, *How The West Came to Rule: The Geopolitical Origins of Capitalism* (London: Pluto Press, 2015), 24.
2. Hannes Lacher, *Beyond Globalization: Capitalism, Territoriality and the International Relations of Modernity* (London: Routledge, 2006); Benno Teschke, *The Myth of 1648: Class, Geopolitics, and the Making of Modern International Relations* (London, Verso Books, 2003) and "Bourgeois Revolution, State Formation and the Absence of International," *Historical Materialism* 13, no. 2 (2005); Ellen Meiksins Wood, *The Pristine Culture of Capitalism: A Historical Essay on Old Regimes and Modern States* (New York: Verso, 1991); *The Origin of Capitalism: A Longer View* (New York: Verso, 2002), 147–181 and *The Empire of Capital* (New York: Verso, 2003).
3. Teschke, "Bourgeois Revolution," 7.
4. Ibid., 13.
5. Teschke, *The Myth of 1648*, 252–255.
6. Lacher, *Beyond Globalization*, 90.
7. Teschke, "Bourgeois Revolution," 17–18. See also Lacher, *Beyond Globalization*, 92.
8. Lacher, *Beyond Globalization*, 93.
9. Theda Skocpol, *States and Social Revolutions: A Comparative Analysis of France, Russia, and China* (Cambridge: Cambridge University Press, 1979).
10. Ellen Meiksins Wood, *The Origin of Capitalism: A Longer View* (New York: Verso, 2002), 147–149.
11. Wood, *The Empire of Capital.*
12. Wood, *The Origin of Capitalism*, 152–156; Wood, *The Empire of Capital*, 78–83.
13. Martin J. Murray, *The Development of Capitalism in Colonial Indochina, 1870–1940* (Berkeley: University of California Press, 1980) analyzes one example of a capitalist "enclave" economy produced by the new imperialism from a framework that owes much to the work of Brenner.
14. See Martin J. Murray, ed., *South African Capitalism and Black Political Opposition* (Cambridge, MA: Schenkmen Publishing, 1980).

15. David Roediger, *Class, Race and Marxism* (London: Verso, 2017), 25–27; Alex Anievas and Karem Nisancīouglu, "The Poverty of Political Marxism," *International Socialist Review* 94 (Fall 2014).
16. Ellen Meiksins Wood, *Democracy against Capitalism: Renewing Historical Materialism* (New York: Cambridge University Press, 1995), 259.
17. Cinzia Arruzza makes a similar point ("Remarks on Gender," *Viewpoint Magazine*, September 2, 2014, https://www.viewpointmag.com/2014/09/02/remarks-on-gender and "Logic or History? The Political Stakes of Marxist-Feminist Theory," *Viewpoint Magazine*, June 23, 2015, https://www.viewpointmag.com/2015/06/23/logic-or-history-the-political-stakes-of-marxist-feminist-theory).
18. Charles Post, "Comments on Roediger's *Class, Race and Marxism*," *Salvage On-Line*, 2017, http://salvage.zone/online-exclusive/comments-on-roedigers-class-race-and-marxism.

Index[1]

[1] Note: Page numbers followed by 'n' refer to notes.

X. Lafrance, C. Post (eds.), *Case Studies in the Origins of Capitalism*, Marx, Engels, and Marxisms,
https://doi.org/10.1007/978-3-319-95657-2

Springer Theses

Recognizing Outstanding Ph.D. Research

For further volumes:
http://www.springer.com/series/8790

Aims and Scope

The series "Springer Theses" brings together a selection of the very best Ph.D. theses from around the world and across the physical sciences. Nominated and endorsed by two recognized specialists, each published volume has been selected for its scientific excellence and the high impact of its contents for the pertinent field of research. For greater accessibility to non-specialists, the published versions include an extended introduction, as well as a foreword by the student's supervisor explaining the special relevance of the work for the field. As a whole, the series will provide a valuable resource both for newcomers to the research fields described, and for other scientists seeking detailed background information on special questions. Finally, it provides an accredited documentation of the valuable contributions made by today's younger generation of scientists.

Theses are accepted into the series by invited nomination only and must fulfill all of the following criteria

- They must be written in good English.
- The topic of should fall within the confines of Chemistry, Physics and related interdisciplinary fields such as Materials, Nanoscience, Chemical Engineering, Complex Systems and Biophysics.
- The work reported in the thesis must represent a significant scientific advance.
- If the thesis includes previously published material, permission to reproduce this must be gained from the respective copyright holder.
- They must have been examined and passed during the 12 months prior to nomination.
- Each thesis should include a foreword by the supervisor outlining the significance of its content.
- The theses should have a clearly defined structure including an introduction accessible to scientists not expert in that particular field.

Andreas W. Rost

Magnetothermal Properties near Quantum Criticality in the Itinerant Metamagnet $Sr_3Ru_2O_7$

Doctoral Thesis accepted by
University of St Andrews, UK

Springer

Author
Dr. Andreas W. Rost
Scottish Universities Physics Alliance (SUPA),
School of Physics & Astronomy
University of St Andrews
North Haugh
St Andrews KY16 9SS, UK
ar35@st-andrews.ac.uk

Supervisor
Prof. Andrew Mackenzie
School of Physics & Astronomy
University of St Andrews
North Haugh
St Andrews KY16 9SS, UK
apm9@st-andrews.ac.uk

ISSN 2190-5053

e-ISSN 2190-5061

ISBN 978-3-642-26619-5

ISBN 978-3-642-14524-7 (eBook)

DOI 10.1007/978-3-642-14524-7

Springer Heidelberg Dordrecht London New York

Softcover reprint of the hardcover 1st edition 2010

Cover design: eStudio Calamar, Berlin/Figueres

Printed on acid-free paper

Springer is part of Springer Science+Business Media (www.springer.com)

Supervisor's Foreword

Our department nominated this thesis for a Springer award because we regard it as an outstanding piece of work, carried out with a remarkable level of independence. Andreas Rost joined us in 2005, as one of the inaugural Prize Students of the Scottish Universities Physics Alliance. Our research group has been working on $Sr_3Ru_2O_7$, in collaboration with our colleagues in the group of Professor Y. Maeno at Kyoto, since 1998. By early 2005 we had tantalising evidence that a novel phase was forming at very low temperatures, in an overall phase diagram dominated by quantum fluctuations.

We knew that comprehensive thermodynamic information would be needed in order to understand how this was happening, and that the demanding constraints of low temperature and high magnetic field meant that bespoke apparatus would need to be constructed. Andreas had studied the specific heat of glasses below 50 mK during his diploma thesis work at Heidelberg, and was brimming with ideas about how to proceed. We gave him advice, and constantly discussed the physics with him, but quickly realised that the best way to proceed practically was to give him a budget, and let him take the main design decisions, double-checking with us from time to time.

Andreas' design is notable for its flexibility. The same apparatus can be used to measure the specific heat by standard relaxation or a.c. methods, as well as the magnetocaloric effect in conditions ranging from quasi-adiabatic to highly non-adiabatic. All four modes were used during his measurements, in order to build up a comprehensive, cross-checked data set which allowed small entropy changes to be measured in absolute units.

The thesis reports three central pieces of new physics. First, the unusual 'liquid crystalline' behaviour of the correlated electrons in $Sr_3Ru_2O_7$ (established in separate work by our group) occurs in a bounded phase in an equilibrium phase diagram. Second, the entropic behaviour in the phase itself is unusual, suggesting the presence of some additional degrees of freedom whose origin is not yet understood. Third, the phase formation takes place against a background of strongly peaking entropy, suggesting that quantum criticality plays a key role in the physics. Some of these key results were published in 2009 as a full-length

Research Article in Science magazine, and several more manuscripts are in preparation. Already, however, the work has led to surprising and intriguing connections beyond our immediate field. The peaking of the entropy is surprisingly strong, and raises the question of whether the phase forms to avoid an entropic singularity. Such a singularity is not predicted by traditional theories of quantum criticality, but is, apparently, a feature of novel approaches in which string theory techniques are applied to the problem. Time will tell if this is a promising scientific train of thought, but Andreas' data being featured in conferences on cosmology is not something that any of us could have predicted when this project began. It illustrates the fact that the rewards for thorough, high precision experimental work are many and varied.

St Andrews, April 2010 A. P. Mackenzie and S. A. Grigera

Acknowledgments

The work presented in this thesis would not have been possible without the help and support from a number of people. First and foremost I am greatly indebted to my co-supervisors Andy Mackenzie and Santiago Grigera, who introduced me to the fascinating field of correlated electron physics and always had an open door for my plentiful questions. Not only did they support me in all aspects of the work but I am particularly grateful for the many opportunities I was given to explore science beyond the necessities of the project. Special thanks are due to Rodolfo Borzi, Naoki Kikugawa and Robin Perry, who helped by introducing me to the experimental equipment in the laboratory and the measurement techniques used by the group. Their patience with me and their help with the day-to-day work in the early parts of my Ph.D. was invaluable. Discussions with them helped me understand many of the small but important details of the scientific research undertaken by the laboratory. I need to particularly thank Robin Perry together with Jean-François Mercure and Alexandra Gibbs for the sample growth and characterisation. The work presented here would not have been possible without this. I shared all the little successes and failures occurring during a Ph.D. with Jean-François Mercure, Andrew Berridge and Jason Farrell, who carried out their Ph.D. studies at the same time as me. Most of the results presented here are crucially informed by long discussions with them and I learned a lot from their insights into $Sr_3Ru_2O_7$ and the work carried out by them. I also benefited from interesting discussions with many other members of the lab and I want to thank Jan Bruin, Demian Slobinsky, Alexandra Gibbs as well as the members of other groups—Ed Yelland, Alex Holmes, Marie-Aude Measson, Felix Baumberger and Anna Tamai—for their time and support. One aspect that made St Andrews a special place for a Ph.D. project was the interaction with other groups in the department. Many hours of discussions on the technical, theoretical and sometimes philosophical aspects of my work were spent in the common room. I am particularly grateful to Chris Hooley, Andrew Green and John Allen for sharing their insights into physics with me. I would also like to use the opportunity to thank the technical staff in the department. Reg Gavine not only ensured the constant supply of liquid helium but also helped with many other aspects of laboratory life, such as failing pumps.

Further thanks are due to Mark Ross in Electronics as well as David Steven and George Robb from the workshop for putting my designs into reality. I especially would like to thank my parents as well as my sister and brother-in-law, who always support me in my studies and often help me to see what is important beyond the work in the lab. Finally and most importantly I would like to thank Alex for accompanying me along the journey of my Ph.D. time. Her constant support, encouragement and understanding are invaluable.

The work reported in this thesis was financially support by the Scottish Universities Physics Alliance (SUPA) Graduate School and the Engineering and Physical Sciences Research Council (EPSRC). I also benefited from the travel grant scheme of the Scottish International Education Trust (SIET), allowing me to visit the laboratories of Y. Maeno at Kyoto University.

Contents

Chapter 1
Introduction

In solid state physics one is in the situation that it is possible to write down the Hamiltonian governing the physics of the systems under investigation. The quantum mechanical Schrödinger equation describing the electrons and nuclei that form the solid contains their kinetic energy terms and the Coulomb interactions between the particles. This situation means effectively that one has a 'theory of everything' available, describing in principle all material properties below the energy scales of solidification. From a reductionist point of view this is a *fait accompli*.

Unfortunately, for the number of particles in realistic solid state systems this 'theory of everything' is a highly complex set of equations that currently is not only insoluble analytically but also beyond the capability of numerical methods in most cases.[1] It is in particular the Coulomb interaction between particles that makes the equations intractable and correlates the motion of all electrons with one another. One of the most radical simplifications of the equation is simply to neglect the Coulomb interaction, leading to the electrons conforming to the theory of the Fermi gas. Surprisingly it is found that the functional form of the properties of a wide range of crystalline materials can be successfully described by this theory. A reason for this was provided by Landau who showed that under certain general conditions the fundamental low energy excitations of an interacting Fermi liquid have the same charge and spin quantum numbers as non-interacting electrons, explaining the similar behaviour to the Fermi gas. However the extraordinary

---

[1] One has to point out though that developments in numerical calculations have made great advances in recent years and are now a useful tool in the understanding of band structures of crystalline materials. Especially the availability of tool sets such as Wien2K [1] and CASTEP [2] make the use of the techniques available to non-experts and become more and more used in the lab environment. However, they are based on certain approximations of the full Hamiltonian and therefore currently unable to treat problems going beyond these approximations.

A. W. Rost, *Magnetothermal Properties near Quantum Criticality in the Itinerant Metamagnet $Sr_3Ru_2O_7$*, Springer Theses, DOI: 10.1007/978-3-642-14524-7_1,

success of Fermi liquid theory makes materials not falling into this category of particular scientific interest.

If the effective interactions between the quasiparticles in a Fermi liquid become strong enough, its basic assumptions can break down and this opens the path to a wealth of unexpected phenomena and the continuing discoveries of new physics. This makes solid state physics an extraordinary field where experimental discoveries lead to effective theoretical descriptions, as happened in the case of superconductivity and BCS theory, and at the same time theoretical developments are guiding experiments, with a recent example being the search for p-wave superconductivity in Sr_2RuO_4 [3]. But the wealth of phenomena extends far beyond unconventional superconductivity to a diverse range of physics such as is observed in Kondo systems [4, 5], the fractional quantum Hall effect [6, 7] or the rapidly growing field of frustrated spin systems [8].

One route to novel physics in metallic systems that has been investigated intensely in recent years is the phenomenon of quantum criticality—the physics related to a zero temperature second order quantum phase transition that can be crossed by tuning an external parameter such as pressure or magnetic field. In the vicinity of this phase transition—called the quantum critical point—the thermodynamic properties are not dominated by classical thermal fluctuations, as are finite temperature second order phase transitions, but by quantum fluctuations. These renormalise the properties of the two competing quantum ground states, potentially giving rise to non-analytic singularities of their thermodynamic properties at the quantum critical point. This allows for novel quantum phases, that are under normal conditions thermodynamically unstable, to emerge in the vicinity of quantum critical points.

An experimentally successful approach to quantum critical points in phase diagrams has been the suppression of a finite temperature second order phase transition to zero temperature [9] by tuning such variables as pressure [10], magnetic field [11] or doping [12]. Figure 1.1 shows the example of $CePd_2Si_2$ studied by Mathur et al. [10]. Here the observed phase transitions in the temperature–pressure phase space are shown. At zero pressure the material undergoes an antiferromagnetic second order phase transition as a function of temperature. If one applies pressure the antiferromagnetic transition temperature T_N is systematically suppressed towards lower temperature. However the quantum critical point that would ultimately be reached at a critical pressure p_C is 'avoided' by the material becoming superconducting inside the indicated dome. What makes this new superconducting phase so interesting is that it is supposed to be mediated by electron–magnon rather than electron–phonon interactions. Quantum criticality is also thought to play a significant role in the overall phase diagram of a range of systems of which two of the most well known are the cuprate high-T_C superconductors and f-electrons in heavy Fermion Kondo systems [9].

The material studied in this project, $Sr_3Ru_2O_7$, is an example of a metallic system thought to be close to a quantum critical phase transition that can be tuned by magnetic field. It has a currently unique combination of properties that make it a particularly interesting example.

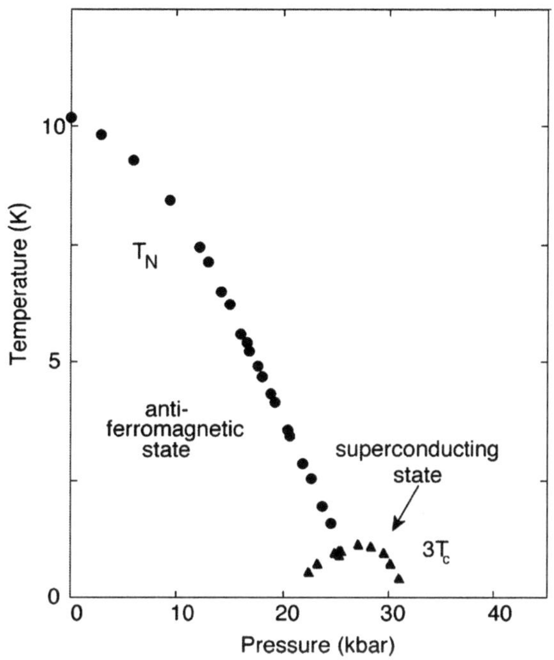

Fig. 1.1 Here the phase diagram of $CePd_2Si_2$ as a function of temperature and pressure is reproduced from Ref. [10]. The transition temperature T_N of the second order phase transition to an antiferromagnetic phase is suppressed towards lower temperatures by applying pressure. Before the quantum critical point is reached the material undergoes a further transition to a state of unconventional superconductivity thought to be mediated by magnons rather than phonons. The transition temperature T_C to superconductivity has been multiplied by a factor 3 for the purpose of presentation

First, quantum criticality in $Sr_3Ru_2O_7$ is approached by suppressing the critical end-point of a line of first order phase transitions to zero temperature leading to a novel class of quantum phase transition—the quantum critical end-point. The tuning parameters here are the magnitude of the magnetic field and its orientation with respect to the crystal structure, with the quantum critical end-point being realised with the magnetic field being applied along the crystallographic *c*-axis.

Secondly, the associated physics can be studied in clean single crystal samples whose electronic structure is quasi-two-dimensional. This allows for a detailed study of the fermiology of the quantum mechanical ground states in the vicinity of the proposed quantum critical point by a range of otherwise not usable experimental techniques such as quantum oscillations, angular resolved photo emission studies (ARPES) or scanning tunneling microscopy (STM).

Last but not least it was found in ultra clean samples with mean free paths of the order of 3000 Å that in the vicinity of the expected quantum critical end-point the material forms a novel quantum phase whose electronic system shows nematic-like transport properties.

This combination of experimental findings makes $Sr_3Ru_2O_7$ an ideal candidate to study the above phenomena in detail. Though a wealth of experimental studies have been performed, so far no direct measurement of the evolution of the entropy of the system across the low temperature phase diagram has been achieved. This is a major gap in our knowledge since the entropy encodes important information on the overall degrees of freedom of the system.

The measurements presented in this thesis have two main purposes. First, the phase diagram of the novel quantum phase is investigated. Here specific heat measurements are used to identify the thermodynamic nature of the surrounding phase transitions as well as to study the temperature dependence of the entropy inside the phase. The second and equally important focus of the project is the change of entropy of the surrounding 'normal' phases upon approaching the critical region as a function of magnetic field. The method normally employed to reconstruct the entropy at a given magnetic field H and temperature T is to integrate the specific heat at H from zero temperature to T. In the case of approaching a quantum critical point this cannot be done since finite temperature specific heat measurements cannot reliably be extrapolated to zero temperature. Therefore, here the less commonly encountered magnetothermal effect was used. In this measurement the entropy of a system is extracted by analysing the temperature changes of a sample during a magnetic field sweep.

In the first part of the following chapter the main assumptions and results for the theory of the Fermi gas and the Fermi liquid are reviewed insofar as they are relevant to this project. This is followed by a brief introduction to quantum criticality and its importance to the study of materials that go beyond the Fermi liquid. The second part will review the physical properties of $Sr_3Ru_2O_7$ and introduce the current experimental evidence for quantum criticality, the existence of a novel quantum phase and the electronic structure in the surrounding 'normal' states. Chapter 3 introduces the relevant aspects of thermodynamics in magnetic fields and the measurement methods for specific heat and the magnetothermal effect. In particular the strong magnetic moment and the requirements for the magnetothermal measurement made it necessary to design and characterise a new experimental setup and calibrate thermometers over the relevant temperature and magnetic field range. In Chap. 4, the details of this experimental apparatus together with characterisation measurements are presented. This is followed in Chap. 5 by the results of the magnetothermal study of the entropy evolution as a function of temperature and magnetic field in the vicinity of the critical region of the phase diagram. In particular, results on the anomalous new phase and the evolution of the normal state upon approaching the critical field will be presented and discussed in relation to previous measurements. Furthermore, the results of a preliminary angular study with the magnetic field being applied at directions different from the crystallographic c-axis are given in Appendix B. The thesis will conclude with a brief summary of the achievements of the project.

References

1. Blaha P, Schwarz K, Sorantin P, Trickey SB (1990) Full-potential, linearized augmented plane-wave programs for crystalline systems. Comp Phys Commun 59(2):399–415
2. Segall MD, Lindan PJD, Probert MJ, Pickard CJ, Hasnip PJ, Clark SJ, Payne MC (2002) First-principles simulation: ideas, illustrations and the CASTEP code. J Phys Condens Matter 14(11):2717–2744

3. Mackenzie AP, Maeno Y (2003) The superconductivity of Sr_2RuO_4 and the physics of spin-triplet pairing. Rev Mod Phys 75(2):657–712
4. Stewart GR (2001) Non-Fermi-liquid behavior in d- and f-electron metals. Rev Mod Phys 73(4):797–855
5. Kondo J (1964) Resistance minimum in dilute magnetic alloys. Prog Theor Phys 32:37
6. Tsui DC, Störmer HL, Gossard AC (1982) Two-dimensional magnetotransport in the extreme quantum limit. Phys Rev Lett 48(22):1559–1562
7. Laughlin RB (1983) Anomalous quantum Hall-effect—an incompressible quantum fluid with fractionally charged excitations. Phys Rev Lett 50(18):1395–1398
8. Diep HP (2005) Frustrated spin systems. World Scientific Publishing, Singapore, London
9. Mathur ND, Grosche FM, Julian SR, Walker IR, Freye DM, Haselwimmer RKW, Lonzarich GG (1998) Magnetically mediated superconductivity in heavy Fermion compounds. Nature 394(6688):39–43
10. Löhneysen Hv, Rosch A, Vojta M, Wölfle P (2007) Fermi-liquid instabilities at magnetic quantum phase transitions. Rev Mod Phys 79(3):1015–1075
11. Custers J, Gegenwart P, Wilhelm H, Neumaier K, Tokiwa Y, Trovarelli O, Geibel C, Steglich F, Pepin C, Coleman P (2003) The break-up of heavy electrons at a quantum critical point. Nature 424(6948):524–527
12. Schröder A, Aeppli G, Coldea R, Adams M, Stockert O, von Löhneysen H, Bucher E, Ramazashvili R, Coleman P (2000) Onset of antiferromagnetism in heavy-Fermion metals. Nature 407(6802):351–355

Chapter 2
Background Physics

In this chapter I will introduce the theoretical concepts and experimental data that are relevant to the study of $Sr_3Ru_2O_7$ presented in this thesis. From a theoretical point of view the fundamental phenomena of a wide class of correlated electron systems are surprisingly well described by a non-interacting 'Fermi gas' theory. One of the first assumptions of this theory is not to take into account any electron–electron interactions besides Pauli's Exclusion Principle. It is thanks to a theory by Landau [1–3] that we understand why the results for the Fermi gas also apply qualitatively to strongly interacting Fermi liquids. Since the properties of the metallic ground state of $Sr_3Ru_2O_7$ in zero magnetic field are well described by the concepts of Landau's Fermi liquid theory I will review its most important results in the first part of this chapter. Indeed the predictions of Landau's Fermi liquid theory are so robust that it is in particular the systems that go beyond that theory and show non-Fermi liquid behaviour that have attracted a wealth of experimental and theoretical, with the high temperature superconductors of the cuprate [4] and recently iron–pnictide families [5] being but two of the most famous examples. In particular, the concept of quantum criticality has been used experimentally as a route to novel quantum states and will be briefly discussed.

The second part of this chapter will review the most relevant experimental data existing to date on $Sr_3Ru_2O_7$. Here I will in particular discuss the thermodynamic evidence for a metamagnetic quantum critical end point as well as the existence of a novel quantum phase in its vicinity. The chapter will finish with a summary of the experimental evidence for Fermi liquid quasiparticle excitations across the phase diagram.

2.1 Itinerant Electron Systems

To give a thorough introduction to the 'Fermi gas' or Landau's Fermi liquid theory is beyond the scope of this thesis. However, in order to put the experimental results

A. W. Rost, *Magnetothermal Properties near Quantum Criticality in the Itinerant Metamagnet $Sr_3Ru_2O_7$*, Springer Theses, DOI: 10.1007/978-3-642-14524-7_2,

and their significance into perspective it is necessary to summarise the most relevant results of the non-interacting theory in the first part of this section. Here particular emphasis will be put on the properties in magnetic fields. This will be followed by a basic introduction to Fermi liquid theory in order to show which concepts form the basis for its successful description of a wide range of itinerant electron systems. For more detailed discussions and derivations of the results presented here the books by Ashcroft and Mermin [6] for the properties of solid state systems in general and by Abrikosov et al. [7] for Landau Fermi liquid theory in particular give a good treatment of the subject and provide further references to the literature.

2.1.1 Non-Interacting Electron Theory

Many metals share a range of similar properties such as a linear temperature dependence of the specific heat at low temperatures. A very important step in understanding the generality of the physical laws applying to a vast range of different materials was Sommerfeld's theory of non-interacting fermionic particles that are constrained by boundary conditions in space. In combination with the study of the effect of a spatially varying periodic lattice potential on these non-interacting fermions, the theory is very successful in explaining many aspects of the properties of crystalline materials, especially at low temperatures. For the discussion in the following sections it is important to review the key concepts and nomenclature used.

The first concepts to mention are those of lattice momentum and the Brillouin zone. Since the periodic potential of the lattice destroys the continuous translational symmetry of real space, momentum is no longer a good quantum number. However, a crystalline system still retains a discrete translational symmetry leading to the definition of a lattice momentum. For the purposes here, one can—with one important exception—treat this lattice momentum the same way as the normal momentum, and the explicit reference to the lattice will be omitted in the reminder of the thesis. The important exception is that the momentum space is finite and can be confined to the first Brillouin zone, the primitive unit cell of the reciprocal lattice related to the real lattice via a Fourier transform. Under these conditions it is possible to show that the resulting single-electron energy–momentum dispersion in a crystalline solid is given by a series of energy bands $\epsilon_N(\mathbf{k})$ in the Brillouin zone. Here ϵ is the energy, $\mathbf{k}$ the momentum vector and N the band index. If one neglects the Coulomb and magnetic interaction between the electrons then these energy levels are occupied at zero temperature according to Pauli's Exclusion Principle up to a maximum energy, the so called Fermi energy ϵ_F. Each energy level is doubly occupied due to the degeneracy in spin space. It can be shown that in the thermodynamic limit ϵ_F is independent of sample size. These concepts are illustrated in Fig. 2.1 for the example of copper [6, p. 289].

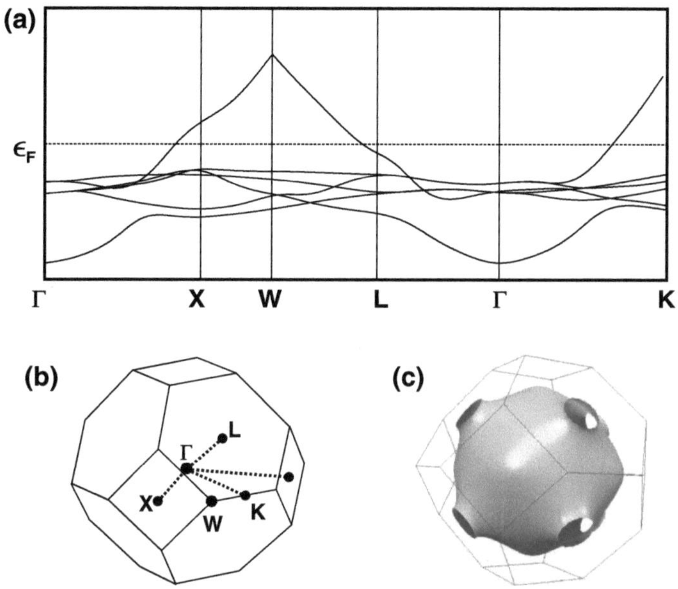

Fig. 2.1 **a** The band structure of Cu close to the Fermi energy ϵ_F is shown (graphic based on [6, p. 289]). The bands are plotted along lines in momentum space connecting points of high symmetry in the Brillouin zone. The position of these points is indicated in **b**, where the first Brillouin zone of Cu is given. The Fermi surface of Cu is shown in **c** [8, 9]

The wave vector in momentum space describing the Fermi surface is called the Fermi momentum $\mathbf{k}_F$. The Fermi surface topology is in general complicated. In particular, more than one band usually crosses the Fermi energy, giving a number of disconnected Fermi surfaces.

Most results of the theory take their simplest form for spherical Fermi surfaces. The magnitude of the Fermi momentum, k_F, is for example independent of direction and equal to the radius. For this reason mathematical results in this thesis are often presented for isotropic Fermi surfaces only. However, these are generally extendable to more complicated topologies.

The elementary excitation of such a system is the occupation of an unfilled level with an electron from a filled level. Whenever an electron crosses the Fermi energy a 'hole' is left behind in the states below the Fermi energy. The resulting symmetry in the number of particle and hole excitations is a fundamental property of a fermionic system as considered here. The typical width in energy of the electronic bands is of several eV. Therefore, any measurement of the system involving energy scales of not more than a few meV probes the physics of the energy–momentum dispersion close to the Fermi surface. As a result many properties of the system can be written in terms of a linearised band structure at ϵ_F. In connection to this an important quantity is the density of states $g(\epsilon)$, with $g(\epsilon)\mathrm{d}\epsilon$ giving the number of electronic states in the energy range from ϵ to $\epsilon + \mathrm{d}\epsilon$ normalised by the sample volume V.

An important class of measurements are thermodynamic experiments at low temperature. Since a temperature of 10 K corresponds to an average thermal energy of the order of 1 meV the above assumption of linearisation is often fulfilled experimentally. In this limit the electronic specific heat c_{el} is linear in temperature T and given by

$$c_{el} = \frac{\pi^2}{3} k_B^2 T g(\epsilon_F), \tag{2.1}$$

with k_B being Boltzmann's constant. The factor $(\pi^2/3)k_B^2 g(\epsilon_F)$ is called Sommerfeld coefficient γ. In the case of an isotropic surface, γ can be written as

$$\gamma = \frac{k_B^2}{3} k_F^2 \left(\left. \frac{\partial \epsilon}{\partial k} \right|_{k_F} \right)^{-1}. \tag{2.2}$$

Comparing this result to the Sommerfeld coefficient of the free electron gas,

$$\gamma_{gas} = \frac{m_e k_B^2}{3\hbar^2} k_F, \tag{2.3}$$

leads to the definition of the thermodynamic effective mass m^* as

$$m^* = \hbar^2 k_F \left(\left. \frac{\partial \epsilon}{\partial k} \right|_{k_F} \right)^{-1}. \tag{2.4}$$

A second class of experiments such as resistivity measurements or the response to strong magnetic fields involves dynamic properties of the electronic states. An appropriate theoretical framework for a discussion of most of the observed effects is the semiclassical theory. The basic components of this theory are electronic wavepackets in real space that represent an excitation of spin 1/2 and charge $-e$ being spread out over several lattice sites. If the analysis does not require too localised a wave function in real space, then one can represent it as a superposition of only a small number of momentum eigenstates around an average Fermi momentum $\mathbf{k}_F$. If one assumes furthermore that the applied electric or magnetic field is varying only slowly over the width of the wave packet, then it is possible to treat the field effectively as a classical force acting on the centre of the wave packet. The above described hierarchy of scales is shown schematically in Fig. 2.2.

An important variable in this theory is the (group) velocity of the wavepacket with which its centre of mass moves. It is given by

$$\mathbf{v}(\mathbf{k}) = \frac{1}{\hbar} \frac{\partial \epsilon}{\partial \mathbf{k}}, \tag{2.5}$$

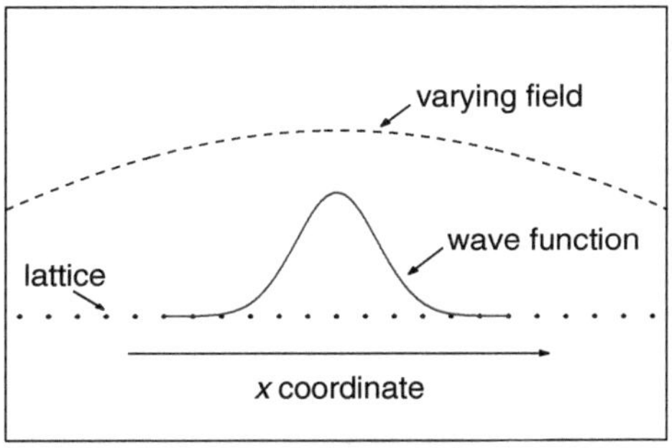

Fig. 2.2 This figure gives a overview of the hierarchy of scales in real space for which the semiclassical description is appropriate. The electron wavepacket described (*blue*) can only be localised to within several lattice site (*black dots*). Furthermore, the variations of the applied field have to be small on the scale of the wavepacket

with $\hbar$ being Planck's constant. The comparison of the momentum $\mathbf{p}$ of a wave-packet given by

$$\mathbf{p} = \hbar\mathbf{k}, \tag{2.6}$$

with the definition $\mathbf{p} = m^*\mathbf{v}$ for the classical momentum leading to a definition of an effective dynamic mass m^* as

$$m^* = \hbar^2 k_F \left(\frac{\partial \epsilon}{\partial \mathbf{k}} \bigg|_{k_F} \right)^{-1}. \tag{2.7}$$

Note here that this is the same definition as has been obtained previously for the thermodynamic effective mass and no distinction between the two will be made in the following.

Within the semiclassical model one can derive the equations of motion for the position $\mathbf{r}$ and momentum $\mathbf{k}$ of a wavepacket under the influence of an electric field $\mathbf{E}$ and a magnetic field $\mathbf{H}$ as

$$\dot{\mathbf{r}} = \mathbf{v} = \frac{1}{\hbar} \frac{\partial \epsilon}{\partial \mathbf{k}} \bigg|_{\mathbf{k}_F}, \tag{2.8}$$

$$\hbar\dot{\mathbf{k}} = -e\left[\mathbf{E} + \frac{1}{c}\mathbf{v} \times \mathbf{H}\right]. \tag{2.9}$$

Here e is the charge of an electron and c is the velocity of light.

After having introduced the fundamental concepts of the theory of a non-interacting Fermi gas I will in the following discuss its results regarding the effects of magnetic and electric fields in more detail.

2.1.2 *Magnetic Field Effects*

Magnetic field effects are generally treated in two regimes. In the first, one assumes that the dynamics of electrons due to the applied field, i.e. electron orbital effects, are negligible. An example for this limit is Pauli paramagnetism. The second case takes full account of the orbital motion leading to such effects as quantum oscillations.

2.1.2.1 Pauli Paramagnetism and an Extension Thereof

If a magnetic field $\mu_0 H$ is applied to an itinerant paramagnetic electron system then each electron can orient its spin parallel ($\uparrow$) or antiparallel ($\downarrow$) to the magnetic field.

Since orbital motion of the electrons will be neglected here the only effect of the field is a shift of the energy levels for the spin-up and spin-down electrons by $\pm\ \mu_B H$. Therefore, in the presence of the magnetic field the density of states for each species of electrons can be given in terms of the zero field density of states $g(\epsilon)$ by

$$g_{\uparrow/\downarrow}(\epsilon) = \frac{1}{2} g(\epsilon \mp \mu_B \mu_0 H). \tag{2.10}$$

The requirement of conservation of number of electrons N in the system then defines implicitly the Fermi energy ϵ_F at zero temperature via

$$N = \int_{-\infty}^{\epsilon_F} (g_\uparrow + g_\downarrow) \mathrm{d}\epsilon. \tag{2.11}$$

In the limit where the magnetic field is small, one can assume that the density of states is effectively constant, resulting in the Fermi energy ϵ_F being field independent. Furthermore, the magnetization M is given in terms of the number of spin up electrons, $n_\uparrow$, and spin-down electrons, $n_\downarrow$, by

$$M = -\mu_B(n_\uparrow - n_\downarrow) = -\mu_B(-\mu_B \mu_0 H g(\epsilon_F)), \tag{2.12}$$

resulting in the familiar expression for the susceptibility of Pauli paramagnetism χ of

$$\chi = \mu_B^2 g(\epsilon_F). \tag{2.13}$$

Two things should be mentioned. First of all the derivation at no point made any reference to the band structure other than the density of states, nor to the orientation of the magnetic field. Pauli paramagnetism is therefore isotropic. Furthermore, for simplicity, the argument was presented only for zero temperature, but it can be shown that χ is, to first order, temperature independent.

The reason the effect was presented in some detail here is because in the following it will be discussed what occurs when the magnetic field is sufficiently strong such that the assumption of the constant density of states breaks down (however orbital effects will still be neglected). This, for example, can happen at experimentally accessible fields if there is a peak in the density of states close to the zero field Fermi energy. This thought experiment is presented in Fig. 2.3.

In part (a), a possible situation in zero magnetic field ($H_0 = 0$) is shown. Here the density of states $g_{\uparrow/\downarrow}(\epsilon)$ are shown as a function of energy for the spin-up (blue) and spin-down (red) electrons. The density of states has a peak below the Fermi energy ϵ_F at the energies $\epsilon_{c\uparrow}/\epsilon_{c\downarrow}$ which are identical in zero field. If one now applies a magnetic field H_1 (part b) the energy of the spin-up band is lowered whereas the energy of the spin-down band is increased. However, whereas the difference in shift between the two bands is given by $\mu_B H$, the

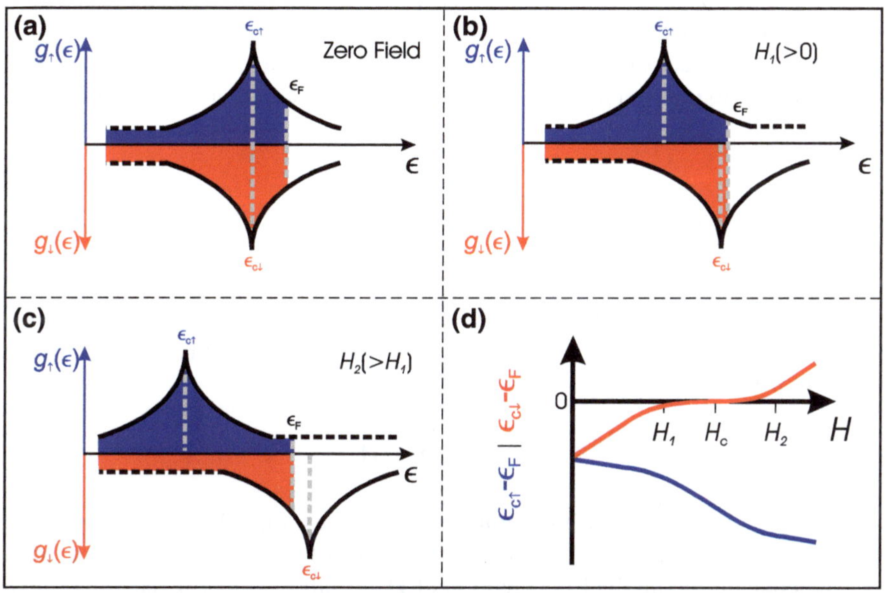

Fig. 2.3 Schematic representation of the effect of a magnetic field on the shift in the density of states of the spin up ($g_\uparrow(\epsilon)$) and spin down ($g_\downarrow(\epsilon)$) Fermi surfaces neglecting orbital effects. In zero magnetic field, as shown in **a**, the density of states of both spin species are the same. In the particular scenario here both density of states have a peak at $\epsilon_{c\downarrow}$ and $\epsilon_{c\uparrow}$ below the Fermi energy ϵ_F. The *filled states* of the two spin species are shown in *blue* (spin-up) and *red* (spin-down). In **b** and **c** it is shown that, when applying successively larger magnetic fields H_1 and H_2, the bands shift relative to each other with the density of states peak of one of the spin species being pushed through the Fermi energy. As discussed in the text the condition of overall number conservation causes the rate of change of the density of states to be a nonlinear function of applied field. This is shown schematically in **d** where the distance in energy of each of the density of states peaks from the Fermi energy ϵ_F, i.e. $\epsilon_{c\uparrow} - \epsilon_F$ and $\epsilon_{c\downarrow} - \epsilon_F$, is given as a function of magnetic field. As shown, $\epsilon_{c\uparrow} - \epsilon_F$ and $\epsilon_{c\downarrow} - \epsilon_F$ are not a linear function of $H - H_C$ where H_C is the critical field at which the peak in the density of states of one of the spin species crosses the Fermi energy

individual relative shift with respect to the Fermi energy is determined by number conservation. The consequence of this is that when the Fermi energy in one of the spin subspecies gets close to a peak in the density of states then the rate at which the Fermi energy approaches the peak as a function of applied magnetic field will slow down.

At a sufficiently high magnetic field the Fermi energy will have crossed the peak in the density of states as shown in Fig. 2.3c. Some careful remarks are necessary here. First, the above discussion completely ignores electron–electron interaction effects. Secondly, here the orbital effects of electronic states, leading for example to the phenomenon of quantum oscillations [10], were neglected. Overall one would not expect necessarily to be able to make quantitatively correct predictions based on this 'Gedankenexperiment'. However, one main qualitative conclusion is expected to hold. Close to a density of states peak one cannot expect that the distance in energy of the Fermi energy to that peak, i.e. $(\epsilon_C - \epsilon_F)$, is directly proportional to $(H - H_C)$, which is the difference of the magnetic field H to the critical magnetic field H_C at which the Fermi energy would lie at the maximum of the density of states peak. This is shown explicitly in Fig. 2.3d, where the relation between the two is shown for the particular scenario discussed here.

2.1.2.2 Quantum Oscillations

In the previous section it was assumed that the only coupling to the magnetic field is via the spin of the electrons. However, according to the semiclassical model introduced earlier, there exists a coupling between the magnetic field $\mathbf{H}$ and the momentum $\mathbf{k}$ of an electron wavepacket:

$$\hbar\dot{\mathbf{k}} = -e\left[\frac{1}{c}\mathbf{v} \times \mathbf{H}\right]. \tag{2.14}$$

On closer inspection of this equation one finds that the trajectory of the wavepacket in momentum space is along a path of constant energy in a plane perpendicular to the applied magnetic field $\mathbf{H}$. In other words, if the wavepacket originates at the Fermi surface its trajectory is a trace along the Fermi surface in a plane perpendicular to the magnetic field. In the following it will be assumed for simplicity that the plane in which the motion takes place in momentum space is the $k_x - k_y$ plane. One consequence of this is that k_x and k_y are not good quantum numbers any more.[1]

In suitable Fermi surface topologies the path of the electron will be closed, resulting in a motion in momentum space and real space that is periodic. Similarly

[1] They are replaced for a spherical Fermi surface by $(k_x \pm ik_y)$.

to the situation of electronic orbits in atomic physics it follows that the motion has to satisfy a quantisation condition which can be expressed in terms of the area a enclosed in momentum space and an integer n as

$$a = \left(n + \frac{1}{2}\right)\frac{2\pi eH}{c\hbar}. \tag{2.15}$$

The above relation is known in the literature as Onsager's relation [11]. A consequence of it is that the eigenstates in momentum space now are lying on tubes (called Landau tubes) whose principle axis is determined by the direction of the magnetic field.

Since the radius of these tubes and, as can be shown, their degeneracy, changes with magnetic field, one expects the properties of the electronic system to vary as a function of field as well. The energy of each tube associated with a definite quantum number n has to vary as a function of field, leading to the the Landau tubes crossing the Fermi energy one by one. This leads to an oscillatory behaviour in the properties of the material that, as can be derived from the quantisation condition, is periodic in $1/H$. A detailed derivation of that dependence is given for example in the book by Shoenberg [10]. Here, I will summarise the main results in the limit of high quantum numbers n.

The first quantity which has to be affected is the density of states. The oscillatory component $\tilde{g}(\epsilon_F)$ of the total density of states $g(\epsilon_F)$ at the Fermi energy ϵ_F as a function of magnetic field H is proportional to [10]

$$\tilde{g}(E_F) \propto \left(\frac{eH}{c\hbar}\right)^{1/2} m^* \sum_{p=1}^{\infty} \frac{1}{p^{1/2}} \cos\left(2\pi p\left(\frac{Ac\hbar}{2\pi eH} - \frac{1}{2}\right) \pm \frac{\pi}{4}\right). \tag{2.16}$$

Several important things have to be noted. First of all, A is an extremal cross sectional area of all possible cuts through the Fermi surface perpendicular to the applied magnetic field H. The contributions of all other cross sections interfere destructively. Secondly the total signal is a sum over all harmonics p of a fundamental oscillation in inverse magnetic field $1/H$. The frequencies F of quantum oscillations are therefore quoted in units of Tesla. Furthermore there is a direct proportionality between F and the area A that depends only on universal constants. By measuring the effect of these oscillations in the density of states on the entropy of the system (magnetothermal oscillations) or the resistivity (Shubnikov–de Haas effect) one can, therefore, obtain information about the size of the extremal areas of a Fermi surface. In particular if the Fermi surface is quasi-two-dimensional (i.e. a tube) the cross section and thereby the oscillation frequency should be proportional to $1/\cos(\Theta)$ with Θ being the angle between the applied magnetic field and the principal axis of the Fermi surface.

If the effect is observed in the longitudinal magnetisation $M_{||}$ or AC magnetic susceptibility it is usually referred to as the de Haas–van Alphen effect. $M_{||}$ can be shown to be proportional to

$$\tilde{M}_{||} \propto \left(\frac{eH}{c\hbar}\right)^{3/2} \frac{m^*}{H} \sum_{p=1}^{\infty} \frac{1}{p^{1/2}} \sin\left(2\pi p\left(\frac{Ac\hbar}{2\pi eH} - \frac{1}{2}\right) \pm \frac{\pi}{4}\right) \tag{2.17}$$

and therefore contains equivalent information on the quantum oscillation frequencies and thereby on extremal Fermi surface orbits.

2.1.2.3 Effect of Temperature on Oscillations

At non-zero temperature the occupation of energy levels does not have a sharp discontinuity at ϵ_F but varies smoothly according to the Fermi-Dirac distribution $f(\epsilon, \mu)$ with μ being the chemical potential. Pippard [12] proposed a simple argument for the effect of temperature on quantum oscillations. He assumed that one can view the smooth Fermi–Dirac distribution as a superposition of a range of systems at zero temperature with slightly different chemical potentials. The overall measured oscillations can therefore be thought of as the phase coherent sum over all these systems. Mathematically, this is equivalent to a convolution of the zero temperature oscillations with the distribution function given by the derivative of the Fermi–Dirac distribution, i.e. $-\, df(\epsilon, \mu)/d\epsilon$. It can be shown that this effectively leads in frequency space to a multiplication of the amplitude of the frequency spectrum with a temperature and field dependent prefactor R_{LK} given by

$$R_{LK} = \frac{x}{\sinh(x)},$$

where

$$x = 2\pi^2 kTm^* c/e\hbar H. \tag{2.18}$$

This is called the Lifshitz–Kosevich (LK) temperature dependence of quantum oscillations. Since the functional form depends on the effective mass m^* one can extract this information from the measured temperature dependence of each of the observed frequencies in the spectrum. Quantum oscillations can therefore be used as a Fermi surface specific probe of the effective mass.

Effect of Impurities

At the end of this section a comment should be made on the impurity dependence of the oscillation amplitude. A crucial component of the theory is the quantisation condition due to closed orbits in momentum space. The presence of impurities means that an orbiting electron will be scattered at a rate τ that is related to the mean free path l of the sample via the Fermi velocity $\mathbf{v}_F = l/\tau$. This is equivalent to a finite lifetime of the Landau levels and results in a phase smearing of the oscillations. It can be shown that the amplitude of oscillations due to this effect depends exponentially on the mean free path l and the magnetic field H. Quantum oscillations are therefore usually only seen in very pure single crystals and/or high magnetic fields. in particular since the dependence on mean free path l is exponential even small improvements in sample quality can significantly improve the signal.

2.1.3 Electric Transport

Empirically it is found that the low temperature resistivity ρ as a function of temperature T for most metals is described by

$$\rho = \rho_0 + AT^2, \tag{2.19}$$

with ρ_0 being a temperature independent constant and A a material specific prefactor. From the semiclassical equations it would follow that the momentum $\mathbf{k}$ of an electron wavepacket is related to an applied electric field $\mathbf{E}$ via

$$\hbar\dot{\mathbf{k}} = -e\mathbf{E}. \tag{2.20}$$

This would imply that the momentum of the electron would grow in time without bounds, implying infinite conductivity. Therefore, in the absence of any inelastic scattering processes, the resistivity would be zero. One obvious source for such processes is impurity scattering, which cause the temperature independent contribution ρ_0 of the resistivity. Since electron–electron scattering cannot take place in the non-interacting electron approximation the only other possibilities for inelastic scattering are electron–phonon processes. These indeed give a temperature dependent contribution, however it is found to generally be proportional to T^5 at low temperatures and not the dominant source of scattering in materials with strong electron–electron interactions. It is one of the failures of the non-interacting electron approximation not to be able to explain the T^2 dependence of the resistivity, since it is dominated by electron–electron processes that are explicitly excluded. I will return to this problem briefly in the context of Fermi liquid theory.

Before finishing this section a brief comment on the magnetoresistance in high magnetic fields should be given.[2] It follows from an analysis of the semiclassical model of a single Fermi surface[3] that, if one applies a magnetic field $\mathbf{H}$ perpendicular to an electric field $\mathbf{E}$, the induced current $\mathbf{j}$ is related to $\mathbf{E}$ via

---

[2] The high field limit here is the same as for quantum oscillations.

[3] The presented equations only hold for closed Fermi surfaces. Open orbit surfaces require a separate treatment discussed for example in [6].

$$\mathbf{E} = \boldsymbol{\rho}_N \mathbf{j}, \tag{2.21}$$

with $\boldsymbol{\rho}_N$ being the resistivity tensor of the Nth Fermi surface. ρ_N has the form

$$\boldsymbol{\rho}_N = \begin{pmatrix} \rho & -RH & 0 \\ RH & \rho & 0 \\ 0 & 0 & 0 \end{pmatrix} \tag{2.22}$$

if the magnetic field is applied the z-axis and the electric field along the x-axis. Here R is the Hall coefficient and ρ is the high field limit of the longitudinal resistivity. It can be shown that ρ saturates in this limit and becomes independent of magnetic field [6]. In a material with N Fermi surfaces each of them can be thought of as a separate conductance channel. Therefore, their resistance tensors $\boldsymbol{\rho}_n$ are added in parallel resulting in an overall resistance of the form

$$\boldsymbol{\rho} = \left(\sum_{n=1}^{N} \boldsymbol{\rho}_n^{-1} \right)^{-1}. \tag{2.23}$$

2.1.4 The Fermi Liquid

All results presented in the previous sections were based on the gross simplification of neglecting electron–electron interactions. Nevertheless, they are found to agree with most of the experimentally observed behaviour of a wide range of metals. In this section a theory of the interacting Fermi liquid will be introduced that was originally developed by Landau in a series of papers [1, 2, 3]. It not only shows how the previous results are stable even with strong electron–electron interactions but also gives insight into some of the previously unresolved issues such as the temperature dependence of resistivity. As the name suggests, Landau's Fermi liquid theory describes the properties of a system of Fermions that are strongly interacting not dissimilar to the strong interactions of atoms in a liquid.[4]

The first important component of Landau's theory is what is now known as the adiabatic continuity principle. Here one assumes that the interactions are 'switched on' from zero and increased continuously to their final magnitude. In this way the eigenstates of the non-interacting problem will evolve in a continuous way to the eigenstates of the fully interacting problem. Therefore, there exists a one-to-one correspondence between the low-lying excitations of the non-interacting and the interacting system. Due to this correspondence it is possible to still label the interacting quantum states with the quantum numbers of the non-interacting eigenstates, keeping in particular the distinction between occupied and unoccupied

[4] Though I will discuss here the theory primarily in terms of electrons it should be pointed out that it applies to all interacting Fermion systems, such as, for example, liquid ^{3}He.

levels. This preserves the concept of the Fermi energy ϵ_F and the Fermi surface. However, even though the elementary excitations which empty an occupied level and fill an unoccupied one obey Fermi statistics, they are no longer single electron excitations but excitation of the whole Fermi liquid. These excitations are therefore often called quasiparticles. An important difference to single particle excitations is that quasiparticle excitations are not independent of each other. An elementary excitation of the Fermi liquid involves a redistribution of the charge density which is the source of a residual interaction between the quasiparticles. This causes the life time of quasiparticles to be finite. It is therefore not a priori clear that they constitute a good description of the system on the timescale of an experiment.

The second important component of Landau's Fermi liquid theory addresses this issue by analysing the lifetime of quasiparticles due to interactions. The main effect limiting the lifetime of a high-energy quasiparticle excitation of energy ϵ is the decay into excitations of lower energy under conservation of the symmetry in the number of particles and holes. It can be shown that the decay rate for a single excitation in the presence of an otherwise filled Fermi sea is proportional to $(\epsilon - \epsilon_F)^2$. Based on this it can be argued that there can always be found a temperature T below which the excitations are sufficiently long lived such that on the time scale of the experiment the quasiparticle picture is an appropriate description of the system. This phase space protection of the scattering rate between quasiparticles is also the origin for the T^2-term in the temperature dependence of the resistivity.

In summary, these two fundamental concepts of the theory show that at sufficiently low temperature the excitations of a Fermi liquid take the form of quasiparticles that obey Pauli's exclusion principle. Furthermore, the concepts of filled and empty states, and therefore of a Fermi surface are preserved. An important consequence is that any property whose derivation in the non-interacting picture only takes into account properties close to the Fermi surface should still hold in the framework of Fermi liquid theory.

What does change contrary to the non-interacting case is therefore not the functional form of most of the physical properties of the system but the absolute values and the range of external parameters, such as temperature, over which it is applicable. This explains why the theory of a Fermi gas is so successful in qualitatively describing properties of a wide range of crystalline solid state systems at low temperatures without taking full account of electron–electron interactions.

The enhancement of the properties of the system with respect to the non-interacting band structure values is phenomenologically described by so-called Landau Fermi liquid parameters. These encapsulate the effect of interactions on the observable quantities in a phenomenological way. They represent, in principle, the prefactors of an expansion of the momentum and spin dependent interaction energy in harmonics of the Fermi surface. For the case of a spherical Fermi surface this can be done explicitly as an expansion in spherical harmonics. Here one finds for the measured effective mass m^* an enhancement over the non-interacting band mass m_{band} given by

$$m^* = \left(1 + \frac{F_1^s}{3}\right) m_{band}. \tag{2.24}$$

Furthermore the magnetic susceptibility is enhanced as

$$\chi = \frac{m^*}{m_{band}} \frac{1}{1 + F_0^a} \chi_{band}, \tag{2.25}$$

with F_1^s and F_0^a being two Landau parameters for an isotropic Fermi surface such as, for example, in the case of liquid ^{3}He at low temperatures. The factor $1/(1 + F_0^a)$ is also often referred to as the Sommerfeld–Wilson ratio of a Fermi liquid. It describes the ratio between the spin susceptibility and the effective mass enhancement and can therefore be thought as a guide to the importance of magnetic quasiparticle interactions.

An interesting observation relating to the prefactor A of the temperature dependent part of the resistivity was made by Kadowaki and Woods [13]. When plotting for a range of materials A versus the square of the Sommerfeld coefficient γ^2 it was found that there is a positive linear correlation between them. The ratio A/γ^2 of a material is referred to as the Kadowaki–Woods ratio. It can indeed be theoretically justified that A is proportional to the square of the effective mass $(m^*)^2$ and therefore γ^2 for a single spherical Fermi surface (see [14] and references therein). However, when considering multiband materials where the different Fermi surfaces act as parallel conductance channels but contribute 'in series' to the specific heat, it becomes apparent that the Kadowaki–Woods ratio cannot hold as a general law when considering the overall material properties but at most for the specific contribution of a single part of the Fermi surface to the overall measurable quantities.

Last but not least, it should be remarked that the electron–electron interaction and therefore the renormalisation of the electronic properties in a real multi band material are often significantly different from band to band and can even vary within a band. This again only affects the quantitative aspect of the renormalisation but does not change the qualitative functional form of those properties, as long as the basic assumptions of Fermi liquid theory such as the adiabatic continuity are not violated.

2.1.5 Beyond the Fermi Liquid

In the previous section Landau's Fermi liquid theory was introduced. Its main implication was that the functional form of the theoretical predictions of the Fermi gas also hold for strongly interacting systems at low temperatures and small excitation energies. Just how robust Landau's Fermi liquid theory is can for example be seen in heavy Fermion systems, where the charge carriers have effective masses of the order of 100 electron masses. The seemingly wide range of applicability the success of Landau's Fermi liquid theory makes the materials in which it fails to describe particularly interesting, not in the least, to say it in Landau's own words (used in a different context), since '*especially [as] the brevity of life does not allow us the luxury of spending time on problems which will lead to no new results*' [15].

There are of course ample examples of non-Fermi liquid behaviour such as BCS superconductivity. Here, the fundamental excitations are not quasiparticles but Cooper pairs. In particular, the Kohn–Luttinger theorem [16] shows that any Fermi liquid at low enough temperatures will become superconducting. However, the theorem does not give a lower bound for that transition temperature and indeed for a number of metals no superconductivity has been observed to date.

From the scientific point of view the materials which attract particular interest are those that exhibit novel properties that do not readily agree with Landau's Fermi liquid theory or BCS superconductivity. Most notably falling into both these categories are the high temperature cuprate superconductors discovered in 1986 [4]. First these materials have an unusual superconducting state at low temperatures. Secondly the 'normal' metallic state above the superconducting transition has many characteristics that are not in agreement with a normal Fermi liquid description. However it should be noted here that this does not exclude the existence of quasiparticles in these materials. In particular, for special representatives of these compounds in which the normally present disorder due to carrier doping is suppressed, it was possible to observe the above described phenomenon of quantum oscillations [17, 18, 19]. There is an exciting range of other materials and concepts that show non-Fermi liquid physics such as the fractional quantum Hall effect systems [20] and Kondo lattice systems [21].

Particular interest in recent years has been caused by systems that can be tuned by an external parameter from Fermi liquid behaviour to non-Fermi liquid behaviour due to their closeness to a so-called quantum critical point. In the following I will introduce both from an experimental and theoretical point of view the concept of quantum criticality and its implications. This can be by no means exhaustive due to the large amount of research existing in the field and the mathematical complexity involved in the theory. More detailed accounts are given in several extensive reviews covering both experimental and theoretical aspects [21, 22, 23].

2.1.5.1 Quantum Criticality

Second order phase transitions at finite temperature usually occur between a high temperature disordered and a low temperature ordered phase. The order is characterised by an order parameter that starts to grow continuously in the ordered phase from zero at the transition temperature. A typical example is the transition from a paramagnetic to ferromagnetic phase with the order parameter being the magnetisation M. An important aspect of second order transitions is that coherent fluctuations in the order parameter diverge both in length and timescales on

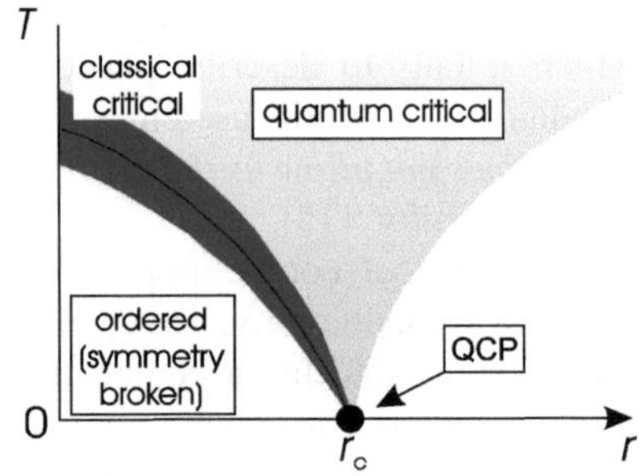

Fig. 2.4 The figure shows a generic scenario of quantum criticality. For details see text

approaching the transition temperature from either side. In particular, the diverging time scale implies that the associated characteristic frequency ω and thereby the energy scale $\hbar\omega$ of these fluctuations goes towards zero. However, as soon as this energy scale is much smaller than that given by the temperature T, i.e. $\hbar\omega \ll k_B T$ they are effectively classical in nature. For classical fluctuations only the spatial dimensions have to be taken into account. Therefore, the critical fluctuations of any finite temperature second order phase transition fall into the universality classes of classical second order phase transitions.

However, if one can suppress the finite temperature transition towards $T = 0$ by using a tuning parameter such as pressure or magnetic field, then the region over which the critical fluctuations are classical in nature also shrinks to zero. This situation is shown schematically in Fig. 2.4. Here the second order transition line between the disordered and ordered state is shown in black with the region of classical fluctuations around the transition being indicated in red. When suppressing the second order phase transition towards zero temperature then the region over which the classical critical fluctuations dominate is reducing. If one crosses the transition at $T = 0$ as a function of the control parameter r then the critical fluctuations associated with the phase transition at r_C have a purely quantum mechanical nature, hence the name quantum critical point. It is here where the description of Fermi liquid theory generally breaks down.

Above r_C one generally observes a finite temperature cross-over towards a Fermi liquid like behaviour at low temperatures. The quantum critical behaviour is expected to become non-universal above sufficiently high temperatures.

This kind of physics has been especially well studied in heavy Fermion compounds, where often occurring ferromagnetically or antiferromagnetically ordered ground states can potentially be suppressed in temperature by the application of magnetic field or pressure.

Two examples are shown in Fig. 2.5. On the left hand side the phase diagram of $YbRh_2Si_2$ is shown in the $H - T$ plane ([25], graphic reproduced from [23]). Here the colour scheme shows the power law of the temperature dependence of the resistivity, with blue being 2 (Fermi liquid like behaviour) and the other end of the colour scale (orange) corresponding to 1. On applying a magnetic field one observes a suppression of the antiferromagnetic phase to below the experimentally accessible range. At the critical field the temperature dependence of the resistivity

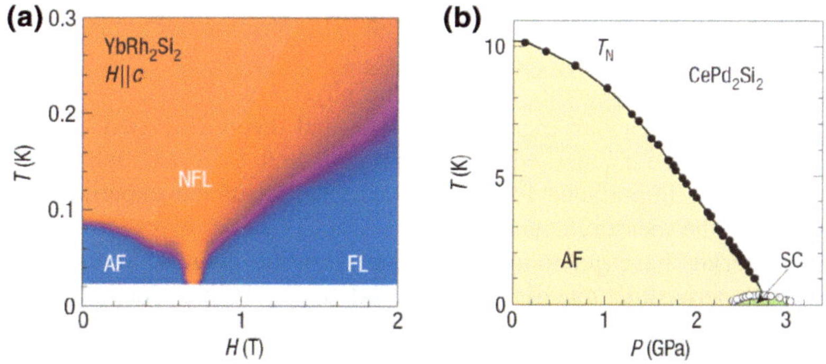

Fig. 2.5 Two examples of materials believed to be close to a quantum critical point (graphics reproduced from [23]). **a** The exponent of the temperature dependent part of resistivity for $YbRh_2Si_2$ as a function of temperature T and magnetic field H as derived from the logarithmic derivative of the resistivity with respect to temperature [25]. The colour scheme runs from 1 (*red*) to 2 (*blue*). The low field/low temperature phase is antiferromagnetic whereas the high field/low temperature phase is consistent with Fermi liquid like behaviour. In between the two states a quantum phase transition is expected to occur at the field where the measured resistivity is linear down to lowest temperatures. **b** The phase diagram of $CePd_2Si_2$ as a function of pressure. Again an antiferromagnetic phase transition is suppressed towards $T = 0$. However, at low temperatures a superconducting phase intervenes. The superconductivity is believed to be unconventional in that it is mediated by magnons rather than phonons

is non-Fermi liquid like over the whole range. At higher fields Fermi liquid behaviour in the resistivity is recovered.

In Fig. 2.5b the phase diagram of $CePd_2Si_2$ under pressure is shown [26] (Graphic reproduced from [23]). Here again the second order phase transition is suppressed towards zero temperature, this time by applying pressure.

In the second example a particularly significant aspect of quantum criticality is realised. What is often observed in the vicinity of quantum critical points is the stabilisation of novel phases with physical properties not usually observed. In $CePd_2Si_2$ for example the superconducting ground state is believed not to be due to electron–phonon interactions but to electron–magnon interactions [26]. This is particularly surprising since conventional superconducting states are destroyed by magnetic interactions.

The currently most successful approach in describing the quantum critical phenomenon was pioneered by Hertz [27] and Millis [28]. This theory is based on a renormalisation group approach similar to the theory of classical critical phenomena and leads to a classification of quantum phase transitions into certain universality classes. The fundamental difference is that for quantum phase transitions it is not only spatial but also temporal fluctuations that are included in the quantum mechanical action describing the system. Discussing Hertz–Millis theory in detail is beyond the scope of this brief introduction to the subject. However good introductions can be found in the aforementioned review articles [21, 22, 23]. Some of the results thought to apply to $Sr_3Ru_2O_7$, the system studied in this project, will be summarised in Sect. 2.2.2.

2.2 The Physics of the Ruthenate Family

Having discussed the general aspects of the physics of metals, this section will concentrate on the relevant experimental data and theoretical models specific to $Sr_3Ru_2O_7$, the material studied in this project, and Sr_2RuO_4, whose physical properties are of importance for the characterisation of the experimental setup developed for the measurements.

Both materials have generated significant scientific interest. Sr_2RuO_4 was the first layered perovskite material isostructural to the high-T_C cuprates that was found to be superconducting [29]. The transition temperature of 1.5 K is rather low compared to the high-T_C's, but it was proposed early on [30] to be one of a few superconducting materials whose order parameter has p-wave symmetry. A detailed presentation of the physics of Sr_2RuO_4 can be found for example in the review article by Mackenzie and Maeno [31].

$Sr_3Ru_2O_7$ is on the other hand in its zero-field ground state a highly enhanced paramagnet with a Wilson ration of ≈ 10 [32]. For comparison, the Wilson ratio of ^{3}He is 4 (see for example [33]). The interest in the material grew dramatically when the magnetic field phase diagram was studied in detail in a series of papers [34, 35, 36], reporting not only signatures consistent with a quantum critical point but also the existence of a novel phase in its vicinity that shows evidence of 'electron-nematic' properties in transport measurements.

2.2.1 Crystal Structure and Synthesis

The materials discussed in this thesis belong to the Ruddlesden–Popper strontium ruthenate series with the chemical formula $Sr_{n+1}Ru_nO_{3n+1}$, of which Sr_2RuO_4 and $Sr_3Ru_2O_7$ are the $n = 1$ and $n = 2$ members respectively. Their ideal crystal structures are shown in Fig. 2.6.

The fundamental building blocks are layers of corner-sharing ruthenium oxide octahedra. The number of adjacent RuO_2 layers is the reason for calling the materials the single-layer and bi-layer members of the series respectively. In between layers, Sr cations are arranged as shown.

The crystal structure of Sr_2RuO_4 with the tetragonal space group *I4/mmm* is faithful to the above ideal representation. The lattice parameters are $a = b = 3.862$ Å and $c = 12.722$ Å [38]. Contrary to that, the octahedra in $Sr_3Ru_2O_7$ show a small counter rotation of the octahedra by 7° [39]. The rotation direction alternates between the planes within a bi-layer. This structural difference causes a $\sqrt{2} \times \sqrt{2}$ reconstruction of the unit cell in the ab-plane and changes the space group of the material to the orthorhombic *Bbcb* with $a \approx b = 5.5$Å [39, 40]. This has significant implications for the electronic structure as will be shown further on.

The first single crystal samples of $Sr_3Ru_2O_7$ were grown by Cao et al. [41] with the flux-growth method. These samples were found to be ferromagnetic

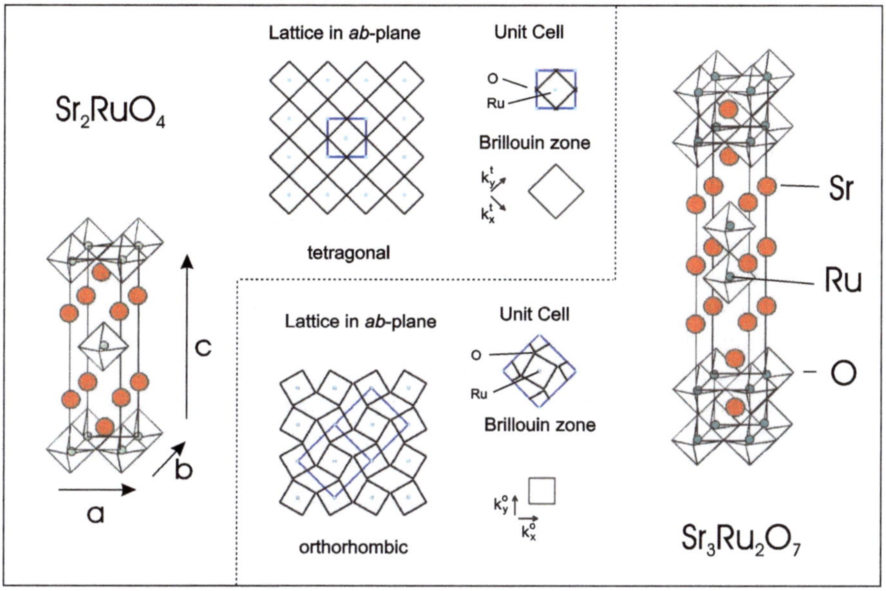

Fig. 2.6 Here the crystal structure is summarised for Sr_2RuO_4 and $Sr_3Ru_2O_7$ (graphics partially reproduced from [37]). Please see text for details

below 100 K. The material was subsequently synthesized in single crystal form by Ikeda et al. [42] by employing infra-red image furnace growth and found to be paramagnetic at low temperatures. The previously observed ferromagnetism was most probably due to inclusions of $Sr_4Ru_3O_{10}$ impurities. Since the image furnace grown crystal have a significantly improved quality they are referred to as second generation samples in the following. The thermodynamic properties, especially in magnetic field, were found to depend significantly on the sample quality and after a detailed growth study by Perry et al. [43] it was possible to reduce the residual resistivity of the materials by an order of magnitude (third generation samples). As will be seen in the following sections one cannot underestimate the importance of working with the highest purity samples available.

2.2.2 Thermodynamic Properties and Magnetic Phase Diagram

In the following I will introduce the phase diagram and the associated properties of the materials as established by previous measurements. I will in particular concentrate on thermodynamic measurements as well as resistivity before discussing the microscopic electronic structure in more detail in the next section.

2.2.2.1 $Sr_3Ru_2O_7$

Zero Field Low Temperature Properties

The crystal structure of $Sr_3Ru_2O_7$ is highly anisotropic, and this anisotropy is reflected in a number of properties such as its resistivity. In Fig. 2.7 the in-plane resistivity ρ_{ab} as well as the resistivity along the c-axis, ρ_c, are shown as a function of temperature T for second generation samples [32]. A pronounced asymmetry not only exists in the residual resistivity at zero temperature (observe the different scales for ρ_{ab} and ρ_c), but also in the A coefficient of the T^2 behaviour, as can be deduced from the gradient of the curves in the inset where the low temperature resistance is plotted against T^2.

The electronic specific heat c_{el} divided by temperature T is reproduced in Fig. 2.8a from [44] (data points not relating to the zero field properties have been

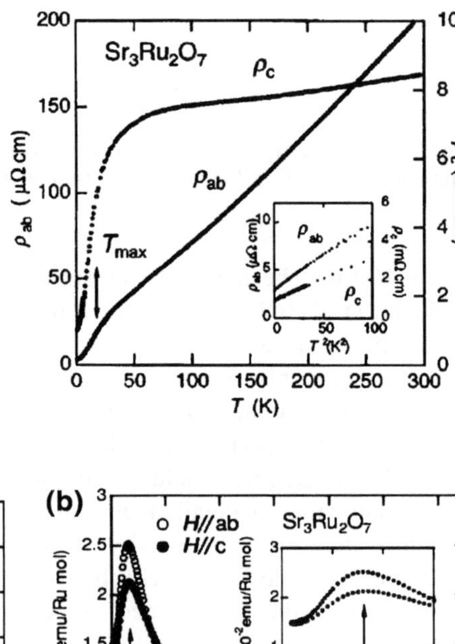

Fig. 2.7 In-plane and c-axis resistivity ρ_{ab} and ρ_c of $Sr_3Ru_2O_7$ as a function of temperature [32] (note the different scales for ρ_{ab} and ρ_c). The *inset* shows the same data in the low temperature range as a function of T^2

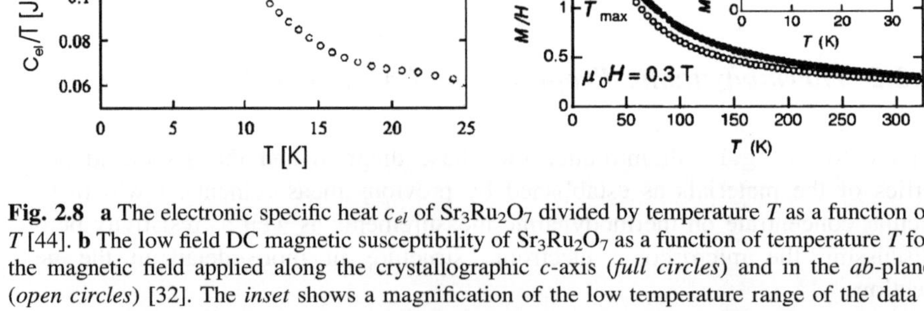

Fig. 2.8 **a** The electronic specific heat c_{el} of $Sr_3Ru_2O_7$ divided by temperature T as a function of T [44]. **b** The low field DC magnetic susceptibility of $Sr_3Ru_2O_7$ as a function of temperature T for the magnetic field applied along the crystallographic c-axis (*full circles*) and in the ab-plane (*open circles*) [32]. The *inset* shows a magnification of the low temperature range of the data

removed for clarity). c_{el}/T has a finite zero-temperature value corresponding to a Sommerfeld coefficient γ of 110 mJ/Ru-mol K^2, which is relatively large in the context of the ruthenates. Furthermore, there is a significant hump in the specific heat at a temperature of the order of 8 K that is in general associated with the metamagnetic feature discussed later on.

As mentioned before, $Sr_3Ru_2O_7$ is found in zero field to be a highly enhanced paramagnet. Figure 2.8b shows the DC magnetic susceptibility as determined by measuring the magnetisation M resulting from a small applied magnetic field H as a function of temperature T for two different orientations of H [32]. Here one can see a remarkably isotropic susceptibility at low temperatures even though the material itself is strongly anisotropic, suggesting that the Pauli term dominates the paramagnetism (see Sect. 2.1.2). From the above measurements a Wilson ration of $\approx$10 can be deduced.

Metamagnetism and Quantum Criticality

The unusually high Wilson ratio can be interpreted as $Sr_3Ru_2O_7$ being a paramagnet close to a magnetically ordered state. Indeed when applying a magnetic field one can observe a rapid superlinear rise in magnetisation at a well defined field. This phenomenological effect is called metamagnetism and is commonly encountered in local moment systems [45] undergoing spin-flip or spin-flop transitions. Figure 2.9a shows the magnetisation of $Sr_3Ru_2O_7$ as a function of applied magnetic field for several temperatures [44]. Here the field is applied in the crystallographic *ab*-plane. The metamagnetic feature at approximately $5T$ is clearly identifiable and is more defined towards lower temperatures.

Grigera et al. [46] studied the AC magnetic susceptibility systematically as a function of temperature as well as magnitude and direction of the applied magnetic field. They found that with the field applied in the *ab*-plane the metamagnetic cross-over turns into a first order phase transition as indicated by a dissipative out of phase component of the AC susceptibility. This first order transition line terminates in a critical end point at approximately 1.2 K. What caused particular interest was that the temperature of the critical end point could be suppressed as a function of angle of the applied magnetic field, leading to the possibility of a new class of quantum critical point—a so-called quantum critical end point [34]. The state of the phase diagram in second generation samples is summarised in Fig. 2.9b. Here, the position of the resulting sheet of first order transitions as a function of magnetic field, field direction and temperature is shown in green. The black line indicates the experimentally determined position of critical end points. The critical field moves towards higher values as the field is rotated towards the c-axis. At $B||c$ the critical endpoint is suppressed to below experimentally measurable temperatures. This particular orientation of magnetic field is the main focus of the project reported in this thesis.

The most precise early evidence for quantum criticality in this system was obtained by a detailed study of magnetotransport. The resistivity data were

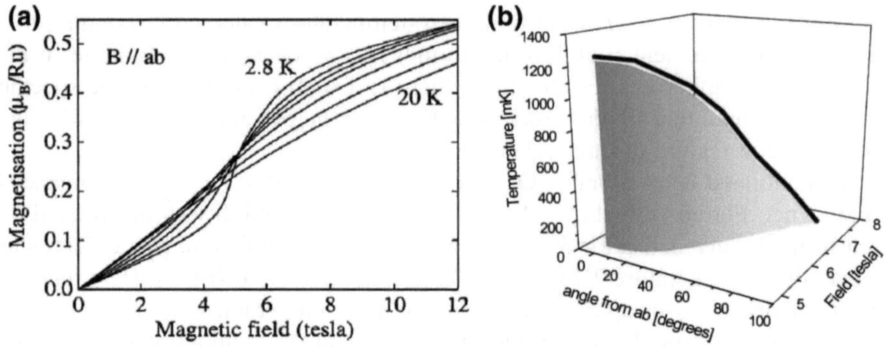

Fig. 2.9 **a** The magnetisation of $Sr_3Ru_2O_7$ as a function of applied magnetic field for a range of temperatures between 2.8 and 20 K [44]. The field is applied in the crystallographic *ab*-plane. The superlinear rise at low temperatures is the metamagnetic feature discussed in the text. **b** The *green* surface denotes the position of the metamagnetic first order transitions observed in second generation samples of $Sr_3Ru_2O_7$ as a function of field magnitude, field orientation (as angle between the magnetic field and the *ab*-plane) and temperature T [46]. The sheet of first order transitions terminates in a line of critical end points shown in *black*. For the field applied along the *c*-axis (90° on the angular scale) the data are consistent with the critical end point being suppressed to zero temperature

analysed at several magnetic fields H under the assumption that ρ is a combination of a temperature independent impurity scattering term, the residual resistivity ρ_{res}, and a temperature dependent power law contribution AT^{α}, i.e.

$$\rho(T,H) = \rho_{res}(H) + A(H)T^{\alpha}. \tag{2.26}$$

In a Fermi liquid scenario α would be 2. Quantum critical theories however predict different power laws for the temperature dependence according to the universality class of the particular transition observed. A study by Millis et al. [47] analysed $Sr_3Ru_2O_7$ in particular and found that the temperature exponent should be 1 at the critical field H_C.

The main results of the experimental study are shown in Fig. 2.10 [34]. In panel (a) the extracted temperature exponent as a function of magnetic field[5] is shown. On approaching the critical field, the range in temperature over which the exponent of 2 consistent with Fermi liquid behaviour is observable, shrinks to below the lowest measured temperature. At the critical field a close to linear temperature behaviour is observed whereas at higher magnetic fields Fermi liquid like behaviour is recovered.

In panel (b) both the extracted residual resistivity ρ_{res} as well as the A coefficients extracted at lowest temperatures are plotted as a function of field in the vicinity of the critical field at $H_C \approx 8\,\mathrm{T}$. The increased A coefficient in the vicinity

[5] To be more precise it is the logarithmic derivative of the temperature dependent part of the resistivity ρ with respect to temperature T, $\partial \ln(\rho - \rho_0)/\partial \ln T$, that is shown. Here ρ_0 is the residual resistivity. For more details see [34].

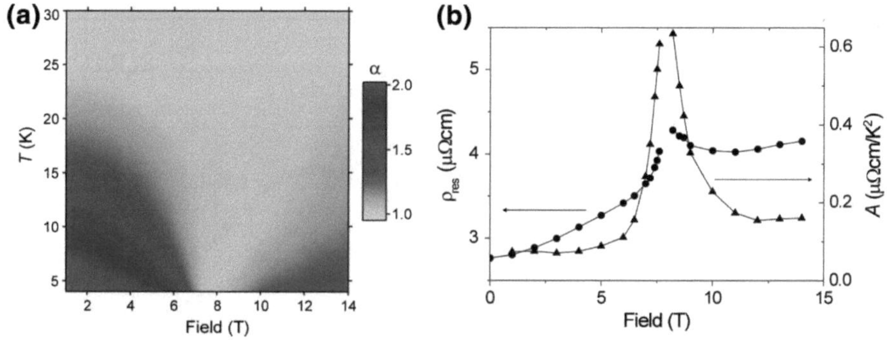

Fig. 2.10 **a** The logarithmic derivative of the temperature dependent part of the resistivity with respect to temperature as a colour scale in the magnetic field and temperature plane [34]. In the case of a pure power law AT^{α} this is equal to α. **b** The residual resistivity ρ_0 as well as the coefficient A of the temperature dependent part of the resistivity as a function of magnetic field and temperature (note the different scales of ρ_0 and A). For details of the parameter extraction from the original data please refer to [34]

of H_C indicates, in conjunction with the Kadowaki–Woods ratio (see Sect. 2.1.4), an increase in the effective quasiparticle mass of at least a fraction of the Fermi liquid excitations. However, a detailed theoretical understanding of this ratio in a realistic multiband system in a magnetic field is not developed completely. Therefore, a thermodynamic study of the specific heat is necessary to address the issue, in particular since the quantum critical scenario makes specific predictions about the temperature and field dependence of the specific heat [47, 48]. Furthermore the peak of residual resistivity at the critical field seems to suggest that the increase of the quasiparticle mass is accompanied by an increase of the impurity scattering. In hindsight this feature is most probably associated with the phase formation observed in the high purity third generation samples as discussed below.

Experimental evidence consistent with a quantum critical scenario was observed in the measurement of the electronic specific heat c_{el} close to the critical field at temperatures above 1.5 K by Perry et al. [44]. The results are shown in Fig. 2.11. Here c_{el} divided by temperature T is shown as a function of T for a range of magnetic fields. The field direction is parallel to the crystallographic c-axis. In particular, the functional form of the data at 7.7 T was found to be consistent with c_{el}/T having a singular component that diverges logarithmically at $T = 0$ consistent with a quantum critical scenario [47].

Novel Quantum Phase and Nematic-Like Transport

The possibility of studying quantum criticality in a clean system motivated a detailed study into the optimisation of the crystal growth parameters by Perry et al. [43]. In the resulting third generation samples, mean free paths of the order of

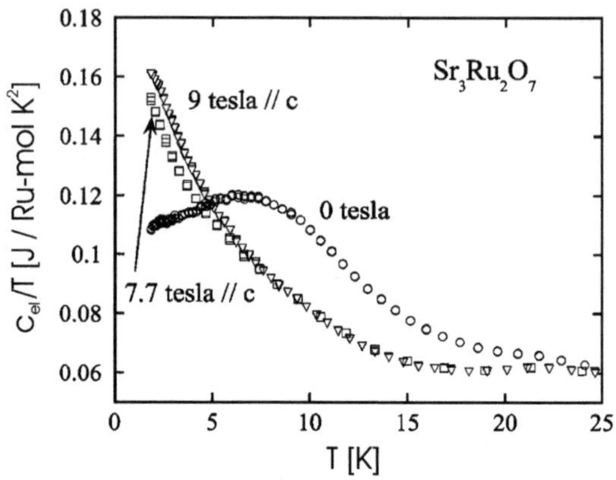

Fig. 2.11 Electronic specific heat c_{el} divided by temperature T as a function of T. Measurements have been done in zero field, 7.7 T and 9 T with the field oriented parallel to the crystallographic c-axis [44]

3,000 Å were observed. In these samples it was found by Grigera et al. [35] that in the vicinity of the proposed quantum critical end point a novel phase is stabilised which consequently is strongly disorder sensitive.

Figure 2.12 presents the experimental evidence for this phase as seen in electric transport and several thermodynamic measurements [35]. Part (a) shows the resistivity as a function of field for several temperatures. The resistance curves describe a distinct region as a function of magnetic field between 7.8 T and 8.1 T in which the resistivity is significantly increased and a much weaker temperature dependence observed compared to the surrounding states.

Experimental evidence that these features indeed mark first order phase transitions is shown in part (b). Here both the in-phase and out of phase components of the AC magnetic susceptibility[6] χ' and χ'' as well as the linear magnetostriction λ are shown as a function of magnetic field H for a sample temperature of 100 mK. The features (1) and (2) coincide with the boundaries of the anomalous resistive region in the previous graph. Furthermore the clear signatures in the loss term χ'' indicate that these are first order transitions. The width of the transitions as seen here is 50 mT. Feature (3) is a metamagnetic cross-over that is much wider in magnetic field and does not show up in χ''. In the inset of Fig. 2.12b a trace of magnetisation M as a function of temperature T is shown at the critical field H_C. Here a clear change in temperature dependence at 1.2 K is an indication for a thermodynamic transition into the new phase. However, further definite thermodynamic proof is needed to establish its exact nature.

Finally in Fig. 2.13 the magnetisation of ultra clean $Sr_3Ru_2O_7$ as a function of applied magnetic field is shown (data provided by R.S. Perry). The field orientation is parallel to the crystallographic c-axis and the sample temperature is 70 mK. The magnetisation is raising very fast at the transitions (1) and (2) and the crossover (3). The labels here correspond to the same used in Fig. 2.12.

[6] Strictly speaking AC magnetic susceptibility is not a thermodynamic probe but frequency dependent.

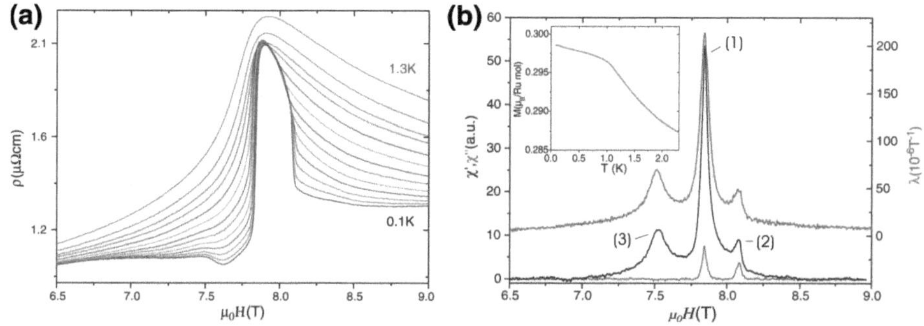

Fig. 2.12 **a** The in-plane resistivity of a third generation $Sr_3Ru_2O_7$ sample as a function of magnetic field *H* for several temperatures between 0.1 and 1.2 K [35]. The field is applied along the crystallographic *c*-axis. **b** Measurements of the components χ' and χ'' of the complex AC magnetic susceptibility as well as the linear magnetostriction λ as a function of magnetic field. Here the sample temperature is 100 mK and the field is applied along the *c*-axis. The *inset* shows the magnetisation of $Sr_3Ru_2O_7$ as a function of temperature at $\approx$8T, a field in between the two first order phase transitions that are observed in the other thermodynamic quantities [35]. Furthermore the two features coinciding with the resistive boundaries in **a** are labelled (*1*) and (*2*)

Fig. 2.13 Magnetisation of third generation $Sr_3Ru_2O_7$ samples as a function of applied magnetic field. The field orientation is parallel to the crystallographic *c*-axis and the sample temperature is 70 mK. The labels (*1*)–(*3*) are explained in the text (data provided by R.S. Perry)

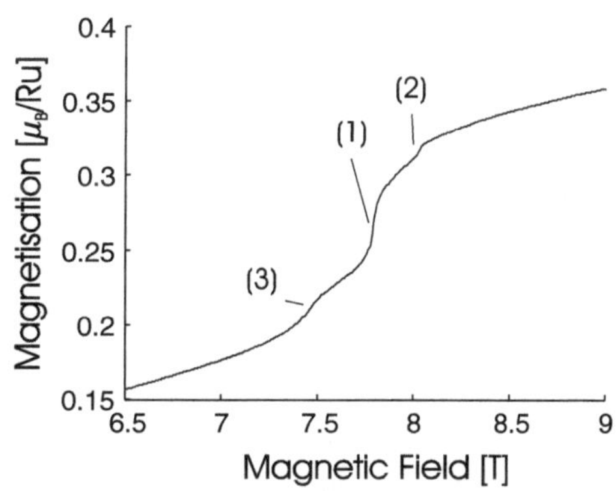

That the novel phase between the boundaries (1) and (2) has indeed highly unusual resistive properties has been established by Borzi et al. [36] in a careful study of the resistivity as a function of not only applied field *H* and temperature *T* but also of the angle between the current *I* and *H*. In particular Fig. 2.9a shows the resistivity as a function of magnetic field *H* with the field applied at 77° from the crystallographic *ab*-plane. This field can be thought of as a linear combination of a field H_c parallel to the *c*-axis and a small added component H_a along the *a*-axis. Here, the label *a* has been chosen instead of *b* arbitrarily since *a* and *b* are interchangeable. The current *I* can now be applied either along ($I_\parallel$—shown in black) or perpendicular ($I_\perp$—shown in red) to the in plane field component H_{ab} as shown in the inset in Fig. 2.14a. While the resulting curves outside the new phase are indistinguishable, their behaviour inside the phase is dramatically different.

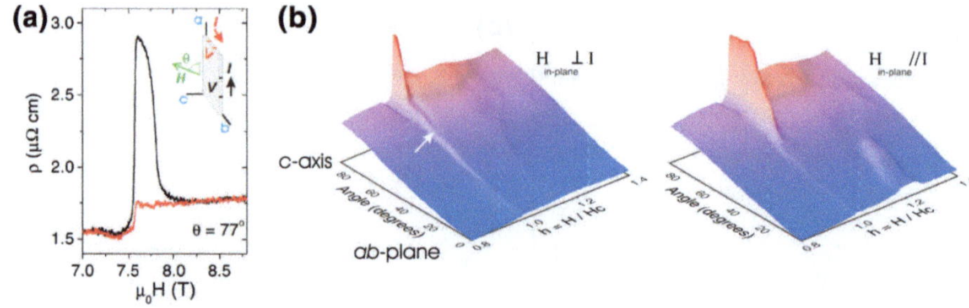

Fig. 2.14 **a** The resistivity ρ as a function of field H with the field applied at 77° from the *ab*-plane (i.e. close to the *c*-axis) [36]. The two traces correspond to the current being parallel to the in-plane component of the field (*black*) and perpendicular to it (*red*) as shown in the inset. **b** The in plane resistivity as a function of orientation and magnitude H of magnetic field. The two graphs correspond to the two different orientations of the current I with respect to the in-plane component of the magnetic field H as indicated. Please note that the field scale is given in H/H_C. Here H_C is the angle dependent position of the main first order metamagnetic transition. Furthermore, on the angular scale 90° corresponds to the magnetic field being applied parallel to the *c*-axis and 0° to the magnetic field being in the *ab*-plane. The *white arrow* indicates the point at which the two first order transitions enclosing the novel quantum phase merge, within experimental resolution

Anisotropic transport in itself is not unusual. Here, however, first of all it has been found in an accompanying neutron study that while the transport is anisotropic one cannot distinguish between the values of a and b within experimental resolution even under an applied in-plane magnetic field. Instead the data indicate that the symmetry breaking revealed by transport is intrinsic and the small applied in-plane magnetic field is merely 'aligning' different regions of domains of an intrinsically symmetry broken phase. In combination the results by Borzi et al. are consistent with the electronic liquid breaking the (discrete) rotational symmetry of the lattice—a behaviour called, in analogy to nematic phases in liquid crystals, *'electronic nematicity'*.

The full angular dependence for $I_{\parallel}$ and $I_{\perp}$ as a function of magnitude of applied field and orientation of the field relative to the *ab*-plane is shown in Fig. 2.14b. Please note that the field magnitude axis is divided by the critical field H_C which is angle dependent as has been discussed in the previous section. In addition to the anomalous phase close to the *c*-axis (at an angle of 90°) a further anomalous region can be identified in the *ab*-plane.

Finally, before ending this section, the most relevant information on the position of phase transition lines and the observance of 'electron-nematic'-like behaviour is summarised in Fig. 2.15. Panel (a) is reproduced from [49] and shows as a function of temperature, magnetic field and orientation of the field the position of the established first order transition lines in green whereas the regions under the blue domes are those in which the anomalous 'nematic' transport characteristics have been observed. In Fig. 2.15b the phase diagram in the *c*-axis as established by magnetisation M, AC magnetic susceptibility χ, linear magnetostriction λ and thermal expansion coefficient α is shown [35, 50]. The position of the first order

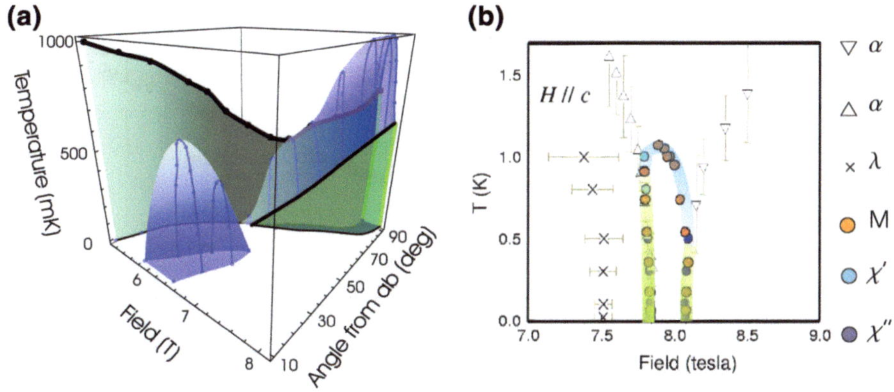

Fig. 2.15 Here the most relevant phase diagram information of high purity single crystal $Sr_3Ru_2O_7$ based on the current experimental data is shown. **a** The observed first order metamagnetic transition sheets as a function of temperature, magnetic field magnitude and orientation are shown in green. The *black lines* represent the lines of critical end points of these sheets. Furthermore the regions inside the *blue domes* have been found to show 'nematic-like' transport features as discussed in the text. On the angular scale 90° corresponds to the magnetic field being applied parallel to the *c*-axis and 0° to the magnetic field being in the *ab*-plane (figure reproduced from [49]). In **b** the phase diagram with the field applied parallel to the *c*-axis is shown. The *green lines* show the position of first order transitions whereas the blue line indicates the position of the putative second order phase transition. The other features are thermodynamic crossovers. The data points shown are extracted from DC magnetisation *M*, the components of the complex AC magnetic susceptibility χ, linear magnetostriction λ and thermal expansion coefficient α [35, 50]

transitions is marked in green as in the previous graph. The true thermodynamic nature of the 'roof' connecting the two first order transitions cannot be determined on the basis of the evidence that existed before the current project began. The other features indicated in this phase diagram are crossovers.

2.2.2.2 Sr_2RuO_4

In this section the thermodynamic properties of Sr_2RuO_4 will only be discussed insofar as they are relevant to the characterisation of the experimental setup developed in this thesis.

In zero field, Sr_2RuO_4 has a superconducting transition at $T_C = 1.5$ K. In Fig. 2.16a the electronic specific heat c_{el} divided by temperature T is shown as a function of temperature [51]. The sharp transition at T_C is clearly identifiable. Furthermore c/T above T_C is consistent with Fermi liquid theory. The magnitude of the Sommerfeld coefficient γ of the normal state is 38 mJ/Ru-mol K^2, approximately a third of the Sommerfeld coefficient observed in $Sr_3Ru_2O_7$. The results for electronic specific heat are usually quoted 'per mole ruthenium' (Ru-mol) since the valence electrons in these systems originate from the Ru 4*d*-shell as will be discussed in the next section.

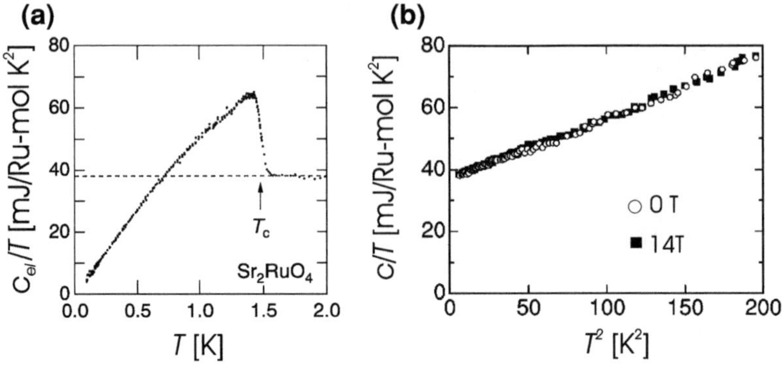

Fig. 2.16 **a** The electronic specific heat c_{el} of Sr_2RuO_4 divided by temperature T as a function of T [51]. The *dotted line* represents the normal state specific heat that would be observed if the transition to superconductivity at T_C would not take place. **b** The total specific heat c of Sr_2RuO_4 divided by temperature T as a function of T^2 with the sample being in zero magnetic field and in a field of 14T [52]

The second important feature for this project is that the specific heat of the normal state of this material is virtually independent of magnetic field. In order to illustrate this, Fig. 2.16b shows the specific heat divided by temperature as a function of T^2, for no magnetic field applied (circles) and with a magnetic field of 14 T applied (squares) [52]. The linear dependence on T^2 is caused by the phononic contribution to the specific heat.

2.2.3 Electronic Structure Properties

In the previous section the macroscopic properties of $Sr_3Ru_2O_7$ and Sr_2RuO_4 were presented. In particular it was shown that in certain regions of the phase diagram their properties are consistent with Fermi liquid theory. In this section the current experimental knowledge of the microscopic electronic structure, that is, the Fermi surface and band structure of these materials will be briefly reviewed. The section will begin with Sr_2RuO_4 since the more complicated band structure of $Sr_3Ru_2O_7$ can be understood more easily by starting from the band structure of Sr_2RuO_4.

2.2.3.1 Fermi Surface of Sr_2RuO_4

Sr_2RuO_4 is a material whose Fermi surface has been studied in great detail using quantum oscillations [54, 55]. The upper part of Fig. 2.17 shows as an example typical de Haas–van Alphen oscillations as a function of the magnetic field [53]. Due to the unusually high signal to noise ratio it is possible to observe the fundamental frequencies as well as higher harmonics as is shown in the frequency

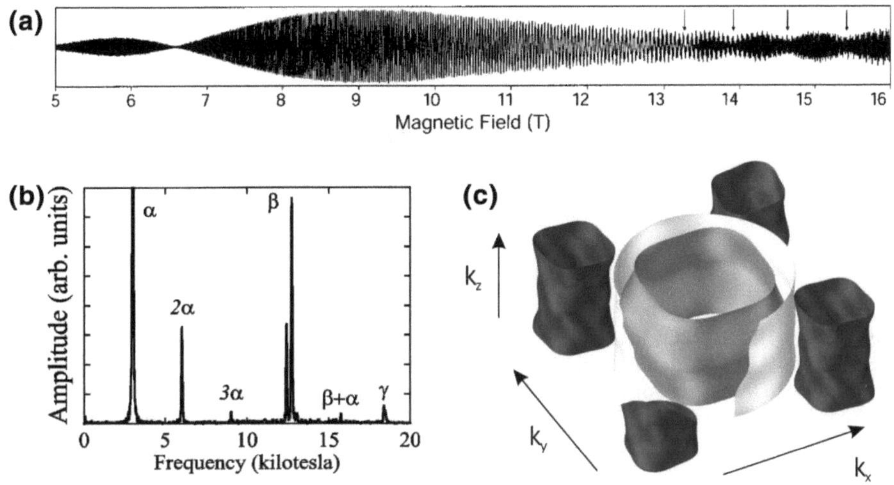

Fig. 2.17 **a** A typical trace of Sr_2RuO_4 quantum oscillations as a function of magnetic field observed in the de Haas–van Alphen effect [53]. **b** The frequency spectrum of quantum oscillation in inverse magnetic field for Sr_2RuO_4 [52]. The magnetic field is applied along the crystallographic *c*-axis. The fundamentals α, β and γ are labelled together with their harmonics and sum frequencies. **c** The Fermi surface of Sr_2RuO_4 as reconstructed from quantum oscillations in combination with LDA calculations [31]. The central surface is the β sheet surrounded by the γ surface. The α surface is centred on the corner of the Brillouin zone and shown four times here. The Fermi surface dispersions along k_z have been amplified by a factor 15 for reasons of presentation

spectrum in Fig. 2.17. In a detailed angular dependence study, Bergemann et al. [55] were able to reconstruct the Fermi surface of Sr_2RuO_4 as shown in Fig. 2.17c. It consists of three quasi-two-dimensional parts, the α, β and γ surfaces, that are relatively weakly warped in the k_z direction. The quasi-two-dimensionality can be readily understood by taking the crystal structure into account. The electronic states at the Fermi surface are derived from Ru 4*d* orbitals. Since these are arranged in layers of RuO octahedra, the hopping integral in a tight binding approach for electronic states close to the Fermi energy is significantly larger within a plane than in between planes. This leads to a very weak dispersion of the energy bands in the k_z direction of momentum space resulting in the observed quasi-two-dimensionality of the Fermi surface.

The quantum oscillation findings have been largely confirmed by ARPES measurements [56] and LDA band structure calculations [57], as shown in Fig. 2.18a and b, respectively.

ARPES and quantum oscillation measurements in $Sr_{2-x}La_xRuO_4$ samples, which are effectively electron-doped, made a definite identification of the α sheet as being of 'hole'-like character and the β and γ sheets as being 'electron'-like [58, 59].

Since the surfaces are quasi-two-dimensional the contribution of a single Fermi surface sheet of effective mass m^* to the Sommerfeld coefficient γ can be shown in the case of Sr_2RuO_4 to be [54]

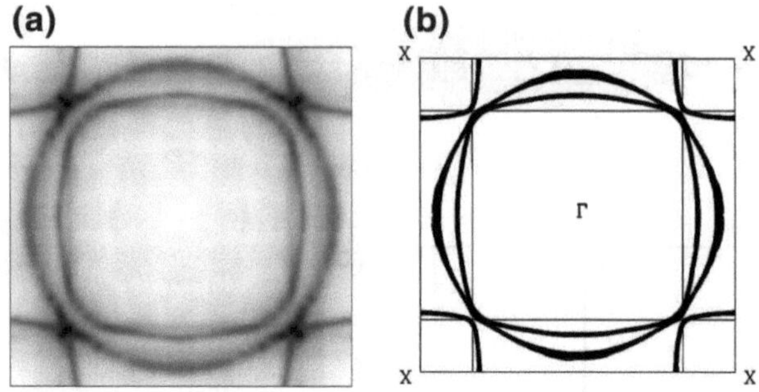

Fig. 2.18 **a** The Sr_2RuO_4 Fermi surface cross section in the k_x–k_y plane of the Brillouin zone as measured by ARPES (graphic reproduced from [31] based on [56]). **b** The same cross section as obtained by LDA calculations [57]. Here the thickness of the lines is indicating the warping of the surfaces in the k_z-direction. Γ labels the zone boundary whereas *X* labels the zone corner

$$\gamma = \frac{\pi N_A k_B^2 a^2}{3\hbar^2} m^* . \tag{2.27}$$

Here, N_A is Avogadro's constant, k_B Boltzmann's constant, $\hbar$ Planck's constant and a the lattice parameter of Sr_2RuO_4. By applying this equation to the measured masses from the de Haas–van Alphen experiments one deduces a total Sommerfeld coefficient of 38.5 mJ/Ru-mol K^2, in good agreement with the value obtained from bulk specific heat measurements.

A further test for the Fermi liquid description of the material is, if the Fermi surface volume can successfully account for all the valence electrons in accordance with Luttinger's theorem [60]. Using the experimental results one obtains a total of 4.05 electrons in the three observed valence bands, in agreement with the four remaining electrons in the Ru^{4+} state of the material.

Overall, one can conclude that the band structure of the normal state of Sr_2RuO_4 can be very well understood in terms of Fermi liquid theory.

2.2.3.2 Fermi Surface of $Sr_3Ru_2O_7$

The Fermi surface structure of Sr_2RuO_4 was discussed in some detail in the previous section because it is a good starting point for understanding the rather more complex Fermi surface structure in $Sr_3Ru_2O_7$.

The first basic assumption for the following line of argument is that in both materials it is the energy bands largely originating from the Ru 4*d* orbitals which cross the Fermi energy. The second assumption is that the change from single layer to double layer material causes a so-called bilayer splitting, i.e. doubling of the number of bands, but does not affect the quasi-two-dimensionality of the Fermi surface. The third assumption is that the rotation of the octahedra in the *ab* plane causes a $\sqrt{2} \times \sqrt{2}$ reconstruction of the unit cell but is otherwise, due to its smallness, only a weak perturbation.

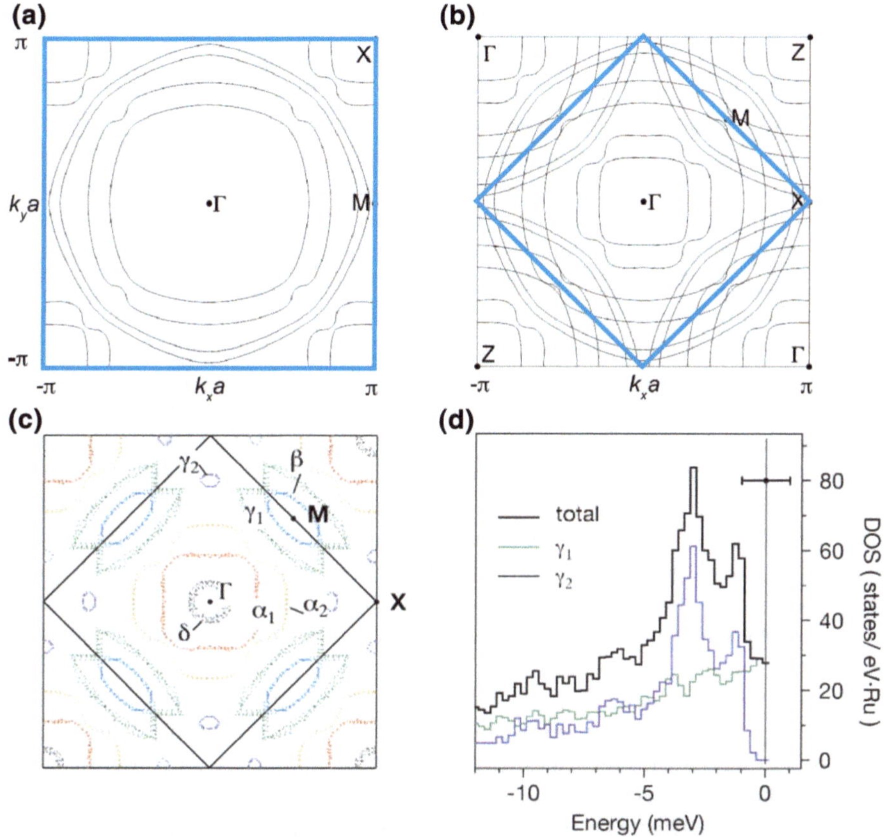

Fig. 2.19 This figure shows schematically how the complex zero field Fermi surface of $Sr_3Ru_2O_7$ can be understood by considering the effects of the differences in structure between the two materials being treatable as perturbations to the band structure. **a** The expected effect of a bi-layer splitting on the Fermi surface. The quasi-two-dimensionality of the Fermi surface is assumed to be retained. If one takes into account the $\sqrt{2} \times \sqrt{2}$ reconstruction of the unit cell due to the rotation of the RuO-octahedra one expects the Brillouin zone to halve and rotate by 45°. This new Brillouin zone is shown in *blue* in **b**. The bands have to be folded into this new zone as indicated. This results in a high degeneracy in the band structure along certain paths in momentum space. These are lifted, leading to a reconstruction of the Fermi surface. **c** The band structure in the k_x–k_y plane as extracted from an ARPES measurement [61]. For details regarding the labelling please see text. **d** The density of states as function of energy relative to the Fermi energy as measured by ARPES for the two γ pockets and their total sum. The error bar in energy represents the experimental uncertainty in the position of the Fermi energy. The plot is reproduced from [61] (labelling changed for consistency)

The effect of these assumptions on the Fermi surface are sketched in Fig. 2.19a and b which are reproduced from [37]. Part (a) shows the k_x–k_y plane of the Sr_2RuO_4 Brillouin zone. Here the previously presented Fermi surfaces are shown doubled due to the bilayer splitting. In part (b) the new Brillouin zone due to the

$\sqrt{2} \times \sqrt{2}$ reconstruction of the unit cell is shown in blue. The bands are 'back-folded' resulting in the shown complex Fermi surface topology.

If one would stop the 'Gedanken experiment' here, then the eigenenergies of the resulting bands would be degenerate along several paths in momentum space. Perturbation theory predicts that in a material these degeneracies are lifted. This in turn would lead to a reconnection of the Fermi surface which in its details is sensitive to the exact prevailing energetics in the material. Figure 2.19c shows the Fermi surface in the k_x–k_y plane as extracted from an ARPES measurements by Tamai et al. [61]. Though different in detail, the overall geometrical similarities between the measurement and the prediction based on a very simple model is remarkable. One can therefore assume as an hypothesis that the above assumptions are a good starting point for an understanding of the band structure of $Sr_3Ru_2O_7$ in zero field. The Fermi surfaces in Fig. 2.19c are therefore labelled in accordance to their relation to the Fermi surface and band structure in Sr_2RuO_4. For example the α_1 and α_2 sheets are mainly derived from the α Fermi surface sheet in Sr_2RuO_4. One obvious difference to the Fermi surface as expected from the simple model presented earlier is the additional δ-surface centred at the Γ point of the Brillouin zone. LDA calculations by Singh [61] indicate that this pocket is derived from a band that did not cross the Fermi energy in Sr_2RuO_4 but also has primarily a Ru $4d$ orbital character (in this case $d_{x^2-y^2}$). Overall, the ARPES measurement observed five sheets that certainly cross the Fermi energy, namely α_1, α_2, β, γ_1 and δ. LDA calculations indicate that δ is indeed bilayer split but that the splitting could not be resolved. The sixth Fermi surface shown, γ_2 is particular in that the energy resolution of the ARPES measurement is not sufficient in its own in order to decide if this pocket is indeed crossing the Fermi energy or is situated just below it. However, the γ_2 surface proves to be critical to the properties of the material. First of all if one excludes it then the observed Fermi surface can only account for $\approx$40% of the total measured specific heat, as will be discussed in more detail below. Secondly ARPES measurements of the band structure below the Fermi energy revealed two peaks in the density of states $g(\epsilon)$ of the γ_2 pocket. This is shown in Fig. 2.19d (the graph is reproduced from [61] with alterations to the labelling for consistency). Here the density of states (DOS) of the two γ pockets and the total sum is shown as a function of energy relative to the Fermi energy. A small peak is situated at ≈ -1 meV and a stronger one related to a saddle point in the band structure at ≈ -4 meV. The error bar shows the uncertainty in the determination of the position of the Fermi energy in the experiment.

The detailed properties of these six Fermi surfaces will be presented at the end of this section together with the results from de Haas–van Alphen measurements. Quantum oscillations in resistivity (Shubnikov–de Haas effect) and magnetic susceptibility (de Haas–van Alphen measurements) in $Sr_3Ru_2O_7$ have been reported in several papers [62, 63]. The most detailed study on the samples with the highest purity has been performed recently by Mercure et al. [37]. On the low field side, with magnetic field applied parallel to the crystallographic c-axis, they were able to observe the same five Fermi surface sheets as the ARPES measurements, namely α_1,

Table 2.1 The properties of the $Sr_3Ru_2O_7$ Fermi surfaces as measured by de Haas–van Alphen (dHvA) and ARPES experiments

	α_1	α_2	β	γ_1	γ_2	δ
dHvA						
F (kT)	1.78	4.13	0.15	0.91	–	0.43
Area (% BZ)	13.0	30.1	1.09	6.64	–	3.14
m^* (m_e)	6.9 ± 0.1	10.1 ± 0.1	5.6 ± 0.3	7.7 ± 0.3	–	8.4 ± 0.7
ARPES						
Area (% BZ)	14.1	31.5	2.6	8.0	<1	2.1
m^* (m_e)	8.6 ± 3	18 ± 8	4.3 ± 2	9.6 ± 3	10 ± 4	8.6 ± 3

F is the observed frequency in $1/H$ of quantum oscillations, BZ stands for Brillouin zone and m^* is the effective mass in units of electron mass m_e. Reproduced from [37]

α_2, β, γ_1 and δ. The angular dependence of the oscillations is consistent with these Fermi surface pockets being quasi-two-dimensional.

The amplitude of the extremely small γ_2 pocket was not identified in the initial de Haas–van Alphen measurements performed in the study. For the other five pockets both the cross-sectional area and the effective mass were measured with relatively high accuracy. Table 2.1 reproduced from [37] gives the detailed results as obtained from both measurements

The overall agreement between the two measurements is good with the de Haas–van Alphen results showing the smaller experimental uncertainty. An important test is if these measurements can explain the experimentally observed bulk specific heat. If one takes only the five Fermi surfaces excluding γ_2 into account than the expected Sommerfeld coefficient from the de Haas–van Alphen experiment is (56 ± 1) mJ/Ru-mol K^2 and from the ARPES measurements (67 ± 12) mJ/Ru-mol K^2, both of which account for only approximately half of the measured specific heat value of 110 mJ/Ru-mol K^2.

The γ_2 pocket on the other hand occurs four times in the Brillouin zone and furthermore is probably bilayer split. The contribution to the Sommerfeld coefficient is therefore eight times the value as calculated based on its effective mass m^* alone. Taking the mass of the γ_2 pocket as measured by ARPES into account would therefore result in revised estimates of the Sommerfeld coefficient of (127 ± 27) mJ/Ru-mol K^2 (ARPES) and (116 ± 16) mJ/Ru-mol K^2 (de Haas–van Alphen). These values would be in broad agreement with the specific heat measurements. Since the size of the γ_2 is negligible on the scale of the size of the Brillouin zone it has a very small effect on the Luttinger sum for the total number of electrons enclosed by the Fermi surfaces.

Contrary to ARPES, the de Haas–van Alphen effect is intrinsically suited to extend the Fermi surface study to high magnetic fields. Here I will summarize the main findings by Mercure et al. [37] as relevant to this thesis.

1. One of the most important results is the absence of any significant effective mass increase in the vicinity of the critical field for any of the five observed frequencies. Figure 2.20a shows this as an example for three of the observed

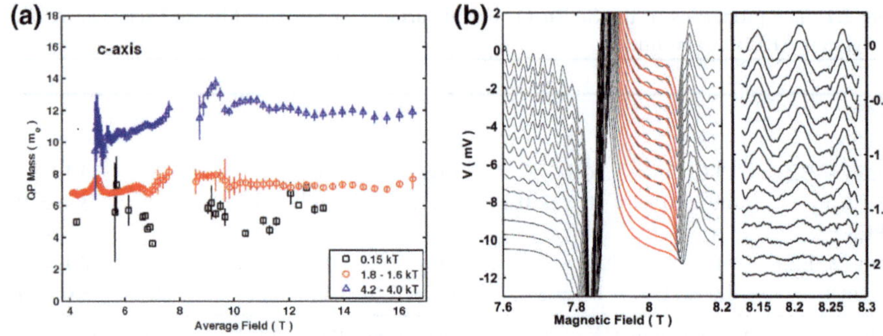

Fig. 2.20 **a** The quasiparticle mass as a function of magnetic field for some of the frequencies observed by de Haas–van Alphen measurements. **b** Data of second harmonic de Haas–van Alphen measurements. The traces which correspond to different sample temperatures have been offset for clarity. In the *right panel* the data inside the novel quantum phase are shown after the background given in *red* in the *left panel* has been subtracted (graphics courtesy of J.-F. Mercure). For more details see [37]

frequencies. Here the effective quasiparticle (QP) mass is plotted as a function of magnetic field applied parallel to the *c*-axis of $Sr_3Ru_2O_7$. Therefore, the specific heat contribution of the five Fermi surface sheets α_1, α_2, β, γ_1 and δ cannot explain the observed peak in the *A*-coefficient of resistivity as discussed in the previous section.

2. Mercure et al. succeeded in measuring quantum oscillations in the region of the new phase as shown in Fig. 2.20b. The left panel shows the second harmonic of an AC magnetic susceptibility measurement as a function of magnetic field for several temperatures. Here the traces have been offset in order of temperature for clarity and the upmost trace corresponds to the lowest temperature. The two strong features correspond to the phase boundaries of the novel phase and the red curves are a polynomial background fit to the data. The right panel shows the data with this background being subtracted. Here the quantum oscillations are clearly identifiable. The phase of the oscillations has no apparent temperature dependence. Furthermore the amplitude dependence on temperature is well described by the Lifshitz–Kosevich formula. One can conclude that at least part of the excitation spectrum in the novel quantum phase is therefore consistent with the existence of Fermi liquid quasiparticles. That does not mean however that all electronic degrees of freedom can necessarily be described as itinerant quasiparticles, with other examples where this is considered to be a possibility being high-T_C superconductors [64] and heavy Fermion Kondo systems [22].
3. The observed frequency structure in the high field Fermi liquid state is highly fractured and the amplitude significantly suppressed. Possible reasons for this can be magnetic breakdown and Fermi surface reconstruction.

The ARPES and de Haas–van Alphen measurements presented here therefore seem to indicate that the physics of $Sr_3Ru_2O_7$ is driven by a single band of the complicated band structure which is associated with the γ_2 pocket. It has to be emphasized that this conclusion is reached by elimination of the remaining Fermi surface and the evidence for a peak in the single-particle density of states associated with γ_2. No direct evidence of the field dependence of this peak or the effective mass of γ_2 exists.

Within the above assumptions only one of the Fermi surfaces would have a significantly field dependent effective mass. In this case the resistivity of only one Fermi surface would show a peak as a function of magnetic field. A commonly raised concern is that this peak should in a simple model not dominate the overall resistance since the conductance channels of all Fermi surface sheets add in parallel. This is seemingly at odds with the results by Grigera et al. [34], where a significant increase of at least a factor of 5 was observed in the A coefficient of the temperature dependent part of the resistivity as a function of magnetic field. However, one has to keep in mind that Grigera et al. have measured the A coefficient of the *magneto*-resistance of $Sr_3Ru_2O_7$. Therefore, one has to take into account that it is not the scalar longitudinal magnetoresistance of the Fermi surfaces but the full resistivity tensor that is added in parallel in order to calculate the overall resistivity of the material as discussed in Sect. 2.1.3.[7] Under these conditions it is possible that the divergence in the resistivity in one of the Fermi surfaces is dominating the total resistivity over a wide field range.

2.3 Summary

In this chapter I discussed the general framework of Fermi liquid theory as well as the concepts of quantum criticality and ‘electron-nematic’ transport. I furthermore reviewed the experimental evidence for a quantum critical end point in the material as well as thermodynamic measurements of a novel quantum phase in its vicinity which shows features of electron nematic like properties in transport measurements. I finally discussed the current knowledge of the zero field Fermi surface and the extent to which measured quasiparticle observations can account for the observed thermodynamic behaviour.

In this thesis several open questions arising from the current available experimental data will be addressed by magnetothermal studies and specific heat measurements.

---

[7] It has to be noted here that the simple addition of the resistivity tensors only holds for closed Fermi surfaces. If open orbits are present, the longitudinal magnetoresistance does not only depend on the magnitude of the applied magnetic field but also crucially on the orientation between the electric field and the open orbit, leading to significant anisotropies in transport. Intriguingly, if domains of different orbital orientations exist in the anomalous phase region that are orientable by a small in-plane magnetic field one would naturally expect ‘nematik-like’ transport properties similar to the ones observed by Borzi et al. To the authors best knowledge though discussed in private communications this path has not been explored in the theoretical literature so far.

The first part of the project is to investigate the entropic properties of the supposed low and high field Fermi liquid states. In particular the question of a peak in the Sommerfeld coefficient that was indirectly inferred from the measured peak in the A coefficient will be discussed. Furthermore data will be presented on magnetothermal oscillations, quantum oscillations in the entropy which can be studied by a method that is particularly sensitive to low frequencies.

The second part of the project relates to the novel quantum phase. Here the main data that will be presented will concern the nature of the surrounding phase transitions as well as the temperature dependence of the specific heat inside the phase.

References

1. Landau LD (1956) The theory of a Fermi liquid. JETP 30:1058
2. Landau LD (1957) Oscillations in a Fermi liquid. JETP 32:59
3. Landau LD (1958) On the theory of a Fermi liquid. JETP 35:97
4. Bednorz JG, Müller KA (1986) Possible high-T_c superconductivity in the Ba–La–Cu–O system. Z Phys B Condens Matter 64(2):189–193
5. Kamihara Y, Watanabe T, Hirano M, Hosono H (2008) Iron-based layered superconductor La[$O_{1-x}F_x$]FeAs ($x = 0.05 - 0.12$) with $T_c = 26$ K. J Am Chem Soc 130(11):3296–3297
6. Ashcroft NW, Mermin ND (1976) Solid state physics. Saunders, Philadelphia
7. Abrikosov AA, Gorkov LP, Dzyaloshinski IE (1975) Methods of quantum field theory in statistical physics. Dover, New York
8. The fermi surface data base (2009). http://www.phys.ufl.edu/fermisurface/jpg/Cu.jpg
9. Choy T-S, Naset J, Chen J, Hershfield S, Stanton C (2000) A database of fermi surface in virtual reality modeling language (vrml). Bulletin of the American Physical Society, vol 45, p L36.42
10. Shoenberg D (1984) Magnetic oscillations in metals. Cambridge University Press, Cambridge
11. Onsager L (1952) Philos Mag 43:1006
12. Pippard AB (1965) The dynamics of conduction electrons. Blackie, Glasgow
13. Kadowaki K, Woods SB (1986) Universal relationship of the resistivity and specific-heat in heavy-Fermion compounds. Solid State Commun 58(8):507–509
14. Hussey NE (2005) Non-generality of the Kadowaki–Woods ratio in correlated oxides. J Phys Soc Jpn 74(4):1107–1110
15. Landau LD (1960) Theoretical physics in the twentieth century, a memorial volume to Wolfgang Pauli. Interscience, NY, 245 pp
16. Kohn W, Luttinger JM (1965) New mechanism for superconductivity. Phys Rev Lett 15:524
17. Doiron-Leyraud N, Proust C, LeBoeuf D, Levallois J, Bonnemaison J-B, Liang R, Bonn DA, Hardy WN, Taillefer L (2007) Quantum oscillations and the Fermi surface in an underdoped high-T_c superconductor. Nature 447(7144):565–568
18. Sebastian SE, Harrison N, Palm E, Murphy TP, Mielke CH, Liang R, Bonn DA, Hardy WN, Lonzarich GG (2008) A multi-component Fermi surface in the vortex state of an underdoped high-T_c superconductor. Nature 454(7201):200–203
19. Vignolle B, Carrington A, Cooper RA, French MMJ, Mackenzie AP, Jaudet C, Vignolles D, Proust C, Hussey NE (2008) Quantum oscillations in an overdoped high-T_c superconductor. Nature 455(7215):952–955
20. Tsui DC, Störmer HL, Gossard AC (1982) Two-dimensional magnetotransport in the extreme quantum limit. Phys Rev Lett 48(22):1559–1562

21. Stewart GR (2001) Non-Fermi-liquid behavior in *d*- and *f*-electron metals. Rev Mod Phys 73(4):797–855
22. Löhneysen Hv, Rosch A, Vojta M, Wölfle P (2007) Fermi-liquid instabilities at magnetic quantum phase transitions. Rev Mod Phys 79(3):1015–1075
23. Gegenwart P, Si Q, Steglich F (2008) Quantum criticality in heavy-fermion metals. Nat Phys 4(3):186–197
24. Grigera SA, Mackenzie AP, Schofield AJ, Julian SR, Lonzarich GG (2002) A metamagnetic quantum critical endpoint in $Sr_3Ru_2O_7$. Int J Modern Phys B 16(20–22):3258–3264 (4th conference on physical phenomena at high magnetic fields, Santa FE, New Mexico, 19–25 October 2001)
25. Custers J, Gegenwart P, Wilhelm H, Neumaier K, Tokiwa Y, Trovarelli O, Geibel C, Steglich F, Pepin C, Coleman P (2003) The break-up of heavy electrons at a quantum critical point. Nature 424(6948):524–527
26. Mathur ND, Grosche FM, Julian SR, Walker IR, Freye DM, Haselwimmer RKW, Lonzarich GG (1998) Magnetically mediated superconductivity in heavy Fermion compounds. Nature 394(6688):39–43
27. Hertz JA (1976) Quantum critical phenomena. Phys Rev B 14(3):1165–1184
28. Millis AJ (1993) Effect of a nonzero temperature on quantum critical-points in itinerant Fermion systems. Phys Rev B 48(10):7183–7196
29. Maeno Y, Hashimoto H, Yoshida K, Nishizaki S, Fujita T, Bednorz JG, Lichtenberg F (1994) Superconductivity in a layered perovskite without copper. Nature 372(6506):532–534
30. Rice TM, Sigrist M (1995) Sr_2RuO_4 - an electronic analog of ^3He. J Phys Condens Matter 7(47):L643–L648
31. Mackenzie AP, Maeno Y (2003) The superconductivity of Sr_2RuO_4 and the physics of spin-triplet pairing. Rev Mod Phys 75(2):657–712
32. Ikeda S, Maeno Y, Nakatsuji S, Kosaka M, Uwatoko Y (2000) Ground state in $Sr_3Ru_2O_7$: Fermi liquid close to a ferromagnetic instability. Phys Rev B 62(10):R6089–R6092
33. Vollhardt D (1984) Normal ^3He—an almost localized Fermi-liquid. Rev Mod Phys 56(1):99–124
34. Grigera SA, Perry RS, Schofield AJ, Chiao M, Julian SR, Lonzarich GG, Ikeda SI, Maeno Y, Millis AJ, Mackenzie AP (2001) Magnetic field-tuned quantum criticality in the metallic ruthenate $Sr_3Ru_2O_7$. Science 294(5541):329–332
35. Grigera SA, Gegenwart P, Borzi RA, Weickert F, Schofield AJ, Perry RS, Tayama T, Sakakibara T, Maeno Y, Green AG, Mackenzie AP (2004) Disorder-sensitive phase formation linked to metamagnetic quantum criticality. Science 306(5699):1154–1157
36. Borzi RA, Grigera SA, Farrell J, Perry RS, Lister SJS, Lee SL, Tennant DA, Maeno Y, Mackenzie AP (2007) Formation of a nematic fluid at high fields in $Sr_3Ru_2O_7$. Science 315(5809):214–217
37. Mercure J-F (2008) The de Haas–van Alphen effect near a quantum critical end point in $Sr_3Ru_2O_7$. PhD Thesis, September 2008
38. Chmaissem O, Jorgensen JD, Shaked H, Ikeda S, Maeno Y (1998) Thermal expansion and compressibility of Sr_2RuO_4. Phys Rev B 57(9):5067–5070
39. Huang Q, Lynn JW, Erwin RW, Jarupatrakorn J, Cava RJ (1998) Oxygen displacements and search for magnetic order in $Sr_3Ru_2O_7$. Phys Rev B 58(13):8515–8521
40. Kiyanagi R, Tsuda K, Aso N, Kimura H, Noda Y, Yoshida Y, Ikeda S-I, Uwatoko Y (2004) Investigation of the structure of single crystal $Sr_3Ru_2O_7$ by neutron and convergent beam electron diffractions. J Phys Soc Jpn 73(3):639–642
41. Cao G, McCall S, Crow JE (1997) Observation of itinerant ferromagnetism in layered $Sr_3Ru_2O_7$ single crystals. Phys Rev B 55(2):R672–R675
42. Ikeda SI, Maeno Y (1999) Magnetic properties of bilayered $Sr_3Ru_2O_7$. Phys B 261:947–948 (international conference on strongly correlated electron systems (SCES 98), Paris, France, 15–18 July 1998)
43. Perry RS, Maeno Y (2004) Systematic approach to the growth of high-quality single crystals of $Sr_3Ru_2O_7$. J Cryst Growth 271(1–2):134–141

44. Perry RS, Galvin LM, Grigera SA, Capogna L, Schofield AJ, Mackenzie AP, Chiao M, Julian SR, Ikeda SI, Nakatsuji S, Maeno Y, Pfleiderer C (2001) Metamagnetism and critical fluctuations in high quality single crystals of the bilayer ruthenate $Sr_3Ru_2O_7$. Phys Rev Lett 86(12):2661–2664
45. Stryjewski E, Giordano N (1977) Metamagnetism. Adv Phys 26:487
46. Grigera SA, Borzi RA, Mackenzie AP, Julian SR, Perry RS, Maeno Y (2003) Angular dependence of the magnetic susceptibility in the itinerant metamagnet $Sr_3Ru_2O_7$. Phys Rev B 67(21):214427
47. Millis AJ, Schofield AJ, Lonzarich GG, Grigera SA (2010) Metamagnetic quantum criticality in metals. Phys Rev Lett 88(21):217204
48. Zhu LJ, Garst M, Rosch A, Si QM (2003) Universally diverging Grüneisen parameter and the magnetocaloric effect close to quantum critical points. Phys Rev Lett 91(6)
49. Berridge AM, Green AG, Grigera SA, Simons BD (2008) Inhomogeneous magnetic phases: a LOFF-like phase in $Sr_3Ru_2O_7$. Phys Rev Lett (accepted). arXiv:0810.2096v1
50. Gegenwart P, Weickert F, Garst M, Perry RS, Maeno Y (2006) Metamagnetic quantum criticality in $Sr_3Ru_2O_7$ studied by thermal expansion. Phys Rev Lett 96(13):136402
51. Nishizaki S, Maeno Y, Mao ZQ (2000) Changes in the superconducting state of Sr_2RuO_4 under magnetic fields probed by specific heat. J Phys Soc Jpn 69(2):572–578
52. Mackenzie AP, Ikeda S, Maeno Y, Fujita T, Julian SR, Lonzarich GG (1998) Fermi surface topography of Sr_2RuO_4. J Phys Soc Jpn 67(2):385–388
53. Bergemann C, Julian SR, Mackenzie AP, NishiZaki S, Maeno Y (2000) Detailed topography of the Fermi surface of Sr_2RuO_4. Phys Rev Lett 84(12):2662–2665
54. Mackenzie AP, Julian SR, Diver AJ, McMullan GJ, Ray MP, Lonzarich GG, Maeno Y, Nishizaki S, Fujita T (1996) Quantum oscillations in the layered perovskite superconductor Sr_2RuO_4. Phys Rev Lett 76(20):3786–3789
55. Bergemann C, Mackenzie AP, Julian SR, Forsythe D, Ohmichi E (2003) Quasi-two-dimensional Fermi liquid properties of the unconventional superconductor Sr_2RuO_4. Adv Phys 52(7):639–725
56. Damascelli A, Lu DH, Shen KM, Armitage NP, Ronning F, Feng DL, Kim C, Shen ZX, Kimura T, Tokura Y, Mao ZQ, Maeno Y (2000) Fermi surface, surface states, and surface reconstruction in Sr_2RuO_4. Phys Rev Lett 85(24):5194–5197
57. Mazin II, Singh DJ (1997) Ferromagnetic spin fluctuation induced superconductivity in Sr_2RuO_4. Phys Rev Lett 79(4):733–736
58. Shen KM, Kikugawa N, Bergemann C, Balicas L, Baumberger F, Meevasana W, Ingle NJC, Maeno Y, Shen Z-X, Mackenzie AP (2007) Evolution of the Fermi surface and quasiparticle renormalization through a van Hove singularity in $Sr_{2-y}La_yRuO_4$. Phys Rev Lett 99(18):187001
59. Kikugawa N, Mackenzie AP, Bergemann C, Borzi RA, Grigera SA, Maeno Y (2004) Rigid-band shift of the Fermi level in the strongly correlated metal: $Sr_{2-y}La_yRuO_4$. Phys Rev B 70(6):060508
60. Luttinger JM (1960) Fermi surface and some simple equilibrium properties of a system of interacting Fermions. Phys Rev 119(4):1153–1163
61. Tamai A, Allan MP, Mercure JF, Meevasana W, Dunkel R, Lu DH, Perry RS, Mackenzie AP, Singh DJ, Shen Z-X, Baumberger F (2008) Fermi surface and van Hove singularities in the itinerant metamagnet $Sr_3Ru_2O_7$. Phys Rev Lett 101(2):026407
62. Perry RS, Kitagawa K, Grigera SA, Borzi RA, Mackenzie AP, Ishida K, Maeno Y (2004) Multiple first-order metamagnetic transitions and quantum oscillations in ultrapure $Sr_3Ru_2O_7$. Phys Rev Lett 92(16):166602
63. Borzi RA, Grigera SA, Perry RS, Kikugawa N, Kitagawa K, Maeno Y, Mackenzie AP (2004) de Haas–van Alphen effect across the metamagnetic transition in $Sr_3Ru_2O_7$. Phys Rev Lett 92(21):216403
64. Damascelli A, Hussain Z, Shen ZX (2003) Angle-resolved photoemission studies of the cuprate superconductors. Rev Mod Phys 75(2):473–541

Chapter 3
Thermodynamic Measurements of Entropy

> "My greatest concern was what to call it. I thought of calling it 'information', but the word was overly used, so I decided to call it 'uncertainty'. When I discussed it with John von Neumann, he had a better idea. Von Neumann told me, 'You should call it entropy, for two reasons. In the first place your uncertainty function has been used in statistical mechanics under that name, so it already has a name. In the second place, and more important, nobody knows what entropy really is, so in a debate you will always have the advantage."'—Claude Shannon (1948) [1].

In the experiments presented in this thesis the magnetic phase diagram of $Sr_3Ru_2O_7$ is studied in detail. Of particular interest are the changes of the entropy of this system with both temperature and magnetic field. Entropy is certainly one of the less tangible concepts of physics, its understanding furthermore complicated by the variety of ways in which it can be defined. This however should not lead one to underestimate its central importance to thermodynamic studies. Not only is it fundamental to the definition of a temperature scale in thermodynamics. It also is one if not *the* quantity linking the field of thermodynamics with the subject of statistical physics via the postulate that the entropy S of a system with N accessible microstates is given in the microcanonical ensemble by

$$S = k_B \ln N. \tag{3.1}$$

Here k_B is as usually the Boltzmann constant. Entropy is therefore the quantity that links the theoretical predictions of microscopic models with the experimentally accessible quantities of thermodynamics.

Furthermore, entropy and its derivatives such as specific heat play an important role in the study of phase transitions. As will be discussed in the following sections entropy usually exhibits a step change across first order transitions leading to the absorption or release of heat—the so called latent heat. Across second order transitions on the other hand entropy evolves continuously but not smoothly, leading to discontinuities or divergences in the derivatives of the free energy such

A. W. Rost, *Magnetothermal Properties near Quantum Criticality in the Itinerant Metamagnet $Sr_3Ru_2O_7$*, Springer Theses, DOI: 10.1007/978-3-642-14524-7_3,

as the specific heat. Measurements of specific heat are therefore fundamental to the study of phase transitions.

In the following I will introduce the necessary theoretical background to thermodynamic measurements under magnetic fields. This will be followed by a description of the measurement methods for the specific heat and magnetocaloric effect used in the experiments discussed in Chaps 4 and 5.

3.1 General Considerations on Thermodynamics in Magnetic Fields

In this section the main thermodynamic concepts relevant to this work will be discussed. The intention is not to give an introduction on thermodynamics, which is well covered in a variety of textbooks. However, there exist differences across the literature regarding the exact definition of such central quantities as magnetic work. Therefore, in the following sections an overview is given of some of the most important aspects of thermodynamics in magnetic fields.

3.1.1 The Laws of Thermodynamics for Magnetic Systems

It is assumed that the reader is familiar with the general aspects of thermodynamics. Here, the laws of thermodynamics will be briefly discussed regarding their specific formulation for magnetic systems and relevant implications for this work.

3.1.1.1 The First Law: Energy Conservation

The first law of thermodynamics is in principle a statement about the conservation of energy. In its mathematical form it is expressed as

$$\mathrm{d}U = đW + đQ, \tag{3.2}$$

where $\mathrm{d}U$ is the change of internal energy during an infinitesimal change of state during which the amount of work $đW$ is done to and the amount of heat $đQ$ is absorbed by the system under consideration.

For magnetic systems it is in particular the magnetic work term $đW$ for which differing definitions are given in textbooks. The fundamental question for the experiments presented in this work is what work $đW$ has to be done to magnetise a sample inside a coil. A very good discussion of this is given for example in the book by Mandl [2]. There it is shown that the total work done is given by[1]

$$đW = \mu_0 H \mathrm{d}M. \tag{3.3}$$

Here μ_0 is the magnetic vacuum permeability. The above definition includes the mutual interaction energy $\mu_0 HM$ between the vacuum field H and the magnetisation M. It is sometimes argued that this is not part of the *physical* system represented by the sample alone and should be excluded. That indeed simplifies many problems from a conceptual and calculational point of view in statistical mechanics. However $\mu_0 HM$ is an energy that has to be changed if one wants to change the thermodynamic state of the sample. It is therefore to be included if one considers the *thermodynamic* system onto which work is done, so that is the definition that will be used in this thesis.

For a purely magnetic system the first law of thermodynamics therefore reads

$$\mathrm{d}U = đQ + \mu_0 H \mathrm{d}M. \tag{3.4}$$

3.1.1.2 The Second Law

> Any method involving the notion of entropy, the very existence of which depends on the second law of thermodynamics, will doubtless seem to many far-fetched, and may repel beginners as obscure and difficult of comprehension.—Attributed to Gibbs (1873) [3].

The second law introduces entropy as a property of the thermodynamic state of a system. It is based on the observation that for any closed reversible thermodynamic path

$$\oint \frac{đQ}{T} = 0 \tag{3.5}$$

holds. Therefore, one can define a new variable S that is a thermodynamic function of state of the system and whose differential is given by $\mathrm{d}S = đQ/T$.

Furthermore, let us assume that a given system in an experiment has as its natural variables temperature T and externally applied magnetic field H. Then the entropy is a function of T and H only.[2] The total differential of the entropy can therefore be written as

---

[1] This expression excludes the vacuum self energy term, which is independent of the thermodynamic state of the system under consideration.

[2] Here I ignore $-P\mathrm{d}V$ terms since all experiments take place at $P = 0$ in vacuum.

$$dS(T,H) = \left.\frac{\partial S}{\partial T}\right|_H dT + \left.\frac{\partial S}{\partial H}\right|_T dH, \tag{3.6}$$

where

$$\left.\frac{\partial S}{\partial T}\right|_H = \left.\frac{C_H}{T}\right|_H \tag{3.7}$$

is the heat capacity of the system at constant magnetic field, C_H, divided by temperature T. This quantity describes how much the heat content of a system changes upon a small change of temperature. Similarly, one can measure the change of entropy while changing the magnetic field at constant temperature. This leads to the magnetocaloric coefficient

$$\Gamma = T\left.\frac{\partial S}{\partial H}\right|_T. \tag{3.8}$$

Both quantities, the specific heat and the magnetocaloric coefficient, enclose similar important information—how the entropy of a system changes as a function of temperature or applied magnetic field.

Finally it should be mentioned that the first and second law of thermodynamics allow us to write down the magnetic version of one of Maxwell's relations

$$\left.\frac{1}{\mu_0}\frac{\partial S}{\partial H}\right|_T = \left.\frac{\partial M}{\partial T}\right|_H. \tag{3.9}$$

3.1.1.3 Consequences of The Third Law

The third law of thermodynamics is the most subtle (and indeed controversial) one. Originally derived in 1906 by Nernst, it is an experimental observation stating that at zero temperature all thermodynamic systems have the same entropy, to be defined as zero. From a theoretical point of view this law has a purely quantum mechanical origin and was contested initially.

Since at zero temperature all entropies are zero, it has in particular to hold that

$$\lim_{T\to 0}\frac{\partial S}{\partial H} = 0, \tag{3.10}$$

and through the Maxwell relation (3.9)

$$\lim_{T\to 0}\frac{\partial M}{\partial T} = 0. \tag{3.11}$$

3.1.2 Phase Transitions

The previous section introduced the basic relations for thermodynamic states of magnetic systems. A further important aspect of thermodynamic experiments is the study of phase transitions between these states.

First and Second Order Transitions

The physics of phase transitions is a very well-studied subject and good introductions can be found in several textbooks. This section will concentrate in particular on the physics of first order transitions in magnetic fields as this is relevant for the analysis in Chap. 5.

Clausius–Clapeyron Relation

The well-known Clausius–Clapeyron relation for a PVT system relates the curvature of a first order phase transition line in the *P*–*T* diagram, dP_C/dT_C, with the difference in entropy $(S_2 - S_1)$ and volume $(V_2 - V_1)$ between the two states 1 and 2 coexisting at the pressure P_C and temperature T_C. The relation is given by

$$\frac{\mathrm{dP_C}}{\mathrm{d}T_C} = \frac{(S_2 - S_1)}{(V_2 - V_1)}. \tag{3.12}$$

Since it is not commonly found in textbooks, the derivation of this relation for the equivalent magnetic transition will be presented in the following.

The starting point for the derivation is the Gibbs free energy *G*, which is the appropriate thermodynamic potential if the natural variables are magnetic field *H* and temperature *T* such as in the experiments discussed here. It can be expressed in terms of the internal energy *U*, temperature *T*, entropy *S*, magnetic field *H* and magnetisation *M* as

$$G = U - TS - \mu_0 MH = \mu N, \tag{3.13}$$

with μ being the chemical potential and *N* the number of constituting particles. At a first order phase transition two phases (1) and (2) are in thermal equilibrium and $\mu_1 = \mu_2 = \mu$ has to hold. Therefore, the Gibbs free energies *G* have to be equal for both phases and the line of first order transitions is given by $G_1(H, T) = G_2(H, T)$.[3] From the definition of magnetic work the form of the

[3] The general principle is, that at the transition the appropriate thermodynamic potential, whose variables are the natural variables of the experimental conditions, has to be identical for the two phases. In the case here the natural variables are magnetic field and temperature, which requires the Gibbs free energies of the two phases to be equal.

differential of the internal energy, $\mathrm{d}U$, was derived in Eq. 3.4. It therefore follows that the differential of the Gibbs free energy for a magnetic system is given by

$$\mathrm{d}G_{1,2} = -S_{1,2}\mathrm{d}T - \mu_0 M_{1,2}\mathrm{d}H + \mu \mathrm{d}N. \tag{3.14}$$

Along the first order transition line both G_1 and G_2 have to change by equal amounts since along the transition line $G_1 = G_2$ holds. It follows therefore together with Eq. 3.14 that

$$-S_1\mathrm{d}T_C - \mu_0 M_1 \mathrm{d}H_C = -S_2\mathrm{d}T_C - \mu_0 M_2 \mathrm{d}H_C \tag{3.15}$$

is true at the transition. Here the index c indicates that the equation only holds for the critical values of the temperature and magnetic field at which the transition occurs. This equation can now be rewritten to give the magnetic form of the Clausius–Clapeyron relation:

$$\mu_0 \frac{\mathrm{d}H_C}{\mathrm{d}T_C} = -\frac{(S_2 - S_1)}{(M_2 - M_1)}. \tag{3.16}$$

Here $\mu_0 \mathrm{d}H_C/\mathrm{d}T_C$ gives the curvature of the first order transition line in the H–T plane of the phase diagram. One direct consequence concerns the curvature of the phase transition line at zero temperature. In combination with the third law of thermodynamics it follows that ΔS is zero at absolute zero. In a first order metamagnetic transition ΔM is in general not zero. Therefore, the curvature $\mathrm{d}H_C/\mathrm{d}T_C$ has to be zero.

3.2 Experimental Consequences

The basis for measuring changes in the entropy of a system used in this thesis is the thermodynamic relation

$$\mathrm{d}S = \frac{đQ}{T}. \tag{3.17}$$

Here $đQ$ is a heat flux in or out of the sample at temperature T resulting in a differential change of entropy $\mathrm{d}S$ in the sample. This simple equation is at the heart of thermodynamics and allows us to extract changes in the entropy during an experiment.

In Fig. 3.1 the schematic setup of an experiment based on Eq. (3.17) is shown. One has to be able to apply heat $đQ$ to the system in a controlled way via a heater and to measure the temperature of the sample via a thermometer. For the purposes of the following discussion it will be assumed that the specific heat of the thermometer and the heater are zero and the thermal link between them and the sample is infinitely good. The temperature of the bath is supposed to be constant. The system is therefore characterised by the specific heat of the sample and the thermal conductance of the link.

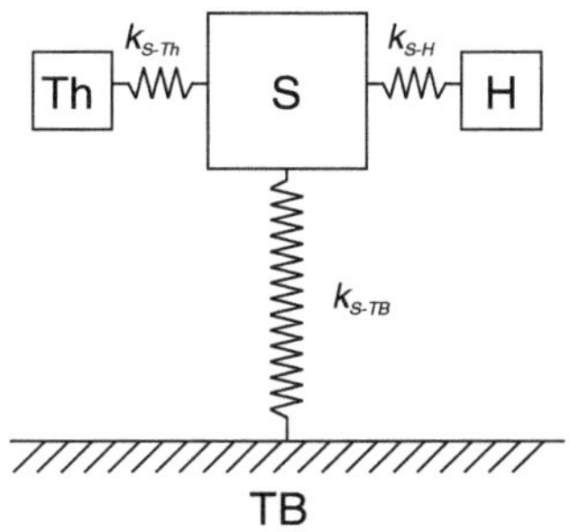

Fig. 3.1 Thermal schematic of a typical caloric experiment showing its main components and their relation to each other. The temperature of the sample *S* is measured by the thermometer *Th*. A controlled amount of heat $đQ$ is applied to the sample via the heater *H*. The thermal bath *TB* provides a heat reservoir at fixed temperature T_0. The components are linked via thermal links of conductances $k_{S\text{–}Th}$, $k_{S\text{–}H}$ and $k_{S\text{–}TB}$ as shown

3.2.1 Principle of Specific Heat Measurements

Heat as a form of energy and the measurement of specific heat of different substances have been at the core of thermodynamics. The original principle of measuring the specific heat by investigating the change of temperature after supplying a well-defined amount of energy to the substance under investigation is still used in so called adiabatic measurements. However, since the 1960s other non-adiabatic methods have been developed, in which the sample is not completely isolated. In the following the three methods employed in this work will be introduced. These are the main methods available and different experiments are often only different in the explicit realisation of the generic components, i.e. the heater, thermometer and thermal links. The interested reader can find more detailed information on specific heat measurements for example in the review by Stewart [4].

3.2.1.1 Adiabatic Measurement

The adiabatic method goes back to the definition of the heat capacity of a thermodynamic system as

$$C_{\text{System}}(T) = \lim_{\Delta T \to 0} \left(\frac{\Delta Q_{\text{input}}}{\Delta T} \right) \tag{3.18}$$

with ΔQ_{input} being a heat pulse applied to the sample at a time t_0 and ΔT being the temperature difference between the initial temperature T_0 and the temperature T_1 to which the sample is heated due to the heat pulse.

Therefore, by applying a small amount of heat ΔQ and measuring the temperature change ΔT one can calculate the specific heat. The characterisation of this method as 'adiabatic' already implies the main technological challenge: the experimental setup has to be thermally decoupled from the bath in order to avoid exchange of heat between the sample and the bath during the experiment.

Temperature differences between the setup and the environment cause constant heat flows which distort the temperature measurement. Therefore the thermal conduction $k_{S\text{-}TB}$ has to be chosen to be small in order to minimize the heat transfer. This applies as well to the additional heat leaks caused by connecting wires for heater and thermometer to the experimental environment. The experimental reality is shown in Fig. 3.2. Here the sample temperature T is plotted in blue as a function of time for an idealised experiment. Initially the sample is at temperature T_0. At time t_0 a heat pulse is applied. This causes the temperature of the sample to rise to T_1. After the jump in temperature the sample decays exponentially back to its equilibrium temperature T_0.

In a realistic experiment the jump has a finite width in time as indicated in red. Its height can be extracted using the so-called midpoint construction by fitting an exponential curve to the later times $t > t_0$.

However, especially at very low temperatures (below 1 K) it becomes increasingly difficult to sufficiently thermally isolate the sample and at the same time to be able to cool it down within a reasonable amount of time. It becomes essentially impossible to measure more than a few data points within reasonable times. A major breakthrough came around 1970 with two important papers by Sullivan and Seidel [5] as well as Bachmann et al. [6] experimentally realising specific heat measurements that did not require a near perfect thermal isolation from the environment. These methods are called 'non-adiabatic' for that reason and are introduced in the following sections.

3.2.1.2 Relaxation Time Method

The most direct extension of the adiabatic method was first introduced by Bachmann et al. [6]. They employed a measurement procedure schematically shown in Fig. 3.3. Here the temperature of the sample is plotted as a function of time during a measurement cycle. Initially (phase I) the sample is in equilibrium with the thermal bath at temperature T_0. At time t_1 a continuous heating is applied and sustained during the whole of phase II. This causes the sample to heat up and reach

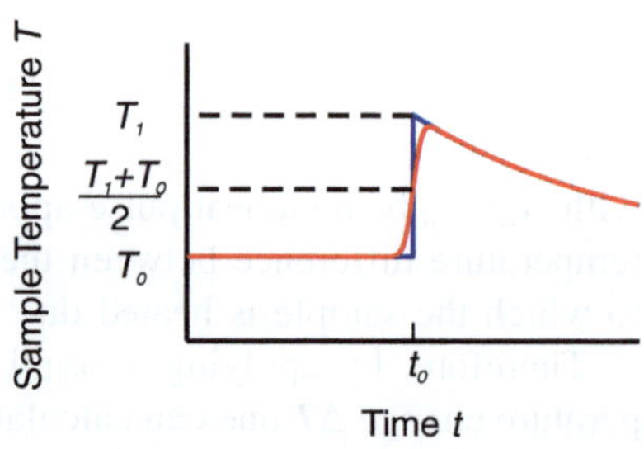

Fig. 3.2 Sample temperature as a function of time during a heat pulse experiment. In *blue* the idealised experiment with instantaneous heat jump is shown. In *red* a more realistic curve in an experiment with a finite width in time for the temperature jump is given

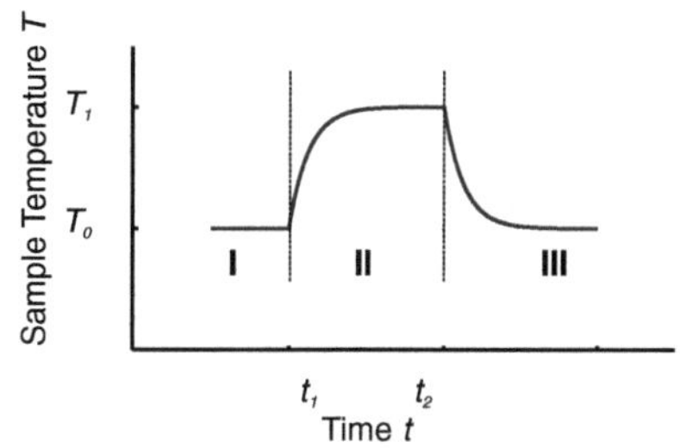

Fig. 3.3 Trace of the sample temperature T as a function of time t during a relaxation time measurement cycle. In phases *I* and *III* no heat is applied whereas during phase *II* the sample is heated by a continuous heat input

a new temperature T_1. When this new steady state is reached, within experimental resolution, the heating is switched off at time t_2 and the sample allowed to relax back to equilibrium with the bath.

It was shown by Bachmann et al. [6] that the following two relations can be derived by solving the differential equations describing the temperature dependence of the sample.

First, the temperature rise at the beginning of phase II is exponential in nature. The temperature T of the sample as a function of time is given by

$$T(t) = T_1 + (T_0 - T_1)e^{-\frac{k}{C}(t-t_1)} \quad \text{for } t_1 < t < t_2, \tag{3.19}$$

with C being the heat capacity of the sample. Equivalently, it has to hold for the temperature decay of phase III that

$$T(t) = T_0 + (T_1 - T_0)e^{-\frac{k}{C}(t-t_2)} \quad \text{for } t > t_2. \tag{3.20}$$

Secondly, the thermal link k of the system is given independently through the applied power $\dot{Q}$ by

$$k = \frac{\dot{Q}}{T_1 - T_0}. \tag{3.21}$$

Together, these two relations allow the measurement of the heat capacity C by extracting the time constant $\tau = C/k$ from the exponential relaxation of the sample together with the independent measurement of the thermal link k. A modification of the above method [7] is the primary technique used by the Quantum Design PPMS system.

3.2.1.3 AC Method

A major disadvantage of the above relaxation time method is that it is still a 'discrete' measurement at a fixed temperature of the thermal bath. It is therefore not very well suited for measuring significant changes in specific heat over small changes of control parameter such as temperature or magnetic field—a situation usually found at phase transitions. The final method presented here is a breakthrough in improvement of the relative accuracy of specific heat measurements and was pioneered by Sullivan and Seidel [5].

The most important change introduced by them was to apply an oscillating heater power to the sample in the form of

$$\dot{Q} = \dot{Q}_0 \cos(\omega t), \tag{3.22}$$

with $\dot{Q}_0$ the amplitude of the oscillation, $\omega = 2\pi f$ the angular frequency and t the time. This can for example be simply achieved by using a resistive heater and applying an AC current of frequency *f*/2.

For the analysis of the experiment a slightly more detailed description of the setup than previously used is necessary. In Fig. 3.4a the basic geometry used in the experiments reported in this thesis is shown. The power $\dot{Q}$ is applied to one side of a sample of length L and cross section A. The temperature is measured on the other side, connected via a thermal link k to the thermal bath.

There are two important time scales in this system. The first is τ_{int} which is the characteristic time scale for heat diffusion inside the sample. The second is τ_2 which is the thermal time constant between the sample and the thermal bath. It is given by the coefficient of the heat capacity of the sample C and the thermal

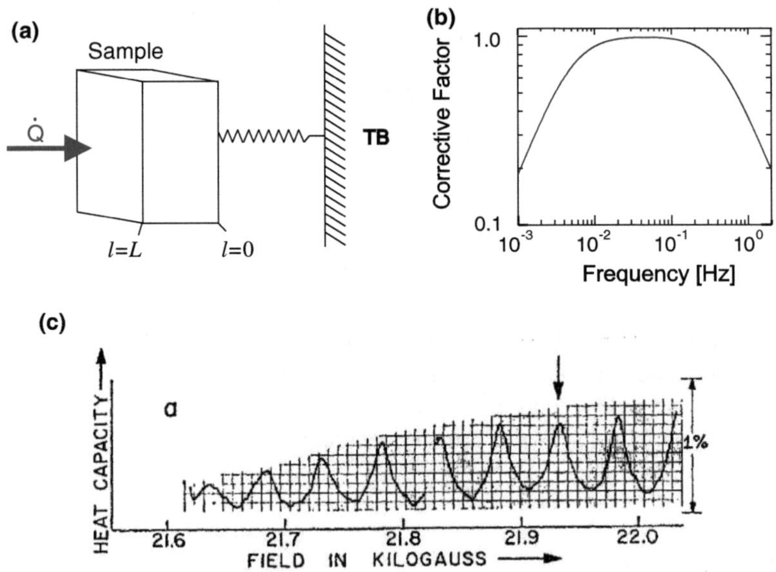

Fig. 3.4 **a** The geometry for the AC specific heat measurements performed in this project. The oscillating heat input $\dot{Q}$ is applied to one side of a sample of thickness L. The temperature is measured on the other side at $l = 0$. This side is also weakly coupled to the thermal bath *TB*. **b** The factor describing the corrections to the amplitude in Eq. 3.23 as a function of frequency $f = \omega/2\pi$ due to the finite time constants τ_{int} and τ_2 of the setup. **c** An example of the possible relative accuracy with this method [5]. Here, quantum oscillations in the heat capacity of a Beryllium sample were resolved as a function of magnetic field

conductance of the link k, i.e. $\tau_2 = C/k$. From the way the experiment is set up it follows that one tries to achieve $\tau_{int} \ll \tau_2$ so that the sample reaches internal equilibrium on much shorter time scales than with the thermal bath.

If the frequency ω of the applied AC heating satisfies the condition $\omega\tau_{int} \ll 1 \ll \omega\tau_2$ one can show that the temperature of the sample is oscillating around an average temperature $T_{average} > T_0$ with the oscillatory component $\tilde{T}$ given by[4]

$$|\tilde{T}| \approx \frac{\dot{Q}}{2\omega C}\left(1 + \omega^2\tau_{int}^2 + \frac{1}{\omega^2\tau_2^2} + \frac{2k}{3k_S}\right)^{-1/2}. \tag{3.23}$$

Here $\dot{Q}^2$ is the amplitude of the heat input oscillating at angular frequency ω and C the heat capacity of the sample. Furthermore, k_S is the thermal link represented by the sample itself.

The terms in the bracket describe several corrections to the amplitude of the oscillations. The second term, containing the internal relaxation time τ_{int}, describes the thermal damping along the length of the sample. The higher the applied frequency ω is, the more effective this damping becomes. The third term, containing the time constant τ_2, corresponds to a correction to the size of the amplitude of the oscillations due to the fact that heat can flow in and out of the system through the thermal link. Finally, the third term is a frequency independent correction depending on the ratio k/k_S, where k is the thermal link between the sample and bath and k_S the thermal link represented by the sample itself. It is included here for completeness but is negligible in the experimental setup discussed later in this work because of $k_S \gg k$.

In Fig. 3.4b the resulting typical frequency dependence of the corrective factor is shown.[5] In an experiment the optimal frequency is that of the maximum of this curve, since here the corrections to the signal are minimal. This furthermore ensures that changes in specific heat have a negligible impact on the overall corrective terms which depend indirectly on the heat capacity of the sample.

Therefore, in the above described limit the amplitude of temperature oscillations is to first approximation directly proportional to the inverse of the heat capacity of the sample C. It is this fact that is used to measure C. By continuously monitoring the temperature oscillations while slowly changing a control parameter such as the thermal bath temperature or the magnetic field it is possible to measure the specific heat of the sample with high relative precision. An example of the achievable precision is given in Fig. 3.4c. Here the heat capacity C of a Beryllium sample is shown as a function of applied field [5]. The observable oscillations are quantum oscillations in C.

---

[4] Here it is assumed as before that the heater and thermometer have a negligible heat capacity and are in thermal equilibrium with the sample.

[5] Values for the time constants are chosen corresponding to the experiment described later.

3.2.2 Magnetocaloric Measurements

In the previous section, measurement methods for the specific heat c of a material were discussed in detail. As shown in Sect. 3.1.1 specific heat effectively gives information on how the entropy of a system changes with temperature. In the following, methods are discussed that measure the isothermal change of entropy while changing an applied magnetic field. In this case one is therefore interested in

$$\left.\frac{\partial S}{\partial H}\right|_T . \tag{3.24}$$

It is often argued that the isothermal change in the entropy S between two magnetic fields H_0 and H_1 can be calculated from measurements of the heat capacity C of a sample. Indeed, according to the third law of thermodynamics, at zero temperature all phases have, independent of magnetic field H, the same entropy $S_{T=0}(H) = 0$ as a function of magnetic field. Therefore, one can in principle write

$$S(H_1, T) - S(H_0, T) = \int_{T'=0}^{T'=T} \left\{ \frac{\partial S(H_1, T')}{\partial T'} - \frac{\partial S(H_0, T')}{\partial T'} \right\} \mathrm{d}T', \tag{3.25}$$

and consequently

$$S(H_1, T) - S(H_0, T) = \int_{T'=0}^{T'=T} \left\{ \frac{C(H_1, T')}{T'} - \frac{C(H_0, T')}{T'} \right\} \mathrm{d}T'. \tag{3.26}$$

This shows that theoretically it is possible to reconstruct the entropy of a system over the whole phase diagram by only measuring the specific heat $C(H, T)$ as a function of the appropriate magnetic fields and temperature. However, it is not possible to measure C to zero temperature. One therefore has to extrapolate high temperature measurements down to absolute zero in order to use the above equation. If the material is in a thermodynamically well understood state such as a Fermi liquid, this is still possible since the temperature dependence can be assumed to be known. However this method breaks down in particular close to magnetic phase transitions and in thermodynamic phases that are not well understood, i.e. in exactly the most interesting cases from a scientific point of view. Here the magnetocaloric effect becomes important since it can, as will be shown below, measure entropy changes as a function of field without requiring experimentally inaccessible information from lower temperatures.

In order to see how this can be extracted from an experimental setup such as that shown in Fig. 3.1 one has to analyse the heat flow occurring during a change of magnetic field at a constant rate in time.

First of all heat $\mathrm{d}Q_{\text{link}}$ can flow in time $\mathrm{d}t$ from or to the sample through the thermal link between the sample and the thermal bath. $\mathrm{d}Q_{\text{link}}$ is given by

$$\frac{\mathrm{d}Q_{\text{link}}}{\mathrm{d}t} = -k(T_S - T_B), \tag{3.27}$$

with k being the thermal conductance of the heat link, T_S the sample temperature and T_B the temperature of the thermal bath. The sign convention here is such that $\mathrm{d}Q_{\text{link}}$ is negative when heat flows from the sample. According to the second law of thermodynamics it is equal to $T_S\mathrm{d}S$, resulting in

$$T_S\frac{\mathrm{d}S}{\mathrm{d}t} = -k(T_S - T_B). \tag{3.28}$$

Furthermore, since the entropy S of the system is a function of temperature T and magnetic field H only, Eq. 3.28 can be rewritten as

$$T_S\left\{\left.\frac{\partial S}{\partial T}\right|_H \frac{\mathrm{d}T_S}{\mathrm{d}t} + \left.\frac{\partial S}{\partial H}\right|_T \frac{\mathrm{d}H}{\mathrm{d}t}\right\} = -k(T_S - T_B). \tag{3.29}$$

If the magnetic field at the sample is changed by $\mathrm{d}H$ in a time interval $\mathrm{d}t$, then one can express the total differential of the sample temperature with respect to time as

$$\frac{\mathrm{d}T_S}{\mathrm{d}t} = \frac{\mathrm{d}T_S \mathrm{d}H}{\mathrm{d}H\ \mathrm{d}t}. \tag{3.30}$$

Applying this relation to Eq. 3.29 gives

$$\left\{T_S\left.\frac{\partial S}{\partial T}\right|_H \frac{\mathrm{d}T}{\mathrm{d}H} + T_S\left.\frac{\partial S}{\partial H}\right|_T\right\}\frac{\mathrm{d}H}{\mathrm{d}t} = -k(T_S - T_B). \tag{3.31}$$

This can further be simplified by using the definition for the heat capacity C, which is

$$C = T_S\left.\frac{\partial S}{\partial T}\right|_H, \tag{3.32}$$

resulting in

$$\left\{C\frac{\mathrm{d}T}{\mathrm{d}H} + T_S\left.\frac{\partial S}{\partial H}\right|_T\right\}\frac{\mathrm{d}H}{\mathrm{d}t} = -k(T_S - T_B). \tag{3.33}$$

The final step is to rearrange the above equation. This results in an expression for the partial differential of the entropy S with respect to the magnetic field H given by

$$\left.\frac{\partial S}{\partial H}\right|_T = -\frac{k}{T_S}(T_S - T_B)\frac{1}{\dot{H}} - \frac{C}{T_S}\frac{\mathrm{d}T_S}{\mathrm{d}H}. \tag{3.34}$$

In the following I will consider two cases. The first is the adiabatic condition. Though not the one used for this experiment it is the one most usually encountered and should be discussed for completeness.

The second is the limit of a good thermal link between the sample and the thermal bath. This limit allows nearly isothermal measurements. It is slightly more complex to implement but overcomes some of the limitations of adiabatic measurements.

3.2.2.1 Adiabatic Conditions

Under adiabatic conditions the thermal link between the sample and the bath can be considered to be zero, i.e. no heat can be exchanged with the environment. Equation 3.34 therefore changes to

$$\left.\frac{\partial S(T_S, H)}{\partial H}\right|_{T_S} = -\frac{C}{T_S}\frac{\mathrm{d}T_S}{\mathrm{d}H}. \tag{3.35}$$

This can be rewritten as

$$\mathrm{d}T_S = -\left.\frac{T_S \partial S(T_S, H)}{C \quad \partial H}\right|_{T_S} \mathrm{d}H. \tag{3.36}$$

In other words a change of magnetic field by $\mathrm{d}H$ will cause a change in temperature $\mathrm{d}T_S$ of the sample that is proportional to $\partial S/\partial H$. This result is often also quoted in a similar form based on the Maxwell equation 3.9 given in Sect. 3.1.1

$$\mathrm{d}T_S = -\mu_0 \left.\frac{T_S \partial M}{C \partial T}\right|_H \mathrm{d}H. \tag{3.37}$$

The two equations above describe the underlying physics in particular of adiabatic demagnetisation refrigeration. Here the temperature of a material such as a paramagnetic salt is changed by changing the applied magnetic field. This can then be used to cool an experimental setup. This well known principle is discussed in several textbooks such as [8] and [9].

The following discussion will concentrate on the use of the effect in studying the phase diagram of a material. One can, for example, consider the case of increasing the magnetic field H applied to a sample linearly as a function of time t, such that at $t = t_0$ the sample passes through a first order transition, as shown in Fig. 3.5a. At that moment a step change in entropy occurs and latent heat is released. In this case a step change in temperature will be observed as shown in Fig. 3.5b.

Therefore, this form of the magnetocaloric effect is well suited to track with high accuracy the phase diagram of a material by simply monitoring the temperature of the sample as a function of magnetic field during a field sweep. A very good example of this is shown in Fig. 3.6 [10].

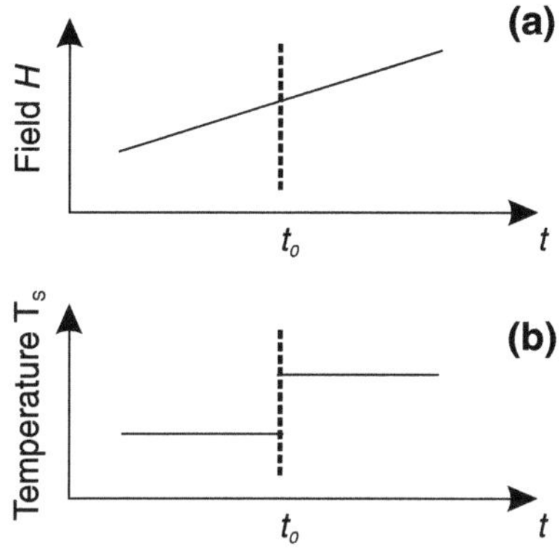

Fig. 3.5 Here the magnetocaloric effect is shown schematically for the case of crossing a first order transition line under adiabatic conditions. The magnetic field is increased linearly as a function of time t as indicated in (**a**). At time t_0 the sample undergoes a first order transition. This results in the release of latent heat associated with the first order transition causing the temperature of the sample to increase step like, as indicated in (**b**)

Fig. 3.6 Phase diagram of URu_2Si_2 in the H–T plane [10]. The traces are the results of magnetocaloric sweeps in nearly adiabatic conditions with different initial sample temperatures

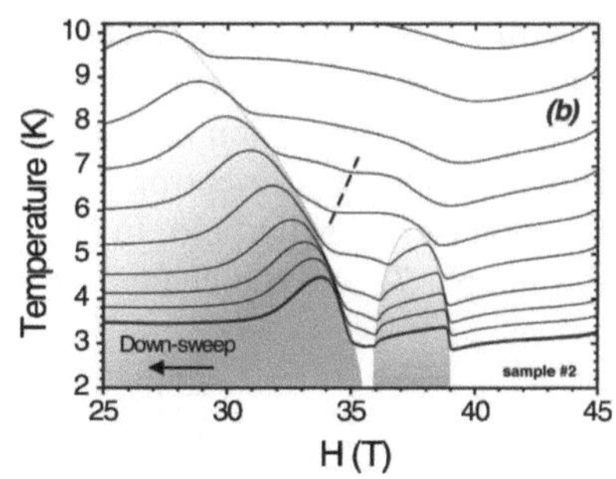

Here the temperature of the sample as a function of magnetic field during a field sweep is shown for several temperatures of the thermal bath. The discontinuities in the temperature traces at the phase boundaries are clearly identifiable.

However, it is less direct to extract further quantitative information about the entropy changes as a function of magnetic field due to the large temperature changes of the sample and the fact that true adiabatic conditions are difficult to achieve at low temperatures. The non-adiabatic method with a finite thermal link discussed in the following addresses these issues in particular.

3.2.2.2 Non-adiabatic Conditions

In Fig. 3.7 the same process as in the previous graph is shown. As indicated in part (a) the magnetic field at the position of the sample is increased as a function of time t such that at $t = t_0$ the sample undergoes a first order phase transition.

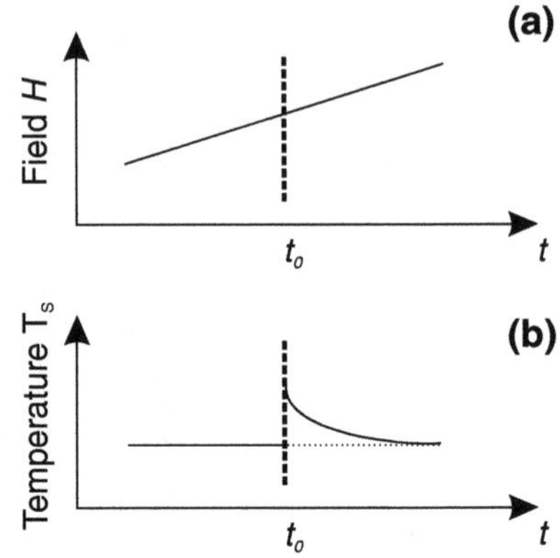

Fig. 3.7 The same experimental process as in Fig. 3.5 is shown for non-adiabatic conditions. Contrary to the previous case the sample temperature relaxes back to the equilibrium temperature after the magnetic field has been increased beyond the point of the first order transition

Part (b) shows the temperature of the sample as a function of time. Similarly to the previous case the temperature of the sample T_S undergoes a jump at t_0. However, contrary to the previous case the sample relaxes back to equilibrium with the thermal bath. Therefore this measurement has the same ability to trace the phase diagram as the previously discussed adiabatic method. It has the added advantage that the measurement is quasi-isothermal if the sample temperature stays sufficiently close to the thermal bath temperature.

So far the discussion has solely concentrated on the effect of phase transitions. However, changes in entropy can also occur inside a thermodynamic phase as a function of magnetic field. In Eq. 3.34 the connection between the temperature of the sample T_S and the change in entropy $\partial S/\partial H$ was derived to be

$$\left.\frac{\partial S}{\partial H}\right|_{T_S} = -\frac{k}{T_S}(T_S - T_B)\frac{1}{\dot{H}} - \frac{C}{T_S}\frac{\mathrm{d}T_S}{\mathrm{d}H}.$$

In the case where the sample is relatively well coupled to the thermal bath the second term can be neglected in the analysis compared to the first. Therefore, in the highly non-adiabatic case, one can write

$$\left.\frac{\partial S}{\partial H}\right|_{T_S} \approx -\frac{k}{T_S}(T_S - T_B)\frac{1}{\dot{H}}. \tag{3.38}$$

Since $\partial S/\partial H$ as well as k are independent of the direction in which the magnetic field is swept, whereas $1/\dot{H}$ is not, the term $(T_S - T_B)$ has to change sign. In other words the temperature trace of a sample during a magnetic field sweep with increasing field is opposite to the temperature trace during a field sweep of decreasing magnetic field.

This situation is depicted in Fig. 3.8a where a temperature trace of a $Sr_3Ru_2O_7$ sample is shown schematically during a sweep of the magnetic field with increasing field (blue) and decreasing field (red). Here the aim is not to give details of the physics of $Sr_3Ru_2O_7$ contained in these traces. This will be done in detail in Chap. 5. However, for the current discussion two things should be pointed out.

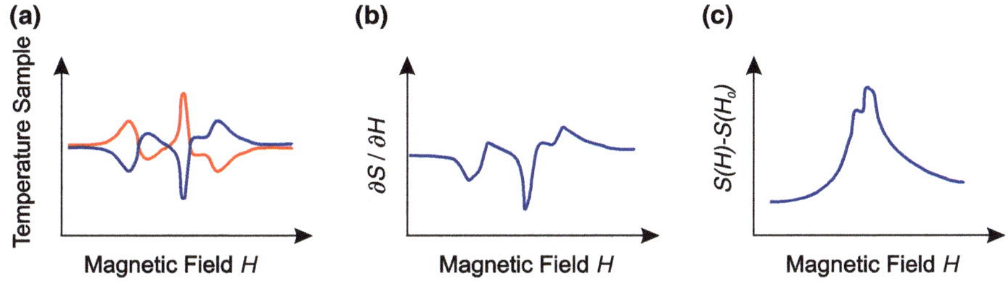

Fig. 3.8 **a** The temperature of the sample as a function of magnetic field during a sweep of the magnetic field for increasing fields (*blue*) and decreasing fields (*red*). Since one is in the well coupled limit the traces are seemingly mirror symmetric about the equilibrium temperature. **b** The reconstructed $\partial S/\partial H$ as a function of magnetic field based on the traces in **a**. **c** The entropy change as a function of magnetic field that results from integrating the trace in **b** with respect to a reference field H_0

First, the position of phase transitions is clearly visible in form of sharp features in the temperature traces. Second, the two traces appear to be reflections of each other about the average temperature. As discussed above, this is a direct consequence of the experiments being conducted in the highly non-adiabatic regime.

At the sharp transition features the temperature of the sample varies rapidly. In these parts of the traces the approximation of neglecting the second term in Eq. 3.34 breaks down. In consequence, in order to reconstruct the entropy of the sample along the whole trace, one has to analyse the full equation. In a first step $\partial S/\partial H$ is calculated based on the additional information of the thermal link k and the heat capacity of the sample C. The resulting $\partial S/\partial H$ as a function of magnetic field H is shown in Fig. 3.8b. This looks very similar to the temperature trace itself due to the fact that the first term that is directly proportional to $(T_S - T_b)$ dominates. The second step is then to integrate $\partial S/\partial H$ as a function of H with respect to a chosen reference field H_0. This way one obtains $S(H) - S(H_0)$ as a function of magnetic field H as shown in Fig. 3.8c.

If the rate of change of the magnetic field $\dot{H}$ during a sweep is chosen to be low enough then one can ensure that the sample temperature does not change more than a few percent around the average temperature. This is comparable to the changes in sample temperature in the previously presented specific heat measurement methods. One can therefore say within experimental possibilities that the reconstructed trace of the entropy change of the sample as a function of magnetic field is isothermal.

3.2.2.3 Magnetocaloric Oscillations

As has been discussed in (Sect. 2.1.2), Fermi liquids show quantum oscillations as a function of applied magnetic field in many observable quantities. Since the effect is created by an oscillatory component in the density of states at the Fermi energy it also has to be observable in the magnetocaloric effect. These oscillations have

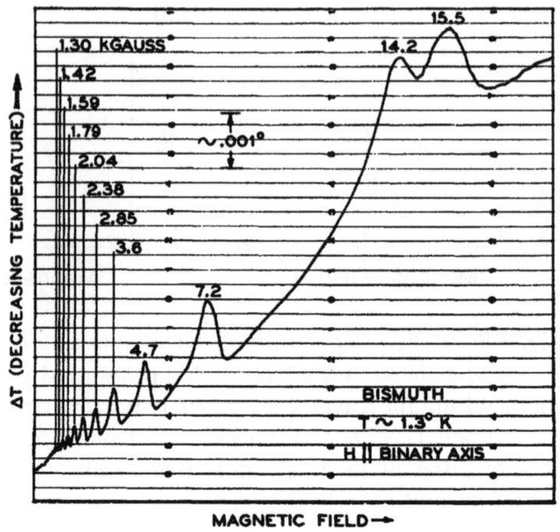

Fig. 3.9 Quantum oscillations in bismuth observed in the change of temperature during a magnetic field sweep [11]

indeed been measured and were found first, to my knowledge, by Boyle et al. [11] for bismuth. Their results are shown in Fig. 3.9.

The first theoretical analysis was published by Condon in his seminal paper from 1966 [12]. In the following, rather than deriving the effect from first principles it will be motivated based on the de Haas–van Alphen effect discussed in (Sect. 2.1.2).

As shown there, the total magnetization $M(H, T)$ of a Fermi liquid as a function of magnetic field H and temperature T can be expressed as the sum of a 'normal' non-oscillating background contribution M_{BG} and an oscillatory component $\tilde{M}$ whose origin is the phenomenon of quantum oscillations.

$$M(T,H) = M_{\mathrm{BG}}(T,H) + \tilde{M}(T,H). \tag{3.39}$$

Furthermore, according to Maxwell's relation (see Eq. 3.9 given in Sect. 3.1.1) one knows that

$$\frac{1}{\mu_0}\frac{\partial S}{\partial H}\bigg|_T = \frac{\partial M}{\partial T}\bigg|_H. \tag{3.40}$$

Therefore, the entropy has to show an oscillatory component $\tilde{S}(H,T)$ that is related to the oscillations in magnetisation via

$$\frac{1}{\mu_0}\frac{\partial \tilde{S}}{\partial H}\bigg|_T = \frac{\partial \tilde{M}}{\partial T}\bigg|_H. \tag{3.41}$$

Furthermore, it was shown in the previous section that during a magnetocaloric sweep under non-adiabatic conditions, the change of entropy S with magnetic field H can be approximated as

$$\frac{\partial \tilde{S}}{\partial H}\bigg|_T \approx -k(\tilde{T}_S - T_B)\frac{1}{\dot{H}}.$$

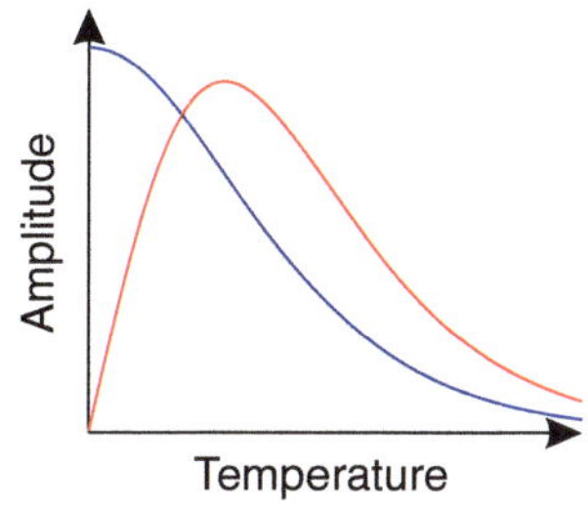

Fig. 3.10 Here the functional form of the Lifshitz–Kosevich formula (*blue*) and its temperature derivative (*red*) are shown as a function of temperature

That this condition is fulfilled can be experimentally checked by the reflection symmetry between of the quantity $(T_S - T_B)$ between a sweep of increasing and decreasing magnetic field.

Therefore, for quantum oscillations in the magnetisation that have a sufficiently low frequency the relation

$$\mu_0 \frac{\partial \tilde{M}}{\partial T}\bigg|_H = -k(\tilde{T}_S - T_B)\frac{1}{\dot{H}} \tag{3.42}$$

holds.

As shown in Sect. 2.1.2, the temperature dependence of the oscillations in magnetisation is given by the Lifshitz–Kosevich factor $R_{\rm LK}$. Therefore, the amplitude of the magnetocaloric oscillations is proportional to the temperature derivative of the Lifshitz–Kosevich factor, i.e. $\partial R_{\rm LK}/\partial T$ rather than $R_{\rm LK}$ itself. The function is given by

$$\frac{\partial R_{\rm LK}}{\partial T} = \frac{\partial}{\partial T}\left\{\frac{x}{\sinh(x)}\right\} = \left\{\frac{1}{\sinh(x)} - x\frac{\cosh(x)}{\sinh^2(x)}\right\}\frac{\partial x}{\partial T}, \tag{3.43}$$

with

$$x = 2\pi^2 k_B T m^* c/e\hbar H \tag{3.44}$$

and

$$\frac{\partial x}{\partial T} = 2\pi^2 k_B m^* c/e\hbar H. \tag{3.45}$$

Figure 3.10 shows the functional form of both quantities, $R_{\rm LK}$ (blue) and $\partial R_{\rm LK}/\,\partial T$ (red), as a function of temperature.

While $R_{\rm LK}$ is a monotonically decreasing function with temperature, its derivative $\partial R_{\rm LK}/\partial T$ shows a pronounced maximum.

References

1. Tribus M, McIrvine EC (1971) Energy and information. Sci Am Magaz 225(3):179–184
2. Mandl F (1988) Statistical physics. Wiley Blackwell, New York

3. Gibbs JW (1873) Graphical methods in the thermodynamics of fluids, Transactions of the Connecticut Academy, I. pp. 309−342, April–May
4. Stewart GR (1983) Measurement of low-temperature specific-heat. Rev Sci Instrum 54(1):1–11
5. Sullivan PF, Seidel G (1968) Steady-state, AC-temperature calorimetry. Phys Rev 173(3):679–685
6. Bachmann R, Schwall RE, Thomas HU, Zubeck RB, King CN, Kirsch HC, Disalvo FJ, Geballe TH, Lee KN, Howard RE, Greene RL (1972) Heat-capacity measurements on small samples at low-temperatures. Rev Sci Instrum 43(2):205
7. Hwang JS, Lin K, Tien C (1997) Measurement of heat capacity by fitting the whole temperature response of a heat-pulse calorimeter. Rev Sci Instrum 68(1, Part 1):94–101
8. Lounasmaa OV (1974) Experimental principles and methods below 1 K. Academic Press, London
9. Pobell F (1992) Matter and methods at low temperatures. Springer, Heidelberg
10. Jaime M, Kim KH, Jorge G, McCall S, Mydosh JA (2002) High magnetic field studies of the hidden order transition in URu_2Si_2. Phys Rev Lett 89(28):287201
11. Boyle WS, Hsu FSL, Kunzler JE (1960) Spin splitting of the landau levels in bismuth observed by magnetothermal experiments. Phys Rev 4(6):278–280
12. Condon JH (1966) Nonlinear de Haas-van Alphen effect and magnetic domains in beryllium. Phys Rev 145(2):526–535

Chapter 4
Design and Characterisation of Novel Experimental Setup

The aim of the project presented in this thesis was the study of the entropic properties of $Sr_3Ru_2O_7$ as a function of magnetic field. The sizable magnetic moment of this material as a function of field leads together with the anisotropy of the magnetisation to a significant torque at the metamagnetic phase transitions in the phase diagram of $Sr_3Ru_2O_7$. Furthermore, in order to carry out the magnetocaloric measurements reported here, a high temperature stability and low noise thermometry under magnetic field is necessary. In order to optimise the experiment for these requirements a new setup was designed, built and characterised by the author. In this chapter first a general overview of the design will be given. An important component is the careful calibration of the thermometry as a function of temperature *and* magnetic field, which will be discussed in the second part of this chapter. Finally, characterisation measurements with Sr_2RuO_4 as well as $Sr_3Ru_2O_7$ will be presented.

4.1 Measurement Environment and Sample Holder

All caloric measurements reported in this thesis have been carried out in an Oxford Instruments 'Kelvinox 25' dilution refrigerator fitted with a superconducting 17 T magnet. This instrument is capable of performing measurements down to a base temperature of 25 mK. The operating principle of a dilution refrigerator is widely described in the literature and details can be found for example in [1] or [2]. In the context of this work two points are important to mention. First, the experiment takes place inside an evacuated space immersed in liquid helium. Second, the cooling is achieved in the so-called mixing chamber shown in Fig. 4.1. The name originates from the cooling process which is based on the low temperature properties of the cooling agent—a ^3He–^4He mixture. As shown in 4.1, this mixing

A. W. Rost, *Magnetothermal Properties near Quantum Criticality in the Itinerant Metamagnet Sr3Ru2O7*, Springer Theses, DOI: 10.1007/978-3-642-14524-7_4,

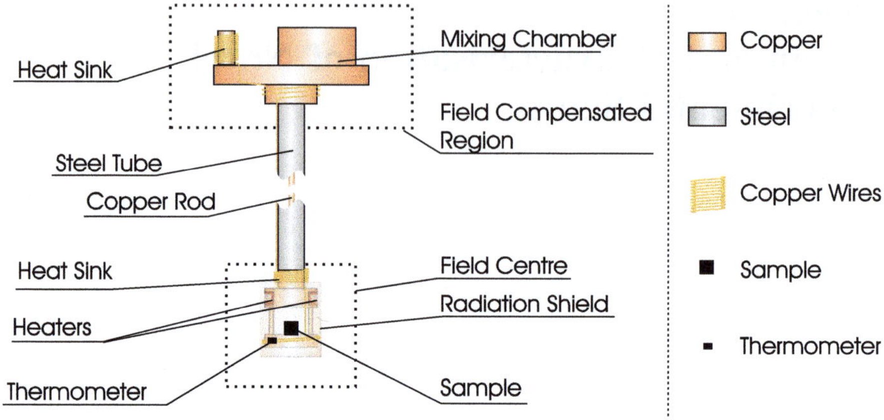

Fig. 4.1 Overview of the experimental environment and the sample holder. Details are given in the text

chamber is installed in a field compensated region.[1] The centre of the magnetic field is approximately 30 cm below it.

In order to position the experimental setup in the field centre an appropriate sample holder had been built. As indicated in Fig. 4.1 it is made of a hollow stainless steel tube with a thin copper rod running along the inside for thermal contact. This combines the structural stability of the steel with the good thermal conductivity of the copper while minimising the possibility for eddy-current heating in the copper during magnetic field sweeps. The tube is terminated by two copper surfaces which connect to the mixing chamber on one end and the experimental setup at the other end. All experimental wiring from the mixing chamber to the experiment is made of twisted pairs of 100 μm insulated copper. The wires are heat sunk at the two positions indicated in Fig. 4.1, which also shows the location of two thin film heaters[2] at the bottom of the probe holder as well as a field and temperature calibrated thermometer.[3] The heaters and thermometer are used to directly stabilise and control the temperature of the experimental setup. Finally, the experiment is shielded by a radiation shield made of 50 μm thin copper foil and screwed into the terminating copper block of the sample holder. This is of particular importance to avoid heating of the thermally isolated sample by thermal radiation from the 4.2 K 'hot' surfaces of the vacuum can.

In the following section, I will describe the experimental setup in the centre of the magnetic field in more detail.

[1] One of the main advantages of this design is the possibility of measuring the temperature of the mixing chamber without the complications of thermometry under magnetic field.

[2] These are 500 Ω strain gauges supplied by Kyowa Electronics.

[3] This is a RuO_2 chip thermometer identical in built to the one used as a sample thermometer and described in Sects. 4.2.3 and 4.3.

4.2 Design of Experimental Setup

As mentioned above, the specific heat and magnetocaloric measurements on $Sr_3Ru_2O_7$ under high magnetic fields reported here impose considerable and often competing requirements on the experimental setup. On the one hand, for example, one wants to minimise the relative contribution of the addenda to the total signal and therefore work with the largest samples possible. That, on the other hand, results in the case of $Sr_3Ru_2O_7$ in a large magnetic moment. The resulting forces in magnetic fields can lead in the best case to the sample detaching from the setup and in the worst case to the destruction of the sample stage. In the following section this and other requirements for each of the components will be discussed, explaining the motivation for the particular implementation of the setup chosen in this project. This will be followed by a section giving a rough estimate of the thermodynamic properties of the setup based on the physical properties of the materials used as given in the literature and summarized in Appendix A.

4.2.1 Design Goals and Experimental Realisation

Chapter 3 gave a general introduction to the principles of the thermodynamic measurements used in this work. In particular, (Fig. 3.1) showed a schematic of an idealised experimental situation. This schematic depicted the sample, heater, thermometer and thermal bath as being abstractly linked without any further support. In reality one often uses a sample platform to which one attaches the sample, heater and thermometer. This sample platform is then linked to the thermal bath. The situation appropriate for the experimental design of this work is shown in Fig. 4.2a. Both the sample (S) and the thermometer (Th) are directly attached to the sample platform (SP). The heater (H) is attached to the sample (S). The thermal resistances between these four components are shown in black. From an experimental point of view these resistances have to be minimised in order to achieve thermal equilibrium between the components. In contrast to that, parasitic thermal links in the experiment between the thermometer (Th)/heater (H) and the thermal bath (TB) are shown in red. These are caused by the electrical connections of these components. Their thermal resistance has to be maximised to minimise the amount of heat flowing through them. This parasitic heat flow could cause either the thermometer or heater not to be in thermal equilibrium with the sample, leading to systematic errors. Finally, the thermal link between the sample platform (SP) and the thermal bath (TB) is shown in green. Its thermal conductance k has to be adjustable so that in combination with the total heat capacity of the sample and addenda (C_{total}) the thermal time constant $\tau = C_{total}/k$ is of the correct order of magnitude.

The particular implementation chosen in this project is shown schematically in Fig. 4.2b and as a graphic in Fig. 4.2c. Here, a copper ring acts as the thermal bath.

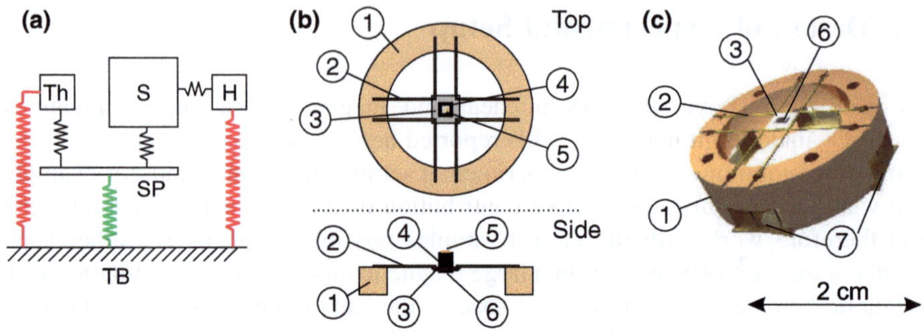

Fig. 4.2 Overview of the experimental setup. **a** Schematic of the thermodynamically relevant components of the setup. These are the sample *S*, the thermometer *Th*, the heater *H*, the sample platform *SP* and the thermal bath *Th*. The components are thermally connected as indicated (for details see text). The setup as implemented in this work is shown in **b** and **c**. The main components are a copper ring *1*, Kevlar strings *2*, a silver platform *3*, the sample *4*, the heater *5*, the thermometer *6* and CuBe springs *7*. Not shown are the electrical contacts and the platinum wire for the thermal link

From this a sample platform made of silver is suspended on Kevlar strings. On one side of the sample platform a RuO_2 thermometer is installed whereas the sample is fixed to the other side. The heater is a thin film strain gauge attached to the top of the sample. The electrical contacts are made via high resistance Manganin[4] wires. Finally, the tunable link is achieved via a thin platinum wire that can be adjusted in length and thickness. In the following each of these components will be discussed in detail.

4.2.2 Sample Platform and Thermal Bath

The sample platform and its support structure have been designed to satisfy two main constraints. First of all, from a thermodynamic point of view, the sample platform needs to have a very good thermal conductivity and small specific heat in order to achieve thermal equilibrium between the thermometer and the sample. Second the support structure between the thermal bath and the sample platform has to have an extremely low thermal conductivity to achieve a high tunability of the thermal link.[5] On the other hand the particular experiment of measuring a material with a strong magnetic moment in high magnetic fields requires good mechanical stability.

[4] All Manganin wires used in this work are 86%Cu/12%Mn/2%Ni wires of 30 μm diameter supplied by Goodfellow.

[5] One can always increase the thermal conductivity if desired.

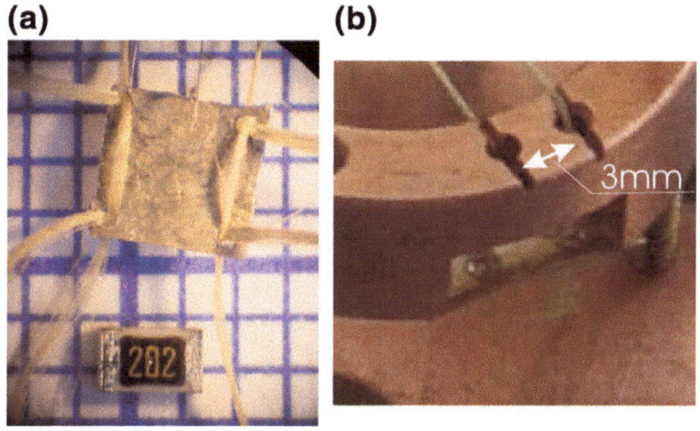

Fig. 4.3 **a** The sample platform (SP) with Kevlar strings and a typical thermometer chip (background is mm paper). **b** The CuBe springs tensioning the Kevlar string

In particular the last condition rules out a standard design where a sample platform is suspended on thin superconducting wires. The design chosen here therefore is to suspend the sample platform on four Kevlar[6] strings as shown in Fig. 4.3a. Each of these strings consists of 35 filaments of a diameter of 17 μm. In order to avoid further addenda contributions by, e.g. epoxy the Kevlar is threaded through holes in the sample platform as shown in Fig. 4.3. The filaments are extremely strong and can be tensioned at room temperature such that the sample platform is fixed in a quasi rigid position.

The platform itself is made of silver.[7] It is approximately 4 mm × 4 mm wide and has a thickness of 0.15 mm. The main consideration here was to use a material of high thermal conductivity that is able to withstand the mechanical stress from the suspension. It furthermore has sufficiently 'soft' edges to avoid damaging the Kevlar strings.

Though the Kevlar strings can be tensioned at room temperature a particular problem is their negative thermal expansion coefficient. This leads to an extension upon lowering of the temperature and without further precautions would cause the sample platform to loosen. Therefore, the Kevlar filaments are fixed with Stycast[8] at the ends to CuBe[9] springs as shown in Fig. 4.3b. This material is elastic to low temperature and keeps the tension of the Kevlar strings. That the platform keeps its rigidity down to 77 K temperatures has been directly tested by immersing it into liquid nitrogen. This is important because most of the total thermal expansion/contraction for materials used takes place between room temperatures and 77 K [3]. A further indirect test is the measured phase diagram of $Sr_3Ru_2O_7$ discussed later (see Sect. 5.1 in Chap. 5).

6 The Kevlar is supplied by Goodfellow.

7 The material was obtained from Goodfellow and has a nominal purity of 99.5%.

8 Stycast is an epoxy supplied by DuPont.

9 The CuBe is a 98% Cu and 2% Be alloy supplied by Goodfellow.

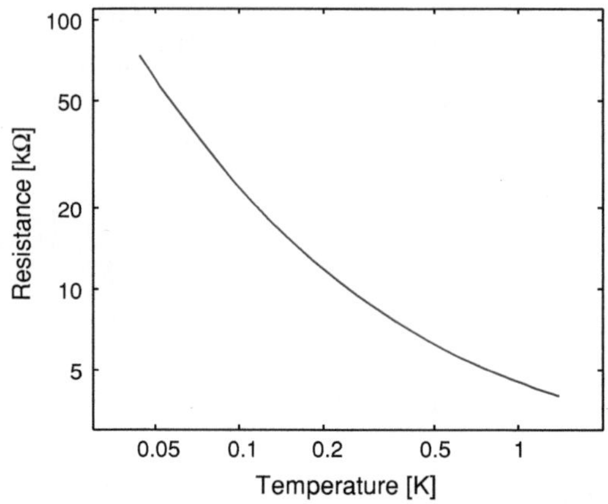

Fig. 4.4 The typical resistance behaviour of a RuO_2 chip as function of temperature

4.2.3 Thermometer

Central to the caloric experiments reported in this work is an exact knowledge of the absolute temperature of the sample over the whole temperature and field region. Since most thermometers have an appreciable dependence on magnetic fields this requires the thermometer to be calibrated as a function of both temperature and field.[10]

The setup presented here uses standard Lakeshore RuO_2 resistance chips[11] with a cross section of 1.45 mm × 1.27 mm and a thickness of 0.3 mm. The resistive material is a thin layer of a RuO_2 based glass deposited on a polycrystalline Al_2O_3 substrate and contacted by platinum pads. In order to reduce the thermal path between the bottom of the substrate and the resistive layer the former was polished down to 100 μm.

Figure 4.4 shows a typical resistance curve as a function of temperature for thermometers of this kind. The exponential increase of resistance towards lower temperature ensures that the sensitivity d $\ln(R)$/d $\ln(T)$ increases towards lower temperatures. The physical basis for the increasing resistance is the fact that the conductance of the material is dominated by variable range hopping of electrons in the RuO_2-glass matrix. The conductance decreases towards lower temperatures since this hopping is thermally activated.

[10] The one type of sensor I am aware of that is field independent is based on the dielectric constant of certain glasses. However these have the problem of long times to reach thermal equilibrium and are in their current form not suitable for the experiment.

[11] Model RX-202

In the experiment the thermometer is attached to the silver platform via Apiezon grease. The electrical contacts for the four-point resistance measurement were made with twisted pairs of Manganin wires with a diameter of 30 μm. These wires could not be attached by solder since heating the thermometers significantly above room temperature would have destroyed their calibration. It was therefore decided to make the contact with a silver based conductive epoxy.[12] Since these contacts are not very strong mechanically they furthermore had to be stabilised with a minimal amount of Stycast.

The details of the thermometer calibration and characterisation carried out for this thesis are discussed in Sect. 4.3.

4.2.4 Heater

The final component of the experimental setup is the heater. As in the case of the thermometer it has to satisfy the condition of having a small thermal mass. Furthermore, one would like to have a resistive element that does not significantly change its resistance as function of temperature or magnetic field. Here, it was decided to use thin film strain gauges. During the course of the experiment two different strain gauges were used, The first is a 120 Ω heater supplied by Kyowa Electronics.[13] The substrate is a very thin polyimide resin of approximately 13 μm thickness. The resistive element of the gauge is a CuNi alloy film. The mass is less than 1 mg.

The second type a 5 kΩ strain gauge supplied by Vishay.[14] Here the film is made of a modified K-alloy (NiCr) on a glass–fibre-reinforced epoxy substrate[15] of approximately 13 μm thickness and a total weight of less than 1 mg.

For the experiment one of these heaters is attached to the sample via conductive silver epoxy[16] in order to have optimal thermal contact. Furthermore, they are contacted by two twisted pairs of Manganin wires of 30 μm diameter to supply the heater current and being able to simultaneously carry out a four point measurement of their resistance. Over the full temperature (100 mK to 1.5 K) and magnetic field range (0–15 T) the heater resistance was found to vary less than ±0.25%.

[12] DuPont 4929 room temperature silver paste.

[13] Model KFG02-120-C1-16

[14] Model SK-06-S022H-50C

[15] As a technical aside it has been found that the solvent used in GE varnish destroys this substrate.

[16] DuPont 4929

4.2.5 Estimates of Thermal Performance

In order to have a guide for the experiment the main thermal characteristics of the setup were estimated. The bases for this are the physical properties of the materials used as found in the literature. A detailed list of the experimental values as well as the original sources is given in Appendix A. Here, the main results for the estimate of the heat capacity of the addenda, the thermal link to the bath, as well as the resulting thermal time constants are given. It should be emphasised that the intention is not to calculate exactly the properties of the setup but rather to provide a guide for the rough order of magnitude of the properties of the setup as well as possible variations with temperature and magnetic field.

4.2.5.1 Addenda Heat Capacity

The specific heat of almost all of the materials used for the experimental setup has been measured previously. Figure 4.5 shows the most significant contributions to the heat capacity C_{add} of the addenda. It is given as C_{add}/T as a function of temperature to be more clearly comparable with measurement results presented later, which are also shown divided by temperature. The shaded regions indicate the contributions of each component leading to the total heat capacity shown by the red curve. These contributions are based on an estimate of the total amount of material in the setup in combination with the literature specific heat values.

The first main contribution (1) comes from the silver platform. Here, the mass of the platform was measured to be 17.3 mg and the source for the specific heat is du Chatenier and Miedema [4]. The physical origin for the heat capacity of the platform at these temperatures is primarily the electronic specific heat of this metal.

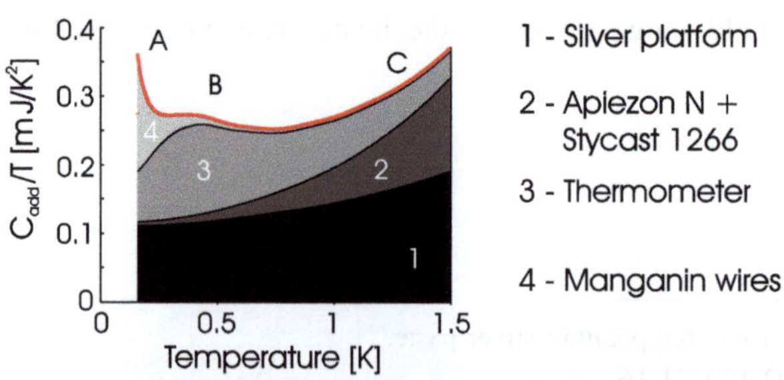

Fig. 4.5 Here, the red curve shows the addenda contribution to the heat capacity of the setup as a function of temperature. The shaded areas under the curve correspond to the contribution of different components (*1*, *2*, *3* and *4*). Furthermore three significant features in the background contribution are emphasised by *A*, *B* and *C*. Further details are given in the text

The second contribution (2) is coming from amorphous materials such as the Apiezon grease (measured by Schink and Löhneysen [5]) used to fix the thermometer to the platform and Stycast (measured by Siqueira and Rapp [6]) that is used to fix the electrical contacts to the heater and thermometer. Since the amount of amorphous material applied is not directly measurable it was assumed here that both components have a mass of less than 1 mg. Furthermore, the specific heat at low temperatures is of the same order of magnitude and has a similar temperature dependence for almost all amorphous materials [7]. The contribution indicated by region (2) can therefore also be understood as a sum total of all amorphous components[17] of a total mass of the order of 1 mg.

Component (3) is an estimate of the heat capacity contribution by the thermometer itself. Unfortunately this particular thermometer has not been measured previously. However Volokitin et al. [8] have investigated the heat capacity of a range of similar resistance chips. The common feature of all was a peak in the heat capacity in the range from 0.3 to 0.7 K. Here, the behaviour of one such resistance chip that is most comparable to the dimensions and resistance value of the one used in this work is shown.

Finally, contribution (4) gives the heat capacity of the Manganin wires that are directly fixed and thereby thermally anchored to the thermometer with Stycast.[18] While the phonon and electronic contribution is negligible, Manganin shows a significant low temperature Schottky anomaly. The data presented here is based on the work by Ho et al. [9]. As in the case of amorphous materials, a Schottky anomaly is a generic feature of magnetic impurities or nuclear magnetic contributions. The contribution shown here is therefore to be understood as being representative for the amplitude of a Schottky anomaly at low temperatures that can be caused by any number of magnetic impurities in the materials used in this experiment.

Finally it should be mentioned that for the first three contributions the magnetic field dependence is not known in detail but can be expected to be weak. Contrary to this it is known that the 'high' temperature tail of a magnetic Schottky anomaly as shown here scales with temperature T and magnetic field H as H^2/T^2.

Overall these four contributions lead to a total heat capacity as indicated by the red curve. In particular, attention should be drawn to the three features in the temperature dependence indicated by A, B and C. These are predominantly caused by a Schottky anomaly in the Manganin wires (A), the peak in the heat capacity of the thermometer (B) and by the contribution of amorphous components (C). As will be seen later two of these features can be clearly identified in the experimentally determined addenda contribution.

[17] This includes small possible additions from the Kevlar strings and the support of the heater.

[18] This is a total length of 12 mm wire of 30 μm diameter. Wire that is not directly glued to the thermometer is assumed to be thermally inert on the timescale of the experiment due to the high thermal resistance of this alloy.

4.2.5.2 Thermal Conductances

The second characteristic property of the setup is the thermal link between the sample platform and the copper ring acting as the thermal bath. There are three materials connecting these two.

First of all there are eight strings of Kevlar each of which consists of 35 filaments of 17 μm diameter and 8 mm length. The thermal conductivity κ_{Kevlar} of Kevlar has been measured by Ventura et al. [10] and found to be well described by

$$\kappa_{\text{Kevlar}} = 3.9 \times 10^{-5} T^{1.17}\,\text{W/cm K}$$

over a range of temperature T from 0.1 to 2.5 K.

The second contribution to the thermal conductivity comes from the electrical contacts to the thermometer and heater. These are four twisted pairs of Manganin wire with a diameter of 30 μm per wire and a length of approximately 1.5 cm. In the work by Peroni et al. [11] the thermal conductivity κ_{Manganin} has been found to follow a similar power law of

$$\kappa_{\text{Manganin}} = 9.5 \times 10^{-4} \times T^{1.19}\,\text{W/cm K}.$$

The final thermal link is that made by a 30 μm thick and 1 cm long platinum wire. Its thermal conductivity was reported by Davey et al. [12] to be

$$\kappa_{\text{Platinum}} = 0.32 \times T\,\text{W/cm K}.$$

The thermal conductance k is given by

$$k = \kappa \frac{A}{L}, \tag{4.1}$$

with A being the cross section and L the length of the thermal link. This gives for our three components at $T = 1$ K the following three values:

$$\begin{aligned} k_{\text{kevlar,1K}} &= 3.1 \times 10^{-8}\,\text{W/K}, \\ k_{\text{Manganin,1K}} &= 3.6 \times 10^{-8}\,\text{W/K}, \\ k_{Pt,\text{1K}} &= 2.2 \times 10^{-6}\,\text{W/K}. \end{aligned} \tag{4.2}$$

A word of caution here should be that the value for platinum had been determined for high purity single crystalline material whereas the wire used as a thermal link in the experiment was not annealed. This can cause the thermal conductivity to be significantly reduced. Experimentally one finds a value which would be expected to be of the order of $k_{1K} = 5 \times 10^{-7}$ W/K with the temperature dependence being close to the expected $k(T) \propto T$.

4.2.5.3 Thermal Time Constants

Finally, I would like to discuss the typical thermal time constants to be expected from the experimental setup. The sample platform to thermal bath relaxation time constant τ is given by

$$\tau(T) = \frac{C_{\text{add}}(T) + C_{\text{sample}}(T)}{k(T)} \tag{4.3}$$

One would therefore expect without any sample on the setup an addenda-only relaxation time of the order of 0.6 s assuming an average heat capacity of $3 \times 10^{-7}\ T$ J/K and a thermal conductance of $5 \times 10^{-7} T$ W/K. A typical sample of $Sr_3Ru_2O_7$ of a total weight of 20 mg on the other hand has in zero field a heat capacity of the order of $7.5 \times 10^{-6}\ T$ J/K giving a typical time constant for the experiment of 15 s.

So far the design as well as theoretical performance of the setup have been discussed. In the final two sections of this chapter experimental results describing its characteristics will be presented. All of these measurements however depend crucially on the thermometer installed on the sample platform being calibrated as function of temperature as well as magnetic field. Therefore, the next section first discusses the details of the thermometer calibration.

4.3 Thermometry

As discussed earlier a central part of the specific heat setup is the thermometry. For this work RuO_2 based thick film resistance chips have been chosen as thermometers and their general properties described in the previous section. Here, the known electrical properties of RuO_2 chips in the low temperature range will be reviewed first. In the second part the details of the calibration are presented.

4.3.1 Physical Properties of Thermometers

4.3.1.1 Low Temperature Resistance

RuO_2 resistive chips have been used for thermometry for over 20 years. Their main advantage is the steep rise in electrical resistance R upon lowering the temperature T. However each individual resistor has a slightly different resistance as a function of temperature requiring individual calibration. In Fig. 4.6 the resistance curve is shown for the calibrated thermometer that was used in this work as the temperature standard.[19]

An important quantity for thermometers is their sensitivity, meaning the relative change in resistance upon a relative change in temperature. This quantity is given by d(ln R)/d(ln T). The log–log plot in Fig. 4.6 shows that this quantity is relatively constant over the temperature range of interest to this experiment.

[19] The calibration was done by Lakeshore and the serial number of the thermometer is U01518.

Fig. 4.6 Low temperature resistance R as a function of temperature T for the calibrated Lakeshore RuO_2 chip U01580 used as the temperature standard for this work

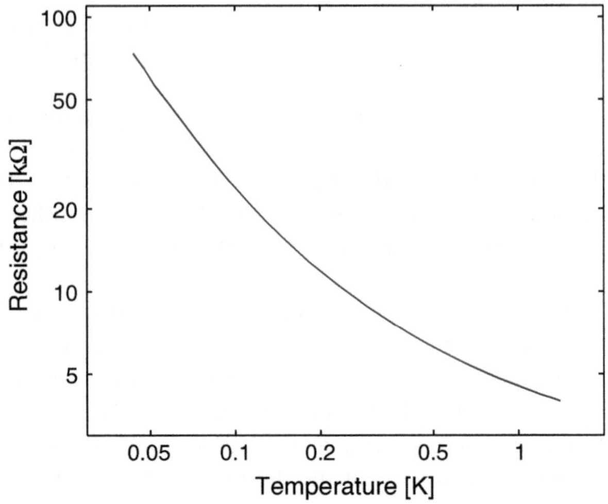

The above calibration by Lakeshore had been performed on 77 logarithmically spaced temperature points between 43 mK and 45 K and has been interpolated in the three temperature regions from base temperature to 800 mK, from 800 mK to 6 K, and from 6 to 40 K by Chebychev polynomials of degree ten. These have the form of

$$T = \sum_{i=0}^{i=10} A_i \cos(i \arccos(X)), \tag{4.4}$$

where T is the temperature, A_i are coefficients provided by Lakeshore and X is given by

$$X = \frac{(\log_{10}(R) - \log_{10}(R_{\text{low}})) - (\log_{10}(R_{\text{high}}) - \log_{10}(R))}{\log_{10}(R_{\text{high}}) - \log_{10}(R_{\text{low}})}. \tag{4.5}$$

Here, R is the resistance and R_{low} and R_{high} the resistance values at the lower and upper end of the interpolation range. This interpolation scheme was used during the calibration measurements to determine the temperature of the calibrated thermometer from its measured resistance.

4.3.1.2 Magnetoresistance

Of particular interest in this thesis is the performance of the developed setup under magnetic fields. The magnetoresistance of RuO_2 chips has been measured by several authors. In Fig. 4.7 the results by Goodrich et al. [13] are presented. Here the relative change of the resistance R as a function of field is shown in a range from 0 to 18 T. The temperature is 28 mK.

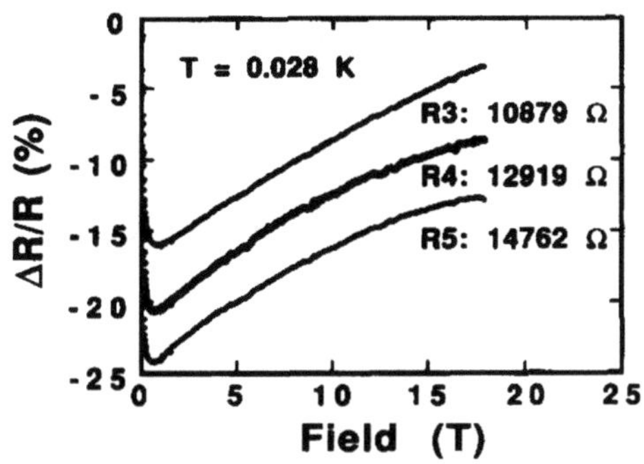

Fig. 4.7 Here the relative change in resistance $\Delta R/R$ as a function of magnetic field is shown for several individual resistors [14]. The temperature during the experiment was 28 mK

The resistance initially drops and goes through a minimum at around 1 T. Above this field the resistance starts raising monotonically. It was shown in the same paper that the change in resistance above 3 T is well described by a linear dependence on $\mu_0 H^{1/2}$ with H being the applied field. However the particular proportionality coefficient is temperature dependent, requiring its measurement over the full temperature range.

Finally, it has been shown that the absolute resistance of RuO_2 chips can change by thermal cycling, which would in principle make a thermometer calibration impossible. It was shown however in [14] that the resistance saturates as a function of thermal cycles. The results of that study are shown in Fig. 4.8. Here in each cycle the five resistors indicated are cooled from room temperature to 4.2 K and their resistance measured. A resistance difference of 10 Ω would correspond to a temperature error of approximately 65 mK or 1.5%. The changes are saturating after approximately 60 cycles. The physical origin of the effect has been ascribed to structural changes (i.e. micro cracks) due to mechanical stresses in the resistance chips.

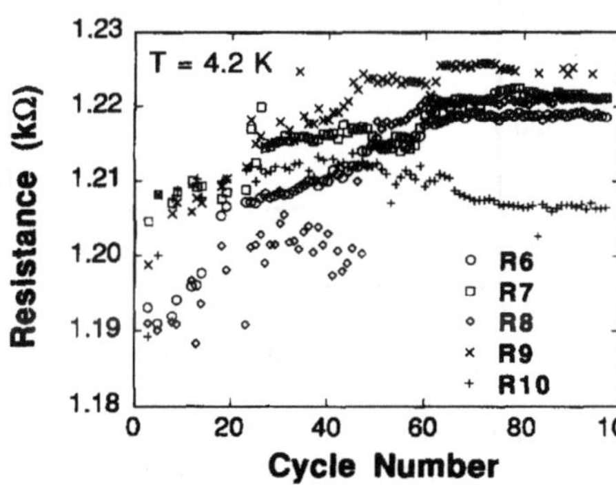

Fig. 4.8 Resistance as a function of thermal cycles to 4.2 K for several resistors [13]

4.3.2 Thermometer Calibration

Having described the relevant resistive properties of RuO_2 chips in the previous section, the calibration procedure itself is detailed here. A total of four chips were calibrated. They are all model RX-102 bare chips obtained from Lakeshore.

4.3.2.1 Thermal Cycling

As mentioned above mechanical stress can alter the resistive properties of the resistive chips. Therefore, they had to be thermally cycled after removing part of the substrate by polishing (see Sect. 4.2.3). This was done with the resistivity probe of a Quantum Design MPMS system. This system allows the programming of temperature cycles between room temperature and 4 K while providing the possibility of monitoring the resistance during the process.

Figure 4.9a shows the resistance of two of the RuO_2 chips as a function of cycle number. As one can see there are variations of the absolute resistance that are correlated with each other. It is assumed that these variations come from systematic errors in the temperature stability of the MPMS system. Already, however, it is possible to determine that the absolute changes are below 0.5%. A better way for looking at resistance fluctuations with thermal cycles is to look at the relative ratio between two of the resistors and thus eliminating to first order the systematic temperature error. This is shown in Fig. 4.9b. Here it is apparent that after 40 cycles the resistance changes are of the order of 0.1%. It was therefore assumed that the resistors were sufficiently cycled.

4.3.2.2 Low Temperature Calibration Probe

For the calibration itself in the previously mentioned Oxford Instruments cryostat a new calibration probe was developed. It is shown schematically in Fig. 4.10.

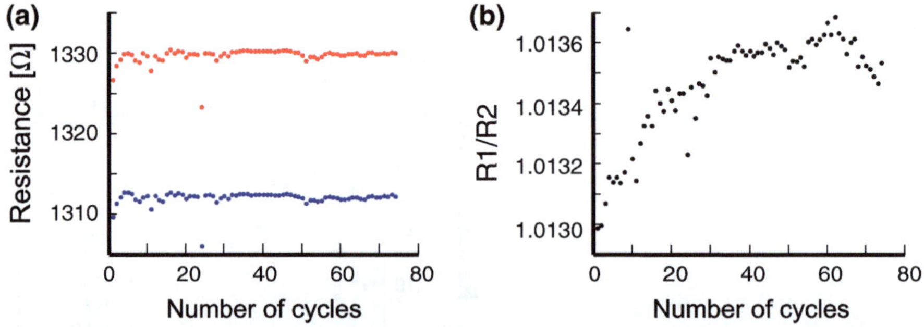

Fig. 4.9 **a** Resistance of two RuO_2 thermometer chips as a function of thermal cycles with base temperature 4 K. **b** The relative resistance of these two chips as a function of thermal cycle in order to eliminate systematic temperature fluctuations of the Quantum Design PPMS system

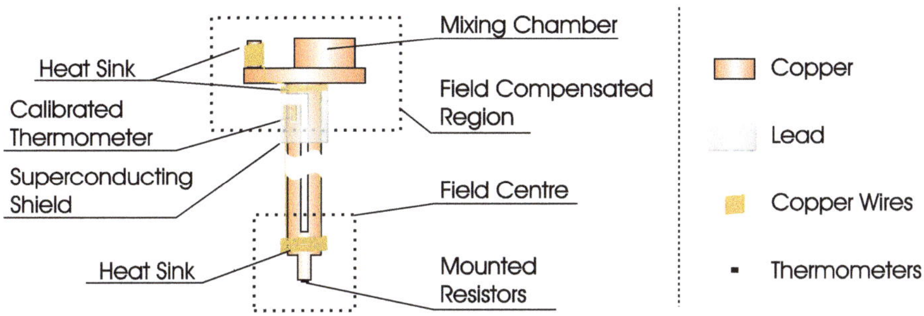

Fig. 4.10 Schematic overview of the calibration probe. Details are given in the text

The thermometers to be calibrated were installed at the bottom of the probe in the centre of the magnetic field. The probe design is primarily driven by the fact that the calibrated thermometer is a RuO_2 chip in itself. To avoid any magneto-resistive effects it had to be installed in the field compensated region at the mixing chamber. Here the magnetic field is smaller than 200 Gauss. To reduce the effect further, the top of the probe was surrounded by a superconducting shield made of lead formed into the shape of a tube.

In order to make sure that the calibrated thermometer is measuring the temperature of the resistors rather than the temperature of the mixing chamber the probe was slit along its length and all wires leading to the calibrated thermometer were carefully heatsunk at the same positions as those of the uncalibrated resistors.

Figure 4.11a shows a schematic of the electrical wiring. On the left hand side the current source is shown. For all experiments reported here a Keithley 6221 AC current source was used. The blue region in the centre indicates the part of the electronics that is inside the cryostat, which is only the measured resistance R and the two twisted pairs for current and voltage leads of the 4-point resistance measurement. On the very right the lock-in amplifier used as a volt meter in this experiment is shown with its effective input impedance. All measurements reported in this work were performed with Stanford Research SR830 lock-ins. The frequency signal for the lock-in process was supplied via an external TTL trigger line from the Keithley current source.

One problem in low temperature thermometry is high frequency noise. While not affecting the lock-in amplifier measurement this noise can cause the resistance thermometers to be internally heated by Joule heating. In order to avoid this, high frequency filters were installed on all lines with the component values given in Fig. 4.11a. The performance for this filter was simulated for a typical resistance value of the thermometer chip of 20 kΩ. In Fig. 4.11b the amplitude and phase shift of the voltage signal as seen by the lock-in amplifier is shown as function of frequency of the AC current. The −3 dB value usually defined as the cut off frequency for a filter is reached at around 20 kHz. This results in a signal loss of less than 0.1% below 20 Hz. After a careful study of amplitude versus frequency for a given excitation current it was decided to use 13.1 Hz as the excitation

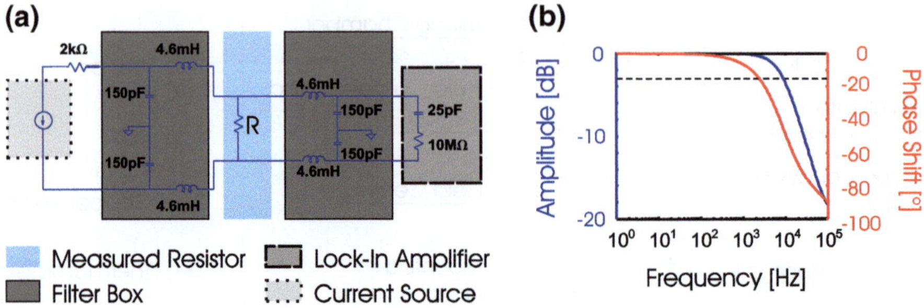

Fig. 4.11 **a** The electric circuit used for all thermometry measurements. The current source and lock-in amplifier are both at room temperature outside the cryostat. Directly at the cryostat filter elements of the given characteristics are installed in a filter box. The blue region marks the part of the electronics inside the cryostat, i.e. the RuO_2 chip thermometer and wiring for a four point measurement. **b** The voltage signal (*blue*) in dB as measured across the effective input impedance of the lock-in amplifier together with the phase shift (*red*) as a function of frequency of the excitation current. 0 dB corresponds to full signal whereas the −3 dB value marked by the dotted line defines the cut-off frequency of the filter

frequency for all thermometry measurements. The excitation current was chosen to be 0.3 nA below 100 mK and 2.5 nA above 100 mK to stay within the recommended regions of power dissipation in the RuO_2 chips in order to avoid self heating of these resistors by the measurement current. It was experimentally verified that this value is well below the excitation current above which self-heating effects become measurable.

All four resistors as well as the calibrated thermometer were driven by the same current source with the voltage measurement being done with five lock-in amplifiers operating in parallel.

4.3.2.3 Calibration Procedure

Figure 4.12a shows a single step of the calibration measurements. The top part shows the temperature of the calibrated Lakeshore thermometer as a function of time t whereas the lower part shows the resistance of one of the RuO_2 chips on the same timescale. At $t = 0$ the temperature set point is changed from 98 to 102 mK. Both the thermometer and the chip stabilise on the same timescale which rules out any significant thermal resistance between them. Over the range where both thermometer and resistor have reached stability the temperature and resistance values are averaged. This average value constitutes a single point in the resistance versus temperature graph shown in Fig. 4.12b for one of the RuO_2 chips. The measurement points are spaced in 5% steps between 50 mK and 1.5 K resulting in a total of approximately 70 data points (twice as many as the Lakeshore calibration over the same temperature range). The gap in data points around 1 K is caused by a thermodynamic instability of the $^3He - {}^4He$ mixture of the cryostat making a sufficiently good temperature stabilisation impossible.

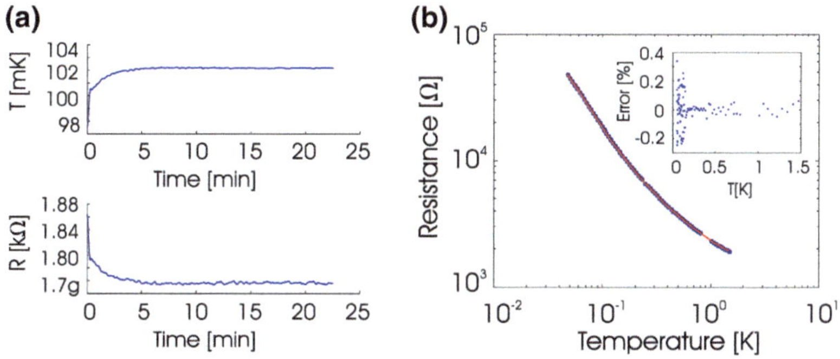

Fig. 4.12 **a** A single step of the calibration procedure. In the *upper graph* the temperature of the calibrated RuO_2 chip is shown as a function of time. The *lower graph* gives the resistance of one of the uncalibrated thermometer chips over the same time. The resistance and temperature for a single calibration point is measured as the mean value over the region where the signals are stable. **b** The resulting calibration curve of the resistance R as a function of temperature T (*blue points*). The *red* curve is an interpolating smoothing spline through this data. In the *inset* the residuals of this fit are shown

The red curve in Fig. 4.12b shows the interpolating smoothing spline that was used to parameterise the data over the given temperature range. The inset shows the relative deviation of the measured resistance of the data points R_{measured} from the interpolating spline $R_{\text{interpolated}}$ as given by Error $= (R_{\text{measured}} - R_{\text{interpolated}})/R_{\text{interpolated}}$ as a function of temperature.

In the region above 100 mK where an excitation current of 2.5 nA has been used the error distribution is smaller than 0.1%. Below 100 mK this error distribution increases significantly mainly due to the lower excitation current of 0.3 nA.

The above described calibration was done at 0 T as well as at 11 fields between 3.5 and 15 T that were evenly spaced as a function of the square root of the magnetic field H, i.e. evenly in $H^{1/2}$ in order to reflect the expected behaviour of the magnetoresistance of the RuO_2 chips. From the data gathered, a surface of the form $a(T) + b(T)H^{-1/2}$ was fitted to the quantity $(R(\mu_0 H) - R(0\text{T})/R(0\text{T}))$ for each of the resistance chips with $a(T)$ and $b(T)$ being fit parameters at each temperature T. The resulting fit surface as a function of magnetic field and temperature is shown in Fig. 4.13a together with the data points used for the calibration. Figure 4.13b shows the relative deviation of all measurement points from the fit surface. The error is less than 0.5% for all points except a few outliers.

The importance of calibrating the thermometer both as a function of temperature and magnetic field is stressed in Fig. 4.14. Here the temperature error that one would make if one would use the zero field calibration for all fields is shown. The blue line indicates the thermometer temperature at 100 mK whereas the red curve is the temperature one would believe the thermometer to be at if using the zero field calibration—an error of the order of 8–16%.

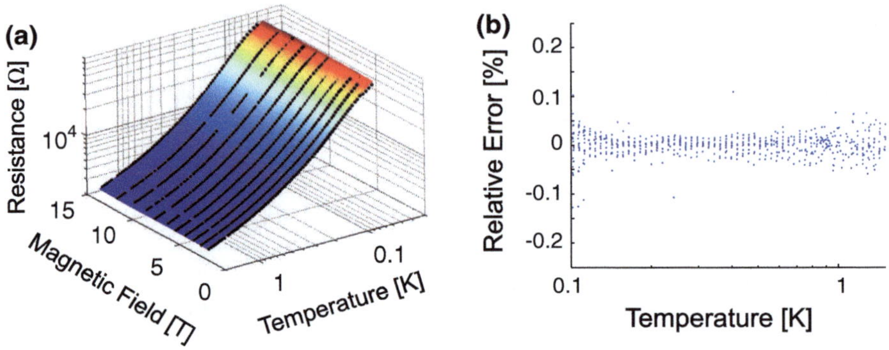

Fig. 4.13 **a** In *black* are shown the calibration points for the resistance of one of the thermometer chips both as a function of temperature and magnetic field. The surface is calculated via the described interpolation scheme. **b** The relative deviation (R_{meas} − R_{calc}/R_{calc}) of the measured resistance R_{meas} from the calculated resistance R_{calc} as a function of temperature for all magnetic fields

4.4 Characterisation Run With Sr_2RuO_4

In order to test the performance of the setup we chose to measure the well established compound Sr_2RuO_4. There are several reasons for this. First of all the compound has a specific heat and thermal conductivity sufficiently similar to $Sr_3Ru_2O_7$ that a realistic test under the final experimental conditions is possible. Second, ultra high purity samples of Sr_2RuO_4 have, as discussed in Chap. 2, several interesting thermodynamic properties in the temperature-field region the setup has been designed for. First high quality Sr_2RuO_4 has in zero field a phase transition to superconductivity at 1.5 K. This allows us to put a lower bound on the intrinsic measurable width of a phase transition. Secondly it has been shown that its specific heat above the critical field for superconductivity is Fermi liquid like and independent of magnetic field. The availability of sufficiently large high

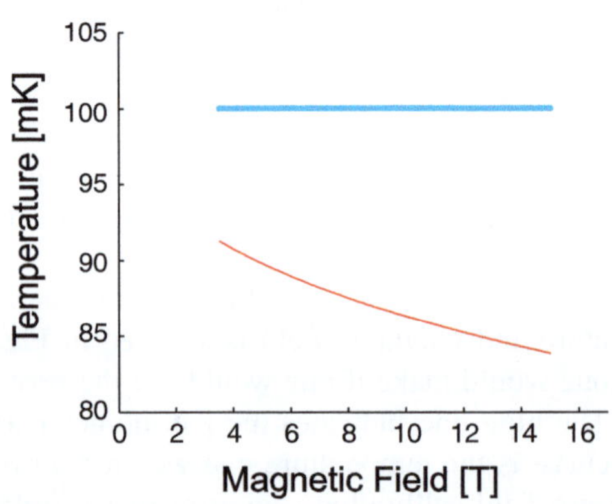

Fig. 4.14 The figure shows the temperature one would wrongly assume (*red curve*) as a function of magnetic field with the thermometer being at 100 mK (*blue curve*) if one does not take into account the field dependent corrections to the calibration

quality single crystal samples in our group particularly allowed to study the possibility of measuring magnetothermal oscillations that occur in the Fermi liquid state.

In this section I will first discuss the relevant properties of the Sr_2RuO_4 sample used in this project. This is then followed by a presentation of the characterisation measurements themselves.

4.4.1 Sample

The sample used in this experiment was cut from a single crystal grown and characterised by A. S. Gibbs in the group of Prof. A. P. Mackenzie. The residual resistivity of the crystal was measured to be 0.12 μΩ cm, corresponding to a mean free path of 3,000 Å. Figure 4.15 shows the superconducting transition in zero field as measured by the out of phase component χ'' of the AC magnetic susceptibility as a function of temperature. Mackenzie et al. [14] have shown that the transition temperature is strongly dependent on impurities present in Sr_2RuO_4 samples. The transition temperature of 1.49 K as given by the peak position in the AC susceptibility places this crystal among the best grown anywhere in the world.

For the experiments reported here an approximately 1.5 mm × 1.5 mm × 3 mm large parallelepiped with a total sample mass of 37.8 mg was used.[20] One of the two square shaped surfaces of the sample was cleaved along the crystallographic *ab*-plane. This allowed for accurate mounting of the sample with the *ab*-plane parallel to the surface of the silver sample platform and therefore perpendicular to the magnetic field.

4.4.2 Specific Heat in Field

First the heat capacity under magnetic field was investigated in order to establish the addenda contribution. Here two of the measurement methods described in Chap. 3 were used—the relaxation time as well as the AC heating method.

Figure 4.16a shows an example measurement for the relaxation time method at 410 mK and a magnetic field of 4 T. Here the temperature change of the sample relative to the temperature at time $t_0 = 0$ is plotted as a function of time. At t_0 an AC current of 0.85 μA and a frequency of 100 Hz is applied to the heater. With a resistance of 4.995 kΩ this results in a power dissipation of 3.6 nW. This causes the sample to heat up by 12 mK. The green line marks the range over which the average temperature before the heating step was measured. The red curve is an exponential fit to the data at times $t > t_0$. From this one extracts a time constant τ,

[20] This corresponds roughly to 1.11×10^{-4} Ru−mol.

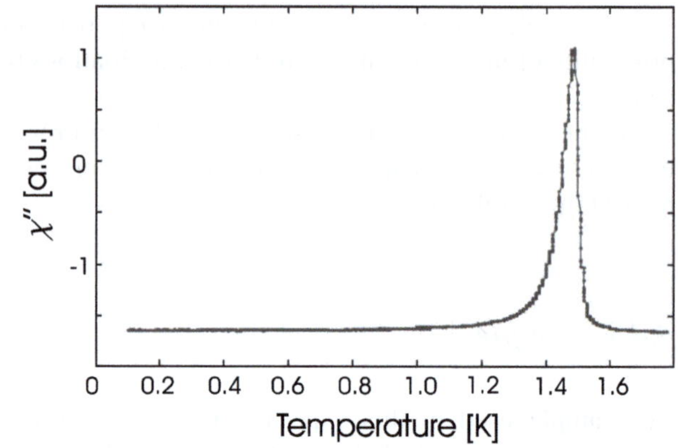

Fig. 4.15 Out of phase component of the AC magnetic susceptibility χ'' as a function of temperature. Graphic courtesy of A. S. Gibbs

typical for all measurements presented, of $\tau = 6.3$ s. As described earlier the temperature step ΔT in combination with the applied heat power $\dot{Q}$ gives the thermal conductance k between the sample platform and the thermal bath as $k = \dot{Q}/\Delta T$. One therefore can calculate the total heat capacity of the setup C as $C = k\tau$ with τ. This has been done for a range of 11 temperatures between 200 mK and 1.2 K. At each temperature the procedure was carried out ten times and the results averaged. The heat capacity C divided by temperature T obtained this way is shown in blue in Fig. 4.16c.

The second method used is the AC heating method. Figure 4.16b shows in blue the temperature trace of the sample while a continuous 40 mHz AC current is applied. The AC measurement starts at a thermal bath temperature of 1.2 K with a current of 4.25 μA. During the experiment both the temperature of the thermal

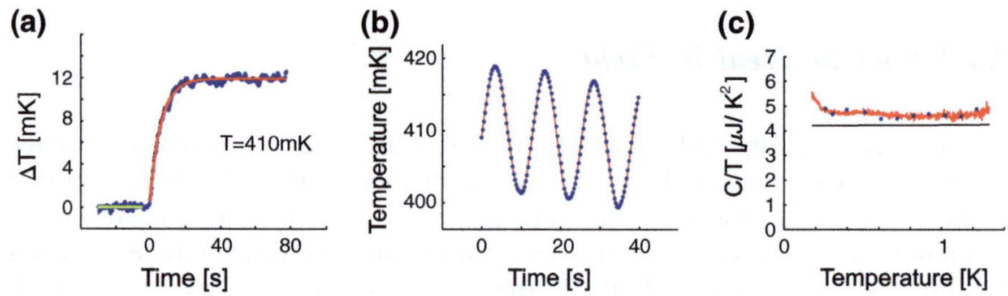

Fig. 4.16 Part **a** Shows the temperature difference ΔT of the sample and addenda as a function of time for a typical relaxation time measurement. From time $t = 0$ continuous heating is applied to the setup. The *green line* shows the fit through the data in order to establish the initial temperature whereas the *red curve* is an exponential fit to the data to times above $t = 0$. Part **b** Shows an analysis step for the AC measurement method. Here in blue the temperature of the setups is shown as a function of time while AC heating is applied and the temperature of the thermal bath is slowly lowered. The *red curve* shows a fit to the data as explained in the text. Part **c** Finally shows the result for the heat capacity divided by temperature as a function of temperature for both the relaxation time method (*blue*) and the AC method (*red*) (further details are given in the text). The *black curve* gives the expected heat capacity of the sample according to literature values [15]

bath and the current are lowered linearly at an approximate rate of 3.9 mK/min and 2.7 nA/min respectively until base temperature is reached. This causes sinusoidal temperature oscillations as a function of time on the background of a linearly decreasing temperature, as shown in the data presented. The frequency f of these oscillations is twice the excitation frequency or $f = 80$ mHz. The amplitude A of the oscillations is extracted from the data by fitting the temperature signal over time intervals of 45 s with a function of the form

$$T(t) = T_0 + at + A\sin(2\pi f + \phi_0), \tag{4.6}$$

where T_0, a and ϕ_0 are free parameters of the fit. Such a fit is shown in Fig. 4.16b in red. As was discussed in the previous chapter the heat capacity C of the sample is then proportional to the inverse of the amplitude A^{-1}.

In Fig. 4.16c the heat capacity C of the setup divided by temperature T is shown as a function of temperature as obtained by the relaxation time (blue) and AC heating method (red).[21] The black curve represents the heat capacity divided by temperature of the Sr_2RuO_4 sample as calculated from literature values. The difference between these is the heat capacity of the addenda. It is plotted in Fig. 4.17a together with the background contribution to the heat capacity at 14 T. Here one can identify three characteristic features labelled (A), (B) and (C). As discussed in Sect. 4.2.5 these can be attributed to a Schottky anomaly (A), the thermometer(B) and a contribution from amorphous materials (C).

The high temperature addenda contribution C_{add}/T for both 4 and 14 T is quasi identical whereas at low temperatures they deviate. Figure 4.17b shows the difference $\Delta C(T) = C_{add,4\ T}/T - C_{add,14\ T}/T$ between these two curves together with a fit of the form $\Delta C(T) = a/(T^2)$ which corresponds to the expected functional form of the change in a magnetic Schottky contribution to the heat capacity between different magnetic fields. Since the fit is a very good representation of the data, it is concluded that the heat capacity of the addenda is independent of magnetic field besides a Schottky contribution. This is a significant finding since it shows that the entropy of the addenda above the characteristic onset of the Schottky anomaly at 250 mK can be considered constant. Therefore, any measured entropy changes in the magnetocaloric experiments presented in Chap. 5 have to come from the sample.

Compared to the absolute value estimated in Sect. 4.2.5 the field independent contribution is a factor 1.5 to 2 larger. Taking into account the uncertainties in the theoretical estimate this can be considered as a good agreement, in particular since they agree qualitatively.

---

[21] As described in 3 the AC heating method though having a better relative accuracy than the relaxation time method tends to systematically overestimate the heat capacity for several reason such as finite sample dimensions. Here a multiplicative correction factor of 0.95 has been applied in order to minimise the mean square deviation of the AC heating data from the more absolute accurate relaxation time measurement.

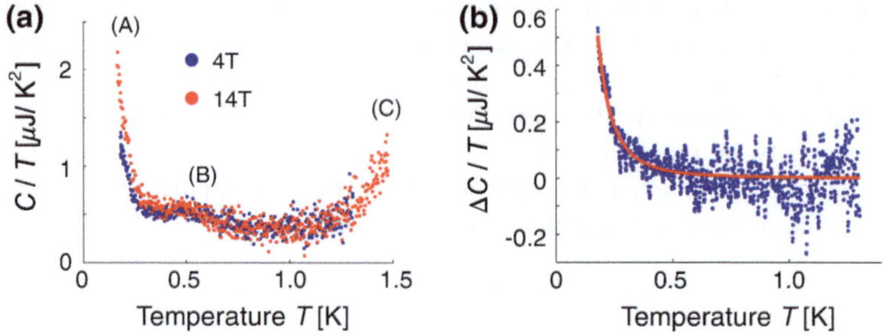

Fig. 4.17 **a** The addenda contribution to the measured heat capacity as a function of temperature for two different magnetic fields as indicated. The expected features of a Schottky anomaly *A*, the thermometer *B* and the contribution from amorphous materials *C* are clearly identifiable. **b** The difference in addenda contribution between 14 and 4 T. This shows that only the Schottky anomaly is field dependent. The *red curve* is a fit through the data

4.4.3 Specific Heat at Zero Field

After having established the addenda contribution to the heat capacity, the specific heat *c* in zero field was measured as a function of temperature. The results, corrected for the addenda contribution, are shown in Fig. 4.18 (blue curve) together with the addenda corrected results at 4 and 14 T. In red, data from the literature obtained by Nishizaki et al. [16] are shown.

The data taken here is in very good qualitative and quantitative agreement. The jump at the phase transition is resolved to within 45(5) mK.

4.4.4 Magnetocaloric Oscillations

Finally, due to the high quality of the sample, it was possible to study magneto-thermal oscillations. As discussed in Chap. 3 these temperature oscillations which

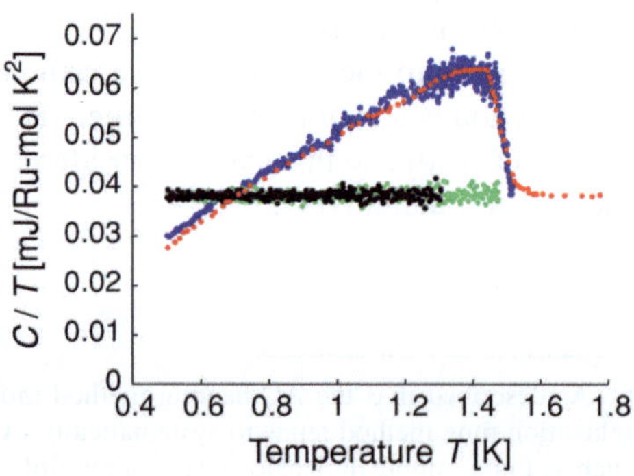

Fig. 4.18 Here the measured heat capacity of the sample in zero field (*blue*) is compared with the literature data (*red*) [16]. In *green* and *black* the specific heat at 4 and 14 T is given for comparison

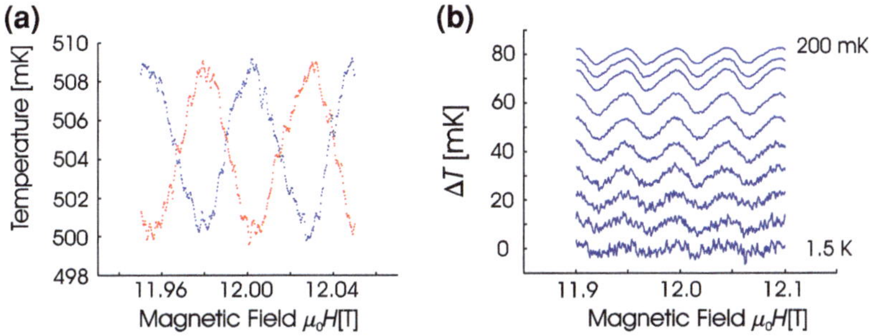

Fig. 4.19 **a** The observed temperature oscillations for an upsweep and downsweep of the magnetic field in *blue* and *red*, respectively. **b** The temperature oscillations of the sample relative to the bath temperature are shown for a number of thermal bath temperatures (the signals have been offset for clarity)

occur while sweeping the magnetic field are caused by oscillation in the entropy of the sample as a function of magnetic field and are a further manifestation of the same effect causing de Haas–van Alphen oscillations.

Figure 4.19a shows the temperature of the sample during an upward (downward) sweep of the magnetic field in blue (red).[22] The sweep rate chosen was + (−)0.05 T/min. The oscillations are clearly identifiable and their relative phase is 180° as one expects from a magnetocaloric signal if the sample is coupled strongly to the thermal bath.[23]

An important characteristic of quantum oscillations is their temperature independent phase. Figure 4.19b shows the temperature variation of the sample as a function of magnetic field during field sweeps with the same sweep rate at the temperatures indicated. The data for different temperatures has been offset for clarity. Here one can clearly see that the maxima and minima of the oscillations do not change position. Furthermore, it is possible to identify a clear temperature dependence of the amplitude $A(T)$ of the oscillations. As previously shown (see Chap. 3) it should be proportional to the temperature derivative of the well known Lifshitz–Kosevich formula.

In order to analyse the temperature dependence in more detail the Fourier transformation of the oscillatory signal between 11.5 and 12.5 T as a function of inverse field was taken for all temperatures shown.

In Fig. 4.20a the frequency spectrum for one such temperature ($T = 500$ mK) is given together with a Gaussian fit to its main peak at 2,975 T, This frequency agrees well with the previously published result of 3.0 kT [17].

---

[22] The curves are corrected for a known hysteresis in the magnetic field sweeps of ± 15 mT.

[23] In particular this phase shift rules out that the oscillations are oscillations in parasitic eddy-current heating due to Shubnikov–de Haas oscillations in the resistivity. These would show a phase shift of 0° due to the fact that eddy-current heating does not depend on the sign of the sweep rate.

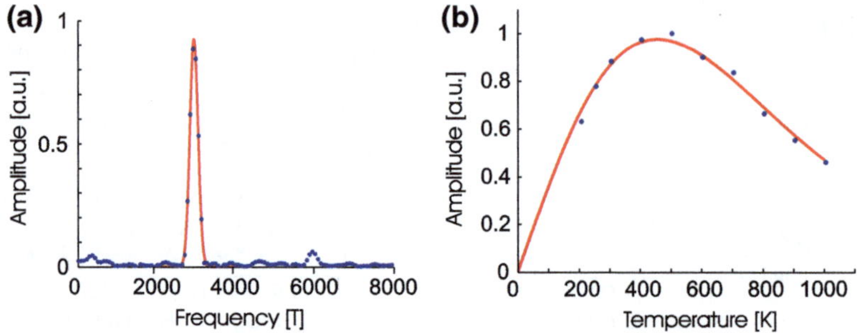

Fig. 4.20 **a** Shows a frequency spectrum of the observed magnetothermal oscillations (*blue*) together with a Gaussian fit to the main peak (*red*). **b** Shows the temperature dependence of the amplitude of the oscillation together with a fit of the temperature derivative of the Lifshitz–Kosevich formula

Figure 4.20b shows the amplitude of the oscillations as a function of temperature as determined from the area under the Gaussian fit to the frequency spectrum. The red curve is a fit of the temperature derivative of the Lifshitz–Kosevich formula giving a mass of (3.0 ± 0.1) m_e. This is slightly lower that the literature value of 3.3 m_e but in good agreement with other experiments conducted on recent samples [18].

4.5 Characteristics and Details of Measurements on $Sr_3Ru_2O_7$

4.5.1 Sample Selection

The samples used in this experiment were grown and characterised in a previous study [19]. Here two samples of that study have been used. Their quality has been determined by several characterisation measurements, the results of which are summarised in Table 4.1. One of the main criteria was a low residual resistivity of the order of 0.5 μΩ cm. Furthermore the content of impurity phases of

Table 4.1 Summary of characterisation measurements for samples C698J and C698K

Property	C698J	C698K
Mass	24.1 mg	23.0 mg
Residual resistivity ρ_0	0.48 μΩ cm	0.51 μΩ cm
Normalised dHvA amplitude	11.6 a.u.	31 a.u.
Impurity Sr_2RuO_4	0.6%	2%
Impurity $SrRuO_3$	0.008%	0.03%
Impurity $Sr_4Ru_3O_{10}$	0.04%	0.05%

The mass is the sample mass used in the experiments here. All other data is reproduced from [19]. For details see text

Sr_2RuO_4, $SrRuO_3$ and $Sr_4Ru_3O_{10}$ as determined from AC magnetic susceptibility studies had to be small.

The main sample on which the magnetocaloric and specific heat experiments were performed is C698J due to its higher purity. It was cut to rectangular dimensions with an *ab*-plane cross section of approximately 1.5 mm × 1.5 mm and a height of $\approx$1 mm in the crystallographic *c* direction. The second sample C698K was a control sample for reproducibility of the experiments. Because of its higher de Haas-van Alphen amplitude it was also better suited to the measurement of magnetocaloric oscillations. Therefore, though the effect has been observed in both samples, oscillation measurements reported here are only those for C698K. Furthermore, this sample has been optimised for an initial angular dependence study of the magnetocaloric signal by being cut in a specific way described in detail in Appendix B.

4.5.2 Thermal Link

An important characteristic of the experimental setup is the thermal link k between the sample platform and the copper ring acting as the thermal bath. In order to know the thermal conductance k both as a function of magnetic field H and temperature T it has been measured in situ during the main experiments on sample C698J. The measurement was performed by applying a constant heat input $\dot{Q}$. Together with the measurement of the sample temperature with heat input T_S and the temperature of the sample without applying additional heat T_0 it is then possible to calculate k via

$$k = \frac{\dot{Q}}{T_S - T_0}. \tag{4.7}$$

In Fig. 4.21a three traces of the thermal conductance k divided by temperature T are shown as a function of magnetic field H. The temperature of the setup during each of these sweeps is $T_{setup} = 200$ mK, $T_{setup} = 500$ mK and $T_{setup} = 1200$ mK as indicated. One can observe a decrease in thermal conductance as a function of magnetic field that can be described by a linear fit within the resolution of the experiment as indicated in red.

Figure 4.21b on the other hand shows a trace of the thermal conductance k divided by temperature T as a function of T. The applied magnetic field is 8 T. The thermal conductance is not a simple constant as expected from a pure metallic link. The anomalies are most certainly coming from contributions to k by the Kevlar strings as well as the Manganin wires. The fit through the curve is a 5th order polynomial. For this experiment one can assume to first order that the magnetic field and temperature dependence of the thermal link are independent from each other insofar as $k(H, T)$ can be expressed as a product of the form $k(H, T) = k_H(H)k_T(T)$. As indicated above, the field dependence is fitted by a

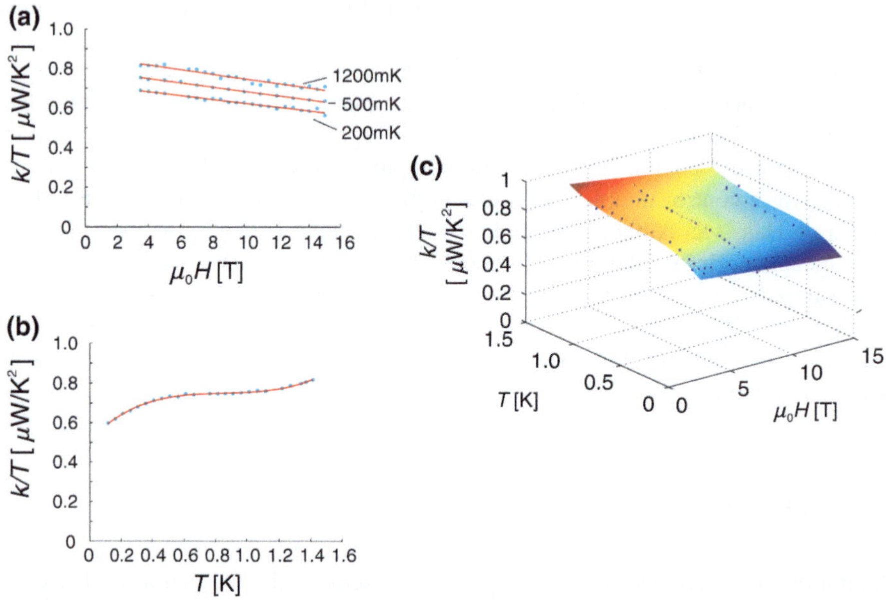

Fig. 4.21 **a** In *blue* is shown the thermal link k divided by temperature T as a function of magnetic field H for three different setup temperatures as indicated. The *red* curves are linear fits through the data. **b** The same quantity but this time as a function of temperature at an applied magnetic field of 8 T. The fit in *red* is a polynomial of fifth order. **c** The fit surface for the thermal link k divided by temperature T as a function of both T and magnetic field H. Also shown as *black dots* are the data points used to create the surface

linear polynomial and the temperature dependence by a 5th order polynomial. Besides the traces already presented, two further temperature dependences were measured at magnetic fields of 4 and 14 T.

Figure 4.21c shows the resulting surface together with the data points used to generate the fit. The standard deviation of the relative error of the measured data points k_{exp}/T from the surface k_{fit}/T, that is the standard deviation of the quantity $(k_{\text{exp}} - k_{\text{fit}})/k_{\text{fit}}$ is found to be $\approx 1\%$. It is this fitted surface for the thermal link that was used in the data analysis presented in the following chapter.

4.5.3 Specific Heat

Finally, an important last part of this chapter is the discussion of the parameters chosen for the AC specific heat measurements presented in this work. As discussed in Sect. 3.2.1 the most important parameter is the choice of excitation frequency. It is unusual in that it is of the order of several tens of mHz contrary to a more common value of above 100 Hz. This extremely low frequency is a consequence of the experiment being optimised for the magnetocaloric sweeps.

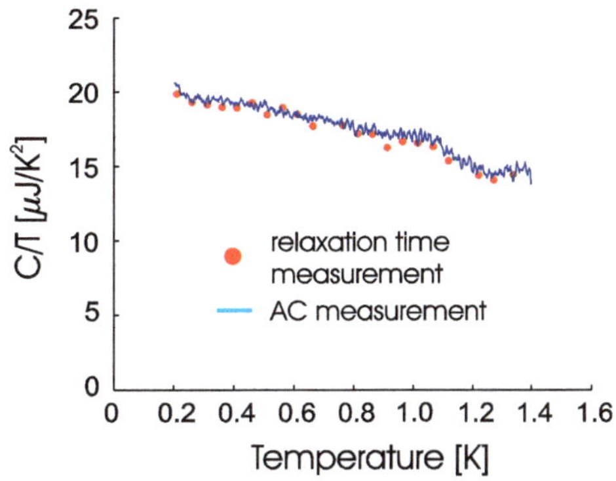

Fig. 4.22 Here the heat capacity C of sample C698J and addenda divided by temperature T as a function of T is plotted. The magnetic field at the sample is 8 T. In *red* the results of the relaxation time method are given whereas in blue the results of the AC specific heat method are shown

The frequency dependence of the AC specific heat measurement has been carried out at several temperatures and magnetic fields in the area of interest of the phase diagram. Overall the optimal frequency for the experimental conditions has been found to be 35 mHz. For this value the variation of the correction factor over the phase diagram is of the order of 1%.

Without wanting to discuss the physical meaning here, I show in Fig. 4.22 the temperature dependence of the heat capacity C of sample C698J and addenda divided by temperature T as measured by the relaxation time method (red) and AC technique (blue) with the above mentioned excitation frequency of 35 mHz. The magnetic field applied to the sample is 8 T.

At the position of the relaxation time measurement points the AC method is found to overestimate the specific heat on average by a factor of 1.01(1). Since this is consistent with 1 and an error of 1% is at the limit of achievable accuracy in this experiment, it was decided not to apply a correction factor to the AC specific heat results.

References

1. Pobell F (1992) Matter and methods at low temperatures, pp 105–137. Springer, Heidelberg
2. Lounasmaa OV (1974) Experimental principles and methods below 1K. Academic Press, London
3. Pobell F (1992) Matter and methods at low temperatures, pp 44–48. Springer, Heidelberg
4. du Chatenier FJ, Miedema AR (1965) Heat capacity below 1 K: observation of the linear term and the HFS contribution in some dilute alloys. In: Proceedings of the 9th international conference on low temperature physics, p 1029
5. Schink HJ, Löhneysen Hv (1981) Specific-heat of Apiezon-N grease at very low-temperatures. Cryogenics 21(10):591–592
6. Siqueira ML, Rapp RE (1991) Specific heat of an epoxi resin below 1 K. Rev Sci Instrum 62(10):2499–2500
7. Pobell F (1992) Matter and methods at low temperatures, pp 40. Springer, Heidelberg
8. Volokitin YE, Thiel RC, de Jongh LJ (1994) Heat capacity of thick film resistor thermometers and pure RuO_2 at low temperatures. Cryogenics 34:771

9. Ho JC, O'Neal HR, Phillips NE (1963) Low temperature heat capacities of Constantan and Manganin. Rev Sci Instrum 34:782
10. Ventura G, Barucci M, Gottardi E, Peroni I (2000) Low temperature thermal conductivity of Kevlar. Cryogenics 40(7):489–491
11. Peroni I, Gottardi E, Peruzzi A, Ponti G, Ventura G (1999) Thermal conductivity of Manganin below 1 K. Nuclear Physics B-Proceedings Supplements 78:573–575, 6th international conference on advanced technology and particle physics, Villa Olmo, Italy, OCT 05–09, 1998
12. Davey G, Mendelssohn K, Sharma JKN (1965) In: Proceedings of the ninth international conference on low temperature physics, p 1196
13. Goodrich RG, Hall D, Palm E, Murphy T (1998) Magnetoresistance below 1 K and temperature cycling of ruthenium oxide-bismuth ruthenate cryogenic thermometers. Cryogenics 38(2):221–225
14. Mackenzie AP, Haselwimmer RKW, Tyler AW, Lonzarich GG, Mori Y, Nishizaki S, Maeno Y (1998) Extremely strong dependence of superconductivity on disorder in Sr_2RuO_4. Phys Rev Lett 80(1):161–164
15. Mackenzie AP, Ikeda S, Maeno Y, Fujita T, Julian SR, Lonzarich GG (1998) Fermi surface topography of Sr_2RuO_4. J Phys Soc Jpn 67(2):385–388
16. Nishizaki S, Maeno Y, Mao ZQ (2000) Changes in the superconducting state of Sr_2RuO_4 under magnetic fields probed by specific heat. J Phys Soc Jpn 69(2):572–578
17. Mackenzie AP, Julian SR, Diver AJ, McMullan GJ, Ray MP, Lonzarich GG, Maeno Y, Nishizaki S, Fujita T (1996) Quantum oscillations in the layered perovskite superconductor Sr_2RuO_4. Phys Rev Lett 76(20):3786–3789
18. Kikugawa N, Mackenzie AP. Private communication
19. Mercure J-F (2008) The de Haas-van Alphen effect near a quantum critical end point in $Sr_3Ru_2O_7$. Ph.D. thesis. September

Chapter 5
Experimental Results and Discussion

The aim of this study is to investigate the entropy of $Sr_3Ru_2O_7$ in the vicinity of the proposed quantum critical end point. Of particular interest are the entropic properties of the material in relation to the phase formation of the anomalous 'electron nematic' [1]. The phase diagram as established before this project was discussed in detail in Sect. 2.2.2. The most important aspects are summarized in the following, in order to be able to put the detailed results presented here in context with the wider phase diagram. For this purpose Fig. 2.15 from Chap. 2 is reproduced below. For more details please refer to Sect. 2.2.2.

In Fig. 5.1a [2] the two first order metamagnetic sheets (green) are shown as a function of temperature, magnitude and direction of the applied magnetic field. The data were obtained from analysis of the out of phase component of the AC magnetic susceptibility. The lines of critical endpoints of these first order sheets are marked in black. Furthermore, the regions enclosed in the blue domes represent the volumes of phase space in which a 'nematic-like' signature has been observed in the resistivity. The main part of this chapter is concerned with the entropy as a function of temperature with a magnetic field applied parallel to the *c*-axis. In the diagram presented in Fig. 5.1a, this corresponds to an angle of 90°. In Appendix B results will be presented of an initial magnetocaloric study with the magnetic field applied at an angle of approximately 70° as well as with the magnetic field perpendicular to the *c*-axis.

In Fig. 5.1b a more detailed view of previous results for the magnetic field parallel to the crystallographic *c*-axis is given. Here the phase boundaries of the anomalous 'nematic' region as seen by magnetisation, AC magnetic susceptibilities and thermal expansion are shown [3, 4]. In particular the first order phase transition lines identified by the out of phase component of the AC magnetic susceptibility are indicated in green. Along the blue line anomalies in thermodynamic and transport measurements were observed. These were suggestive of a second order phase transition, but no proof of that exists in the literature. This line of anomalies will be referred to in the following as the 'roof' feature. Furthermore,

A. W. Rost, *Magnetothermal Properties near Quantum Criticality in the Itinerant Metamagnet $Sr_3Ru_2O_7$*, Springer Theses, DOI: 10.1007/978-3-642-14524-7_5,

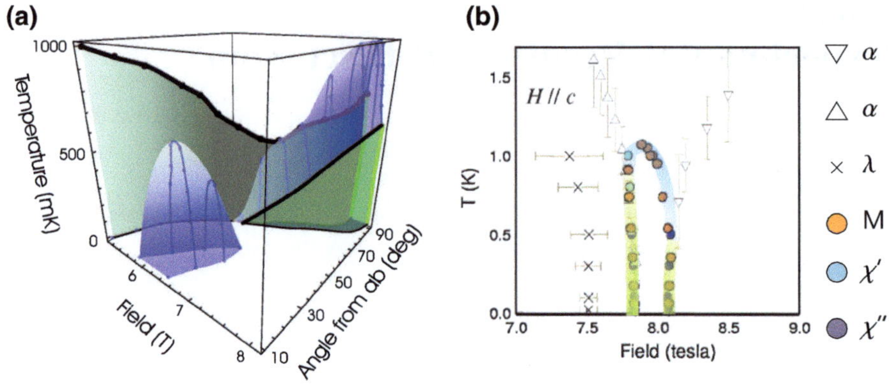

Fig. 5.1 This figure is a reproduction of Fig. 2.15 in Sect. 2.2.2. **a** The *green* surfaces give the position of the metamagnetic first order sheets in the phase diagram of $Sr_3Ru_2O_7$ as a function of temperature, magnitude of magnetic field and its direction as a function of angle from the crystallographic *ab* plane [2]. In *black* the line of critical endpoints is shown. In the regions under the *blue surfaces* 'electron nematic' behaviour has been observed [1]. **b** The phase diagram of $Sr_3Ru_2O_7$ as a function of temperature and magnetic field with the field applied parallel to the *c*-axis is shown. In particular the position of the phase transition lines (*green*) and thermodynamic anomalies (*blue*) enclosing the anomalous phase as seen by magnetisation M and AC magnetic susceptibility χ are presented. Furthermore, the position of thermodynamic crossovers as measured by linear magnetostriction λ and thermal expansion α are given [3, 4]

the positions of thermodynamic crossovers are indicated in the phase diagram (white triangles and crosses) based on magnetostriction, thermal expansion and AC susceptibility measurements.

5.1 Caloric Studies of Magnetic Phase Transitions in $Sr_3Ru_2O_7$

In this section I present the results of caloric studies of the magnetic phase transitions observed in $Sr_3Ru_2O_7$ with the magnetic field applied parallel to the crystallographic *c*-axis.

5.1.1 Evolution of Entropy across Phase Transitions as a Function of Field

5.1.1.1 Magnetic Field Sweeps at 250 mK

In order to investigate the entropy in the important temperature-field region of the phase diagram of $Sr_3Ru_2O_7$, both specific heat and magnetocaloric measurements were performed. In Fig. 5.2a, the result of a single AC specific heat measurement

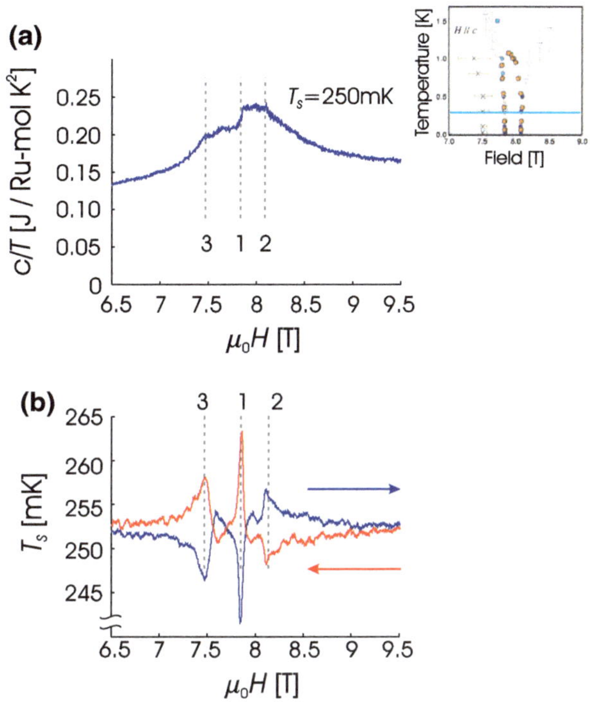

Fig. 5.2 **a** An isothermal sweep of the specific heat *c* divided by temperature *T* as a function of magnetic field *H*. The temperature of the sample is $T_S = 250$ mK. Further labelled are the positions of the two first order transitions (*1*) and (*2*) as well as the metamagnetic crossover (*3*). In the *inset* the position of the sweep measurement in the phase diagram is shown in *blue*. **b** The temperature of the sample during a sweep of the magnetic field at a rate of 0.02 T/min (*blue*) and –0.02 T/min (*red*) as a function of magnetic field. (*1*), (*2*) and (*3*) again mark the position of the first order transition lines and the metamagnetic crossover, respectively

as a function of magnetic field is shown for a sample temperature of $T_S = 250$ mK.[1] Here one can clearly identify the two features (1) and (2) expected to be first order phase transitions as well as the low field crossover (3) as points of abrupt changes in the field dependence of the specific heat *c* (the details of which will be discussed later on). Transition (1) in particular shows a clear sharp rise in *c* within the intrinsic width of the transition of the order of 50 mT. This transition width is consistent with other experiments such as, for example, magnetic susceptibility [3] and is most probably due to impurity effects. However, it is not possible to infer anything about the change of entropy, i.e. latent heat, associated with these transitions from the specific heat measurement.

In order to investigate the transitions further, magnetocaloric measurements were performed. Figure 5.2b shows the temperature of the sample as a function of magnetic field while sweeping the same field at a rate of 0.02 T/min (blue) and −0.02 T/min (red).[2] The temperature change of the sample during an up and down

[1] The measurement was performed with a temperature modulation at a frequency of 70 mHz and an oscillation amplitude not exceeding ±3% of the sample temperature. The sweep rate was 0.01 T/min in order to keep the temperature variation due to the magnetocaloric effect to below ±1.5%. The data were analysed as discussed in Sects. 3.2.1 and 4.4.2.

[2] The magnetic fields for all magnetocaloric measurements have been corrected for a known hysteresis in the field sweep of ±15 mT.

sweep is symmetric about an average temperature of approximately 250 mK, as expected for the magnetocaloric effect in the strongly non-adiabatic limit (see Sect. 3.2.2).

Following the blue curve from low fields one can clearly identify the two transitions (1) and (2) as well as the metamagnetic crossover feature (3) at lower field. At transition (1), upon entering the anomalous phase from lower fields, an abrupt cooling of the sample to below the average temperature is observed. Equally, one can see that the sample temperature increases above the average temperature at transition (2). From this it is already possible to conclude that the sample has an increased entropy inside the phase compared to the surrounding normal states. The quantitative analysis will be given further on.

This result is in particular remarkable for transition (1) since here the magnetisation of the sample is increasing with increasing magnetic field. Intuitively an increase in magnetisation is associated with magnetic order, i.e. a lowering of the entropy. This suggests a significant change in the internal degrees of freedom when entering the anomalous 'nematic' phase region.

5.1.1.2 Clausius–Clapeyron Relation

Counterintuitive as the result may seem, it is consistent with the well known Clausius–Clapeyron relation. As discussed in Sect. 3.1.2, this law relates the curvature of the phase transition line in the $H - T$ diagram, i.e. $\mathrm{d}H_C/\mathrm{d}T_C$ where H_C is the transition field and T_C is the transition temperature, with the change in entropy ΔS and magnetisation ΔM across the transition:

$$\frac{\mathrm{d}H_C}{\mathrm{d}T_C} = -\frac{\Delta S}{\Delta M}. \tag{5.1}$$

Magnetisation measurements have shown that M increases monotonically with magnetic field (see for example Fig. 2.13 in Sect 2.2.2). Furthermore $\mathrm{d}H_C/\mathrm{d}T_C$ is negative/positive for the first order transition (1)/(2). A sign analysis of the Clausius–Clapeyron relation would therefore qualitatively predict an increase of the entropy ΔS across transition (1), which is in agreement with the measurements presented. Similarly, it holds that across the second first order transition (2) a decrease of the entropy would be predicted due to the difference in curvature of $\mathrm{d}H_C/\mathrm{d}T_C$, again in qualitative agreement with the temperature change of the sample at the transition during a field sweep.

An important aspect of the Clausius–Clapeyron relation is its dependence on only two underlying assumptions, namely that it relates to (i) first order phase transitions between (ii) two thermal equilibrium phases (see Sect. 3.1.2). A quantitative agreement of the data with this relation is therefore a necessary condition to show that the observed transitions are true equilibrium transitions. In order to verify this it is necessary to calculate the change of entropy $S(H) - S(H_0)$ as a function of magnetic field H relative to a reference field H_0 from the magnetocaloric sweeps and specific heat measurements.

As shown in Sect. 3.2.2, this is given by

$$S(H) - S(H_0) = -\int_{H_0}^{H} \mathrm{d}H \left\{ \frac{k}{T_S} \frac{T_S - T_{\mathrm{bath}}}{\dot{H}} + \frac{C(T_S, H)}{T_S} \frac{\mathrm{dT_S}}{\mathrm{d}H} \right\}. \tag{5.2}$$

Here k is the thermal conductivity of the heat link between the sample platform and the copper ring, as discussed in Sect. 4.2. T_S is the measured sample temperature during a sweep, T_{bath} is the temperature of the copper ring as measured, C is the heat capacity of the setup (including addenda) and $\dot{H}$ the sweep rate.

Therefore, in order to establish the entropy jump along the phase transition line, one has to first carry out the magnetocaloric sweep over a range of temperatures and secondly to know the heat capacity C of the setup over the important range of the phase diagram. Figure 5.3a shows the temperature change of the sample as a function of magnetic field for a range of thermal bath temperatures. All curves have the same scale as shown but were offset from each other for clarity of presentation. The offset is in proportion to their temperature difference. Figure 5.3b shows the heat capacity of the setup divided by temperature as a function of magnetic field. The curves again are offset for clarity but have the same scale. The data are dominated by the heat capacity of the sample with a small contribution from the addenda. These measurements were used to create an interpolation surface in order to be able to approximate the heat capacity of the setup over the whole temperature-field regime.

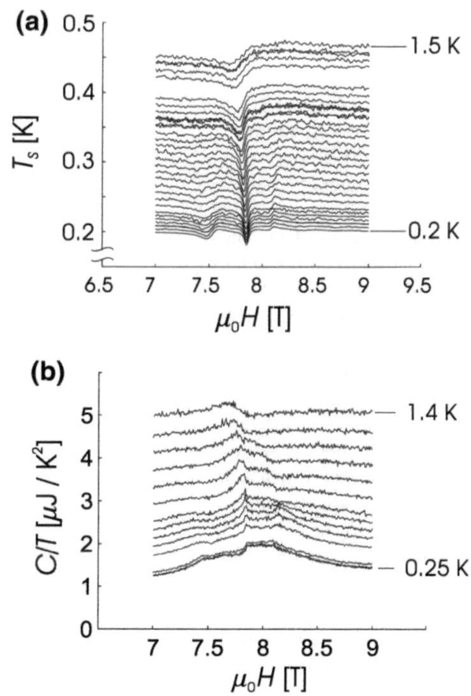

Fig. 5.3 **a** The temperature of the sample T_S during the sweeping of the magnetic field is shown as a function of magnetic field H. The temperature scale corresponds to the lowest trace at 200 mK whereas all other traces are offset in proportion to the difference of the thermal bath temperature during the sweep. **b** The AC heat capacity C of the setup including a small addenda contribution divided by temperature T as a function of magnetic field H for several sample temperatures. The specific heat scale corresponds to the lowest temperature trace of 0.25 K. All other traces have the same scale but are offset in proportion to their temperature difference for clarity

Based on these measurements and using equation 5.2 one can calculate the field derivative of the entropy dS/dH, and from there, the relative change of the entropy ΔS with respect to a reference field $S(H_0)$, i.e. $\Delta S(H) = S(H) - S(H_0)$. Furthermore, since in Sect. 4.4.2 it was established that the entropy change of the addenda as a function of field is negligible in the temperature-field regime studied here, it follows that the calculated entropy changes are those of the sample.

The resulting field derivatives of the entropy as a function of magnetic field are shown in Fig. 5.4a. The curves have been offset for clarity (please note the inverted offset direction compared to previous graphs). These curves look very similar in appearance to the magnetocaloric sweeps themselves. The reason for this is that the integrand in (5.2) is dominated by the first term which is proportional to the temperature deviation of the sample from the thermal bath. The maxima and minima in these curves at the transition correspond to the fastest changes in entropy. These extrema can therefore be used to extract the position of the phase transitions in the $H - T$ plane.

In Fig. 5.4b the resulting changes in entropy with respect to 4 T, $\Delta S = S(H) - S(4\text{T})$, divided by temperature T are shown as a function of magnetic field. The transitions (1) and (2) are clearly identifiable as sharp features in the entropy. The metamagnetic crossover (3) on the other hand is a relatively smooth feature in the entropy. In particular for transition (1) the jump in entropy is clearly visible and it will be this transition that is analysed in more detail in the following discussion.

Figure 5.5a shows the entropy as a function of magnetic field around transition (1) for $T = 450$ mK (blue curve). In red are shown a third order polynomial fit to

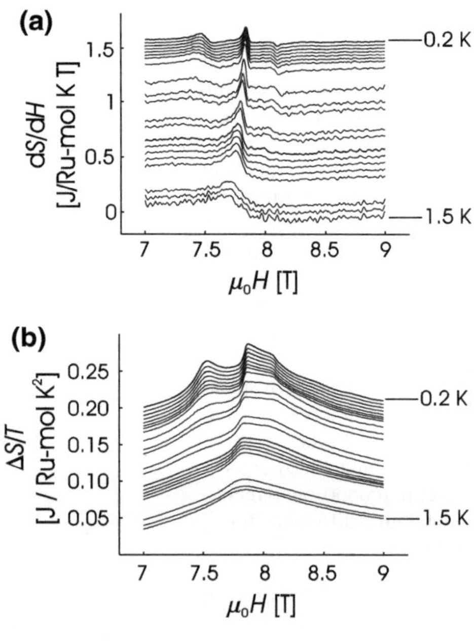

Fig. 5.4 In **a** the derivative of entropy S with respect to magnetic field H is given as a function of magnetic field. The curves are reconstructed from the previous data. The scale on the left corresponds to the highest temperature trace at 1.5 K. The other traces have the same scale but are offset in proportion to their difference in sample temperature for clarity. In **b** the change in entropy S divided by sample temperature T is shown as a function of magnetic field H. The entropy scale corresponds to the trace at 1.5 K. All other traces have the same scale but are offset in proportion of the difference in sample temperature as before

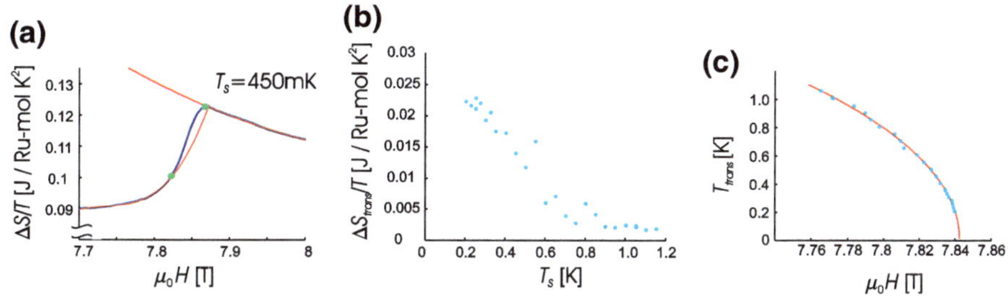

Fig. 5.5 **a** shows the entropy change ΔS divided by temperature T as a function of magnetic field H (*blue curve*) across the main first order metamagnetic transition marked as (1) in Fig. 5.2. The sample temperature is $T_S = 450$ mK. In *red* are shown polynomial fits to the entropy of the thermodynamic phases below and above the transition. The *green points* are marking the range over which the transition occurs determined by a deviation of the entropy from the polynomial fits as described in the text. The difference in entropy between these two points is giving ΔS_{trans}. This quantity divided by temperature is shown in **b** for a range of sample temperatures T_S. Furthermore in **c** the position of the first order transition in the $H - T$ diagram is shown (*blue*) together with a power law fit (*red*) through the data as explained in the text

the low field entropy and second order polynomial fit to the high field entropy. The magnetic field range for the phase transition is determined by the points where the entropy starts deviating from the polynomials significantly. The cut-off value here has been chosen to be a deviation above 0.4 mJ/Ru-mol K^2 which is approximately three times the standard deviation of the data from the polynomial fit. These points of deviation are marked in green in the plot. The difference in entropy between them is taken as the jump in entropy across the transition, whereas the difference in magnetic field as the width of the transition at this temperature. Figure 5.5b shows the entropy jump divided by temperature as determined by the above procedure as a function of bath temperature. As one can see, the entropy jump decreases continuously from its maximum value of 22.5 mJ/Ru-mol K^2 at low temperatures to zero at around 800 mK. This is consistent with previous measurements that traced the out-of-phase component in the AC magnetic susceptibility as an indication of a first order transition to around the same temperature [3]. The remaining 'jump' in entropy at temperatures above 0.9 K is an artefact of the still rapid change in entropy in combination with the 'blind' application of the procedure described above to extract the jump.

In order to compare this jump in entropy to the jump one would expect from the change in magnetisation across the transition according to the Clausius–Clapeyron equation one needs the quantity $\mathrm{d}H_C/\mathrm{d}T_C$, i.e. how the critical field of the transition changes as a function of temperature. For this the midpoint of the transition is extracted from the data as the point of fastest change in entropy as a function of field. The result of this is shown in blue in Fig. 5.5c. Furthermore, in red a power law fit of the form

$$H_C = aT_C^b + c \tag{5.3}$$

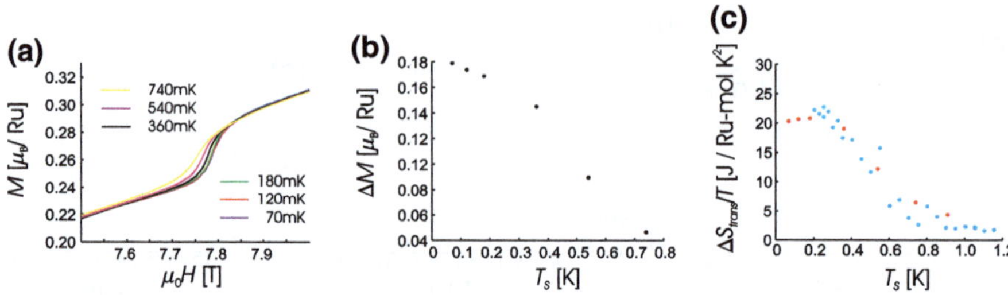

Fig. 5.6 **a** The magnetisation M of $Sr_3Ru_2O_7$ as a function of magnetic field H across the main metamagnetic first order transition for several temperatures as indicated by the colour scheme. The data has kindly been provided by R.S. Perry. **b** The extracted jump in magnetisation ΔM across the transition for the sample temperatures T_S (see details given in text). Finally **c** is giving in *red* the entropy jump $\Delta S_{\mathrm{trans}}$ across the first order transition divided by sample temperature T as calculated by the Clausius–Clapeyron equation from the magnetisation jump ΔM shown in the previous figure. In *blue* is given for comparison the entropy change across the transition as already shown in Fig. 5.5b

is given, with a, b and c being free parameters. The fit results in $a = -0.069(2)$ T/K, $b = 2.1(2)$ and $c = 7.842(2)$ T. It is this fit that is used to evaluate $\mathrm{d}H_C/\mathrm{d}T_C$ at appropriate temperatures.[3]

The final quantity needed is the jump in magnetisation across the transition. Here data for the magnetisation as a function of magnetic field across the transition were kindly provided by R.S. Perry. This is shown in Fig. 5.6a. In order to be consistent with the previous analysis, the midpoint of the transition at the given temperature was first established as the point of fastest rise in magnetisation.[4] Then the change in magnetisation over a width identical to the width extracted from the entropy change at the appropriate temperatures was measured. The resulting magnetisation jumps as a function of the transition temperature are shown in Fig. 5.6b. From these and the quantity $\mathrm{d}H_C(T)/\mathrm{d}T$ it is now possible to calculate the entropy jump one would expect according to the Clausius–Clapeyron relation. These are shown in red in Fig. 5.6c. The overall agreement with the entropy jump directly measured across the transition as shown in blue is very good within the accuracy of the presented analysis.

It can therefore be said in summary that the results presented here are in good qualitative as well as quantitative agreement with the Clausius–Clapeyron relation. This not only confirms that the entropy of the anomalous phase is higher than that of the surrounding 'normal' phases, it also shows that the entropic data of the

[3] Though a power law fit over a limited region with three free parameters cannot be considered very reliable it is worth pointing out that according to the Clausius–Clapeyron relation the fact that the fit of the power b is consistent with 2 results in the entropy jump divided by temperature, i.e. $\Delta S/T$, to be proportional to the jump in magnetisation across the transition, ΔM.

[4] These were found to be approximately 50 mT lower than measured in the magnetocaloric sweeps. This is an indication that during the magnetisation measurements by R.S. Perry the magnetic field was applied at a small angle with the c-axis.

observed transitions are quantitatively in agreement with that expected from equilibrium first order thermodynamic phase transitions.

5.1.2 Specific Heat Signature of Phase Transitions

In the previous section the changes in entropy as a function of magnetic field were studied in detail primarily with the magnetocaloric effect. This allowed in particular an investigation of the two first order transition line boundaries of the anomalous phase. However, in order to investigate the 'roof' feature and in particular to discuss its thermodynamic nature a specific heat study as a function of temperature is more suitable.

In Fig. 5.7a, traces of AC specific heat measurements at four different fields are shown as a function of sample temperature T_S.[5] The position of these

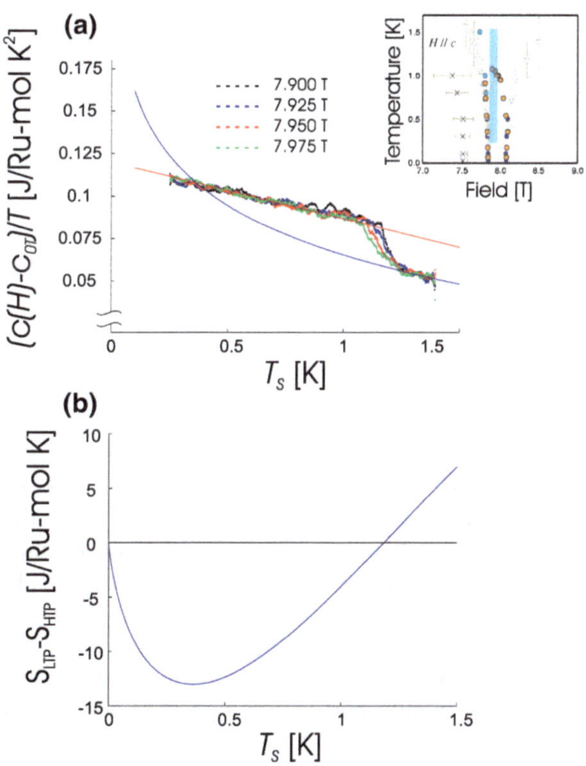

Fig. 5.7 **a** The specific heat $c(H)$ minus the specific heat at zero field $c_{0\,\mathrm{T}}$ divided by temperature T as a function of temperature for four magnetic fields. The position of these measurements in the phase diagram is indicated by the *blue line* in the *inset*. The *continuous red curve* in **a** is a linear fit to the data in the low temperature phase (LTP) and the continuous blue curve is the extrapolation of the high temperature phase (HTP) specific heat divided by temperature. **b** The difference in entropy $S_{\mathrm{LTP}} - S_{\mathrm{HTP}}$ between these two phases as a function of temperature based on the fits shown in **a**

[5] The same temperature modulation as discussed in the previous section has been employed. Furthermore the magnetic field was kept constant and the temperature of the copper ring was continuously lowered at a rate of 2.25 mK/min.

measurements in the phase diagram is indicated in the inset. To be more precise, the difference between the specific heat $c(H, T_S)$ at field H and temperature T_S and the zero field specific heat $c(0, T_S)$ divided by temperature T is plotted. Since $Sr_3Ru_2O_7$ is a Fermi liquid in zero field, this differs from $c(H, T_S)/T_S$ only by a constant offset. The continuous red and blue lines are fits to, respectively, the high temperature and low temperature specific heat data as discussed later on.

At the position of the 'roof' a sharp rise in specific heat is observed upon lowering the temperature. Furthermore, the feature disperses with field as expected, i.e. it moves to lower temperatures as the magnetic field is increased. The width in temperature for the transition at 7.9 T is approximately 75 mK. In Sect. 4.4.3 it was shown that the experimental setup is capable of resolving the superconducting transition in Sr_2RuO_4 to within 45 mK. It therefore has to be concluded that at least some of the width of 75 mK of the feature observed here is due to the properties of the sample rather than of the instrument.

Intriguingly, the specific heat divided by temperature of the anomalous phase, c/T, keeps rising approximately linearly to even lower temperatures. An important question is whether this linear rise extends to lower temperatures. Since at the observed phase transition the entropy of the high temperature phase is the same as that of the low temperature phase the following equality has to hold,

$$\int_0^{T_C} \left\{\frac{c_{\mathrm{LTP}}}{T}\right\} \mathrm{d}T = \int_0^{T_C} \left\{\frac{c_{\mathrm{HTP}}}{T}\right\} \mathrm{d}T, \tag{5.4}$$

with T_C the transition temperature, c_{LTP} the specific heat of the low temperature phase and c_{HTP} the theoretical specific heat of the high temperature state. This can be rewritten as

$$\int_0^{T_C} \left\{\frac{c_{\mathrm{LTP}} - c_{\mathrm{HTP}}}{T}\right\} \mathrm{d}T = 0. \tag{5.5}$$

This therefore gives a possibility of checking the consistency of the assumption of the mathematical form of the low temperature phase specific heat provided one knows sufficiently well the theoretical behaviour of the specific heat of the high temperature phase. As has been shown previously by Perry et al. [5], close to the critical field the specific heat divided by temperature, c/T, has a singular contribution that is logarithmically diverging to lower temperatures. For this project, PPMS measurements were repeated with a small single crystal at the exact field of 7.9 T.[6] The measurements were performed between 0.5 mK and 30 K. The singular part of the high field state between 1.2 and 5 K is found to be well described by

[6] The weight of the $Sr_3Ru_2O_7$ sample used is 2.4 mg and was cut from a piece directly adjacent to the single crystal used primarily in this work.

$$\frac{c_{\text{sing}}(T)}{T} = -a \log(T/1K), \tag{5.6}$$

with $a = -0.42(5)$ J/Ru-mol K^2. In Fig. 5.7a this singular part plus an offset for the normal Fermi liquid contribution is shown as the blue curve. The red curve furthermore is a linear fit to the specific heat of the low temperature state. One therefore has all necessary quantities to evaluate the left hand side of equation 5.5. The resulting curve is shown in Fig. 5.7b. This entropy difference curve crosses zero at approximately 1.2 K. Based on the assumptions that (a) the high temperature phase specific heat has a logarithmic singularity at zero temperature and (b) that the 'roof' feature is a true second order phase transition, one can conclude that the data are consistent with the low temperature state specific heat divided by temperature, c_{LTP}/T, to rise linearly to zero temperature.

Finally, the specific heat as function of temperature was measured for several magnetic fields close to or at the two first order boundaries of the anomalous phase. Figure 5.8a shows three traces of $(c(H, T) - c(0, T))/T$ as a function of temperature for 7.83, 7.84 and 7.8475 T. Coming from high temperatures, the anomaly upon entering the anomalous phase at 1.2 K is clearly visible [indicated by (A)]. Then towards lower temperatures, between 0.4 K and 0.7 K, the first order transition is crossed upon going out of the anomalous phase. It appears relatively wide in temperature. This is due to the combination of the intrinsic width

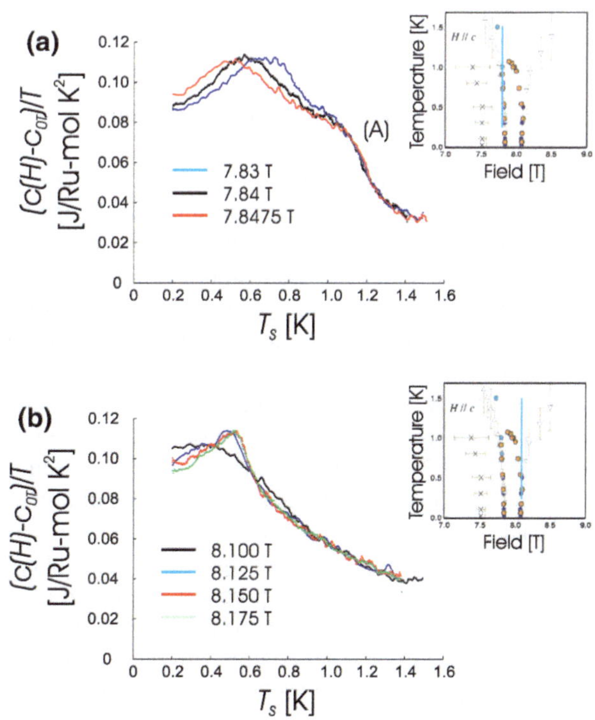

Fig. 5.8 The difference between the specific heat c at magnetic field H, $c(H)$, and the zero field specific heat $c_{0\text{ T}}$ as a function of temperature for the magnetic fields indicated in the graphs. The *insets* in **a** and **b** are indicating the position of the measurements in the phase diagram via the two blue lines. The letter (*A*) in **a** is marking the position of the 'roof' feature as discussed in the previous figure

in magnetic field of 50 mT of the transition and the steep slope of the transition line in the $H - T$ diagram.

Figure 5.8b on the other hand shows $(c(H, T) - c(0, T))/T$ for magnetic fields close to the second first-order transition. Since the slope of the transition line in the $H - T$ diagram is even steeper than for the transition previously discussed, it is not possible to resolve the features coming from the 'roof' and the transition line.

In summary, it was shown in this section that the 'roof' signature as observed by other experiments is also reflected in specific heat measurements as an anomaly, which is consistent with a second order phase transition for the magnetic field applied along the crystallographic c-axis. If one furthermore assumes that the high temperature phase specific heat has a logarithmic singularity at zero temperature, than the data are consistent with the specific heat of the anomalous low temperature phase divided by temperature, c_{LTP}/T, to be linearly increasing towards zero.

5.1.3 Discussion

In this section I have given the results of a detailed investigation of the anomalous phase and the surrounding phase transitions. In the following I will summarize the most important results and discuss their relevance and relation to other experiments.

5.1.3.1 Phase Transition Characterisation

In the first part of the chapter, I showed the results of a detailed entropy study of the proposed thermodynamic transitions in $Sr_3Ru_2O_7$ via a series of magnetocaloric experiments. In particular the features surrounding the new anomalous phase region for the magnetic field applied parallel to the c-axis were investigated. In Fig. 5.9 the results of this study are compared to the phase diagram established in previous experiments. In **a** Fig. 2.15b is reproduced. **b** on the other hand shows a colour contour plot of the derivative of the entropy S with respect to magnetic field H, $\partial S/\partial H$, divided by temperature T, in the temperature field region studied in the work presented here. The smoothed surface has been reconstructed from the data obtained in the magnetocaloric sweeps presented in this section.

Finally, in Fig. 5.9c the graphical overlay of both with no further adjustments to the data is shown. The features in the change of magnetic entropy are coincident with the previously established signatures in the phase diagram. The two first order transitions correspond to sharp positive (red end of the colour scale) and negative (blue end of the colour scale) peaks in $\partial S/\partial H$. This is consistent with the interpretation of latent heat associated with these features. However, it is also clear that these proposed first order transitions are not infinitely sharp but have a finite width

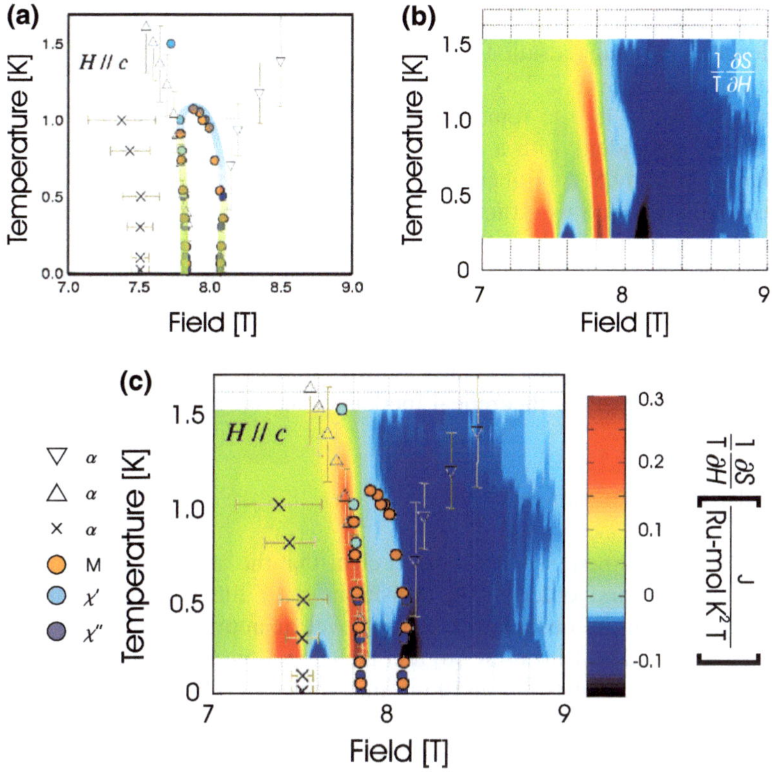

Fig. 5.9 **a** Reproduction of Fig. 2.15b showing the phase diagram of $Sr_3Ru_2O_7$ as a function of temperature and magnetic field based on previous measurements of magnetisation M, complex AC magnetic susceptibility χ, linear magnetostriction λ and thermal expansion α [3, 4]. *Green lines* represent proposed first order transitions whereas the *blue line* represents the 'roof' feature, proposed to be a second order phase transition. **b** The colour scale represents the partial derivative of entropy S with respect to magnetic field H, $\partial S/\partial H$, divided by temperature T over the same temperature-field region as **a**. Finally in **c** the two graphics are overlaid in accordance to their field and temperature axes without further adjustment to the data

of the order of 50 mT, consistent with previous data from, for example, AC magnetic susceptibility.

The signature of the 'roof' feature in the magnetocaloric data is a sudden change in the field derivative of the entropy. In particular the anomalous phase is characterised in this data by a significantly smaller magnitude of $\partial S/\partial H$ than the surrounding 'normal' states. This is equivalent to saying that the field dependence of the entropy in the anomalous phase region is weaker than in the surrounding region in phase space. According to the Maxwell relation 3.9 (see Sect. 3.1.1)

$$\left.\frac{\partial S}{\partial H}\right|_T = \left.\frac{\partial M}{\partial T}\right|_H \tag{5.7}$$

the entropy result is consistent with the previously reported reduced temperature dependence of the magnetisation M inside the anomalous phase region [3], see also inset in Fig. 2.12b, Sect. 2.2.2).

Finally, I would like to remark that the crossover feature at 7.5 T is at low temperatures coincident with a sign change in $\partial S/\partial H$, which is equivalent to a maximum in entropy S. At higher temperature the exact position of the crossover is less easily defined due to difficulties in separating background effects from the feature.

In the following, I will in detail address several questions regarding this phase diagram. First I will discuss whether the observed features bounding the anomalous phase in magnetic field are indeed first order. Secondly the nature of the 'roof' feature will be investigated. Finally, I will discuss the consequences of the observed specific heat for theoretical models concerning the novel phase.

First Order Phase Transitions

Though widely assumed, it is not a priori clear that the anomalous phase region is indeed bound by first order phase transitions as a function of magnetic field. Indeed, after the initial observation of the novel quantum phase by Grigera et al. [3], it was proposed by Binz et al. [6] that the anomalous region is a mixed state of domains of low magnetisation and high magnetisation phases in an extension of the concept of Condon domains [7]. In other words, the region would not be a thermodynamic equilibrium phase. It was shown that even in this scenario the phase would be bounded as a function of magnetic field by superlinear rises in the magnetisation. In this theoretical model the width in magnetic field of the anomalous phase region as well as the size of the magnetisation jumps depend on the demagnetization factor n of the sample and therefore ultimately on sample shape. However, previous studies did not find such a significant shape dependence making this particular theoretical proposal unlikely to be realised in $Sr_3Ru_2O_7$. Nevertheless, it highlighted the possibility of non-equilibrium phenomena in the magnetic phase diagram of $Sr_3Ru_2O_7$.

Two further characteristics of the transition features motivate a further experimental investigation. First, they are not sharp but have a finite width in magnetic field of the order of 50 mT. Small variations in this width are observable for different samples. This finite width could be caused by several effects. Most likely among them is a broadening of the transitions due to a finite impurity content in these ultra clean samples. This is supported by the observation that the phase, which has a width of approximately 0.3 T, is not observable as a well defined region in samples that have an in-plane residual resistivity that is still low (3 $\mu\Omega$ cm) but an order of magnitude higher than in the ultraclean samples studied here ($\rho_0 \leq 0.5\,\mu\Omega\,\mathrm{cm}$) [8]. This indicates that the anomalous phase and its bounding phase transitions are highly sensitive to impurities. A second possibility is a distribution of transition temperatures in the sample due to demagnetisation effects. This effect, though related to the demagnetisation factor n, is fundamentally different from the above discussed formation of Condon domains across the whole anomalous phase region.

Secondly, even though the transitions are metamagnetic in nature there is no true divergence in the AC magnetic susceptibility at the proposed critical end-points [9, 10] as one would expect in the thermodynamic limit and as has been observed in other metamagnetic materials [11]. One possible reason for this is the above discussed finite width of the transition. A second possibility is that the metamagnetic transition is not occurring at $q = 0$ but at a small but finite q. In this case the jump one observes in the $q = 0$ longitudinal magnetisation is a reflection of the finite q singularity [10]. A possibility for such a scenario is the formation of a spin-spiral state which has a transverse magnetisation component as discussed by Berridge et al. [2]. Together, the theoretical possibility of non-equilibrium phenomena and the unusual experimental observations made a further investigation of the metamagnetic features necessary.

In the work presented in this thesis I set out to investigate whether the experimentally observed change in entropy ΔS and in magnetisation ΔM across the width of the proposed first order transition features as well as the curvature of the transition line in the temperature-field phase diagram are qualitatively and quantitatively consistent with the Clausius–Clapeyron relation. As discussed in Sect. 3.1.2 the only two assumptions that have to be fulfilled in order for this relation to hold are that the observed features are (a) first order phase transitions between (b) equilibrium states of the material. If any of these two assumptions do not hold then the Clausius–Clapeyron relation does not have to be followed.

In the data presented here it is found that both transitions bounding the anomalous phase as a function of magnetic field are qualitatively consistent with this relation, i.e. that the sign of the curvature of these transition lines is consistent with the observed changes in entropy and magnetisation. A quantitative test was only possible for the first of the two transitions at 7.8 T which has a much stronger experimental signature. Here it was shown that the data are also quantitatively consistent with the Clausius–Clapeyron relation.

This result puts important constraints on theoretical proposals for the physics of $Sr_3Ru_2O_7$. First, any model assuming that the observed features are not true first order transitions between equilibrium states has to address the issue of why the Clausius–Clapeyron relation is observed to hold within experimental resolution. Secondly, if one assumes that $Sr_3Ru_2O_7$ is in thermal equilibrium across the whole phase diagram as studied in this thesis, then the direct consequence of the magnetocaloric measurements presented is that the entropy of the anomalous phase is higher between the first order transitions than that of the 'normal' states at lower and higher magnetic fields. This indicates that the novel quantum phase has additional degrees of freedom compared to the surrounding 'normal' states. In particular, it has to be pointed out, that the low field limit of the entropy jump divided by temperature, $\Delta S/T$, is of the order of 25 mJ/Ru-mol K^2, corresponding to 20% of the Sommerfeld coefficient at zero field of 110 mJ/Ru-mol K^2. Therefore, a significant part of the electronic degrees of freedom of $Sr_3Ru_2O_7$ has to be involved in the phase transition.[7] To my best knowledge, none of the proposed microscopic theoretical models for the physics of $Sr_3Ru_2O_7$ has reproduced the particular sign of the curvature of the phase transition lines and therefore the equivalent observation of a higher entropy inside the anomalous phase region as compared to the low and high field 'normal' states.

Finally, it should be remarked that the above discussion does not exclude the existence of domains in the anomalous phase. Particularly, if the domains are characterised by an order parameter that couples only weakly to the longitudinal magnetic field, it can be assumed that the effect of the existence of domains on the physics of the phase transitions does not alter their properties to first order and represents a weak perturbation. One such order parameter could for example be the transverse magnetisation. The entropy associated with domain walls can also be assumed to contribute a negligible part to the overall entropy of the system if the domains are of sufficient size. This is most likely the case in $Sr_3Ru_2O_7$ since Mercure et al. [12] were able to show that if domain walls are restricting the electron orbits at the centre of the quantum oscillation phenomena, than they should have an average separation of 0.5 μm within the plane. Each domain would therefore contain at least of the order of 10^6 unit cells.[8]

Characteristics of the 'Roof' Feature

In the discussion so far it has not been shown that the anomalous region in phase space is indeed a well defined novel quantum phase that is separated in the $H - T$ plane of the phase diagram by phase transitions from the surrounding 'normal' states. This would only be the case if the thermodynamic features at the 'roof' of the anomalous phase region are indeed due to a second order phase transition and not a crossover. I will therefore in the following discuss the extent to which the observed anomaly in specific heat is consistent with a second order phase transition.

At the observed transition at 7.9 T and 1.19(1) K the specific heat shows as a function of temperature a rapid increase of 25(5) mJ/Ru-mol K^2 over a range of approximately 75 mK. This is reasonably sharp to identify it as a thermodynamic feature. However, in Sect. 4.4.3 it was shown that the second order superconducting transition of Sr_2RuO_4 in zero field at 1.5 K can be resolved in the experimental setup under comparable conditions to within 45(5) mK. This indicates that the

[7] Another way of stating the significance of the jump of entropy ΔS is that at its maximum at around 400 mK its absolute value is of the order of 0.1% of $R\ln(2)$/Ru-mol, with R being the gas constant and the '2' a somewhat arbitrary choice representing the degrees of freedom of a high temperature system of fluctuating independent spins.

[8] The in-plane a and b lattice constant of the unit cell are approximately 0.4 nm. A domain is therefore expected to contain of the order of $(0.5\ \mu m)^2/(0.4\ nm)^2$ unit cells if one assumes that the domains are quasi-two-dimensional due to the quasi-two-dimensional character of the electronic system.

observed width of 75 mK in $Sr_3Ru_2O_7$ is due at least in part to the properties of the sample.

There are several possible causes for this. First, the intrinsic second order phase transition can be broadened by impurities. If one assumes that the energy scale of the observed broadening of the first order transitions given by $\mu_B \Delta H = \mu_B \times 50$ mT is also the energy scale of broadening in temperature, than one would expect an intrinsic width of the order of $\Delta T = \mu_B \Delta H / k_B = 33$ mK. However, this purely energetic argument assumes that there is no dispersion of the phase transition temperature as a function of magnetic field. Indeed, as has been shown in Fig. 5.7, the midpoint of the feature in specific heat moves to lower temperatures as a function of field at a rate of the order of 0.8 K/T. This implies, that the overall width of the 'roof' feature includes contributions of broadening in both temperature and field. What is meant by this is most easily seen at the two first order transitions in $Sr_3Ru_2O_7$ (see for example Fig. 5.9). Here the transition temperature changes rapidly as a function of magnetic field. This leads to very broad features in the specific heat as a function of temperature due to the finite width of the transitions in magnetic field of the order of 50 mT. In the case of the 'roof' feature this would lead to a broadening of the order of 50 mT $\times$ 0.8 K/T $=$ 40 mK. Of course, this effect and the energetic broadening of 33 mK are not expected to simply add. However, in total they should account for at least half of the observed width of the transition. A more detailed study of the transition in temperature and magnetic field is necessary for a more quantitative analysis.

The second possibility for the observed broadening relates to the physics of the novel quantum phase. If one assumes that for the magnetic field applied parallel to the crystallographic *c*-axis, the 'roof' represents a true second order phase transition, then a symmetry breaking thermodynamic order parameter will be associated with it. The transport measurements reported by Borzi et al. indicate that this symmetry can also be broken by a small magnetic field component in the crystallographic *ab*-plane. Such a component can be present in the experiment here due to a possible misalignment of the sample of the order of 1°. This situation would then be very similar to a ferromagnetic second order phase transition with a small but finite magnetic field applied to the sample. In this case, no true sharp second order phase transition is observed but a crossover from the paramagnetic to the ferromagnetic state. The width in temperature of this crossover is increasing with increasing field. In analogy, what one would expect for the 'roof' feature in $Sr_3Ru_2O_7$ in this scenario is that the second order phase transition turns into a crossover of finite width if the magnetic field is not applied perfectly parallel to the crystallographic *c*-axis. This proposed explanation for the experimental result predicts that if one increases the in-plane magnetic field component deliberately in an angular study, the width in temperature of the feature in specific will increase. This will have to be investigated in a future study.

The assumption that the observed specific heat feature is a broadened second order phase transition is also consistent with the magnetocaloric experiments presented in this thesis. They show that the field derivative of the entropy $\partial S / \partial H$ changes significantly at the 'roof' feature but no peak associated with latent heat is observed. Since entropy is a first derivative of the free energy, this is therefore an observation of an effective non-analyticity of a second order derivative of the free energy within the width of the observed feature with the first derivative being continuous over the same range. This is effectively the definition of a second order phase transition.

In summary, the above presented arguments show that even though the observed specific heat signature of the 'roof' has a small but finite width in temperature, it is nevertheless consistent with a true second order phase transition for the magnetic field applied parallel to the c-axis. The novel quantum phase in this scenario is a region in phase space that is distinct from the surrounding 'normal' states in that it is completely separated from them by first and second order phase transitions as a function of applied magnetic field in the case of the field oriented parallel to the c-axis.

Properties of the Novel Quantum Phase

The above conclusion of the 'roof' feature being a second order phase transition has the important implication that at the transition temperature the entropy of the high temperature phase is identical to that of the anomalous low temperature phase. The implication is that the integral of the specific heat of the low temperature phase from zero temperature up to the transition temperature has to be equal to the integral of the hypothetical specific heat of the high temperature phase over the same temperature region. In this section it was shown that the experimental data is consistent with this if one (a) assumes that the specific heat of the high temperature phase has a logarithmic singularity at zero temperature and that (b) the specific heat c of the low temperature phase as a function of temperature has the form

$$c = aT - bT^2 \tag{5.8}$$

with the quadratic correction b to the linear specific heat of standard Fermi liquid theory being $b = 33(1)$ mJ/Ru-mol K^3. This means that the value of the specific heat divided by temperature at 1 K is 33 mJ/Ru-mol K^2 smaller than the zero temperature Sommerfeld coefficient which is of the order of 230 mJ/Ru-mol K^2. This is on the one hand a significant deviation from standard Fermi liquid theory. On the other hand Mercure et al. [12] have conclusively proven the existence of quantum oscillations in the novel phase indicating the existence of fermionic Landau quasiparticles and the associated Fermi surface. In the following two possible explanations reconciling these experimental observation will be discussed.

First, the anomalous contribution to the specific heat could be due to non-Fermi liquid electronic degrees of freedom. Well known examples of groups of materials in which the possibility that part of the electronic system can be described by fermionic itinerant quasiparticles and others not is considered theoretically, are the normal state of the cuprate high-T_C superconductors [13] or Kondo systems in the regime in which they contain coexisting localized and itinerant electrons [14]. However, I am not currently aware of microscopic theories for $Sr_3Ru_2O_7$ predicting additional degrees that result in the particular form of the observed specific heat.

The second scenario is that the T^2 term in the specific heat has its origin in finite temperature corrections to Fermi liquid theory. One possible theory discussed by Chubukov et al. [15] describes non-analytic quantum field corrections to Fermi liquid theory. Here the authors predict that the specific heat c divided by temperature T of a two-dimensional Fermi liquid is given by

$$\frac{c}{T} = \gamma - B\left(\frac{m^*}{k_F}\right)^2 T\left(f_C^2(\pi) + 3f_S^2(\pi)\right), \tag{5.9}$$

where γ is the usual Sommerfeld coefficient and $f_C(\pi)/f_S(\pi)$ are the backward scattering amplitudes in the charge (C) and spin (S) channel. Discussing the details of the theory is beyond the scope of this thesis. The first important aspect relevant to the discussion here is that it predicts a correction to the specific heat of a two-dimensional Fermi liquid that is quadratic in temperature. It is furthermore quadratic in the effective mass. It was also shown in [15] that $f_S(\pi)$ depends crucially on the Wilson ratio, with large Wilson ratios resulting in large backward scattering amplitudes in the spin channel. $Sr_3Ru_2O_7$ is a material that first of all has a quasi-two-dimensional Fermi surface. Secondly its Fermi surfaces have relatively large effective masses m^* of the order of 10. More importantly the material has a zero field Wilson ratio R_W of the order of 10 [16]. It is therefore at least a possibility that the anomalous specific heat contribution represents a finite temperature correction to Fermi liquid theory. However, the data discussed in the next section regarding the 'normal' states surrounding the novel quantum phase show that the quadratic correction to the specific heat is only measureable in the novel quantum phase and is therefore, if existing, significantly smaller in the surrounding 'normal' states. In order to reconcile this with the theoretical model by Chubukov et al. one has to assume that the backward scattering amplitudes in the charge or spin channel, $f_C(\pi)$ or $f_S(\pi)$, are significantly enhanced in the anomalous phase compared to outside the phase, since the difference in effective mass between the phases is only of order one. This would indicate a fundamental difference in the residual interactions between the Landau Fermi liquid quasiparticles in the novel quantum phase compared to the low and high field states of $Sr_3Ru_2O_7$.

Finally it should be mentioned that several theoretical proposals for the nature of the novel phase based on microscopic properties of $Sr_3Ru_2O_7$ have been put forward. Examples are spin-spirals [2], Pomeranchuk-type instabilities of the Fermi surface [17, 3] and the formation of electronic 'nematic-like' phases [18, 19]. Though these theories in general predict the overall topology of the phase diagram and are in principle consistent with anisotropic transport by showing a change in symmetry of the Fermi surface, none of them predict the above discussed corrections to the Fermi liquid specific heat nor the curvature of the first order phase transition lines.[9]

5.2 The Low and High Field States of $Sr_3Ru_2O_7$

5.2.1 The Low Field Fermi Liquid State

In this section the results of caloric studies of the low field state will be presented. In particular the question of what happens to the entropy and specific heat upon approaching the critical region will be discussed. The second part of the section then concentrates on observed magnetocaloric oscillations in order to further investigate the Fermi liquid contribution to the entropy of the system.

5.2.1.1 Divergence in Entropy and Specific Heat

As discussed in the previous section it is possible to reconstruct the entropy change as a function of magnetic field from the measurements performed in this work. In Fig. 5.10 the entropy change ΔS relative to 5 T divided by temperature T is shown as a function of magnetic field. The traces are offset for clarity where the offset scales with the temperature difference between the traces.

The most striking feature of the entropy in the low field state is the rapid increase towards the critical region. In previous work, both experimentally [8] and

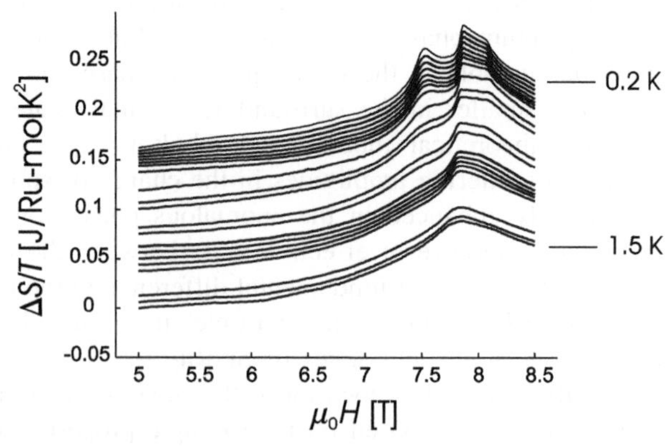

Fig. 5.10 Here the entropy change ΔS relative to 5 T divided by sample temperature T as a function of magnetic field H is shown for several temperatures between 0.2 K and 1.5 K. The entropy scale is that of the 1.5 K curve. The other data have the same scale but are offset in proportion to the difference in sample temperature

9 Though the experimentally observed 'nematic-like' resistivity properties of the anomalous novel phase are not a direct subject of this thesis it should be noted that no explicit calculation of the transport properties has been carried out to my knowledge.

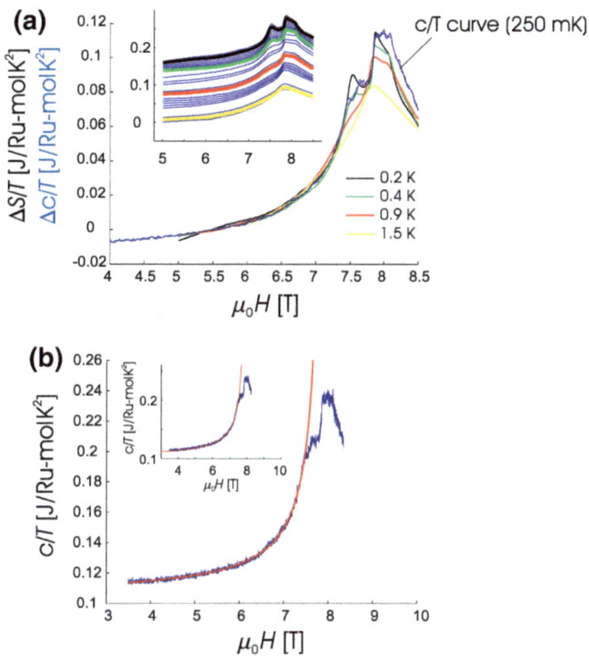

Fig. 5.11 **a** The change in entropy ΔS with respect to 5 T divided by temperature as a function of magnetic field. The sample temperature is 0.2 K (*black*), 0.4 K (*green*), 0.9 K (*red*) and 1.5 K (*yellow*). In the *inset* the previously shown graph of Fig. 5.10 is shown with the position of the *curves* highlighted in the same colours. Furthermore, overlaid in *blue* is the change relative to 5 T of the specific heat Δc divided by temperature T as a function of magnetic field. Here the sample temperature is 250 mK. N.B. both quantities, entropy and specific heat, have the same units and scale. In **b** the specific heat trace of **a** is shown together with a power law fit with an exponent of -1 (*red curve*). In the *inset* the same specific heat trace is shown. However, this time the *red curve* represents a simulation of the specific heat based on a Fermi liquid single particle density of states peak having a power law singularity with an exponent of $-1/2$. For further details see text

theoretically [20] it has been argued that upon approaching the critical region in magnetic field from the low field Fermi liquid state the quasiparticle effective masses should increase for at least part of the quasiparticle excitation spectrum. Such an increase in effective mass would cause an increase in entropy and low temperature specific heat upon approaching the critical region from the low field side as observed.

In Fig. 5.11 the field and temperature dependence is analysed in detail. Part (a) shows four traces of the change in entropy S divided by temperature T as a function of magnetic field for the temperatures 0.2 K (black), 0.4 K (green), 0.9 K (red) and 1.5 K (yellow). The inset shows these curves highlighted in the graph shown in the previous figure. Furthermore in blue is shown a measurement of the AC specific heat c divided by temperature T as a function of field for a sample temperature of 250 mK. The curve is offset such that its zero is at 5 T and therefore represents the change in c/T relative to this field.

The entropy curves are in agreement (within experimental error) between 5 and 7.2 T. It is therefore reasonable to assume that over the temperature and field range represented by these curves the entropy is consistent with a Fermi liquid state that has an increasing quasiparticle mass with increasing field. This is furthermore confirmed by the agreement of $(S(H) - S(5T))/T$ with $(c(H) - c(5T))/T$ since for a Fermi liquid at low temperature the identity $S/T = c/T = const$ holds.

Since the relative accuracy of the AC specific heat measurement is better than that of the magnetocaloric sweeps it is this curve that is used for the further analysis of the divergence in entropy.

It was found that the behaviour is best described by a power law divergence of the form

$$c/T = c_0/T + b\left[\frac{H - H_C}{H_C}\right]^d. \tag{5.10}$$

This fit (red curve) is shown together with the specific heat trace (blue curve) in Fig. 5.11b. The fit has been performed over the maximum field range from 3.5 to 7.4 T and parameters are the non-singular contribution to the specific heat $c_0/T = 106.5(5)$ mJ/Ru-mol K^2, the critical field $H_C = 7.90(5)$ T, the exponent $d = -0.98(10)$ and the prefactor $b = 5.3(1)$ mJ/Ru-mol K^2.

This result indicates that the singular part of the entropy is diverging with a power law consistent with the power -1. However, one has to be careful in the interpretation of this exponent. One scenario for example would be that the peak in entropy is caused by a peak in the single particle density of states of the band structure of $Sr_3Ru_2O_7$. In this case applying the magnetic field would split the Fermi surface into a spin-up and spin-down contribution with the spin-down surface for example being moved through the density of states peak. However, due to number conservation the distance of the chemical potential $\mu_\downarrow$ surface from the peak position e_C in the density in states, i.e. $(\mu_\downarrow - e_C)/e_C$ is not proportional to the distance in magnetic field from the critical field, i.e. $(H - H_C)/H_C$ as has been discussed in Sect. 2.1.2. Important for the discussion here is that for the particular value of -1 of the power law divergence in the underlying density of states singularity would have to diverge with a power of $-1/2$. In other words the singular part of the density of states would have to be proportional to

$$\left(\frac{\mu_\downarrow - e_C}{e_C}\right)^{-1/2}. \tag{5.11}$$

This is shown in the inset of Fig. 5.11b where in blue the measured specific heat is shown together with the calculated specific heat (in red) for an example density of states that has a singular part with an exponent of $-1/2$.

In summary, the measurements show that the low temperature specific heat is consistent with that of a Fermi liquid whose density of state is increasing as a function of magnetic field and has a singular contribution at a critical field of 7.9 T. However, it should be emphasised that it is not possible to draw any firm conclusion upon the cause of the increase in entropy towards the critical region. The observed behaviour can be interpreted within several scenarios, such as quantum criticality and an unusual density of states peak. A more detailed discussion will be given at the end of this section.

5.2.1.2 Quantum Oscillations in the Magnetocaloric Signal

One feature of a Fermi liquid is the possible observation of quantum oscillation phenomena at low temperature and high magnetic fields. As discussed with the example of Sr_2RuO_4 in Sect. 4.4.4, it is possible to observe these quantum oscillations in the magnetocaloric sweeps and gain information on the Fermi surface such as size and effective mass.

Figure 5.12a shows an example of a magnetocaloric sweep at $T_{bath} = 150$ mK. Here the blue curve is a measurement of the sample temperature while increasing the magnetic field at 0.04 T/min and the red curve while decreasing the magnetic field at −0.04 T/min.[10] The oscillatory component is out of phase by 180° as expected for quantum oscillations. An in-depth study of quantum oscillatory phenomena in $Sr_3Ru_2O_7$ has been done using the de Haas–van Alphen effect by J.-F. Mercure and co-workers [12]. In Fig. 5.12b a comparison is shown of the frequency spectrum observed in this work[11] (black curve) with a spectrum

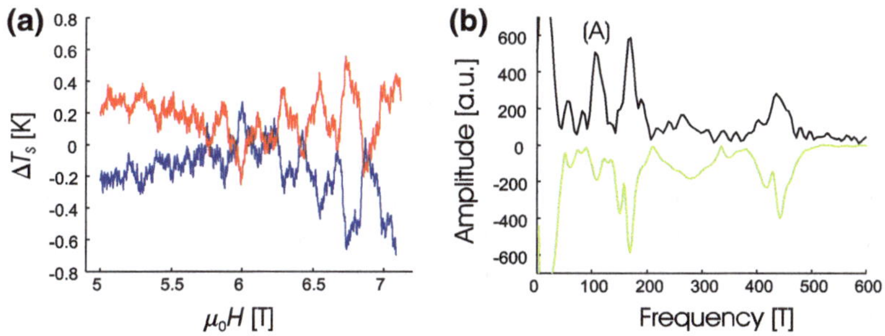

Fig. 5.12 **a** is showing the change of sample temperature ΔT_S during a sweep of the magnetic field at 0.04 T/min (*blue*) and −0.04 T/min (*red*) as a function of magnetic field *H*. The average temperature is 160 mK. **b** shows in *black* the Fourier transform in 1/*H* of the *blue trace* in **a**. In *green* is given the Fourier transform of a de Haas–van Alphen measurement over a comparable magnetic field region at base temperature. The samples used in both experiments were of similar quality. The label *A* indicates the new frequency found at 110 T

[10] All measurements on magnetocaloric oscillations presented in this work were performed on sample C698K with a mass of 23 mg. This is the same sample as used for the angular study reported later on. Quantum oscillations were observed in all samples used during the measurements.

[11] The temperature of the sample for this spectrum is 150 mK and the field range over which the Fourier transform was done is 3.6 T–7.1 T.

obtained at base temperature in the de Haas–van Alphen experiments (green curve) over a similar field range (the sign of the latter spectrum is changed for clarity). The two quantum oscillation experiments are in good agreement in their frequency spectrum. At higher frequencies the magnetocaloric oscillations are thermally damped and the de Haas–van Alphen experiment has a far better sensitivity. However, the magnetocaloric effect is in particular sensitive to oscillations at low frequencies due to a low background contribution and the above mentioned damping of higher amplitude high frequency oscillations. In fact the frequency at 110 T [labelled (A) in the graph] was first clearly observed above the noise level in the magnetocaloric measurements. The frequency was absent in a test experiment of a magnetocaloric sweep without a sample, confirming it to be part of the $Sr_3Ru_2O_7$ quantum oscillation spectrum. After an optimisation of the experimental parameters it was subsequently confirmed by de Haas–van Alphen measurements.

In order to establish the contribution to the specific heat of this part of the Fermi surface a temperature study of the oscillations was performed. This was limited by the highest temperature at which oscillations were still sufficiently observable (approximately 200 mK) and the lowest temperature achievable with the current setup (90 mK). Figure 5.13 shows the amplitude of the oscillations as a function of temperature for measurements of both increasing and decreasing magnetic field sweeps. The amplitude was obtained from a Gaussian fit to the frequency spectrum between 80 and 130 T. The red curve represents a fit of the temperature derivative of the Lifshitz-Kosevich formula for the temperature dependence of the oscillations (see Sects. 3.2.2, 4.4.4). From this fit an effective mass of $8(1)m_e$ is deduced, with m_e being the free electron mass. The result was subsequently confirmed by a detailed de Haas–van Alphen study [12]. The size of the pocket together with the effective mass makes plausible an identification of this part of the Fermi surface with the γ_2 pocket as reported by Tamai et al. in ARPES measurements (see Sect. 2.2.3). According to their measurement, this pocket occurs four times in the first Brillouin zone and is furthermore most probably bilayer split. Any contribution based on the measured effective mass has therefore to be multiplied by a factor of eight to give the total specific heat contribution of this part of the Fermi surface.

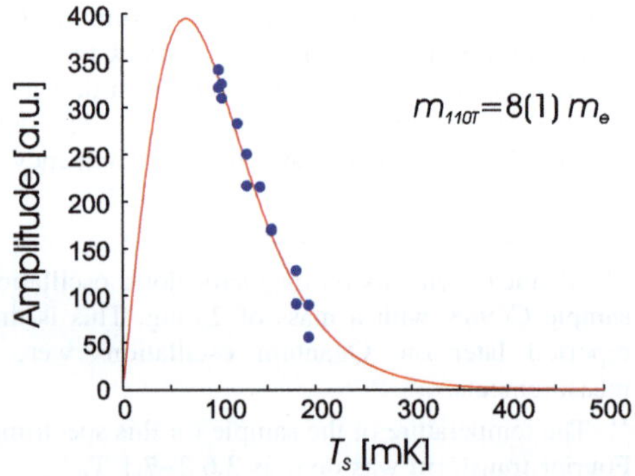

Fig. 5.13 The data in *blue* gives the amplitude of the 110 T peak in the Fourier transform of the data in **a** as a function of sample temperature T_S. In *red* is shown a fit of the temperature derivative of the Lifshitz–Kosevich function to the data. This fit gives a mass $m_{110\ \mathrm{T}}$ for the newly observed frequency of $8(1)m_e$, with m_e being the free electron mass

For a quasi-two-dimensional Fermi surface, the specific heat contribution is directly proportional to the effective mass of an orbit. Here the newly observed frequency is in total contributing 47(6) mJ/Ru-mol K^2. The other five orbits as measured by J.-F. Mercure contribute a further 56(1) mJ/Ru-mol K^2, giving a total of 103(7) mJ/Ru-mol K^2. This is very close to the measured average of 120 mJ/Ru-mol K^2 over the field range of 4–7 T as shown in Fig. 5.11b. It therefore appears that the low frequency observed in this experiment is contributing approximately 45% of the total specific heat.

In this section it was first of all shown that magnetocaloric oscillations are observable in the samples used for this project. Furthermore, this way of measuring quantum oscillations is particularly sensitive to low frequencies and revealed for the first time a clear signature of a small Fermi surface contributing a significant part to the overall specific heat.

5.2.2 The High Field Fermi Liquid State

In this section results on the entropic properties of the high field state above the critical field will be presented.

5.2.2.1 Magnetocaloric Measurements

The analysis of the data for the high field phase of $Sr_3Ru_2O_7$ above the critical phase was done analogously to the data presented in the previous section. Figure 5.14 shows the isothermal change of entropy as a function of magnetic field with respect to 5 T. The curves have been offset as previously from each other for clarity, the offset scaling with the temperature difference.

The most significant feature is, as for the low field side, the strong increase in entropy upon approaching the critical field region. Also clearly identifiable is the entropic signature of a previously reported metamagnetic crossover at approximately 12.5 T [21]. Finally, clearly observable are low temperature quantum oscillations. The combination of these features makes a detailed quantitative analysis of the divergence in entropy as in the previous section impossible. However, in the field region from 8.2 to 10 T the data are consistent with the increase in entropy being such that, for a given magnetic field, S/T can be assumed to be a constant of temperature over the phase space explored by the experiment. Therefore, the conclusion that the observations are consistent with the high field state being a Fermi liquid in this region of magnetic field follows equivalently. Above 10 T deviations assumed to be associated with feature (A) become important.

Finally, I would like to draw attention to the oscillatory component at low temperatures. These again are quantum oscillations being directly observed in the entropy of the system. The observed oscillations are discussed in more detail in the following section.

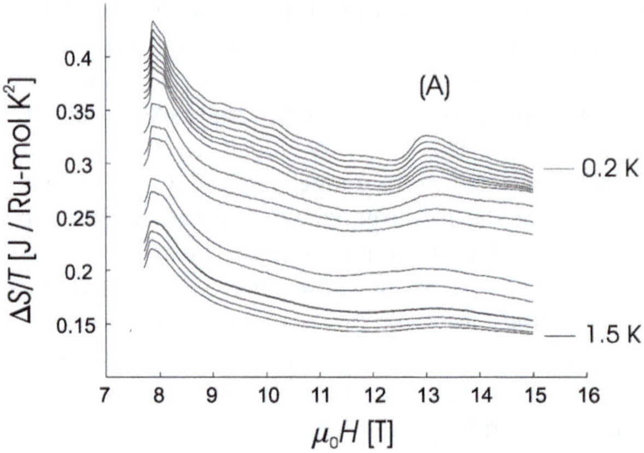

Fig. 5.14 In this figure, analogous to Fig. 5.10, the entropy change ΔS relative to 5 T divided by sample temperature T is shown as a function of magnetic field H. The curves correspond to several temperatures between 0.2 K and 1.5 K. The entropy scale is the same for all curves, which are offset in proportion to the difference in sample temperature (there is no offset for the 1.5 K curve). The label A indicates the position of a further metamagnetic crossover which has been reported previously [21]

5.2.2.2 Quantum Oscillations in the Magnetocaloric Signal

Figure 5.15a shows a trace of the sample temperature during a magnetic field sweep of 0.04 T/min (blue) and −0.04 T/min (red) with a second order polynomial background subtracted. The temperature of the thermal bath was 160 mK.

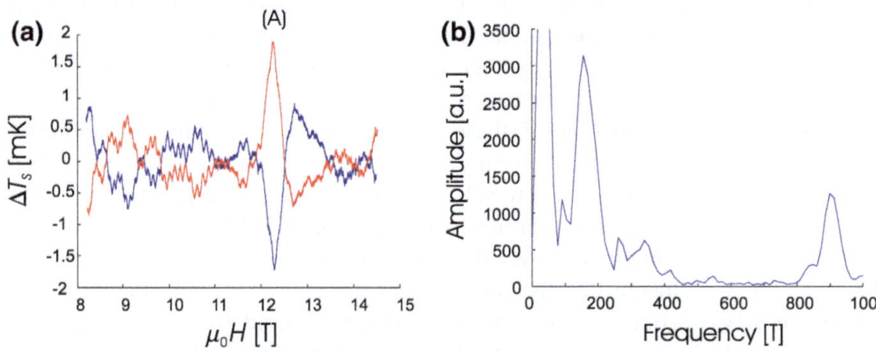

Fig. 5.15 **a** The change in temperature relative to the average temperature during a sweep of the magnetic field at a rate of 0.04 T/min (*blue*) and −0.04 T/min (*red*) on the high field side of the critical field region. The feature labelled with (A) is not part of the oscillatory signal but the magnetocaloric signature of a thermodynamic crossover. The sample average temperature is 160 mK. **b** The frequency spectrum given by the Fourier transform in inverse magnetic field $1/H$ of the *blue trace* shown in **a**

The strong feature at 12.5 T is not part of the oscillatory signal but the previously mentioned signature of a metamagnetic crossover. Figure 5.15b shows the Fourier transform of the signal for the frequency region where the experiment is most sensitive. There is significant spectral weight between 100 and 200 T. Unfortunately it is not possible to resolve if this is a combination of several frequencies or if, for example, the 110 T frequency corresponding to the γ_2 surface has vanished. A temperature analysis of the oscillations showed the measured effective masses to be consistent with the de Haas–van Alphen measurements by Mercure et al. [12].

5.2.3 Discussion

In this section results of magnetocaloric and specific heat measurements in the low and high field phases of $Sr_3Ru_2O_7$ have been presented. Figure 5.16 shows the overal results for the entropy S divided by temperature T (Fig. 5.16) and the specific heat c divided by T (Fig. 5.16) as a function of magnetic field H and temperature T, including the novel quantum phase. Both quantities, the entropy

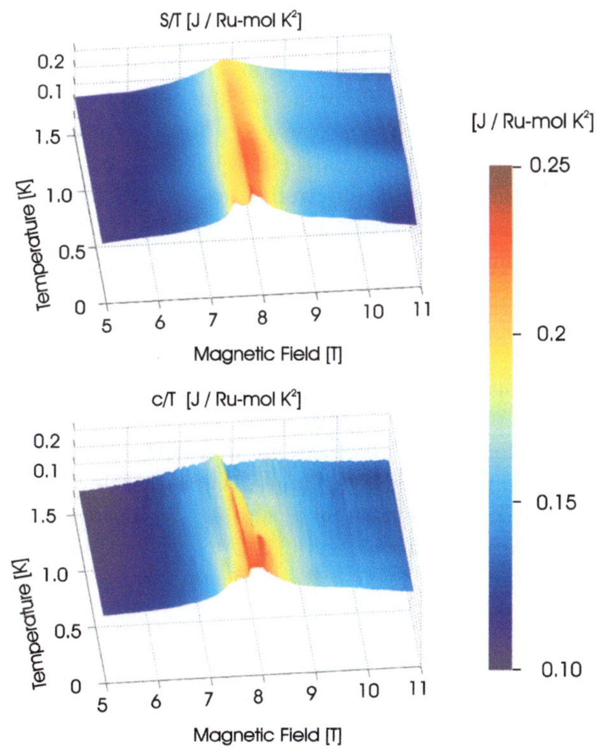

Fig. 5.16 Smoothed surfaces of the entropy S and specific heat c of $Sr_3Ru_2O_7$ divided by temperature T as a function of magnetic field and temperature. The lowest temperature shown in the data is 200 mK. The colour scale is identical for both quantities. The entropy surface is based on the assumption that $Sr_3Ru_2O_7$ has a Fermi liquid like specific heat at 5 T, justified by c/T being constant at that field as shown

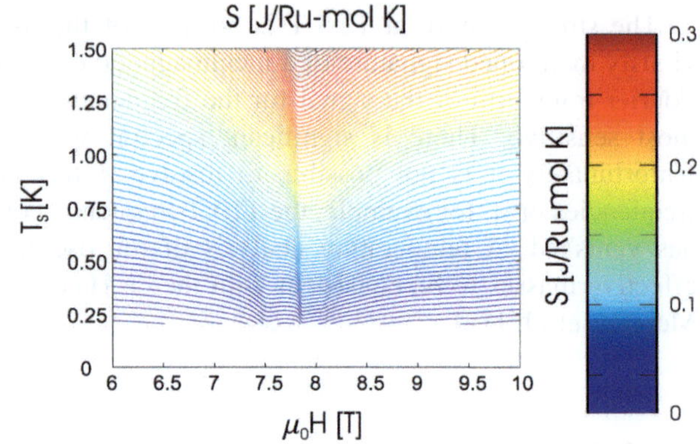

Fig. 5.17 The isoentropes of $Sr_3Ru_2O_7$ in the $H - T$ plane. The corresponding colour scheme is given on the right hand side

and the specific heat, show a pronounced peak structure centred on the critical field of 7.9 T.

By plotting both the entropy and the specific heat divided by temperature one emphasises in particular the Fermi liquid like character of the low and high field phases, since both quantities are consistent with being constant as a function of temperature in these regimes.[12]

However, it is equally informative to plot the entropy itself. This is done in Fig. 5.17 in form of equidistant isoentropes of $Sr_3Ru_2O_7$ in the $H - T$ diagram.

In principle, the isoentropic plot contains exactly the same information as the plot in Fig. 5.16. The physical meaning of these curves is that the temperature of the sample would evolve along them in a perfectly adiabatic magnetocaloric measurement. Upon approaching the critical region from the low or high field side the entropy is 'dragged' towards lower temperature, supposedly resulting in a singularity at the critical field. That this does not violate the third law of thermodynamics can be inferred from the fact that at the same time isoentropes at lower temperature have a smaller curvature than isoentropes at higher temperature, permitting $S(T = 0) = 0$ to hold for the low and high field states of $Sr_3Ru_2O_7$ at all fields.

The three thermodynamic features, i.e. the two first order transitions (1) and (2) as well as the thermodynamic crossover (3) are clearly identifiable. Both the isoentropes between the thermodynamic crossover (3) and the phase transition (1) as well as the isoentropes inside the anomalous phase have a much weaker curvature than in the the low and high field states of $Sr_3Ru_2O_7$.

From the qualitative features one is therefore tempted to assume the physics of $Sr_3Ru_2O_7$ to be driven by a possible singularity in the entropy at zero temperature with the material undergoing a series of transitions as a function of field in order to

[12] The deviations as a function of temperature in the high field state are due to systematic errors when integrating up the magnetocaloric traces as a function of magnetic field. Since this integration is done with reference to 5 T a small random error in any of the quantities can accumulate over the integration range.

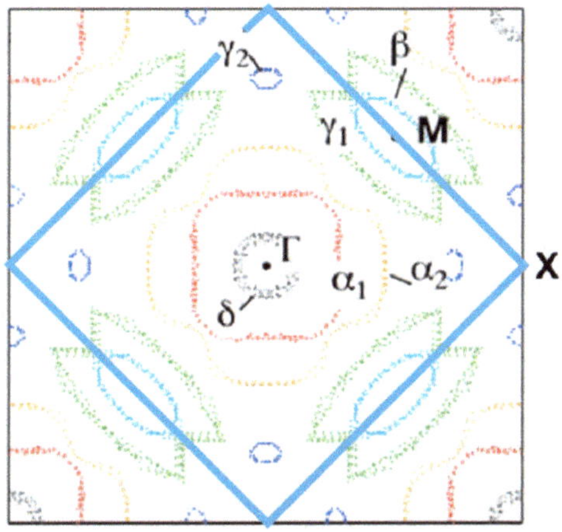

Fig. 5.18 Reproduction of Fig. 2.19c. This shows the Fermi surface of $Sr_3Ru_2O_7$ in the k_x–k_y plane as measured by ARPES [24] with the first Brillouin zone given by the blue diamond outline. M, X and Γ are points of high symmetry in the Brillouin zone. Also labelled are the Fermi surfaces as explained in the text

avoid this singularity. However, the wealth of experimental information, in particular of the zero field phase of $Sr_3Ru_2O_7$ and its evolution as a function of magnetic field, make a far more quantitative discussion possible. In the following I will therefore first analyse the extent to which the single particle density of states of the zero field Fermi liquid could explain both qualitatively and quantitatively the observed peak in entropy. In a second part I will then discuss how other phenomena which are expected to play a significant role in the material, such as for example quantum criticality, can change the properties of $Sr_3Ru_2O_7$ as a function of magnetic field.

First, I will summarise the current experimental evidence for the electronic structure of the low field state. Several authors have conclusively shown the existence of quantum oscillations in both the low field and high field state of $Sr_3Ru_2O_7$ [22, 23, 12]. The inferred existence of a Fermi surface and quasiparticle excitations has furthermore been confirmed at zero field by angular resolved photoemission spectroscopy (ARPES) [24]. In Fig. 5.18 the Fermi surface in the k_x/k_y plane as reconstructed from ARPES measurements is shown (this is the same figure as 2.19c in Sect. 2.2.3). The angular dependence of the frequencies in quantum oscillation measurements show that these Fermi surface sheets are quasi-two-dimensional in character with their primary axis being parallel to k_z. The main characteristics of the zero field Fermi surface as deduced from these measurements were presented in Table 2.1 in Sect. 2.2.3 and reproduced here in Table 5.1. This summary also includes the γ_2 pocket whose existence at the Fermi energy was first demonstrated conclusively by the study presented in this thesis.

The ARPES measurements together with local density approximation (LDA) calculations allowed for an identification of the multiplicity of each Fermi surface part in the Brillouin zone [24]. This information is given in the last two rows of Table 5.1. Here 'Symmetry' refers to the multiplicity due to the symmetry of the Brillouin zone. The γ_2 pocket for example occurs four times. Furthermore 'Bilayer Split' refers to the bilayer split of some Fermi surfaces that has to be taken into account when calculating the physical properties of the material, but, if small,

Table 5.1 The properties of the $Sr_3Ru_2O_7$ Fermi surfaces as measured by quantum oscillation and ARPES experiments [12, 24]

	α_1	α_2	β	γ_1	γ_2	δ
dHvA						
F (kT)	1.78	4.13	0.15	0.91	0.11	0.43
Area (% BZ)	13.0	30.1	1.09	6.64	0.31	3.14
m^* (m_e)	6.9 ± 0.1	10.1 ± 0.1	5.6 ± 0.3	7.7 ± 0.3	8 ± 1	8.4 ± 0.7
ARPES						
Area (% BZ)	14.1	31.5	2.6	8.0	< 1	2.1
m^* (m_e)	8.6 ± 3	18 ± 8	4.3 ± 2	9.6 ± 3	10 ± 4	8.6 ± 3
Symmetry	1	1	2	2	4	1
Bilayer split	1	1	1	2	4	2

F is the observed frequency in $1/H$ of quantum oscillations, BZ stands for Brillouin zone and m^* is the effective mass in units of electron mass m_e. This table contains the same information as Table 2.1 in Sect. 2.2.3 with the addition of the effective mass of the γ_2 pocket first conclusively measured in the work presented in this thesis

would be experimentally unresolvable by quantum oscillation measurements. Together with the γ_2 pocket the specific heat calculated from the effective masses of all Fermi surfaces assuming the above multiplicities is 103(7) mJ/Ru-mol K^2 and consistent with the experimentally measured zero field specific heat of 110 mJ/Ru-mol K^2 [5].

A very important result from the quantum oscillation measurements is the measured field dependence of the effective mass m^* of the identified frequencies. Since m^* for each quasi 2D Fermi surface is directly proportional to its contribution to the overall specific heat one would expect at least part of the Fermi surface to show a significant peak in its effective mass in the vicinity of the critical field of 7.9 T if this peak is caused by quasiparticle excitations. Mercure et al. showed that one can exclude this peak in effective mass for all of the identified frequencies except that corresponding to the γ_2 pocket, for which the analysis was not possible. In other words, these Fermi surface parts cannot explain the observed peak in the specific heat. Therefore, any explanation of the metamagnetism in $Sr_3Ru_2O_7$ based primarily on the zero field density of states has to assume that γ_2 is the Fermi surface pocket at the centre of the unusual physical effects observed.

Importantly, ARPES measurements by Tamai et al. [24] showed that the electronic band associated with the γ_2 Fermi surface pocket has a density of states peak associated with a saddle point energetically close to the Fermi energy. The authors argue that this can in principle be the cause for the observed metamagnetism by spin-splitting the Fermi surface and shifting the chemical potential for one of the spin species through the observed density of states peak.

The most important question arising from the data is therefore if the zero field band structure $Sr_3Ru_2O_7$ can both qualitatively and quantitatively account for the observed peaks in entropy and specific heat presented in this thesis. In a first scenario I will assume the hypothesis that the observed singular contribution in the entropy S divided by temperature T at the critical field of 7.9 T is indeed due to the band structure at zero field. I will discuss the available experimental data under the constraint of this assumption and point out possible inconsistencies. It has to be mentioned here that this part of the discussion is primarily based on the assumption that indeed all relevant Fermi surface parts of $Sr_3Ru_2O_7$ have been identified and their multiplicities correctly assigned. In the second part of the following discussion possible other contributions to the peak in entropy will be presented. In particular the possibilities of either a change in the single particle density of states as a function of magnetic field (as for example predicted by theories for quantum criticality in $Sr_3Ru_2O_7$) or of non-Fermi liquid degrees of freedom will be addressed.

5.2.3.1 Single Particle Density of States Peak

ARPES measurements such as those performed by Tamai et al. [24] are among the few experimental methods able to probe the density of states of a Fermi liquid not only at the Fermi surface but also as a function of energy below the Fermi energy. In Fig. 5.19 the measured density of states for the energy bands resulting in the γ_1 and γ_2 Fermi surfaces as well as the sum total are shown as a function of energy relative to the Fermi energy.[13]

The specific heat at zero field of 110 mJ/Ru-mol K^2 corresponds to 47 states/Ru eV [24]. Of these, 26 states/Ru eV are accounted for by the five Fermi surfaces α_1, α_2, β, γ_1 and δ. These five bands cross the Fermi energy ϵ_F such that the density of states does not vary significantly within several meV of ϵ_F, consistent with the observed weak changes in effective quasiparticle masses in de Haas–van Alphen measurements [12]. γ_2 on the other hand not only is close to a van Hove-singularity

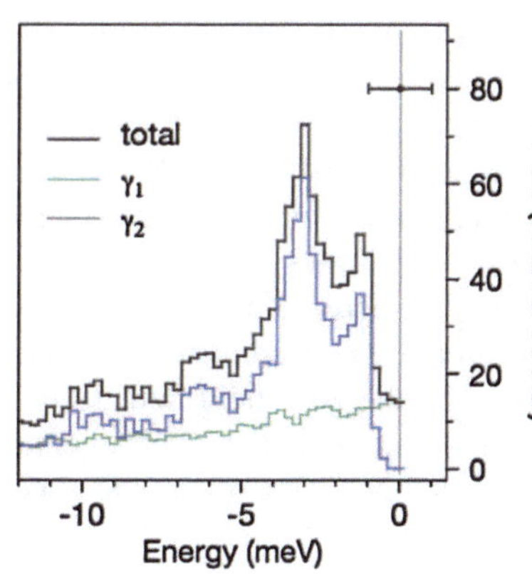

Fig. 5.19 Density of states as a function of energy of the bands associated with the γ_1 and γ_2 Fermi surface as well as the sum total. The figure differs from that in the original publication by Tamai et al. due to a corrected error that overestimated the density of states of the γ_1 associated band by a factor 2

[13] This is not the graph originally published by the authors. The data shown here is corrected for an error in the density of states for the γ_1 band which was overestimated by a factor of 2.

but also to the top of the band. Therefore, the density of states of the band associated with the γ_2 pocket varies rapidly within ± 5 meV of the Fermi energy. A combination of uncertainty in the exact position of the Fermi energy of ± 1 meV and a possible relative shift of the bands due to surface effects[14] makes it impossible to perform an accurate calculation of the exact contribution to the specific heat on the basis of the ARPES measurements alone. However, from the magnetothermal oscillations presented in this thesis it is possible to extract the expected specific heat contribution to be of the order of 47(6) mJ/Ru-mol K^2 or 22 states/Ru eV. Therefore, the Fermi energy is expected to lie at least 1–2 meV below the one shown in Fig. 5.19. Here it is important to note that it is currently not possible to study a potential effective mass divergence of the γ_2 Fermi surface as a function of magnetic field. This is due to the fact that in order to sufficiently resolve this low frequency one has to Fourier transform the oscillation signal over the whole range of available magnetic field from 4 T to 7 T. It remains to be seen if these difficulties can be overcome in future high resolution measurements in combination with advanced data analysis.

The maximum height of the density of states of the band associated with the γ_2 pocket is of the order of 60 states/Ru eV including spin degeneracy, 40 states/Ru eV above the zero field value. This implies that the maximum number of states per Ru per eV that can be gained per spin species is 20 states/Ru eV. In the most simple scenario, applying a magnetic field lifts the degeneracy in spin resulting in the spin-up band being lowered in energy while the spin-down band is raised in energy. This would lead to the spin-up band to being such that the Fermi energy can pass through the density of states peak, gaining at most of the order of 20 states/Ru eV in density of states. The spin-down band on the other hand has a density of states that in the most simple scenario will be constant to first order or drop significantly if the top of the band is reached. Therefore, the zero field density of states as measured by ARPES can at most account for an increase of 20 states/Ru eV in the density of states or 47 mJ/Ru-mol K^2 in the Sommerfeld coefficient as a function of magnetic field. The specific heat measurements presented in this thesis on the other hand show an increase in the Sommerfeld coefficient of the order of 100 mJ/Ru-mol K^2 up to a magnetic field of 7 T. Therefore, a calculation of the increase of the specific heat as a function of field based on the zero field density of states as measured by ARPES underestimates the experimentally measured increase in the specific heat by a factor of 2. This can be assumed to be a large enough discrepancy to conclude that the simple model presented so far, based on the zero field density of states of $Sr_3Ru_2O_7$ as measured by ARPES, is inconsistent with the experimental observations. There are several possibilities however how to reconcile the zero field ARPES and field dependent specific heat measurements.

[14] ARPES is not a bulk but surface probe. It is always possible that a small surface reconstruction results in small changes of the band structure at the surface relative to the bulk. This however, is assumed in first order to only shift the bands relative to each other but not actually to affect the amplitude of the single particle density of states.

First, it could be that the dominant effect of applying the magnetic field is not a splitting of the spin-up and spin-down Fermi surface but a shift of both spin-up and spin-down bands through the van Hove singularity. However, such a shift is not a direct result of a simple single particle band structure effect and would require a rigorous theoretical justification.

A further possibility is a second density of states peak just above the Fermi energy, not being measureable by ARPES. In this case the spin-down bands could also contribute to the specific heat enhancement. Indeed, scanning tunneling microscopy experiments by Iwaya et al. [25] seemed to indicate the existence of two peaks above and below the Fermi energy in the local density of states as measured by the current-voltage characteristic of the tunneling current. However, the density of states extracted in their measurements at the Fermi energy as a function of magnetic field did not show any discernable peak around 8 T but simply a monotonic increase over the measured field region. Therefore, their results are fundamentally inconsistent with the interpretation of an electronic single particle density of states peak causing the observed peak in entropy and specific heat as a function of magnetic field. It is consequently not directly obvious how the features observed by Iwaya et al. can be related to the band structure.

One further possible experiment to probe the band structure above the Fermi energy is by electron doping. In the strontium ruthenate family this can be achieved by replacing Sr atoms in the 2+ oxidation state chemically with La atoms that are in the 3+ oxidation state. This was successfully achieved by Kikugawa et al. in the case of Sr_2RuO_4 [26]. In this study a series of $Sr_{2-y}La_yRuO_4$ samples were prepared and the authors succesfully showed that the effect of La doping is filling the original band structure of Sr_2RuO_4 with electrons, in a so-called ‘rigid

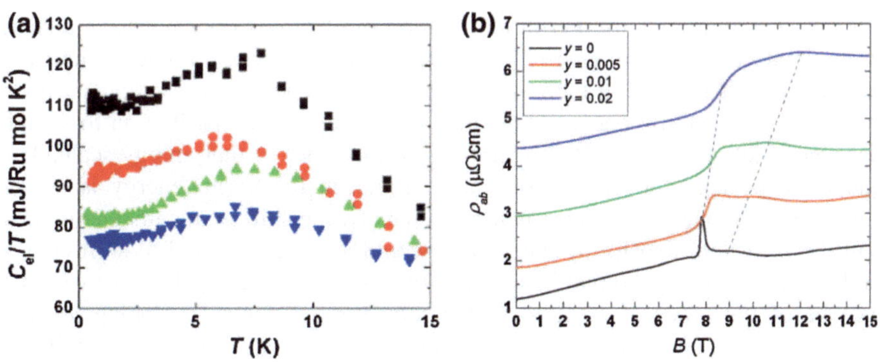

Fig. 5.20 Figures reproduced from Farrell et al. [27]. In the *left panel* the electronic specific heat C_{el} divided by temperature T as a function of T is given for different doping levels of La in $Sr_3Ru_2O_7$ as detailed in the *inset* in **b**. In the *right panel* the in-plane magnetoresistance ρ_{ab} as a function of magnetic field is given for the same doping levels. The field is applied along the crystallographic c-axis. The *broken lines* represent the trend of the metamagnetic features with doping

band shift' of the Fermi level. A similar study for $Sr_3Ru_2O_7$ has been performed by Farrell et al. [27].

In Fig. 5.20 the most important results are presented. First, as is shown in (a), with small amounts of doping the zero field Sommerfeld coefficient rapidly falls from 110 mJ/Ru-mol K^2 with no doping to 78 mJ/Ru-mol K^2 at $y = 0.02$. Furthermore, one observes that with increased doping the metamagnetic features shift to higher fields as is shown in Fig. 5.20b. Here the in plane resistivity ρ_{ab} is shown as a function of magnetic field for several doping levels as indicated in the inset. The broken lines indicate the trend for the features associated with the metamagnetic transitions to shift to higher fields with higher doping. The broadening in these features is ascribed to impurity scattering. In the scenario discussed here it is assumed that La doping is simply adding electrons to the band structure and thereby shifting the Fermi energy through the single particle density of states, as it does in the case of Sr_2RuO_4. Therefore, from the first observation of the sharp drop in the Sommerfeld coefficient one would conclude that the Fermi energy ϵ_F is very close to sharp drop in the density of states above ϵ_F. This is qualitatively consistent with the observation in ARPES that the Fermi energy is close to the top of the band associated with the γ_2 pocket. From the second result, the shift of the metamagnetic features to higher magnetic fields with higher doping, one would conclude that the dominant feature in the single particle density of states causing the metamagnetic transitions is situated below the Fermi energy, again consistent with the ARPES data as discussed before. This does not exclude a further density of states peak above the Fermi energy since it only indicates that the dominant feature is below the Fermi energy.

However, the data also include features that contradict a simple interpretation of the doping study. The most significant is a pronounced peak in the zero field specific heat at 8 K as shown in Fig. 5.20a. In a simple band structure model this peak is associated with the density of states peak in the band structure as follows. At finite temperature T the Fermi distribution of electrons does not have a sharp discontinuity at the Fermi energy but changes smoothly over a range in energy of the order k_BT. Therefore, if there is a density of states peak at an energy $\Delta\epsilon_F$ away from the Fermi energy one would expect the Fermi–Dirac distribution to sample that density of states peak at temperatures of the order of that energy scale. This leads to a peak in the density of states. If indeed the Fermi energy is moved significantly through the band structure, as seen by the shift in metamagnetic field, than the zero field density of states peak would also be expected to shift consistently. In [27] it is argued that in a simple band structure picture this shift would at least be of the order of 10 K to higher temperatures for a La doping level of $y = 0.06$. This, however, is not consistent with the data shown in Fig. 5.20a. It follows that the simultaneously observed shift of the metamagnetic critical field and the unchanged position in temperature of the zero field specific heat peak as a function of La doping are seemingly contradictory features if interpreted within the assumption of a simple shift of the Fermi energy through a rigid single particle density of states. This issue will have to be addressed by further detailed studies of these samples by, for example, ARPES.

Finally, the observed functional form of the peak in the low temperature specific heat c of $Sr_3Ru_2O_7$ has to be discussed. As has been shown in Fig. 5.11b the increase in specific heat c in the low field state is consistent with a singular contribution to c, which is proportional to

$$(H - H_C)^{-1}. \tag{5.12}$$

As discussed previously this implies that if the peak in specific heat is dominated by a peak in the density of states $g(\epsilon)$ of the band structure at a critical energy ϵ_C, then the singular contribution to $g(\epsilon)$ is proportional to

$$(\epsilon - \epsilon_C)^{-1/2}. \tag{5.13}$$

In a three dimensional band structure no true divergence of the density of states is possible. However, in two dimensions logarithmic divergences at saddle points are possible. Therefore, if the band structure of a solid state material is quasi-two-dimensional, it is possible that the density of states in the vicinity of a saddle point peaks sharply, with any divergence ultimately being cut off due to the true three dimensionality of the material. If one assumes that this is the case in $Sr_3Ru_2O_7$ then one would expect the observed divergence to be of logarithmic form as shown in Fig. 5.21a, but not the particular power law given in 5.13. Attempts to construct a density of states with a logarithmically divergent contribution whose magnetic field dependent specific heat agrees with the experimental results on the same level as the density of states with a power law divergence have not been successful.

In order to reconcile these two points, one has to assume that the peak in the density of states looks like a power law over the energy range probed here. In this

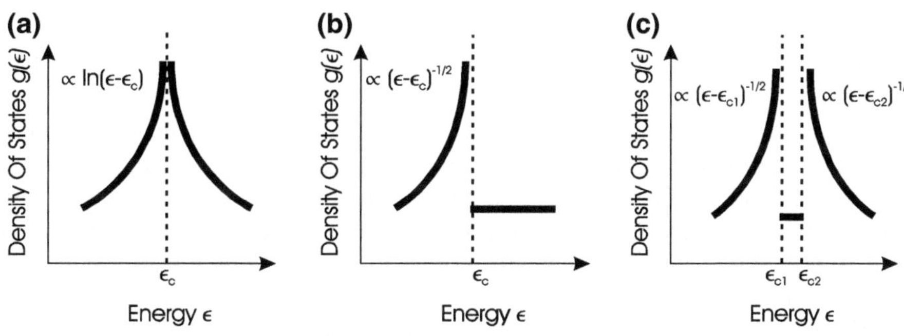

Fig. 5.21 In this figure possible scenarios for divergences in the density of states $g(\epsilon)$ as a function of energy arising generically from band structure features are given. **a** In two dimensions $g(\epsilon)$ can have a singular part proportional to a logarithmic divergence at a critical energy ϵ_C. The divergence is symmetric in field. **b** For one dimensional bands the density of states can diverge at the top of a band as shown. This divergence is proportional to a power law with exponent $-1/2$ but asymmetric, since there are not states above the band edge. The same analogous divergence can appear at the bottom of a band. If the band structure is such that the top of a one dimensional band is at a critical energy ϵ_{C1} just below the bottom of a one dimensional band at a slightly larger energy ϵ_{C2}, then a symmetric situation can arise in a band structure as shown in **c**. Here the density of states diverges in the form of a power law with the exponent $-1/2$ on both sides

case one has to postulate that this form is not due to a generic effect but to particular circumstances in $Sr_3Ru_2O_7$. It is possible in quasi-one-dimensional band structures at the top of a band to have a singular contribution to the density of states of the form of 5.13. However, as shown in Fig. 5.21b this kind of density of states shows the power law divergence only on one side of the singularity, whereas the other side is constant in energy. Therefore, in order to explain the symmetric peak in entropy as measured in this experiment one would have to postulate two quasi-one-dimensional bands in $Sr_3Ru_2O_7$ that are such that energetically the top of one of them is very close to the bottom of the other (Fig. 5.21c). This again would require the postulate of a very specific form of the band structure in order to explain the functional form of the peak in the density of states.

In summary the observed symmetric power law divergence in entropy as a function of magnetic field is not a feature that arises generically from a van Hove singularity in a quasi-two or one-dimensional band structure. One possibility is to postulate a particular non-generic band structure of $Sr_3Ru_2O_7$ that results in the observed specific heat as a function of magnetic field. The other possibility is that the functional form of the observed peak in the entropy cannot be explained only in terms of a band structure feature crossing the Fermi energy.

An alternative possibility discussed in the following is that the zero field density of states as measured by ARPES is significantly changed as a function of field due to field dependent quasiparticle interactions.

5.2.3.2 Alternative Scenarios

An alternative scenario to a rigid shift of the spin-dependent density of states as a function of magnetic field is that the zero field density of states as measured by ARPES is significantly changed due to magnetic field dependent quasiparticle interactions.

One possibility of enhancing the density of states of an electronic band structure is a renormalisation due to quantum fluctuations. A well known example is the electron–phonon coupling leading to an increased effective mass. In principle any fluctuation mode coupling to the Fermi liquid quasiparticle excitations can lead to such an effective mass enhancement. In order to explain in the case of $Sr_3Ru_2O_7$ the above described discrepancies between the zero field band structure observed by ARPES and the magnitude of the increase in the Sommerfeld constant, the fluctuation enhancement would have to be magnetic field dependent. Grigera et al. [8] established that the material is close to a quantum critical endpoint in phase space. The critical fluctuations associated with such a point in phase space would naturally give rise to a magnetic field dependent renormalisation of the band structure as a function of magnetic field. Most importantly, the mass renormalisation is expected to peak at the critical field. The fact that only part of the Fermi surface is significantly affected can in principle be understood if the critical fluctuations have a finite lattice momentum $\mathbf{q} \neq 0$ and couple only to part of the

Fermi surface. Indeed incommensurate spin fluctuations with finite **q** have been observed by Capogna et al. [28] in neutron studies.

Quantum criticality in itinerant systems is a theoretically challenging subject. The best current approach to this field is the theoretical framework developed by Hertz [29] and Millis [30]. Two studies have applied the theory to the case of $Sr_3Ru_2O_7$ [20, 31]. Both predict the qualitative increase in the specific heat as a function of magnetic field, however, the detailed functional form differs. The exact behaviour of the specific heat as a function of magnetic field depends on the universality class of the quantum critical end point. Both papers predict a power law divergence of the Sommerfeld coefficient with the exponents being $-1/3$ [20] and $-1/2$ [31]. However, none of them treats the problem under the constraint of two spin species and number conservation, making a direct comparison to experiment impossible. It can be concluded that a quantum critical scenario would be generically consistent with the experimental observation of the onset of a power law divergence as a function of magnetic field as well as a mass enhancement of the single particle density of states peaked at the critical field of 7.9 T.

Finally, it has to be mentioned that another possibility of the observed enhancement of the specific heat is a thermal population of fluctuation modes. The resulting specific heat contribution would have to have a linear dependence on temperature. This would be from a theoretical point of view very unusual insofar as fluctuations give in general a specific heat with a non-linear temperature dependence due to their bosonic character. I am not aware of examples to the contrary in the literature, but cannot absolutely exclude this possibility.

In summary, in this section I discussed possible scenarios explaining the observed symmetric peak in the entropy of $Sr_3Ru_2O_7$ as a function of magnetic field around the critical field of 7.9 T. It was shown that without postulating a specific density of states containing very unusual features it is not possible to explain the magnitude and functional form of the singular contribution to the entropy solely in terms of the zero field density of states measured by ARPES. I furthermore discussed that allowing for critical fluctuations associated with the metamagnetic features one can naturally explain the existence of a power law as well as the significant enhancement of the electronic density of states as a function of distance from the critical field. More importantly, if these fluctuations are found not to significantly alter the electronic structure of $Sr_3Ru_2O_7$ then this places potentially strong constraints on theories regarding itinerant quantum critical end points.

References

1. Borzi RA, Grigera SA, Farrell J, Perry RS, Lister SJS, Lee SL, Tennant DA, Maeno Y, Mackenzie AP (2007) Formation of a nematic fluid at high fields in $Sr_3Ru_2O_7$. Science 315(5809):214–217
2. Berridge AM, Green AG, Grigera SA, Simons BD (2009) Inhomogeneous magnetic phases: a LOFF-like phase in $Sr_3Ru_2O_7$. Phys Rev Lett 102(13):136404

3. Grigera SA, Gegenwart P, Borzi RA, Weickert F, Schofield AJ, Perry RS, Tayama T, Sakakibara T, Maeno Y, Green AG, Mackenzie AP (2004) Disorder-sensitive phase formation linked to metamagnetic quantum criticality. Science 306(5699):1154–1157
4. Gegenwart P, Weickert F, Garst M, Perry RS, Maeno Y (2006) Metamagnetic quantum criticality in $Sr_3Ru_2O_7$ studied by thermal expansion. Phys Rev Lett 96(13):136402
5. Perry RS, Galvin LM, Grigera SA, Capogna L, Schofield AJ, Mackenzie AP, Chiao M, Julian SR, Ikeda SI, Nakatsuji S, Maeno Y, Pfleiderer C (2001) Metamagnetism and critical fluctuations in high quality single crystals of the bilayer ruthenate $Sr_3Ru_2O_7$. Phys Rev Lett 86(12):2661–2664
6. Binz B, Braun HB, Rice TM, Sigrist M (2006) Magnetic domain formation in itinerant metamagnets. Phys Rev Lett 96(19):196406
7. Condon JH (1966) Nonlinear de Haas–van Alphen effect and magnetic domains in beryllium. Phys Rev 145(2):526–535
8. Grigera SA, Perry RS, Schofield AJ, Chiao M, Julian SR, Lonzarich GG, Ikeda SI, Maeno Y, Millis AJ, Mackenzie AP (2001) Magnetic field-tuned quantum criticality in the metallic ruthenate $Sr_3Ru_2O_7$. Science 294(5541):329–332
9. Grigera SA, Borzi RA, Mackenzie AP, Julian SR, Perry RS, Maeno Y (2003) Angular dependence of the magnetic susceptibility in the itinerant metamagnet $Sr_3Ru_2O_7$. Phys Rev B 67(21):214427
10. Grigera SA. Private communication
11. Stryjewski E, Giordano N (1977) Metamagnetism. Adv Phys 26:487
12. Mercure J-F (2008) The de Haas–van Alphen effect near a quantum critical end point in $Sr_3Ru_2O_7$. PhD Thesis, University of St. Andrews
13. Damascelli A, Hussain Z, Shen ZX (2003) Angle-resolved photoemission studies of the cuprate superconductors. Rev Mod Phys 75(2):473–541
14. von Löhneysen H, Rosch A, Vojta M, Wölfle P (2007) Fermi-liquid instabilities at magnetic quantum phase transitions. Rev Mod Phys 79(3):1015–1075
15. Chubukov AV, Maslov DL, Gangadharaiah S, Glazman LI (2005) Thermodynamics of a Fermi liquid beyond the low-energy limit. Phys Rev Lett 95(2):026402
16. Ikeda S, Maeno Y, Nakatsuji S, Kosaka M, Uwatoko Y (2000) Ground state in $Sr_3Ru_2O_7$: Fermi liquid close to a ferromagnetic instability. Phys Rev B 62(10):R6089–R6092
17. Yamase H, Katanin AA (2008) Theory of spontaneous Fermi surface symmetry breaking for $Sr_3Ru_2O_7$. International Conference on Strongly Correlated Electron Systems (SCES 2007), Houston, TX, MAY 13–18, 2007. Phys B Condens Matter 403(5–9):1262–1264
18. Kee HY, Kim YB (2005) Itinerant metamagnetism induced by electronic nematic order. Phys Rev B 71(18):184402
19. Raghu S, Paramekanti A, Kim EA, Borzi RA, Grigera S, Mackenzie AP, Kivelson SA (2009) Microscopic theory of the nematic phase in $Sr_3Ru_2O_7$. Phys Rev B 79:214402
20. Millis AJ, Schofield AJ, Lonzarich GG, Grigera SA (2002) Metamagnetic quantum criticality in metals. Phys Rev Lett 88(21):217204
21. Ohmichi E, Yoshida Y, Ikeda SI, Mushunikov NV, Goto T, Osada T (2003) Double metamagnetic transition in the bilayer ruthenate $Sr_3Ru_2O_7$. Phys Rev B 67(2):024432
22. Perry RS, Kitagawa K, Grigera SA, Borzi RA, Mackenzie AP, Ishida K, Maeno Y (2004) Multiple first-order metamagnetic transitions and quantum oscillations in ultrapure $Sr_3Ru_2O_7$. Phys Rev Lett 92(16):166602
23. Borzi RA, Grigera SA, Perry RS, Kikugawa N, Kitagawa K, Maeno Y, Mackenzie AP (2004) De Haas–van Alphen effect across the metamagnetic transition in $Sr_3Ru_2O_7$. Phys Rev Lett 92(21):216403
24. Tamai A, Allan MP, Mercure JF, Meevasana W, Dunkel R, Lu DH, Perry RS, Mackenzie AP, Singh DJ, Shen Z-X, Baumberger F (2008) Fermi surface and van Hove singularities in the itinerant metamagnet $Sr_3Ru_2O_7$. Phys Rev Lett 101(2):026407
25. Iwaya K, Satow S, Hanaguri T, Shannon N, Yoshida Y, Ikeda SI, He JP, Kaneko Y, Tokura Y, Yamada T, Takagi H (2007) Local tunneling spectroscopy across a metamagnetic critical point in the bilayer ruthenate $Sr_3Ru_2O_7$. Phys Rev Lett 99(5):057208

26. Kikugawa N, Mackenzie AP, Bergemann C, Borzi RA, Grigera SA, Maeno Y (2004) Rigid-band shift of the Fermi level in the strongly correlated metal: $Sr_3Ru_2O_7$. Phys Rev B 70(6):060508
27. Farrell J, Perry RS, Rost A, Mercure JF, Kikugawa N, Grigera SA, Mackenzie AP (2008) Effect of electron doping the metamagnet $Sr_3Ru_2O_7$. Phys Rev B 78(18):180409
28. Capogna L, Forgan EM, Hayden SM, Wildes A, Duffy JA, Mackenzie AP, Perry RS, Ikeda S, Maeno Y, Brown SP (2003) Observation of two-dimensional spin fluctuations in the bilayer ruthenate $Sr_3Ru_2O_7$ by inelastic neutron scattering. Phys Rev B 67(1):012504
29. Hertz JA (1976) Quantum critical phenomena. Phys Rev B 14(3):1165–1184
30. Millis AJ (1993) Effect of a nonzero temperature on quantum critical-points in itinerant Fermion systems. Phys Rev B 48(10):7183–7196
31. Zhu LJ, Garst M, Rosch A, Si QM (2003) Universally diverging Grüneisen parameter and the magnetocaloric effect close to quantum critical points. Phys Rev Lett 91(6):066404

Chapter 6
Conclusions and Future Work

In this thesis a detailed study of the entropy of the itinerant metamagnet $Sr_3Ru_2O_7$ was presented. With the experimental setup specially developed for this work it was possible to study isothermal changes of the entropy as a function of magnetic field with the magnetocaloric effect as well as performing specific heat measurements. In the following, the main results of this project in relation to the physics of $Sr_3Ru_2O_7$ will be summarised. Particular attention will be paid to data relating to the novel quantum phase as well as the proposed quantum critical point and its effect on the surrounding normal states. The chapter will conclude with a brief discussion of planned future work and the wider relevance of the results.

$Sr_3Ru_2O_7$ has been intensely studied in recent years because of a proposed quantum critical point in its magnetic phase diagram [1] and the discovery of a novel quantum phase [3] which shows 'nematic-like' transport properties in its vicinity [2]. The first part of the results presented in this thesis particularly concerned the entropic properties of this new phase and the surrounding phase transitions. For clarity of the discussion I show again in Fig. 6.1 the magnetic field and temperature phase diagram for the magnetic field applied along the crystallographic *c*-axis. Its details are discussed in Sect. 2.2.2 (Chap. 2). Here it is only important that the data points are marking the position of proposed first (green) and second (blue) order phase transitions and crossovers as a function of magnetic field. In Chap. 5 it was shown that the entropy change and the jump in magnetisation across the first order transition (1) together with the curvature of the transition line in the H–T diagram are quantitatively consistent with the magnetic version of the Clausius–Clapeyron relation. This indicates that it is indeed a first order transition between two equilibrium phases. The same holds for the evolution of the entropy across transition (2) qualitatively. It was furthermore shown that the entropy of the anomalous phase region is higher than that of the surrounding low and high field states, indicating the existence of additional degrees of freedom.

A. W. Rost, *Magnetothermal Properties near Quantum Criticality in the Itinerant Metamagnet $Sr_3Ru_2O_7$*, Springer Theses, DOI: 10.1007/978-3-642-14524-7_6,

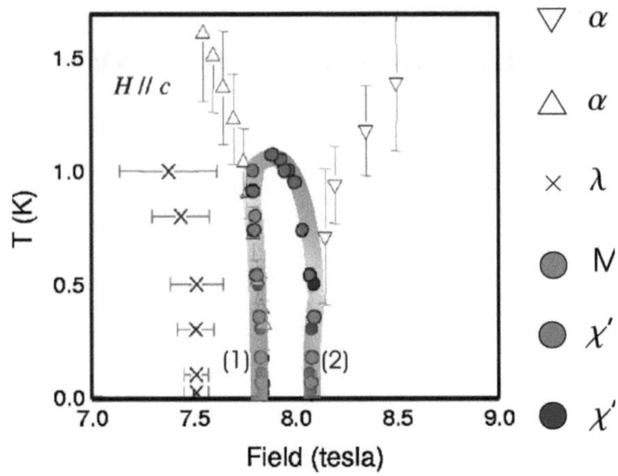

Fig. 6.1 Phase boundaries of $Sr_3Ru_2O_7$ in the *H*–*T* plane with the magnetic field applied along the crystallographic *c*-axis. The data shown are extracted from magnetisation *M*, the complex AC magnetic susceptibility χ, linear magnetostriction λ and thermal expansion α [3, 4]. The *green lines* indicate first order transitions [(*1*) and (*2*)] and the *blue line* represents a second order phase transition. The other data represent crossovers

Furthermore, measurements of the specific heat as a function of temperature across the 'roof' feature, indicated by a blue line in Fig. 6.1, were performed. These results showed that it is consistent with a second order symmetry breaking phase transition at least for the case of the magnetic field being aligned parallel to the crystallographic *c*-axis. It was shown in previous experiments [5], that the high temperature state above the 'roof' is unusual in that its specific heat *c* divided by temperature *T* is consistent with having a logarithmically diverging contribution with a singularity at zero temperature at a critical field in the vicinity of 8 T. The experiments presented here showed that the low temperature novel quantum phase also has a highly unusual specific heat with c/T increasing linearly towards lower temperature and therefore being expressible as $c/T = \gamma - bT$. This is in particular significant since Mercure and co-workers [6] have established the existence of quantum oscillations inside the new phase indicating the existence of a Fermi surface and Landau Fermi liquid quasiparticles. However, the linear contribution to c/T to lowest temperatures seems inconsistent with standard Fermi liquid theory. It is therefore proposed here that either (a) finite temperature corrections to Fermi liquid theory [7] are important in this novel phase or that (b) additional non-Fermi liquid contributions to the specific heat exist. On the one hand, the detailed knowledge of the thermodynamic and microscopic properties of $Sr_3Ru_2O_7$ should enable a quantitative comparison of theoretical models of Fermi liquid corrections with experimental data. On the other hand, if the additional degrees of freedom of the second proposal are for example magnetic in nature, they are potentially measurable in neutron experiments.

Two important future experiments directly related to the ones presented here should be carried out to further study the points raised. First the measurements of specific heat in the novel quantum phase should be extended to below the minimum temperature of 200 mK. Though the experimental setup developed in this thesis can perform measurements in this temperature regime a reliable data analysis is constrained by the existence of a Schottky-type anomaly in the experimental addenda. This can potentially be removed in the next generation of the design. Secondly one should further extend the specific heat study to different angular orientations of the magnetic field. In Appendix B an initial angular study is presented that was carried out by the author. Here a specially cut sample with surfaces along different crystallographic orientations allowed the use of the same setup without the need of a rotation mechanism. This revealed a complex phase diagram for the magnetic field being applied at different angles within the *ab*-plane.

A detailed angular study is also required in order to study the angular dependence of the specific heat signature corresponding to the 'roof'. One way of achieving this is by adopting the setup for a novel three-axis vector magnet system currently being developed for the University of St Andrews. This will allow a smooth rotation of the magnetic field without friction heating as observed in more conventional rotation mechanisms. Here it should in particular be possible to address the question of whether an in-plane field changes the nature of the 'roof' from being a second order phase transition to a thermodynamic crossover.

The second part of the work presented here concerned the entropy of the low and high field states surrounding the anomalous phase. In Sect. 5.2 it is shown that both the specific heat and entropy increase significantly upon approaching the critical region in the phase diagram from either low or high magnetic field as has been inferred from previous measurements [1, 4]. However, at constant magnetic field, c/T is consistent with being a constant as a function of temperature over the temperature range explored. The data therefore indicate that the low and high field phases are Fermi liquids whose Sommerfeld coefficient sharply peaks at 7.9 T. It is scientifically important to address the issue of whether this peak can be understood solely in terms of a shift of the spin-up/spin-down Fermi energy through an otherwise rigid single particle density of states or if the single particle excitation spectrum is dominated by quantum fluctuations renormalising the quasiparticle properties as function of distance from the critical field at 7.9 T.

One of the main contributions of this thesis in relation to this issue is the discovery of a small Fermi surface pocket in quantum oscillations of the magnetocaloric effect contributing approximately 45% to the zero field specific heat. Inconclusive evidence for the existence of this pocket at the Fermi surface had also been seen in ARPES [8] together with the discovery that it is associated with a density of states peak originating in a saddle point van-Hove singularity energetically close to the Fermi energy. In particular the fact that no other Fermi surface sheet was observed in quantum oscillation measurements by Mercure and co-workers [6] to have a significant increase in effective mass and therefore specific heat contribution makes this new Fermi surface pocket the best candidate for being the primary cause of the metamagnetism and of the peak in entropy at the critical field.

The highly detailed measurements allow to show that the magnitude of the specific heat increase is at least 100% larger than estimated from the zero field density of states as measured by ARPES. Furthermore, from a qualitative point of view, the onset of divergence is consistent with a singular contribution to the entropy in the form of a scale invariant power law diverging at the critical field of 7.9 T. Such a power law does not naturally arise from a single feature in the band structure.

The results of this thesis therefore indicate that the peak in the entropy is significantly influenced either by a renormalisation of the quasiparticle properties due to quantum fluctuations or additional non-Fermi liquid degrees of freedom contributing to the specific heat. Both of these possibilities have their origin potentially in the underlying quantum critical point. Especially the first scenario of a peak in the density of states that is enhanced as a function of field would naturally produce a singularity in the entropy as a function of magnetic field having the form of a power law.

An important question is whether one can experimentally distinguish between the different scenarios. One possible experiment that has the potential to do so is the probing of the local density of states by scanning tunneling microscopy (STM) in magnetic fields. If indeed there is a peak in the electronic density of states of $Sr_3Ru_2O_7$ that is fluctuation enhanced as a function of distance from the critical field, then both the existence of the peak and its field dependent change in magnitude should in principle be observable in the current–voltage characteristic of a STM measurement. In the case of no fluctuation enhancement one should at least still observe a peak of the current–voltage characteristic near zero bias corresponding to the proposed van Hove singularity.

The work presented in this thesis should be considered in its wider context. The detailed knowledge of the thermodynamic properties of $Sr_3Ru_2O_7$ in combination with its suitability for nearly all major microscopic solid state probes make the material an exceptional example in which the effect of electron correlations can be studied. In particular it can serve as an important quantitative test case for theories relating to the physics of itinerant quantum critical end points and 'electron-nematic' phases.

Furthermore, from an experimentalist's point of view the method of extracting the isothermal changes in the entropy of a system as a function of magnetic field with the magnetocaloric effect in the non-adiabatic limit has been very successful. First of all, it allowed the careful study of entropy changes across magnetic first order transitions and to quantitatively test the Clausius–Clapeyron relation. Secondly, the technique allowed for the quantitative measurement of entropy changes in a sample as a function of magnetic field without the extrapolation of specific heat measurements to zero temperature and the uncertainties involved with this. This experimental method should easily be applicable to a range of other materials whose magnetic phase diagrams indicate the presence of a quantum critical point or have novel quantum states such as $YbRh_2Si_2$ [9] or URhGe [10]. In doing so it will be possible to study a range of different classes of quantum critical points for which the experimentally measured evolution of entropy with magnetic field can be tested against theory.

Finally it should be mentioned that the observation of quantum oscillations in the magnetocaloric effect has been shown to not only reproduce the results of other quantum oscillation measurements but also be particularly suited to the investigation of low frequency signals and the detection of small Fermi surface pockets with frequencies below 1 kT. It should therefore be extended to materials where such small Fermi surface areas are predicted by band structure calculations or otherwise suspected to be crucial to the material properties, such as the recently observed small Fermi surface pockets in the cuprate high temperature superconductors [11–13].

References

1. Grigera SA, Perry RS, Schofield AJ, Chiao M, Julian SR, Lonzarich GG, Ikeda SI, Maeno Y, Millis AJ, Mackenzie AP (2001) Magnetic field-tuned quantum criticality in the metallic ruthenate $Sr_3Ru_2O_7$. Science 294(5541):329–332
2. Borzi RA, Grigera SA, Farrell J, Perry RS, Lister SJS, Lee SL, Tennant DA, Maeno Y, Mackenzie AP (2007) Formation of a nematic fluid at high fields in $Sr_3Ru_2O_7$. Science 315(5809):214–217
3. Grigera SA, Gegenwart P, Borzi RA, Weickert F, Schofield AJ, Perry RS, Tayama T, Sakakibara T, Maeno Y, Green AG, Mackenzie AP (2004) Disorder-sensitive phase formation linked to metamagnetic quantum criticality. Science 306(5699):1154–1157
4. Gegenwart P, Weickert F, Garst M, Perry RS, Maeno Y (2006) Metamagnetic quantum criticality in $Sr_3Ru_2O_7$ studied by thermal expansion. Phys Rev Lett 96(13):136402
5. Perry RS, Galvin LM, Grigera SA, Capogna L, Schofield AJ, Mackenzie APChiao M, Julian SR, Ikeda SI, Nakatsuji S, Maeno Y, Pfleiderer C (2001) Metamagnetism and critical fluctuations in high quality single crystals of the bilayer ruthenate $Sr_3Ru_2O_7$. Phys Rev Lett 86(12):2661–2664
6. Mercure J-F (2008) The de Haas–van Alphen effect near a quantum critical end point in $Sr_3Ru_2O_7$. Ph.D. thesis, September 2008.
7. Condon JH (1966) Nonlinear de Haas–van Alphen effect and magnetic domains in beryllium. Phys Rev 145(2):526–535
8. Tamai A, Allan MP, Mercure JF, Meevasana W, Dunkel R, Lu DH, Perry RS, Mackenzie AP, Singh DJ, Shen Z-X, Baumberger F (2008) Fermi surface and van Hove singularities in the itinerant metamagnet $Sr_3Ru_2O_7$. Phys Rev Lett 101(2):026407
9. Custers J, Gegenwart P, Wilhelm H, Neumaier K, Tokiwa Y, Trovarelli O, Geibel C, Steglich F, Pepin C, Coleman P (2003) The break-up of heavy electrons at a quantum critical point. Nature 424(6948):524–527
10. Lévy F, Sheikin I, Grenier B, Huxley AD (2005) Magnetic field-induced superconductivity in the ferromagnet UR1hGe. Science 309(5739):1343–1346
11. Doiron-Leyraud N, Proust C, LeBoeuf D, Levallois J, Bonnemaison J-B, Liang R, Bonn DA, Hardy WN, Taillefer L (2007) Quantum oscillations and the Fermi surface in an underdoped high-T_c superconductor. Nature 447(7144):565–568

12. Sebastian SE, Harrison N, Palm E, Murphy TP, Mielke CH, Liang R, Bonn DA, Hardy WN, Lonzarich GG (2008) A multi-component Fermi surface in the vortex state of an underdoped high-T_c superconductor. Nature 454(7201):200–203
13. Yelland EA, Singleton J, Mielke CH, Harrison N, Balakirev FF, Dabrowski B, Cooper JR (2008) Quantum oscillations in the underdoped cuprate $YBa_2Cu_4O_8$. Phys Rev Lett 100(4):047003

Chapter 7
Appendices

7.1 Appendix A: Material Properties

The form and dimensions of the materials in the experimental setup are detailed in Table 7.1. Silver is used for the sample platform. The Kevlar strings are supporting the sample platform with electrical contacts to the thermometer and heater made via the Manganin wires. The platinum wire is used as a tuneable thermal link between the sample and the thermal bath. Furthermore listed are the approximate dimensions of the sample used as well as the various amorphous materials necessary for positioning thermometer, heater and sample.

Relevant literature values for the low temperature specific heat and thermal conductivity of materials used in the experimental setup are given in Table 7.2. The thermal conductivities of silver and platinum depend significantly on the impurity and defect concentration of the material and can differ from sample to sample.

7.2 Appendix B: Angular Dependence of the Magnetocaloric Signal

In Chap. 5, I presented the main results regarding the entropic properties of $Sr_3Ru_2O_7$ as a function of magnetic field and temperature with the field applied parallel to the crystallographic *c*-axis. However, as previously discussed, $Sr_3Ru_2O_7$ also has a very interesting phase diagram for other field orientations. Here I will give an overview of the most significant results as obtained from a preliminary angular study. In order to achieve this with the current setup the specially cut sample C698K was used.

Figure 7.1a shows the sample dimensions. The surface marked with (A) is parallel to the crystallographic *ab* plane and has an octagonal cross section. The

A. W. Rost, *Magnetothermal Properties near Quantum Criticality in the Itinerant Metamagnet $Sr_3Ru_2O_7$*, Springer Theses, DOI: 10.1007/978-3-642-14524-7_7,

Table 7.1 Form and dimensions of the materials in the experimental setup

Material	Length l (mm)	Cross section A
Silver (cuboid)	0.15	$4\ \text{mm} \times 4\ \text{mm} = 16\ \text{mm}^2$
Kevlar (eight strings of 35 filaments)	16	$8 \times 35 \times \pi \times 0.017\ \text{mm}^2 = 0.25\ \text{mm}^2$
Manganin (four twisted pairs)	20	$4 \times 2 \times \pi \times 0.030\ \text{mm}^2 = 0.023\ \text{mm}^2$
Platinum (one wire)	20	$\pi \times 0.025\ \text{mm}^2 = 0.0020\ \text{mm}^2$
$Sr_3Ru_2O_7$ (cuboid)	1.5	$1.5\ \text{mm} \times 1.5\ \text{mm} = 2.25\ \text{mm}^2$
GE 7031		overall < 1 mg
Apiezon N		overall < 1 mg
Stycast		overall < 1 mg

Table 7.2 Relevant literature values for the low temperature specific heat and thermal conductivity of materials used in the experimental setup

Material	Specific heat c	Thermal conductivity κ
Silver	7×10^{-4} J/mol K [1]	25 W/m K [2]
Kevlar	–	αT^n [3] $\alpha = 3.9 \times 10^{-5}$ W/cm K^{1+n} $n = 1.71$
Manganin	$sT^{-2} + aT + bT^3 + cT^5$ [4] $s = 36$ μJ K^2/g $a = 56$ μJ/g K^2 $b = 6.02$ μJ/g K^4 $c = -0.029$ μJ/g K^6	αT^n [5] $\alpha = 9.5 \times 10^{-4}$ W/cm K^{1+n} $n = 1.19$
Platinum	–	3 W/m K [2, 6]
Stycast	$aT + bT^3 + cT^5$ [7] $a = 2.91$ μJ/g K^2 $b = 15.7$ μJ/g K^4 $c = 8.98$ μJ/g K^6	$aT^{1.98}$ [8] $a = 4.9 \times 10^{-4}$ W/cm K^2
Apiezon N	$aT + bT^3$ [9] $a = 1.32$ μJ/g K^2 $b = 25.8$ μJ/g K^4	–

surface opposite to (A) is cut such that its normal forms an angle of 19° with the crystallographic *c* axis. Figure 7.1b shows a reflection Laue pattern taken of surface (A). The borders of the surface are not parallel to the crystallographic axes. Nevertheless one is closer to the *a* or *b*[1] direction (these are equivalent in $Sr_3Ru_2O_7$) and one is closer to the 45° direction. This sample can now be mounted in the three additional ways on the setup as shown in Fig. 7.1c allowing magnetocaloric sweeps at an angle of 19° between the magnetic field and the *c*-axis as

[1] The crystallographic axes here are not those of the orthorhombic structure but of the idealised tetragonal unit cell. In particular they are along the direction of the nearest neighbor *Ru–O–Ru* bond and therefore at 45° to the true crystal axes of the orthorhombic unit cell. This notation is chosen in order to be consistent with the paper by Borzi et al. [10].

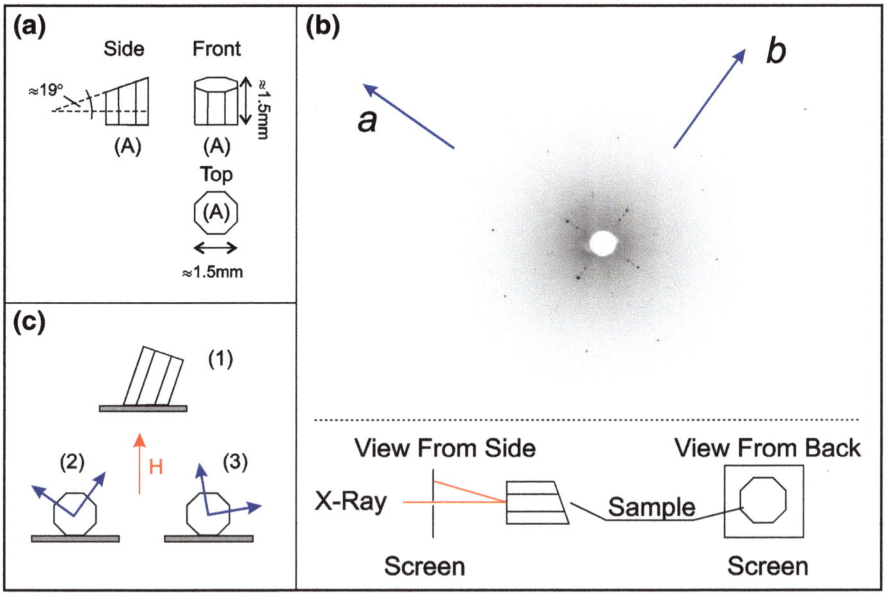

Fig. 7.1 Overview of sample C698K, which has been specially prepared for an initial angular dependence study of the magnetocaloric signal. **a** The front, side and top view of the sample. The base is a regular octagon that is parallel to the crystallographic *ab* plane. The top of the sample has been cut such that the normal to the resulting surface is forming an angle of 19° with the crystallographic *c*-axis. The overall dimensions are as given in the figure. **b** A reflection Laue picture of the sample. The geometry of the X-ray beam, screen and sample are given below the photograph. One can clearly identify the crystallographic *a* and *b* axis. The sides of the octagon are rotated by approximately 10° with respect to the crystal axes. **c** The three different ways in which the sample can be mounted on the sample platform (*grey*). The *blue arrows* are indicating the crystallographic axes and the direction of the magnetic field H is shown in *red*. In orientation (*1*) the applied magnetic field is at 19° to the *c*-axis. In orientation (*2*) on the other hand the field is in the *ab* plane and 35° off the *a*/*b* axis. Finally in orientation (*3*) the magnetic field is again in the *ab* plane but this time 10° off the *a*/*b* axis

well as two measurements with the magnetic field perpendicular to the *c*-axis but at different angles in the *ab*-plane.

7.2.1 Study at 19°

Figure 7.2 shows the temperature of the sample as a function of magnetic field during a field sweep at 0.02 T/min (blue) and −0.02 T/min (red) at a sample temperature of 160 mK. The inset on the upper right is showing the orientation of the sample. Coming from low fields the metamagnetic crossover is still clearly identifiable but has moved to 6.9 T compared to 7.5 T in the case of the magnetic field being applied parallel to the *c*-axis.

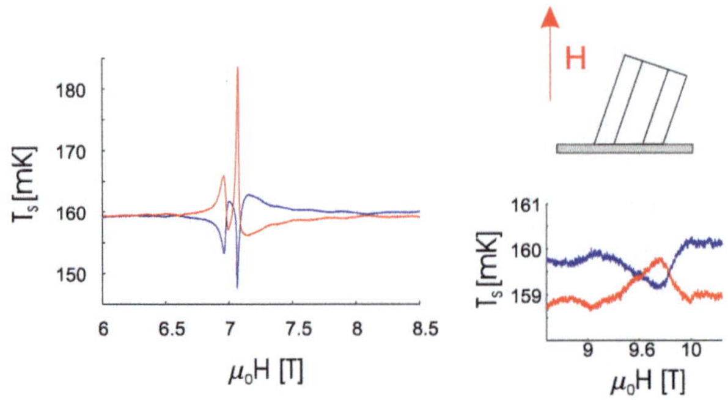

Fig. 7.2 The graph is showing the temperature T_S of the sample during a sweep of the magnetic field H at 0.02 T/min (*blue curve*) and −0.02 T/min (*red curve*). The orientation of the sample during the sweep is shown in the *upper right inset*. The *lower right inset* is showing the same property as the main graph but in the field range of the high field crossover

Similarly the main first order transition has changed from 7.9 T to 7.1 T. The second first order phase transition is no longer identifiable.

The second inset on the lower right shows the position of the high field magnetocaloric crossover that has moved from 12.5 T to 9.5 T.

7.2.2 Study in the ab*-Plane*

Two experiments were conducted with the magnetic field being applied in the *ab* plane. The first shown in the upper right part of Fig. 7.3a is such that the magnetic field is oriented in the same plane as is defined by the crystallographic *c*-axis and the orientation of the '19°' experiment reported above. The second orientation shown in the upper left part of Fig. 7.3b is achieved by rotating the crystal by 45° around its *c*-axis. It is this second orientation where the applied magnetic field points closer along a crystallographic *a* or *b* axis.[2]

In Fig. 7.3a the temperature of the sample during an up (blue) and down (red) sweep of the magnetic field for orientation (2) is shown. The analogous Fig. 7.3b is showing the equivalent sweeps for the orientation (3). The difference in the measurements reveal a significant anisotropy of the phase diagram for field orientations in the *ab*-plane.

First of all, although both show signatures of the expected metamagnetic first order transition (I), this is situated at different fields, namely 5.3 T for orientation (2) and 5.1 T for orientation (3). Furthermore while the magnetocaloric

[2] As discussed earlier these are not distinguishable by the experiments reported here, which is why the labelling is to some extend arbitrary.

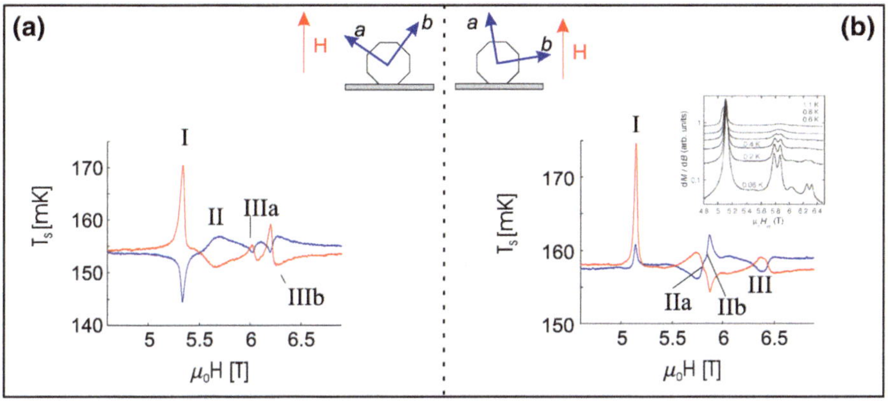

Fig. 7.3 In both figure **a** and **b** the temperature of the sample T_S during a sweep of the magnetic field at 0.02 T/min (blue) and −0.02 T/min (*red*) is shown as a function of magnetic field *H*. The schematics in the centre are giving the orientation of the magnetic field (*red*) relative to the crystallographic *a*/*b*-axis (*blue*). Furthermore the *inset* of figure **b** is showing a previous measurement of d*M*/d*B* as a function of magnetic field for a similar field orientation as the presented magnetocaloric sweep [11]

signal for the up and down sweep in orientation (2) is approximately symmetric as expected for a magnetocaloric signal, it is highly asymmetric in case (3). This implies that in orientation (3) there always occurs heating of the sample independent of the direction in magnetic field in which the transition is crossed. One explanation of this effect would be that due to magnetostriction in the material friction heating is caused either by dislocations in the sample or at the interface between the sample and the sample holder. However, no ageing effect could be observed after repeating the experiment at the same temperature for several times. Neither does the relative size of the signature between up and down sweep change significantly by changing the sweep rate by a factor of 4. The fact however that there is a strong asymmetry between the up and down sweep indicates that there is nevertheless a significant latent heat contribution associated with the transition.

Secondly between 5.5 T and 6.5 T several peaks in the sample as a function of magnetic field indicate a series of phase transitions or crossovers. Though a definite identification without further angular studies is not possible, the most likely is the one indicated in the two graphs. In this scenario, feature (II) in Fig. 7.3b is upon changing the orientation of the magnetic field split into features (IIa) and (IIb) in Fig. 7.3c. Features (IIIa) and (IIIb) in Fig. 7.3b on the other hand are nearly merged into one feature in Fig. 7.3c. Finally, the inset in Fig. 7.3c shows a susceptibility measurement published by Perry et al. for the magnetic field applied along the crystallographic *a* direction. This is close to orientation (2) reported here and as can be seen the position of features in the current experiment are well reflected in the susceptibility measurement.

7.2.2.1 Discussion

These measurements represent a clear indication that the magnetic phase diagram of $Sr_3Ru_2O_7$ has a strong dependence on the orientation of the magnetic field direction in the crystallographic *ab*-plane. Whereas experiments cannot distinguish between the magnetic field being applied along the *a* (*[100]*-direction) or *b* (*[010]*-direction) directions it is clear that the physics for the field applied along the *[110]*-direction is systematically different. In [12], Mercure and co-workers determined that the results for the angular dependence of the de Haas-van Alphen measurements with the magnetic field close to the *c*-axis (*[001]*) can best be described by assuming that the strength of the coupling between the spin and the magnetic field is anisotropic at high fields. Mathematically this can be done by assuming that the usually scalar Landé *g*-factor, describing the strength of coupling between the spin $\mathbf{S}$ and the magnetic field $\mathbf{H}$ via the term $\hat{H}_{\text{mag}} = -g\mathbf{SH}$, is replaced by a positive definite 3×3 matrix $\mathbf{G}$, leading to a revised contribution to the Hamiltonian of the form $\hat{H}_{\text{mag}} = -\mathbf{S}(\mathbf{GH})$. One has to remember that experiments at low fields showed an isotropic Pauli paramagnetism [13] and that the above description can only be valid in high fields. The experiments here however suggest, that the magnetic field positions of transitions in the zero temperature limit are not simply scaled by an anisotropic $\mathbf{G}$ factor, but rather that the phase diagram is affected in a fundamentally nonlinear way.

There are several possible reasons for this behaviour. First of all it is known that there is a strong magnetoelastic coupling present in the material. Therefore, applying the magnetic field along different symmetry axes of the crystalline structure can in principle lead to small but different structural distortions. Since this affects the electronic structure of the material, it is a possible source for the observed anisotropy. This would also explain why the anisotropy is absent at zero field, since the energetic effects of such Fermi surface distortions are undoubtedly of higher order in magnetic field. A second possible reason for the observed anisotropy is spin orbit coupling. This effect has in particular been discussed for the two single layer compounds Sr_2RhO_4 [14, 15] and Sr_2IrO_4 [16], which are isostructural to Sr_2RuO_4.

However a more detailed angular study for the magnetic field being aligned in the *ab*-plane is necessary to study this complex and rich phase diagram in detail. For this purpose a vector magnet system is currently being put in place and an advanced version of the setup presented in this thesis is being developed.

References

1. du Chatenier FJ, Miedema AR (1965) Heat capacity below 1 K: observation of the linear term and the HFS contribution in some dilute alloys. Proceedings of the 9th International Conference on Low Temperature Physics, p 1029
2. Pobell F (1992) Matter and methods at low temperatures. Springer-Verlag,Heidelberg

3. Ventura G, Barucci M, Gottardi E, Peroni I (2000) Low temperature thermal conductivity of Kevlar. Cryogenics 40(7):489–491
4. Marklund K, Bystrom S, Larsson M, Lindqvis T (1973) Low-temperature heat-capacity of Manganin wire and Woods metal. Cryogenics 13(11):671–672
5. Peroni I, Gottardi E, Peruzzi A, Ponti G, Ventura G (1999) Thermal conductivity of Manganin below 1 K. Nuclear Physics B—Proceedings Supplements 78:573–575. 6th International Conference on Advanced Technology and Particle Physics, Villa Olmo, Italy, October 05–09, 1998
6. Davey G, Mendelssohn K, Sharma JKN (1965) In: Proceedings of the Ninth International Conference on Low Temperature Physics, p 1196
7. Siqueira ML, Rapp RE (1991) Specific heat of an epoxi resin below 1 K. Rev Sci Instrum 62(10):2499–2500
8. Armstrong G, Greenberg AS, Sites JR (1978) Very low temperature thermal conductivity and optical properties of Stycast 1266 epoxy. Rev Sci Instrum 49(3):345–347
9. Schink HJ, Löhneysen Hv (1981) Specific-heat of Apiezon-N grease at very low-temperatures. Cryogenics 21(10):591–592
10. Borzi RA, Grigera SA, Farrell J, Perry RS, Lister SJS, Lee SL, Tennant DA, Maeno Y, Mackenzie AP (2007) Formation of a nematic fluid at high fields in $Sr_3Ru_2O_7$. Science 315(5809):214–217
11. Perry RS, Tayama T, Kitagawa K, Sakakibara T, Ishida K, Maeno Y (2005) Investigation into the itinerant metamagnetism of $Sr_3Ru_2O_7$ for the field parallel to the ruthenium oxygen planes. J. Phys. Soc. Jpn 74(4):1270–1274
12. Mercure J-F (2008) The de Haas-van Alphen effect near a quantum critical end point in $Sr_3Ru_2O_7$. PhD Thesis. September 2008
13. Ikeda S, Maeno Y, Nakatsuji S, Kosaka M, Uwatoko Y (2000) Ground state in $Sr_3Ru_2O_7$: Fermi liquid close to a ferromagnetic instability. Phys Rev B 62(10):R6089–6092
14. Haverkort MW, Elfimov IS, Tjeng LH, Sawatzky GA, Damascelli A (2008) Strong spin-orbit coupling effects on the fermi surface of Sr_2RuO_4 and Sr_2RhO_4. Phys Rev Lett 101(2):026406
15. Liu G-Q, Antonov VN, Jepsen O, Andersen OK (2008) Coulomb-enhanced spin-orbit splitting: the missing piece in the Sr_2RhO_4 puzzle. Phys Rev Lett 101(2):026408
16. Kim BJ, Jin H, Moon SJ, Kim J-Y, Park J-Y, Leem CS, Yu J, Noh TW, Kim C, Oh S-J, Park J-H, Durairaj V, Cao G, Rotenberg E (2008) Novel J_{eff}=1/2 Mott state induced by relativistic spin-orbit coupling in Sr_2IrO_4. Phys Rev Lett 101(7):076402

MIX
Papier aus verantwortungsvollen Quellen
Paper from responsible sources
FSC® C105338

If you have any concerns about our products,
you can contact us on
ProductSafety@springernature.com

In case Publisher is established outside the EU,
the EU authorized representative is:
Springer Nature Customer Service Center GmbH
Europaplatz 3, 69115 Heidelberg, Germany

Printed by Libri Plureos GmbH
in Hamburg, Germany